Praise for *Noble Savages*

"One of history's greatest anthropologists—and a rip-roaring story-teller—recounts his life with an endangered Amazonian tribe and the mind-boggling controversies his work ignited. *Noble Savages* is rich with insights into human nature, and an entertaining interlude with a remarkable man."

—Steven Pinker, Harvard College Professor of Psychology,
Harvard University, and the author of *The Better Angels of Our Nature:
Why Violence Has Declined*

"*Noble Savages* is an epic—not only of one of the most extraordinary physical and intellectual adventures ever experienced by a major scientist, but also the history of one of the most significant events in the early, often turbulent meeting between evolutionary biology and the social sciences."

—E. O. Wilson, Pellegrino University Professor Emeritus,
Harvard University, and the author of *The Social Conquest of Earth*
and *Sociobiology*

"A beautifully written adventure story. . . . *Noble Savages* is a remarkable testament to an engineer's 35-year effort to unravel the complex working of an untouched human society."

—Nicholas Wade, *The New York Times*

"One of the most interesting anthropology books I have ever read. . . . [Chagnon's] portrayal of society's origins has so much to say about the nature of our species that it should be examined thoughtfully."

—Charles C. Mann, *The Wall Street Journal*

"An important contribution to the debates over the methods and theories used to understand humans in anthropology and evolutionary sciences—and to debates over how visionaries become the targets of those who do not share their vision."

—Douglas William Hume, *Nature*

"Very few people have led lives as fascinating as Napoleon Chagnon's, or have lived among people as dangerous as the Yanomamö, and fewer still have his courage or his honor. *Noble Savages* is a page-turning masterpiece. You don't need to know anything about anthropology to read it. By the time you finish, you'll know a lot."

—Elizabeth Marshall Thomas, author of *The Old Way* and *The Harmless People*

"*Noble Savages* is Napoleon Chagnon's equal-time response to the libels that were piled upon him by reckless journalists and irresponsible colleagues. For those who followed the debate it is a welcome summary, and for those who did not it is a brilliant introduction to the innocent nobility of the fierce Yanomamö and the petty savagery of the mean-minded savants who saw their outworn ideologies under attack. Chagnon was always himself a fighter, and this book is his final knockout punch in a fight he didn't pick but has most assuredly won."

—Robin Fox, University Professor of Social Theory, Rutgers University, and author of *The Tribal Imagination: Civilization and the Savage Mind*

"Engaging. . . . A fascinating portrayal of the discomfort and danger that anthropologists working in remote areas face. The book is at its most entertaining when documenting the challenges of everyday life in the jungle—how to sleep fitfully in a hammock among enemies who might attempt to assassinate you in your sleep or how to net a juicy tapir for your dinner."

—Rachel Newcomb, *The Washington Post*

"[*Noble Savages*] stands out primarily for its portrayal of how science is done. . . . Chagnon's career has been opinionated, aggravating, courageous, intelligent, and marked by a rarely equalled commitment to the highest ideals of science. . . . Chagnon comes across as I have long thought of him: a cantankerous, brilliant, and noble scientist."

—Daniel L. Everett, *New Scientist*

"Fascinating reading for anyone interested in native peoples, history, and where we all came from."

—Curt Schleier, *The Seattle Times*

"This memoir, Chagnon's first book for a general audience, recounts with confident prose and self-effacing humor his intense immersion, from 1964 onward, within this fascinating people and their jungle environment. . . . In this invaluable book, Chagnon delivers a gripping adventure travelogue. His take on the corrupting relationship between politics and science is as likely to re-stoke the flames of debate as settle outstanding accounts."

—*Publishers Weekly*

"It's not hyperbole to call Chagnon the most controversial and famous anthropologist in America. . . . [*Noble Savages*] is a memoir that offers a highly readable mixture of adventure, science, and scandal."

—Nick Romeo, *Daily Beast*

"A hundred years from now, after the dust has settled, the case of renowned anthropologist Napoleon Chagnon will surely rank high in the annals of science for the systematic persecution of scientific conclusions. . . . Chagnon could arguably be considered the most influential anthropologist of all time."

—*Huffington Post*

ALSO BY NAPOLEON A. CHAGNON

Yanomamö: The Last Days of Eden

Yanomamö: The Fierce People

Studying the Yanomamö

NOBLE SAVAGES

My Life Among Two Dangerous Tribes—
the Yanomamö and the Anthropologists

NAPOLEON A. CHAGNON

SIMON & SCHUSTER PAPERBACKS

NEW YORK   LONDON   TORONTO   SYDNEY   NEW DELHI

Simon & Schuster Paperbacks
A Division of Simon & Schuster, Inc.
1230 Avenue of the Americas
New York, NY 10020

First Simon & Schuster paperback edition February 2014

SIMON & SCHUSTER PAPERBACKS and colophon are registered
trademarks of Simon & Schuster, Inc.

For information about special discounts for bulk purchases,
please contact Simon & Schuster Special Sales at
1-866-506-1949 or business@simonandschuster.com.

The Simon & Schuster Speakers Bureau can bring authors
to your live event. For more information or to book an event,
contact the Simon & Schuster Speakers Bureau at
1-866-248-3049 or visit our website at www.simonspeakers.com.

Designed by Ruth Lee-Mui
Maps by Paul J. Pugliese

Manufactured in the United States of America

1   3   5   7   9   10   8   6   4   2

The Library of Congress has cataloged the hardcover edition as follows:
Chagnon, Napoleon A., date.
Noble savages : my life among two dangerous tribes—the Yanomamö
and the anthropologists / Napoleon Chagnon.
p.   cm.
Includes bibliographical references and index.
1. Yanomamö Indians.   2. Sociobiology.   3. Human behavior.
4. Social evolution.   I. Title.
F2520.1.Y3.C49   2013
304.5—dc23   2012012413
ISBN 978-0-684-85510-3
ISBN 978-0-684-85511-0 (pbk)
ISBN 978-1-4516-1147-2 (ebook)

All photographs are courtesy of the author.

I dedicate this book to two biologists who have been my colleagues and friends for many years and whose view of life on earth—and how we go about explaining and understanding it—ultimately rests on the scientific method and on Darwin's theory of evolution by natural selection. They are

RICHARD D. ALEXANDER

of the University of Michigan, whose career was largely spent studying crickets, and

EDWARD O. WILSON

of Harvard University, whose career was largely spent studying ants.

But they both eventually applied their understanding of the principles of evolution by natural selection to humans and raised questions in my mind about my own profession, anthropology, the study of man. Anthropology had no meaningful answer to the fundamental question about the very subjects of their profession: Why are humans social?

That question cannot be answered by anthropology because it is a biological question. Anthropologists simply assume that it is "natural" to be social. But sociality is something that itself must be explained because not all animals are social.

Once a cultural anthropologist begins thinking about this question, he or she has taken the first bite of a forbidden fruit.

As I write these words, a new issue is reemerging over the level at which natural selection most effectively operates. In several recent publications, especially his 2012 book, *The Social Conquest of Earth*, E. O. Wilson has argued in favor of group selection, thus calling into question some of the most widely accepted views of Hamilton, Williams, Dawkins, Alexander, Trivers, and many others. He has provoked a major reaction by prominent theoreticians in evolutionary biology.

Contents

Introduction

In the Beginning

This is a book about the Yanomamö Indians and my lifelong study of them, particularly their culture, ecology, demography, and their social and political behavior. They were the last major tribe living free from interference of any government when I lived among them. Some of their 250 villages have yet to be visited by outsiders even today, but the number of such villages is dwindling.

The Yanomamö straddle the largely unexplored border between Venezuela and Brazil. Indeed, most of the time I lived among the Yanomamö these governments had very little information about them and paid them no attention.

Until the 1940s and 1950s the Yanomamö were largely unknown to the outside world because they were so isolated, difficult to reach, and lived in an unexplored pocket of the Amazon Basin. There were over twenty thousand of them living in some 250 different, small, independent villages but it took many years and many field trips for me to discover this. During my time among the Yanomamö the Venezuelan and Brazilian frontiers gradually expanded into the Yanomamö area and exploration by adventurers, explorers, missionaries, and a few anthropologists slowly began.

When I arrived among the Yanomamö in 1964, the Venezuelan government's only representation in this remote area was a handful of frontiersmen who worked for the Venezuelan malaria control service (Malarialogía). These men—many of Native Amazonian ancestry

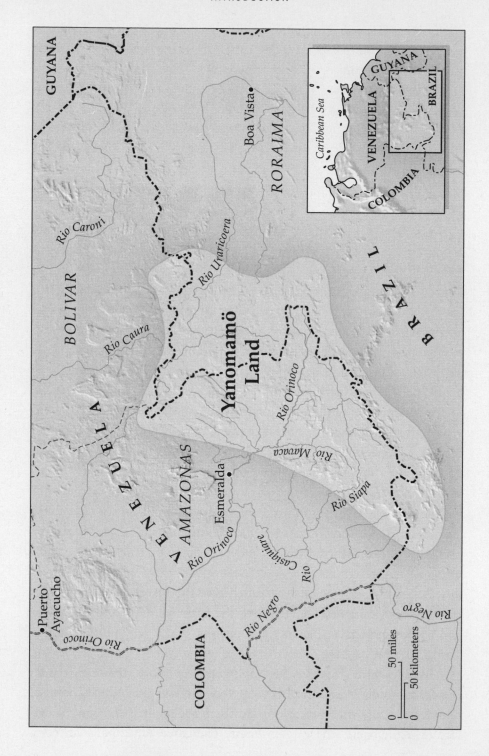

themselves—lived in tiny thatched huts with their wives and children and made very long canoe trips up small rivers to dispense antimalaria pills to the Yanomamö they would encounter.

Almost all the Yanomamö lived away from the larger rivers, so the initial contacts with them necessitated travel up smaller rivers and streams in native Ye'kwana dugout canoes, followed by walking deep into the interior. (The Ye'kwana are a different and neighboring native people.) It was this aspect of Yanomamö cultural geography that kept them isolated and uncontacted for so long and that explains why most of them were still demographically intact when I began studying them.

By 1964, when I arrived, members of a few Yanomamö villages had been attracted out to navigable stretches of some of the larger rivers in the southernmost portion of Venezuela and had settled next to the newly arrived mission groups who came to convert them to Christianity. There were other Yanomamö villages at various distances from these mission posts—a day's walk, two days' walk, or even several days' walk—whose members began visiting the newly contacted villages to see the strange foreigners from the outside world.

When I first arrived I made a small mud-and-thatch hut next to one of the recently contacted villages and started to learn the Yanomamö language. After a few months I began visiting the more remote villages, reaching them either by walking directly from my hut or by taking my small dugout canoe upstream via the smaller rivers and then walking inland from there.

Since that time I have spent some thirty-five years of my academic life studying the Yanomamö in the jungle and writing academic articles and books about them. Anthropologists normally have teaching appointments in colleges and universities. Most of us try to get back to the field at least once to revisit the tribesmen we originally studied for our doctoral research. The field research was the aspect of anthropology I most enjoyed because it was a constant process of discovery and learning. Thus I returned to the Yanomamö some twenty-five or so times over the course of my thirty-five-year research career and I ultimately spent a total of approximately five years living with them. The longest single stretch of time that I spent was my initial field trip, from November 1964 through March 1966, some seventeen months. Thereafter my trips were much shorter, usually two or three months at a time. A few trips were just a couple of weeks or so. I visited and lived among them during all months and seasons, but I preferred to take my field trips during the months of January through early April, the dry season, because travel through the jungle on foot was much easier and more comfortable.

My fieldwork entailed many adventures and risks not commonly encountered in typical anthropological field situations. Today most anthropologists can call home regularly, but I was completely isolated for months at a time with no contact with the outside world. My communication with the outside world was sporadic or, in some cases, not even possible, as when I went inland to visit the more remote villages. While I was at my hut at the mouth of the Mavaca River where it joined the Orinoco, I was able to take occasional trips downstream several hours to a Salesian mission post at the mouth of the Ocamo River and get brief messages out to my wife by shortwave radio. To do this I had to travel six hours in my canoe and stay overnight at the mission. Frequently there was no time left for me to talk to my wife because their contact in Caracas was only able to help them make phone contacts for an hour or so.

The Yanomamö were fascinating, wild, and very difficult to live with, especially when you were the only one of your kind in one of their isolated villages. At one of the three mission posts in Venezuela, at Mavaca, Platanal, and especially at Ocamo, where a few permanent mission personnel lived, they quickly learned to modify their habits and could be very cooperative and even charming in small numbers when visitors from Caracas and other cities occasionally visited the charismatic, jovial priest stationed there, an Italian named Padre Luigi Cocco.

I originally intended to do what most graduate students in anthropology do: spend about a year doing my doctoral research to collect data for my Ph.D. thesis, write it up, publish a few articles, maybe a book for the academic audience, and then do the routine and conventional thing by going back a few years later for a week's visit. That would be the topic of my second book: a popular book about my reflections on how their culture had lamentably changed for the worse since my first visit and how they were now being ruined by creeping civilization and increased contact with the "outside world."

But when I walked into my first Yanomamö village, I realized that

Some Earlier and Current Yanomamö Villages

BRAZIL

VENEZUELA

Padamo

Matacuni

• La Esmeralda

Rio Orinoco

• Mision Padamo

Ocamo

Ocamo •

Buuta

Parima B •

• Bisaasi-teri
Boca Mavaca •

Mahekodo-teri •

Haoyabö-wei

Platanal •

Koyowa-teri •

• Konata

Rio Orinoco

Parima Highlands Hashimo-teri •

• Aramamisi käkö

Patanowä-teri •

Shanishani

Kedebaböwei

Dorita-teri •

• Kreiböwei-teri

Washäwä

Konabuma-teri •

Rahuawä

Hasuböwa-teri •

Paruritawä-teri •

Iwahikoroba-teri •
Örata

Shimakäräba

Mavaca

Mishimishimaböwei-teri •

Siapa

• Doshamosha-teri

Siapa

Moota

• Abruwä-teri

BRAZIL

| 0 | 10 | 20 miles |
| 0 | 10 | 20 kilometers |

these were very special people and that I would have to spend a long time among them learning and documenting their social behavior, their population expansions and migrations, their oral history as the older people recalled it, and the many wars they had fought with their neighbors. The Yanomamö were one of the last remaining large tribes that were still locked in intervillage warfare, struggling to maintain their independence, security, and safety from the ever-possible unexpected attacks by their Yanomamö neighbors. They sometimes made a stand and fought, but other times they fled and settled in adjacent, unpopulated new areas that were safer, gradually moving outward from the center of their homeland.

I would be one of the last eyewitnesses to the political, social, and military struggles that repeatedly occurred among the Yanomamö while I lived with them, but I also learned about many more wars that had occurred in the recent and distant past. I discovered that over time their culture was getting more complex and their villages were growing larger and more cohesive. This process undoubtedly occurred many times in human history as tribal peoples elsewhere—Europe, Africa, the Middle East—made the transition from a hunting-and-gathering way of life to one based on agriculture. Each step they took in that direction made it more likely they would never revert back to how they lived in earlier times. These people were involved in a barely perceptible transition from "primitive" to "complex." This crucial transition is known only from historical archaeological studies in most parts of the world, but in the Yanomamö area I could actually detect and try to document it. This was the last chance for an anthropologist to observe this fascinating social and political transition that terminated with the development of the political state and "civilization."

That is why I decided very early in my fieldwork that I would have to go back repeatedly to continue documenting this rare event.

My initial fieldwork among the Yanomamö began in the mid-1960s when few Yanomamö had any enduring contact with the outside world. Today things are very different. A great deal of change has taken place. Latecomers denounce me because the Yanomamö they visit at Salesian or other missions today are not the same kinds of Yanomamö I first met. And anthropology itself has changed *politically*. It is now acceptable to denounce earlier anthropologists in the name of political advocacy of native rights and to deny what earlier anthropologists like me saw because this older image of the Yanomamö does not conform to what the activists want to see. I will discuss this important development in the final chapters of this book.

What I Discovered

The Ubiquity of Terror. We now live in a world where anxiety about terrorists and terrorism are facts of life in many countries, including the United States. We might think that this is something new in human history, an evil inflicted on us because civilization has broken down. Some might even lament the loss of pristine innocence and wish we could recapture some of the virtues that were lost when cultures became more complex and evolved into nations, empires, and industrialized states. We might even lament how good it would be if we could return to the innocent condition when people were Noble Savages as Jean-Jacques Rousseau and his followers imagined them.

Rousseau never used the phrase "noble savage" (or "the good savage," as it is sometimes translated) in his best known work, *The Social Contract* (1762), but the concept he described—that humans in the state of nature were blissful, nonviolent, altruistic, and noncompetitive and that people were generally "nice" to each other—was soon given that name.

One point I emphasize in this book is that our assumptions about the alleged social tranquility of the past may be idealistic and incorrect. Worse yet, these assumptions appear to be increasingly unsustainable the further back in time we go. Life in the societies of ancient past—the "Stone Age"—appears to have been decidedly uncertain and fraught with danger, mostly from neighboring peoples who seemed to be ever willing to fall upon you when you least expected it—and this possibility was never very long out of your mind. The distant past of humanity may have been more like what Thomas Hobbes had in mind, a life that was short, nasty, and brutish. Perhaps we might want to consider this possibility as we learn more about the nature of human life in a "state of nature."

Security. There are many "maximizing" theories in the social and biological sciences that argue about functions or ultimate purposes of institutions, human motivations, even life itself. In economics, for example, maximizing profit is one example and maximizing access to strategic material resources is another. In political philosophy it might be maximizing the greatest good for the largest number of people. In biology it might be maximizing reproductive survival.

I discovered that maximizing *political and personal security* was the overwhelming driving force in human social and cultural evolution. My observation is based not only on what we have thus far learned from political science and anthropological field reports, but also on a lifetime of experience living with native Amazonian tribesmen who chronically live in what Hobbes called in his major treatise, *Leviathan* (1651), a condition of war. He likened war to foul weather—not just a shower or two, but a persistent condition for extended periods of time, something chronic. The Yanomamö among whom I lived were constantly worried about attacks from their neighbors and constantly lived in fear of this possibility.

Neither Hobbes nor Rousseau ever saw people like Yanomamö tribesmen living in a "state of nature." Their philosophical positions about Man in a state of nature were derived entirely from speculation. It is therefore astonishing that some cultural anthropologists cling to the Noble Savage view of human nature when ours is the profession that collected almost all of the empirical data on tribesmen and what social life was like under "pristine" or "Stone Age" conditions. Thus anthropologists should be the most likely people to arrive at a highly informed, empirically defensible view of human nature using the evidence from generations of anthropological research.

But most anthropologists have never lived among people who are really primitive. Many learn about such people the same way the readers of this book do—by reading about them in the ethnographic reports written by the anthropologists who have actually lived among these people.

During most of my fieldwork the Yanomamö lived as close to the "state of nature" as one could in the twentieth century. I have chosen to call this book *Noble Savages* in part because the Yanomamö I lived among had a certain kind of nobility that most anthropologists rarely see in acculturated and depopulated tribes that have been defeated by and incorporated into the political states in whose jurisdiction they reside.

For many anthropologists who cling to Rousseau's view of mankind rather than Hobbes's, I am a heretic, a misanthrope, and the object of condemnation by politically correct colleagues, especially those who identify themselves as "activists" on behalf of native peoples because I describe the Yanomamö as I found them.

Sociality and the demographic facts of life. The ability to live cooperatively in social groups is not "natural" and therefore not something to be taken for granted or merely assumed. Rather, it is something that must be *explained*.

Not all organisms live permanently in socially organized groups. Why some do is a fascinating question, one that cannot be explained by the social sciences. It is a biological and evolutionary matter, so it falls outside the scope of this book, outside the scope of cultural anthropology. This does not mean, however, that anthropologists can ignore this question.

Several major theoretical breakthroughs in evolutionary theory occurred just prior to or during the time I began studying anthropology at the University of Michigan. One of these breakthroughs should have had a major impact on anthropological theory but, puzzlingly, it did not. The longtime reluctance of anthropological theoreticians and field researchers to take ideas from biology seriously was the most likely reason.

This breakthrough in theoretical biology consisted of a pair of papers that William D. Hamilton, an English biologist, published in 1964 in the *Journal of Theoretical Biology*, a journal that most anthropologists were not familiar with and did not read. But Hamilton's papers quickly entered the more general literature in biology and evolution and at least some scientific anthropologists who were prominent in the profession should have recognized their importance for understanding the frequently noted amity and favoritism characteristically found in kinship interactions among tribesmen in a kinship-dominated society. In a very real sense, these "kinship behaviors" were in fact *reproductive* behaviors.

Hamilton called his new concept "inclusive fitness," but it is now generally known as "kin selection" in today's literature. His general argument was that since related individuals share genes with each other, an individual could get copies of his or her genes into the next generation by favoring close kinsmen and not reproducing sexually at all. For example, individuals share on average half (50 percent) of their genes with their siblings, they share one-fourth (25 percent) with their half-siblings, an eighth (12.5 percent) with their full cousins, etc. Thus if they engage in certain kinds of "favors" that enhance a full cousin's reproductive success, then, to the extent that those favors enabled that kinsman to find a mate and produce offspring, their favoring of that kinsman helped them to get some of *their own* genes into the next generation. As one theoretical geneticist, J. B. S. Haldane, is rumored to have said: "I'd lay down my life for eight cousins. . . ." That's because eight cousins would carry, on average, 100 percent of the genes that the person who laid down his life carried.

This oversight in anthropology is all the more astonishing in view of the fact that much of the first one hundred years of anthropology as an emerging academic and putatively scientific discipline was given over to discussions of the important role that kinship and the "meaning" of kinship played in the formation of that discipline. Accordingly, I will include here some of the relevant demographic facts of Yanomamö life and show how these relate to their struggles to maximize political security. It is easy to get along with your neighbors when there are only a few dozen of them in your band or village and most of them are close kin—brothers and sisters, or dependent juveniles like your children, nephews, and nieces. But it is not so easy to get along when your village grows to be several hundred people and includes people whose kinship ties are increasingly remote—second and third cousins, or strangers who join the village. Arguments and fights then become chronic. Some people have to leave and form their own new, tiny communities because the only rules of cooperation and social amity are kinship rules, and kinship rules cannot maintain social order in large groups.

Large, politically complex societies emerged only after—or as a consequence of—the replacement of kinship institutions and nepotism by other institutions, by what Hobbes called the power that keeps men in awe, namely, the political state and law. That is also why almost all early anthropologists were lawyers or were interested in the development of law from vague customs. They were appropriately astonished by the obvious fact that most of the peoples in the newly discovered worlds of central Africa, Polynesia, Melanesia, Australia, and the Americas lacked what we have come to know as the political state and the law.

But what if when you move there are other people "over there" who don't want new neighbors and who oppose you with violence and threats of violence? This is the problem the Yanomamö face, as have human communities throughout our history. Thus the presence of potentially hostile neighbors inhibits village fissioning, keeping people at home where disputes and arguments increase, but also helping the village to survive as a group in a political situation where an advantage in village size—larger villages are more secure than smaller ones—is valuable whenever other groups are a constant threat.

Leadership and social cohesion. The internal cohesion of a small group of co-resident kinsmen derives mainly from rules, obligations, and expectations about kinship. But as the group increases in size from, say 40 to 80 people, the role that political leaders (headmen) must play in keeping order increases. Since the headmen come from the largest kinship group, most of their "subjects" are blood relatives and their tasks are relatively easy. The tasks become more difficult as village sizes get larger—150 people or so—and headmen must then become more insistent in their injunctions and begin to use threats and physical coercion to maintain order and peace within the group. When villages get even larger, say 200 people, headmen can become oppressive and tyrannical. Some of the Yanomamö villages I lived in contained close to 300 people and one group contained nearly 400 people immediately before I first visited them. The political leaders in these villages were extremely harsh men, and I shall describe some of their activities and characteristics in the pages that follow.

Political evolution. It is unusual—and perhaps even unwise—for an anthropologist to attempt to relate his own ethnographic fieldwork to broader issues like the evolution of political society. Part of the reason is that a study of a specific culture like the Yanomamö Indians represents just a single example in a much larger set of existing ethnographic examples that, collectively, compose the larger picture. However, I would argue that there are two general exceptions to this rule. The first is that selected data from specific ethnographic studies like mine are often (and legitimately) used in traditional anthropology to inform general theoretical issues and guide further research in many other cultures. The second exception is that some tribal societies are larger, include multiple communities, and therefore this larger sample of villages of the same tribe can indicate probable cultural evolutionary trends. Variations found in these villages strongly suggest how socially adaptive features within the larger sample of communities might logically lead toward increased social and political complexity. Thus the relatively small but distinctive differences among the wider spectrum of Yanomamö villages I have studied can plausibly be interpreted as "micro-evolutionary" changes toward greater social and political complexity in a relatively unacculturated, multi-village, large tribal society.

The key variables and causal factors among the Yanomamö that I am referring to include:

1. Isolation and independence from political states
2. Demographic integrity—a "healthy" age/sex distribution with continuing population growth
3. Geographic and ecological features that provide both constraints on and opportunities for political change
4. Multiple villages that show political and social differences that correlate with local group size, ecological features of their landscape, and the "personality" characteristics of charismatic leaders
5. The chronic threat of lethal attacks from other groups

The Yanomamö I studied seem to have made a few halting steps toward greater social complexity in what I describe as the fertile crescent region of Yanomamöland (chapter 11). Understanding how and why larger, more complexly organized Yanomamö villages came into existence from smaller, less complexly organized villages will shed light on how some of the first steps toward the political state may have been taken by many other tribesmen and, I hope, this will improve our understanding of the evolution of cultural and social complexity in general.

I have written, co-authored, or co-edited five books, some one hundred articles, and some twenty-one documentary films, most of them about specific and technical aspects of Yanomamö culture, demography, and social behavior. Few of my publications were intended for the general public, such as my several contributions to the *National Geographic* and *Natural History* magazines.

This book is my first publication on the Yanomamö for a wider, more general reading audience. While it contains many of the facts and incidents I have discussed elsewhere in technical publications, especially in my college-level monograph, they are presented here in a less technical and, I hope, more easily comprehensible way. Some of the information presented here has never been published before, such as data on female sexuality, infanticide, and statistical aspects of the abductions of females.

Visitors at a feast, dancing for their hosts

1

Culture Shock

My First Year in the Field

The First Day

My first day in the field—November 28, 1964—was an experience I'll never forget. I had never seen so much green snot before then. Not many anthropologists spend their first day this way. If they did, there would be very few applicants to graduate programs in anthropology.

I had traveled in a small aluminum rowboat propelled by a large outboard motor for two and a half days, cramped in with several extra fifty-five-gallon gasoline barrels and two Venezuelan functionaries who worked for the Malarialogía, the Venezuelan malaria control service. They were headed to their tiny outpost in Yanomamö territory—two or three thatched huts. This boat trip took me from the territorial capital, Puerto Ayacucho, a small town on the Orinoco River, into Yanomamö country on the High Orinoco some 350 miles upstream. I was making a quick trip to have a look-see before I brought my main supplies and equipment for a seventeen-month study of the Yanomamö Indians, a Venezuelan tribe that was very poorly known in 1964. Most of their villages had no contact with the outside world and were considered to be "wild" Indians. I also wanted to see how things at the field site would be for my wife, Carlene, and two young children, Darius (three years old) and Lisa (eighteen months old).

On the morning of the third day we reached a small mission settlement called Tama Tama, the field "headquarters" of a group of mostly American evangelical missionaries, the New Tribes Mission, who were working in two Yanomamö villages farther upstream and in several villages of the Carib-speaking Ye'kwana, a different tribe located northwest of the Yanomamö. The missionaries had come out of these remote Indian villages to hold a conference on the progress of their mission work and were conducting their meetings at Tama Tama when I arrived. Tama Tama was about a half day by motorized dugout canoe downstream from where the Yanomamö territory began.

We picked up a passenger at Tama Tama, James P. Barker, the first outsider to make a sustained, permanent contact with the Venezuelan Yanomamö in 1950. He had just returned from a year's furlough in the United States, where I had briefly visited him in Chicago before we both left for Venezuela. As luck would have it, we both arrived in Venezuela at about the same time, and in Yanomamö territory the same week. He was a bit surprised to see me and happily agreed to accompany me to the village I had selected (with his advice) for my base of operations, Bisaasi-teri, and to introduce me to the Indians. I later learned that *bisaasi* was the name of the palm whose leaves were used in the large roofs of many Yanomamö villages: *-teri* is the Yanomamö word that means "village." Bisaasi-teri was also his own home base, but he had not been there for over a year and did not plan to come back permanently for another three months. He therefore welcomed this unexpected opportunity to make a quick overnight visit before he returned permanently.

Barker had been living with this particular Yanomamö group about four years at that time. Bisaasi-teri had divided into two villages when the village moved to the mouth of the Mavaca River, where it flows into the Orinoco from the south. One group was downstream and was called Lower Bisaasi-teri (*koro-teri*) and the other was upstream and called Upper Bisaasi-teri (*ora-teri*). Barker lived among the Upper Bisaasi-teri. His mud-and-thatch house was located next to their village.

Left to right: James V. Neel, Napoleon Chagnon, and James P. Barker, 1966

We arrived at Upper Bisaasi-teri about 2 P.M. and docked the aluminum speedboat along the muddy riverbank at the terminus of the path
used by the Indians to fetch their drinking water. The Yanomamö normally avoid large rivers like the Orinoco, but they moved there because
Barker had persuaded them to. The settlement was called, in Spanish,
by the men of the Malarialogía and the missionaries, Boca Mavaca—the
Mouth of the Mavaca. It sometimes appeared on Venezuelan maps of
that era as Yababuji—a Yanomamö word that translates as "Gimme!"
This name was apparently—and puckishly—suggested to the mapmakers
because it captured some essence of the place: "Gimme" was the most
frequent phrase used by the Yanomamö when they greeted visitors to the
area.

My ears were ringing from three dawn-to-dusk days of the constant
drone of the outboard motor. It was hot and muggy, and my clothing was
soaked with perspiration, as it would be for the next seventeen months.
Small biting gnats, *bareto* in the Yanomamö language, were out in as-
tronomical numbers, for November was the beginning of the dry season
and the dry season means lots of *bareto*. Clouds of them were so dense

in some places that you had to be careful when you breathed lest you inhale some of them. My face and hands were swollen from their numerous stings.

In just a few moments I was to meet my first Yanomamö, my first "primitive" man. What would he be like? I had visions of proudly entering the village and seeing 125 "social facts" running about, altruistically calling each other kinship terms and sharing food, each courteously waiting to have me interview them and, perhaps, collect his genealogy.

Would they like me? This was extremely important to me. I wanted them to be so fond of me that they would adopt me into their kinship system and way of life. During my anthropological training at the University of Michigan I learned that successful anthropologists *always* get adopted by *their* people. It was something very special. I had also learned during my seven years of anthropological training that the "kinship system" was equivalent to "the whole society" in primitive tribes and that it was a moral way of life. I was determined to earn my way into their moral system of kinship and become a member of their society—to be accepted by them and adopted as one of them.

The year of fieldwork ahead of me was what earned you your badge of authority as an anthropologist, a testimony to your otherworldly experience, your academic passport, your professional credentials. I was now standing at the very cusp of that profound, solemn transformation and I truly savored this moment.

My heart began to pound as we approached the village and heard the buzz of activity within the circular compound. Barker commented that he was anxious to see if any changes had taken place while he was away, especially how many Yanomamö died during his absence. I found this somewhat macabre, but I later came to understand why this was an important concern: among the Yanomamö it is offensive—and sometimes dangerous—to say the name of a dead person in the presence of his close relatives, so it is important to know beforehand, if possible, who is no longer living to avoid asking about them.

I nervously felt my back pocket to make sure that my nearly blank field notebook was still there, and I felt more secure when I touched it.

The village looked like some large, nearly vertical wall of leaves from the outside. The Yanomamö call it a *shabono*. The several entrances were covered over with brush and dry palm leaves. Barker and I entered the opening that led to the river. I pushed the brush aside to expose the low opening into the village.

The excitement of meeting my first Yanomamö was almost unbearable as I crouched and duck-waddled through the low passage into the open, wide village plaza. I looked up and gasped in shock when I saw a dozen burly, naked, sweaty, hideous men nervously staring at us down the shafts of their drawn arrows! Immense wads of green tobacco were stuck between their lower teeth and lips, making them look even more hideous. Strands of dark green snot dripped or hung from their nostrils—strands so long that they drizzled from their chins down to their pectoral muscles and oozed lazily across their bellies, blending into their red paint and sweat.

We had arrived at the village while the men were blowing a greenish powder, a hallucinogenic drug called *ebene*, up each other's noses through yard-long hollow tubes. The Yanomamö blow it with such force that gobs of it spurt out of the opposite nostril of the person inhaling. One of the side effects of the hallucinogen is a profusely runny nose,

Green nasal mucus laden with hallucinogenic *hisiomö* snuff powder

hacking and choking, and sometimes vomiting. The nasal mucus is always saturated with the green powder, and the men usually let it run freely from their nostrils.

My next discovery was that there were a dozen or so vicious, underfed growling dogs snapping at my legs, circling me as if I were to be their next meal. I stood there holding my notebook, helpless and pathetic. Then the stench of the decaying vegetation, dog feces, and garbage hit me and I almost got sick.

I was shocked and horrified. What kind of welcome was this for the person who came here to live with you and learn your way of life, to become friends with you, to be adopted by you? The Yanomamö put their weapons down when they recognized and welcomed Barker and returned to their chanting, keeping a nervous eye on the village entrances.

We had arrived just after a serious fight. Seven of the women from this *shabono* had been abducted the day before by a neighboring group, and the local men and their guests had just that morning recovered five of them in a brutal club fight that nearly ended in a shooting war with arrows. The neighboring abductors, now angry because they had just lost five of their seven new female captives, had threatened to raid the Bisaasi-teri and kill them with arrows. When Barker and I arrived and entered the village unexpectedly, they suspected or assumed that we were the raiders.

On several occasions during the next two hours the men jumped to their feet, armed themselves, nocked their arrows, ran to the several entrances, and waited nervously for the noise outside the village to be identified. My enthusiasm for collecting ethnographic facts and esoteric kinship data diminished in proportion to the number of times such an alarm was raised. In fact, I was relieved when Barker suggested that we sleep across the river for the evening, adding "because it would be safer over there." I disconsolately mumbled to myself, "Christ! What have I gotten myself into here?"

As we walked down the path to the boat, I pondered the wisdom of having decided to spend a year and a half with these people before I had even seen what they were like. I am not ashamed to admit that had there been a diplomatic way out, I would have ended my fieldwork then and there. I did not look forward to the next day—and months—when I would be alone with these people. I did not speak a word of their language, and they spoke only their own language. Only a few of the young men knew a handful of words in Spanish—not enough to utter even a short comprehensible sentence.

The Yanomamö were decidedly different from what I had imagined them to be in my Rousseauian daydreams. The whole situation was depressing, and I wondered why, after entering college, I had ever decided to switch my major to anthropology from physics and engineering in the first place. I had not eaten all day, I was soaking wet from perspiration, the *bareto* were biting me, and I was covered with snot-laden red pigment, the result of a dozen or so complete examinations I had been given by as many very pushy, sweaty Yanomamö men.

These examinations capped an otherwise grim and discouraging day. The naked men would blow their noses into their hands, flick as much of the green mucus off as they could in a snap of the wrist, wipe the residue into their hair, and then carefully examine my face, beard, arms, legs, hair, and the contents of my pockets. I asked Barker how to say, "Don't do that. Your hands are dirty." My admonitions were met by the grinning Yanomamö in the following way: They would "wash" their hands by spitting a quantity of slimy tobacco juice into them, rub them together, wipe them into their hair, grin, and then proceed with the examination with "clean" hands.

Barker and I crossed the river, carried our packs up the bank, and slung our hammocks in one of the thatched huts belonging to a Malarialogía employee. When Barker pulled his hammock out of a rubber bag, a heavy, damp, disagreeable odor of mildewed cotton and stale wood smoke wafted out with it. Even the missionaries are filthy, I thought to myself. But within two weeks, everything I owned smelled the same way, and I lived with that odor for the remainder of my fieldwork. My several field hammocks *still* smell faintly like that—many years after my last trip to the Yanomamö and after many times through a washing machine.

After I had adjusted to the circumstances, my own habits of personal cleanliness declined to such levels that I didn't protest anymore while being examined by the Yanomamö, as I was not much cleaner than they were. I also realized that it is exceptionally difficult to blow your nose gracefully when you are stark naked and the invention of tissues and handkerchiefs is still millennia away.

I was now facing the disappointing consequences of what, at the time, was a logical conclusion to a sequence of decisions I had made in college. When I had decided to study anthropology, I had to pick a specialization within it. I chose cultural anthropology. The next choice was to pick some kind of society—tribesmen, peasants, or industrialized existing cultures. I picked unknown tribesmen, which limited the parts of the world I could study: there are no unknown tribesmen, for example, in the United States, so I would have to consider more remote places. One of the possible places was South America, and there most of the unknown tribesmen were in the Amazon Basin.

So, here I was, my blank notebook in hand, preparing to dig in for seventeen more months of fieldwork. I was the proverbial blank slate incarnate.

My Life in the Jungle

It isn't easy to plop down in the Amazon Basin for seventeen months and get immediately into the anthropological swing of things. You have been told or read about quicksand, horrible diseases, snakes, jaguars, vampire bats, electric eels, little spiny fish that will swim into your penis, and getting lost. Most of the dangers—diseases, snakes, jaguars, spiny fish, eels, getting lost—are indeed real, but your imagination makes them more ominous and threatening than many of them really are.

Most normal people have no idea how many of the simple things in life just do not exist in the field—something as simple as a flat surface to write on or put your coffee cup on. What my anthropology professors never bothered to tell me about was the mundane, unexciting, and trivial stuff—like eating, defecating, sleeping, or keeping clean. This, I began to suspect, was because very few of my professors had done fieldwork in uncomfortable circumstances remotely similar to what I now faced. These circumstances turned out to be the bane of my existence during the first several months of field research. After that they became merely the unavoidable, inconvenient, but routine conditions of the life of a fieldworking anthropologist who unwittingly and somewhat naively decided to study the most remote, primitive tribe he could find.

I initially set up my household in Barker's vacant mud-and-thatch house, some thirty yards from Bisaasi-teri, and immediately set to work building my own mud-walled, thatched-roof hut with the help of the Yanomamö. Meanwhile, I had to eat and try to do my field research.

I soon discovered that it was an enormously time-consuming task to maintain my hygiene in the manner to which I had grown accustomed in the relatively antiseptic environment of the northern United States. Either I could be relatively well fed and relatively comfortable in a fresh change of clothes—and do very little fieldwork—or I could do considerably more fieldwork and be less well fed and less comfortable.

I quickly learned how complicated it can be to make a simple bowl of oatmeal in the jungle. First, I had to make two trips to the river to haul my water for the day. Next, I had to prime my kerosene stove with alcohol to get it burning, a tricky procedure when you are trying to mix powdered milk and fill a coffeepot with water at the same time. My alcohol prime always burned out before I could turn on the kerosene, and I would have to start all over. Or I would turn on the kerosene, optimistically hoping that the stove element was still hot enough to vaporize the fuel, and start a small fire in my palm-thatched hut as the liquid kerosene squirted all over my makeshift table and mud walls and *then* ignited. Many amused Yanomamö onlookers quickly learned the English expletive *Oh shit!* They actually got very good at predicting when I would say this: if something went wrong and I had a clumsy accident, they would shout in unison: "Say 'Oh shit!' " (*Oh Shit a da kuu!*) Later, and once they discovered that the phrase irritated the New Tribes missionaries, the Yanomamö used it as often as they could in the missionaries' presence, or, worse yet, mischievously instructed the missionaries to say "Oh shit!" whenever they also had a mishap.

I usually had to start over with the alcohol prime. Then I had to boil the oatmeal and pick the bugs out of it. All my supplies were carefully stored in rat-proof, moisture-proof, and insect-proof containers, not one of which ever served its purpose adequately. Just taking things out of the multiplicity of containers and repacking them afterward was a minor project in itself. By the time I had hauled the water to cook with, un-

Medium-size village on the banks of the Siapa River

packed my food, prepared the oatmeal, powdered milk, and coffee, heated water for dishes, washed and dried the dishes, repacked the food in the containers, stored the containers in locked trunks, and cleaned up my mess, the ceremony of preparing breakfast had brought me almost up to lunchtime!

I soon decided that eating three meals a day was simply out of the question. I solved the problem by eating a single meal that could be prepared in a single container, or, at most, in two containers; washed my few dishes only when there were no clean ones left, using cold river water; and wore each change of clothing at least a week to cut down on my laundry, a courageous undertaking in the tropics. I reeked like a smoked jockstrap left to mildew in the bottom of a dark gym locker. I also became less concerned about sharing my provisions with the rats, insects, Yano-mamö, and the elements, thereby reducing the complexity of my storage system. I was able to last most of the day on *café con leche*—heavily sugared espresso coffee diluted about five to one with hot milk reconstituted from powder. I would prepare this beverage in the evening and store it in a large thermos. Frequently, my single meal was no more complicated than a can of sardines and a package of salted crackers with peanut but-

A small village in a remote area

ter. But at least two or three times a week I would do something "special" and sophisticated, like make a batch of oatmeal or boil rice and add a can of tuna fish and tomato paste to it. I also ate a lot of food that I obtained from the Yanomamö—especially bananas, plantains, and potato-like tubers—by trading fishhooks and nylon fishing line.

As to recurrent personal needs let me just say that the Yanomamö have not yet worked out a suitable sewage system. Barker mentioned to me on the first day that people just go off a ways into the jungle to do number two, and to watch where I stepped. "If you run into some of it you'll probably run into a lot of it," he added. The environs immediately surrounding a Yanomamö village of two hundred people are a hazardous place to take an idle stroll. We've all been on camping trips, but imagine the hygienic consequences of camping for about three years in the same small place with two hundred companions without sewers, running water, or garbage collection, and you get a sense of what daily life is like among the Yanomamö. And what it was like for much of human history, for that matter.

I barely recall these things now. They come to mind only when I read over old notes taken in the early days of my fieldwork, or the early letters

I wrote to my wife from the field. They also come to mind when I take out one of my old, smoky field hammocks to string between two trees in my yard.

Beginning to Doubt Some Anthropological Truths

There were two things I learned that first day that would dominate much of my field research life for the next thirty-five years.

The first discovery was that "native warfare" was not simply some neutral item on an anthropological trait list, equivalent to other traits like "they make baskets with vines" or "the kinship system is the bifurcate-merging type." Among the Yanomamö native warfare was not just occasional or sporadic but was a *chronic* threat, lurking and threatening to disrupt communities at any moment. The larger the community of people, the more one could sense its foreboding presence.

Warfare and the threat of warfare permeated almost all aspects of Yanomamö social life: politics, visits between villages, tensions among people, feasts, trading, daily routines, village size, and even where new villages were established when larger communities subdivided, a process I called village fissioning. This martial condition is not often discussed in the anthropological literature because there were few places in the world where populations of tribesmen were still growing by reproducing offspring faster than people were dying and were fighting with each other in complete independence of nation states that surrounded them. Yanomamö history is a history of wars, as Karl Marx claimed of the history of all peoples.

The second discovery I made that first day was that most Yanomamö arguments and fights started over women. This straightforward ethnographic observation would cause me a great deal of academic grief because in the 1960s "fighting over women" was considered a controversial explanation in "scientific" anthropology. The most scientific anthropological theory of primitive war of the 1960s held that tribesmen, just like members of industrialized nations, fought only over scarce *material* resources—food, oil, land, water supplies, seaports, wealth, etc. For an anthropologist to suggest that fighting had something to do with women, that is, with sex and reproductive competition, was tantamount to blasphemy, or at best ludicrous. Biologists, on the other hand, found this observation not only unsurprising, but normal for a sexually reproducing species. What they *did* find surprising was that anthropologists regarded fighting over reproductive competition as ludicrous when applied to humans. Competition among males vying for females was, after all, widespread in the animal world.

I was stunned by the reaction to this finding by some of the most famous anthropologists of the day. There was immediate and serious professional opposition to my rather innocent description of the facts when I published them in 1966 in my doctoral thesis. I was still wet behind my ears in an academic sense, and found myself, at the ripe age of twenty-eight, already controversial for saying that the Yanomamö, a large, multivillage Amazonian tribe, fought a great deal over women and marital infidelity.

That's when I started to become skeptical about what senior members of my profession said about the primitive world. I began suspecting that

Young, beautiful *moko dude* (post-pubescent girl)

senior anthropologists believed that it was their solemn responsibility to "interpret" for the rest of the world what they regarded as the recondite meanings of the customs of other cultures.

In other words, what I didn't know then was that if some serious, well-trained anthropologist who spent more than a year living in the midst of a warring tribe reported that much of the fighting he witnessed was "over women," that is, was rooted in reproductive competition, then such an informed conclusion opened the possibility that human warfare had as much to do with the evolved nature of man as it did with what one learned and acquired from one's culture. Most anthropologists, by contrast, believed that warfare and fighting was *entirely* determined by culture. My fieldwork raised the anthropologically disagreeable possibility that human nature was also driven by an evolved human biology. This idea was extremely controversial in the 1960s and angered many cultural anthropologists.

Thus, my very first published statements and descriptions of Yanomamö violence would constitute an allegedly dangerous challenge to the received wisdom of many senior cultural anthropologists. More immediately worrisome for me was that some of the most prominent of these anthropologists were my own teachers at the University of Michigan and several of them would serve on my doctoral committee.

The Intellectual and Political Climate of the 1960s

It is a truly curious and remarkable characteristic of cultural anthropology, as distinct from other subfields of anthropology, that any time native people are said to do something risky for reasons other than "maximizing access to material resources," leading figures in the profession grow uneasy and suspicious. One well-known cultural anthropologist—an Englishman named Ashley Montagu—wrote angry book-length rebuttals whenever someone prominent made such a claim. He seemed convinced that people might get the wrong impression that biological factors help explain what humans do, or, worse yet, that humans might have something called "human nature" as distinct from a purely *cultural* nature or, more precisely, that their behavioral characteristics might have evolved by some natural process, such as what Darwin called "natural selection."

My career began with the uneasy feeling that cultural anthropology was one of the last bastions of opposition to Darwin's theory of evolution by natural selection. The University of Michigan's anthropology department was, however, the major center of the Theory of Cultural Evolution, whose proponents distinguished it sharply from biological evolution or organic evolution, that is, the evolution of biological organisms.

The standard, almost solemn, epistemological position in cultural anthropology when I was in graduate school was that humans have only a cultural nature. Thus, our physical or biological characteristics as an evolved primate are irrelevant to whatever we do as members of society. The biological properties of humans, as my professors taught me, have to be factored out of any anthropological explanation of what we do.

Among my professors were Leslie A. White, Elman R. Service, Marshall D. Sahlins, Eric R. Wolf, and Morton H. Fried, who were among the most prominent cultural anthropologists of the day and important architects of the anthropological view I have just described.

Anthropology by definition is the science of man. Isn't it strange that this science factors out its central subject's biology in pursuit of understanding its subject?

This rather odd but axiomatic view has deep—and widespread—roots in several of the social sciences, sociology and anthropology in particular. Briefly put, the distinguished nineteenth-century French sociologist Emile Durkheim struggled to establish a "science of society" (what today we call sociology) at a time when it was intricately bound up and intertwined with psychology and social psychology. He felt that there were irreducible facts that were purely and exclusively social in nature and could be studied in their own right, divorced from any psychological and/or biological attributes of the human organisms whose activities were the subject of study. The study of these facts, he argued, deserved to have its own science.

A similar rebellion occurred in cultural anthropology, beginning with the efforts of Herbert Spencer and perhaps culminating in the works of Leslie A. White, one of my major professors, and, later, Marvin Harris, who would become one of my most outspoken critics. White and Harris spent their lifetimes trying to create a "science of culture" ("Culturology" as Leslie White called it: the study of cultural facts). And, like Durkheim before them, they insisted that the biological aspects of human beings were not relevant to "the culture process."

My observation that Yanomamö men fought mostly over women, and, equally important, that these conflicts and their outcomes had important consequences for understanding Yanomamö culture and society, disturbed some of my fellow cultural anthropologists. Why? As I look back on the history of my research, I was saying not just one, but two things that deeply concerned these anthropologists and that were considered to be controversial at the time.

The first was that warfare was common among the Yanomamö and that it was apparently not caused by capitalist exploitation, nor was it a reaction to oppression by Western colonial powers. This raised the possibility that warfare was, in a sense, a "natural" or "predictable" condition among tribesmen who had not been exposed to or corrupted by capitalistic, industrialized, and/or colonial cultures.

The second possibility my research raised was that lethal conflicts between groups might not be explicable by citing "shortages of scarce strategic material resources," considered by anthropologists and other social scientists to be the only legitimate "scientific" reason for human conflict and warfare.

On my return to Ann Arbor in 1966 from my first field trip, a University of Michigan professor, Norma Diamond, invited me to give a lecture in her large introductory class. I spoke about my field research and how important warfare was in Yanomamö culture. The students were fascinated. After my lecture Diamond thanked me for my presentation in front of her class. But, as we walked back to the Anthropology Department, she cautioned me: "You shouldn't say things like that. People will get the wrong impression." When I asked her what she meant, she added: "About warfare. We shouldn't say that native people have warfare and kill each other. People will get the wrong impression."

When I reported in one of my first articles that the Yanomamö fought a great deal over women, one prominent anthropologist, David Schneider, then at the University of Chicago, wrote a sarcastic letter to me that said something to the effect, Fighting over women? Gold and diamonds I can understand. But women? Never! And, as a last-minute addendum to a major book he was about to publish on the history of anthropological theory, prominent anthropologist Marvin Harris described my 1966 doctoral dissertation as giving credence to "the more lurid speculations" of John McLennan, a nineteenth-century Scottish anthropologist and jurist who wrote a book about primitive marriage and viewed "marriage by capture" as a "primitive stage" in human social history. I would ultimately debate this issue with Harris from 1968 until his death in 2001. Several of his disciples try to carry on this debate—or some version of it—today. Harris defended a Marxist "cultural materialist deterministic" anthropological view, while I was among a small minority of anthropologists struggling to develop a more Darwinian, more evolutionary view of human behavior. I saw no difficulty in incorporating both views into a comprehensive theory of human behavior, but Harris (and many other anthropologists) adamantly insisted that a scientific theory of human behavior had no room for ideas from biology, reproductive competition, and evolutionary theory. Many of these anthropologists argued that cultures and societies were not merely *analogous* to living, sexually reproducing organisms, but were *homologous* with them and therefore interchangeable in Darwin's theory of evolution by natural selection. Biologists found this argument implausible and unpersuasive. One of the participants in this long debate who held to the biological point of view asked his opponent in exasperation: "Does your piano menstruate?"

Ironically, Harris and I both argued for a *scientific view* of human behavior at a time when increasing numbers of anthropologists were becoming skeptical of the scientific approach and were even antiscientific. However, Harris was adamantly opposed to a Darwinian perspective on human behavior—which I thought was itself an antiscientific view.

During the weeks, months, and years I spent among the Yanomamö I began to explore and document their lives in statistical and demographic ways—and my doubts about much of what I had learned about anthropology from my professors only grew.

One lesson that I eventually learned from the history of my own anthropological research and the controversies it caused was that cultural anthropology did not fit a traditional scientific definition where facts are established by observations that are verified by others to establish patterns and, if empirical observations by others do not verify the original observations, then efforts must be made to account for the differences in the observations. Instead, anthropology is more like a religion. Indeed, the organizational and intellectual structure of a large fraction of cultural anthropology is best understood if viewed as an academic fraternity that intimidates and suppresses dissent, usually by declaring that the dissenter is guilty of conduct that is unethical, immoral—or Darwinian.

Many cultural anthropologists today are afraid to make even timid challenges to this authority and are very careful to describe their findings in cautiously chosen words that are frequently vague so as not to give people "the wrong impression" or, more important, not to invite the suspicion or condemnation of the ayatollahs of anthropology, the Thought Police who guard the received wisdoms.

How I Chose to Study the Yanomamö

The Yanomamö were not my initial choice for fieldwork. I wanted to study a newly contacted tribe in the central Brazilian highlands, a group called the Suyá, one of several tribes whose members spoke a native language belonging to the Gê language family. I did the necessary library research to write a grant proposal and focused on several of the then-timely theoretical problems in anthropology. I applied for and was awarded a National Institute of Mental Health research grant on the basis of this proposal, a small grant that would cover my travel and living expenses for one year.

Unfortunately, a few weeks after I learned that my NIMH grant was awarded, the Brazilian military overthrew the democratically elected government. From talking with experienced field researchers who had worked in the Amazon area I learned that it was a bad idea to try to get anything done in a country that had just undergone a military coup. Furthermore, it might even be dangerous to try to get into some areas of the country.

I decided to pick a different tribe in a different country, ideally a tribe that straddled the border between two countries. I figured that if one of the countries had a revolution, I might be able to get into the *same* tribe from the *other* country and continue my fieldwork there. Hence, the Yanomamö, who live in Venezuela and Brazil.

Human Genetics

About the time I was doing the library research for my NIMH proposal on the Suyá tribe, I made an appointment to meet with Dr. James V. Neel, head of the University of Michigan Medical School's Department of Human Genetics. Neel was the founder and the chairman of that department and an internationally prominent figure in human genetics. He and several of his colleagues, Dr. William J. Schull in particular, had studied the long-term genetic effects on survivors of the atomic bombings of Hiroshima and Nagasaki. Also, Neel had collaborated in the field with Dr. Frank Livingston, who was now on the faculty in the Anthropology Department and one of my teachers. Their study focused on several native African tribes and the phenomenon of sickle-cell anemia.

I was more intrigued by some of Neel's recent research among the Xavante (Shavante) Indians in collaboration with anthropologists, in particular, David Maybury-Lewis. The Xavante were a Brazilian tribe in the Gê-speaking language group located close to the area where I intended to study the Suyá tribe. I was interested in learning whether Neel would consider a similar collaboration with me after I had lived with the Suyá for a year or so. Many of my own anthropological interests were compatible with and even overlapped extensively with his—genealogies, marriage patterns, demographic patterns, and the social organization of reproduction. His interest in these topics was medical, while mine was anthropological and behavioral. For example, Neel wanted to know the amount of genetic variation that existed between tribes and, more important, between communities of the same tribe, a scientific question that was just starting to be explored in the mid-1960s as human geneticists and anthropologists began to document in a more sophisticated and comprehensive way the extent of human variability by using newly discovered genetic markers in, especially, easily collected blood samples.

I had taken human genetics courses in the Anthropology Department from James Spuhler, whose graduate course included some of Neel's own graduate students and, to my surprise, even a few faculty members in Neel's department.

After an initial and fruitful discussion, I agreed to collaborate with Neel in a short-term biomedical/anthropological research study after I had spent a year among the Suyá and learned their language and the intricacies of their social organization.

However, Neel was also in the process of developing a collaborative relationship with Venezuelan colleagues who were doing similar research among several native tribes in that country, Dr. Miguel Layrisse in particular. Layrisse was internationally known for his serological studies among Venezuelan Indians, much of it done in collaboration with the German-born cultural anthropologist Johannes Wilbert. Layrisse had, for example, discovered a genetic marker known as the "Diego factor," a group of genes found only in people with Native American ancestry and in certain Mongolian populations in Asia. The Diego factor was initially used tentatively to classify Native American tribes into putative "early arrivals" to the New World and "later" populations. Layrisse and Wilbert had begun collecting blood samples to document the genetic characteristics of all the tribes in Venezuela and the variations found among them.

In view of the practical difficulties I would face as a result of the military coup in Brazil, Neel suggested that I consider doing my field research in a Venezuelan tribe that was close to the Brazilian border, a possibility that, as I mentioned, I was already considering. Such research was suddenly all the more possible and attractive because of Neel's recently established connections with Layrisse in Venezuela.

There were a number of Venezuelan tribes whose territories extended into Brazil—the Pemon in the savannah region and the Amazon tropical forest Ye'kwana, for example. There were yet other Venezuelan tribes on the Colombian border that were found in both countries that I also considered, but because they were relatively easy to get to, they were more acculturated by contact with Venezuelan and Colombian nationals. I wanted to study a tribe that had had minimal contact with Western culture.

The most attractive group to me was the apparently numerous but largely unknown group, then known as the Waika. In my general reading in preparation for my comprehensive examinations for the anthropology doctoral program I had read the scant literature that existed on the Waika Indians, who were rumored to be very numerous, warlike, and isolated in the largely unexplored area on the border between Brazil and Venezuela. There were a few recently published firsthand accounts for the Venezuelan Waika, among them several articles by an American missionary named James P. Barker, who had recently begun evangelical mission work in this area.

Layrisse and Wilbert had also recently done blood-sampling work among almost all of the tribes in Venezuela, including a few visits to small villages of Waika (sometimes called Sanema) Indians who periodically moved out of the deep forest and were in sporadic contact with the Ye'kwana Indians and the missionaries who were working with the Ye'kwana. Both the tribal names *Waika* and *Sanema* turned out to be other names for the Yanomamö. Johannes Wilbert had published brief descriptions of his encounters with these somewhat mysterious Indians, but apart from Wilbert's initial and brief reports, there was nothing substantial from anthropologists on any groups of Venezuelan Waika Indians. Indeed, the field of cultural anthropology based on fieldwork in Venezuela was scarce in the mid-1960s.

After a few meetings with Neel and discussions of his developing collaborative agreements with Layrisse in Venezuela, I decided to take Neel's recommendation and begin my research among the Waika in the headwaters of the Orinoco River, a region of Venezuela called the Territorio Federal Amazonas. It was not yet a state, but rather a federal territory. In a strange sense, I felt a little like Lewis and Clark accepting Thomas Jefferson's commission to explore the newly purchased Louisiana Territory.

Things then happened very quickly. In November 1964, my wife, our two small children, and I departed from New York on a Venezuelan freighter. We had a large amount of personal and field equipment packed into five large fifty-five gallon metal barrels, so taking a freighter was much less expensive than flying. I was among the Yanomamö ("Waika") Indians about two weeks after we reached Venezuela and remained there for the next seventeen months, except for two trips of ten or so days out of the jungle to see my wife and our children.

The Waika called themselves Yanomamö, but so little anthropological research had been done among them that this fact either was overlooked or people simply continued to call them by a somewhat derogatory name that had been used by the few locals who came into occasional contact with them. (The word *Waika* seems to be derived from a Yanomamö word, *waikäo*, meaning to "dispatch a wounded animal (or person)," in other words, administer the death blow.)

My contact with the world outside ceased almost entirely for the next seventeen months. For example, I was vaguely aware when I went into the Yanomamö area in late 1964 that the United States had sent several hundred military advisors to South Vietnam to help train the South Vietnamese army. When I returned to Ann Arbor in 1966 the United States had some two hundred thousand combat troops there.

In early 1966, as my initial anthropological field research drew to an end, Neel and a team of his medical researchers joined me in the Yanomamö area for some two weeks as we had planned. Layrisse brought them into the Mavaca area, where I had my mud-and-thatch hut, and we worked from there. Apart from Layrisse, the only Venezuelan in the medical group that initial year was a young dentist, Dr. Charles Brewer-Carías, who had published a short monograph on the dentition of the Ye'kwana Indians. Brewer was also an avid explorer, a self-trained naturalist, and a gifted photographer.

Layrisse left the next day and returned to Caracas while Neel and a small team of medical doctors and Ph.D. candidates from his department and in other departments of the University of Michigan Medical School remained with me for some two weeks. They collected blood samples, urine, feces and saliva samples, made dental casts, and performed physical and dental examinations of all the Yanomamö in each village we visited, including detailed anthropometric information. To make certain that everyone's data records could be pooled, I used a black felt-tip marker to put on everyone's arm an ID number that was linked to the genealogies I had collected during my fieldwork.

The medical team began every day by attending to those Yanomamö who were sick and could be treated in the village with antibiotics and other medications found in the supplies Neel's team brought with them from the University of Michigan.

The analytical results from the blood and other samples the medical team obtained during the brief time they spent with me in 1966 pleased Neel immensely and he subsequently offered me a position in the Department of Human Genetics to participate in additional future field trips to the Yanomamö. Although this kind of postdoctoral position would be an academic dead end for an anthropologist, the short-term benefits were very desirable: I could analyze my field data and publish extensively without the time-consuming tasks of simultaneously preparing and teaching courses—the standard career trajectory of new Ph.D.s in anthropology.

But an additional attractive aspect to the appointment was that it provided me with the opportunity to return to the Yanomamö as a member of a well-funded research program and continue my own anthropological field research. Finding money for relatively costly social science research—especially for foreign travel, as is common in anthropology— was a time-consuming and frequently disappointing process. Sometimes a young, unknown researcher had to apply to several different agencies several different times to obtain funding.

When I returned to Ann Arbor I wrote my doctoral dissertation, took two foreign language examinations (German and Spanish), completed the remainder of my doctoral course requirements (two courses in statistics), and successfully defended my thesis before my doctoral committee in time for the December 1966 university commencement. I was already on the University of Michigan Medical School faculty by the time I received my Ph.D. degree.

2

Discovering the Significance
of the Names

I knew immediately on that first day among the Yanomamö that they
were different from what my academic training had prepared me to find.
The Yanomamö were unusual, and I knew I couldn't describe their society adequately by doing the minimally acceptable fieldwork characteristic of the 1960s. They were too pure, too pristine, and too special. They
had not been decimated by introduced diseases nor by colonists on the
fringe of an expanding frontier. Not even Christian missionaries had had
an impact on them beyond a handful of their numerous villages. Most
of their villages were so isolated that nobody knew for sure how many
there were, let alone the total number of people in them. It was an almost
unique anthropological situation at the time—an extraordinary opportunity to study possibly the last large, warring, isolated tribe left on the
planet.

They were special in many other regards. For example, they struck me
as being more self-confident—even somewhat arrogant—and startlingly
indifferent to the "outside world" shortly after seeing it—or parts of it—

for the first time. I would have expected that they would be more shocked and the shock would last longer on seeing some remarkable new thing for the first time. For example, they were not awed for very long by some of our technology, such as outboard motors, machetes, or flashlights. To be sure, they found them curious and remarkable at first, but they quickly became very matter-of-fact about them.

They also had a very noticeable quality that is hard to explain, a "subjective" quality that my professors and the anthropology books I read never mentioned—nor seemed to even be aware of. For example, I knew immediately when I saw my first Yanomamö what "wild" Indian meant compared to an "acculturated" one. The wild ones had a kind of glint in their eyes and a haughty look about them that the acculturated ones had seemingly lost. There is a wonderful scene in the film version of Peter Matthiessen's fine book *At Play in the Fields of the Lord* that conveys what I'm trying to say. An evangelical missionary couple are working among some recently contacted Amazonian natives and trying to make first contact with the more remote, uncontacted "wild" ones. They string up trinkets, steel tools, and other items, hoping to lure the uncontacted ones to their mission. They wait for days, weeks, months. One day their young son suddenly rushes into his parents' hut, eyes very large, and blurts out in apprehensive, hoarse whispers: "They're here! They're here! The *wild* ones are here!"

My anthropological training probably would have served me adequately had I chosen a native Amazonian group to study that was already accustomed to many years of contact with Venezuelans, Brazilians, or other national populations and could speak some European language tolerably well. But the people I was now living with knew only a few words of Spanish, like *sí* and *no*, and most of them didn't even know these two words. James P. Barker, the New Tribes missionary who came with me the first day, left the following day, and I would not see him again for several months.

I was nevertheless grateful for the small list of phrases he had given me—common phrases that would be useful as I began learning the Yanomamö language, phrases like "Stop that!" or "No, you can't have my machete!" or "Help me find firewood!" or "Give me bananas and I will give you these fishhooks!"

I didn't realize until he left that his phrasebook really was not the language learning aid I expected that it would be. It might have been adequate if I were sitting in a room alone with some sympathetic, cooperative Yanomamö who was interested in teaching me his language, but this kind of situation almost never occurred. Rather, I would usually be surrounded by groups of Yanomamö—dozens—each clamoring to be heard and, when I didn't respond to them in a normal Yanomamö fashion, they assumed that I was hard of hearing and would speak louder, more emphatically, or simply shout impatiently at me.

The field notes I took during the early days and weeks of my fieldwork are very peculiar, incomprehensible, and, frankly, embarrassing as I now look at them. In an effort to learn the language, I would write down what some individual said to me and have him repeat it several times until I had the whole statement. But a phrase uttered in a language you don't understand comes out, in written form, something like this (using English as the example):

tomorrowiplantotakeatripdownstreaminmycanoetocatchsomefishandiwillgiveyousomeifyougivemesomematchesinreturn.

Imagine trying to make sense of a phrase like this in Yanomamö or any unknown language. My early field books contained "sentences" that sometimes ran for a whole page.

How do you separate a jumble of phonemes—sounds—into minimal meaningful elements, morphemes or grammatical units? Or, to put it in simple terms: where does one word stop and the next word begin?

One of my major ethnographic "triumphs" during the first several months of my work was to teach a young man named Rerebawä, who eventually became one of my best informants, what a word was and have him help me break the long strings of Yanomamö sounds I would write down into discrete words. This might seem like a trivial accomplishment, but it is huge when you are trying to learn an unwritten language from people for whom notions of verb, adjective, noun, tense, and so forth don't exist.

Rerebawä was a young man who had recently taken a wife in Bisaasiteri and moved into the village from Karohi-teri, his own village some six

Rerebawä

or so hours upstream and across the Orinoco. Young men from distant villages who marry into another village must work for the wife's parents for around six months to a year before they can take their new wife back home. This is called bride service in the anthropological literature. The Yanomamö name for it is *siohamou*. Rerebawä was a *sioha* in Bisaasi-teri, that is, a young man doing compulsory bride service.

He was not enthusiastic about bride service, so he often hung around me all day and gradually began helping me with the Yanomamö language and other tasks. He eventually became my nearly constant companion, guide, and friend during my initial seventeen months of fieldwork.

Rerebawä would say a sentence in Yanomamö, and I would write it down as I heard it. Then I would ask him to say it slowly. Gradually the boundaries between the sounds would appear, what I assumed were separate words. I would ask Rerebawä to repeat the whole phrase several times slowly, hoping that by doing it slowly, he would pronounce each word *separately* for me so I knew where the word started and ended.

He, of course, knew where each Yanomamö word began and ended, but he had no formal concept of what a word was because Yanomamö did not have a written grammar or dictionary—or a system of writing.

Rerebawä was one of the few informants who realized what I was trying to do and caught on quickly. He was an exceptionally bright young man.

Despite the fact that Yanomamö is not a written language, I had to adopt some alphabet—linguists call it an *orthography*—that represented the basic sounds of the language. My course work in anthropological linguistics was helpful to me here. An anthropologist or missionary with basic training in linguistics can develop a writing system for any unwritten language and after discovering its underlying grammar and structure, can write it on paper. This was an essential requirement before I could even begin the anthropology part of my field research.

The Yanomamö language had a few sounds that do not occur in the English language, so I had to decide on symbols for them. For example, the Yanomamö have a frequently used phoneme that sounds to English speakers like the *oe* or *ö* in the name of the famous German poet Goethe. This sound is, however, difficult for speakers of the Romance languages to hear. What they hear is more like the sound /e/ in the English words *tree, me,* or *see.* At least that is how they choose to write this phone: I chose to use *ö* for this sound because this symbol was more frequently found in publishers' fonts than the more standard *ɨ* (i with a slash through it) that is used in international linguistics conventions.

Thus, I not only had to learn the Yanomamö language, I also had to develop a way to write it so I could, for example, make a dictionary and take notes in their language, or at least write down their names for things so I could refer to a dictionary when I forgot some word in their language.

Some years after I had gotten my Ph.D., I met a prominent American anthropologist who had done his fieldwork in India using native informants who were fluent in English. He casually mentioned that his major informant decided to earn his own Ph.D. in anthropology at Cambridge University. His informant, no doubt, had long since lost the glint of wildness in his eye.

This chronic fact of my fieldwork had an indelible effect on me: I had recurring dreams for two or three years in which I would accidentally stumble upon a Yanomamö who spoke fluent English. I would detain him for hours, bring out my dictionary, and ask him if I had translated their words accurately into English! Hell, I would have settled for one who spoke fluent Spanish or Portuguese.

There is also an unusual problem with the Yanomamö language: it is not apparently demonstrably related to any of the indigenous languages found in the Americas.

The fact that no other native group speaks a related language seems to suggest that the Yanomamö have lived in isolation for a very long time, hidden away in a remote pocket of the vast Amazon jungle that was explored by Europeans only in recent times and only after the Yanomamö themselves began expanding out of their mountainous redoubts into the adjacent lowlands.

The process of learning the Yanomamö language was further complicated by the fact that I was also learning Spanish. I would say things to Venezuelans, for example, that would include words from four different languages in the same sentence. Most of the sentence would be in Spanish, but it would sometimes include words from English, Yanomamö, and German. My mind seemed to have a module that told me *the word you are trying to say is not Spanish* and, therefore, it must be a non-Spanish word from one of the other languages I knew (English and German) or was just learning (Yanomamö). People would look very puzzled whenever this happened but in most cases I never even realized what I had said because it sounded perfectly intelligible inside my brain.

The Physical Appearance of the Yanomamö

On my initial trip into Yanomamö territory we stopped periodically along the Orinoco River. At each stop the communities were smaller and the people began to look more like Amazonian Indians. In fact, many of them were of mixed Spanish and Native American ancestry. Some places where we stopped had hardly more than a couple of families with a few chickens that were kept for the eggs they produced. These people lived primarily on the manioc and plantains they cultivated and the fish and local game they hunted. Their chickens were so wild that on one occasion we purchased one for our dinner: our *motorista* had to chase it around the homestead and shoot it with his shotgun.

I gradually got to know some of these creoles, the ones who worked for the Venezuelan Malarialogía. They were always courteous to me, but when they realized that I was interested in the language and customs of the Yanomamö and treated the Yanomamö with respect, a few of them confidentially told me they were Baré or Kuripako Indians from the Rio Negro area. When they realized that I was enthusiastically trying to learn Yanomamö kinship usage and didn't think it was quaint or backward, some of them, also somewhat secretly, told me they still used kinship terms in their own native language. Their cautious attitudes were understandable. A not uncommon request I periodically got from middle-class Venezuelans in Caracas, when they heard I spent a good deal of time in "Indian country," was, "Bring me back an *india* if you have room in the plane! I could use another *domestica*!" It was as if they thought that Native Venezuelan Indians could simply be taken against their will and put into the domestic employ of someone's household.

The New Tribes Mission post of Tama Tama was approximately the beginning of Yanomamö territory. When I first reached Tama Tama I saw a young man standing on one of the giant rocks that jutted into the Orinoco. I knew as soon as I saw him that I was looking at my first Yanomamö. He had not lost the "wild" look in his eyes.

He was rather stocky but had slender legs and arms. He wore badly faded and tattered pants and a shirt and both were much too large for his frame. He was slightly shorter than the people we had met along the Orinoco on our trip, perhaps five feet, four inches tall. He looked like he weighed about 120 pounds. His jet-black hair was cut pudding-bowl-style. What I could see of his skin was surprisingly light compared to that of the people we saw along the river who spent much of the time fishing in canoes, their skin exposed to the equatorial sun many hours per day.

The Venezuelan men in the boat tried to ask him questions in Spanish. He seemed to understand them, but his responses consisted of mostly nods, two Spanish words (*sí* and *no*) and pointing toward the houses up on the hill above the rocks. I later learned that he was from Mavaca, where I was going. His name was Wakarabewä and he became a good friend during the fieldwork that followed.

The other Yanomamö I met during my first year of fieldwork were, like Wakarabewä, very handsome people. A few of the men even resembled

Wakarabewä

some North American Indians whom I had seen in photographs taken by Edward S. Curtis.

My anthropology training and common sense made me aware of the fact that certain kinds of anthropological data like myths could not be collected immediately and would have to wait until I learned more of the Yanomamö language. However, there were things I could see with my own eyes and describe without knowing much of the language—things like how the Yanomamö cleared gardens, collected roofing materials, when they ate, how they made material items like bows, arrows, or bamboo quivers to carry extra arrow points, what they did to various kinds of game animals to prepare them for eating, etc. These activities did not require a sophisticated ability to communicate with the Yanomamö, who would often hold up objects as they worked so I could see them as they would tell me what they were. I happily jotted these names down—or recorded them on my small tape recorder and later entered them into my three-by-five vocabulary cards and, eventually, into my growing dictionary.

Discovering the "Name Taboo" and the Structure of Yanomamö Society

There were things I could *try* to learn as I learned new words and phrases, but this was somewhat hazardous in the sense that (1) the Yanomamö were practical jokers and would play mischievous tricks on me, and (2) they would sometimes get me into trouble by having me repeat things aloud that angered others within earshot.

Let me give some examples to illustrate one dimension of Yanomamö humor. Their word for pubic hair is *weshi*—the word means to have substantial amounts of hair in your pubic area. It is not something that is taboo to discuss if you are talking about men, no more so than discussing the fact that some men have more hair in their armpits than others do. But whenever I showed them photographs of women—even photos of women from their own village—the first thing that drew their attention was the relative amount of hair the women had around their pubic area. They found women with an abundance of pubic hair sexually provocative.

The Yanomamö have another word that is similar to *weshi* that can easily be confused with it, especially when you are just learning the language. That word is *beshi*, which means "to be horny." You don't admit in public that you are horny and you don't ask people in public if *they* are horny.

One day a young man asked me what I thought was a question about the hair on my body, especially the hair on my pubic area. We were resting on a trail en route to a nearby village. He knew that I sometimes confused these two words. He asked me, *"Wa beshi rä kä?"* ("Are you horny?"), which I mistakenly heard as *"Wa weshi rä kä?"* ("Do you have pubic hair?"). There was a small crowd of young men with me. They all watched and listened attentively. When I said, *"Awei! Ya beshi!"* ("Yes, I'm horny!") they broke into uproarious laughter because they had set me up to confuse the two words—and I fell into their trap.

Strangely—at least to me—the Yanomamö think it is appropriate to verbally insult a nearby person by having *someone else*—a stranger—say the offensive words. The offended person then becomes angry with the person who was commanded to utter the insult or offensive word. For example, if Kumamawä wanted to tell Wakupatawä that he is really ugly, Kumamawä would say to me, the stranger, "Say to Wakupatawä, *'Wa waridiwa no modahawa!'* ('You are really ugly!')" I, of course, would have no idea what I was told to say and would innocently repeat what Kumamawä told me to say to Wakupatawä. But instead of getting angry with Kumamawä, Wakupatawä would get angry with *me*! It is as if getting someone else, especially a stranger, to say the insulting phrase the initiator of the insult is mysteriously invisible and not culpable: he is not an active agent in the sequence of verbal events that results in the insult.

The most common way they did this to me was to tell me to say someone's name aloud in front of them, especially very early in my fieldwork. Someone would say to me, "Say to that guy next to you, *'Buutawä! Koa asho a dahiyo!'* ('Fetch me some firewood!'')," I would say that. Buutawä would get angry at me because I used his name publicly. He would become angry because I disrespected him in public and failed to acknowledge his high status (I will explain the complicated subject of names shortly).

For the better part of the first year I focused on learning how to speak Yanomamö and making my dictionary of words and phrases as I learned them, as well as observing and describing things that did not depend on an intimate knowledge of their language.

As my language proficiency increased I gradually began collecting facts about their kinship rules, beliefs, social relationships, and, generally, the kinds of things you can't learn simply by looking with your eyes.

What I really had to find out was how the Yanomamö organized themselves socially and how their "political system" worked.

The one thing I learned in my anthropology classes that was absolutely true was that tribal societies are fundamentally kinship-based societies and that for tribesmen like the Yanomamö "social organization" was embedded within the complex matrix of kinship, descent from common ancestors, and marriage arrangements.

This might be more easily understood if you imagine a Yanomamö village as a large spiderweb. Where any two strands of the spiderweb cross, imagine that this little node is a person. Let's say the vertical strands of web are "lines of genetic descent" and the horizontal strands of web are "ties caused by marriage." Then imagine that some pieces of the web are thicker and stronger than others and can pull or restrain each node with different amounts of force, that is, sometimes the marriage pieces of web are thicker (stronger) than the crisscrossing lines of descent and the node has a tendency to be pulled more by marriage ties than by descent ties. Finally, imagine that the spiderweb is constantly exposed to the wind, which varies over time and fluctuates by direction, and it is anchored to rigid sticks. So, the web is constantly being stretched by the forces of the wind and restrained by the rigid sticks that sway and bend in the wind, putting different amounts of stress on portions of the web—and the nodes within it.

Therefore in order to discover how each individual in the village—each node in the spider web—was pulled or restrained socially, I had to determine the genealogies of each person to show the constraints set by descent from ancestors and the marriage histories of each adult—to show the constraints and obligations established by marriages.

This rather complex task required that I know the names of every individual, as well as the names of each parent, each grandparent, etc. Then I had to determine who married whom and, when multiple spouses were found, the sequence of the marriages (which was first, which second, etc.), as well as the names of each child by each set of parents. This information would constitute only a portion of the matrix about the human nodes: just the ties of descent, kinship, and marriage among them.

Both men and women remarry when their spouses die or are killed. In addition, many men have several wives at the same time (polygyny) or several wives that they divorce ("throw away") and then replace. Finally, in some cases, a few men share the same wife (polyandry) until one of them can find a wife for himself.

I will discuss Yanomamö polygyny in more detail later, but a brief comment is necessary here. All Yanomamö men would like to have multiple wives but not all of them are able to. Marriage success is largely dependent on how many ascending generation patrilineal male relatives a young man has: these men can help younger men in their own lineage find wives—usually after the older men find wives for their own sons. Although the father is probably the most important person in helping a young man find a wife, the size of his father's patrilineage—and thus its prominence in village politics—is also important because other men want or at least prefer to give their daughters to men in prominent lineages. Village size also plays a role in a man's marital success—larger villages are able to retain more of their women because they have to promise fewer of them to allies and they are able to coerce more women from smaller allied villages.

Ties of kinship, descent, and marriage were only part of the puzzle of how their social and political system worked. I also had to establish two additional dimensions of this puzzle: the spatial or geographical dimension and the historical dimension.

Geography: I had to collect the names of the villages (or abandoned gardens) where each life historical event took place, that is, where each person was born, where older females had their first menstrual period, where each person lived when each marriage took place, and where, if dead, they died.

History: Over time the members of any given Yanomamö village have moved from one garden to another as they construct new *shabonos*, meaning establish new villages. Relationships among villages are an important political fact of life for the Yanomamö, as I discovered soon after my arrival at Mavaca.

Social Intricacies of Name Avoidance

Within a few months of settling in at Mavaca I learned specialized phrases to collect genealogies—phrases like "what is his/her name?" or "what is the name of X's father (mother)?" or "what is the name of X's spouse?" or "what garden was he/she born in?"

I soon realized that I could not have picked a more recalcitrant and uncooperative group of people to study.

The Yanomamö have what anthropologists call a name taboo. Not many anthropologists have had to deal with such a taboo, and I was surprised when I later realized how few anthropologists knew what it actually meant in specific cases, how widely it varied from tribe to tribe, and the "sociopolitical" content it had in specific tribes.

Among the Yanomamö, strangers are generally suspect and viewed with distrust because the Yanomamö believe that they are likely to inflict supernatural harm on them. To know someone's personal name is, in a sense, to "possess" some kind of control over that person, so the Yanomamö initially do not want strangers to know their personal names. However, the Yanomamö name taboo is a very complex set of practices and expectations, not just a simple prohibition on the use of someone's name in public, as many anthropologists assume. For example, there are some circumstances where using another's name publicly is both permissible and commonplace. The longer the stranger remains among them, the less concerned they are about the outsider learning their names and, of course, the less able they are to prevent him from learning them. By that time the stranger will have caught on to the fact that, to be courteous and polite, one should generally avoid using someone's name in public and, instead, use the *kinship term* that inevitably is adopted between the stranger and *every* individual in the village.

For example, if some Yanomamö decides to call me by the term that means "brother," then I am expected to call *him* brother in return. I must also call all of his brothers by the same kinship term—and all of his sisters by the kinship term used for sisters.

What frequently happens is that the headman of the village adopts some fictitious kinship relationship with you. Usually (if you are male) it is the kinship relationship that means brother-in-law that is most frequently chosen. In the Yanomamö language this term is *shori* or, more formally, *shoriwä*. It is an especially "friendly" relationship, because it implies that you must be generous with your possessions with your *shori* because you and he are expected to give each other your respective sisters in marriage. Thus, on first meeting male strangers, the Yanomamö males keep shouting repeatedly *"Shori! Shori! Shori!"* to emphasize their friendly intentions, expecting the strangers to reciprocate in a friendly way by yelling back *"Shori! Shori! Shori!"* This occurred so frequently when early contacts were being developed between strangers and the Yanomamö that outsiders began calling the Yanomamö the *Shori* tribe. Most of the Catholic missionaries and their Venezuelan employees up to about 1990 referred to the Yanomamö as *los Shoris,* as did some of the evangelical missionaries I knew.

So, when someone comes into a Yanomamö village to live there for a long period of time—as I did—they must somehow or other become incorporated into the social group by an extension of kinship ties. This does not mean that the Yanomamö "like" you or accept you in some special way. It simply means that they have their own way of dealing with you on their own terms—their *kinship* terms. Naïve visitors often report that "The natives 'liked' me so much that they adopted me." The natives, however, extend this practice even to people they *dislike.* It has nothing to do with liking someone or "adopting" someone.

Yanomamö villages comprise a small number of what we would call very large extended families. Nearly everyone in the village is a blood relative to everyone else. The example I just used for brothers and sisters applies across the board for other kinship relationships. If I call someone "sister" then her children must call me "uncle" and I must call them "nephew" and "niece."

Every time I went to a village I had not visited before, the headman would greet me with the term *shori* and I would respond by calling him *shori* in return. Then for the next hour or two most of the members of the village would make it a point to announce who they were by approaching me and calling me some kinship term that would be consistent with what the headman and I called each other—and everyone would automatically become one kind or another of my blood relative.

The Yanomamö system of kinship classification does not have any kin terms that mean "relatives by marriage," people we call our "in-laws." Everyone is, by kin term, a blood relative. I translated their word *shori* as brother-in-law, but it also and more accurately means "my male cross cousin," a blood relative. The Yanomamö in fact are *obliged* to marry their female cross cousins or a woman that falls into the kinship category that means "female cross cousin." So, the headman of a strange village and I become potential matrimonial allies, each expecting to be given the other's sister in marriage—as well as material wealth such as dogs, clay pots, arrows, and, more recently, steel tools. These goods are almost always foremost in mind in the headman's apparently altruistic but actually avaricious and selfish expectations.

So, in the early months of that first year of fieldwork I was faced with a big problem that had several dimensions. First, the Yanomamö didn't want me to know their names because I was a stranger, a *nabä:* a subhuman. Second, if I learned their names they didn't want me to use them in public. Third, I had to collect accurate genealogies even to begin to understand how their social system functioned and this *required* knowing the names of all individuals including dead individuals in each person's ancestry.

A major obstacle emerged. I was determined to figure out their social system, which required knowing their individual names and genealogical relationships, but they were just as determined to conceal these facts from me. A fascinating and complicated process then emerged, one that was invisible to me over the initial months of my fieldwork as it played itself out.

For example, I determined, by simply listening to their conversations, that it was acceptable to use the names of young children in many circumstances, like wanting to get the attention of some adult whose name you didn't want to use aloud in public. It was acceptable to yell out something like "Hey! Go get Nakabaimi's mother!" Nakabaimi being a child. Ethnographically this common practice is called *teknonomy*—to use the name of one person to attract the attention of someone or to refer to someone whose name you do not want to say aloud.

I could, in this fashion, at least begin genealogies that would be based on a child called, for example, Nakabaimi with parents called "Nakabaimi's mother" and "Nakabaimi's father." Needless to say, this quickly became cumbersome when I tried to determine who the parents and siblings were of Nakabaimi's mother and Nakabaimi's father.

But I also determined by listening to Yanomamö conversations that you should not use a child's name if he or she is sick—it might attract the attention of malevolent spirits who might then steal the child's soul and cause it to get more sick or even die. The same is also true for adults who would normally be able to use each other's names aloud. When they are sick it is considered hazardous to do so and it is therefore avoided.

The name taboo has several functions in the Yanomamö status system. Among other things it is strategically implicated in and central to understanding the Yanomamö social and political systems.

It was difficult for me to think about the Yanomamö as having a "status system" because, according to the picture I had gotten from my anthropology training, people like the Yanomamö were "egalitarian" and nobody had higher status than anyone else his or her age, except, possibly, for the short-lived times that a "chief" spoke for the group in dealings with other groups—as in trading or chance meetings. Then, after these brief circumstances, the chief would revert in status from first among equals to just another male of his age group. "One word from the chief and everyone does as he pleases," as an early Russian anthropologist described the "government" of one of the Siberian tribes he studied.

When I was a graduate student, my more advanced graduate classes on primitive social organization informed me that differences in status in all human societies were basically determined by "differential access to scarce, strategic material resources." We were taught that this condition did not obtain in tribal societies because there was no wealth as such, and thus there were no status differences other than sex and age. This meant that older people had more prestige than younger ones simply because they were older, and males were more important than females simply because they were males. Individuals of the same age and same sex have the same social and political status. Kinship had nothing to do with biology.

This was a fundamental message of Marxist social science that dominated most departments of anthropology in the 1960s, especially those departments that were considered to be "scientific." For reasons I've never understood, "science" and "Marxism" were linked together. One implied the other because, I suppose, both were materialistic and involved a logic of cause and effect, which I understood and accepted. What I didn't accept was the subtle "Marxist" message that academics who found cause-and-effect important in science also had to actively advocate a social agenda of egalitarianism or socialism. Science as such did not advocate anything.

What I found from my fieldwork was that the political leaders in all Yanomamö villages almost always have the largest number of genetic relatives within the group. I also found that some people, in addition to political leaders, had higher status than others, and that political status among the Yanomamö depended to a very large extent on the numbers and kinds of biologically defined (genetic) relatives one has in the community and was entirely unrelated to "control" one had over allegedly "scarce strategic resources." In short, it was apparent to me as an observer of their daily behavior that material things mattered much less to the Yanomamö than biology, for example, genetically related kinsmen—contrary to the prevailing anthropological wisdom derived from Marxism.

My training at Michigan led me to believe that people like the Yanomamö had virtually no status differentials other than age or sex. One could not add to one's status by, for example, striving to be bigger, more influential, more likely to be listened to. Thus the Yanomamö name "taboo" was an integral part of their status system and not simply some kind of mysterious avoidance custom. It should be stated at the outset that Yanomamö males are concerned about their status and they strive for esteem. You can see this develop as a boy matures. It is acceptable to use a boy's name aloud when he is a toddler, but as he matures and starts tying his penis to his waist string, as a *yawäwä*, or pubescent male and later when his muscles start to become hard (*yiiwä*) as the Yanomamö classify a male of this age, he begins to *demand* a measure of respect, and he publicly objects when his name is used aloud, because doing so indicates publicly that he is just a child.

The Yanomamö have a rich vocabulary to describe stages of life during human maturation, which can be roughly used to calculate approximate ages. Here are just a few:

ihiru, ihirubö	An infant of either sex
horeaö	To creep, as an infant learning to walk
oshe	a young child of either sex
suhebä ukaö	a girl whose nipples are beginning to enlarge
yawäwä	a young boy who is tying his penis to his waist string
yiiwä	an adolescent male whose muscles are getting hard
suwa härö	a female who is about the age of puberty
moko dude	a recently post-pubescent female who has not had a child

suwa pata	a mature woman
waro pata	a mature man
patayoma	an old woman
rohode	an old man; an old person

Objecting to the public use of your name is a kind of status conscious-ness among the Yanomamö, and those who can compel others to desist from doing this acquire higher status earlier in life. By extension, some young men can be a pain in the neck to other Yanomamö (and were to me, too) because they quickly get angry and unpleasant when someone uses their name aloud and disrespects them by ignoring their "high" status. These kinds of reactions occur not because some taboo has been violated, but because some politically ambitious young guy is merely testing his status in preparation for later and larger political bouts.

In this sense, the taboo on using names serves to endorse and rein-force the differential status system among males—and this might be its *central* function in their political system. The so-called name taboo is not simply some unusual custom that possesses supernatural attributes the violation of which provokes offense among others. Among males, it is also a way of showing deference to another, an acknowledgment of the high status of another male, and a display of awareness of an individual's social clout, which, by definition, is what politics boils down to.

We also have name taboos. See what happens when, on your next visit to your family doctor, you address him/her by their given name—or call the judge at a trial by his or her first name, or when an enlisted sol-dier calls his commanding officer by name rather than rank.

Yanomamö girls and women, on the other hand, have very little sta-tus compared to boys and men of the same age. The Yanomamö are male chauvinists. Thus the names of young girls are more frequently used than the names of young boys: "Go call Jennifer's mother" is more common than "Go call Joey's mother" if a woman has young children of both sexes. The sex of the child eventually trumps the respective ages: if Joey is twelve and Alice is sixteen, people will probably use "Go call Al-ice's mother" to avert a possible snit by Joey, who is now tying his penis to his waist string and becoming aware of the status system and how to use it.

The Yanomamö "Sabotage" My Genealogy Research

In my early attempts to learn everyone's names I inadvertently set into motion a bizarre and clandestine counterresponse by the mischievously inclined among them. Had I not been the victim I might have found their elaborate scheme rather funny, even admirable in a mischievous way.

It had to do with a different aspect of the name taboo and it went like this. When a person dies, his or her name is not supposed to be used aloud again in that village. This aspect of the name taboo is intended to avoid reminding the close kinsmen of the death of a loved one, which would provoke sadness and grief. The longer the person has been dead, the less angry (*hushuwo*) their kin would be if their name were inadvertently mentioned aloud in their presence. Because of this name taboo the Yanomamö try to name people in such a way that the loss of that name in their language does not create a linguistic hardship. They try to name people with minute aspects or attributes of commonly used names of plants, animals, environmental features, etc. For example, instead of naming someone "deer" they would name that person "hair of the deer" or "hooves of the deer" or "skin of the deer." When that person died, they could still use the word for "deer" but would have to avoid saying, for example, "hooves of the deer." But sometimes—usually by chance—a commonly used word in the language is also the name for some person.

Sometimes the name of an important foodstuff or animal is used so frequently for a person when they are young that, when they suddenly die, that name has been associated with that individual—"stuck" to that individual—so intimately that they have to stop using it and must then use a clumsy circumlocution to refer to the original important foodstuff or animal, like the "red things" instead of "the fruits of the rasha palm."

A very prominent man in Bisaasi-teri was named *Rashawä* after the economically important palm tree and its staple fruit *rasha*. He was killed by an enemy group and his name could no longer be used publicly within his village. Instead, they used a rather clumsy circumlocution when they wanted to say the name of the tree or its fruit: "the tree that produces the edible round red things."

Complicating the problem of collecting genealogies was the fact that a large number of Yanomamö have two (or even more) names. This makes it difficult to cross-check one informant's story with another informant's. If you find a disparity and confront your original informant, the informant will most likely say: "Oh! He has two names; I gave you the one *we* know him by." Then you have to go back to the second informant to verify what the first one just told you. This is very time-consuming because in many cases the two informants live in different villages. If you do not accurately establish the correct name, then all descendants of that incorrectly named person become part of a lineage they may not belong to and you may misrepresent and misunderstand their political and marriage system. Because my study ultimately involved so many different villages, there were numerous cases of individuals from widely separated villages having, by chance, the same name.

Usually in cases where there are several names, one is the "true" name and the other(s) are nicknames or derogatory names that people use behind the person's back or in distant villages, which, in general, denigrate their neighbors when they are out of earshot.

One of the most prominent and famous men in the area where I worked was named *Matakuwä*—translated as "Shinbone." He sired forty-three children by eleven wives and was the past headman of his group. Due to his prodigious reproductive accomplishments many people in several different villages were either his direct descendants or collateral blood relatives. But people in other, unrelated villages who were either disrespectful or contemptuous called him by an equally well-known derogatory name: *Bosikomima*—"Plugged-up Anus" or "Mr. Constipation."

I quickly learned that I had to do my genealogical work privately—informants would be unwilling to say the names of adults who lived in their village if others were listening. And, even then, they would pull my head close to their mouths and whisper the name into my ear. Bear in mind that this was very early in my fieldwork—two or three months after I arrived—and I was still, in their eyes, a stranger who shouldn't be told these things.

I deliberately and systematically used older people for most of this work. Younger people tended to invent names (and relationships) to impress me with how much they knew, whether or not the information was accurate. All of my informants soon realized that I would, as a matter of policy, find other informants and cross-check what each of them told me so I would be able to detect the dishonest among them. They also quickly learned that I rewarded them more for accurate information, or, simply stopped using them altogether if I caught them in fabrications, in which case they would get no payment.

My payment scale started with small items—small fishhooks, nylon fish line, spools of thread, a box of matches—and as their information consistently withstood cross-checking, I gave larger and more valuable trade goods like knives and machetes if they worked for several information sessions. The Yanomamö in this region near Mavaca and Ocamo had had relatively frequent access to steel tools for many years before I arrived because they lived on a major river, but still prized these items because knives and machetes wore out or broke and had to be replaced. More important, individuals from remote inland villages would visit them and beg for steel tools.

I used many informants and often worked late into the night. Some informants exhibited all the correct signs of telling the truth when they told me the names of deceased parents and grandparents: they would grab me by the head, pull my ear close to their mouths, and barely audibly whisper the person's name into my ear. I would dutifully write it down next to one of the circles (for women) or triangles (for men) and put brackets around the name to signify "dead" and fill in the circle or triangle to indicate the person was dead. These precautions would remind me to be extra careful about this name—and to remind me to make sure I didn't say it in front of people who might be closely related to that dead person. Of course, I had to keep a "mental" list of names that I could not say aloud for most of the informants I planned to use in the future— names of their deceased close kinsmen like father, mother, siblings, offspring, etc.

I was elated after these kinds of information sessions, not only because I was making progress on the genealogies and understanding their social system, but also because it seemed that my informants were beginning to trust me enough to share this somewhat taboo information with me in increasing confidence. I felt like they were accepting me as I hoped they would from the very first day I came into their community and their lives.

The drudgery of long hours collecting genealogies deep into the night went on for weeks and months. I used many different informants—males and females—from Upper and Lower Bisaasi-teri whose *shabonos* were just a few hundred yards apart, separated by the Mavaca River. I would test each new informant I worked with by cautiously asking them questions about remotely related deceased ancestors of a set of people that many earlier informants had repeatedly and independently given me identical answers to. If they independently confirmed what many other older informants had secretly told me, they passed the test and I would continue working with them . . . and ask them questions about new people, or about another generation of ancestors.

In this fashion and with this tedious and usually unpleasant drudgery my notebooks filled and overflowed . . . thousands of circles and triangles, many names and many with brackets around them, lines showing descent over the generations and others showing marriages, and how everyone was related to everyone else in this system of kinship. My spiderweb was getting larger and more complex and this gave me a sense of great satisfaction because I was now seeing patterns that suggested why some people acted as a group and favored or disfavored people both within their village or in other villages.

Discovering the Elaborate Sabotage

About four or five months after living in Bisaasi-teri I was invited by some young men to visit one of the closer Shamatari villages, a village called Mömariböwei-teri. The Bisaasi-teri referred to all the villages to their south as Shamatari villages to emphasize that they were slightly different Yanomamö groups with distinct histories. The Yanomamö are very ethnocentric and seize on the slightest of differences to make invidious distinctions between "them" and "us." To the Bisaasi-teri, the Shamatari were "them," distinguished from "us."

The word Shamatari might derive from *shama* which means tapir and *tari* which implies a group of historically related peoples, i.e., the "Karawatari" as a group of related people who are distinct from the "Shamatari." The affixes *teri* and *tari* imply that *tari* is a larger group. The affix *teri* often means just a single village whereas *tari* implies or means a collection of related villages.

It was on this visiting trip that the scales fell off my eyes. Months after I had filled my notebooks full of individual names, living and deceased parents and grandparents, husbands and wives, children, etc., I discovered how the Bisaasi-teri had systematically deceived me.

Some of the prominent men in Bisaasi-teri had gotten wives from Mömariböwei-teri and, consequently, there was sporadic visiting of people from both groups to each other's village. In addition, a few young men from Mömariböwei-teri had been promised wives in Bisaasi-teri and were living there to do bride service—and they would be coming with me on this trip to visit their families in their home village. One of these was Wakarabewä, the young man I had met on the rocks at Tama Tama several months earlier, the first Yanomamö I saw with a wild glint in his eyes.

The trip was an eight-hour walk through swamps, hills, shallow streams, and a few low mountains if we traveled with just light loads—our hammocks and a few trade goods like fishhooks, fish line, matches, and perhaps a machete as a gift for the headman.

I, of course, had more equipment than my young male companions—a backpack that contained a dozen tins of sardines and manioc flour for my companions, soda crackers for me, my field notebooks, a small tape recorder, two cameras, extra film, and my double-barreled twelve-gauge shotgun to shoot game.

The Yanomamö normally make a trip this short with just their bow, arrows, a vine hammock and a bamboo quiver about fifteen inches long that dangles down their backs on a neck cord to hold extra bamboo arrow points, an agouti-tooth knife to sharpen arrow points, and a fire drill kit.

There were two reasons I wanted to visit this particular village. First, I wanted to see the entire population at home in their village in order to make a complete census with ID photographs and estimated ages for everyone—and the sex of all children. I had already met many of them when they visited Bisaasi-teri but to do an accurate census I had to go to their village. Second, I planned eventually to move to one of the Shamatari villages and make that village the focus of my study. This annoyed the people in Bisaasi-teri—they hoped I would stay with them and keep my *madohe* (trade goods) in their village for their privileged use.

The Bisaasi-teri insisted the Shamatari were different from them but I couldn't tell any difference. They were different, as it turns out, because their immediate ancestors were different.

The Bisaasi-teri used *Shamatari* to categorize some half-dozen inter-related and little-known villages to their south, but acknowledged that they were true Yanomamö who, according to their Creation Myth, were descendants of the Blood of Moon. As this story goes, Peribo (Moon) was an ancient Spirit who lived on the Sky Layer. He would periodically descend to This Layer (earth) to cannibalistically devour Yanomamö between pieces of cassava bread. Two Yanomamö archers, also Spirit Ancestors, Suhirina and Uhudima, decided to shoot Peribo with arrows. They came upon him as he was ascending back up into the Sky after de-vouring Yanomamö (Spirits). Uhudima decided that he would shoot first. He shot many arrows at Peribo but missed every time. He was *sina*, a "poor marksman." To be *sina* is undesirable, a defect in male Yanomamö.

Suhirina then stepped forward just as Peribo was almost out of arrow range. He shot a single arrow, which struck Peribo in the belly. Peribo let out a terrible scream. Blood began to drip from his belly and fell down to This Layer. Peribo's blood immediately turned into People when it hit the ground, People who were extremely violent and fierce and constantly made war on each other. Their wars were so incessant that they extermi-nated each other. But where Peribo's blood mixed with water, it thinned a little. The Yanomamö created by thinned blood were also fierce and fought a great deal—but not as much as the first ones, so they survived and left descendants. As Peribo's blood got thinner by mixing with more water and flowed outward to the periphery of This Layer, the people cre-ated from this mixture became less and less warlike.

The Shamatari were also created from the thinned blood of Peribo and are also fierce—perhaps not as fierce as the Bisaasi-teri, but fierce nevertheless. They do, however, speak a little "crooked," according to the Bisaasi-teri.

As always on trips through the jungle we walked single file to get to Mömariböwei-teri. Despite the fact that the walk was difficult and I had to constantly concentrate on where I stepped, my sense of excitement increased the closer we got. It was my first visit to this village.

I kept asking my companions: "How much farther?" They would usu-ally reply with the same answer: *"A brahawä shoawä..."* ("It is still a long way off.") Eventually one of them turned around and whispered to me that we were getting close to the village. My companions stopped talking and began walking slowly as if they were stalking some game animal—silently, attentively, and cautiously. They stopped and quickly tended to their coiffure and decorations. They combed their pudding-bowl bangs with their fingers, donned their monkey-tail headbands, washed their legs and arms in the stream, and quickly applied the red *nara* paint and a few brilliant feathers they carried in the bamboo arrow point quivers (*toras*) that dangled down their backs. Then they urged me, with whispers and gesticulations, to "clean myself up"—wash the mud off my legs and put on a red loincloth to make myself presentable as a visitor. I obliged, somewhat dumbfounded at this hasty but ceremonial preparation for a short visit to a group of people they already knew quite well and had seen very recently, and who were their close relatives. The Yanomamö love drama, ceremony, and the attention they command on just a mere visit to a village they grew up in and had left just a few months ago.

The Bisaasi-teri gave a short, collective burst of high-pitched whistles almost simultaneously with our sudden entry into the *shabono*. An instant, loud, collective hoot erupted from the residents, who excitedly took our whistle signal as a sign of peace and that we were friendly visitors, not raiders.

The seniormost young man among my young companions motioned to me to move up to the front, beside him, and we proudly, if not haughtily, led the procession into the center of the circular plaza. It was surrounded by the twenty-five-feet-high, almost vertical roof of the *shabono*. We formed a semicircle in the middle of the plaza, stood motionless, heads erect and in our befeathered silent splendor. We waited a few moments in our best pose. Then the excited male hosts inspected us, remarked on how beautiful we looked, and excitedly welcomed us, rattling their upright bows and arrows in our faces. Then they led each of us individually to his specific portion of the *shabono*, to his and his family's house, where we were given hammocks and cooked food.

While a Yanomamö *shabono* may look like a communal circular dwelling—especially from the air—it is in fact composed of individual family houses constructed by the families, who cooperate to make the roof boundaries between them seamless.

We all rested for a courteous half hour or so and my companions gradually began to visit friends and relatives and resume normal activities as if they were at home. Indeed, some of them actually *were* at home—the ones who originally came from Mömariböwei-teri but who now lived in Bisaasi-teri as *siohas* doing bride service.

Word soon spread that I was going to take identification pictures of everyone in family groups in order to see how many people lived in Mömariböwei-teri. Knowledge of what I invariably did in other villages as my "work" (*ohodemou*) spread to all nearby villages long before I visited them. The Mömariböwei-teri were already aware of what I was about to do in "my work."

I announced that I wanted everyone to stay at home and not go off hunting or to their gardens. My request was largely unnecessary—this was my first visit to their village and those who had never seen me in person wanted to take this opportunity to do so. Visitors—especially a *nabä* like me—cause a lot of excitment, so everyone stays home when visitors arrive lest they miss something worth seeing, like, perhaps, a third arm or an extra eye of the subhuman *nabä*.

I had previously gotten the names of most of the residents of Mömariböwei-teri from people living in Bisaasi-teri who came from Mömariböwei-teri—but I had to determine approximately how old each one was by inspection. In addition, informants sometimes do not know the sex of newborns if children are born when they are away, so in those cases I also had to determine that with my own eyes.

The villagers cooperated enthusiastically and happily. I explained to them I wanted to know who lived in each house and who was a member of that family. The Yanomamö have a notion of nuclear family very similar to ours—unmarried sons and daughters usually lived at home, but married ones lived in different households within the same village. Most males usually come back home if they marry a girl in a different village, but they often marry someone in their own village. Most Yanomamö girls want to be given in marriage to someone in their *own* village—because they will have brothers who will protect them from a possibly cruel husband. But the major strategy of intervillage political alliances is to get your allies to give you marriageable females—and to promise to give some of your girls in the future as a quid pro quo. These relationships strengthen ties among the villages and provide additional security, despite the fact that some of the strength is based on "credit." Thus, some girls are, as part of the price of alliance, required to live among strangers in the villages of their new husbands, who can and often do inflict severe punishments on them for their suspected or imagined infidelities.

I started my census late that day in the household of the Mö-mariböwei-teri headman, Shiitawä. I would start all censuses with the headman's family in every village. Headmen are usually very cooperative—they quickly learned that I always brought a bigger gift for them than for other men and this news spread from village to village. They also encourage all the others to be cooperative and usually, in a loud voice, order everyone in the village to follow my instructions. Sometimes they do this at night if I arrive late in the afternoon and do not plan to begin my census work until the next day. The headman will *kawa amou*—give a loud, lengthy, and somewhat poetic monologue after dark, after people have settled into their hammocks for the night. He tells them that he wants everyone to be friendly and cooperative with me, his *shori*, and everyone will be pleased with the gifts I have brought.

As is the case with just about every Yanomamö headman, Shiitawä had a large polygynous family—the largest family in the village. He got them to arrange themselves in a straight line and situated each of his wives with her babies (in arms) and her older offspring huddled next to her. Finally, he took his own place and I took two pictures of them: a Polaroid, for instant availability, and a 35 mm black-and-white that I would later, back in Michigan, develop and have printed as a four-by-six image onto which I would transfer the information I had written on the Polaroid. By then the Polaroid prints would be soiled—full of red pigment and smudges from dozens of fingers. The Yanomamö loved to look at these pictures, run their fingers over them, and discuss them for hours; I would let them pass my "album" around in my hut for everyone to see their own images—as well as the images of the other families.

After photographing the headman's family I would move to the next household and repeat my procedure. Sometimes the headman would come along to assist me, but most of the time people caught on to what I wanted to do and the headman's assistance was not needed.

I learned a great deal about their social and political organization just by making a census in this fashion. For example, the households immediately next to Shiitawä's belonged to his married brothers and their wives and children. Thus, all adult males in the same lineal descent group—a patrilineal lineage—lived side by side in one section of the *shabono*— they all had the same father. Where Shiitawä's brothers' houses ended, the next group of men would belong to a different patrilineage—they would be a different set of brothers with a different father. Shiitawä's village had (at that census) 119 residents—men, women, and children—but they fell into four patrilineages of about equal size: about twenty-five to thirty people in each lineage group.

By contrast, Bisaasi-teri had two large patrilineages in their village of 127 people that dominated social and political life, plus two or three much smaller lineages. But, just across the river from Bisaasi-teri were another ninety-four people in Lower Bisaasi-teri, downstream from where the Mavaca River flows into the Orinoco River. As mentioned earlier, they were originally part of the larger Bisaasi-teri village, but they split away in a big fight over a woman. But their kinship composition was a mirror image of the main village: they had the same two large patrilineages just as the main group had.

It took several hours to make my initial census in Mömaribowei-teri. This census was easy because I already knew the names of most of the residents before I got there—the young men from that village who were doing bride service in Bisaasi-teri had given me most of this information. Later, back at Bisaasi-teri, I would add additional information about each person with these same young informants—which young girl was promised in marriage to which young man, where new babies had been born, etc. But, I would use much *older* informants to get the names of the parents and ancestors of the Mömaribowei-teri.

There are, however, some young men who go out of their way to learn these facts if they have political aspirations and want to become leaders when they grow older. Rerebawä, the informant I mentioned above who helped me learn his language, was such a man. He intended to return to his natal village and, he hoped, would become the headman there.

This is where I learned I had been deceived. After my census work— the main purpose of my visit—was over in Mömaribowei-teri, I strolled around the village and visited with the residents, making small talk. To show them how much I knew about Yanomamö people and places, I softly mentioned the name of the Bisaasi-teri headman and some incident that involved both of us. Several adults were listening when I made my comment:

> *Mömariböwei-teri resident:* [snickering] Who? I don't recognize that name!
> *Chagnon:* The headman there! [whispering his name again]
> *Mömariböwei-teri resident:* [outright ribald laughter] Who is he married to?
> *Chagnon:* Her name is Nakaweshimi. You should know her . . .
> *All nearby Mömariböwei-teri residents:* [Side-slapping laughter until tears
>   run from their eyes]

My face flushed with embarrassment and anger as the word spread around the village and everybody was laughing hysterically.

The name I had been given for the wife of the Bisaasi headman, *Nakaweshimi*, translated to something very vulgar like "Hairy Cunt." It seemed that the Bisaasi-teri had collectively conspired to tell me a bunch of whopping lies about people's names. Each Bisaasi-teri informant would relate to my other informants the specific false names he had given me for other residents. They had come up with "new" names for almost all of the adult residents there . . . and most of the older kids as well. It must have been a somewhat time-consuming and elaborate hoax since it involved people in both the Upper and Lower Bisaasi-teri.

Hairy Cunt was married to the headman, Long Dong, their youngest son was Asshole, and so on. All of these names had been given to me solemnly, with a straight face, whispered into my ear softly and followed by the solemn whispered warning: "Don't tell anyone I gave you this name!"

If I had not gone to another village and innocently mentioned these "secret" names, I would have been totally ignorant of the elaborate hoax the Bisaasi-teri had played on me. I made this discovery some *six months* into my fieldwork!

What if I had gone home before that point and written my doctoral dissertation using this information? Many anthropologists do their fieldwork in less time than that—and usually in a single village, which means they cannot cross-check their information with people in other villages. Most anthropologists also report that the social organization in the tribe they studied was all about kinship but few of them report how they determined this and whether this conclusion was based on the genealogies they collected to support their conclusions.

This incident radically changed my field methods. Thereafter, when I wanted to learn something about Village A, I would go to Village B and ask people there what I wanted to know. I didn't have to engage in this strategy for all classes of information, but I learned to predict rather accurately what kinds of information they would most likely falsify (for example, the true names of any close kin they had in that village, names of famous dead headmen, etc.) or otherwise conceal from me (cases of incest involving their own kinsmen) and I simply avoided asking about those things in the villages for which I wanted the information.

It was more inconvenient to do some of my work this way, but in the long run it saved me a great deal of time trying to reconcile inconsistencies that originated in mischievous falsehoods told to me not simply to avoid revealing taboo names, but also because the Yanomamö have a wicked humor. They enjoyed duping others, especially the unsuspecting and gullible anthropologist who lived among them.

3

Raids and Revenge

Why Villages Fission and Move

The First Vengeance Raid

For the first several months of my field research I tried to make sense of what happened that first day when I duck-waddled into the *shabono* and was greeted by armed and angry men.

I learned that there had been a bloody club fight the day before I arrived. Matowä, the hotheaded Monou-teri headman, had provoked it. He and his men had captured seven Patanowä-teri women and taken them to their village several hours to the south. The angry and determined Patanowä-teri men, who that week were visiting Bisaasi-teri where I was making my first visit, had quickly recovered five of their seven stolen women in this club fight. Matowä then vowed to shoot and kill the Patanowä-teri, apparently to teach them a lesson for having recovered five of their seven stolen women. More important, the recovery raid had embarrassed him and possibly called his renown into question.

The village of Patanowä-teri had split into several groups. One of the groups continued to be known to its neighbors as "Patanowä-teri" but other groups assumed new names that would rapidly change as their leaders tried to distinguish themselves from their congeners, i.e., from the collective group known originally as Patanowä-teri. Both the Bisaasi-teri and Monou-teri were originally "factions" in Patanowä-teri, but by the time I arrived they had taken on the identities of "Bisaasi-teri" and "Monou-teri" and lived in separate villages. The name changes were made to help them deny culpability for wrongs they wanted to associate with a group with a different name and dissociate from—even though all of the groups were closely related.

Squabbling and club fighting over women caused the Bisaasi-teri, Patanowä-teri, and Monou-teri to separate and move away from each other. Now the Patanowä-teri lived more than two days away from both the Bisaasi-teri and the Monou-teri, whereas the latter two villages were only a few hours' walk from each other.

I found this very puzzling: why should these three closely related groups be fighting with each other and threatening to kill each other? It didn't make any sense if I looked at this situation in terms of what I had been trained to expect: kinsmen should be *nice* to each other, but yet on my first day in the field, they had bloody heads from clubbing each other in the recovery raid—and now they threatened to kill each other. I knew I had to find out more about how these groups were interrelated and the specific reasons why they broke up.

The most inexplicable thing to me in all of this was that they were fighting over *women*. My anthropology textbooks and my professors had taught me that on the "rare" occasions that tribesmen fought, it was inevitably over some scarce material resource like cultivable land, water supplies, rich hunting areas, etc. Yet the Yanomamö said they were fighting over *women*. I anticipated skepticism when I reported this after I returned to my university.

The headman of Bisaasi-teri—Kaobawä—was trying to make peace with the Patanowä-teri when the abductions occurred. After the abduction and recovery he appeared to have, at least in principle, preferred that the Monou-teri leave things as they were. After all, the Monou-teri were ahead by two women and nobody was killed.

But Matowä was an incorrigible hothead and wanted to intimidate the Patanowä-teri, even humiliate them. He was known to seduce the wives

of other men in his *own* small village, and on one occasion, he even seduced the wife of one of his younger brothers. The young man was afraid
to stand up to him and challenge him, so in his anger and frustration,
he shot his *own* wife with an arrow. He meant only to wound her, but
his arrow struck her in a vital area and she died from the wound. She
was from a different and weaker village, so nobody sought to avenge her
death.

For a few years after separating from the Patanowä-teri, Matowä's
entire group lived among the Bisaasi-teri, but his chronic philandering
eventually caused a major club fight there and he and his group fissioned
away from Kaobawä's Bisaasi-teri group to form Monou-teri. They moved
up the Mavaca River, several hours' walk, but remained on relatively
peaceful terms with the Bisaasi-teri.

Matowä knew that the Patanowä-teri had many enemies to their north
and east and were looking for new friends and allies—that is why they
had visited the Bisaasi-teri in the first place. In the characteristic Machiavellian way that most Yanomamö headmen seem to think, Matowä decided that this would be a good time to harass them, despite the fact that
his village was very small compared to Patanowä-teri. Matowä's group
was about 60 people, and the Patanowä-teri group was about 225 at that
time. If the Patanowä-teri did not have so many active enemies, Matowä
would not have dared to do what he did next: he organized a raiding
party against the powerful Patanowä-teri and set out to attack them by
stealth and kill one or more of them. His raid took place at the beginning
of the dry season—in January 1965, less than two months after I began
my field research.

The Monou-teri raiders left from their own *shabono* on their lagoon
some four or five hours by trail south of Bisaasi-teri. They had to travel
at least two full days to reach the Patanowä-teri in the dry season. They
traveled quickly and the second day brought them close to the village
and they spent the night just short of their destination. They later told
me they did not make campfires that night, lest the smoke betray their
location. They said they ate cold leftover plantains that night, painted
their bodies black with masticated charcoal, shivered in their vine hammocks, and waited silently for the dawn to come. (Even in the Amazon
rainforest, one becomes chilled at night when sleeping without clothes

or a campfire.) They said that they split into two groups and slowly approached the village, hiding in the underbrush.

Eventually people in the Patanowä-teri *shabono* awakened, and daily activities began apprehensively and cautiously, as is always the case when members of an isolated village like Patanowä-teri know that they are likely to be attacked at any time by enemies.

The attacks usually come at dawn, giving the raiders a long period of daylight in which to retreat. In these apprehensive conditions the local residents usually try to leave the *shabono* in armed groups—the men with their bows and arrows guarding the women as they go about their gardening tasks or collecting wild foods.

It is also usually too dangerous for the men to hunt, because small parties of hunters are vulnerable when they are at a considerable distance from their village and can be easily overwhelmed by a larger group of raiders. Thus in times of war there is much less meat at Yanomamö hearths.

The Monou-teri raiders waited in the shadows of the underbrush very near the enemy's *shabono*. Eventually a man named Bosibrei wandered a short distance outside of the *shabono* to harvest the fruits from a cultivated *rasha* palm tree that stood just a few yards from the *shabono*. Nobody thought that raiders would get this close to the *shabono*, so he went about his task nonchalantly and without undue concern.

Rasha trees have thousands of four-inch-long, rigid, very sharp spines sticking out from the entire length of their trunks. In order to climb a *rasha* tree to reach the cluster of fruits some thirty or forty feet above, the climber has to construct a climbing frame from poles and vines and inch his way cautiously up the tree a few feet at a time to avoid being punctured by the spines. Once a short way up the tree, the climber is extremely vulnerable to archers on the ground.

Bosibrei was near the top of the *rasha* tree when the Monou-teri raiders crept out of their concealment, nocked their war arrows, and shot a volley at him. He was pierced by several arrows, fell some thirty feet from the tree, and died almost instantly. After ascertaining he was dead, the Monou-teri raiders retreated hastily without being detected. Astonishingly to me, one of the raiders who shot an arrow into Bosibrei was married to one of his daughters!

Rerebawä making climbing frames in preparation for climbing a *Rasha* tree.

Weeks before this raid—and anticipating an inevitable new war—the Monou-teri had already begun clearing new gardens in a more defensible location. They decided to put an obstacle—the Mavaca River—between their new *shabono* and the Patanowä-teri. They made their new *shabono* and cleared their new gardens several hours across the Mavaca River from (west of) their existing village site. This would become their new, permanent village site once their gardens began producing.

Clearing new gardens is an extremely labor-intensive undertaking. However, moving meant that any Patanowä-teri raiders would have to cross the Mavaca, a major obstacle. To do so they would expose themselves and would lose the advantage of surprise.

The new gardens were also in the direction of their recently acquired allies—the Shamatari villages of Mömariböwei-teri and Reyaboböwei-teri (the former was the village where I discovered that most of my genealogical information on the residents of Bisaasi-teri was utter nonsense). The close proximity of Monou-teri's two new allies would most likely further deter a Patanowä-teri raid.

But the Patanowä-teri's revenge was swift, extraordinary, and lethal.

They deliberately targeted Matowä and went after him on their retaliatory raid. They caught Matowä a short distance from the new gardens, searching for honey with two of his wives. It was in late January or early February 1965 . . . just a few weeks after he and his raiders had killed Bosibrei.

Matowä's older wife related the story to me. Matowä was peering up a tree, looking for the bees' nest and honey when his assailants found him. He apparently didn't even see them in the gray shadows of the dim forest. There was a sizable number of raiders. They quietly nocked their arrows and released them simultaneously in a single volley. At least five arrows struck Matowä in his chest and abdomen. Although he was probably mortally wounded, he nocked one of his own arrows, cursed his assailants defiantly, and feebly shot back at them. One of the raiders, a man named Bisheiwä, then nocked a second arrow, resolutely aimed it at Matowä, and released it. It flew true, striking Matowä in the neck, just below his ear. He fell to the ground and died while the raiders solemnly surrounded him and watched. Then they hastily and silently departed, leaving the two frightened women. Taking the two women as captives would have impeded their safe retreat back to Patanowä-teri. They had to cross the Mavaca River again and then travel two full days.

Bisheiwä, who shot the fatal arrow into Matowä's neck, was one of Bosibrei's sons. The raiders also included two men who called Matowä by the kinship term meaning brother; they were in his lineage, not brothers, but cousins on the male side of the family. Three of the raiders, including Bisheiwä, were Matowä's brothers-in-law (shoris). This underscores the fact that kinship is not an impediment to lethal violence, although the shoriwä relationship is usually a very amicable one. Finally, one of the raiders was a Shamatari who, with his mother, had been abducted many years earlier by the Patanowä-teri from a Shamatari village to their south.

Matowä's wives fled back to the village and told the others what had happened, which is also how I first learned the details of this raid.

The Monou-teri were shocked and disturbed by the swift and lethal retaliation of the Patanowä-teri. But instead of giving chase, they unraveled in a political sense: they were stunned and thoroughly demoralized by the death of their leader, their waiteri.

They mournfully cremated Matowä's body the next day and held a small mortuary ceremony in their village, consuming some of Matowä's ashes in plantain soup. They would hold a larger, more elaborate *reahu* (mortuary ceremony) later and invite the members of allied villages to a big feast for that purpose.

Matowä's two wives were taken by his brothers as additional wives, according to Yanomamö custom, the same custom of the Levirate that we know from the Bible. Many tribal peoples all over the world observe this same rule.

The Monou-teri then fled deep into the jungle to hide.

This cowardice disgusted Matowä's patrilineal relatives in Bisaasi-teri—including Kaobawä, the village headman and a classificatory brother of Matowä. The Bisaasi-teri were furious that the Monou-teri displayed unforgivable cowardice by not pursuing the raiders and trying to kill at least some of them. To show fear and timidity is an invitation to others to further intimidate and exploit your group and it gives *all* groups related to you the stain of cowardice. The Monou-teri's decision to flee reflected on Kaobawä.

Kaobawä then assumed the responsibility of organizing a revenge raid against the Patanowä-teri. He did so just as the dry season was at an end, in early April, which would make a counterraid by the Patanowä-teri unlikely: the rainy season would make the two days' travel through flooding jungle very difficult or even impossible.

Kaobawä invited the Monou-teri to move into his village temporarily, an invitation they gratefully accepted. As mentioned earlier Kaobawä had been attempting to make peace with a major faction of the Patanowä-teri when Matowä initiated all these tragic events. Peace between Kaobawä's faction of Bisaasi-teri and Patanowä-teri was now a very remote possibility because of Kaobawä's invitation to the Monou-teri.

Kaobawä had an adult son by a previous marriage, Shinahewä, who lived in Patanowä-teri, and Kaobawä wanted to make it possible for this young man to visit freely between their two estranged villages. Despite the fact that Yanomamö villages at war are like modern nations at war, there is concern for kinsmen when they live in a village that is now a belligerent. The distinction between warrior and civilian is fuzzy in the Stone Age. In most cases, no harm will come to the noncombatant rela-

A hunting camp containing several *yanos*—temporary huts made with poles, vines, and leaves.

tive, but sometimes a few residents, moved by grief, will try to harm or even kill that person. That is the reason some people choose to flee to a safer (but related) village when hostilities break out. In fact, a sizable faction of the Patanowä-teri did flee to and rejoin the Bisaasi-teri group shortly after this war began.

The impending war set in motion a number of activities that helped me to understand more fully the histories of the various villages I had become familiar with in the short time I had been living there, as well as their political strategies.

First, Kaobawä took immediate steps to make his village more defensible: the Upper Bisaasi-teri had two *shabonos* located immediately next to each other, just a few yards apart. They were, as the Yanomamö say, living *he borara*: "separate, but close to each other." This phrase kept coming up when I collected accounts from old informants about the various village movements they and their parents had made in the past. To live *he borara* is pretty good evidence that the two groups were having a local squabble and wanted to have their own, independent, village, but could not move too far away from each other because they were involved in a war with a distant larger village whose leaders would regard them *both* as enemies—and would more easily kill them if they separated and moved away from each other. The obvious lesson is that there is safety in numbers, so Yanomamö groups conscientiously attempt to maximize the size of their villages and try to quash internal squabbles before they lead to antagonisms that can split the village into two hostile smaller groups. This is why they often choose to live *he borara* for security and safety reasons.

Kaobawä had to persuade the members of the two *he borara* groups to consolidate into one larger *shabono*—a palisaded *shabono*. Moreover, when the Monou-teri—some sixty people—temporarily moved in with them, the greater village would number over two hundred people and could field a much larger raiding party to deal with enemies. The Monou-teri would help with the construction of the new *shabono* and palisade,

A large Yanomamö garden with two *shabonos*, indicating that the village is splitting into two separate groups but living *he borara*—close to each other. When the second and smaller group establishes a producing garden elsewhere, it will move there and make a new *shabono*.

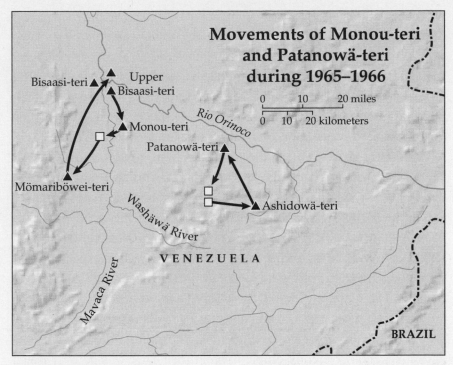

Movements of Monou-teri and Patanowä-teri during 1965–1966

Successive movements of the Monou-teri and Patanowä-teri with respect to their new gardens and allied villages during 1965–66 as they attempted to avoid raids from each other.

an upright wall of eight-foot-high posts that were buried into the ground a foot or so and then lashed together with strong vines.

The Patanowä-teri had to undertake defensive preparations. The Monou-teri and Bisaasi-teri were now their most active enemy. Thus the Patanowä-teri also abandoned their existing village and gardens and moved to the south to establish new gardens and construct a new, heavily palisaded *shabono*. They also took enormous numbers of plantain cuttings from their old garden and transplanted them to their new gardens. And, like the Monou-teri, they were now dependent on allies for refuge, food, and a respite from the now-increased number of raids on their group by both their traditional old enemies *and* their new enemies, the Monou-teri.

Historically powerful groups like the Patanowä-teri have a special kind of problem: they become powerful by intimidating and harassing their neighbors, raiding them, driving them out of the region, abducting women from them, bullying them, and occasionally killing some of them. However, these old enemies never forget and never forgive: they simply feign friendship and trust when they sporadically meet. So, when the powerful groups find themselves embroiled in new wars on a new front, all their previously dormant enemies seize this opportunity to strike at them while they are militarily and politically vulnerable—or perceived to be.

For these reasons, during the first seventeen months of my field research the Patanowä-teri were raided some twenty-five times by their older enemies and by the new enemies such as the Bisaasi-teri and their recently acquired Shamatari allies.

Even though I was living with the Bisaasi-teri, I was politically neutral and could move between the warring factions at will in this particular war. But my visits to the Patanowä-teri during this period were nerve-racking. The Patanowä-teri were always agitated, jumpy, constantly peering into the shadows of the forest for signs of raiders—and grabbing their weapons on hearing any unidentified noise from the forest. Fights and arguments frequently erupted within their large village over trivial things, and the two Patanowä-teri headmen would quickly descend on the troublemakers with clubs, threatening harsh actions if they failed to desist from their squabble.

When I visited, they made me stack up pieces of firewood and my backpacks around my hammock at night to protect myself from arrows that nocturnal assassins might shoot at me. They also insisted that I keep my shotgun loaded and next to my hammock within reach, to shoot at anyone who came into the village after the entrances were blocked shut for the night.

All of this seemed perfectly reasonable and quite logical to me at that time. But I gradually realized that my fieldwork situation had imperceptibly become very different. To a certain extent I was no longer simply an outside observer looking into their culture, as if it existed in some kind of test tube. I had, in a sense, become part of what I was there to observe: I had become an element in their neolithic world. At night, in the dark shadows of a *shabono,* all men are Yanomamö. In this specific case, all men were Patanowä-teri.

The Patanowä-teri embarked on what I considered to be a brilliant military strategy. Instead of spending time attempting to raid *all* of the relatively minor groups that were now attacking them with undeserved boldness, they concentrated their efforts on just a few of their more notable adversaries, like the large village of Hasuböwä-teri, just a day and a half to their east. They had previously once rendered the Hasuböwä-teri militarily impotent by systematic raids that targeted their political leaders, their *waiteri*—men with reputations of ferocity. They boasted to me that they killed most of them and regarded the others there with contempt because they were cowards. When I first met the Patanowä-teri in early 1965, they scoffed at the mere mention of the Hasuböwä-teri; they sardonically dismissed them by saying that they were now "like women" because the Patanowä-teri had killed all their *waiteris*. Now, with the Bisaasi teri hostile toward the Patanowä teri, the Hasuböwä-teri were trying to reassert themselves. To deal with this the Patanowä-teri conducted what contemporary military analysts might call preemptive strikes: they killed the remaining few Hasuböwä-teri *waiteris,* thus neutralizing, in their view, this possible threat. That enabled them to concentrate on the Bisaasi-teri/Monou-teri/Shamatari alliance to their west because all was now relatively quiet on their eastern front.

The Bisaasi-teri raid against the Patanowä-teri organized by Kaobawä took place in April 1965. Kaobawä expected his two Shamatari allies to the west—the Mömariböwei-teri and Reyaboböwei-teri—to send contingents of warriors to participate in this raid, but it seemed that they were reneging on their promise. In Yanomamö politics, allies often need each other but do not always deliver on their promises of aid and do not often trust each other.

Kaobawä delayed his raid for a few days because he suspected that his Shamatari allies were simply waiting for his raiding party to leave so they could then descend on Bisaasi-teri and steal women. But at the last minute a few men from each of the two allied Shamatari villages finally did show up, and the concern over allied treachery was put to rest, at least on that occasion.

On the afternoon before they left on the raid Kaobawä held a small *reahu* mortuary feast. Ripe plantains were cooked and mashed into a sweet, thick soup contained in a large bark trough staked to the ground to prevent the soup from leaking out—it was like a massive banana pudding stored in a bark canoe. Although I had been living with them for five months I was still apprehensive about trying to get close to the group of mourners, who seemed to be in an emotionally volatile mood. Thus I remained a comfortable distance away while the women drank gulps from small gourds of plantain soup into which some of Matowä's ashes had been mixed, and everyone wept loudly, and plaintively called to their fallen kinsman with endearing kinship terms. It was very sad.

Later in the day the raiders conducted a mock raid, a ceremonial rehearsal of what they hoped to do when they reached Patanowä-teri.

They constructed an effigy—a *no owa*—to represent a specific Patanowä-teri man they intended to kill. In this case the *no owa* was a pithy log about five feet long with the bark removed. The pale, stripped log was painted with dark red *nara* pigment—wavy lines to represent maleness—and a few colorful feathers were attached to the head end. It was placed in a hammock, as if the victim were resting and *mohode*— unaware. Kaobawä then organized the raiders into several groups. Each group slowly crept—duck-waddled—toward the *no owa* from different directions. When they were close, they silently rose to a shooting position, drew their bows, and on a signal from one of them, simultaneously let their arrows fly. The *no owa* shuddered and bounced in the hammock as the dozen or so arrows thudded into it. Then the raiders hastily retreated from the *shabono* and retreated a short distance into the forest. After a few moments, they silently returned to the *shabono* and retired to their hammocks to wait for nightfall.

The *shabono* became eerily quiet after dark. I could tell that something was about to happen. The normally crying babies were shushed by the mothers. I could hear people moving around but I could not see them. Their hearth fires had been deliberately allowed to die down to embers and it was very dark inside the *shabono*.

It is a strange feeling to know that something dramatic is about to happen—something deeply primitive and frightening—but not knowing what it might be. My eyes kept darting around, trying desperately to see what was making the soft, muffled noises. People were moving and almost gliding past me quietly but I couldn't see them. Maybe they were surrounding me and planned to shoot me for trying to witness some prohibited sacred ceremony that outsiders were not allowed to see?

A *no owa*, or effigy, of some intended male victim. This one is made from a log with the bark removed and painted with a long serpentine design. It has a monkey-tail headband covered with white buzzard down. The man hovering over it is spitting on it to insult the enemy it represents.

The stillness was suddenly shattered by a blood-curdling scream—a man's voice that sounded like part animal growl and part wail. He emerged from the darkness of the *shabono* interior to my right, clacking his six-foot-long war arrows against his heavy palm-wood bow stave as he marched slowly out to the dim center of the village clearing, making frightening screams and growls as he mimicked various ferocious carnivorous animals and insects. I could barely make him out as he turned and stood menacingly with his face to the southeast, toward the enemy village of Patanowä-teri—but also toward me! He rested the fletched ends of his arrows on the ground near his feet, next to his stout bow. He then stared silently toward the southeast—over my head. I still thought he was staring at me. I was thinking, You're next, *nabä*!

Then the village grew unsettlingly quiet again. Presently another man, from a different part of the village, stepped out of the dark shadows of the *shabono* roof, noisily clacked his arrows against his bow stave, and, like the first man, proceeded slowly toward the center of the plaza. And like the first man, he uttered piercing, shrill noises mimicking carnivorous animals and biting insects.

I felt goose bumps on my arms. I imagined myself being present at a time ten thousand years in the past and thought about how utterly strange that I was to be one of the last members of my profession to experience an event that had, by the 1960s, become nearly unique. These were the last of the Stone Age warriors assembling to wreak mayhem and death on distant enemies. Their enemies waited anxiously, not knowing when they would come, but anticipating their terrible wrath.

The warriors were painted black but looked in other regards like they did normally, naked with their penises tied to their waist string. Only their bows and arrows proclaimed them as *yahi tä rimö*—humans who dwelt in houses—and not *urihi tä rimö*, wild and beastly animals who lived in the forest. Their anger, aggression, and determination were premeditated and resolute, not spontaneous like the sudden, aggressive bite or attack of a feline or canine predator.

Each raider repeated this process until they were all standing in a straight line, facing toward the southeast. It took only some thirty minutes for the lineup to be completed, but it seemed like several hours. I later learned that I was watching a ritual that the Yanomamö call *wayu itou*, the ritual pre-raid assembly of the raiders. This ritual is conducted

A warrior line-up—*wayu itou*—just before departing on a raid. The group includes Matarawä, a young boy going on his first raid to avenge his father's death at the hands of raiders a month earlier.

only on the eve of a raiding party departing to kill enemies. I have subsequently witnessed several others and all caused goose bumps to appear on my arms and neck.

The murmurs and whispers of the women and children suddenly ceased and the village again became very quiet. I continued to squat at the edge of the plaza, trying to be as inconspicuous and unobtrusive as possible. What I was witnessing clearly provoked awe and powerful emotions among the Yanomamö—but I was worried that it was something that might also provoke *anger* among them because I was watching and tape-recording it.

Again the silence was suddenly broken, this time by a deep baritone voice slowly singing, "I am meat hungry! I am meat hungry! Like the carrion-eating vulture, I am hungry for flesh!" I recognized the voice as Torokoiwä's, one of Matowä's brothers, who was an exceptionally skillful singer and chanter. The stanzas of the Vulture song, as it is called, changed radically from deep, methodical baritone phrases to nearly falsetto ones within a single phrase. I still get chills when I play my tapes of this song—it is truly frightening and has, for want of more precise words, an undeniable primordial quality.

The rest of the raiders repeated the lines of the song, ending the final word with a disturbing high-pitched scream.

Torokoiwä then led a second chorus of the song, varying the words slightly, referring this time to the voracious meat hunger of a type of carnivorous wasp, instead of the vulture in the first chorus. Specific men interjected descriptions of violent deeds they intended to inflict on enemy warriors—bashing their brains out, splattering their blood all over their wives' possessions, making their children tremble and weep, and other despicable violent things.

When the singing of the last stanza terminated, the entire line of warriors coalesced into a tight formation and shouted three times in unison, getting louder each time: "Whaaaa! Whaaaa! WHAAAA!" Then suddenly they became silent and listened for the echo of their last shout, which would portend success. When the echo was heard, they became frantic and excited for they knew then that their enemy would be found at home. They hissed, growled, and clacked their weapons together excitedly, dancing in place.

Eventually Kaobawä calmed them down and they reassembled. They repeated the shouting two more times in almost precisely the same fashion. But at the end of the third repetition they scattered and ran back to their respective houses, making a sound like *bububububububu* as they ran. On reaching their hammocks, they all began to vomit and retch symbolically, making disgusting, loud puking noises. They were vomiting out the "rotten flesh" of the enemy whose body they had symbolically devoured like carrion during the *wayu itou.*

They then retired for the night. Hearths were given more firewood and the flames danced and flickered as they came back to life. Babies periodically whimpered and cried until their mothers gave them a breast, and a few dogs let out sharp yelps as their owners hit them with pieces of firewood for moving in too close to the hearth to keep warm. The *shabono* interior described a nearly perfect circle of campfires spaced a few yards apart. Only the first few feet of the roof over the campfires was illuminated, where the roof met the earth, and I could see a hundred or more hammocks, strung low to the ground, some motionless, some swinging gently. Several of Matowä's brothers murmured and sang sad, melancholy songs, mourning for him deep into the night. The smoke of many campfires lofted slowly upward following the interior of the slanted roof and then silently disappeared into the black sky.

At daybreak it was cold. The women went quietly to the gardens and cut bunches of plantains and tied them into bundles. The men would, in turn, bind them to their vine hammocks and carry them on their backs by a shoulder thong. They would eventually roast them over hot coals and eat them en route to the Patanowä-teri, the enemy.

The Patanowä-teri were at least two days away, but they might be even further: they were in the process of moving to a new, more defensible garden at a place where their enemies would least expect them to be. Thus the raiders were uncertain of their precise location and, therefore, how much food they should bring to sustain themselves.

The raiders repainted their legs, arms, faces, and torsos in black pigment (masticated charcoal) in the dimness of the first light. They inspected their weapons, changed arrow points if necessary or simply out of nervousness, and made sure their bowstrings did not have any weaknesses that might cause them to break at a crucial moment.

At dawn Kaobawä passed the word for them to repeat the *wayu itou*, but this time it would be in daylight and I could see more clearly what had been so terrifying to me in the dark.

The warriors slowly and with resolute determination marched one at a time to the center of the village and stood in a line, facing southeast as they did the night before. This time they did not sing the Meat Hungry Vulture song, but simply shouted in unison toward their enemy. When they heard their echo, they marched dramatically out of the village single file, picked up their vine hammocks and plantains that were placed on the trail by the women, and silently disappeared into the jungle. Their mothers, sisters, wives, and daughters wept, and as they disappeared they apprehensively enjoined the warriors to be careful, to come back home safely—as women everywhere do when their sons, brothers, husbands, and fathers go off to war.

Kaobawä had not been well for several months prior to this raid. He was suffering from what he kept describing to me as a pain in his lower back, urinary tract, and lower abdominal areas. I could not tell if the pain was inside, perhaps like kidney stones, or outside, caused by some trauma or injury. In any event, he sometimes had difficulty walking long distances. He nevertheless insisted on leading this raid. I suspect that he was worried that if he did not, his enemies would interpret the village's collective failure to avenge Matowä as cowardice.

Let me emphasize the Yanomamö view that when members of a group acquire a reputation of timidity and cowardice, their neighbors take ruthless advantage of them, push them around, insult them publicly, and take their women. Thus it is strategically important to react decisively to any affront, no matter how trivial. If a group is small, the men try to make up for their numerical disadvantage by acting as if the group is bigger, nastier, more ferocious, and ready to fight on a moment's notice. Feigning to be "larger than life" is a deception that is widespread in the animal world but is usually a characteristic displayed by *individual* combatants. The Yanomamö, however, engage in this masquerade *as members of social groups*. I often deliberately avoided visiting small villages because they were predictably very aggressive and unpleasant to be around in order to compensate for their actual military weaknesses.

The raiders were not gone a half day when a few of them began to return to the village. They complained of pains in their legs, or thorns in their feet. Most of these were younger men of dubious valor, men who enjoyed displaying their alleged ferocity in the safety of their own *shabono* during the *wayu itou* and in front of the young women, but who were keenly aware of the risks they would endure when they got close to their enemy's village and the arrows started flying.

The ones who pushed on to the enemy's village traveled slowly the first day, looking for signs of recent footprints leading toward or from the southeast. These would be evidence that Patanowä-teri raiders had crossed through the area. They also carried plantains for several days' meals, which were heavy and slowed them down at first. On this raid they also paced themselves so they would arrive in the general vicinity of Patanowä-teri's most recent village near or at dusk of the second day. They would camp just an hour or so from the village and reconnoiter the area, hoping to find positive signs of recent local travel along the footpaths. They knew this area well, since they themselves had lived here when they and the Patanowä-teri had been one large village some dozen years earlier.

The raiders later told me they spent the last night close to the village and could not make campfires to keep themselves warm. Every member of the raiding party I spoke to made a point of telling me about how uncomfortable it was sleeping without a campfire. I could empathize with them. When I traveled through the jungle and camped for the night I would change into my sleeping attire: a clean, dry set of clothes that included a T-shirt, dry underpants, socks, long pants, a long-sleeve shirt—and an insulated, lightweight nylon blanket. I always felt very cold whenever the fire went out at any altitude, and it was much worse at higher elevations. The Yanomamö have no clothes or blankets, so they shivered uncomfortably all night long, naked in the damp, cold night air. Yes, I could understand how cold and uncomfortable it must have been without fire. Fire is what makes Yanomamö *yahi tä rimö*—different from beasts.

The raiding party leaders also confided to me another problem: their concern that the younger men might defect and turn back. The excuses would be fear of a nocturnal jaguar attack without a campfire, the cold, the sore feet—and any other plausible justification, including a bad dream that portends disaster. Most of them were simply frightened, but to show or admit fear is a sure invitation to be branded a coward, an accusation that tends to remain forever in the memories of others. It is acceptable to use as excuses injury, the cold, jaguar threats, sore feet, etc. and not admit you were afraid.

Their plan from the outset was to split up at dawn and approach the village in several small groups of about four men each. They hoped to shoot one or more of the enemy and retreat in a defensive pattern: while two defenders remained on the trail with their weapons ready, the others would hastily retreat past them. Then the first two would retreat while two of the former group would take places down the trail to cover them against any pursuers. They would repeat this pattern until they were at a safe distance from the village and then all would literally run toward home and safety.

If there were any novices on the raid they would make another *no owa* out of leaves or a log and rehearse the retreat for their benefit.

On this particular raid they brought along a boy of about twelve years. He was Matarawä, Matowä's oldest son. He was the youngest raider I ever saw on any of the raiding parties I witnessed. This would be his first raid: they wanted him to taste and enjoy the cold dish of revenge for the death of his father. But they protected him, always making sure he had experienced raiders in front of and behind him—and they planned for him to be the first to retreat to safety after they killed an enemy.

While the raiders were gone those who remained behind were tense and nervous, constantly on the lookout for other raiders—especially men from erstwhile friendly villages. Raiders might take this opportunity to visit the village and seize with relative impunity some of the now poorly defended young women and girls.

The women were nervous and irritable, and several bitter arguments broke out among them over trivial issues. One woman became very angry when her sister left her baby with her to babysit for a brief time. When she returned, the babysitter picked up a stout piece of firewood and bashed the mother along the side of her head, knocking her unconscious and causing a bloody scalp wound. The few adult men in the village had difficulty preventing the fight from escalating and involving more of the village women and possibly some of the men.

The raiding party had been gone almost a week when Kaobawä and his youngest brother, Shararaiwä, staggered into the village and collapsed silently into their hammocks. They were exhausted.

Kaobawä's groin pains had worsened on the trail and he had great difficulty walking: he would have been a liability to the group as they retreated, so he reluctantly dropped out of the raid and planned to head slowly for home. When they turned back they were getting close to Patanowä-teri. Shararaiwä accompanied him to make sure he could make it all the way back. But shortly after they dropped out and were headed home, Shararaiwä stepped on an *arowari*—a very poisonous snake—and was bitten by it. The rainy season had already begun, and the snakes were concentrating in the higher areas—where the Yano-mamö trails usually were. Snakebites are much more common in the rainy season for this reason.

Shararaiwä's leg began to swell up immediately and he could not walk. Kaobawä, barely able to walk himself, then had to carry his brother on

his back—or leave him where he lay, close to the enemy village. Kaobawä carried Shararaiwä for the better part of two days, in great pain,
until they finally reached the banks of the Orinoco River. He intended to
make a crude bark canoe and float downstream for the remainder of the
trip because he could carry Shararaiwä no farther.

But they had the good fortune of discovering a concealed dugout
canoe that one of the men from another village had hidden in the brush.
The man was on a visit to Bisaasi-teri and had had to cross the Orinoco
to get there.

The next morning the main group of raiders marched silently into the
village. Word quickly spread that they had reached the Patanowä-teri and
succeeded in killing one of them with their arrows. The Patanowä-teri gave
chase, managed to get ahead of them as they retreated, and were able to
shoot one of the raiders, a Monou-teri man named Konoreiwä.

Two men were carrying Konoreiwä in his vine hammock, strung on a
pole between them. He was unconscious and had been for some time.
He had been shot with an arrow that was tipped with a lanceolate-
shaped *rahaka* point. It had gone completely through his chest, just
above his heart, and the tip of the point had protruded out of his back.
They managed to pull it out on the trail, but it was a very bad wound.
They told me that one of them was able to bite the end of the protruding
arrow point and pull it out with his teeth. They also told me that before
they got back Konoreiwä was coughing up blood filled with air bubbles,
and he wheezed with each breath. The arrow had torn through a lobe of
his lungs—almost always a fatal wound.

When they reached the Bisaasi-teri *shabono* they transferred Konoreiwä into a more comfortable, larger, cotton hammock that was strung
close to and above a fire to keep him warm.

They asked me to "cure" him, that is, "treat" his wound. I thought
Konoreiwä's chances without major surgery were poor. I had learned, on
the spot so to speak, how to stitch up injured Yanomamö, mostly head
wounds from club fights, but properly treating Konoreiwä's arrow wound
was way out of my league. The crowning achievement of my first-aid
skills had been putting about ten stitches into the mangled foot of Shi-
imima, one of Kaobawä's brothers. He had wanted to see if there was a
caiman in a submerged den he found in the bank of a small stream. He

quickly found out that, indeed, there was a caiman in that hole, one who was ferociously protecting her newly hatched eggs.

The Yanomamö believe that when you are wounded with a *rahaka*-tipped arrow you can drink only minute quantities of water until you recover. Most of their folk beliefs are almost the opposite of what sound medical practice recommends.

Konoreiwä lay silently in his hammock for several days, eating little, and drinking less. He was slowly wasting away, mostly from dehydration. I did what my modest medical knowledge and medical supplies permitted, which was keeping the entry and exit wounds clean and giving him antibiotics in an attempt to prevent infection.

Finally, I could not bear to watch him wasting away and decided to take matters into my own hands, Yanomamö customs and taboos that proscribed water be damned. I made a conscious decision to interfere in their culture—and I do not feel the least bit guilty for doing so. Some anthropologists would say I did something unethical because this act *might* give them hope and therefore make them *dependent* on modern medicine and, when I left, my medicine would no longer be available. This would most likely cause them psychological harm. According to such logic it is better not to give them hope and make them dependent on modern medicine, to let them die. I disagree.

I ceremoniously made Konoreiwä a large batch of extremely sweet lemonade, proclaiming loudly that it was *mönasönö*. The Yanomamö don't have a word for what we call medicine so I used the Spanish word for it, *medicina*, which they knew about in Bisaasi-teri. The Yanomamö pronounce it *mönasönö* and it is usually taken to be something nearly magical that *nabäs* are able to make to cure themselves and cure the Yanomamö. *Mönasönö* includes such things as antimalarials, penicillin, anti-worm medicine, aspirin, measles vaccine (after 1968), and so on.

Their taboo did not prohibit a wounded warrior from taking *mönasönö* for his near-lethal *rahaka* wounds, even when it came in a watery (and clandestinely sweetened) form.

When my batch of *mönasönö* was finished, I brought it over to Konoreiwä's hammock and very publicly announced that I was going to give him some of my *mönasönö*. Several men who had been on the raid gathered around me. I made a point of holding up several aspirin pills, crushed them in a pair of spoons in front of their eyes, and dropped the powder into the aluminum pot containing the *mönasönö* and stirred it for a few moments into the liquid, thus increasing its magical potency. I then took a Yanomamö spoon of sorts—a small gourd cut in half along its length—and dipped it into the *mönasönö* and, lifting Konoreiwä's head slightly up from his hammock, counseled him to drink the *mönasönö*. His face lit up as he swallowed it. The others probably assumed that it was some sort of shock reaction he had from the power of the *mönasönö*. But I had to smother a grin, for now *two* of us knew that it was very sweet lemonade, masquerading as *mönasönö*. A knowing glance of acknowledgment and an imperceptible flicker of his eyebrows told me he also knew that this was not ordinary *mönasönö*.

I admonished the others that this *mönasönö* was to be drunk *only* by the victim—it would potentially harm anyone else—and they were to continue giving it to him during the night and into the next day, at which time I would make another batch of it.

Thanks to his inherently superior constitution, and with a generous ration of *mönasönö*, Konoreiwä slowly recovered. My reputation as a curer increased further. By the time I left for home that year the Bisaasi-teri had a great deal of trust in me and confidence that my *mönasönö* was tendered in good faith, usually worked, and tasted rather like *buu*, their word for honey and for sugar water.

The raiders who shot fatal arrows into their Patanowä-teri victim were both brothers of Matowä. Since they were now *unokai*—killers of men—they had to ritually purify themselves by undergoing a special ritual: the *unokaimou*. Both had undergone this purification before for earlier killings.

It was because of this specific raid that I began to learn about the existence of an important, permanent, and earned status position in Yanomamö society: *unokais*. It was a high status that did not emerge because of "differential control" over the strategic resources available in Yanomamö culture, nor control over the material means of production. This was the sort of argument textbooks claimed about status positions in "egalitarian" societies, a status that all individuals of the same sex and same age would more or less automatically acquire just by being there. Not all men were willing to endure the risks and expose themselves to the dangers that Yanomamö *unokais* did—and *unokais* held a special, earned, and respected status that only some men achieved.

The two *unokais* were given a special space in Kaobawä's *shabono*, where they strung their hammocks. Their space was separated from the adjacent areas with a seven-foot-high wall made of palm fronds. The *unokais* had their food brought to them for the week they were in ritual confinement. The two men used sharp sticks, not unlike chopsticks, to pierce their food and take it into their mouths: they were not allowed to touch the food lest they contaminate it with the pollution their fingers and bodies exuded. If they did so, this pollution would enter them and cause them to become sick. They also had to be careful to scratch their bodies, when they itched, with similar (maybe even the same) sticks they used to eat with. Their hands and fingers were especially polluted. They had to keep their voices low and speak in whispers. They were also pro-hibited from cutting their hair and had to let it grow for the better part of the year. And they had to refrain from sex for a lengthy period.

The *unokaimou* ceremony was, in almost all respects, nearly identical to the ceremony that pubescent girls went through when they had their first menses—the *nyöbömou,* which marked their transition into woman-hood.

After about a week in ritual confinement the two *unokais* emerged. Their vine hammocks—the ones they were sleeping in and the ones they used on the raid—were then taken down and tied with vines to a specific kind of tree about six feet above the level of the ground. Their vine ham-mocks were spaced about a foot apart on the trunk of this tree. The tree was on the bank of the Orinoco, perhaps by chance, hidden in the under-brush. Their scratching sticks were also attached to the hammocks and to the tree. When this was done, the two men were free to resume their normal activities—except for cutting their hair and resuming sexual ac-tivities. I don't know how long the sexual abstinence requirement lasted. Most anthropologists, me included, know very little about the sexual lives of the people they study.

Unokais have an unusual status in their villages. Most outsiders do not know about them, or about the unpretentious and rarely discussed high status they have. Even a diligent, curious anthropologist might not learn about them if he studied a village that has not engaged in warfare

Rare photo: the vine hammocks of the *unokais*

or where no individuals in that village had killed another human in the recent past.

Unokais are both respected and somewhat feared because they have demonstrated a willingness to kill people and are likely to kill again. In a political context, the military credibility and strength of a village can be measured by how many *unokais* it contains—with the caveat that village size is extremely important as well. But, if two equal-sized villages are compared, the one with the largest number of able-bodied *unokais* will be the stronger, the more feared, and the more formidable opponent.

Many men acquire a reputation for being *waiteri*, fierce. But someone who is an *unokai* has demonstrated his willingness to inflict lethal harm on an opponent and to actually behave in an ultimately fierce manner. Publicly and socially, such men can be extremely placid and calm in their outward demeanor, and even very pleasant and charming. By contrast, many men who are not *unokais* seem to be compelled to behave in such a way as to *imply* that they are killers of men. Such men can be very obnoxious and unpleasant in their public lives—ordering people around, intimidating them, threatening to hit them with their machetes or axes, even threatening to kill them. But if an *unokai* threatens to strike or to kill someone, he usually means what he says. When an *unokai* gives an order to some man in the village, that man had better do what is asked of him. That is how power, authority, and coercive force by leaders emerges, adds to, and goes beyond the kind of solidarity and cohesion that inheres in the lesser cohesiveness associated with kinship amity. This is the quality that leads ultimately to the power behind law: the odiousness of sanctions. Without law, political states cannot exist.

Kaobawä's raid against the Patanowä-teri achieved several important things in the arena of regional Yanomamö politics. In the first place the killing of Matowä was, in a sense, a Patanowä-teri test of the strength of the blood ties between the Bisaasi-teri and the Monou-teri: they had killed Matowä, a close patrilineal kinsman of Kaobawä, a man whom he called brother. The Patanowä-teri also knew that Kaobawä had many kinsmen in Patanowä-teri as well, but could not accurately predict his actions when they killed Matowä. Would Kaobawä favor his brothers-in-law (*shoris*) in Patanowä-teri over members of his patrilineal lineage (*mashi*)? Kaobawä acted swiftly and unhesitatingly by raiding the Patanowä-teri, perhaps with the larger (and longer-term) military implications in mind: his actions made the Patanowä-teri keenly aware that he would defend and stand up for the Monou-teri—and the Monou-teri members of his own patrilineage, his own *mashi*. This meant that the Patanowä-teri would not be safe in the Bisaasi-teri area: they would have to approach the Monou-teri by a more circuitous southern route to raid them, a route that would expose their raiding parties to the two Shamatari allies of the Monou-teri and the Bisaasi-teri. Moreover, Kaobawä was previously an *unokai*—as were a rather large number of other men in both Monou-teri and Bisaasi-teri.

It began to be clearer to me that patrilineal descent—acknowledging membership in a patrilineal descent group called *mashi*—was important in Yanomamö political relationships. Lineages are an evolutionary step toward greater social complexity in tribal societies, where kinship relationships structure most social interactions. Patrilineages are defined by genealogical relationships up from and down from some male ancestor and including in the group thus defined *all* males who are related via the male line. For example, my father's father was also named Napoleon Chagnon. If I consider all males up from and down from him in the male line, they would all be members of my patrilineal lineage—my *mashi*. In many situations, especially in political and military ones, we would act as a single group because our survival and well-being would depend on it.

Forming and acknowledging the existence of patrilineal descent groups in your society are important steps in the development of political complexity. Patrilineages are not evident in monumental architecture, sophisticated pottery, conspicuous trappings of office like fancy decorations or staffs of authority, but more subtle things that are more difficult to detect—like the *numbers* and *kinds* of genetically related kinsmen who will support your decisions and are willing to die doing so. But, as these patrilineal descent groups and the larger societies in which they are found become larger and more complex than the Yanomamö, these descent groups become identified with real property and with material possessions. Among the Yanomamö, this second step has not yet been achieved. The first step—the most important step—emerged independently of control over scarce, strategic material resources.

What these Yanomamö descent groups control and defend are reproductive rights in nubile females and the male kin who give these women to you and take them from you according to rules of incest and marriage-ability. All additional "functions" of patrilineages are secondary and derived from these initial functions.

The Monou-teri Raid

Just as the rainy season was ending in early 1965—in about late July or early August—the Monou-teri initiated another raid against the Patanowä-teri. The Monou-teri raid occurred several months after Kaobawä's raid. This was the only raid the Monou-teri went on that year without the help of at least one of their allies.

I was staying with the Monou-teri in the *shabono* on their lagoon.

On the day before the raid they conducted a very special ceremony, one that I had not seen before and have not seen since. Perhaps it was a ceremony reserved for *unokais* who have fallen in war.

They assembled in front of the house of Torokoiwä, one of Matowä's brothers. There they placed several gourds that contained the ashes of Matowä's cremated body into a shallow basket. They were in an extremely distressed and almost violent mood known as *hushuwo*.

Matowä's bamboo arrow point quiver—his *tora*—was taken down from the rafters of Torokoiwä's house and placed on the ground next to the gourds. All the adults in the village crowded in close to the artifacts, squatting on their haunches, weeping and singing very sad songs, calling to Matowä by endearing kinship terms. I was gently and gradually pushed out of the crowd to the periphery and had difficulty seeing exactly what they were doing. I dared not stand up to see better because this would be offensive to the Monou-teri and they were in an extremely volatile mood.

Matowä's adult brothers were each given several of his lanceolate *rahaka* arrow points. The men fondled them gently and wept aloud. They would put them on their arrows the next day and use them on this raid. They hoped to kill one or more Patanowä-teri with arrow points that had belonged to their beloved kinsman, a victim of the Patanowä-teri.

Then one brother smashed Matowä's *tora* by pounding on it with an ax. The shattered pieces of bamboo were put into a small pile and burning coals from the hearth were mixed into the splinters to ignite them. As they burned, the mood of the women turned into a state of frenzy: they pulled their hair, struck their bodies with their hands and fists, and wailed loudly.

One of Matowä's brothers then filled a snuff tube with *ebene* and gently blew it into several of the gourds containing his ashes, a postmortem aliquot of hallucinogen—possibly to enable the deceased Matowä to make one last contact with his beloved *hekura* spirits. Then the snuff tube itself was broken in half, the breaking point being measured off from the end by the length of one of Matowä's *rahaka* arrow points. The broken snuff tube and the gourds were gently wrapped in leaves, tied with vines, and placed back into the structural roof poles, presumably for later ceremonies. It was growing dark when this ceremony ended. People slowly returned to their hammocks, added firewood to their hearths, blew on the coals until their fires danced, and retired for the night.

It was one of the saddest ceremonies I ever witnessed, because I knew these people well and I identified with them, and had great empathy for them. I was deeply moved by what they had just done.

Torokoiwä and other men began quietly singing very melancholy songs to their fallen kinsman, softly, sadly, as they sobbed out the words. I lay in my hammock and listened, not bothering to tape-record it, take photos, or write down notes. One of them asked me aloud why I was not making a nuisance of myself as I usually do. I quietly replied by saying, "Ya buhii ahi." It means something like "my innermost being is cold because I am in mourning and sad."

My words were whispered around the village, and as each person heard them, he or she looked over knowingly, approvingly at me. The children, who inevitably gather around my hammock, were told to go home and not bother me. The adults told the children that I was hush-uwo, in a state of emotional disequilibrium, and that my soul was cold. To them I was finally acting like a human being, like a Yanomamö. The ones whose hammocks were close to mine quietly reached over to me, looked at me, and touched me gently. And we wept together.

The raiders assembled at dawn, performed the wayu itou, shouted toward the direction of Patanowä-teri, and listened for the echo to return. They left the shabono silently, in a single file.

The raiders never reached the village of the Patanowä-teri. All the trails were flooded and they had to make many detours. They eventually gave up and returned to their village after about a week.

During that one year of war the Monou-teri managed to capture just two women from the Patanowä-teri, but at the price of many blows to their heads in a brutal club fight and the killing of their charismatic and audacious headman, Matowä. The Patanowä-teri, in turn, had two men killed by raiders from Monou-teri and their allies, but managed to recover five of the women taken from them by force on that first day.

During that same time period the Patanowä-teri were raided some twenty-five times, mostly by villages other than Monou-teri and Bisaasi-teri.

The incident that took place the day before I arrived had precipitated a set of hostile actions based on smoldering grievances held by other enemies of the Patanowä-teri who then seized the opportunity to settle earlier scores and began raiding them to kill.

In Yanomamö warfare the time to strike a new blow is when an enemy is temporarily down and struggling—and has many new enemies. Machiavelli could have written *The Prince* about the political strategies of Yanomamö headmen and villages.

But for me, the larger lesson of what I witnessed had to do with what this single war revealed about the unknown history, the social and political dynamics, and the regional geographical movements of the several parties to the conflict. I couldn't understand this war—or any Yanomamö war—until I knew the details and deep history of the several villages that were the major belligerents.

Again, I realized that my anthropological training was wide of the mark. It was obvious to me that the "field study" of contemporary tribal groups was too narrowly focused on a single village and a time period that was too shallow. The standard anthropological paradigm or model seemed to assume that tribal villages were frozen in time, had no history to speak of, and rarely changed position in a fixed sociopolitical matrix. The standard social anthropology model I grew up with was severely limited and therefore inadequate to explain what I was witnessing and, I would argue, inadequate to explain much of the history and political dynamics of the Paleolithic era, or what has recently come to be called the EEA—the environments of evolutionary adaptedness, the Environments of History, or the ARE, the adaptively relevant environments that humans lived in prior to the political state and civilization.

4

Bringing My Family to Yanomamöland and My Early Encounters with the Salesians

My Wife and Children Among the Yanomamö

I planned to bring my wife, Carlene, and our two young children into the jungle during my fieldwork. Our son, Darius, was three years old and our daughter, Lisa, was eighteen months in late 1964 when we arrived in Venezuela. Naturally, I would go in ahead of them and scout things out and, so to speak, set up camp for a year's stay. Our plan was that my family would join me after I had been there a few weeks.

While my graduate studies didn't cover things like family living while doing fieldwork, I knew of a few anthropologists who took their wives into the field with them, but few of them had families with young children. I also knew from a two-day meeting with James P. Barker in Chicago before I went to Venezuela in November 1964 that some of the New Tribes missionaries, including Barker himself, who worked in Venezuela's Amazonas region had their families with them at a few of their remote posts.

Soon after I made my first trip to Mavaca I contacted my wife by shortwave radio from the Salesian Mission at Ocamo and explained the field situation to her (except for the green snot and club fighting). I informed her that conditions were a little more "primitive" than I had initially expected and that it would take me some extra time to make improvements—like building a mud-and-thatch hut just outside the village where we could live close enough to the Yanomamö to hear them, but far enough from their *shabono* so we could have some privacy when we wanted it. I added that Barker, the New Tribes missionary, said we could share his outhouse—I was trying to put an optimistic twist on his generous offer.

The field situation during that first year didn't improve to the extent that I was willing to bring Carlene and our children in for a protracted period of time like six or seven months. Malaria, for example, was especially bad that year, and many of the Yanomamö were suffering from it. Several of them died, despite the efforts of the Malarialogía, whose personnel had abundant quantities of antimalarial pills and who were ever-willing to go to the widely scattered *shabonos* and treat the sick Yanomamö. Dysentery and diarrhea, especially among the Yanomamö children, was also a serious problem, as were periodic outbreaks of upper respiratory infections like common colds. All of these were present when I reached the field and, according to Barker, were a constant hazard of life in the jungle, not to mention the very serious problem of the diurnal gnats that made life hell by day and the thousands of malaria-carrying mosquitoes that made it hell by night.

Padre Cocco

After the first day I was alone with the Yanomamö. Barker had returned to Tama Tama downstream, and I would not see him for three months.

I found it very difficult to live among the Yanomamö at first. I was the only non-Yanomamö in the Upper Bisaasi-teri village, which had some 130 or so people in it. For the first month I could not even cross the river to visit with the Malarialogía personnel because I had no dugout canoe or motor. I finally purchased both of these. This made it possible to go downstream some two hours to the Salesian Mission at Ocamo to make contact by shortwave radio with my wife, who was now staying at IVIC, the Venezuelan Research Institute in the mountains above Caracas. The

Padre Cocco

one *civilizado* I could talk to at that point in my fieldwork was Padre Luiz (Luigi) Cocco, the Italian Salesian priest who had established the mission at the mouth of the Ocamo. He was a jolly, kind man who looked a bit like Santa Claus. He spoke by radio every morning at six to an older Venezuelan man who lived in Caracas, named Don Teodoro. Padre Cocco would contact Don Teodoro, who would patch me through by telephone to my wife's apartment at IVIC, but these attempts were successful only about half of the time. Then I would have to spend another night at Padre Cocco's mission and try again the next morning.

Later my first year another Salesian priest, Padre José Berno, arrived at Mavaca about two hours by motorized canoe upstream from Ocamo to start another Salesian mission. He brought his own shortwave radio with him. Padre Berno offered to help me contact my wife via Don Teodoro, an opportunity that I enthusiastically and gratefully accepted. But the first time I tried to take advantage of his offer, he attached a condition: he wanted me to take Yanomamö language materials from James Barker and give these items to him. Barker had developed a Yanomamö dictionary and a basic grammar in order to produce school materials to teach Yanomamö children how to read and write in their own language, and in Spanish as they learned it from the Salesians. I never saw these language items, but Barker mentioned them to me.

I refused to do this for Padre Berno and preferred to take the inconvenient trip downstream to continue to use Padre Cocco's radio. Because of my regular visits, Padre Cocco and I got to know each other quite well, and I overnighted at his mission regularly that first year.

We would have long talks, and my command of Spanish improved. Although Padre Cocco's native language was Italian, he spoke Spanish quite well. He said he was writing a book on his experiences as a missionary among the Yanomamö and asked me to help him with some of the aspects of Yanomamö culture, settlement patterns, and how the group near his mission—Iyäwei-teri—was related to the villages farther up the Ocamo River. He also wanted to use some of my color photographs to illustrate his book, which I happily provided.

He was astounded, for example, when I told him the Yanomamö called their female cross-cousins by the same term they used for "wife" but distinguished their female parallel cousins from their cross-cousins and called them by the same term they use for "sister." At first he didn't believe me and insisted that we go to the *shabono*, where he questioned one of the young Yanomamö men, "Carlito." Padre Cocco was flabbergasted when Carlito corroborated what I had told Padre Cocco. Padre Cocco had spent ten years with the Yanomamö and had never noticed this practice.

Padre Cocco told me a story about his life as a young priest in northern Italy. He was from Turin. During World War II, he said, he took great risks to save downed Allied pilots from the Germans, hiding them in his church and helping them eventually to get to safety. Later, he told me how he saved Axis pilots by hiding them in his church and helping them to get to safety. In both cases he said he could have been executed by firing squad for what he had done. Then, with a twinkle in his eye, he whispered to me that after the war ended he began receiving a pension from both the Allied and Axis powers for what he had done to save their respective pilots.

On one occasion he told me that he had just read in his recent Salesian newsletter a message from the pope that Catholic priests could have fruitful social dialogues with people of other faiths—including atheists. He added, "This means that I don't have to feel guilty for being friendly with you." Padre Cocco had correctly decided that I was an atheist.

The Sinister Side of the Salesians

During 1965 a disturbing incident took place that became an intricate component in later problems that developed between the Salesians and me. It was something Padre Cocco asked me to do. One day in 1965 Padre Cocco paid me a visit at my mud-and-thatch hut at Mavaca. I was surprised but delighted to see him—he had never visited me although I had visited him many times.

Napoleon Chagnon (left) with Hmno. Iglesias (right). An unidentified Salesian priest stands in the background.

He was very disturbed when he showed up. He told me that he had just learned that Hermano (Brother) Iglesias, who had been sent to the most remote Salesian Mission post, had been having an affair with a Yanomamö woman for several years. In fact he had sired several children by her at the mission in Platanal. (This was the village of the Mahekodoteri.) Padre Cocco was angry, ashamed, and bitterly disappointed, not so much because Iglesias had violated his vows of celibacy but because he had brought great shame on the Catholic Church and created a potentially embarrassing public scandal. Padre Cocco seemed desperate to keep this shameful act out of the Venezuelan media. Hermano Iglesias would eventually be dismissed from his duties, would return to Spain, and would no longer be affiliated with the Salesian Missions.

I listened quietly. Then Padre Cocco proposed a solution to the problem that would avert publicity and spare the church any embarrassment. He told me that Iglesias spoke very highly of me and trusted me because he and I shared an interest in photography. Padre Cocco suggested that I approach Hermano Iglesias and invite him to go fishing with me. He was an avid fisherman. But this would be a very special fishing trip. I would be the only one to come back from it and I would report that a tragic accident had taken place: Iglesias had bumped his head on a tree branch, had been knocked out of the boat, and drowned in the swift current.

Padre Cocco then said, with pointed emphasis: "I can assure you that there will be no investigation of the accident, neither by the Venezuelan National Guard nor by the territorial government."

He left shortly after that and returned to Ocamo. I was a bit shaken by this suggestion but concluded that Padre Cocco was upset and didn't expect me to do as he proposed. I assumed that the issue would eventually be quietly handled when Padre Cocco's anger subsided.

But several days later Padre Cocco paid me a second visit, traveling at night from Ocamo to my hut. Since it is not safe to travel alone in a motor-driven dugout canoe at night, the trip had to be about something important. Astonishingly, he repeated his proposal and again emphasized that there would be no investigation by the military and territorial authorities.

I declined his invitation, preferring to believe that Padre Cocco's anger and concern had still not dissipated.

Despite my affection for Padre Cocco, my view of the Salesian Missions changed markedly. I realized that they were not an entirely benevolent group but that they were capable of some rather draconian actions so long as these actions were surreptitious.

I was at Ocamo the day that Hermano Iglesias left Amazonas with his children by the Yanomamö woman. He was defiant, complaining about how much money the Salesian organization owed him for services rendered. Padre Cocco and other representatives of the missions were obviously angry with him. I avoided them and departed as quickly as I could.

IVIC and My Family

IVIC (Instituto Venezolano de Investigaciones Científicas) was the Venezuelan academic research facility that served as my "institutional" host. It was the official institutional host and Venezuelan collaborator of the University of Michigan medical researchers from the Department of Human Genetics, James V. Neel's group. Although I had no formal relationship to Neel's department for the first seventeen months of my fieldwork and had my own National Institute of Mental Health research grant, I was considered by Neel's Venezuelan medical collaborators at IVIC as part of the official "Michigan team." Miguel Layrisse, Neel's most important collaborator at IVIC, had already sent one of his lab technicians, Esperanza Garcia, to Ann Arbor, where she was getting special training in new laboratory techniques in Neel's department. This interinstitutional agreement was very fortunate for me, because my family could stay in one of IVIC's faculty apartments while I was in the jungle. The downside of this arrangement was the severe logistics problems my wife had as a near prisoner in this mountainous redoubt that had no grocery store. She had no transportation to go shopping in Caracas for household necessities. Fortunately, there was a family there from Switzerland—the Munzes—who graciously and generously invited her and the children to go shopping with them in Caracas about once a week.

I managed to get out of Amazonas twice during my first year in the jungle and was able to spend about a week each time with Carlene and our children. During these brief trips I replenished my food and other supplies, had my film processed, and ate ravenously of green tossed salads, French baguettes, cold beverages like beer and fruit juices—and other foods for which I hungered and dreamed regularly during the long months in the jungle.

But the longer I spent with the Yanomamö, the more I failed to notice the inconveniences and difficulties of living among them.

For example, I had become so accustomed to the constant stinging bites of the *bareto*—the diurnal gnats—that I barely noticed them anymore. Their bites no longer left burning, red, itchy welts on my skin because my body had grown accustomed to them, as everyone does after a month or so. When I finally brought my wife and children into Mavaca they reacted strongly to the bites, and it would be weeks before their bodies would adjust. Consequently they immediately became sick and feverish from the *bareto* bites.

Bringing one's wife and children into Amazonas in the mid-1960s involved major logistics and planning problems. For example, travel to the interior, especially to Venezuela's Amazonas, had to be by river and involved very long trips using native dugout canoes.

Few people in the United States realize how difficult and frustrating it can be to do routine things in a country with few large cities, where most of the country is referred to with some kind of word that means outback, interior, campo, or forest. The more improbable it is that some routine task can be done in such a place, the more sincerely it is promised by Venezuelans, who find a need to think of their country as being everywhere a highly developed, civilized, and modern republic.

There was only one landing strip in the Yanomamö area when I first arrived in 1964. It was an unimproved dirt airstrip at a place called La Esmeralda, a natural savannah that was underwater—or too wet to land on—during the peak of the wet season (April to August). At most other times large airplanes could land at Esmeralda, including C-47s (the military equivalent of the commercial DC-3) and C-123s, military transports with a drop-down door large enough to load and unload jeeps, small trucks, bulky cargo, or airborne troops, who could parachute out of the rear of this cargo plane. In 1964 La Esmeralda had a resident Salesian missionary, Padre Sanchez, who had a tiny chapel and living quarters, and a small Ye'kwana community of some fifty people who had previously been converted by members of the New Tribes missions. They ignored Padre Sanchez and never attended services at his chapel.

By 1965 the Salesian Missions in Amazonas had persuaded the Venezuelan government to provide them with regular military flights to fly in certain kinds of bulky and heavy supplies to their more remote missions. Otherwise, the only other way to bring in supplies was by hiring Venezuelans in Puerto Ayacucho to bring them up the Orinoco in large dugout canoes, which the missions also did for transporting things like gasoline, diesel fuel, metal roofing, cement, etc.

The Salesian bishop in Puerto Ayacucho, the territorial capital, wanted the government to promise them at least one flight per month to La Esmeralda during the times of the year when the rains did not interfere with these cargo flights. La Esmeralda (or simply Esmeralda, as the Venezuelans called it) was just on the edge of Yanomamö territory, about two to three hours by motorized canoe downstream from Padre Cocco's mission at Ocamo.

At Esmeralda a gigantic basalt mountain, Cerro Duida, rose abruptly from the savannah to some ten thousand feet, and beyond Duida there were other, even taller craggy basaltic mountains. This area was the heartland of the Carib-speaking Ye'kwana, whose territory lay mostly north of the Yanomamö region but overlapped with it in places. The military flight negotiations between the Salesian bishop and the Venezuelan air force were under discussion about the time I began my work among the Yanomamö.

The air forces of most Latin American countries at this time were used primarily to provide freight services to their remote interiors—and especially to the various groups of the Catholic Church in the several countries. In Venezuela, this meant the Salesian Missions. The Salesians boasted, for example, that "every President of Venezuela was educated in a Salesian Catholic School." In a sense in the remote interior region, the Venezuelan air force might be regarded as the "Salesian air force." Ironically the Salesians cynically viewed the evangelical New Tribes missionaries as mostly American, mostly capitalistic, and always seditious: one of the proofs of their sedition, for example, was that "they even had their own air force." The "New Tribes air force" was actually a group of civilian pilots belonging to the Mission Aviation Fellowship (also known as Alas de Socorro in some countries) who flew mostly for evangelical mission groups—but were always willing to make flights for functionaries of the national governments where they operated and in some countries afforded the only safe and reliable air transportation into the remote areas of those countries.

The Salesians in Venezuela were politically powerful, especially in rural areas like the Federal Territory of Amazonas and in its capital city, Puerto Ayacucho. The highest civil office was held by the governor, who was appointed by the president of Venezuela. But the Salesian bishop of Amazonas was easily as powerful politically as the governor, if not more powerful. In fact, the territory of Amazonas was basically a theocracy—a political entity ruled by the Catholic Church. I met one of the former governors of Amazonas many years later at a reception in New York. He mentioned that his chronic problem as governor was carrying out his policies when the Salesian bishop was opposed to them. He added that "this was the single most important problem of all of my predecessors as well." (In 1996 Amazonas ceased to be a federal territory and was granted statehood.)

Early in my career the Salesians considered me harmless (after they determined I had been raised as a Catholic) and thus I got along amicably with them. I would bring them, for example, special foods—like large ten- to fifteen-pound pieces of Parmesan cheese and bottles of rum or Scotch whisky. In addition to allowing me to use their radio at Ocamo, they permitted me to store some of my gasoline at their missions when I was away from the Yanomamö area.

New Tribes Mission and Salesian Politics

The serious battle for Yanomamö souls in the Venezuelan Amazon had begun in the 1950s. The area was ignored by the Venezuelan government because of its remoteness from the capital, Caracas. In fact, the national government left many of the social services that are normally a function of the secular government, such as education, or recording of marriages, births, and deaths, to the Catholic Church. It was probably much cheaper to do it that way and, of course, the church was granted some important legal privileges. The 1915 Venezuelan Law of the Missions gave the Salesians extraordinary powers with respect to the native peoples in Venezuela's remote areas. This law enabled the Salesians to "attract" and "reduce" the Indians to their mission by just about any means they could.

In 1964 when I arrived, Puerto Ayacucho had only a few paved streets and a population of about three thousand. A very large fraction of the people were government employees and military personnel. Puerto Ayacucho was essentially a government administration town.

The Salesian bishop's headquarters in Puerto Ayacucho was large. It had various buildings for schools and dormitories for resident students from more remote areas who lived there during the academic year. Most of the children were from nearby tribes.

The Salesians ignored the tribes whose members lived more than forty miles or so from Puerto Ayacucho because they were too difficult to reach and lived in widely scattered small villages. Most of these native villages were far up small rivers that eventually joined the Orinoco, for example, the Carib-speaking Ye'kwana. The Yanomamö were not even known to most residents of Puerto Ayacucho until the 1950s, and the Salesians ignored them until the New Tribes Mission began to establish contact with them in the Upper Orinoco.

In 1950 James P. Barker started the first permanent New Tribes station among the Yanomamö. He told me that he had been in the U.S. Army and, when he got out after World War II ended, decided to become a missionary for the New Tribes Mission, an organization that focused on some of the world's most remote, little-known tribal groups in places like highland New Guinea, the Amazon Basin, and other remote areas.

Barker said that he decided to work in Venezuela and specifically on the Upper Orinoco River where a few New Tribes missionaries had begun to evangelize a few years earlier. There were no Yanomamö villages on or even close to a navigable portion of any Venezuelan river in those days, so he and a colleague named Gene Higdom eventually paddled a canoe up the Orinoco from the last outpost of civilization, probably at the rapids where the Ventuari River flows into the Orinoco. There was a small community of Venezuelan creoles there—settlers of mixed ethnic background—European (Spanish and Portuguese), African, and Native Amazonian. Their tiny community there was called Santa Barbara.

Barker and Higdom paddled upstream many miles in a small dugout canoe until the Orinoco River was narrow enough for people to cross it without canoes. By that time they had paddled their canoe past three major tributaries of the Upper Orinoco—the Padamo River, the Ocamo River, and the Mavaca River, in that order. None of these sites was occupied in 1950. Where the Mavaca entered the Orinoco they found a Yanomamö community of approximately 125 people, the village known as Mahekodo-teri. They established their mission at this village.

Thus began the first sustained European contact with any Yanomamö village in Venezuela.

Higdom apparently remained for less than a year, leaving to get married in August 1951. Barker left Mahekodo-teri some time after that and returned to the United States to try to raise money for his mission and to rest and recuperate.

Until then the Salesians had ignored the Yanomamö, but the thought of a non-Catholic religious mission anywhere in this vast territory seemed to be unacceptable to them. They immediately dispatched one of their brothers to Mahekodo-teri to establish a Salesian presence and stake their claim to this and all surrounding Yanomamö villages. When Barker returned to Venezuela he learned that the Salesians had started a Catholic mission and had given it the Spanish name *Platanal*. Barker could not return there.

Barker was relatively fluent in the Yanomamö language at that point. He was aware that a village on the lower Ocamo River called Iyäwei-teri was keen on having a *nabä*—a non-Yanomamö—come and live with them. They wanted the steel tools that *nabäs* almost always brought with them, as well as other manufactured items. Thus he established a new New Tribes Mission post among the Iyäwei-teri, who were eventually persuaded to move down the Ocamo several miles to where it flowed into the Orinoco. That place was subsequently named *Boca Ocamo*—the "mouth" of the Ocamo.

When Barker left for the United States a few years later, the Salesians once again sent one of their missionaries to establish a mission among the Iyäwei-teri at the mouth of the Ocamo River. This was Padre Luigi Cocco.

When Barker returned, he had to find yet another Yanomamö group to evangelize.

This time it was the Yanomamö village of Bisaasi-teri. Some ten years earlier they had been massacred in a devastating *nomohori*—a "dirty trick"—instigated by their Shamatari enemies. In 1950, while still at his original mission at Mahekodo-teri, Barker had witnessed the procession of the Bisaasi-teri survivors of that massacre move into Mahekodo-teri, where he got to know them.

The Bisaasi-teri, as Barker explained to me, were willing to move out to the mouth of the Mavaca River where it joins the Orinoco, and that is where I found the Bisaasi-teri in 1964, some five years after Barker had persuaded them to settle there.

Bisaasi-teri was a large village and it was experiencing growing pains and internal political struggles. When the village moved to the mouth of the Mavaca, it subdivided into "Upper" and "Lower" as previously described. The Lower Bisaasi-teri made gardens and their *shabono* on the west side of the Mavaca River, where it joins the Orinoco, that is, a few hundred yards down the Orinoco from the other group. The Upper Bisaasi-teri made their gardens and *shabono* on the east side of the Mavaca River—up the Orinoco. The downstream group referred to themselves as *koro-teri* (downstream village) and the other group called themselves *ora-teri* (upstream group). But they both called themselves Bisaasi-teri. Together they numbered some 250 people, one of the larger Yanomamö villages known at that time.

The New Tribes Mission took steps to safeguard its Bisaasi-teri mission: they had New Tribes families living in both groups lest the Salesians try to establish their own mission in one of the Bisaasi-teri groups.

Barker built his mud-and-thatch house next to the *shabono* of the upper group, and a different New Tribes family, the Janks (from Canada), built their house on the southwest area next to the *shabono* of the Lower Bisaasi-teri group. Several other New Tribes Mission families also stayed periodically among the Lower Bisaasi-teri to make it difficult for the Salesians to move in if any of the evangelical families left for longer than a few weeks.

Sure enough, the Salesians showed up at this New Tribes Mission location almost immediately. They located themselves *across* the Orinoco River from the two communities of the Bisaasi-teri where the few thatched huts of the Malarialogía families were located. The Salesians began first by establishing a *comedor* (a communal eating place), and then by sending a Dutch lay brother, Hermano Pedro, and subsequently one of their priests, Padre José Berno, to Mavaca to build a church and a mission compound.

These activities were just beginning when I arrived in 1964. Padre Berno had not yet arrived, but Pedro was there. The *comedor* was not functioning yet, but for a time Pedro lured some of the Yanomamö children from the two villages across the Orinoco to his *comedor* with food, particularly highly sugared oatmeal. However, they stayed only for breakfast and returned across the river. Hermano Pedro had a Venezuelan employee—a *motorista*—who would pick up and return the Yanomamö children.

Not long after that the Salesians became even more aggressive in their mission efforts—what the 1915 Law of the Missions called *atrayer y reducir*: *attract* the native people to the mission and *reduce* them to living there. Sometime in the early 1970s the Salesian missions at Ocamo, Mavaca, and Platanal began removing Yanomamö children from their villages—often isolated villages at some distance from these three missions—and sending them far downstream to Isla Ratón, a small island in the middle of the Orinoco near Puerto Ayacucho. There the children were put into dormitories, taught Spanish, and discouraged from using their own language. They were away from their parents and their villages for months at a time.

The Salesians would "persuade" the parents to give up their children by offering them steel tools, like machetes and axes. Since the Salesians were only minimally competent in the Yanomamö language and could not clearly explain to the Yanomamö what they were doing, and since the Yanomamö in these remote villages knew no Spanish, this activity effectively amounted to purchasing the children and taking them away from their parents.

Eventually complaints by the Yanomamö provoked the Salesians to change their policy. The Salesians then built the same kind of dormitory facility at Esmeralda and lodged the Yanomamö children there, once again against their will and against the wishes of their parents.

Eventually, in the mid-1970s, the Salesians provided schooling for the Yanomamö children at their Ocamo, Mavaca, and Platanal missions so the children could at least remain in their own villages close to their parents.

By then I had long since committed myself to studying the several villages south and west of Mavaca and away from the Salesian missions. These were the groups that the Yanomamö referred to as Shamatari because they had a slightly different migration history and genealogical origins. I tried to ignore the changes that were going on in and near the Salesian missions because there were so many Yanomamö villages that were remote and largely outside the sphere of the mission influence. I felt that studying these more remote villages was my best opportunity for understanding the issues on which I focused my research.

The New Tribes Mission decided to abandon their mission at Mavaca about 1973 and concentrated their efforts on Yanomamö communities that were more difficult to reach and where the Salesians were unlikely to follow them and force them to leave.

Guns and Germs

But even the remote Yanomamö villages were not outside the range of Salesian influence. As early as 1960 the Salesians were providing shotguns to the Yanomamö at Ocamo. They may have given shotguns to the Mahekodo-teri at about the same time. By 1967 Padre Berno had introduced shotguns at Mavaca, using them to lure about half of the Lower Bisaasi-teri to "his" side of the Orinoco. To the Yanomamö, shotguns are powerful incentives to move. Guns are more efficient at killing game— and defenseless neighbors—than arrows.

I first became aware of the shotguns in 1965 while collecting genealogies and making a census of several remote villages north of the Orinoco and east of Padre Cocco's mission at Ocamo. Part of my demographic efforts entailed obtaining causes of death of all deceased people I encountered in the genealogies I collected. Several very recent deaths were attributed to raids by the Iyäwei-teri at Padre Cocco's mission. My Ma-

korima-teri informants insisted that Padre Cocco's group used shotguns
to kill several of their village's men.

I made a special trip to Padre Cocco's mission and told him what my
informants said about the shotgun killings by men from his village. He
readily admitted that he had provided the shotguns and ammunition but
vehemently denied that "his people" would use them to kill other people.
He insisted they used them only for hunting game, the purpose for which
he had provided them. He was, in fact, incensed that I would even suggest that the shotguns were used in lethal raids against others.

As we were talking about this, one of the adult men was walking by
and Padre Cocco called him over to ask him about my outrageous account. Padre Cocco had given him the Spanish name Carlito. In the mission pidgin he asked Carlito if they had gone to the distant villages along
the Höräta River and killed people with their shotguns. Carlito responded
in a matter-of-fact way: "*Sí, Padre*. We killed this many with our shotguns," holding up several fingers.

Padre Cocco was shocked, then outraged. He read the riot act to Carlito and immediately went to the *shabono* with Carlito and confiscated
all the shotguns he had given to them, some half-dozen or so as I recall.

Padre Cocco thanked me for making him aware of this situation and
we continued to be friends. But he later returned the shotguns to the
Iyäwei-teri, who solemnly assured him that they would use them only for
hunting, a promise that was soon and predictably broken. The Iyäwei-teri
just became more secretive about their raids.

When I returned to Venezuela in 1968 to do fieldwork and reached
Mavaca, I learned about Padre Berno's decision to give the Lower
Bisaasi-teri several shotguns, the first of many, along with dugout canoes
and several outboard motors. He had "purchased" half of the Bisaasi-
teri to get them to move to his side of the river. I remember the haughty
and conniving headman named Paruriwä (also known as Hontonawä)
swaggering down to my canoe as I pulled up to the riverbank to give my
regards to Padre Berno. He carried his shotgun conspicuously across his
shoulder, making sure I could see it.

I got out of my canoe and walked up to the mission. Padre Berno
came out to greet me. Next to him were a Yanomamö man and his wife,
friends of mine. They were now fully clothed with used garments that

some charitable organization had contributed to the Salesians. The garments were filthy and in tatters. The man didn't know how to use the zipper on his trousers, so he cut a large hole in the crotch of his pants. His wife had a young baby and was breastfeeding it. Since her dress was not designed to breastfeed an infant on demand, she had cut holes where her pendulous breasts were more accessible to the baby. There they stood, grinning at me, delighted to see me: he with the crotch cut out of his trousers exposing his genitals and she with holes cut out for her breasts. The parts of their anatomy Padre Berno most wanted to conceal with the new clothing were now more prominently visible.

It was not long before Padre Berno's faction of the Lower Bisaasi-teri put their new weapons to use in their wars. Over time they harassed, threatened, and intimidated the Mömariböwei-teri, a day's walk to the south, so mercilessly that the latter fled from the area and made an extremely long migration to the Casiquiare River and, from there, upstream to where it met the Orinoco close to Tama Tama. There they were now within sight of the New Tribes Mission headquarters settlement and effectively outside the mainstream of Yanomamö politics, alliances, and warfare.

Over the next several years the Salesians gave more shotguns to the Yanomamö. In about 1969 the Lower Bisaasi-teri now living at Padre Berno's mission raided the Patanowä-teri and killed one of the two headmen there, Kumaiewä, and one of his adult sons. They shot Kumaiewä at very close range, nearly blowing his head off. The previous year I had made my first documentary films on the Yanomamö. Kumaiewä is shown in this film ceremoniously chanting with Shinanokawä, the headman of Mahekodo-teri, who, along with his co-villagers, were guests at this feast in Kumaiewä's village.

Two other Mahekodo-teri men were also prominent in this film, both sons of Shinanokawä: Asiawä and Heawä. Both of these men now had obtained shotguns from the Salesian mission at Platanal and they used them ruthlessly in raids against their enemies. For example, Asiawä killed the headman of Makorima-teri, Säsäwä, by shooting him in the head. Asiawä's younger brother, Heawä, once raided a distant village and killed a man there with his shotgun. When I asked one of my informants, Rerebawä, about this shooting and why Heawä would raid a village so distant and kill someone he didn't seem to know and whose village had done nothing to him or anyone in his village, Rerebawä replied: "Heawä is very fierce. When you give a fierce Yanomamö a shotgun he wants to use it. He killed this man *bädao*," meaning "without cause."

Heawä and Asiawä killed a large number of people with their shotguns, including a woman in Lower Bisaasi-teri, where I worked when I first arrived. I only know the details on Heawä's and Asiawä's shotgun victims who lived in villages that my own work focused on, but the Bisaasi-teri claim that they killed many other people in other villages with their shotguns.

My demographic research was beginning to annoy the Salesians. I was not attempting to discredit or denigrate them or their efforts to convert the Yanomamö, but my investigations invariably uncovered things they would have preferred to be left undocumented. I could feel the tension build between me and the Salesians at Mavaca.

Getting My Family In

Late in 1965 I came out to IVIC to get my wife and children and took them with me to my base of operations at Bisaasi-teri at the mouth of the Mavaca River. Before this, I built a small mud-and-thatch house for us. Before we reached Mavaca, though, we stopped at Ocamo. The Yanomamö village of Iyäwei-teri was at Ocamo, some 120 people. They had gotten to know me quite well because I regularly passed through Ocamo and spent nights at Padre Cocco's mission.

It was here that my wife saw the Yanomamö for the first time. They were quite excited to see her: *"Möbraö! Shakiwä bä suwabö kuwä kure! Kama käkäba ihirubä akai!"* ("Look! There stands Chagnon's wife! And his two children as well!") They caressed and fondled the children and immediately wanted to know their names. I said their names softly, as is the Yanomamö way of being polite and circumspect when the person whose name is being used is within earshot. This custom is usually not observed for young children, but it was my way of informing them that my children had so much "value" that even I, their father, was circumspect in their presence and would only whisper their names to others. Loud, excited tongue clicks and gasps filled the air as they repeated their names aloud softly, acknowledging the high status I conferred on my children and wife by simply whispering instead of saying their names aloud.

I wanted to push on to Mavaca by nightfall. I had left my dugout canoe, gasoline tanks, and outboard motor at Ocamo when I had gone to Caracas nearly two weeks earlier to pick up my family. I hurriedly mounted the motor on the canoe and loaded it with our possessions. My wife carefully got into the canoe and made sure the children were securely fastened in, then we departed upstream. Mavaca was some two hours away and would be my family's new home in the jungle.

I was quietly anxious to see my wife's reaction to the marvelous hut I had built for her and the children, sheltered from the elements and more-or-less safe from the hazards of the jungle. In fact, I secretly felt a bit smug about—indeed, even proud of—the handyman accomplishments I could soon reveal to her. I even privately thought to myself, Not many wives of anthropologists enjoy such luxuries on the field trips they take with their husbands!

I had long since forgotten how pleasant and relaxing a river trip in a dugout canoe could be, but Carlene several times told me afterward how much she enjoyed that trip.

When you sit near the front of a long dugout canoe, the incessant drone of the outboard motor is barely noticeable. What is more audibly apparent is the constant and soothing whisper of the dugout's prow cutting through the water. The speed of the canoe creates a cooling breeze on your body and the *bareto* are swept away with the wind. It is usually quiet enough to hear the exotic calls of macaw parrots and the jabbering of the parakeets as they wing overhead in pairs or in small flocks, seemingly in a hurry to cross over the river. Colorful swarms of yellow and white butterflies flitted around the emerging sandbars. The dry season was beginning, the sky was clear, and the air was pleasantly warm.

By contrast, much of the time I had spent on the rivers of Yanomamö-land was at the helm of, and therefore right next to, a noisy outboard motor. Most of the time I was in narrow, winding rivers, crouched over in an uncomfortable standing position so I could quickly raise the propeller out of the water, searching the ripples for telltale signs of hidden rocks or submerged deadfalls immediately ahead of my prow. Most trips in my dugout were usually hard work for many boring hours on end, but river travel was always better than hacking your way through the jungle on foot.

The soothing, pleasant trip for my wife and children came to an end when I slowed my canoe and eased it into my landing, a tiny machete-hewn niche I had had the Yanomamö dig into the muddy bank of the Mavaca River some twenty-five yards from where it joined the Orinoco.

The hordes of *bareto* appeared as soon as I stopped the outboard motor. We got out of the canoe and walked up to the house that I had glowingly described to my wife many times by radio and in letters to her from the field. Several dozen Yanomamö were there to greet us, mostly women and their babies; the men were in the *shabono* taking hallucinogenic drugs and chanting to their personal spirits—their *hekura*—as they did every afternoon. As at Ocamo earlier that day, the local Bisaasi-teri women were excited and pleased at long last to meet my wife and children. They knew them only by the photographs I had shown them and by their names.

The Bisaasi-teri women felt my wife all over, marveling at her fair complexion and complimenting her on how *riyahäwä* (beautiful) she was. The women ran their hands under her blouse to make sure she was built like them and had breasts. They also affectionately fondled the children and kept exclaiming about their blond hair. They wanted me to give the children to them—especially our daughter.

It was the second day of November 1965 when my family moved into my mud-and-thatch home adjacent to the Yanomamö village of Bisaasi-teri.

Although it never became a specific point of conversation, I knew that my hut was somewhat less elegant than I had led my wife to believe. But that's only because it is quite difficult to make an elegant mud hut.

Life in Our Mud-and-Thatch Hut

The hut was of simple design—a rectangular structure about 20 feet by 20 feet. I had built it as an extension to Jim Barker's much larger house by prior agreement, primarily to save me the effort of building one of the walls. Barker was delighted to have it as an extension to his own house and said he would later use it as a guest quarters when other mission families visited. He himself had moved back into his own house about six months earlier, bringing his wife and young daughter with him.

I made my walls with a line of log posts buried upright into the clay earth, spaced about two feet apart and connected horizontally with many narrowly spaced thin strips of palm wood—makeshift lath—that were lashed to the upright logs with vines. Ordinary clay soil, mixed with sufficient water to make the consistency of wet concrete, was packed into the spaces between the upright logs. After this mud dried for a week or so, an initial finish coat of thinner mud was applied to the inside and outside surfaces. When this mud dried out in a few days, it would shrink and leave a rough, cracked surface that looked like what a pool of muddy water leaves behind when it dries up. A second and third coat of thin mud eventually produces a more-or-less smooth surface, but the inside walls of the house—where the sun can't get to—are usually very dark and this surface never gets completely dry. Mold and mildew are big problems in an equatorial mud house because of high humidity.

My floor was made from crumbled moist clay pounded flat with a heavy log to compact it and make it relatively smooth. Needless to say, any liquid that spills onto such a floor produces a lingering, slippery mud puddle. As flooring goes, a mud floor is more difficult to keep clean than, say, linoleum or tile. Washing the floor with a mop is not an option.

My house had only one entrance; there were no windows on the ground floor. My single window was in the 6-foot-high end-gable in the roof area, that is, in the thatch. My door was standard in dimensions, but made from round poles and a few scraps of rough-sawn boards that I obtained from Barker. I put two latches on it so I could lock it from both the inside and outside. Nevertheless it wouldn't have taken much effort to break through it, as the Yanomamö would easily do several times while I was away on some trip to visit other Yanomamö villages.

I partitioned the ground floor into two rooms by erecting another wall of logs and mud daub. The partition created a small, enclosed space that was basically a storage area where I kept canned foods, motor oil, tools, canoe paddles, and other goods, as well as the kinds of possessions the Yanomamö coveted: my small cache of "trade goods." These were the things like small spools of thread for making arrows, small knives, fishhooks, fish line, etc. I paid the Yanomamö for informant work, for roofing thatch, and for helping me cut and haul the timbers, collect the vines, and do the mud work that went into constructing my house.

There were few architectural luxuries, but one I did include was an indoor shower. I made a privacy mud wall in one of the corners to box off a small area to stand in. I ran a plastic hose through the roof thatch into an empty but clean gasoline barrel, which I supported on a stout scaffold. The shower end was a cheap plastic showerhead that had a pinch-type stopcock. I had older Yanomamö boys fill the barrel with buckets of river water, which would become pleasantly warm in the barrel in the sun. I finished the shower stall with a small platform to stand on, made from vines and small sticks, and fashioned a drain of sorts in the mud floor. The drain was just a small but rather deep hole directly underneath the stick-and-vine platform to stand on and keep your wet feet elevated above the mud.

One had to be careful to not leave the water trickling for very long or else the small shower area would fill up and overflow into our living quarters. Primitive, dank, mildew-covered, and disagreeable as it was, the shower allowed my wife and children to keep relatively clean in privacy, and it was much safer to bathe the children in the shower than in the deep, swift Mavaca River. Several years before I arrived, a Yanomamö child disappeared while bathing in the Mavaca River right in front of where my hut stood. The grief-stricken Yanomamö concluded that an anaconda had taken him.

But by far the best part of my house was the *troja* (pronounced "tro-ha"). There is no English word that accurately conveys what this Venezuelan Spanish word means. It refers to the large area immediately above the ceiling of a room, what we might roughly translate as an "attic." But our "civilized" houses have many supporting rafters separating the ceiling from the attic, whereas my mud hut had, instead of multiple two-by-eight rafters spaced two feet apart, just a few stout, round logs spaced some six feet apart that served to hold the outer walls together. Most huts built like mine leave these round logs exposed, and from the packed mud ground floor, a person normally sees the bottom side of the leaves that are used to thatch the roof. But if you place some kind of wood or other rigid material *across* these round logs, you have a *troja*: an aboveground storage (or living area) with a dry floor. Access to my *troja* was a crude ladder I made from poles and vines.

My *troja* floor was made from long pieces of split palm wood. Several of the many palm tree species in the Amazon can be easily split length-wise into strips. When you shave off the interior pithy material with a machete you get a long, springy board that is relatively flat on one side and rounded on the other, rather like wide pieces of lath. Palm wood is brittle but extremely hard and durable. It is also hazardous to handle be-cause the edges are extremely sharp and can cause painful cuts and even more painful splinters. It is also difficult, for example, to pound nails into. But, when one places these long pieces flat-side down, the palm wood perpendicular to the round rafter logs and lashed together with vines, one can fashion a perfectly suitable wood floor. The sharp edges are on the lower edges of the rounded hump that sticks up.

The *troja* floor is a bit springy if the round supporting logs are far apart, but it certainly beats a mud floor. You can actually put things down on the palm wood floor and they won't get damp.

We slept in our *troja,* separated from the elements above and outside by scores of thin rafter poles to which the palm thatching of our roof was attached. These rafter poles were stout enough to tie our hammocks to, so we slept suspended, just above the *manaca* palm wood floor, dry, rela tively cool, and protected from malaria-transmitting mosquitoes by our mosquito nets.

Our youngest child, Lisa, was not yet two years old, too small to sleep by herself in a hammock. I borrowed a "cage" for her to sleep in from Barker, a box that was covered on all sides with metal mesh screen to keep out the mosquitoes and other biting things.

Almost all cultures distinguish sharply between nature and culture, a theme elaborated in many ways in the works of the famous French an-thropologist Claude Lévi-Strauss. The Yanomamö, for example, focus on this distinction in their conception of their villages and the very nature of man as distinct from animals. Their word for house is *yahi,* a place where human beings dwell. Their word for jungle is *urihi,* the place where wild things—things that are not human—live. Their communal dwellings—*shabonos*—are a collectivity of individual *yahis*—individual houses. Thus a *shabono* represents *culture* and cultural things—things that they call *yahi tä rimö*. In sharp contrast, wild things—nonhuman things—are natural, components of *nature: urihi tä rimö*. For them, culture ends at the outside surfaces of the *shabono* roof and walls. My house was supposed to embody this inflexible Yanomamö principle and keep the jungle outside of our personal, cultural area.

After several days I noticed that my wife was dozing off frequently during the day. It was then that I discovered that she was not sleeping at night. She said she was keeping the rats away from the children by shining her flashlight on them all night long. I had forgotten that, by night, a dozen or so jungle rats would come into the house and live in the roof thatch, moving from place to place along the many poles that held the thatch, rustling the thatch as they moved. The boundary between culture and nature represented by my mud hut was not as firm as it was supposed to be.

My wife could see and hear the rats in the thatch, but when they reached the hammock ropes and began to climb down to our hammocks, she became especially alarmed. I had gotten used to them during the year and ignored them much as New Yorkers learn to ignore sirens when they sleep at night. I simply thought of them as jungle rats, just part of the background noise.

Rats, of course, are sometimes reported in our newspapers as attacking sleeping children and chewing on their faces and extremities, but these reports are invariably from the slums in crowded industrial cities. But my poor wife was staying awake at night to make sure the rats wouldn't harm the children, maintaining vigil over them with her clutched flashlight, shooing them away if they got too close to the children.

I solved this problem by hiring several young Yanomamö boys to sleep in the *troja* with us. They were delighted to provide a rat-exterminating service, using their miniature bows and arrows; to their amazement and delight, they also got to use our prized flashlights. Flashlights were still novel in 1965 and regarded by the Yanomamö as extremely useful and almost magical.

I paid these intrepid young hunters per rat with fishhooks, fish line, and other small items. Their two-foot arrows were made of the rigid, stiff spine of a palm leaf, sharpened to a needle point at one end and fletched with two tiny feathers at the other end. Their tiny bows were fashioned

A child with a small bow and arrow of the
kind our *troja* "hunters" used.

from a wiry branch about thirty inches long. The arrows had enough ve-
locity to go completely through the body of a rat when they actually hit
one, causing it to fall from the rafters, to be dispatched with a stick by the
gleeful young hunters when it hit the *troja* boards. They didn't get many
rats, but their constant shooting harassed the rats enough to keep them
nervously moving about.

My Magnificent Shower and Other Disasters

For reasons that still baffle me, the arrival of my wife and children coincided with a particularly dramatic increase in the insect problem. I
always had insect problems, but some very unusual ones materialized
when my family joined me.

The first time my wife took a shower she let out a shriek: she found herself face-to-face with a large, hairy black spider about the size of a small saucer. It was crawling down the wall from the thatch just above her. It wasn't a tarantula, but it was almost the size of one, but skinnier. I dispatched it with a stick. It made one of those yucky squish sounds when I did, like the sound when you step on a very large, juicy cockroach. (We had an abundance of large, juicy cockroaches.)

The next morning when I put on my damp trousers I felt something crawling in them—and scrambled to get out of them as quickly as possible. There were three or four spiders inside the pants legs, similar to the one my wife had confronted the previous day, but not as large. While I always gave my trousers and long-sleeve shirts a vigorous shaking before putting them on to rid them of insects and vermin, these spiders had a more tenacious grip on the inside of my trousers than ordinary spiders and did not dislodge with an ordinary shake.

We always had to carefully examine our clothing before putting anything on and were especially diligent about our children's clothing. Shoes, of course, had to be examined carefully, pounded on a rigid surface and shaken before putting them on: spiders and scorpions crawl into them at night, perhaps because they are attracted to the warmth. Once, when I took a long trip on foot between two villages, a sizable colony of termites decided to make my soaked tennis shoes their new nesting place. I had hung my shoes on a tree limb before retiring for the night, as I always did. The next morning there must have been several hundred termites in my shoes; it took me about fifteen minutes to reclaim them and get all the termites out of them. Fortunately, my mud hut didn't have termites.

Not only did we have to be careful when dressing in the morning, but we also had to be careful about eating. Small insects and maggots invariably appear in all your foods when you bring them into the jungle and try to store them there for more than a few days, as I had already discovered. Meals took a great deal more time in the jungle than they did back home because we had to carefully spread the food apart and search each spoonful of oatmeal, rice, beans, etc. before allowing the children to take it into their mouths and swallow it.

Daily Circumstances for the Family

In general, it was very unpleasant to be outside during the day—for any-one, and especially for the Yanomamö, who had no clothing and were at the mercy of the *bareto*. The Yanomamö traditionally avoid large rivers, and I suspect that the *bareto* problem is one reason why they do. I once took some 16 mm motion picture film of Yanomamö children playing at the riverbank, and when I later had it developed and viewed it I was as-tonished at what I saw: the children were incessantly striking their arms, legs, faces, torso, and bodies to keep the *bareto* from biting them, like child flagellants engaged in some ritual. In general, the larger the river, the more the *bareto* are a problem, especially in the dry season. There are accounts by early anthropologists and explorers of tribes along the Amazon River who would only come out of their smoky huts for a few hours a day to work and hunt—just after dawn and just before dusk. The reason? Biting insects were so much of a problem and these people had no clothing. A few hundred yards inland from the larger rivers—like the Mavaca—the diurnal *bareto* are much less of a problem.

Cold, frozen regions like the Arctic could not have been colonized by humans until warm clothing was invented. My hunch is that most of the Amazon Basin adjacent to large rivers was uninhabitable until some kind of clothing—like tunics made from woven cotton or twined bark fibers—was eventually developed, as it was in pre-Columbian times in the Andes and some parts of Amazonia.

The Children's Playground

Our hut was too close to the river to let our children out of the house without constant supervision. The Mavaca River was deep and swift, not a place you would want your small children to be near unattended.

The small yard of sorts between the river and our hut was cleared of trees but had lots of knee-high weeds covering it—the kind of place where poisonous snakes would be difficult to see. And there were lots of poisonous snakes. Several Yanomamö were bitten and died the first year I lived at Mavaca. Before I arrived, snakebite victims, if they sur-vived, usually lost an arm or a leg. The limb would become gangrenous, wither, and finally just fall off. Sometimes the bone would have to be cut or chopped off, without anesthesia. One of my early informants, a young man named Karödima, had only one leg. He had lost the other to a snakebite and had to hop around on one leg, supported with a long stick he always carried.

Barker had a side yard that he invited us to use so our children could play in it. It was fenced off from the jungle with chicken wire and the surface was covered with about two inches of sand. He had had the Yanomamö haul sand up from the river during the dry season when sandbars would appear. Thus his sand-covered small side yard was safe in the sense that snakes would be immediately visible so long as the children remained where the sand was.

But Barker had several chickens that also used this fenced-off area—it was primarily to keep the chickens in, but served also as a safe but small play yard for his daughter. When my wife examined the sand that the children were playing in she discovered that it was full of gooey chicken droppings—and so the "sandbox" was now off-limits.

The only relatively clean area for our children to play in was our hut with mud walls and mud floors that were always damp and covered with mildew or mold. It was not a suitable place to let the children crawl around, and we had no furniture to speak of for them to play in and keep off the damp floor. In addition, a sizable area of our hut was walled off for the Yanomamö who came to visit us every day. They had to stay on *their* side of the low wall for a number of reasons, the main one being that without this barrier our tiny house would become home to forty or fifty Yanomamö whose sense of what we call personal space was essentially nonexistent.

Another reason was that some of the Yanomamö were not frequent bathers and many of them had open sores and lesions on their bodies. Finally, the Yamomamö had a sense of personal hygiene that would disgust most Westerners and not a few non-Westerners. They were constantly chewing tobacco—men, women, and children—and, of course, spitting frequently on our floor. They also had the rather unpleasant habit of blowing large quantities of slimy snot out of their noses into their hands and then wiping it onto any nearby surface, as I described earlier.

While the *troja* was cool and pleasant after dark and an ideal place to sleep, it was hot and uncomfortable during the day, so the children couldn't play there, either. In short, our children didn't have much fun at Mavaca.

By contrast, the Yanomamö children had much more fun, but they paid a price in terms of dysentery, insect bites, and skin infections.

Getting Out of Yanomamöland

Within a day of getting my wife and children into the field I realized that I had made a colossal mistake. They were miserable from the heat, insect bites, unsanitary conditions, sheer boredom, anxiety, and frustration at not being free to move around as a normal space would have afforded them.

I did almost no fieldwork while they were with me. My mud hut was not the pleasant, clean sanctuary I thought it would be, mainly because I hadn't considered the part of the equation that the Yanomamö represented. In an empty jungle or a jungle with just about any other tribe living in it, our situation might have been tolerable and possibly even pleasant. If my house had been larger—or if I had made the floor out of cement and the walls from wood—things might have been more tolerable and the children would have had more clean space in which to play. But it was almost immediately clear to both my wife and myself that the conditions were unsuitable.

Mistake or not, in the Venezuela of 1965 you couldn't just decide to get out and go back to Caracas—or anywhere else, for that matter— unless you planned to travel by canoe and had a huge amount of fuel cached along your intended route. You were at the mercy of scheduled or unscheduled airplane flights into this area. Sometimes the flights were separated by many weeks or months, as they were when I brought my family into the area.

I learned on my small shortwave radio receiver that—to my immense relief—there was another military flight scheduled to come into Esmeralda in about three weeks. And so not many days after joining me at Mavaca, my wife and I were planning—and hoping—to get her and the children onto that military flight.

A day or two before the plane was scheduled to land the Yanomamö discovered and captured three infant river otters. The parents had probably been illegally killed for their fur by employees of the Venezuelan Malarialogía, who could sell the pelts to Colombians at one of the several border outposts near Puerto Ayacucho. We persuaded the Yanomamö to give us the baby otters to take back to Caracas and give them to the national zoo, where they would be properly cared for and might survive. The otters were still nursing, so my wife had to fashion some kind of makeshift baby-otter bottle—and a powdered whole milk mixture—and feed them almost hourly. Ironically and mercifully, efforts to save the baby otters took our minds off our own situation.

I loaded my canoe with the supplies and items she needed to get back to Caracas with our children—and the baby otters. By now, the missionaries at Ocamo knew I was putting my family on the military flight and they thoughtfully contacted people at IVIC by shortwave radio to have them send transportation to pick her and my children up at the military base at Palo Negro.

I would have—and probably should have—gone back with Carlene to deal with any unanticipated problems that might come up. But nobody knew when another flying opportunity would arise to get me back to the Yanomamö area. It might be many weeks. My first year of fieldwork was drawing to an end, and I still had many things to do.

We arrived at Esmeralda, three hours downstream from Ocamo, several hours before the flight landed. It was difficult saying good-bye to my wife because I felt very guilty, even ashamed, for having brought her and our children into the Yanomamö area in the first place and then not escorting her back. They were now exhausted and sick from the many insect bites. I was relatively certain that her flight back to Palo Negro would be routine, and she would be safely back at IVIC by nightfall. Somebody from IVIC would be there to meet her.

I later learned that the military flight was not routine. It seems that the cargo plane had landed at some very muddy airstrip earlier in the day and one of the retracting landing gears had gotten clogged up with mud and was jammed. The pilots discovered this as they tried to land at Palo Negro and had to abort the first attempt at landing. As the plane circled to make another attempt, the crew struggled to free the landing gear and, ultimately, had to crank it down by hand. My wife later said all the members of the crew were very nervous—they weren't sure the landing gear would lock and hold up for the landing. She said they were furiously and rapidly making repeated signs of the cross as the plane touched down—safely—at Palo Negro.

The baby otters died the next day at the Caracas zoo.

5

First Contact with
New Yanomamö Villages

The probability is close to zero that any contemporary anthropologist will have the opportunity to be the first representative of his or her culture to contact tribal peoples who have never seen outsiders before or who have had fleeting encounters with outsiders. In the Amazon Basin, for example, remaining uncontacted tribes consist of a few families who are hiding out in the remaining hidden pockets of unexplored difficult-to-reach areas. The Yanomamö were the last large, multivillage tribe left in the mid-1960s when I went there. At that time they were about 25,000 people living in 250 or more separate villages.

Fewer anthropologists study tribesmen anymore. The very mention of the word *tribe* in anthropology has, in the past fifteen or twenty years, become an embarrassment to politically correct cultural anthropologists.

Into the Mysterious Interior

As I said earlier, my intent from the very beginning was to study the Shamatari groups to the south of the Bisaasi-teri. Although many of the Shamatari were uncontacted, members of two Shamatari villages—Mömariböwei-teri and Reyaboböwei-teri—sporadically came out of the jungle and visited the Bisaasi-teri on the Orinoco River to acquire steel tools after about 1960. The first village was a full day's walk inland through swamps, mud, and steep hills; the second was another whole day beyond that over escarpments that were two thousand feet or so high.

I got to know many of these people from their visits to Bisaasi-teri—and my own several visits to their villages on foot. As with the vast majority of Yanomamö villages, the only way to get to them was by walking.

My original plan in 1964 was to spend sufficient time in Bisaasi-teri to learn enough Yanomamö to communicate with and then initiate work among the two Shamatari villages. I wanted to get away from villages that had direct contact with the outside world, even though Bisaasi-teri was just entering into regular contact with the "civilized" world when I began my fieldwork. There were so many pristine Yanomamö villages when I began my work, why should I study the ones who were already being acculturated?

I made no attempt to conceal my interest in the Shamatari, and this, I later came to realize, bothered the Bisaasi-teri because they did not want me to visit these villages, convinced that I would bring some of my valuable trade items, or *madohe*, to them. They also considered it rather discourteous: they had received me amicably and why, therefore, should I want to go live with lesser people?

It soon became known to the members of the two Shamatari villages that I was interested in living with them for a lengthy period and that I intended to visit other, even more remote Shamatari villages farther to their south. I was especially interested in a village that was rumored to be very large, one that everybody referred to as "Sibarariwä's village"—which I eventually discovered was called Mishimishimaböwei-teri. It was also known by several other names as well, making it difficult to know whether there was just one village or several interrelated villages. I gradually learned to sort through the problem of multiple names of villages by focusing on who the headmen were.

Sibarariwä was the acknowledged headman of the Mishimishimabö-wei-teri group, and a man with a reputation for duplicity and ferocity. He was said to have been the mastermind of a treacherous feast that claimed the lives of many Bisaasi-teri men. This was the reason that the Bisaasi-teri despised him and wanted to kill him.

I eventually discovered that most of the men in the two closest Shamatari villages also despised Sibarariwä, who had begun raiding them because they tried to help the Bisaasi-teri get revenge on Sibarariwä's group just before I arrived in 1964 . . . and would try again later, about 1969. I was initially puzzled by the fact that these three villages had, until very recently, been one village—just as Bisaasi-teri, Monou-teri, and Patanowä-teri had been a single village. In both cases the villages split because of fights among them over the possession of some woman.

Thus, while the people in all three of these Shamatari villages were closely related, chicane and treachery had turned them against each other because of the ambitions of a few political leaders.

It was not difficult for me to get guides in Bisaasi-teri to take me to the first Shamatari village, Mömariböwei-teri, since a considerable number of young men from that village were living in Bisaasi-teri as sons-in-law (known in Yanomamö as *siohas*) while they were doing bride service— working for and living with their in-laws. Moreover, the Bisaasi-teri had managed to obtain a number of young women from Mömariböwei-teri by, for want of a more delicate description, political coercion verging on out-right theft: stronger villages constantly try to coerce women from smaller weaker allied villages.

The young in-married Shamatari men were more than willing to take me to their natal village if the pay were a machete or a knife. But once I reached the first Shamatari village—about a ten-hour walk—my guides would be coerced by their elders in that village to terminate the trip there: they did not want me to continue on to the second, more distant village of Reyaboböwei-teri because they were certain that I would give valuable *madohe* to them.

The avariciousness of the Yanomamö is immediately apparent to all outsiders in their constant begging for your possessions, begging that becomes annoying, coercive, and very depressing if you are the target of the demands, as I was during almost all of my fieldwork. Because I visited and studied so many villages, the constant begging became so oppressive that to escape it I had to periodically get into my canoe, go out into the middle of the river, and just float for an hour or so away from the Yanomamö. I was living alone with them and had no one else to talk to or listen to.

Thus, once I reached the first village, the older men usually told me that the second, more distant village was *very far away*, the trails were terrible, the jungle was flooded and, besides, nobody was home: "They all went on a long camping trip far, far away . . ." was a common story, and it usually worked. The thought of walking nearly two more days through hills, swamps, and jungle to an abandoned village is not an exciting one. In fact, the only way I managed to get to the second village was to hire young men in Bisaasi-teri who were *from* that village and who would not be persuaded to stop at the first village.

During my first year in the field I managed to accumulate a rather large amount of demographic, historic, and genealogical information on the two closest Shamatari groups by talking with visiting Shamatari from these two villages and by conducting long, private interviews with the in-married residents from those villages. In addition, there were several old women in both Bisaasi-teri groups who, as young women, had been abducted from these Shamatari villages or the predecessors of these villages.

It soon became clear from these data that I had to visit Sibarariwä's village, far to the south, to fill in many gaps. My genealogies showed that the residents of Sibarariwä's group were intimately related to the residents of Reyaboböwei-teri and Mömariböwei-teri, and informants repeatedly told me that the three groups had a common origin, which the genealogies clearly confirmed. It was also becoming clear that following the standard field research model in anthropology—residing in a single village for the duration of your fieldwork—would have yielded an inadequate understanding of the Yanomamö. Every village was intimately tied to other villages by genealogy, political history, language dialect, common settlement patterns, and the constantly changing patterns of alliance, feasting, and raiding as groups betrayed each other—and then were forced to ally again as circumstances changed.

The Bisaasi-teri and the two closest Shamatari groups used an additional ploy to discourage me from visiting Sibarariwä's village, which was said to be located somewhere on the Shukumöna River, not far beyond the headwaters of the Mavaca. They recited to me gruesome tales of treachery and violence that characterized their own dealings with Sibarariwä's people and assured me that Sibarariwä would surely kill me and my guides if I ever went there.

These stories impressed and sobered me enough to cause me to reconsider my intentions, particularly because these tales were borne out in the life-history data I collected on causes of death. Sibarariwä's village had a well-deserved reputation for violence and raiding. Many Bisaasi-teri, Mömariböwei-teri, and Reyaboböwei-teri had died at the hands of Mishimishimaböwei-teri archers.

In any event, I knew in advance that I would have difficulty finding guides to take me to Sibarariwä's village. Most of the young men from Bisaasi-teri would find it too risky because they might get shot by the Mishimishimaböwei-teri. The in-married young Shamatari men would be under pressure from the Bisaasi-teri to decline my invitations to take me to contact Sibarariwä's village. The Bisaasi-teri began putting pressure on the in-married Shamatari *siohas* to clam up whenever I tried to discuss a visit to the more remote villages.

I finally found a candidate named Wakarabewä, about eighteen years old, from Mömariböwei-teri. He had been promised a young wife in Lower Bisaasi-teri and was doing his bride service there—some five hundred yards downstream from my mud hut in Upper Bisaasi-teri. As a son-in-law—a *sioha*—he was expected to do all manner of onerous tasks for his parents-in-law, and as a Shamatari he was also subjected to a considerable amount of derision and insult: the Bisaasi-teri had a low opinion of the Shamatari and treated them as inferiors.

Wakarabewä's father-in-law was particularly unpleasant to him and, coincidentally, was also the headman of Lower Bisaasi-teri. He denied Wakarabewä sexual access to his daughter while at the same time he allowed some of the local men of the village to have sex with her. Wakarabewä could not complain publicly about it, but he privately related his bitterness to me.

He eventually told me in private that he didn't think Sibarariwä would kill me if I went to his village, provided I was with him or his father—who, it turned out, was one of Sibarariwä's many brothers! I concluded that a trip there was possible, but I had an uneasy feeling about accepting the word of a young lad when the consensus of the older male Bisaasi-teri was precisely the opposite.

About ten months after I had been in Bisaasi-teri a group of young men from Reyaboböwei-teri visited. As usual, when their visit was over they stopped at my hut to beg for *madohe*. They mentioned that a group of men from Sibarariwä's village had recently visited them. They also told me that Sibarariwä's group had recently moved north, away from the Shukumöna River, had crossed the mountains, and was now living very close to the headwaters of the Mavaca River. After carefully questioning them I concluded that it was possible to ascend the Mavaca in my dugout canoe to a point very close to the putative new location of Sibarariwä's village. The rivers were high now because of recent rains, so I decided to plan immediately for the trip.

I was very excited about this. It was in late 1965, in the first year of my work, and I felt comfortable enough with my Yanomamö language skills to risk a visit into the unknown and unexplored large area to the south.

Wakarabewä agreed to come with me and suggested the names of a few more young Shamatari men who might be amicably received by the Mishimishimaböwei-teri. I then spoke privately with these young men and secured their promises to come with me.

Enter the Dragon

Word soon spread through Bisaasi-teri that I was planning to ascend the Mavaca to try to find Sibarariwä's village. My hut was then visited by party after party of concerned Bisaasi-teri who strongly advised me against such a foolish thing. When their stories of lethal treachery failed to frighten me into canceling my plans, they began a new tactic: they told me about the much-dreaded *raharas*.

Raharas, they explained to me, were created when Man (Yanomamö) was in his infancy. Few living Yanomamö have ever seen a *rahara* up close, but they all knew of men who met other men who had allegedly seen them from a great distance, men who tremble even today when they speak in whispers about these sightings. *Raharas* are associated with the Great Flood and with deep, enchanted water. When the Great Flood receded, the *raharas*—terrifying, dragon-like serpents something like the Loch Ness Monster—originally took up residence in the Orinoco River, somewhere near its headwaters. But since they have never been seen in the Orinoco, the presumption is that they migrated to other rivers after the Flood and now live in those rivers.

Even though few people admit they have ever actually seen *raharas*, their behavior is quite well-known to the Yanomamö. They rise up out of the water and devour those who are foolish enough to attempt to ascend or cross the rivers, especially the headwaters of lesser-known larger rivers. Furthermore, it is alleged that an *underground* river connects the Orinoco with the Mavaca headwaters, and that a number of the *raharas* migrated into the Mavaca headwaters and now lie in wait for unsuspecting travelers who innocently come in canoes up this river. My guides and I would almost certainly fall victim to these savage and voracious beasts.

The *rahara* story nearly sabotaged my intended trip up the Mavaca. Since none of the Bisaasi-teri or Shamatari had ever ascended the Mavaca very far in a canoe, the assertion that it teemed with *raharas* was as good as true in the imagination of my Bisaasi-teri hosts.

Delegations of Bisaasi-teri repeatedly came to my hut to dissuade me. Kaobawä, the headman, and Shararaiwä, his youngest brother, took it upon themselves to relate to me the dangers posed by the *raharas*. For example, Shararaiwä told me (and my Shamatari guides) that the *raharas* would surely rise up and devour us—canoe, motor, gasoline, and paddles. The others nodded and clicked their tongues to indicate their agreement with Shararaiwä's claim, the clicking of tongues being the Yanomamö way to endorse and underscore a claim made orally. My would-be guides, who were also being privately badgered in the village by the Bisaasi-teri, looked gloomily at the ground and remained silent. I could see that the *rahara* story was eroding their confidence.

I was growing very annoyed with the Bisaasi-teri for going to what I considered to be ludicrous ends to prevent me from reaching Sibararíwä's village. I had a long, heated argument with Kaobawä and Shararaiwä on the existence of *raharas* but concluded that any further discussion along this line would be fruitless. Just as you don't argue with the missionaries about the existence of God, you don't argue with the Yanomamö about the existence of *raharas*. Some things are simply a matter of faith.

I thought about it for a while and decided to change tactics. "Yes," I conceded, "there probably are *raharas* near the Mavaca headwaters!" Moreover, I already knew that *raharas* existed in other regions and I had, in my youth and in my native Michigan-urihi-teri, seen many of them and had killed my fair share of them with my shotgun. I had just not been aware that they were also found in the headwaters of the Mavaca River and my skepticism was initially based on this misunderstanding.

Yanomamö logic, fortunately, permits such inconsistencies: it is not so much a matter of *what* you assert as it is *how* you assert it and the kinds of details you give to support your claims. Take the upper hand, give particulars, be assertive, talk about specific *raharas* you have known.

I knew *raharas* very well indeed. As a matter of fact, I was also known in Michigan-urihi-teri as a good shot when it came to *raharas* and I would most certainly be able to employ these skills should we run into any *raharas* on the upper Mavaca. I would keep my double barreled shotgun loaded at all times with my special *rahara* shot to be ready for them.

My young guides perked up, listened attentively, and seemed less gloomy as I continued my argument.

"Didn't I explain these magical cartridges to you?" I went on. I knew from my vast experience while hunting *raharas* in Michigan-urihi-teri precisely where one had to hit a *rahara* in order to kill it with just one shot. I gave an anatomical demonstration to underscore my authority, pointing my finger below my right ear: "You've got to shoot it right here, in the neck! Just below the head! This area is especially lethal if you shoot the *rahara* there!"

I assured them that I also brought with me a very special kind of cartridge called *rahara brahaishaömodimö* ("something made for killing *raharas* at a long distance") and showed them several cartridges with rifled slugs protruding from the plastic jackets. They clicked their tongues in amazement, for they had never seen a *rahara brahaishaömodimö* until now.

Shararaiwä flushed with annoyance and chagrin when I shifted my argument and asserted that I had special knowledge about the fabulous beasts. He and Kaobawä held the advantage only so long as they had a monopoly on knowledge, and since neither of them had ever seen a *rahara*, let alone killed one, I immediately gained the upper hand. Shararaiwä stalked off in a huff, muttering that he was sure the *raharas* on the Mavaca were bigger and fiercer than those in Michigan-urihi-teri.

One of my several guides backed out the next morning and another asked me if it wouldn't be more prudent for him to come on my *second* trip, after I exterminated all the *raharas* found in the waters of the upper Mavaca.

My canoe was already loaded for the trip, and I knew I had to get under way immediately: the risk of losing the rest of my guides increased the longer I remained in Bisaasi-teri.

Thus we hurriedly left Bisaasi-teri with my dugout canoe heavily loaded with provisions, the roar of my outboard motor drowning out the shouts and rejoinders of the men who were still attempting to prevent me from finding the Mishimishimaböwei-teri. They were annoyed with me and with my guides: "You'll see! They'll kill you all! They will pretend friendship at first, and when you are off your guard they will fall on you with bow staves and spear you to death!"

We ascended the Mavaca River for two full days, chopping our way through logs and deadfalls for much of the second day. We were now in unknown Shamatari territory. When we pulled up along the bank to make camp for the second night, the river was so narrow that it was difficult to negotiate the hairpin curves in the current without touching the riverbank on one side or the other.

When my guides set about collecting vines, leaves, and poles for our temporary hut, they returned hastily to the canoe where I was cleaning game, their faces ashen with fear. They had found a recently traveled trail a few yards away from the river. It was a Shamatari trail.

I was elated about the discovery and quickly went to investigate. As we examined the trail and speculated about its origin and terminus, two of my three guides anxiously insisted that we leave for home immedi-

ately: they were sure we were very close to the village and they were not
going to go any farther. Only Wakarabewä indicated that he was willing
to go on. The two others were adamant about going home and were visibly frightened. I had no choice but to turn back.

I was furious with them and later asked why they decided to come in
the first place. Their answer? "For a machete, an ax, and a large cooking
pot!" They had been so certain that we would never get close to the village that they came along just for the payment I had promised them, and
it was an extremely large payment! They also knew that on such trips I
always shot a great deal of game and gave most of it away to the families
of my guides. For them, the trip was basically a paid hunting trip and
they had no intention of reaching the Shamatari village or, incidentally,
allowing me to do so.

Perhaps I was foolish and perhaps it was fortunate that I did not make
it to the Shamatari village. Maybe the Shamatari were every bit as treacherous as the Bisaasi-teri made them out to be and I was not experienced
enough to predict their behavior. I decided to put Sibarariwä's village out
of my mind for the remainder of my first field trip and concentrate on im-
proving the data I had on the Bisaasi-teri and the two closest Shamatari
villages.

Just before I left for home at the end of my first field trip I was again
visited by young men from Reyaboböwei-teri. They told me that a small
group of men from Sibarariwä's village had visited them shortly after my
aborted trip with Wakarabewä. They had learned about my trip through
the jungle grapevine. I asked the Reyaboböwei-teri what the reaction
was among them, and their reply was, in effect, that Sibarariwä's group
wanted me to come and visit them. The visitors from Sibarariwä's group
had, in fact, asked the Reyaboböwei-teri to pass this information on to
me. Unfortunately this information got to me too late to do anything
about it that field season because I was already making plans to go
home.

My 1967 Field Research

My fieldwork the following year, in January 1967, took me to Brazil and
to some dozen or so Yanomamö villages that were located immediately

across the border from Venezuela in the Brazilian state of Roraima. I had just gotten my Ph.D. degree in anthropology from Michigan's Rackham School of Graduate Studies a month earlier and now held a joint appointment as assistant professor in Michigan's Anthropology Department and as a research associate in the Department of Human Genetics in the University of Michigan Medical School, James V. Neel's department.

It was on this field trip that Neel and his biomedical team determined that the Yanomamö had little or no exposure to measles, a disease that has caused lethal epidemics in many Amerindian populations. (Thus began the fieldwork that more than thirty years later would lead to horrible accusations against Neel and me, which I will discuss in the final chapters of this book.)

When my Brazilian trip ended in March, I returned to Venezuela again to make an attempt to contact Sibarariwä's village. This time I intended to have Wakarabewä's father, Shabreiwä, guide me. Because he was one of Sibarariwä's many brothers, he was able to move freely between Mömariböwei-teri and Mishimishimaböwei-teri, despite an overall condition of hostility between the two villages. But, as luck would have it, he had been bitten by a snake recently and could not walk. So, I again had to postpone my attempt to contact the Mishimishimaböwei-teri.

While I had been thwarted twice, these setbacks filled me with an even greater resolve to visit Sibarariwä's group.

1968 and Karina

I returned to Venezuela in 1968 to resume my fieldwork, which had now become an annual January-to-March routine by agreement with Neel.

I had met a boy named Karina in the closest Shamatari village in 1967. Karina was then about eleven years old. He had lived all of his life in Sibarariwä's village, but in 1967 he and his mother had returned to Mömariböwei-teri—her natal group. Karina's mother had been abducted from Mömariböwei-teri years earlier and had decided to return. Karina had never seen a foreigner before and he was then frightened of me, avoiding me all the time I was in Mömariböwei-teri.

When I saw Karina again in 1968 he had lost his fear of foreigners, most likely because he had met Neel and members of his expedition.

Karina (right) as a 10-year-old boy.

Karina even seemed to seek out opportunities to be around them, to get to know them, and, perhaps, do some favors-for-pay for them. He had become a long-term visitor in Bisaasi-teri by early 1968.

He was now about twelve years old, about that age when pubescent Yanomamö boys like to show their elders that they are bold and fearless. At this age they begin to show resentment when people use their names in public—especially those who are younger, lesser Yanomamö—which is how they advertise their increasing maturity and, they hope, their growing political importance.

I knew that Karina had grown up in Sibarariwä's village. When I casually asked him if he was willing to take me to Sibarariwä's village, I was giving him an opportunity to show the others that he was important, an opportunity that he enthusiastically accepted. I planned to have one or two older guides, young men who were *huyas*, bachelors who liked to show their keenness for adventure, perhaps even adventure with some exciting risks involved—as young men everywhere are wont to do.

I worked privately with Karina for about a week on genealogies and the identities of the village residents. I had already collected names and partial genealogies on Sibarariwä's group during the previous two years, but it was clear that Karina was very knowledgeable—he had lived there for ten years, almost his entire young life. There were more than two hundred people living in Sibarariwä's village by my count from the genealogies, and I knew from experience that this had to be an underestimate: collecting these kinds of data "from a distance" invariably leads to underestimates of group size. It was clear that Karina knew everyone there, but probably did not tell me the names of all of them because even the most willing, cooperative informants invariably forget to mention some of the people who live there.

My two guides and I left for Sibarariwä's village several times shortly after I got to the field in 1968, but we had to turn back every time. Once it was bad gasoline. Another time it was a motor problem. A third time something else went wrong with the motor. On two of these aborted attempts we had traveled two full days up the Mavaca River before turning back, which was annoying and frustrating to all of us because it was so time-consuming. When I made yet another attempt, my older guide failed to show up, leaving me with just Karina.

At dawn the day we left my hut at the mouth of the Mavaca River, Karina said he wasn't feeling well and didn't feel like coming. He was getting frustrated because of our several false starts. I covered him with my shirt to keep him warm and set a small aluminum boat over the top of the larger canoe to protect him from the rain and the sun, reassuring him that he would feel better in a day or so. We would eventually leave the larger dugout behind and make the last part of the trip in the smaller aluminum boat that was perched on top of our dugout.

I was also feeling a little under the weather from a severe skin infection—a fungus—around my groin. Some three weeks earlier I had visited the village of Patanowä-teri and, as is customary, entered the village as a Yanomamö visitor, resplendent with feathers, red paint, and a scarlet loincloth. Unfortunately I did not have my own loincloth with me, so I borrowed one from a Yanomamö. He happened to have a contagious and virulent fungus infection of his crotch. Soon afterward I didn't need a red loincloth: I was naturally scarlet from my knees to my navel, itching and burning like crazy. My skin infection was further aggravated by sitting in the rain in wet clothing for days, operating the outboard motor. The only remedy I had with me was a can of Desenex foot powder. You can't imagine the hilarious reaction of the Yanomamö watching the resident fieldworker in a most indescribable position trying to sprinkle foot powder onto his crotch, using gravity as the propellant.

By now I was down to the last of my gasoline supplies and I was very tired. I had spent countless hours running an outboard motor during the past several weeks and had not gotten enough sleep. I vowed that this would be my last try at reaching the village. If I did not make it this time, I decided I would give up. I had wasted far too much time chasing this phantom, and my luck up until this point was unbelievably bad.

I had never gotten to the headwaters of the Mavaca on previous trips, so I did not know if I would encounter rapids or waterfalls. If I did, I would need another guide because Karina was too small to help drag the heavy dugout canoe over logs or through rapids.

A few young men appeared at the canoe to see us off for the umpteenth time. I asked one of them, Bäkotawä, a *huya* of some eighteen years, if he would be interested in coming along with us. He thought about it for a second and then said he would be willing to—provided I would pay him an ax, a machete, and a cooking pot. I agreed to his price and added, "Will you be afraid—like my guides were before—and want to turn back when we get close to the village? If you do get frightened, I am not turning back and you will have to walk home if you refuse to come with me to the village."

He scoffed and said, with an air of annoyed defiance, "I am not capable of being afraid!" He went on and said that he was already a man, and a fierce one at that. He added that he would deceitfully tell the Mishimishimaböwei-teri that he was actually from Patanowä-teri, not from Bisaasi-teri, to thwart any possible harsh treatment once we got there.

I then asked Karina if he would go along with Bäkotawä's story. He somewhat sullenly indicated by a whimpered grunt that he would. So, Bäkotawä hastily went back to the *shabono*, got his weapons and hammock and joined us, and we three intrepid explorers set off for the headwaters of the Mavaca River.

We traveled eight hours the first day and made camp on the right bank of the Mavaca. Karina was feeling much better that evening. He was hungry and mischievous—and began teasing Bäkotawä, reminding him that *he* was a real Mishimishimaböwei-teri, not a mere Patanowä-teri, as Bäkotawä would deceitfully claim to be.

The second day brought an unwelcome surprise. We had gone only about two hours when we ran into two huge, partially submerged trees that blocked our passage. The river had dropped enough during the week to expose about a foot of the immense trunks above the water, far too large an obstacle to drag the heavy dugout over. Moreover, the trees were submerged too deeply in the river to try to cut through them with axes. We reluctantly had to leave the bigger dugout canoe behind at this point and transfer the outboard motor and our gear to the smaller aluminum canoe, which had been, up to now, tied to the top of my dugout. We couldn't go as fast in the aluminum canoe as we had been going in the dugout because the aluminum craft was overloaded with our equipment, food, and gasoline, and was not nearly as streamlined as a long, heavy dugout.

We traveled nine and a half hours the second day. The river had dropped at least five feet since my trip of a week earlier, but we had fewer problems with deadfalls. One advantage the small canoe had was that it was light enough so that we could easily drag it by hand through or over most of the obstacles or unload it and portage around them.

At about eleven o'clock on the third day, after we had been traveling since dawn, Karina suddenly turned around and motioned me over to the right bank, shouting: "There! Over there! I know this place! I've been here before!"

He excitedly jumped out of the canoe and disappeared into the jungle. Bäkotawä and I followed quickly behind him. There was a large, conspicuous trail a few yards from the river. Karina calculated that we were within a day's walk of Sibarariwä's village, and that this was a trail they used when they visited the Iwahikoroba-teri, who, he said while pointing, lived almost due east of this spot.

I suddenly got goose bumps: I was definitely now in unknown Shamatari territory and my chief guide knew where their village was!

Karina also said that the river turned west from here and that it would be quicker for us to walk to the village from this spot than continue in the boat. Sibararïwä's village, he said, lay to the south of us. Karina and I were very excited and pleased about reaching this familiar point, but Bäkotawä became strangely moody and said nothing.

The riverbank was steep and high. I was afraid that if we left the boat in the river, a sudden rain would swell the river enough to wash it away. I insisted that we put the boat and motor up on the bank, knowing that we would have been in serious trouble if our boat got loose and floated away while we were inland trying to find Sibararïwä's village.

The load in the boat had been reduced considerably by this time. We had used up much of the gasoline and had periodically dropped off most of the remaining fuel along the way for the trip home. We were essentially down to our food, hammocks, trade goods for Sibararïwä's people, my cameras, tape recorder, notebooks, film, two shotguns, and a small transistor shortwave radio receiver.

Everything but the bulky trade goods (several aluminum cooking pots and some dozen machetes) fitted comfortably into my two backpacks. Since Karina assured me we were within a day's walk of the village, we decided to leave all but a few trade goods behind and later send the Shamatari down to the canoe to get them. We also decided to leave some of the food here for the trip home since it would be silly to carry it into the village and then carry it back.

In making a quick inventory at this point I was surprised to discover how little food we actually had with us. I had been so preoccupied with motor problems, gasoline, and guides that I had paid too little attention to our food. The box was the same one I had packed for the first trip, and I had not added anything to it after the three aborted attempts, yet several of us had eaten on those aborted attempts for several days. Our food at this point consisted of about three pounds of rice, two pounds of manioc flour, one pound of sugar, a dozen or so cans of sardines, two chocolate bars, three cups of powdered milk, a quarter pound of salt, and one pound of coffee. It was not anything to worry about if Sibararïwä's village was only a day away: we could expect to be fed by our hosts. And, as long as I had shotgun cartridges, meat would be no problem if it took us longer to get to the village. I still had *all* of my *rahara* cartridges left over from last year (some half-dozen twelve-gauge rifled slugs for tapir), plus the more numerous No. 4 birdshot cartridges I always carried for small game like *pajui*, the ubiquitous wild turkeys. I left the sugar, milk, manioc, coffee, some rice, and half of the sardine supply at the river for the trip home, bringing some rice, chocolate, and the remaining sardines with us plus a small cooking pot in which I could cook the rice.

It took us about an hour to store our supplies and load the packs. We started off shortly after midday.

Although it had not rained much downstream for the past week, the trail here was unusually slippery and wet. We followed the base of a large hill most of the time, gradually getting higher and higher. I was surprised to find swamps and water-filled potholes so high above the river elevation. At about three o'clock a violent thunderstorm hit and we huddled together under a small nylon tarp for almost an hour trying to keep the packs from getting soaked. We resumed walking after the rain stopped, eventually reaching a Yanomamö resting place on the trail. We stopped there.

Well-traveled Yanomamö trails have these resting spots every three hours or so. They are usually flat places where the trees are thin and widely scattered and, ideally, some of the sky can be seen so the Yanomamö can tell the time. The Yanomamö stop to rest on long trips and usually fall into the habit of using the same places over and over. Some even have names. As they sit around and chat, their hands are always busy, breaking branches, chopping on logs with machetes or axes, snacking, repacking the loads in their baskets, etc. The resting stops soon take on the character of Paleolithic junkyards: battered, hacked trees, worn-out baskets, empty seedpods, wilting banana and plantain peelings, and other debris scattered around.

Karina told us about the last time he was at this spot, on a trip from Iwahikoroba-teri. He showed us the log that Börösöwä, the most prominent Iwahikoroba-teri headman, sat on, where the others sat, what they talked about, who threw away the worn-out pack basket that was lying there rotting, and so on. For the first time since I had been trying to contact these Shamatari groups they seemed real. The people were no longer just names in a genealogy or a dot on my field maps. I was certain for the first time that I was actually going to *reach* Sibarariwä's village.

Karina told us that there was a large, more permanent camping site ahead of us and, a few hours beyond that, the village of his people, who were now known as Mamoheböwei-teri—after the name they gave to their most recent garden.

It was around four o'clock by the time we reached the second camping site. It had not been used for at least a year. Karina said that Sibarariwä made this camp after a fight in the village with Möawä, his younger rival and nephew. Afterward part of the group moved here temporarily until tempers cooled off. It was a fairly large campsite, large enough to accommodate over a hundred people. What impressed me most were the mildew and dampness of the area, and the thousands of termite grubs that were now hatching in the dilapidated, rotting *yanos*—the temporary huts the Yanomamö make for short stays.

We decided to sleep here for the night. If we pushed on, we would arrive at the village after dark. I preferred to have as much daylight as possible during my first day's visit to a hitherto uncontacted village, a general Yanomamö policy when they themselves visit a group for the first time.

We were famished. Our only meal that day had been some dry, smoked caiman left over from the day before. We decided to eat a big meal before pushing on, knowing that our visit would cause such a sensation in the village that we were not likely to have much time for cooking or eating. We boiled enough rice for both supper and breakfast and gorged ourselves with it.

As dusk gathered Karina was in a mischievous mood and began bantering and teasing Bäkotawä. He recounted from hearsay, for example, the treacherous feast in 1950 that Sibarariwä had engineered for the Bisaasi-teri, and the revenge event that the Bisaasi-teri held in return. He told him of the anguish of the Shamatari over the deaths that resulted, and implied that he *might* accidentally let it slip that Bäkotawä was *actually* from Bisaasi-teri, not from Patanowä-teri. He talked about how sneaky the people in this village were, how many raids they had gone on, who they killed, and how much they hated the Bisaasi-teri. I finally had to shut him up because Bäkotawä was becoming visibly frightened.

When I turned in for the night I made the mistake of not hanging my shoes or the packs up off the damp ground, over the fire. The next morning they were covered with squirming termite grubs inside and out. It took me fifteen minutes to get them all out by banging my shoes against trees, each other, or throwing them on the ground to knock the termites loose.

And on that gloomy dawn Bäkotawä announced that he was too frightened to go on and said he wanted to go back to the boat. I was angry, mostly about Karina's mischief, but I was determined not to turn back this time. Silently, so as to not reveal my anger, I unpacked the food and gave Bäkotawä a share of the rice in a waterproof small plastic bag. There were matches and cooking pots at the boat and he could use these when he made camp there. I had two shotguns, although neither Bäkotawä nor Karina knew how to use one. I had brought the extra one along to make them feel more secure. I gave one of them to Bäkotawä along with a dozen or so cartridges and a quick lesson in how to load and shoot a shotgun. There were also fishhooks at the boat, so he would be able to keep himself fed while Karina and I pushed on. I sternly warned him not to put my boat in the water for *any* reason, including fishing. He explained that although he was frightened now because we were so close to the village, he would not be frightened at the boat. He said he would make a camp there and wait for us to return. I told him we would be gone about three or four sleeps, and he assured me that he would wait for us.

Karina and I left for the village about 7 A.M. We soon began running into fresh signs of Yanomamö travelers: we saw footprints in the mud that were made after the previous day's rain and found several ripe *rasha* fruits on the trail. Someone had passed through the area the day before while carrying bunches of *rasha*. After about an hour we came upon an abandoned garden and an old village site, one that had been deserted for many months. Someone had been foraging in the nearby garden and had cut the *rasha* from the still-producing trees. My skin began to tingle: we were very close to Sibarariwä's group.

At nine-thirty we crossed a small stream at the base of a hill. Karina said it was the stream that the villagers bathed in and got their water from, but since there were very few footprints in the sand he was sure the village was deserted. A few minutes later we crossed over the peak of the hill and found ourselves in a modestly large Yanomamö plantain garden. We cautiously stopped and listened but heard only the raucous sounds of black *kobari* birds in the distance. Karina pointed out the ridgeline of the *shabono* roof over the tops of the banana plants. We continued down the trail and walked into the village. It was completely deserted and all but one small section had been burned down. We walked over to this section and laid our packs down in the shade.

Karina seemed more disappointed than I was. We sat there, discussing the possible location of the group. Karina pessimistically suggested that they had gone to one of their several camping areas on the Shukumöna River but hesitated to guess which one. The Shukumöna was a long walk from here, across a steep mountain ridge.

We decided to look around in the garden to see if anyone had returned to it recently. We soon found many fresh signs of life: the residents could not be very far away because they were periodically returning to the garden to fetch food. We found a stalk of ripe plantains and ate several of them.

We decided to follow their trail along the Mavaca River to the southwest, toward a camping area Karina said they preferred to others. We left everything behind except our hammocks and our weapons and traveled quickly. It was soon apparent that we were on the right trail, for the signs became fresher and more numerous as we went along. We had followed the trail for about an hour and a half when Karina suddenly stopped and motioned for me to be quiet. Ahead of us we could faintly hear babies crying and people talking and we could see the smoke of their fires wafting through the trees. We had found them!

I suddenly felt very limp and helpless. What the hell had I gotten myself into? I was down to my hammock, my sneakers, my Speedo-style swimming trunks, a borrowed loincloth, my shotgun, and a small hip pack to carry my shotgun cartridges. The farther I had come, the fewer accoutrements of civilization I had to distinguish me from Adam. I felt naked and, as a matter of fact, I very nearly was.

Karina hissed at me as I reflected on my pitiful situation: "Stay here. They will be frightened of you—they have never seen a *nabä* before and they might shoot you with arrows! They will be scared of your shotgun, so give it to me and take my arrows." Not thinking clearly and without hesitation I gave him my shotgun and took his bow and arrows. We quickly washed the mud from our legs to look presentable and I put on my borrowed loincloth and stashed my swimming trunks in my hip pack. Before I could think about what I had just done, Karina was gone. Now

I *really* felt naked and defenseless, clutching a few skinny arrows and a palm wood bow.

Karina disappeared down the trail a few score yards, entered the temporary camp, and announced himself with a series of short, high-pitched whistles. The voices stopped for a second and the jungle was quiet. Then explosive loud cheering and hooting erupted as they recognized him and welcomed him into camp. He had left them as a boy, a *yawawä*, but returned as a young man, a *huya*, now some twelve years of age and more mature.

It suddenly got very quiet again. Then there was a moment of excited buzzing and I knew they had been informed of my presence. I suddenly felt very self-conscious. I wiped the mud off my legs and straightened my loincloth. Karina soon reappeared and beckoned me toward him. I nervously walked into the clearing in proper Yanomamö fashion and stood there in the formal visitor's pose, clutching Karina's bow and arrows while the men ran screaming about me, waving their own bows and nocked arrows, pointing them at my face. My head was whirling and I felt dizzy. My mouth was dry, but I knew I was one of very few anthropologists who were privileged to experience this custom. Out of the corner of my eye I could see women and children frantically running, making for the jungle and safety. It was simply too much for them. Finally, one of the older men cautiously grabbed me by the arm and led me to a hut, motioning me to lie down in the empty vine hammock that was strung there.

They were as nervous and apprehensive as I was. Each time I moved, even slightly, they jumped away from me. I lay in the hammock as a visitor should, one hand behind my head and one hand over my mouth, with my legs crossed and eyes fixed on some invisible object above the heads of everyone, staring blankly into space, pretending that this is how I normally lay in a hammock when I was in strange, new villages whose residents had never before seen a foreigner.

In the hammock next to me lay a man of obvious importance—visitors are always given a hammock next to someone of rank. He was about thirty-five years old and his face showed no emotion, hard and cold. He was far too young to be Sibarariwä.

After a while I managed to attract Karina over to my hammock and whispered softly to him: "Is this Sibarariwä?" Karina whispered back: "No! He is someone else. But he is very big!"

I later learned that his name was Möawä and his renown had eclipsed that of Sibarariwä—his father's brother. They had fought recently, perhaps within the past year. Sibarariwä left the village with the largest faction following him. Möawä, because of the sheer force of his character, was now beginning to attract them back into his fold and back to his village. At this point he had most of Sibarariwä's followers in his own group. Thus the old leader whose name and reputation had struck fear and hatred in the minds of the Bisaasi-teri was replaced and eclipsed by a younger, even fiercer man. One could only imagine how terrible the younger man must be to have replaced such a renowned leader.

By and by Karina told them that we had left our packs at the *shabono*, and two men were dispatched to get them.

It is impossible to describe the noises they made on seeing me for the first time. The Yanomamö are noisy people to begin with, but when they are excited, they are *really* noisy. They hissed, clucked, clicked, hooted, and screamed. The adult men shooed the younger ones away and crowded around my hammock, each trying to elbow his way in for a better look. Soon they were all around me and I was surrounded by a large mass of sweaty, painted bodies.

According to their own courtesy protocols, they are not supposed to approach a visitor for several minutes, or at least a time long enough to be polite, and they should not stand upright directly over the hammock where the visitor reclines. The Yanomamö etiquette system collapsed completely on that day. Only Möawä in the hammock next to mine remained aloof and silent, eyeing us all with an expressionless, indifferent, cold stare.

Finally, one of the squatting men duck-waddled closer to me and cautiously reached out and touched my leg. He jerked his hand back, as if he had touched a red-hot cast iron stove. He clicked his tongue and let out a long, low growl. Another tried it, and then another. They all grunted and clicked their tongues, implying that just touching my skin was a weird and sensational experience.

They kept exclaiming "Whaaa! Look at how hairy he is! He is covered with hair, like a *basho* monkey!" They gradually got bolder and soon there were dozens of hands rubbing up and down on my body, feeling the hair on my legs, arms, and chest. Finally, one of the men in the front row yelled at a young man: "Go out to the other camp and get your father and the others! Your father has to see this!" The young man quickly bolted out into the jungle but reappeared within seconds with a sheepish look on his face: he had forgotten his bow and arrows in his excitement.

The examination went on for nearly an hour as new people duck-waddled in closer and wiggled in to have their feel. I felt like a plump chicken being pinched and rubbed by dozens of chefs to determine how I might taste when cooked.

At first they observed some of the code of etiquette by not asking me any direct questions, but finally their excitement and curiosity just overwhelmed them and they began to ask me things, trying to be as courteous as they could. Until now I had remained completely silent.

The first thing they wanted to know: "Why did it take you so long to come and visit us? We've been waiting for you a very long time!" They said that they had repeatedly sent me messages via the Reyaboböwei-teri and Mömariböwei-teri who came to visit Bisaasi-teri—ever since they learned that I was trying to ascend the Mavaca to find them for the past two wet seasons.

They also had an incredible repertory of stories about me and my activities from the very first year I came to the Yanomamö four years earlier. Some of their stories were hilarious, and I marveled at what must have been an extraordinary system of selective retention of the facts available to them. For example, they related to me in considerable detail an incident that happened about a year earlier on a two-day inland trip I had taken into Reyaboböwei-teri. They acted out in detail how I had slipped on a rock, fallen backward into the river, and injured my arm. They even mimicked amusingly well the explicative I blurted out: "Oh shit!" They wanted to see the scar they knew I had on my arm from the fall and, when I showed it to them, they hooted and growled with approval. Then they rubbed it gently and told me they knew how much it must have hurt and whined how "sad" they were when they learned of my mishap. I was dumbfounded.

Then they asked me a strange thing. They wanted me to take the "skins" (tennis shoes) off my feet so they could examine my feet. I didn't understand why they would make such an unusual request, but it quickly became apparent. They had heard through the jungle grapevine that I wore sneakers "to cover up my tender feet." When they saw them they exclaimed: *"Whaaa! Wa mami kä duku no modahawä!"* ("Your feet are really and truly tender and pink, just as we heard they were!")

They sent for the women who had fled into the jungle—and scolded them for running away. A few of the older women apprehensively came over and touched my arms, legs, and pink feet because the men made them do it—to show me that everyone there was friendly. The women weren't very enthusiastic about having a hairy *nabä* in the camp, because he frightened the children.

Finally, Karina interrupted the discussion and suggested that I might be hungry, knowing that I hadn't eaten since dawn. A few of the *huyas* quickly left and returned a few minutes later with ripe bananas and plantains and other leftover vegetable morsels.

I had barely begun to eat when I heard shouting and hooting just outside the camp. A dozen or so well-armed naked men marched into the camp, looking and searching excitedly with their eyes: "Where is he? Where is he? Where's the hairy *nabä?*" By this time the Yanomamö had heard the evangelical missionaries, the Salesians, and the employees of the Malarialogía use my names—Napoleon and Chagnon, but in Venezuela my last name was pronounced the French way—"sha-ñon" which the Yanomamö could not pronounce, because it did not end with a vowel. The closest they could come to "sha-ñon" was *shaki,* their word for a particularly noisome bee that would crawl on one's perspiring skin. So, that's what they called me: *Shaki* or, with a masculine ending, *Shakiwä.*

They, of course, had to do their own examinations of me. The new examinations took well over an hour, at the end of which most of my body was covered with *nara*—the red pigment they smear on their own bodies. It gets on everything and is difficult to get off your body and, if you have any, your clothing.

It was getting late. The crowd began to thin out as people went to their own huts to prepare food for the late-day meal. The din of excited conversation kept on as they went about these tasks.

Thus the people of Mishimishimaböwei-teri had finally seen their first foreigner. He was larger and hairier than they imagined.

A steady rain began falling, slowly but growing more intense as darkness fell. People scurried to find extra leaves from the nearby jungle to patch leaks in their roofs. I was relieved that their attention had turned back to humdrum activities and away from me. I got up, opened my pack, and slung my own hammock. This caused a minor sensation because my hammock was made of nylon mesh, and they had never seen one like this. It was also about three times as large as their hammocks, which amazed them. They all wanted to try it out, red pigment and all.

A lone figure approached the camp. He emerged quietly from the rain, an older man. He was carrying a long walking stick but was not hobbling. He made directly for my hut. A man in a nearby hammock quickly got up and left. The older man leaned his walking stick against the hut. He wiped the rain from his face, unceremoniously got into the vacated hammock, and settled in without saying anything. A woman in the next hut over immediately brought him some roasted plantains and departed quietly. The camp became strangely silent.

I knew immediately that it was Sibarariwä, the fabled and notorious headman of the Mishimishimaböwei-teri.

Karina had told me earlier that I should address him as either *shoriwä* (brother-in-law) or *shoabe* (father-in-law, grandfather, or mother's brother). This would relate us to each other in the best possible way according to Yanomamö kinship principles. It would automatically create between us a bond that implied certain modes of behavior and mutual obligations that other kinship terms did not convey. I decided that I would call him *shoabe*, since it implied more obligations on my part, and put him in a superior social position, a generation above mine.

The village was no longer the same after Sibarariwä entered. It had become tense and strained, and I began to feel uncomfortable. The few stragglers who were sitting around my hammock got up and left, saying nothing, leaving the two of us lying in adjacent hammocks conspicuously trying to ignore each other, each waiting for the other to make the first move. Since I was the visitor I expected him to break the ice. But he was silent and poker-faced and pretended I was not even there.

So I decided I would initiate the conversation. I turned in his direc-

Sibarariwä, sitting in background, behind the line of children,
and William Oliver, University of Michigan pediatrician, 1987.

tion, and called to him: "Father-in-law! I have come to your village to
visit you and bring *madohe*. Is it true that your people are poor and in
need of machetes?" I could hear low whispers of excitement around us
after I spoke—the very word *madohe* stirs people. After a while he replied
sarcastically: "Yes! We are poor in machetes," implying that I ought to
know better than to ask such a stupid question when I could plainly see
that they were poor in machetes.

I remember being surprised by the sound of his voice—it was rather
high-pitched for a man of such great renown, sounding almost like the
voice of a child or a woman.

Apart from that, his tone of voice did not inspire any warm feelings
in me. We chatted halfheartedly for a while. I could tell that things were
not going too well and that this old goat was not going to be friendly. I
concluded by telling him that I would give him the small cooking pot I
had with me and one of my small knives, but that I would bring him a *big*
gift on my next visit. I explained that this visit was primarily to discover

if they were friendly and if they were in need of *madohe*, as the rumors had it.

Sibarariwä's solemn arrival and cool demeanor threw a cloud of gloom over an otherwise enthusiastic welcome. After a while I decided to ignore him and struck up conversations with people in the other huts.

He and Möawä ignored each other as well. Eventually a modestly large crowd of men was around my hammock again, and the mood reverted to the excitement of mid-afternoon.

I explained to them that I came to see how many people there were in their village and told them I already knew what their names were, and who their wives and children were, but I wanted to see them with my own eyes. I would speak to each of them in the morning and find out what kind of small gift he or she would like me to bring on my next visit.

I showed them my field ledger and where their names were written. They would point to a name and ask me who that was. I would whisper the name into the ear of one of them and he would relate it to the others by some teknonymous or kinship reference, and they would roar with laughter, amazed that my scribbles were their real names.

That night I got my shortwave transistor radio out of my pack and tuned in a news broadcast. They were fascinated by the strange contraption but immediately recognized male and female voices. They insisted on listening to a station with a female voice, and crowded around attentively to hear a woman talking in a language they did not understand. (As I recall, it was a missionary broadcast in Dutch, and I didn't get much out of it, either.) Every once in a while I would try to find a station more to *my* liking but they insisted on hearing a female voice. Most of them went home when I turned the radio off, but a few of them hung around just to stare at me—and periodically ask me if I were sleeping yet. They had the annoying habit of waking me to ask if I were sleeping yet.

I fell asleep worrying about what Bäkotawä would do when he got back to the boat. What if he were so frightened that he could not bear to wait for us to come back? What if he took the boat and left us? I decided that I had to go to the river soon and check on him. Thanks to Karina the Mishimishimaböwei-teri already knew about Bäkotawä and insisted on inviting him to the camp, assuring me they would not harm him.

The next morning I began the task of identifying everyone by name, writing a number on their arms with a felt-tip marker to make sure each person had only one name and one identity number. More accurately, I had to associate the names I had learned from Karina and other informants with the faces I could now see in the flesh.

I estimated their ages and identified their spouses if my information was incomplete in this respect. Some of them had gotten married since Karina last lived there. I found out where everyone had been born (the name of the garden and/or village) and where post-pubescent females had their first menses. I had the names of 270 living people in my field ledger, but the camp contained only about eighty people. There had been a recent fight over a woman, and the village had temporarily split into two. I had found only the smaller part. The others were across the mountains on the Shukumöna River, living in another garden. My hosts were mad at them and did not want to take me there. But they were not mad enough to raid them.

I systematically identified everyone on my list, whispering the names into Karina's ear, who then translated them into kinship circumlocutions so as to avoid as much as possible saying their names aloud.

By ten o'clock I had numbered everyone in the group and the census was as complete as I could make it for the time being. I had also noted after each name the item that person wanted me to bring on my next visit, and they were surprised at the total recall I had when they decided to check me. I simply looked at the number I had written on their arm, looked the number up in my field book, and then told the person precisely what he had requested me to bring for him on my next trip. They enjoyed this, and then they pressed me to mention the names of particular people in the village they would point to. I would look at the number on the arm, look it up in my field book, and whisper his name into someone's ear. The others would anxiously and eagerly ask if I got it right, and the informant would give an affirmative quick raise of the eyebrows, causing everyone to laugh hysterically: they didn't even have to have the name mentioned aloud—all that was necessary was to have the person into whose ear I whispered the name confirm it by raising his eyebrows to indicate, "He got it right!"

With this task finished, I had essentially completed the major objective of this first trip and passed the remaining time visiting with my hosts, doing what they wanted me to do—strange and exotic things that *nabä* are rumored to do.

They wanted me to shoot my shotgun, as they had never seen one before. I had them fill a gourd with water and throw it up into the air and I would blow it to pieces at fifteen yards, splattering water and shattered gourd all over. This really impressed them, especially the loud report of the exploding cartridge.

They wanted to see how strong I was, and we lifted each other, or bent arms to show our muscles, and made other silly displays. They also wanted to show me how close the Mavaca River was to their camp, so we went for a walk to the river. The path we took terminated at a small, shallow rapids. When I asked what it was called, they replied, "It has no name. We just call it 'the rapids.' " They decided, on the spot, to name it for me to commemorate my first visit to them.

By mid-afternoon we were back at the camp, and it was raining hard.

They now knew I had *madohe* at the boat and were anxious to have it. They badgered me constantly until I agreed to go to the boat to check on the trade goods. This meant, of course, that I had to leave for home because visitors distribute their trade goods immediately before departing.

Most of the adult men decided to come along just to see my boat, but Sibararïwä was not among them. He had quietly left at dawn and returned to the small camp he and a few others had made some distance away, taking the small cooking pot and knife I had given him as gifts.

We left for the canoe about three o'clock, using a much better trail than the one Karina and I had followed to get to their camp. It rained hard all the way, and we traveled at a very fast pace, suspecting that we would not make it to my boat by dark. We intercepted the trail I had come in on about an hour before reaching the river.

There we found spent cartridges every few hundred feet. Bäkotawä had been playing around with the shotgun, probably shooting at everything from tiny birds to strange sounds. There was no telling how many cartridges he had shot before he got to this point, but at the rate we were finding the spent hulls he was probably out of ammunition by the time he reached the boat.

None of the men brought food or their hammocks with them. They apparently planned to take me to the boat, trade bows and arrows for the machetes I had cached there, and return home early the following morning. They would be hungry, but they were too excited to think about food. They could make hammocks from bark strips in a few minutes and would sleep in these makeshift contraptions for the night.

Karina was in the lead, followed by several men and me. The main body followed behind us. About 6:30 P.M. darkness fell, and we had trouble following the trail well before we reached the spot where I left the boat.

My greatest fears were realized. Bäkotawä had taken the boat, motor, trade goods, food—*everything*.

At first I refused to believe my eyes. Bäkotawä did not know how to run the motor, so why would he want to take the motor? Besides, the motor was not even mounted on the canoe. And why take the trade goods? He knew that the villagers would be furious if I had promised them fifteen machetes and then been unable to deliver them. It was as if he were trying to get me into the most unpleasant of all possible jams. He had not even spent the *night* there. There was no sign of a temporary hut, no fire, nothing. At first I thought we were at the wrong place, but on close inspection and after Karina insisted, I agreed. I was suddenly very depressed because I knew that I was in a very difficult situation, a possibility that I had been trying to suppress in my mind, but one that I secretly feared would be realized.

The river had come up several feet since we had left the boat three days ago and the spot did not look the same. But our tracks were there. My first suspicion was that Bäkotawä had moved everything across the river and downstream a little to get off the main trail and conceal himself. I fired my shotgun two times, but no reply came. Perhaps he knew I had Shamatari with me and he was too afraid to return my signal.

We made our camp in darkness and in a cold drizzle. I had a piece of nylon tarpaulin with me and draped it over some branches. When the drizzle changed to rain all twenty of my companions huddled and squatted together around my hammock and spent the night in that position, shivering, naked, slumped over, and partially *in* my hammock.

At dawn I gave Karina my shotgun and two cartridges and a quick lesson in how to fire each chamber. I told him to walk along the river until midday and then fire the cartridges just before he turned back. He was to wait to see if Bäkotawä would reply. Meanwhile, some of the young men were sent back to the garden, some four hours behind us, to fetch food. I spent the morning in my hammock, contemplating my plight and trying to weigh the alternatives in the event that Bäkotawä could not be found. I was almost out of food and had only five or six cartridges left. I could get vegetable food from the Yanomamö in case I had to walk back, but I would have to have them carry it: our packs already contained just about as much as two men would want to transport over that distance—my notes, medicine, food, tape recordings, our hammocks, etc.

My base of operations was due north of us at the confluence of the Mavaca and Orinoco rivers, a fact that I also confirmed with the Mishimishimaböwei-teri. I had no idea how long it might take to walk there from here.

There were two possible ways to walk out. The trail to the northeast would take us to Iwahikoroba-teri, two or three days' walk from our present location. The Iwahikoroba-teri were uncontacted and, according to the Bisaasi-teri, a very treacherous group. My Mishimishimaböwei-teri companions were not anxious to have me find out where the Iwahikoroba-teri lived, probably because they suspected that I would visit them in the future and bring my *madohe* there. From Iwahikoroba-teri it was another four or five days' walk to a new garden made by the Patanowä-teri. I had spent two weeks with them a month earlier, but at their old garden. I knew that if I reached their village I could get some of them to take me to Bisaasi-teri, a further three- or four-day trip.

The arguments against this plan, besides the reluctance of my potential guides to consider going this way, were several. First, the rainy season had now started and most of the jungle was inundated. Many detours would be required and walking would be slow through the swamps. If it were eight or ten days' walk in the dry season, it could easily become fifteen or more days' walk in the wet season. Second, my only pair of tennis shoes would not last that long, and my feet were too "soft" to make such a trip barefooted. I never imagined that a Yanomamö guide would abandon me in some unexplored area, steal my canoe and supplies, and leave me to fend for myself. If I could have predicted this I would have packed more tennis shoes! Third, if anyone heard about my plight and tried to find me, I would be too far away from the river to hear them and an embarrassingly large "rescue" operation might develop unnecessarily.

The alternative trail was to the northwest, to Reyaboböwei-teri. It was almost a week's walk to that village in this weather, according to my companions, and two or three days from there to Bisaasi-teri, depending on how fast you walked. I had made this trip in two and a half difficult days earlier in the year.

All of the above arguments applied against the second alternative, in addition to two further disadvantages. The distance between reliable provisions was greater and there was a war developing between my present hosts and the Reyaboböwei-teri. Wadoshewä, a prominent Mishimishimaböwei-teri man, told me that he had recently visited the Reyaboböwei-teri and was chased out of the village by their headman, Idahiwä, who threatened to kill anyone from Mishimishimaböwei-teri who visited there in the future.

The possibilities of walking out seemed remote at best, and I would consider doing so only as a last resort. I could, after all, live indefinitely with the Mishimishimaböwei-teri if I had to, and I was confident that someone would sooner or later realize I was missing and come looking for me. But I was not sure that anyone among the missionaries knew that I had left to try to contact the people in Sibarariwä's village and had taken only two Yanomamö guides with me.

While waiting for Karina to return, and convinced that Bäkotawä was gone for good, I had what I thought was a splendid idea: I would make a *bark* canoe with the help of the Mishimishimaböwei-teri and descend the Mavaca River in that!

Whenever the Yanomamö have feasts they make bark troughs to hold the many gallons of plantain soup consumed at these feasts. The troughs are similar to crude canoes and are occasionally used that way. They are so clumsy and poorly made that they are usually discarded after a single voyage, almost invariably a downstream trip because you can't paddle them against the current. The bark softens, deteriorates rapidly, and loses its resiliency after a few days. It then collapses like a post-Halloween jack-o'-lantern and rots quickly. But such a canoe would last long enough for me and Karina to make it back to the large dugout canoe I had left downstream.

When I asked my companions to help me find an *arapuri* tree, the tree whose bark is used for the trough, they insisted that *arapuri* trees could not be found in this area.

This was depressing news. Making the bark canoe and going downstream in it would have been merely an inconvenience and I was largely viewing my plight as exactly that. Now that I learned that the bark canoe idea was completely out of the question, I began to realize that my situation was likely a bit more serious.

I thought about it for a while and it hit me: I'll make a *log* raft! The Yanomamö groups near the Orinoco all know how to make them, and I assumed that the Mishimishimaböwei-teri would also know how to do it. The Mishimishimaböwei-teri knew what I meant when I asked about log rafts but confessed that they had never made one.

Log rafts are simple to make, and I knew that they could do it with a little help. In fact, the palisades they erect around their villages for defensive purposes are essentially vertical log rafts.

We had my single machete to work with and spent most of the morning cutting logs and collecting lianas with which to lash them together. I was not exactly happy about this alternative, since any raft is very clumsy compared to a boat, and Karina was by no means an accomplished gondolier. We would have great problems guiding a log raft through the snags and curves in the river, but it was still a much better option than walking.

I instructed them to cut only light, pithy trees. I helped pick out the trees, measured off the proper length, cut them, and hauled them to the river. My companions took turns chopping with my machete. By midday we had assembled the logs at the river's edge and were ready to lash them together. My spirits lifted a bit as we tied the logs together with vines. By early afternoon the raft was as wide as I dare let it get and still be navigable. I called the work to a halt.

The Mishimishimaböwei-teri gathered at the bank to witness the test run. I gingerly stepped onto the crude craft—and it promptly sank! It would not even hold *my* weight, let alone mine plus Karina's. My companions tried hard to look concerned and disappointed, but many of them turned their faces so I could not see their grins.

I went back to my hammock to wait for Karina to return and thought once again about walking out. I wondered out loud: perhaps we could make it back to the spot where we had left the large canoe, which I calculated to be about halfway between our camp and Bisaasi-teri. But we would have to follow the river for the greater part of the way in order to be sure that we did not inadvertently pass by the canoe without seeing it. The major argument against this plan was that I could not predict Bäkotawä's behavior: since he took with him virtually everything I left at the river, there was little reason to believe that he would pass the big canoe by without also appropriating *that* as well.

Later in the afternoon Karina and his companions returned silently to the camp and flopped into their hammocks. They eventually explained that they had walked all day, reaching the spot where Karina, Bäkotawä, and I had made our last camp. Karina told all of us that not only was Bäkotawä *not* there, but he had even stopped there to collect the empty gasoline tank we left behind! Karina had fired the shotgun twice but Bäkotawä had not returned the signal.

The rest of the Mishimishimaböwei-teri learned of my situation and people began streaming into our camp all day long, bringing food and hammocks. A more substantial camp gradually took form. All the huts were covered with *kedeba* leaves to keep the rain out. At least everyone would be dry, fed, and rested.

While I was lying in my hammock contemplating my situation, one of the men confronted me with the following proposition. He was very logical and began his argument as follows:

"You are a *nabä*. Don't *nabäs* know how to make canoes?"

"Yes," I replied, adding, "but I don't have the right tools to make a canoe. You need axes to make canoes and Bäkotawä took my axes."

He then excitedly exclaimed: "We have two axes back at the village! We could use these to make a canoe!"

My spirits lifted once again. I told him that if he would send for the axes and help me hollow out a tree, we could make a canoe. In fact, I was the best damned canoe-making foreigner they would ever meet!

Several young men were immediately dispatched back to the village to fetch the axes and more bananas. They must have run all the way to the village and back, for they returned a few hours after dark. They covered the round-trip distance in about six hours, almost the time that it took

Karina and me to walk it just one way! While they were gone we went looking for a suitable canoe tree.

The Ye'kwana Indians, who live just north of the Yanomamö, are superb dugout canoe makers. The Yanomamö do not know how to make canoes—they live in the interior and avoid larger rivers, so they don't need canoes. The Ye'kwana are a "river people" and the Yanomamö a "foot people"—a standard ethnographic classification for Amazon Basin tribes.

I knew what kinds of trees the Ye'kwana used for canoes but had no idea how to identify them in a forest or whether this was the kind of forest where such trees were found. I decided that the safest bet would be to ask the Mishimishimaböwei-teri to find a tree about "this big around" (about thirty inches in diameter) that was pithy on the inside; it would be easer for us to hollow it out if it were pithy. They soon found one that they claimed had pithy characteristics. We marked it and would return to fell it when the axes arrived.

We all retired that night in much better spirits, listening to female voices on my shortwave transistor radio, munching on roasted plantains and boiled *rasha* fruits that the women had brought to us.

We began working on the tree about eight in the morning. The axes were so badly worn and dull that progress was quite slow. These axes had been traded inland to the Mishimishimaböwei-teri after having been used by many previous owners until they were nearly worn out and had been reduced to only half their original size.

The good news was that the tree indeed was pithy in the center, a factor that contributed as much to our progress as the axes did.

I measured off the length I thought would be sufficient to carry Karina and me—about twelve feet—and we cut off the trunk at that point. Next I scratched an outline of the area we were to hollow out and we set about removing the pith.

It was hot and humid, and we soon were puffing and sweating profusely. The men were in excellent spirits and cooperated happily, making a game out of the project. I was delighted with their enthusiasm, but I had to watch them diligently since, in their enthusiasm, they chopped recklessly, making the canoe too thin at spots.

By early afternoon it was taking shape. It resembled a giant cigar with a deep gouge cut out of its center, but it looked as though it might float. I decided that I did not know enough about canoe making to attempt to spread it open with heat, as the Ye'kwana do. This would have made it flatter on the bottom and therefore less likely to roll over, but flattening it with fire would risk splitting the log in half.

At about 2 P.M. I concluded that any further effort to make it thinner with the axes and machete would risk splitting the log in two. There were already several serious cracks appearing in the bottom. To correct this we had to wrap vines tightly around the ends of the log.

We dragged it to the river, some hundred yards away, where we planned to test its seaworthiness. I was a little worried that the canoe would be like the raft—buoyant enough to float by itself, but not buoyant enough to hold me and Karina.

We had gotten almost to the river when the lead man spotted a tree with honey in it and the work came to an immediate halt. There is nothing that will excite the Yanomamö more than a cache of honey, and they immediately set about smoking the bees out of the nest and digging the sweet liquid out of it with sticks and leaves. A crude basket was made from leaves and the honey was put into it and mixed with water. The Yanomamö are not very particular about what gets into their mead. They end up with a brew that is about 5 percent honey, 80 percent water, and 15 percent debris consisting of half-dead bees, wiggling larvae, leaves, honeycomb, and dirt. It is consumed with great gusto, the container being passed from hand to hand, each man taking a deep draught before having it snatched by the next man. They usually blow most of the debris off the surface and drink under it, using their lips like shallow straws.

As luck would have it the honey tree was right next to the spot where we planned to launch the canoe. Most honeybees in this area are stingless, but these were not. Soon the canoe and the riverbank were covered with groggy insects that attacked us furiously, but the men didn't seem to mind. They just swatted their ankles and dipped larva-filled honeycombs into the mead and munched on them. The bees were too much of a nuisance for us to do much more work on the canoe that afternoon.

I wanted to see if the canoe would float and so cautiously put it into the river. To everyone's delight—especially mine—it stayed on top of the water. However, like any round log, it promptly rolled over. We even

tested it with one man inside while the others held it to keep it from rolling. I breathed easily for the first time: it still floated.

I managed to talk a few of the more enthusiastic workers into cutting
two long poles for an outrigger, and to find one of the buoyant trees we
used earlier for the raft. I cut two pairs of notches on each gunwale and
tightly lashed in the outrigger poles with vines across the canoe. Then we
lashed the outrigger log to the end of these outrigger poles and tried the
canoe once again. This time it remained afloat without rolling over, but
the outrigger log was not very buoyant and would sink if too much weight
was put on that side of the canoe. I called for a volunteer to find a more
buoyant log. But by this time my companions were understandably tired
of raft and canoe manufacturing and insisted that there was not a more
buoyant log in the jungle.

I had difficulty talking them into helping me make canoe paddles, but
some of the older men volunteered to help me and ordered a few young
men to join in. That night we whittled three crude paddles by the dancing firelight, one being a reject that had been thinned too much on the
handle. I decided to take it along anyway as a spare.

I listened to the mission broadcasts in the morning, but still no word
about Bäkotawä or any evidence that the missionaries were aware that I
was missing. Bäkotawä had been on the river for over four days by now.

We went to the new canoe, which was moored with vines a few hundred feet below our camp. We carried the packs to it, including a number
of bamboo arrow point cases (toras), bows, and arrows for which I had
traded some small knives with the Yanomamö.

The bees had regained their strength overnight and inflicted revenge
on us for robbing the honey. Karina wanted to be the first to try the
canoe, an honor I conceded to him without argument. One of the men
swam the short stretch across the Mavaca with the long vine that was
tied to the canoe. Karina got in with one of the paddles and the man
pulled him out into the river and across by the vine. Trying unsuccess-
fully to look like an expert boatman, he paddled the clumsy log with his
equally clumsy paddle. From the difficulty he had keeping his balance
in the canoe I could tell that this was going to be a very challenging trip.

Karina weighed about seventy pounds and the canoe was just barely
afloat. I weighed more than twice as much, and our gear—not count-

ing the bows and arrows I obtained in trading—probably accounted for another fifty pounds. With some difficulty Karina managed to maneuver the canoe back to port, and we carefully loaded the equipment in, tying everything down with vines, including my shotgun.

The cracks that I noticed yesterday were worse, and my friends tried to caulk them with mud. I managed to convince them that mud would quickly wash out and gave them one of my shirts to tear up and use as caulking. The repairs took just a few minutes and seemed to be temporarily adequate.

The moment of truth was now upon us: would it keep us afloat? I bade my companions good-bye and told them I would be back in the following dry season with many trade goods to repay their kindness. They assured me that they would reunite with the others who had separated from them and rebuild the *shabono* at the spot where the old one was burned down. I instructed Karina to sit in front and to exercise great caution when paddling: the canoe was very unstable. I then climbed into the back.

Much to my disappointment I discovered that the water came to within a half inch of the gunwales. We were floating, but just barely. Then Karina took one small dip with his paddle, shifting his weight over so slightly from center. The left gunwale dropped below water level—and we sank instantly, not having gotten one foot offshore. Everything got soaked except the few items—cameras, lenses, tape recorder, film, field notes, etc.—that I had put into a waterproof rubber bag. We frantically tried to grab the packs before they went under, but it was too late. The canoe slowly sank and settled on the bottom; only our heads were above water. We must have looked very stupid indeed.

Again, our friends turned their faces to conceal their grins. But it *was* funny, and I had to laugh, too.

We dragged the canoe out to the bank again, bailed it out, unpacked everything, and resorted it. The *toras* full of curare arrow points were the first to go. Möawä ordered a number of young men to make a small hut across the river in which I could store the items I would leave behind. I took only those items that were absolutely essential for survival and those that had scientific value, keeping my field notes and leaving behind things like antivenin for snake bites. The Mishimishimabowei-teri transported the excess equipment to the other side of the river, using the canoe as a ferry. They were wise enough to swim alongside the canoe rather than try to ride in it.

After reloading the canoe, we went through the motions of farewell one more time, but this time only halfheartedly. We all expected that the canoe would capsize as soon as we got into the current and we'd have to bail it out again.

Karina and I climbed into the canoe for the second time. The water came to within two inches of the gunwales and my hopes revived slightly: we were a whole inch and a half higher than before!

The canoe was in a shallow backwater adjacent to a sharp bend in the river. There were several large logs blocking the way, but we pushed off into the current anyway—and promptly got hung up in the snags and again sank instantly. Fortunately, we were able to stand on a sunken log and refloat the canoe while the others chopped the logs out of our way. I could tell that paddling was going to be almost out of the question: Karina was too clumsy. Each time he took a stroke, he leaned way over, and the water rushed into the canoe. While we were waiting for the Shamatari to clear this deadfall, I asked one of them to cut us two long poles.

My hand-hewn canoe, Karina standing next to it after we reached our camp downstream and our second canoe.

I tied the paddles down with vines and bailed the canoe with a gourd, which its friendly former owner had suggested I might find useful for this purpose and presented to me as a farewell token. I tied that down, too.

We climbed into the canoe again and were immediately caught up in the current. We were so precariously balanced that we couldn't turn around to wave farewell to our companions. We were off in the swift current and our friends disappeared from sight when we rounded the first bend.

I do not know how many times we swamped that first day. I had no idea that a boy so small could be so inept and so clumsy. Each time he moved his weight he caused the canoe to ship water. But, instead of trying to rebalance the canoe or jumping out when he saw that we were sinking, he froze up, hung on for dear life, and sank both of us with the canoe. Had he jumped over the side, as I was doing when water started coming in, the canoe would have continued to remain afloat and we could have bailed it out with no problem before it filled up and sank.

It turns out that there may have been a logical reason for Karina's reluctance to jump out of the canoe into the river. He explained to me earlier that he was afraid of *yahediba*—electric eels. I insisted that there were none, like there were no *raharas*, and urged him, whenever the canoe started to swamp, to jump out to keep the canoe from going under.

About midday, as we were bailing out after one of our mishaps, I stepped on a log beneath which was hiding an electric eel. I didn't know what hit me, but I felt a sharp pain in my leg and was knocked flat on my back from the jolt. When I got to my feet I saw the eel swim slowly into deeper water. The electric shock was remarkably strong—strong enough to knock me down. And so I forgave Karina under my breath.

My outrigger was a good idea but had one built-in disadvantage: it acted as a snag-catcher and caused us to sink many times. We invariably capsized whenever it got caught on a snag, which would hold us fixed to some tree branch. The current was strong enough to turn us sideways in the river; the water would then rush over the edge of the canoe and swamp us.

Sharp bends were a problem, too. Unless we managed to keep to the inside of the bend, the current would force us against the bank on the opposite side. When the outrigger touched the bank we would go under again—in the deepest water. It is a hopeless feeling to see a sharp bend ahead of you and try to delicately pole such a clumsy canoe to the inside of the curve. The immediate reaction is to pole harder, but when you do, your weight shifts just enough to cause you to ship water. Once water starts coming over the edge, you almost always swamp and sink.

The natural hazards were not nearly so frustrating as the one sitting in the canoe with me. Yanomamö are not river people, and if Karina may be taken as a typical example, they might have gone extinct had they opted for canoes instead of foot travel. By the end of the first day of travel Karina still did not know which side he had to pole on to make the canoe go to the left or right. By the time it was dark that first day I was so hoarse from screaming "to the left," "to the right," and so on, that I could barely talk. He would sulk conspicuously but then turn away as an uncontrollable smile lit his face, a soaking wet Indian dwarfed by the undershirt I had given to him. I had to choke down an occasional smile myself.

It rained most of the day, and the river was rising quickly. Most of the exposed sandy spits and sandbars were now underwater. We had to be careful to make our camp that night well above the current water level, for the river could rise as much as five or six feet overnight and carry away our camp and any equipment that wasn't stashed in the canoe, which I carefully lashed to a stout tree on the riverbank.

When it came time to cook our rice for supper, another unfortunate realization hit me. I had been conserving the rice for the trip home and had not eaten any since the evening before contacting the village. But, I had given my only cooking pot to Sibarariwä! There we were—no pot to cook our only food in. Fortunately, I had stored our rice in a small powdered milk tin, so we could at least use that as a makeshift pot. It was nothing but luck that I had given Bäkotawä his share of the rice in a plastic bag. We would have gotten pretty hungry had I kept the plastic bag and given Bäkotawä the tin.

Our hammocks and clothing were soaked, and it was uncomfortable even to be in them. But the fire soon warmed us up and the steaming hot rice drove the shivers away. The thing that really picked up our spirits was the evening broadcast from the New Tribes Mission reporting that Bäkotawä had arrived in Bisaasi-teri late that afternoon and that he had apparently abandoned me and Karina in the Mavaca headwaters. So, at least I knew that someone was aware that I was missing. The mission also reported, for my benefit in case I could hear it, that Bäkotawä had lost much of my equipment but did save the motor and dragged it out of the river onto a bank somewhere. They also mentioned that when he got to about an hour above Bisaasi-teri, he unloaded all my axes, machetes, and cooking pots and hid them in the jungle "because they were heavy" and he was tired of paddling their dead weight. He had paddled them four and a half days and decided, one hour away from his destination, that they were too heavy for the canoe to transport or for him to paddle their weight?

I decided that it was best to push on the next day. It might be some time before help came and we were getting low on food. Our fire went out during the night and at dawn we woke up shivering, cold and still wet. We ate the leftover rice, packed the radio and hammocks, and pushed off once again.

The river was broader and deeper now, and our poles were only marginally useful. It was not long before we had to abandon them entirely—we could no longer touch the bottom with them. When we switched to our paddles we had a rapid series of misfortunes. We had gotten fairly efficient with the poles and could keep from tipping the canoe after some practice, but the paddles required more exertion, and as a result we capsized several times before we could get the hang of it again. Then we lost our spare paddle on one of our sinkings. Later in the day we got snagged in an overhanging tree and capsized again, losing another paddle. At about three o'clock that afternoon, shortly after losing the second paddle, we reached the big canoe and were immensely relieved that it was still there. Even the nest of cooking pots I had left in the canoe was still there, so we could now cook a meal larger than a cupful.

I had hoped that Bäkotawä would have put the motor in the big canoe as he went by, but he had discarded it somewhere upstream from here. We transferred our equipment to the big canoe and cut more poles for pushing.

The river was now very deep, but the poles enabled us to keep away from the banks and overhanging brush, keeping the bugs from falling onto us as they had been doing for the past two days. Our single paddle was too short and the blade too small to be of much help in the big canoe. We were thus largely at the mercy of the current. I remembered that our original first camp was only about two hours downstream by motor from the big canoe. I had hoped we could reach it by nightfall because if help did come, they would probably camp there at the end of their first day. It was one of those inviting camping places—well above the normal river elevation and with a wide, appealing, sandy beach.

Now that we were in the big canoe, we could stand up, walk around, and in general, revert to our old, clumsy ways. More important, we could unlash the shotgun and shoot game for supper.

I had not looked at the shotgun for almost three days. I had tied it under my seat and it had spent much of the past three days underwater. The barrels were badly rusted and the breech opened with considerable difficulty. I loaded it and kept it handy. Before long we floated past a relatively large caiman, which I killed with one shot.

Caiman meat is pretty grim fare. Its white, firm flesh looks like boiled lobster and it even slightly resembles lobster in taste. But caiman is as tough as shoe leather, no matter how you cook it. However, we were both pretty hungry for meat at that point, and the thought of even a piece of roasted caiman made our mouths water. The Yanomamö eat a lot of caiman meat, since the animals are found in even tiny streams.

By nightfall we could see that we were not going to reach our earlier campsite, so we made camp at the mouth of a small creek. I shot another, smaller caiman, so we had plenty of meat for the remainder of the trip. The last few hours with the big canoe convinced me that we would have to whittle another paddle before going on in the morning. The canoe was just too heavy to control with our single small paddle or with our poles.

We were now at a point on the Mavaca where we could make it all the way back to Bisaasi-teri in about twenty-four hours of continuous floating. From here on the river was broad, and all we had to do was keep the canoe in the middle of the stream and the current would do the rest.

We boiled rice and roasted more of the caiman for supper. We were both dog-tired and fell asleep as soon as we finished eating. And, at last, we were finally dry.

The next morning I learned by radio that one of the New Tribes missionaries and a Ye'kwana Indian were planning to come up to look for us right away. The radio message also gave the approximate location of the spot where Bäkotawä had put my motor. We had already gone past it and would have to go back upstream to get it when the missionary got here. We decided that it was better to remain in our camp all day, since we had to go back upstream to find my motor anyway.

We spent the day lying in our hammocks. I was not feeling very well and needed some rest. My numerous scratches and insect bites were infected and the fungus on my groin was flaring again. The combination of starchy food, tropical fungi, and hard work was wearing me down physically.

We came to life when we heard the soft humming of wild turkeys in the jungle behind us. Karina went ahead of me and quickly pointed one out. I shot it and ran on to see if there were more. Karina was still ahead of me, excitedly pointing out another bird. I was down to my last cartridge. When I closed the badly rusted breech the chamber fired accidentally: the firing pin had rusted so badly that it did not retract when I opened the breech after the previous shot.

Karina stood there in shock, gaping at me as a three-inch sapling toppled over—just a few feet from his head. I had almost shot him. I was very badly rattled from this experience.

By late afternoon we had forgotten about the close call and were waiting for the turkey and rice to cook. We dined in great comfort and style that evening, although we were both disappointed that the boat had not reached us. Perhaps we were farther upstream from my old campsite than I thought.

By nine o'clock that night we were convinced that the boat would not reach us until the next day, so we went to sleep. But a shotgun blast just a few feet from our hammocks got us to our feet in a second: it was the Ye'kwana Indian named Antonio, and Rerebawä, my Bisaasi-teri friend. They had made it to my old camp and were out hunting for their supper. They were unaware that Karina and I were sleeping just a few feet above the caiman they had just shot, and our shouts to them were as startling as their shotgun blast was for us. They paddled over to us, and Rerebawä and I hugged each other happily. He was nearly convinced that the Shamatari had killed me and was relieved to see me alive and well. He told

me that he would never let me go on another trip without him, despite
the dangers to which he might be exposed. Karina begged half of Rerebawä's wad of chewing tobacco and collapsed back into his hammock,
sighing. "I nearly died of poverty!" he exclaimed as he lay in his hammock, contentedly sucking on the used wad of tobacco.

I was so delighted to see the "rescue" team that I presented Antonio
and Rerebawä with my cooking pot of boiled *pajui*: turkey and rice. They
took it back to their own camp, a few minutes downstream, to share with
the missionary. As it turned out, I had as much food as they! They had
left in such a hurry that they brought only enough manioc flour to last
them one day, plus the shotgun I had loaned to Bäkotawä. Had I remained upstream, they would have gotten pretty hungry within the next
day, especially if I had remained in the village. They could have eaten
caiman or turkeys for a long time, but meat without vegetable food is
not very satisfying. I fell asleep thinking about the Yanomamö verbs that
describe eating, particularly the verb *dehiaö*: "to eat a bite of meat and
then a bite of vegetable food and chew both together and swallow them."
Their language captures so many interesting and fundamental aspects of
life.

The next morning at dawn they returned the empty cooking pot, and
we left to collect the equipment I had left behind and to look for my
motor. We found the motor late that morning. It was in poor condition
from being submerged in the river several times. Both cylinders were full
of water. We worked for about an hour before we got all the water out. In
attempting to start it we accidentally set it on fire, but we put the fire out
before too much damage was done to the wiring. It finally started, and we
were on our way again.

We were able to travel at full throttle most of the way up to the cache
of equipment I left behind where Karina and I had launched our hand-
hewn dugout canoe. By dusk we had found the cache, turned around,
and were on our way back home. The river was now full enough that we
could safely travel by the motor at night.

When we reached the spot where we met our rescue team, Karina and
I transferred my motor over to the large dugout and we came the rest of
the way down to Mavaca—and home—by ourselves.

Thus, in the wet season of 1968 I came to visit and begin to know the people of Mishimishimaböwei-teri, who were located in a distant place that was difficult to reach. With the passing years I visited them many times and got to know them even better and grew very fond of almost all of them. But there was one man that I never grew fond of, indeed, I grew to dislike intensely. That was Möawa. He would later try to kill me.

6

Geography Lesson

Maps of the Yanomamö Region in the 1960s

I first reached the Yanomamö area by boat, which was, at that time, the only way of getting there. There were no airstrips closer than Esmeralda, and that one was just an unimproved dirt strip and too wet to land on for some six months of the year.

I could not have picked a location in the Western Hemisphere that was more poorly mapped in the mid-1960s than southern Venezuela and adjacent portions of northern Brazil.

I sought and got copies of the standard maps that were publicly available from sources like the major encyclopedias, government mapping services in both the United States and Venezuela, and the authoritative National Geographic Society in Washington, D.C.

Most of the maps I assembled from these various sources generally agreed on major items such as geopolitical boundaries, large rivers, general terrain, and large cities. But the devil must have been in charge of many important details because either these were not found on the maps or no two maps agreed on them. Most depressing were the cases where they were wrong on all maps regarding key features of T. F. Amazonas in Venezuela.

One of the major problems was that I never saw this area from an airplane and had only a vague notion of elevation differences. I knew the eastern border of southern Venezuela adjacent to Brazil was a chain of low mountains called Sierra Parima. Because of the way I entered the area and the way I traveled—by dugout canoe—I could canoe right by a mountain and not even realize it was there. From a canoe in a relatively narrow river, you can't see beyond the immediate treetops on either side.

Consequently I had the naïve impression that the Yanomamö area was basically a flat, featureless, low-lying jungle, except for the Parima Mountains.

The largest river in Venezuela is the Orinoco—one of the world's major rivers—whose largely unknown (in the mid-1960s) upper reaches lay in the heart of the Yanomamö tribal distribution. One of the sizable tributaries of the Upper Orinoco is the Mavaca River, the southernmost of the major Orinoco tributaries. It was here at the confluence of the Mavaca and Orinoco that I made my "base camp"—my mud hut—and from this citadel I would intrepidly make the Yanomamö known to anthropology and the world at large.

The mouth of the Mavaca River was accurately represented on all the maps. But when I began making trips up the Mavaca or walking inland to hunt game with the Yanomamö, I suspected that something was wrong with my maps. At first I could easily ignore my suspicions so long as I didn't wander too far inland or ascend smaller streams in my canoe. But the more I traveled and visited isolated Yanomamö villages and tried to map them, the harder it was to ignore my suspicions: either the Yanomamö didn't know where they lived—a preposterous idea—or the best maps were dead wrong.

For example, the National Geographic Society map indicated that the Orinoco River split into two streams in the Yanomamö area. One of the streams flowed northward through the heartland of Venezuela, turned to the east, increased in size, and then flowed into the Atlantic Ocean near Trinidad. But the other stream turned to the south and was named the Casiquiare Canal. After winding and snaking its way some 250 miles, it joined the Rio Negro—a large tributary of the Amazon River.

This meant that most of Venezuela, Guyana, Suriname, French Guiana, and the northeastern portion of the Brazilian Amazon—the entire northeastern portion of South America—was technically a very large island. One could enter the Orinoco River at its mouth from the Atlantic Ocean and canoe all the way to the Amazon River, to emerge again in the Atlantic Ocean again near the Brazilian city of Belém.

Even more astonishing was the fact, shown in very small print on the National Geographic Society map, that the Casiquiare Canal *changed directions every season:* in the wet season it flowed in one direction, but in the dry season it flowed in the *opposite* direction. I found that alleged fact preposterous.

But, nevertheless, I had to check it out. Who knows what wonders the earth conceals? You can't imagine how stupid I must have seemed to the local Ye'kwana Indians, the few local Venezuelan creoles, and the Yanomamö whom I repeatedly asked, in all sincerity, "Does the Casiquiare change directions in the wet season?" The polite ones pretended they didn't understand such a stupid question; those who did understand it would sarcastically say things like "Of course! And at other times of the year it goes straight up—into the sky!" and turn their faces to conceal their cynical grins.

An even bigger problem for me was that all of the most authoritative maps showed the Mavaca River headwaters originating near the Orinoco headwaters, flowing to the west, then gradually changing directions and flowing almost due north until it joined the Orinoco.

The Yanomamö insisted otherwise: they invariably told me (by pointing when I asked) that the Mavaca's headwaters were *due south* of my mud hut at the mouth of the river.

Thus I had to figure out a way to determine where the several villages south of the Orinoco—which meant all of the then-known Shamatari villages—were located on my map, and, more important, where they were located with respect to each other and with respect to my base camp at the mouth of the Mavaca.

My Initial Mapmaking Efforts

Astonishing as this sounds, I had to try to make my own maps of this area and ignore the published maps. Satellite imagery, GPS instruments, and Google Earth were yet some thirty years into the future.

I had worked my way through Michigan's undergraduate program as a college-trained route surveyor, initially for the state and later for a private road construction company. This background turned out to be very useful in my efforts to make reasonably accurate field maps.

There were a number of reasons why accurate maps were important—and even central—to my work. No existing map of the day showed the locations of *any* Yanomamö village in either Venezuela or Brazil and yet there were more than two hundred fifty such villages. Minimally, I had to know how to map the locations of those villages that were important in my fieldwork.

While there were Yanomamö villages at the mouth of the Ocamo and the mouth of the Mavaca, not even these Yanomamö villages were shown on any maps, nor were the Catholic or evangelical missions found on the maps. One had to go there in person to know that there were any human beings there at all.

Since these river junctures—where the Ocamo and Mavaca rivers joined the Orinoco—were accurately shown on all maps, it was easy to indicate on the same maps the names of the Yanomamö villages located there. The Yanomamö village at the mouth of the Ocamo was called Iyäwei-teri and the village at the mouth of the Mavaca was called Bisaasi-teri, as I have mentioned.

There were a few other Yanomamö villages located on or near the Orinoco. Once I had canoed up and down the local stretch of the river I could more or less accurately locate them on a map. I would guess that they were, for example, "about halfway by canoe between Ocamo and Mavaca," and so forth.

Inland Areas Away from the Rivers

One of the villages I discussed earlier was Patanowä-teri, the group from whom the seven women were abducted on the first day I was in the field.

I visited them at their inland location several times during my first year of fieldwork. This involved taking a trip up the Orinoco in my dugout canoe, portaging around a rapids known as Raudal Guaharibo (shown on some maps), and proceeding upstream several more hours to the mouth of a tiny stream known as Shanishani kä u (rarely shown on any maps and never with the Yanomamö name). The men who worked for the Malarialogía called it Caño Bocon after a fish by that name that was commonly found there. I pulled my canoe into the mouth of this small river and secured it to a tree with a rope. Then I would call my guides over to determine how far away and in what directions various villages and abandoned gardens were, especially, on the initial trip, where Patanowä-teri was.

One of my favorite traveling companions was Rerebawä—the man who helped me learn the Yanomamö language. I would take out my handheld surveyor's compass and ask him to point to the direction of the Patanowä-teri village. Then I would write down the magnetic bearing from the point where I was standing to the village. I would then ask him to tell me how far away the village was, as well as other abandoned gardens and village sites used in the recent past by the Patanowä-teri. He knew this village well, having gone there frequently with Bisaasi-teri visitors.

The Yanomamö express distance by the number of "sleeps" it takes to get somewhere. If a place can be reached without sleeping, they point to where the sun comes up and describe an arc with a slow sweep of their arm and stop where the sun would be when they reached their destination. If the sun is straight up, one would reach it by midday, around noon. Since they begin traveling as soon as there is enough light to see, that would mean about five or six hours of travel. But there is a lot of inaccuracy in this measuring system. For example, midday might be anytime from 10:30 A.M. to 1:30 P.M. Or if the trail is wet and crisscrosses small streams and rivers, travel takes extra time. If the Yanomamö run into a game animal and chase after it, that also adds to the travel time. But by and large, they tended to give average travel times based on a large number of trips to that village. After I made the trip myself, I would know how long it took to get from place A to place B under normal circumstances.

But when you ask about *distant* villages that you will probably never walk to, you have to rely on what your informant(s) tell you about distances in sleeps. Sometimes the village is so far away that the informant would sit down in order to use his toes to supplement his fingers to indicate that it is "more than twenty sleeps" away. However, the Yanomamö cannot count accurately beyond 2. They do not have "numbers" for anything larger than 2. So, when they have to sit down to express a long distance by using their toes, it could be a long way away or it might be a shorter distance away, but they don't want to take you there because they don't like the people there or don't trust them, or they don't want you to give them your valuable trade items that they themselves covet.

I would also ask my guides to point to locations that I knew well just to check on the accuracy of their spatial awareness. I was always stunned by how accurate their pointing was over even very large distances. For example, I once took Rerebawä to Caracas, more than five hundred air miles away, and then later asked him to point to Caracas when we got back to his village. Without hesitation he pointed accurately in the correct direction.

On the many hunting trips I took with the Yanomamö—sometimes in areas they had never been in before—they would rarely get lost. If we shot some kind of game animal early in the day and they didn't want to carry it all day, they would conceal it in some thicket or high tree branch and we would then hunt for five or six more hours. When it was time to return to our camp, they would walk directly to where the dead animal was concealed, retrieve it, and take it back to our camp. Their sense of direction and ability to navigate in otherwise unexplored jungle is nothing short of phenomenal. I'd be willing to bet that I could take a Yanomamö man into the heart of the Congo in Africa and he would be as skilled as any Congo native at finding his way around after just a few days and a few trips in the local jungle.

There were other reasons I needed accurate maps. One was that a large portion of the history of each individual and of each community was remembered by them in terms of *where* they lived at particular times in their lives. Thus geographical space, not time, seemed to be their calendar.

There is a branch of human theoretical biology that deals with "life histories" and much of the data I wanted was of this kind. This is non-geographical data that covers significant biological life events, such as birth, puberty, marriage, child-bearing, death, etc. Place of birth, places where females had their first menses, places where people died, were the things I learned to ask about when I took my censuses. The Yanomamö are extraordinarily aware of specific geographical locations where important things happened to them as individuals and as members of some group. I realized this early in my fieldwork and began recording in my notes every reference they made to geographical locations, which were always named: old gardens or earlier villages, waterfalls, specific hills, etc. Thus, in the absence of an accurate time scale, I used what they used: a geographical framework to relate to others the significant events in their lives. In their scheme the significant life-historical events for every individual were associated with specific locations.

When I inquired about group locations like old villages and tried to get the histories of where they originated, where they moved to after abandoning gardens, where they split into two or more groups, etc., these histories were always expressed as places and the sequence of "placed events" was usually confirmed by informants from other villages. Geography was central to the lives of the Yanomamö in a way that time was not.

Hunting, Traveling, and Camping with the Yanomamö

During my first year in the field I spent a lot of my time learning about the life-historical events in the personal histories of every Yanomamö I met—as well as the personal histories of their living and deceased ancestors. When I wasn't at Mavaca, I was traveling with groups of hunters, or groups of young men going to some distant village, or groups of people on *waiyumö*—extended camping trips that could last several days or several weeks. But I was always recording or writing things into my notebooks about people and places and documenting what people were doing while we traveled.

On one trip with the Bisaasi-teri we were camped about a day south of the village, hunting game and collecting seasonal palm fruits. Kaobawä, the headman, ran across some *obo* (armadillo) dens that were fresh. There was a cluster of small flying insects hovering around the entrance hole. When I asked about the insects, they said something like, "You wouldn't understand this." They assumed that I would not be able to understand the notion of specific parasites that are attracted to certain animals and how the Yanomamö use this information to decide that the animal is at home in the burrow. The specific flying insects are always present when there are armadillos in a den, so the Yanomamö do not waste their time digging up what looks like a fresh burrow if these insects are not flying around the entrance.

The Yanomamö were excited at the prospect of fresh meat for dinner. Several young men scurried around to find old termite nests. The brittle, dry termite nest material gives off dense clouds of smoke when set on fire, and it burns and smolders for a long time. They stuffed the burrow entrance with the material, lit it, and then looked around the nearby jungle. After a while the other entrances to the underground burrow began giving off smoke. They quickly plugged up these entrances with dirt to keep the smoke inside the burrow and proceeded to crawl on their hands and knees between the burrow entrances with their ears to the ground, listening for armadillo movements. They put little sticks in the ground each time they heard noises, which would give them a general idea of where the armadillo was. Eventually the smoke would asphyxiate the animal and it would die underground.

The little sticks used to mark the approximate place they heard the last armadillos burrowing noise belowground was not necessarily the exact place where the animal died. It might have moved back or forward from the last spot that they detected its noise. So, to determine the exact spot to dig down into the dense clay to the burrow, they cut a long vine from a nearby tree. They then tied a knot at the end of the vine and began spinning the vine into the burrow entrance with their palms after removing the smoldering termite nest materials. They slowly spun the vine—knot first—into the long burrow: the knot, as it thumped against the sides of the burrow, was audible to the Yanomamö, whose ears were pressed to the ground, following it as it inched along. When it would go no further, they marked the place on the vine where the mouth of the burrow was and withdrew the long vine. They laid the vine on the ground along the general axis of the subterranean burrow, following the sticks that stuck out of the ground. The knot told them where to start digging into the dense clay. Using their bow staves, they dug into the ground some eighteen inches to two feet and hit the armadillo on the first try and dragged him by the tail out of the den. They found several more by the same techniques that afternoon.

The Yanomamö gutted the armadillos and placed them onto a *babracot*—a small platform made from sticks about three feet above the campfire. There the armadillos smoked and slowly roasted for several hours.

I had never eaten armadillo before. I found smoked armadillo to be delicious; tender and succulent. Later that year I spent the night at Padre Cocco's mission and joined him in a delicious meal of something I couldn't identify. The nuns had prepared it in a light cream sauce, maybe with some wine. After dinner I asked him what kind of meat we had just eaten. *Cachicama*, armadillo. It was even more delicious than the smoked version I had shared with the Yanomamö.

Spider monkey (*basho*) hunting is one of the most rigorous activities I engaged in while living with the Yanomamö. This species is the largest monkey they hunt—and a very desirable game animal. *Basho* travel through the jungle canopy at amazing speeds, so the hunters must be constantly on the run to keep up with them. I always hoped that we would *not* run into a troupe of *bashos* when I traveled in the jungle with the Yanomamö because if we did, the Yanomamö would shout at me, urging me to keep up with the monkeys so I could shoot some of them with my shotgun. The Yanomamö used curare arrow points, which would usually break off inside the monkey, then slowly paralyze and eventually kill it.

The points are made from a pencil-like piece of thin palm wood about a foot long. The points are weakened every few inches by transverse cuts made from a steel knife or machete so they will break and lodge in the animal. About a dozen of the points are stuck into a tight bundle of leaves and propped over a bed of glowing wood embers. They are then painted with multiple coats of thin curare liquid while positioned over the bed of glowing coals until the curare thickens and becomes sticky. The curare itself is derived from plants that grow in the Yanomamö homeland.

Three other species of monkey are also hunted for their meat: the red

Dedeheiwä (right) painting curare on palmwood tips.

howler monkey (*iro*), the black monkey (*wisha*), and the capuchin monkey (*howashi*). These species are not as difficult to hunt because they tend to stay in the same group of trees and do not flee like the spider monkeys. The Yanomamö frequently keep young capuchin monkeys as pets and let them roam around the *shabonos* at will. They are very mischievous and pesky and seemed to perceive that I was a stranger. They usually focused their attentions on me—swatting me on the head as I passed under the pole they were sitting on, and then scurrying just out of range to watch me. When I turned away they would quickly come back and swat me again.

The tail of the black monkey has an important ceremonial use. The Yanomamö take the bone out of the tail, open the tail to spread the skin, dry it, and fashion it into a furry headband that is usually worn by men for festive occasions. I think my first attempt at humor among the Yanomamö occurred early in my fieldwork on the occasion that I shot two black monkeys. I usually gave the meat to the Yanomamö, but in this case I wanted to keep the tails to make headbands. A disagreement ensued. They thought I should just keep one of the tails and give the other to one of them. I managed to get the point across that the reason

I wanted both was that I intended to give them both to Pau (Jim Barker) so he could be properly decorated for feasts. Their response: "But Pau only needs one of them!" I then replied: "He needs two of them. He is bald!" They thought about this for a second and broke into hysterical laughter. They retold the story back in the village because they thought it was clever. I've never seen a bald Yanomamö, although some older men often have thinning hair. Among the Yanomamö, it is somewhat impolite to allude to another person's head, especially the forehead. Indeed, the most vile and vulgar insult you can utter in Yanomamö is *"Wa bei kä he shami!"* ("Your forehead is filthy!") Any allusion to blemishes, warts, pimples, etc., on someone's skin, especially on or near the forehead, is potentially insulting.

I was shocked the first time I saw how they prepare monkey meat. They smoke almost all their game—birds, fish, reptiles, and mammals—if they have more than they plan to eat when they bag it. They build a frame from slender poles stuck into the ground. They then build one or more horizontal platforms of smaller saplings—strong enough to hold the game animals they plan to cook—as I described above for the armadillos. Then they place the animals on these racks and let them cook slowly over a smoky fire until the meat is well done. They can preserve meat in this fashion for about seven or eight days, but it becomes charred and dried if left on the smoke rack long enough to preserve that well.

On the first day I entered a Yanomamö village—the day after the clubfight over women—I saw a half-dozen charred monkeys on the *babracot*, their dried smoked hands sticking out. I immediately thought, My God! They've killed some babies and are cooking them over a smoky fire! Barker must have anticipated my reaction. He calmly noted that they would be having smoked monkey meat for dinner.

The Yanomamö would beg me to go hunting with them, especially when they wanted to get a lot of game in a short time immediately prior to a feast they would be holding for their allies from another village. They knew that I always gave almost all the meat to them and kept only a small amount to last me a day or so. This had some implications for their own self-interests because there are only a few kinds of "ceremonial quality" meat that are worthy enough to give to visitors at a feast. These are: (1) tapir (*shama*), the most desirable game animal of all; (2) *wara*, the large-collared peccary; (3) *boshe*, the smaller white-lipped peccary; (4) *obo*, the armadillo; (5) *basho*, the large spider monkey; (5) *paruri*, the wild turkey–like bird (*guan*); (6) *iwa*, the caiman. These are the most desirable meats in the Mavaca area where I worked, but there might be others in the highland areas like the Parima Highlands to substitute for the lack of some species, like caiman and tapir, which are more commonly found in lowland areas.

The Anaconda

One of these hunting trips turned out to be especially productive. We had to leave one of the men at camp to tend to the meat smoking and keeping enough firewood handy because after our first day we had an abundance of meat.

At midday on the second or third day we stopped to rest at the bank of a small stream. It was humid and hot. Walking, stalking, and running to shoot at game had gotten all of us—some ten young men and me—sweaty and thirsty.

The small streams that eventually fed the larger streams and rivers were mere trickles in the dry season, but they usually carried enough water to flow all year long. In the wet season, many of these small streams would become deep and swift, sometimes even too violent to cross safely by trying to walk armpit-deep across or through them.

We were at an outside bend in the stream where, in the wet season, the force of the rushing water had cut a deep hole adjacent to the bank, a hole so deep that in the subdued light of the deep jungle one could not clearly make out what was at the bottom. It was perhaps six feet deep compared to the six or so *inches* depth across the stream on the other side.

I laid my double-barrel twelve-gauge shotgun on the bank next to me and bent over to take a drink from the otherwise sparkling, gently flowing stream. As I was drinking I noticed something moving deep down in the murky bottom. I sat up to take a better look, and as soon as I moved my face and head away from the stream the water *exploded* in front of me: a very large anaconda head shot out of the water and whizzed just inches away from my face. I immediately went into a rage: this son-of-a-bitch of a snake was trying to kill me!

I can't explain why my first reaction was anger and rage instead of fear. I grabbed my loaded shotgun and fired both barrels into the huge snake at nearly point-blank range. While these rounds were probably fatal, the snake was still writhing and twisting violently in the water. I reloaded my shotgun and fired another volley into the snake, reloaded, fired another, and reloaded again. I think I shot this snake some ten or twelve times, maybe more. All that I recall was how angry I was that this powerful snake had hidden at the bottom of a murky hole and tried to grab me, drag me into the water, and kill me. For some reason I felt that it wasn't "honorable" to kill someone by deceit.

After I calmed down I decided to take the skin and asked my Yanomamö companions to give me a hand at skinning the anaconda. It was about fifteen feet long.

I got out my hunting knife and instructed my several helpers to hold the snake as straight as they could so I could cut a straight line along its belly from its anus to its head. As soon as my blade touched the serpent it twitched and coiled abruptly. Several of the men holding on to it went flying off into the stream because of this tropistic but relatively minor twitch. After some effort I managed to skin the snake and took it back to Mavaca after the hunt was over.

The Yanomamö ignored the 150 or so pounds of perfectly good snake meat and left it to rot. They did, however, scrape off and put into leaf packages some three or four pounds of anaconda belly fat. They brought this back to camp and tossed the leaf packages into the edge of the glowing coals of our fire. At dinner that evening they dined on roasted plantains dipped in the hot, liquified belly fat of the anaconda. Plantains au jus.

The more serious snake problem the Yanomamö face is from poisonous snakes. I had my fair share of close calls with these. Perhaps as many as 50 to 60 percent of all Yanomamö get bitten by a poisonous snake at some time in their life, but most of them recover. I never made an attempt to quantify this problem precisely although early in my fieldwork I did gather statistics on how many died of snakebite in one of the populations I studied. Some of my Yanomamö friends tragically died from snakebite. One who survived was a young man named Karödima, who lived in Upper Bisaasi-teri. His leg got gangrenous, withered, and rotted off. I hoped to get him a prosthetic device, but the medical people I consulted at the University of Michigan Medical School told me that he would have to be fitted in person, which was impossible for me to arrange.

On one trip during the wet season I was nearly bitten by a *Bothrops atroy* (the fer-de-lance, the most common snake that causes fatalities among the Yanomamö) that had fallen unnoticed into my dugout canoe when I brushed through an overhanging tree limb. The snake slithered underneath my gasoline tank next to my bare feet. I reached down to shake the gas tank to see how much fuel was left and, when I lifted the tank, I was staring at a relatively large, coiled poisonous snake about twelve inches from my bare feet. I carefully and slowly placed the gasoline tank back over the snake, stepped up onto my higher seat, slowly picked up my machete, and then again lifted the gasoline tank carefully, my machete poised to strike. As soon as I saw the snake I chopped the machete down on him with as much force as I could. The tightly coiled snake became a bunch of writhing snakefurters.

After what I considered to be too many close calls I decided to shoot every snake I saw. When you regularly travel in very remote jungles and are many miles from possible help this is probably a good adaptive strategy.

Jaguars

I once took Rerebawä with me far up the Mavaca River to get compass bearings from a known spot to a large number of old garden sites and former village locations. The known spot was the mouth of a small river that flowed into the Mavaca from the east. It wasn't named but several maps showed its location. I planned to ask Rerebawä to give me directions and estimated distances from this location to a lot of places that my accumulating data on "places of birth" and so forth had revealed. We decided to make camp on a small island in the middle of the Mavaca adjacent to the mouth of this small river.

We had to cut some poles on the nearby bank to make a triangular

Yanomamö hut from which to hang our hammocks. We covered the pole frame with a small tarp in case it rained that night, collected some firewood, and made camp under the tarp. It was the beginning of the rainy season and the river was rising; I was worried that a sudden heavy rain would swamp the sandbar and our campsite, in which case we would have to jump into our nearby canoe and find a new sleeping place on higher ground.

As darkness came we settled in for the night. We kept feeding wood into the fire, lazing in our hammocks and chatting.

At about 10 P.M. we heard the first ominous noise. It was a muffled cough, between the riverbank and our flimsy hut: the animal was on our tiny island. Rerebawä quickly got to his feet and moved our small supply of firewood closer to the fire. He whispered hoarsely, *"Öra."* Jaguar. I immediately loaded my double-barreled shotgun and kept it on my lap for the rest of the night. The beast didn't go away and he knew we were there. We heard him emit low coughs periodically during the night, always between us and the riverbank, always very close by. Only our fire kept him at a distance. Needless to say, we didn't get any sleep that night. It is when you can't hear jaguars, though, that you are probably in the most danger.

The Mavaca Basin seems to have more than its share of jaguars or I tended to run into them more frequently than others. On one trip into Mishimishimaböwei-teri, again with Rerebawä as my guide, we were followed all the way from our canoe to the edge of the village by a jaguar, a walking distance of four hours. Rerebawä thought he heard something shortly after we left the canoe and began walking. We therefore retraced our footsteps and almost immediately found jaguar tracks in the muddy path, right over our own tracks that we had made just minutes before. We then kept looking back—jaguars attack silently from behind and kill an unwary human with one bite to the back of the head. We retraced our steps every fifteen or so minutes and kept finding fresh jaguar tracks on top of ours. We never saw it, but it stalked us all the way to the village.

On another occasion, a group of visitors from the remote village of Yeisikorowä-teri were approaching Mishimishimaböwei-teri. They were walking single file, maybe some ten yards separating each man in the visiting party. A single jaguar managed to silently kill three of the men in rapid succession—within minutes—and was about to pounce on a fourth when the intended victim turned, saw the jaguar, and shot him with an arrow.

One time I was almost attacked in my hammock by a large jaguar. I was traveling up the Mavaca River with two young men from Mömaribö-wei-teri. We were going to Mishimishimaböwei-teri. When we camped the first night one of them woke me to ask if he could borrow my flashlight to go off in the woods to urinate. He had never seen a flashlight before and was fascinated with it. It took him a long time to come back and when he did, the batteries were almost dead. He had been shining it on every insect, tree frog, etc. and wore down the batteries. Shortly afterward my other companion woke me up and asked to borrow my flashlight for the same reason.

We camped again a second night, this time close to the trail from the river inland to Mishimishimaböwei-teri. Anticipating their nocturnal bodily needs I gave them my flashlight (with new batteries) as we were settling in for the night so they didn't have to wake me up to ask for it.

At about dawn I felt several strong tugs on my hammock rope and heard one of my guides frantically and hoarsely shouting at me: *"Öra! Öra! Öra!"* My hammock was strung so low that my back was nearly touching the ground. My nylon mosquito net was about two feet above my face and illuminated by the bright beam of the flashlight I had given to one of them. The beam also showed the head and face of a very large jaguar peering down at me with his enormous canine teeth bared. As soon as I shouted at him, the jaguar bounded off into the jungle and disappeared.

During the night our fire had died down to embers and the jaguar walked into our campsite. He apparently stopped at my hammock intending to attack me, but my mosquito net puzzled him when his whiskers touched it. At this same instant the guide with my flashlight turned it on, saw the jaguar, frantically tugged on my hammock rope, and awakened me.

It was sheer luck that the jaguar didn't kill all three of us and sheer luck that I had given my flashlight to one of my guides before going to sleep.

The Yanomamö have two cautionary sayings about dangers after the sun sets and *mididi* (darkness) comes. *Mididiha Wayu käbä huu,* and *Mididiha Öra käbä huu.* Raiders go by night. Jaguars hunt by night.

These incidents happened along or near a river called *Örata kä u,* Jaguar River. I concluded that this river is aptly named.

River of Parakeets

The Yanomamö told me as early as 1965 that there was a high but narrow mountain ridge separating the Mavaca headwaters from a "very big river called *Shukumöna-kä u,*" river of the Parakeets, a river they insisted was as large as the Orinoco at the place where the Mavaca flowed into it. They claimed that this river was very close to the Mavaca headwaters.

This constituted the major geographical problem that plagued my research during the first year because this river was not indicated on maps of this region.

On one of the few trips I made back to Caracas during my first year of fieldwork, I sought out and met with an American cartographer associated with the U.S. embassy and told him about this "large river" I had learned about from the Yanomamö. He listened politely and commented something to the effect that this was highly unlikely, but he would "look into it" as more geographical data became available.

Then in early 1968 I had an opportunity to fly up the Mavaca to its headwaters with a bush pilot hired by the University of Michigan's Human Genetics Project to take out the Yanomamö blood samples that were collected in the third season of that project.

I recall how nervous and excited I was. I would at last be able to confirm or reject the huge amount of information the Yanomamö had given me by then about the more significant geographical locations that described their migrations, population expansion, and occupation of new lands. They had told me that their migrations out of the Parima Mountains took them down into the Orinoco Basin, and then into the "Parakeet" river basin they had mentioned on the other side of the ridge of mountains I was about to see with my own eyes.

They didn't know that the Parakeet River—the Shukumöna—had a foreign name: Siapa. But this name was used only for the downstream portion of the river near the Casiquiare. The rest of the Siapa was thought to be the headwaters of the Mavaca River.

It was a clear day. We took off from the newly completed dirt airstrip at Ocamo, flew up the Orinoco to the mouth of the Mavaca River, then flew due south up the Mavaca.

I was giving directions to the pilot and owner of the light single-engine Cessna, a Yugoslav expatriate named Boris Kaminsky. My instructions were what the Yanomamö had told me during the previous eighteen months about this area. The Mavaca eventually narrowed to a stream so small that it became difficult to follow as it disappeared into the misty vegetation. The jungle canopy started to obscure its course the farther south we flew—but to my delight, its course was consistently almost 180 degrees due south, just as the Yanomamö had insisted.

A ridge of mountains immediately to our south appeared dead ahead—it was perpendicular to our bearing and ran east-west. The Mavaca below appeared only occasionally as shiny strips of water between increasingly large areas of jungle canopy. Kaminsky turned to me and said, "We have to climb—those mountains ahead are pretty high." I knew the elevation of the confluence of the Mavaca and Orinoco was approximately five hundred feet above sea level, but we were now some hundred miles south. I had repeatedly taken elevation readings with a precision altimeter during the year. The main course of the Mavaca through its entire length was a meandering, slow river with no waterfalls until near its headwaters. I would guess that these small falls were no more than about six hundred feet in elevation and they were very near the looming mountains ahead of us. As Kaminsky climbed high enough to clear the mountains, he mentioned to me that we were at about 2,700 feet.

I looked down out the window and suddenly began screaming aloud, over and over again: "There it is! There it is! The *Shukumöna*! Just like the Yanomamö said! And it is bigger than the Orinoco!" I frantically shot pictures of it with my Nikon, frame after frame. I jabbered excitedly into my tape recorder as if I had discovered a new planet or moon. Everything was just as the Yanomamö repeatedly told me it was! And the facts were entirely different from what the published maps said. What these maps showed as the headwaters of the Mavaca River were actually the headwaters of a different and poorly known major river. The Venezuelans know the lower reaches as the Siapa. The Yanomamö know the entire river as Shukumöna-Kä-u—River of Parakeets.

The Siapa appeared immediately at the base of the ridge of sharp mountains that separated the Mavaca headwaters from the Siapa Basin. Kaminsky commented: "The land below is pretty high." His altimeter indicated that it was at about 1,700 feet above sea level. This was a broad plain, lying some 1,200 feet higher than the Mavaca and Orinoco basins.

The Siapa flowed in a nearly straight line from the east-northeast to the west-southwest along the ridge of low mountains labeled Unturan on the few Venezuelan maps that showed them. This geography explained why those Yanomamö groups that had crossed over the mountains into the Siapa Basin remained there for only short periods of time before they moved farther south into the adjacent lower lying areas of Brazil. The highlands did not contain the environment that was familiar to the Yanomamö.

We flew just a few hundred feet above the Siapa River heading upstream toward the east northeast. After about fifteen or so minutes we spotted a Yanomamö *shabono* on the south bank of the river. I asked Kaminsky to circle it so I could get some photos. We flew around it twice. Naked Yanomamö men, women, and children ran out of the traditional *shabono*, apparently frightened of the airplane, perhaps the first one they had ever seen. Given the size of the *shabono*, I guessed that it housed approximately ninety to one hundred people. They must have been completely uncontacted. I knew eventually I had to go there.

In my excitement at seeing the river for the first time I apparently stripped the sprocket holes on the roll of film I had hurriedly put into my Nikon, so the roll was completely blank—it had not advanced a single frame as I was furiously taking pictures. My next discovery was that my tape recorder's batteries were dead and not a single comment I made was recorded as I thought it was when I was documenting one of the most exciting moments of discovery in my fieldwork.

I have thought about this irony on the several times since then that

I have flown over this ridge of mountains separating the Orinoco and Siapa basins. It both saddens and pleases me. This was one of the last major geographical-ecological mysteries that my research on the Yanomamö investigated and solved. I felt strangely empty because I had learned a secret, and once this secret was known, the unexplored Amazon seemed to be a little diminished.

7

From Fieldwork to Science

As early as the summer of 1966, after my first collaborative field study with James V. Neel and his biomedical researchers, I could see signs of change taking place in the Yanomamö area. In 1965 Padre Cocco had hired the Yanomamö men from several nearby villages along the Ocamo upstream from his mission to clear the jungle for an airstrip. They came for a week or so at a time and stayed at Ocamo, where Padre Cocco fed them with sardines, plantains, and manioc flour purchased from the Ye'kwana. After working for a few weeks they went home. They came back again and again, cutting trees and pulling stumps by hand until the dirt airstrip was long and wide enough for a small plane to land on and take off from his mission at the mouth of the Ocamo.

Neel and his research team joined me in the Yanomamö area for their first field studies in January 1966, the peak of the dry season. They flew in to Padre Cocco's new airstrip at Ocamo in a small Cessna, the first plane to land on this new airstrip. Neel had hired Boris Kaminsky, the Yugoslavian immigrant who would later fly me over the Siapa River. I picked them up at Ocamo and brought them to Mavaca, my base camp. My wife and children had returned to Ann Arbor a few months earlier.

Padre Cocco continued to expand and lengthen the airstrip with Yanomamö labor. Within a year, the Venezuelan air force was landing DC-3s (C-47s) and, eventually, larger twin-engine *Barrigones*—"fat-belly" cargo planes, C-123s.

The airstrip made it possible for other visitors to conveniently and easily fly into the Stone Age from large cities like Caracas and even farther away. Padre Cocco soon discovered he had many well-to-do friends in Venezuela who had private airplanes, and they began to visit him. He was a cordial and accommodating host. He would, for example, take visitors to nearby more isolated villages, and they would usually express their gratitude by leaving generous cash contributions to his mission work as they departed for home. I once counted five light airplanes on Padre Cocco's airstrip, all Venezuelan visitors with their families who had come to see "wild" Indians.

The Role of the U.S. Atomic Energy Commission in Yanomamö Research

During Neel's first visit in 1966 I was still a graduate student and still being supported entirely by my predoctoral NIMH research grant. I became a salaried member of Neel's department in January 1967, just after I was awarded my Ph.D. in December 1966, as I have mentioned.

Neel had a large multiyear research grant from the U.S. Atomic Energy Commission, which supported human genetics research projects in many other universities as well. Neel had founded the Human Genetics Department at the University of Michigan Medical School and was its longtime chairman. Prior to that, he was part of the U.S. Atomic Bomb Casualty Commission, the medical division of the Atomic Energy Commission, which was formed after World War II. It was composed mainly of medical doctors and researchers, and its assignment was to treat the survivors of the Nagasaki and Hiroshima atomic bombings and, in Neel's case as a geneticist, monitor the offspring of the survivors for possible long-term genetic consequences. Neel designed research projects to fulfill this assignment.

Neel was a masterful grantsman, the kind of academic who is able to persuade funding agencies to support new kinds of research that extend and build on his previous research. For example, administrators of his AEC grant were pleased with the results of his earlier grants to investigate possible genetic effects of the atomic bombings in Japan, so Neel approached them with a new large project. Since the traditional "marriage structure" of the residents of Nagasaki and Hiroshima was literally destroyed, the best way to understand the possible ramifications of long-term genetic damage in Japan would be to make a comprehensive study of the traditional Japanese family and its reproductive customs—courting, engagement, marriage, etc. To understand what might be happening in Hiroshima and Nagasaki, he proposed a major study of some Japanese population not affected by these bombings, ideally a Japanese population that was minimally affected by World War II. The AEC funded his proposal to study the entire population of a small (but populous) island off the main Japanese islands. This study would pay a large part of the salaries of many of his department's faculty, research associates, and secretarial staff for several years, sparing the University of Michigan's Medical School much of the expense of paying these people from general operating funds.

I met Neel just as his research grants from the AEC were in their final phases. But he managed to secure additional funding for a small pilot study of South American Indians before his AEC funds ran out. He argued that because we now knew a lot about the population that was exposed to the atomic bombings of Hiroshima and Nagasaki, and we increased our understanding by studying the marriage and reproductive systems of an unaffected large Japanese population, what was now needed was a study of a primitive baseline human population that was not Japanese and not affected by a world war. Since the proposed size and costs of this study were very small, the AEC permitted him to include this study in his annual grant renewal.

My initial participation in Neel's pilot project was funded by my own grant from the U.S. National Institute of Mental Health, not the AEC. NIMH was traditionally a major source of funding for predoctoral anthropological field research like mine. My NIMH predoctoral grant lasted from 1964 until about November 1966, when I finished the formal requirements for the Ph.D.: finishing all required course work, passing language examinations in two foreign languages, submitting an acceptable doctoral thesis, and defending it before my thesis committee. My first field collaboration with Neel took place in 1966, while I was still on my NIMH grant and working on my Ph.D. I didn't begin receiving a salary from Neel's department until late 1966.

The Brazilian Yanomamö Villages

In 1967, about three months after I joined Michigan's Human Genetics Department, I went to Brazil as part of a collaboration with one of Neel's former Brazilian Ph.D. students, Francisco Salzano. Neel and Salzano had collaborated previously on a brief study, also funded by the AEC, of the Xavante Indians of Brazil's Mato Grosso region, a study that included David Maybury-Lewis, a British anthropologist associated with Harvard University. It was because of the initial publications of this collaboration that I became aware of Neel's interests in South American Indians and decided to contact him, as discussed in chapter 1. The Xavante Indians were Gê speakers, as were the Suyá, the tribe I initially planned to study before switching to the Yanomamö.

Our Brazilian trip would take us to a large number of Yanomamö villages along and immediately east of the Parima Mountains, which defined the border between Venezuela's Amazonas territory and Brazil's Roraima state. I would get to see how varied the Yanomamö were and what other kinds of terrain they lived in. It became immediately apparent to me that the government in Brazil was much more aware of the Yanomamö than was its Venezuelan counterpart.

We stayed in each of several villages for only about a week. Most of them were smaller than the villages I had gotten to know across the border in Venezuela, and many of them seemed to have nearby *shabonos* with satellite communities living *he borara* and from whom they had recently fissioned. This usually happens when the members of the several groups are on strained terms, which is to say, squabbling with each other.

Neel's medical and scientific goal in studying Amazonian Indians was to document the magnitude of genetic variability that was used to distinguish one "tribe" from another, and the amount of genetic variation that existed between villages of the same tribe, an empirical question that had not been adequately discussed in the medical and genetics literature about indigenous peoples. Other observations on the Yanomamö he and his medical team made were secondary and, to a certain extent, a kind of showmanship for anthropological onlookers. Medical doctors do better and more "scientific" research than physical anthropologists do.

Neel often scoffed at and showed no small amount of contempt for studies done on native peoples by an underfunded, isolated individual researcher (often an anthropologist) working on a Ph.D. in some remote tribal place. His Yanomamö expeditions by contrast were very well funded and involved highly trained medical experts from several different medical fields. He took immense pride in making an admirable and comprehensive biomedical study of tribesmen—and he largely succeeded in outshining his competitors in this new and rapidly developing biomedical field of studying native peoples. He was able, because of an abundance of funding, to outshine those similar anthropology projects that were typically underfunded.

By the mid-1960s there were several biomedical research groups beginning to make elaborate studies of native peoples all over the world—in Melanesia, sub-Saharan Africa, Polynesia, and the Amazon Basin. Previous inadequately funded anthropological studies of indigenous peoples were being replaced by elaborate well-funded studies by researchers from prominent medical schools at major universities whose extramural grant access was heavily weighted in favor of research in the medical, biological, and mathematical sciences as distinct from the social sciences.

Most of the genetic markers of interest were alleles that could be identified in various components of blood samples. Neel was also interested in other measures that would help define a biomedical baseline that could be used to understand pre-industrial human populations who yet lived in relative isolation, by helping to answer questions about population migrations, "genetic distances" between various "tribes," and a variety of questions concerning individual versus group differences.

Research into the demography of small-scale populations like the Yanomamö was also a growing field in anthropology at the time. This was the "overlap of interests" that I shared with Neel that made our collaboration desirable from my perspective. But Neel's biomedical interests could be satisfied with short field trips and a collection of blood and other medical samples. Indeed, Neel himself didn't even have to go on these field trips: anybody could collect blood samples for his laboratory. For example, Miguel Layrisse, our Venezuelan collaborator, left the field after one day and collected none of the blood or other samples in our collaborative multiyear study of the Yanomamö. But Neel wanted a hands-on intimate experience with "the American Indian" and enjoyed the added authority that such experience afforded him. That, I suppose, was the reason he stayed in the field for at least two weeks each year. However, I got the impression that the "American Indian" seemed to be, for him, an *idea* about Indians more than the highly variable individuals he was systematically documenting with the meticulous data his various team members were compiling.

My interests in anthropological-demographic data required long-term residence among the Yanomamö—learning their language, gaining their trust and acceptance, and spending hours, weeks, and months painstakingly speaking in whispers to many informants from many villages, piecing together genealogies, histories of wars and their mortality consequences, deaths by various diseases identified by Yanomamö informants, village fissions, and so forth, and placing much of this information on the questionable maps I had to work with while making my own, more accurate maps. This was not the kind of research effort one could send an assistant into the field to do.

But in many respects Neel seemed to regard me as just another assistant, subordinate in the field as well as in his department after I accepted a position in the latter. Neel had a decidedly patronizing and condescending view of anthropology compared to what "scientists" like him did. In his view anthropologists should confine their interests to things like taboos, customs, beliefs, myths, how to live in the jungle. They should learn the native language in order to assist the scientists in the expedition. When, however, the anthropologist collects important data like statistics on births, deaths, marriages, mortality rates, etc., as I did, he should dutifully turn them over to the scientist he is working for.

Technically, after I joined his department Neel was paying my salary, and I agreed to do many of these things. But there was a fundamental

James V. Neel photographing two Yanomamö girls.

misunderstanding between us from the outset. Much of my data was demographic information that "scientific" anthropologists like me collected in order to explain social patterns and longer-term historical trends. I regarded these data as mine and whatever similar data I collected after becoming a member of his department as something we should share in joint publications.

Our collaboration also and quickly began to get lopsided in terms of the amount of time I could spend on my own research interests and data collecting. A pattern emerged. Each year when Neel and his medical team were exhausted after about two weeks of intensive fieldwork among the Yanomamö, they would leave the field, taking the most recent set of blood and other tissue samples with them on the plane out of the jungle from Esmeralda or Ocamo. But that same plane would bring in a *new*, fresh group of biomedical researchers from Neel's department who were eager to spend the next two weeks furiously collecting additional blood samples at other, more remote Yanomamö villages and, of course, I would have to be their guide and gofer. So I had to spend much of my field time attending to the interests of the various medical people associated with Neel who came in fresh waves. Our collaboration did not leave me much time to do my anthropological fieldwork and collect new data on topics that were important to me—and to anthropology as a science.

Finally, Neel expected all the members of his "team"—regardless of their own religious convictions or absence thereof—to participate in group singing of evangelical gospel songs when we were invited to do so at New Tribes missions. I refused to do this. I also refused to participate in Salesian religious activities. Although I was on friendly terms with the missionaries (and continued to be for years after leaving Neel's project), I did not want to compromise my independence in the eyes of the Yano-mamö by appearing to be identified with mission groups, whether New Tribes or Salesian. I felt that my own work and relationships with the Yanomamö had to be sharply distinguished from the objectives of the mission groups. I insisted on remaining neutral in what would predict-ably become an uncomfortable competition between *católicos* and *evan-gélicos*.

A Trip to the Brazilian Yanomamö

The first of the Brazilian Yanomamö villages I visited under Neel's aus-pices was Yaröhä-teri, on the Toototobi River. These Yanomamö were similar to the Venezuelan Yanomamö I had studied, but their dialect was different enough to make it a bit difficult for me to communicate easily with them during the first several days. The other villages we visited that year spoke Yanomamö dialects even more difficult for me to understand at first, but we managed to understand most of what we said to each other.

We spent about a week in the Yaröhä-teri group—it was actually sev-eral small villages living *he borara* along the Toototobi River. The blood samples we collected in this and other Brazilian Yanomamö villages that year led to the discovery in Neel's lab that almost none of the Yanomamö had measles antibodies in their blood and had never been exposed to this devastating disease. When Neel returned to Ann Arbor in late Febru-ary 1967 he contacted Parke-Davis pharmaceuticals, which had a facility in Ann Arbor, and persuaded them to contribute two thousand measles vaccines for our scheduled January 1968 return to Venezuela. But when we arrived in the Yanomamö area in January 1968, an epidemic of measles had already started. We spent many days attempting to vaccinate a barrier around the places where it most likely would spread.

Neel had sent half of the two thousand doses to Brazil, along with a sufficient amount of gamma globulin to ameliorate the reaction to the vaccine, with William J. Oliver, head of the Pediatrics Department at the University of Michigan Medical School. Oliver hand-carried them to make certain they did not get lost or left unrefrigerated en route. Those of us going to Venezuela carried the remaining measles vaccine and the gamma globulin for those. Our vaccine was Edmonston B, which had been administered to some 15 million people by that time, including many third-world isolated groups and native peoples.

Our team that year split into two groups when we reached Caracas and we repacked our equipment and supplies accordingly. Neel took most of the members of the biomedical team into the upper Caura River, a Ye'kwana area, on one plane with approximately half of the medical supplies and vaccines, while I proceeded alone to the Yanomamö area with the other half. By sheer coincidence, all of the gamma globulin was packed in a container that went with Neel's group. I had half of the measles vaccines, but none of the gamma globulin.

Our field trip in 1968 happened to coincide with a Venezuelan/French expedition that Dr. Marcel Roche, the head of IVIC, had organized. They brought their own anthropologist, a Frenchman named Jacques Lizot. This was his first trip to the Yanomamö.

Neel had also arranged for one of the young men in the New Tribes Mission, Danny Shaylor, to work with his medical team and help with translating both Spanish with the creoles we would run into at the Salesian Missions and Yanomamö when we were in their villages. It turned out that Danny couldn't meet us as scheduled because he had to take back to a village midway on the Ocamo River the cremated remains of a young man who had just died in Tama Tama of measles—one of the first fatal cases. Information had reached us even before we left Ann Arbor that a measles epidemic had broken out in some Brazilian Yanomamö villages, including the one in which Neel's team had discovered that the Yanomamö had never been exposed to this disease.

The origin of the epidemic was in the rural Brazilian population along the Amazon River, with one known focus at the city of Manaus. An evangelical missionary family visited Manaus in early 1968, and their young daughter was unknowingly exposed to measles there. Because there is an incubation period, she did not exhibit the clinical signs of measles until after the family reached Yaröhä-teri. Apparently the Yaröhä-teri then got measles from this child.

Measles then rapidly spread along the riverways by Brazilians coming from the Rio Negro area. These Brazilian men had sought out the Salesian missions in the Upper Orinoco that were known to provide work, even if just short-term. As a consequence, the epidemic reached Tama Tama, Ocamo, and Platanal in nearby Venezuela before we got there in early 1968.

The Brazilian Yanomamö had many more—and more serious—threats to their cultural and demographic survival than the Venezuelan Yanomamö after approximately 1970. In Brazil, the colonists, gold miners, lumbermen, cattle ranchers, military, and land developers seemed poised to pounce at the boundaries of the Yanomamö area after the mid-1960s, when the construction of a major road through uncharted Amazon jungle, the Perimetral Norte, was underway. In Venezuela the situation was far different, because the Venezuelan Yanomamö were not threatened by lumbermen or gold miners. The Venezuelan military did not establish a sustained presence in Yanomamöland until about 1987, when Brazilian *garimpeiros* (gold miners) suddenly overran the Yanomamö area on the Brazilian side of the border and a few of them reached the headwaters of Venezuelan streams and rivers in the Upper Orinoco region before being repelled by the Venezuelan military.

Anthropologists who worked in each country were differently affected. On the Brazilian side, they were politically radicalized. They became militant as native rights activists and seemed always to be fighting the forces of acculturation rather than actually studying the Yanomamö. Anthropologists who worked among the Yanomamö on the Venezuela side seemed to be more focused on purely anthropological issues. Ironically, none of these anthropologists was Venezuelan.

Most Venezuelan anthropologists were not interested in doing fieldwork, even though their country contained some of the least acculturated native peoples in South America. Some of the Venezuelan anthropologists seemed to resent the presence of anthropologists from other countries, especially the United States. In my case, many of them put political obstacles in my way to prevent me from getting research permits to continue my fieldwork among the Yanomamö in Venezuela. This went on almost constantly throughout my research career.

My Expanding Theoretical Interests

One technological advantage in Neel's department in the late 1960s was that it had one of the few computers on the University of Michigan campus. This enabled me to enter my growing demographic and genealogical information into an easily accessible form. Two people in Neel's department, William J. Schull and his graduate student Jean MacClure, helped me with a specific program to analyze my genealogies, a formula developed by geneticist and statistician Sewall Wright, to calculate "inbreeding" or "relatedness" from genealogies, a so-called "f" statistic or "inbreeding coefficient." Schull and MacClure were already using this statistic in their studies of the Japanese survivors of the atomic bombings.

To put this issue in simple terms, you share (approximately) half of your genes with your brothers or sisters—and also with your parents and children. One half is 50 percent, or 0.5000, the "f" value of your relationship to them. But, you only share one-fourth of your genes with a half brother or half sister because you have only *one* parent in common. The corresponding "f" value is 0.2500. It is thus possible to express the degree of relationship between any two genetic relatives by the "f" statistic. For your full siblings, $f = 0.5000$, for half siblings $f = 0.2500$, for first cousins $f = 0.1250$, etc. Thus, in complex genealogies like those I collected among the Yanomamö, any known common ancestor contributes to how closely you are related to your (genetic) kinsmen, both to your ancestors and to your descendants.

The principal reason I wanted to analyze kin relationships was the fundamental role that kinship has played in societies, as understood in anthropology. For example, one of my former professors, Elman Service, published a book in 1985 titled *A Century of Controversy: Ethnological Issues from 1860 to 1960*. It addressed what kinship means in the primitive tribal world and, by extension, what earlier anthropologists did or did not do with the genealogies they collected. The so-called genealogical method in anthropological research was much touted but seldom practiced in a serious quantitative way.

Astonishingly, almost none of the kinship studies that Service wrote about used a metric like Sewall Wright's "f" statistic or some other measure to characterize "closeness" and "remoteness" of kinship ties in tribal societies that anthropologists had studied. Yet many anthropologists explained things in the societies they studied by invoking such variables as "closeness of kinship" or "distant or non-kin." I intended to put kinship "closeness and remoteness" into a precise, quantitative, standard form.

Yanomamö men are very concerned about paternity and spend a great deal of time "mate guarding" to prevent other men from impregnating their wives. Often, men take their wives along with them while they, for example, clear and burn timbers to make gardens, especially if the wives are young and nulliparous (have not had a child), or they make sure their wives are in a large group of people most or all of the time. If the man goes away on a several-day trip, he asks some trustworthy man—a brother, for example—to keep an eye on his wife. They seem to assume that women will be seduced or raped if left unguarded for long. Much of the mistreatment of women is caused by male sexual jealousy. A man may beat his wife when she has been alone and out of sight for more than an hour or so because he suspects that she has been seduced by some co-villager. Women who married into the village and women abducted from other villages are especially vulnerable to seduction attempts because they have few or no male kin in the village to look after their interests.

Smaller villages have fewer such problems because they tend to be composed of close kinsmen who cooperate more reliably. By "close kinsmen" I could specify, using the "f" factor, precisely how close the degree of kinship relatedness is within a village.

My field research and analytical approach were part of what anthropologist Robin Fox and sociologist Lionel Tiger referred to as the "zoological perspective" in the social sciences, a reawakening of interest in man's evolved nature as distinct from his purely cultural nature.

I hadn't fully realized in the late 1960s that the mere suggestion that Homo sapiens had any kind of "nature" except a "cultural nature" caused most cultural anthropologists to bristle. What Tiger and Fox—and a small but growing number of scientific anthropologists—were interested in was the question of how precisely evolution by natural selection—Darwin's theory of evolution—affected Homo sapiens socially, behaviorally, and psychologically.

Long-term studies of nonhuman primates and primate social organization were affecting cultural anthropology. Many earlier anthropological "truths" were beginning to crumble, such as claims that Homo sapiens alone among animals shared food, made tools, or cooperated with other members of the group who were genetically closely related. More generally, findings from the field of ethology and animal behavior were beginning to work their way into the literature of anthropology. Predictably, cultural anthropologists began to resist these trends, often by denigrating the academics who were taking the first steps in that direction or by attempting to discredit the emerging contributions by criticizing the most sensational work, often by nonexperts (for example, Robert Ardrey's *African Genesis*).

My hope in the 1960s was to make a contribution to a major controversy that was then important in cultural anthropology by "quantifying" kinship relatedness and descent patterns using my $F\hat{g}$ statistic, where the subscript "g" means that the coefficient "F" is calculated on genealogies resulting from informant interviews.

One approach to understanding the basis of social solidarity or social amity that holds groups together is often called structuralism and is identified with French anthropologist Claude Levi-Strauss. This approach emphasized marriage exchanges between groups and regarded descent from some ancient ancestor as the most important source of solidarity in tribal societies. Another approach, often frequently associated with South African–born anthropologist Meyer Fortes, emphasized that "kinship" was the irreducible, rock-bottom foundation of social amity and solidarity. The assumption by partisans of both sides seemed to be that larger communities of tribesmen had a tendency to fall apart if they became too large. My Yanomamö data seemed to be a perfect test case of marriage versus kinship because their villages fissioned into smaller groups once they reached a certain size and the number of villages on which I had data was large for comparative purposes.

I contributed a number of papers to this interesting issue. I originally believed that lineage and descent were important in holding together tribal communities like the Yanomamö, but as I examined my extensive genealogies, I began to change my mind. Kinship, especially closeness of genetic kinship, seemed to be more important than descent. I could demonstrate with my genealogies that some individuals were related to many of their kinsmen by up to a dozen different ways! (My first presentation on this issue occurred at the annual physical anthropology meeting in 1974 and was published in 1976.) But there was something new looming on the horizon, something called *sociobiology*. Without my knowing it, much of my work attempting to understand and explain the solidarity generated by Yanomamö kinship relationships was subsequently considered to be sociobiology.

I will discuss this subject further in a later chapter, because my innocent and early association with sociobiology became inextricably linked to controversies and criticisms of my Yanomamö research. These controversies became complex because they became largely political and nonscientific. These were early days in what would soon become a controversy and eventually a virtual war over the role of evolutionary science within the field of anthropology.

The Measles Epidemic

I went to the Yanomamö area in a plane that carried a French research team led by Dr. Roche, the head of IVIC. We landed at Padre Cocco's Ocamo mission and spent the night there. We planned to go on to Mavaca the next day, some two hours upstream by large dugout.

That night the Salesian nuns asked me, Roche, and some of the French medical doctors to come over to the building where the Yanomamö lived because several of them were running high fevers and were sick. Roche examined several of the adults and concluded that they appeared to have measles. He decided that the Ocamo Yanomamö had to be vaccinated immediately, even though I had no gamma globulin to reduce fevers. The French doctors vaccinated all of the adult Yanomamö and the older children in the village.

I took the group to Mavaca the next day. They would stay on the side of the Orinoco River where the Salesian mission was located. Roche made sure the French researchers had everything they needed or wanted, including their own shortwave radio and a Venezuelan radio operator.

Roche had also arranged with the Venezuelan military to have one flight per week flown into Ocamo with supplies for the French team, including fresh green vegetables, bread, steaks, and cases of beer that would be cooled in two large kerosene refrigerators that IVIC had also supplied for their "research."

My small mud-and-thatch hut was on the opposite side of the Orinoco, a few yards up from where the Mavaca River entered the Orinoco. Since Neel's group had already done its study of the Upper Bisaasi-teri village located there in 1966, my hut was merely a jumping-off point for our planned 1968 work of vaccinating the local Bisaasi-teri and vaccinating and sampling the Yanomamö groups farther up the Orinoco and inland, ending up in Patanowä-teri. By the time we reached Patanowä-teri we had used most of the thousand vaccines and gamma globulin injections that Neel had brought in for the vaccination program. We planned to use our remaining measles vaccines and gamma globulin at the Salesian mission at Platanal, from whose residents, the Mahekodo-teri, Neel's team had collected blood and other tissue samples in 1966. Because the exposure to outsiders and the diseases they might unknowingly carry is greater at mission posts, Neel's priority was to vaccinate those at the missions first. But when we reached this Salesian mission at Platanal—the most remote one on the Orinoco River—we discovered that the Yanomamö residents had all departed because they were en route to visit the Patanowä-teri to participate in a feast there. We spent the night at the mission, then left for Patanowä-teri the next day. I had taken guides who had been vaccinated for measles at Mavaca, but they couldn't find the trail into Patanowä-teri, so I had to go back to Mavaca to get another vaccinated guide who knew the way. When I got Neel's medical team into the village, they immediately vaccinated some ninety adults and older children and began taking blood, stool, urine, and other samples. After a few days I took Neel's team back to the mouth of the Shanishani River, some four hours away, where we arranged to have a large dugout waiting to take Neel, his medical team, and their samples to

Esmeralda to fly to Caracas. Tim Asch and I remained in Patanowä-teri
to film *The Feast*.

Several days after Neel's team left, I had to make a quick trip to Platanal to pick up supplies and mail. While I was there, Padre Sanchez, a
Salesian priest who was temporarily assigned to Platanal from his regular
post at Esmeralda, asked me to look at a Brazilian man who had just arrived there from the Rio Negro area looking for work.

I took a deep gulp when I looked at this man. He showed all the
signs that I had seen at Ocamo several weeks earlier when Roche and I
looked at the sick Yanomamö there, signs that he was coming down with
measles.

I urged Padre Sanchez to send this man downstream to either Mavaca
or to Ocamo, where we had vaccinated everyone; nobody there now had
active, communicable cases of measles. I had heard on the short-wave
radio that measles was still spreading to remote inland Yanomamö villages north of the Orinoco, but by now I had also heard on the radio

Padre Sanchez.

that the Venezuelan health officials were acquiring measles vaccines and were reportedly sending them into the Yanomamö area along with medical personnel. I repeatedly emphasized to Padre Sanchez that the Mahekodo-teri would be coming home after the feast was over, and, if this Brazilian man had measles, he would communicate it to the Yanomamö. Everyone would get sick, and possibly many of them would die.

Padre Sanchez assured me that he would send the sick Brazilian man downstream on the next *voladora* that he would be sending to Mavaca. I then returned to Patanowä-teri to continue filming *The Feast*. When the filming was finished, Asch and I packed our equipment and had a few Patanowä-teri carry it out to my canoe. Any reactions from the vaccinations that Neel's team had administered two weeks earlier were so mild that we didn't detect them. Nobody complained of fevers that sometimes accompanied measles vaccinations. We then left for Mavaca, some six or seven hours downstream. As we approached Platanal en route, we stopped to let Padre Sanchez know we were leaving the area. I asked about the Brazilian man who was sick with what appeared to be measles. Much to my horror, Padre Sanchez had failed to send him downstream and now he had an active case of measles! I insisted that Padre Sanchez allow me to take the man with me, explaining that the Mahekodo-teri were now en route to their home near Platanal. Padre Sanchez refused my offer.

As soon as I reached Mavaca I went to the Salesian mission and urged Padre Berno to contact Padre Cocco or someone at Ocamo to explain that there was a Brazilian man at Platanal with an active case of measles. Between these two Salesian missions, I hoped that they could persuade Padre Sanchez to send the sick Brazilian downstream to prevent a new outbreak of measles at Platanal.

But not long afterward Padre Sanchez showed up in the mission at Mavaca, and I learned that the Mahekodo-teri had contracted measles from the sick Brazilian. Some of them fled to Patanowä-teri and exposed many in this village to measles, although Neel's team had vaccinated as many of the Patanowä-teri as the remaining vaccines permitted. French medical personnel who were at Mavaca immediately sent a team to Platanal to treat the sick, but many Mahekodo-teri had died by that point.

Padre Sanchez did not act, despite several warnings from me that the

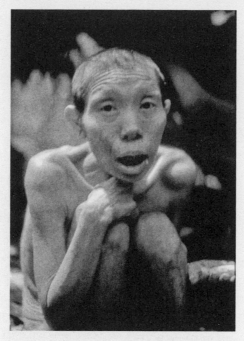

Yanomamö woman with measles, Mana-
viche area.

Brazilian man he harbored at Platanal would start a measles epidemic if
he didn't send him out. He may have been responsible for the measles
epidemic at Platanal that took as many as twenty-five or thirty lives,
mostly residents of Mahekodo-teri.

I don't know if Padre Berno at Mavaca or any of the Salesians at
Ocamo contacted Padre Sanchez by radio to demand that he get the sick
Brazilian out of his mission. If not, then these Salesians could bear the
responsibility for these deaths. Later that year Padre Cocco confided in
me that he was angry with rumors, which he blamed on the New Tribes
Mission, that the Salesians were guilty of complicity in Yanomamö
deaths from measles. I never heard these rumors and assured Padre
Cocco that I doubted that the New Tribes Mission spread them. But if the
rumors referred to the actions of Padre Sanchez at Platanal, as far as I
was concerned they *were* unfortunately true.

8

Conflicts over Women

Archaeological Evidence That Earlier People Fought over Women

The archaeological record reveals abundant evidence that fighting and warfare were common prior to the origin of the political state and, in much of the Americas, prior to the coming of Europeans. Females appear to have been prized booty in those cases where large numbers of skeletons—victims of massacres—have been found together.

One of the most important archaeological sites containing this kind of evidence is located in South Dakota—the Crow Creek site. The site was excavated in the late 1970s. A terrible massacre occurred there in about AD 1325, some 175 years before Columbus reached the Americas.

The Crow Creek people lived in a large village on the Great Plains and, like the Yanomamö, were heavily dependent on cultivated foods, especially corn, beans, sunflowers, and squash. At the time of the massacre they must have suspected something ominous because they were erecting a new palisade around their village next to a newly excavated fortification ditch. (The Yanomamö, about 70 percent of whose food is cultivated, also palisade their villages when they suspect raids from their neighbors.)

The community consisted of a large number of houses (lodges) made from earth, packed over wooden pole frames. These probably contained extended family units consisting of a senior married couple and their children and, perhaps, adult brothers or sisters and their families. The village was defensively located on a bluff overlooking the Missouri River. The residents had to climb down and then back up a steep bank to reach their gardens and bring produce, firewood, and water back to their lodges.

It is believed that a large force of enemy warriors appeared on foot without warning one day, breached the unfinished palisade, burst into the village, and showered the residents with arrows, stones, and fire-brands.

The raiders might have been a temporary coalition of a number of smaller, more nomadic groups: nomadic groups tend to collaborate periodically and victimize more sedentary, larger farming groups in the Plains area. The raiders killed most of the residents and burned their houses to the ground. Dismembered and mutilated corpses were strewn amid the burned lodges. Their enemies were clearly very vicious, the kind of neighbors you would like to keep on the *other* side of your palisade and moat.

Later, wolves and dogs came to scavenge the bodies. The survivors eventually returned cautiously and dragged the mutilated corpses of their kinsmen into the fortification ditch and hastily buried them there. They apparently never returned to this tragic place.

There were approximately five hundred victims. Their cultural artifacts indicate that they were the immediate ancestors of the Arikara Indians, one of the major Upper Missouri tribal groups, presently located in North Dakota.

The attackers mutilated many of the bodies and took trophies from them, such as scalps, hands, and feet. One of the skulls showed lesions from an earlier scalping, but the wounds had healed prior to this massacre. Many of the skeletons indicated that nutritional deficiencies were common. That their village site was chosen with defense in mind is also suggested by the many broken bones that had healed, probably caused by falls when climbing down and then back up the steep bank to and from their gardens. Or, perhaps, these injuries were caused by fights with other members of their own group—or neighboring groups.

On that fateful day the raiders took more than just scalps, hands, and feet as trophies after the massacre. A demographic analysis of the some five hundred skeletons indicated that many young women between the ages of twelve and nineteen years and young children of both sexes were missing, most likely having been taken away as captives. The young women presumably became extra mates for their captors, as would the pre-reproductive female children.

A More General Pattern?

We don't know *directly* how common fighting over women or the practice of taking females as captives was in the past—archaeological sites like Crow Creek are rare and ethnographic accounts are often silent about fights over women even if they take place while the anthropologist is there.

But eyewitness accounts by early travelers and accounts by Europeans who lived many years as captives of tribesmen suggest that the practice was rather widespread. For example, the early Spanish conquistadors commonly reported that on the larger islands in the Caribbean the men spoke the Carib language and their wives spoke Arawak—because a large fraction of the women had been captured from the weaker Arawakan tribes on nearby, smaller islands.

On the other side of the globe, in Australia, capturing women from other tribes was a nearly universal practice and the cause of much fighting prior to European colonization. A particularly gripping account of how chronic this practice was can be found in the very readable, if not sensitive, biography of William Buckley, an English convict who was sent to Australia, then an English penal colony, at the beginning of the nineteenth century to serve out his sentence.

Buckley managed to jump ship in about 1803 and escape into the then-unknown and unexplored interior, where he lived for the next thirty or so years with many different groups of aborigines. When he was eventually discovered and repatriated, he told his life story to one John Morgan, who subsequently published it.

Violence, treachery, and killings were common, almost everyday occurrences in the many groups among whom Buckley lived. In a very high fraction of the cases the conflicts began over women, sexual jealousy, and abductions of women, who, according to Buckley, were the "source of almost all of the mischief in which the men engaged." A man's status and prominence were measured, according to Buckley, by the number of wives he had. His account makes it clear that aboriginal men actively competed to acquire them and took many of them by force from weaker neighbors whenever possible—whenever the apparent costs were lower than the perceived gains.

Warfare in the Stone Age: An Evolutionary Assessment

Acquiring additional females of reproductive age has probably always been the most prized outcome of intergroup conflict in the long history of our species and the purpose for which these conflicts most often arose. Polygyny was relatively inexpensive for most of that history because acquiring the material ability to support extra wives or mates depended less on first obtaining wealth itself and more on the ability to manipulate male alliances that effectively deployed lethal violence and the threat of lethal violence to this end. Perhaps if we viewed the human ability to harness, control, and prudently deploy violence for reproductive advantage, we could consider this skill the most important of all strategic resources. In my view, recent emphasis in the social sciences on wealth and control of scarce, strategic material resources in the political evolution of Homo sapiens applies only to the most recent era of human history, perhaps only the last eight thousand or so years. Indeed, the whole purpose and design of the social structures of tribesmen seems to have revolved around effectively controlling sexual access by males to nubile, reproductive-age females: the purpose or function of "social organization" among tribesmen (and many nonhuman animals) seems to have been the efficient regulation of *sexual access to females by males* and *the role that male coalitions play in this process*. Most of this regulation and control is expressed by the systems of descent, kinship classifications, marriage rules, and incest proscriptions that humans have developed, practices that have been the central—and increasingly ignored—subject of cultural anthropology.

My many hours of taped interviews of old Yanomamö informants who told me about their immediate and distant past and of the many wars they fought before they moved to the villages in which I found them are very clear about the importance of women in their conflicts. One of my old informants, Dedeheiwä, a renowned shaman from Mishimishimaböwei-teri, is typical. After days and days of interviews during which I kept asking him about the cause of the fight at every place where a village split into several hostile villages, he said in exasperation: "Don't ask such stupid questions! Women! Women! Women! Women! Women! They screwed all the time and made a noise like wha! wha! wha! when they screwed. Women!"

Yanomamö Conflicts, Fighting, Warfare, and Abductions

Most outside observers notice that the Yanomamö fight a lot, particularly in villages that number a hundred or more people. In small villages they don't fight nearly as much because there are usually just two or three extended families that have gotten wives from each other for generations and most of the residents in a demographically normal village are children or teenagers.

Many people are also surprised to learn that some Yanomamö men often mistreat their wives—they beat them with pieces of firewood, shoot them with barbed arrows in a nonfatal part of their bodies, chop their arms and upper bodies with axes and machetes, press burning chunks of firewood against their bodies, and do other things that most of us would find revolting and vile.

Yanomamö men are intensely jealous of their wives and always seem to be tracking them, always aware of what they are doing—and what sexually active males in the village are also doing. The men spend a good deal of time mate guarding, especially when their mates are not pregnant and the husbands might be cuckolded. The married men are especially concerned about the possibility that one or more *huyas*—

young men—might sexually molest their wives or they imagine that their wives might be easily and willingly seduced by them. The men seem to have the fatalistic view that an unguarded woman will invariably be seduced by some *huya* if left unattended for very long, and therefore the men assume the worst if their wives are out of sight and not with groups of other women.

Throughout history and in many societies men have been sexually jealous of their wives, so these Yanomamö practices should not surprise us. There is a large literature on female claustration—what men do and have done to prevent their women from being inseminated by other men.

One of the well-documented accounts of fighting over women comes from New Guinea. After World War II, many eager young anthropologists flocked to New Guinea to do field research among the very primitive tribes of the Highlands, an area with large numbers of completely unknown peoples and where tribal warfare was known to be common. When I was considering my own field plans in 1963, the Highlands of New Guinea was the only part of the world other than the Amazon where relatively unacculturated tribesmen could be found. One of the major Highlands tribes that received considerable anthropological attention in the late 1950s and early 1960s was the Dani. The percentage of adult male deaths due to warfare among the Dani is approximately 25 to 30 percent.

One subgroup of the Dani, the Dugum Dani of the Grand Valley, held spectacular "fighting tournaments" that entailed masses of elaborately painted and decorated warriors charging against and retreating from each other on grassy hillsides, shooting arrows and hurling insults at each other. Their warfare was indelibly and artistically captured in one of the most stunningly beautiful and elegant ethnographic films ever made: *Dead Birds*. Karl Heider, the principal ethnographer for the filming and research team, attributed Dugum Dani conflicts to three basic causes: "Among the sources of conflict, pigs and women are primary, and land rights run a poor third."

In 1987 Gordon Larson, an anthropologist and missionary associated with the Summer Institute of Linguistics (SIL), filed his doctoral dissertation at the University of Michigan. By that time he had lived among one of the subgroups of the Dani for some thirty years and had collected very detailed data on their "disputes" and the stated causes of the 179 cases he investigated. He broke these down into four causes: women, loss of life (revenge), property, and land. The most frequent cause of these disputes was women, some 73 of the 179 cases (41 percent).

Of these disputes 104 were resolved by some form of violence: brawls, feuds, and feuds that led to war. Again, the most common cause of fights in each of these four categories was women, which accounted for 40 percent of them. Surprisingly, fighting over land was the least common reason given by Larson's informants for their violence, accounting for only 6 percent of it.

In any event, there is ethnographic evidence of the role that "fighting over women" plays in the political lives of unacculturated tribes. Indeed, the ethnographic evidence that a major cause of warfare among tribesmen is the desire for women is so obvious that it is remarkable that so many anthropologists dismissed my reports that most Yanomamö fights start with arguments over women.

While fighting over women is common among the Yanomamö, the frequency and severity of the disputes are basically a function of village size. The Yanomamö characteristically want to appropriate young women from neighboring villages and, if their village is stronger (that is, they have a larger village), they will coerce smaller groups into giving women, usually in exchange for the promise of a woman in return at some indefinite time in the future. But they sometimes forcibly take women from their weak neighbors.

Disputes and fights over women are a major cause of Yanomamö fighting and warfare, but they are not the only causes. If I had to specify the single most frequent cause of lethal conflicts, it would be revenge for a previous killing. However, what constitutes a killing is a matter of forensic opinion. If a snake bites a man and he dies, this is not necessarily an unfortunate bit of luck. The Yanomamö sometimes decide that the death was caused by witchcraft—an enemy in a distant village *sent* the snake, and therefore this enemy is now a legitimate target for a revenge killing.

In order to understand what tribal conflicts are like, one must take a broader view of violence and warfare than social scientists are accustomed to doing. Warfare, club fights, wife-beating, etc. are conflicts over resources that are useful or necessary for survival and reproduction, which is to say, useful in an evolutionary sense. The theory of natural selection is not simply a theory about survival, but a theory about *reproductive* survival.

Humans have conflicts of interest because, like all creatures, we must appropriate resources from our immediate environment to survive and reproduce. Consuming or using an item necessarily deprives another creature from utilizing that item. Thus conflicts are inevitable. For humans, conflicts of interest change over time as cultures become increasingly complex and evolve; the available relevant resources are affected by many variables. These include the physical environment, the political and social environment, population density, sex ratio of the adults, maximum sizes of permanent groups, history of previous conflicts, and many other factors. Some are "natural" and some are "social."

Human conflicts throughout history can be traced to conflicts over two fundamentally different kinds of resources: *somatic* resources and *reproductive* resources. The first kind satisfy bodily needs like growth and physiological maintenance; the second—members of the opposite sex—make it possible to leave descendants.

Putting it crudely, "somatic" resources are the near-exclusive focus of attention of those who try to explain war in terms of scarcities of strategic material resources—"gold and diamonds," for example. This social science approach focuses heavily on group survival in the physical sense.

A more sophisticated—and comprehensive—approach draws attention to the biological dimensions of natural selection and the importance of *individual* survival. Reproductive resources include not only members of the opposite sex (mates) but also those immediate neighbors and allies who take risks (and sometimes suffer costs) helping you to acquire and protect your mates. These allies are useful, if not crucial in a social sense. Historically, these useful allies have mainly been kin: genetic relatives or individuals whose reproductive interests overlap with your own. Brothers (genetic kin) and brothers-in-law (wife givers) are two examples. They sometimes pool their abilities to wield violence on your behalf and, in this sense, cooperative violence and its deployment can be thought of as a kind of biosocial or sociobiological resource that differs from purely somatic resources.

The Yanomamö have frequent fights over women but it would be inaccurate and misleading to say that they "go to war" over women. They also fight when someone's honor or status is challenged or called into question, but it would be inaccurate to claim that they go to war over breaches of honor. They sometimes kill an innocent visitor to their village because of suspicion of witchcraft, but it would be equally misleading to say that their wars are caused by witchcraft. Their wars are generally the result of cumulative grievances of many kinds that pit specific men against each other (and their kin), starting sometimes with trivial disagreements, and then escalating into increasingly more serious confrontations. These can include incidents like stealing bananas or tobacco, accusations of sorcery, and suspicion of infidelity. For example, a discovered (or suspected) affair leads to a club fight. The village splits into two new ones. Suspicion of the new group grows and resentments build and smolder. An untimely and inexplicable death is sufficient evidence that your neighbors are practicing harmful magic against you. An innocent visitor from the suspected village visits and is killed. Revenge killings follow and a new cycle of war begins, sometimes pitting now distantly related kin against each other. Unless you know something about the etiology of this particular war, it would be misleading to leap to the conclusion that it was caused by, say, witchcraft. The process of trivial incidents growing into a war is long and complex and an inattentive or uninformed observer might not even be aware of the many connections, especially if one's observations are short-term and occur in a small village.

In my opinion, it is best to consider war as one kind of conflict, very often a conflict that has grown out of and is an extension of many earlier and often trivial disagreements. While it is possible to find a specific cause—an insult, a failure to repay an earlier favor, theft of an object, assumed or real illicit seductions, etc.—for each of the intervening and sometimes trivial conflicts, it is usually a gross oversimplification of the complex developmental process of conflicts to cite the immediate provocation as the reason for an act of lethal violence between groups. (This approach goes back to F. Barth and some of the British sociologists.)

Sex Ratios

There are more males than females in the Yanomamö population. I became aware of this during my first year of fieldwork. Not only were there more Yanomamö males than females in the overall population, but especially in the younger age categories. I made this demographic finding a theoretical issue for understanding social and political relationships in tribal societies in most of my early publications.

Sex ratio deviations from an even split are characteristic in all human populations. For example, the sex ratio at birth in most large postindustrial populations is about 105 to 107 males to every 100 females. Among the Yanomamö the overall sex ratio is in the range of 125 to 130, depending on which clusters of villages are used to calculate it. In small populations like Yanomamö villages, short-term mortality rates can have significant effects on sex ratio. At one time, a village of a hundred people might have an adult sex ratio of 130, but an epidemic (or a sudden war) in a small population might change it to, say, 110 overnight, because there are so few adults and the deaths of just a few of them can have a great effect on the sex ratio.

The study of sex ratio and the reasons why there are more males than females in human populations (and among sexually reproducing species in general) is a complex problem in biology.

I initially believed that the imbalance that I observed and recorded was caused by preferential female infanticide, that is, that the Yanomamö killed more female babies at birth than male babies. What I knew for sure by my own observations was that: (1) there was a demonstrable shortage of females, (2) the Yanomamö engaged in infanticide (which I will discuss later in this chapter), and (3) informants said they preferred male newborns to female newborns because "male babies are more valuable." Preferential female infanticide was frequently reported in the technical anthropological literature. I postulated this theoretical model of Yanomamö warfare in one of my early publications.

But I soon backed away from this explanation once I began reading the literature in theoretical biology and discovered how flexible and malleable sex ratio was in human populations. I assumed that an at-birth sex ratio of 105 was a biological universal, but I was wrong.

The main difficulty in sex-ratio studies is population size. Although I included a number of villages in my study sample and thought this was statistical overkill, I was still studying a small population of Yanomamö: 4,000 is a small population for sex-ratio studies. To statistically demonstrate that a sex ratio of 115 was significantly different from a sex ratio of 107 would require a much larger population size—and I would have to interview women simultaneously in every one of the widely scattered, difficult-to-reach villages even to get the necessary census data.

It is for these kinds of reasons that demographers and sex-ratio researchers use very large populations. In many countries, Venezuela being one of them, a national census is produced in a single day: everyone is required to stay at home that day to be counted by hordes of census takers employed by the government. Try doing that among the Yanomamö. (Their numbers in Venezuela and Brazil are still only "estimates" in the current censuses of both countries.)

However, the shortage of females among the Yanomamö is real, apart from the absolute numbers of the two sexes. The reason has to do with polygyny, the marriage of one man to two or more women. Many Yanomamö men have multiple wives—as many as five or six wives simultaneously. This means that many other men will have no wives.

Therein lies the principal reason why there is so much fighting among the men for the available women. This would be true even if the Yanomamö at-birth sex ratio were 100, or even if there were a modest excess of females.

Discovering the shortage of females was a surprise to me, but I was intrigued by this discovery. I didn't recall any anthropological study of a tribal people where a shortage of females was discussed in terms of its potential impact on social and political relationships among men and women, let alone its implication in warfare and politics. I became keenly aware that first year that many of the club fights in each village and arguments and disagreements between men in different villages revolved around women: failure to cede them in marriage as promised, illicit sexual trysts involving a married woman and her short-term lover, or attempts to recover some woman who had been seized earlier by men in a neighboring village. Fighting over women might appear to be a "lurid activity" to some cultural anthropologists, as Marvin Harris put it, but it has important implications for understanding wars in pristine tribal societies. Biologists think that acquiring females is an effective reproductive strategy in sexually selected populations—including humans—and is not just "lurid speculation."

Yanomamö Abduction of Females

"Dragging away" is how the Yanomamö describe some abductions and it is an apt characterization in many cases: the victim is grabbed by her abductors by one arm, and her protectors grab the other arm. Then both groups pull in opposite directions. Even other women get involved, particularly women from the victim's group who don't want strangers to take her. The victim invariably screams in agony, and the struggle can last several long minutes until one group takes control of her. But in the majority of cases women are taken when they, with their husbands and children, are visiting a different village. The perpetrators simply force the females into a group of local males who, brandishing their weapons, tell their husbands to leave "or else!" This usually happens when a small group of men and their wives and children visit some large but untrustworthy ally and are woefully outnumbered. The husbands have very little choice but to head for home—and try to recruit a large group of male supporters who are willing to go back and help them recover the abducted women. This almost always leads to violence, usually club fights or shooting with arrows.

It is always strong groups taking women from weak groups, that is, men in large, powerful villages taking women from men in smaller, politically weak villages—even on the occasion of feasts that one group has invited the other to. This possibility is universally understood among the Yanomamö, at least by their political leaders, and it is the reason why the men of each group attempt to convince the others by boasting or acting *waiteri* (fierce) to show that their group is at least as large or as fierce as the other.

When both groups are of approximately the same size and therefore have approximately the same potential for inflicting harm on each other, the temptation or likelihood of an abduction is greatly reduced. It is always a good idea to be as big as your neighbors, and if you are not, to accept their invitations to feast or trade with considerable caution. Such an invitation might be a trap. Because of the ever-present possibility of raiding, allies need each other, but they cannot trust each other.

When a Yanomamö group is starting a new alliance with another whose members they do not know well (or might even suspect), usually in the context of a ceremonial feast, the men sometimes hide their women and children deep in the jungle near their own village and attend the feast by themselves. They do this in order to get to "know" their potential allies better. But this is a potentially hazardous course of action because the hosts immediately confront them with accusations that their guests are "suspicious" and "wary" and don't trust their friends: "We are sincere people, your trustworthy friends! You offend us by implying that we have bad intentions!" But the costs of not accurately detecting a village of cheaters are potentially very high. The hosts might even have a sinister long-term plan. They might invite the other group to several feasts, be friendly to them, make them feel confident, and encourage them to bring their women the next time. And then when the others bring their women, they turn on them, they pull a dirty trick, a *nomohori*.

A small fraction of abducted women are taken by raiders who are at war. This is usually an unexpected "bonus": the raiders go to kill male enemies and retreat for home before the victim's body, riddled with arrows, is even discovered. On their retreat the raiders sometimes come across a group of women at a distance from the village and if the risks seem low they will take one or more of them. Women abducted this way are usually gang-raped by the raiders en route home, and once reaching the home village, gang-raped by any and all willing males there, sometimes by visiting men from allied villages if any are present. The raping can go on for many days.

The unfortunate captives are eventually taken as wives by local men. Headmen frequently take them as wives and, I discovered, sometimes do so to terminate the raping and eliminate this disruptive source of sexual frenzy and chaos in the village. Headmen sometimes "share" them with younger brothers for a while and might later give the women to them as their own exclusive wives.

Rapes also occur independently of abductions. Men from larger, more powerful villages—a group of hunters for example—will occasionally

find a man and his wife in the jungle and, while some of them restrain
the husband, the others rape her. Subsequent retaliation depends, once
again, on the relative sizes of the two villages. It would be imprudent for
a group of hunters from a small village to do this to a man and his wife
who are from a much larger nearby village.

A very curious thing about abductions is that in the majority of cases
the victim is well-known to her abductors—and might even be related to
them. This is an expectable consequence of how the kinship-dominated
Yanomamö villages grow and fission. In most areas, the members of
neighboring villages were once members of the same village some years
earlier—but were separated when the larger group subdivided and went
different ways. Even though they are kin, over time their respective
groups become estranged and sometimes even hostile to each other,
and with passing generations, they become less closely related. Another
way of saying this is that the Yanomamö frequently abduct women they
know—and may even have grown up with as children. Indeed, they
even abide by their incest prohibitions when the captive female is given
to some man as a wife—the man who acquires the woman should not
be related in ways that violate their incest prohibitions. (I do know one
case, however, where a village fissioned and separated a man from his
half sister. They grew up in different villages. She was later captured and,
ultimately, taken in marriage by her half brother, who was the headman
of the new village.)

If a man is really fierce, as most headmen are, he can commit incest
with impunity. One of my dearest friends among the Yanomamö once
boasted to me about his five-year-old son: "He's going to be fierce when
he grows up! He'll even commit incest!"

Measuring or calculating the rate or frequency of abductions is difficult because one must know the history of each village accurately,
including when specific families separated when the village split apart.
Village size and relative political strength at any given point in its history complicate the matter. For example, a large, powerful village of 225
people might, over time, abduct a relatively large number of women from
its smaller neighbors and then fission into two or three smaller villages of
70 or so people each. You might be able to determine that before it fissioned 20 percent of the adult females were abducted from neighboring

groups. After it fissioned into three groups, disproportionate numbers of the abductees may end up in the respective new villages: one of the three might have few, the two others might have most of them. Or, for example, a large village might have spent a long period of time in one area and include many abducted women, but it is gradually forced out of the area into a less desirable peripheral area and must fission into smaller groups. It "carries" its history of previous abductions for a while—and might be conspicuous among its neighbors for having disproportionately more abducted women compared to them.

Frequency of Female Abduction

In my early publications I reported that some 20 percent of the adult women in the "core" villages I worked in were abducted from other villages. This estimate did not change appreciably as a consequence of the fieldwork I did after that. The core villages I studied had a total population of 769, and an average of 22.6 percent abducted females in them.

General Treatment of Women

The life of an abducted woman is not invariably worse in the village of her captors than it was before. In some cases, her life is even happier, more tranquil, and most important, safer and more secure. Yanomamö women who are battered by their husbands have no authorities to which they can turn for protection except relatives in the village who are bigger and nastier than their husbands. The lives of a few women are so miserable, in fact, that they willingly run away from their home village and seek refuge in another village where a new husband might treat them better.

A woman who does this is called a *shuwahi*—she flees, usually from a cruel husband, and throws herself at the mercy of the men in a different village. In many cases she knows these men and might even be related to them. Since her previous husband and his friends are almost certain to pursue her and punish her severely—perhaps even kill her—the woman tries to flee to a village that is more powerful than the one she leaves behind.

Not much scientific attention has been given to the role that brutality and battering of women probably played in human behavioral evolution or "the environments of history," as Richard Alexander called this era. Even sociobiological theory, now frequently called evolutionary psychology, seems to have a very Eurocentric flavor to it—implying that women in the Paleolithic wanted or sought basically the same kinds of things that women today want: a handsome man with lots of material resources; a man who has no other wife; a man who won't philander and will put all his efforts into being faithful to the wife and invest heavily in her offspring; a man with good genes; a man who has prestige and commands power. Most of the data behind such beliefs were collected from female college students from middle- and upper-class homes, not from Stone Age women. This view that we can project such contemporary attitudes into the past is probably also somewhat Rousseauian because it assumes an equality of the sexes that likely did not exist in historical environments but is approximated to varying degrees on contemporary large college campuses.

The Yanomamö women I interviewed seemed to want only to be free from beatings and severe punishment by their husbands, who sometimes only "suspected" them of the deeds for which they were being mistreated.

Many Yanomamö women bear horrible scars from injuries inflicted on them by their husbands, as I mentioned earlier. I witnessed several such incidents. In one that was particularly revolting a man bludgeoned his philandering wife with a piece of heavy firewood, delivering many sickening blows to her head and face. Even after she was lying unconscious on the ground with blood streaming from her ears, nose, and scalp, he continued to bash her with potentially fatal blows while all in the village ignored the scene. Her head bounced off the ground with each ruthless blow, as if he were pounding a soccer ball with a baseball bat. The headman and I intervened at that point—he was killing her. I later sewed up her wounds after getting permission to do so from her still violently angry husband.

This woman had a tragic life in other respects. Some years after the beating just described, her newborn infant slipped from her arms as she slept in her hammock over her hearth. The infant burned to death in the glowing embers before the mother heard her faint cries and woke up. Not long afterward the mother was bitten by a snake and died.

In some cases, a violently angry man will shoot his wife with an arrow, usually aiming at a nonfatal part of her body such as her thigh or buttocks. But in his rage and with her attempts to protect herself, he sometimes will hit her in a vital spot and kill her. The arrow of choice is tipped with an *adari* point—a long barbed point (ten to twelve inches) to the tip of which is attached a sharp sliver of monkey femur. It is difficult and very painful to extract this type of arrow point from your flesh. In the area I lived in during most of my research career, some 30 percent of the deaths among adult males was due to violence, mostly victims shot with arrows, many like these. About 5 percent of the deaths among adult females were also due to violence, mostly from husbands who beat them to death or shot them with an *adari*-tipped arrow that missed its mark.

But the most horrible of wounds inflicted on women are from steel tools, like axes and machetes, or from glowing pieces of firewood held against some part of their body. The assailants are almost always their husbands.

A number of my anthropological detractors accused me of inventing or exaggerating Yanomamö violence—and a few of them even claimed that I was the cause of much of it. They argued that my allegedly unpleasant demeanor provoked the Yanomamö to do violent things they never before did. But often I witnessed violence directed at wives whom I barely knew, and I frequently saw many horrible scars that resulted from machete blows or arrow wounds. Missionaries and Malarialogía employees described to me similar instances in Yanomamö areas I only occasionally visited.

Mark Ritchie describes an episode of Yanomamö male violence toward women in his fascinating 1996 book *Spirit of the Rainforest*. Ritchie is a businessman who befriended a group of evangelical missionaries working among the Yanomamö just north of the area I worked in. Ritchie visited the Dawson Mission on the Padamo River six times over the course of thirteen years, beginning in the early 1980s. He documented, with the translation help of one of the missionaries, the life of one of the political leaders in the group.

Yawalama was out of the garden and onto the jungle trail when Longfoot caught her and threw her to the ground. She jumped to her feet and he chopped one leg out from underneath her. With her back on the ground she used her arms to protect herself from his machete. He chopped her like a mad animal and left her to die . . . It took five people to carry her because so many extra hands were needed to hold the parts that were nearly cut off. . . . Keleewa [a missionary] and his wife and sisters spent the rest of the night cleaning her wounds and putting muscles back on arms and legs. . . . The knee cap was cut off and tendons stuck out. They stuck it back and taped it together. (Ritchie, pp. 221–22)

This girl was only thirteen years old at the time.

In a different incident among the same group of Yanomamö, one of them reflected on an incident during which a brutal husband punished his wife with a glowing piece of firewood:

He remembered that horrible smell the day a man got mad at his wife. He had knocked her to the ground and stood on one of her ankles. Then he picked up her other ankle with his hands and with her legs apart he held a stick from the fire up between them. "If you don't want to have me, you won't have anyone for a while." . . . He held it there until it made the whole place stink from the burning flesh. (pp. 223–24)

Ritchie's description of violence in Yanomamö culture is consistent with my own reports. There are other observations, too, that fit the general theoretical framework that violence and warfare play a central role in Yanomamö culture.

These accounts lead to the same conclusion: life in the tribal world is hard and often punctuated with extreme violence. The Yanomamö are probably a typical example of what life is like in a state of nature, in the absence of the institutions of the political state, what Hobbes characterized as the "Powere that keeps men in Awe." While it is also true that tribesmen spend many happy hours hunting, fishing, gathering, and telling wonderful stories and myths around the campfire, one of the most salient features of their social environment is the threat of attack from neighbors. Seemingly ubiquitous in this social environment is the avarice men display for the women in both their own group and those in neighboring groups. Women in the contemporary tribal world—the so called ethnographic present—are the objects of male possessiveness and aggression, and I suspect that they were always so in our Paleolithic past.

The tokens of wealth that we civilized people covet are largely irrelevant to success and survival in the tribal world and were irrelevant during most of human history. But women have always been the most valuable single resource that men fight for and defend. As Aristotle Onassis, who married Jackie Kennedy after President Kennedy was assassinated and was one of the twentieth century's wealthiest men, noted, "If women didn't exist, all the money in the world would have no meaning."

Anthropologists who collect the traditional kinds of data among tribesmen now find themselves in the peculiar position of being censured simply for reporting their observations in academic journals because these data will offend some group that believes in the concept of the Noble Savage. Never mind that this concept is inconsistent with ethnographic facts. This virtual Noble Savage is a construct based on faith: in that respect anthropology has become more like a religion—where major truths are established by faith, not facts.

The Sexual Life of Yanomamö

Field-working cultural anthropologists are (or should be) aware of two kinds of "truth" that they eventually report from their field studies: (1) what the natives say they do, and (2) what the natives actually do. Sometimes these are nearly identical, but more often the discrepancy between them is very large.

Our own Ten Commandments might illustrate my point. The Ten Commandments do not accurately describe how most people from a Judeo-Christian heritage go about their business in daily life. Many people lie, cheat, and covet when they think they can get away with it. These are cost-benefit kinds of activities: if the benefits are high and the costs or penalties small (or if they are unlikely to be caught), people often violate society's rules. The Yanomamö are just like us—not only rule makers, but rule *breakers*.

Let's examine how this works in Yanomamö culture and society. Let's see how, for example, Yanomamö rules about sex and reproduction comply with or deviate from observable practices.

Let me first summarize some of the more general statements I have published that illustrate the differences between what the Yanomamö say they do and what they actually do. Most Yanomamö men and women would agree with my statements about the following several Yanomamö customs.

Rule 1: Yanomamö women are not supposed to have sex when they are pregnant.
Both men and women have occasionally mentioned to me that the unborn fetus would be harmed or in some way jeopardized if the woman ignored this proscription. Although they all knew of women who had sex during pregnancy, I had the impression that they disapproved of this.

Rule 2: Yanomamö women are not supposed to have sex when they are nursing infants, a period that lasts up to two years.
The occasional discussions I had with women in particular about this rule indicated that resumption of sex too soon after the birth of a child was dangerous for the health and survival of the child. I have also heard, in unrelated contexts, women speculate that a recent death of some woman's nursing child was a consequence of her violating this rule.

On the other hand, some women become pregnant and have babies while they are still nursing a previous child, so, clearly, the proscription is sometimes violated. In addition, a number of infanticides were explained to me in the following terms: the mother elected to kill the newborn because she could not nurse two offspring and, in effect, elected to save the older one, whom she dearly loved and into whom she had already put a large amount of maternal investment.

Rule 3: Pre-pubescent girls should not engage in sexual activities.
This rule seems to be fairly robust, but I know that it is occasionally violated. There appears to be no odious sanction for the females, but a male *allegedly* has to go through a somewhat rigorous act of ritual purification in a ceremony called *unokaimou* if he has sex with a pre-pubescent girl. *I know of no instance of this happening where I worked.* The only *unokai* ceremony I witnessed followed the killing of another human being, which happens when raiders attack members of another village or when an

Yanomamö Divorce Rates Compared with Those in Other Societies (from Chagnon and Hames, 1984)

Group	Rate	Location	Group	Rate	Location
Kanuri	64	Africa	Huli	**33	New Guinea
Ndembu	61	Africa	Raiapu Enga	**33	New Guinea
Kofyar	*48	Africa	Ngoni	29	Africa
Malaysia (rural)	48	SE Asia	Elti	29	New Guinea
Java (rural)	47	SE Asia	Somali	28	Africa
Yoruba	46	Africa	Mambwe	28	Africa
Konda Valley Dani	45	New Guinea	Tonga (Plateau)	28	Africa
Luvale	45	Africa	Ganda	27	Africa
Lamba	42	Africa	Tonga (Gwembe)	26	Africa
Bakweri	42	Africa	KyakaEnga	23*	New Guinea
Irigwo	*40	Africa	Yanomamö	20	S. America
Herero	40	Africa	Kawelka	19	New Guinea
Gonga	38	Africa	South Fore	**14	New Guinea
Ngoni (Fort Jameson)	37	Africa	Telefolmin	**15	New Guinea
Yao	35	Africa	Shona	11	Africa
Soga	*35	Africa	Palestinian Arabs	8	Middle East

United States Rates

Year	Rate	Source Author	Source Date
1920	***13	vandenBerghe	1979
1940	***17	vandenBerghe	1979
1960	***26	vandenBerghe	1979
1970	***33	vandenBerghe	1979
1975	***43	vandenBerghe	1979

Notes:

*Our estimate based on available quantitative data.

**Mean of male and female rates.

***Proportion of divorce rate per 1000 to marriage rate per 1000. Barnes's 'C' ratio is rarely, if ever, calculated for modern societies. Our measures here should very closely match a 'C' ratio.

intravillage club fight turns lethal. I have documented many of these killings and have witnessed several *unokai* ceremonies. Some Yanomamö allegedly claim that someone who kills a harpy eagle (*mohomö*) must also go through the *unokai* purification ceremony. *I have never heard about or documented cases of men going through the* unokai *ceremony for killing a harpy eagle.*

Rule 4: Marriage for females is almost universal after puberty; that is, nearly all post-pubescent women are married for nearly their entire reproductive life spans.

This rule is in part derived from what the Yanomamö say, and what I as an observer have documented. In that regard it is different from the first three rules above. In general, when I ask broad questions like "who do you marry?" their answers are not specific about the age people have to be when they marry, but their answers indicate that females can be married at very young ages—and even be promised in marriage before they are born. Thus the married life of females begins when they are very young—toddlers in some cases—and can last until they are very old. Most women have had a large number of husbands—upwards of five or six—during their lifetimes, in part due to high mortality rates among males and in part due to the dissolution of marriages, what we would call divorce. Page 234 shows the comparative "divorce" rate among the Yanomamö in the area where I worked.

Rule 5: Yanomamö women should be faithful to their husbands.

This rule is the most frequently broken. Yanomamö men are like men in almost all other societies: they are excessively proprietary about their wives and are intensely jealous, often to violent extremes. Most disputes, fights, and wars can be ultimately traced back to conflicts among men over alleged or actual infidelity by wives. Yanomamö social order (and disorder) is shaped primarily by the sexual relationships and reproductive interests of adult men and women.

Statistical Findings from My 1986 Expedition

The table below shows how well my proposed rules compare with the empirical data summarized in the chart.

This chart is based on information provided by individuals whose reliability as informants I had established on multiple previous trips. Many of them were men who were familiar with (and were co-villagers of) the females about whom I inquired, and to whom most of them were related and whom they had grown up with. The majority of my informants were adult men between thirty and forty years old, although I also asked the same questions of a smaller number of female residents. I mention this because the gender/sex of the anthropologist might introduce a bias into the inquiry; that is, the reported answers to some questions might be different if the anthropologist had, in this case, been a woman. I doubt that this is true for most of the kinds of questions because these are simple matters of observation—the sex of the person, approximate age of the person, marital status of the person, whether the person was post-pubescent, pregnant, or lactating. These facts are observable.

The only question that *might* prompt a different response to a male anthropologist is the question "Is this female sexually active at the present?" I do not know for sure if responses to the same question asked by a female anthropologist would change the results I report below, but my hunch is that they would not. A male anthropologist working with male Yanomamö informants might get more reliable information on this question because male Yanomamö are keenly interested in this topic. It is central to their reproductive and sexual interests and so they "track" this part of their social environment attentively.

Reproductive Status of 302 Yanomamö Females (Based on Unpublished Data from 1986)

AGE CATEGORY	0–10	11–19	20–44	> 45	TOTALS
NUMBER OF FEMALES	91	53	118	40	302
SEXUALLY ACTIVE	1	43	93	25	162
MARRIED	10	46	116	22	194
POST-PUBESCENT	0	39	118	40	197
PREGNANT	0	4	9	0	13
CURRENTLY NURSING	0	15	77	3	95

The data summarize the answers that male (and a few female) informants gave me to a series of inquiries I made regarding *all* the females in twelve small villages—which amounted to 302 females, ranging in age from newborn infants to the oldest living female residents, some of whom were in their seventies.

Let's compare these data to the five rules I mentioned above.

Rule 1. Pregnant women should not have sex.
The data in this table indicate that only thirteen women (about 4 percent) in the sample were pregnant at the time of the sample.

Pregnancy rates at any given time are very sensitive to immediate health and morbidity patterns, particularly the sometimes irregular and unpredictable appearance of a sickness that sharply increases infant deaths. Not all of these should be defined as "epidemics" as such. Malaria, for example, is endemic in Yanomamöland. Its incidence waxes and wanes, depending often on rainfall. Thus after a period of high malaria infection rates that lead to larger-than-average numbers of infant deaths, women who have lost infants tend to become pregnant in "clusters" and the pregnancy rate after such period of infant mortality might be very high. At other times in the same population, the pregnancy rates might be much lower. This is one reason why a once-only short-term visit to a single community might result in data that misrepresent the larger pattern. Therefore, the thirteen pregnant women in this sample might reflect a rate that is near the low end of a fluctuating rate. While 302 females constitute a relatively large sample for many anthropological studies, for biosocial inquiries it may be too small.

The thirteen pregnant women fall exclusively in the two middle age categories: women who are at least eleven years of age but no older than forty-four years of age.

Eleven of the thirteen pregnant women (85 percent) are currently engaged in sex, so the proscription against sex during pregnancy is not very robust. The only two pregnant females who were *not* having sex were the two *youngest* pregnant females, leading one to suspect that some sexual taboos are intended to apply only to the youngest, least experienced, or most naïve. I think the sample size is too small to warrant anything other than the recommendation that "further research is needed"—as all scientific findings implicitly invite us to do. Another possible explanation for what I observed is that the stage of pregnancy affects this proscription—

sex early in pregnancy, for example, might not be as strenuously proscribed as it is in late pregnancy.

Rule 2. Nursing females should not be sexually active.

Again, this rule does not seem to be followed in a rigorous fashion and
the statistical evidence indicates that it is often ignored:

1. In the second age category (ages 11–19) there are 15 nursing females,
   10 of whom are actively engaged in sex—67 percent of them.
2. In the third age category (ages 20–44) there are 77 nursing females,
   49 of whom are actively engaged in sex—64 percent of them.
3. Of *all* the nursing females in these two age categories, 59 of 95—also 64
   percent—are engaged in sex.

Finally, of the 40 females in the oldest age category (45+), there are 3
nursing females—and all of them are sexually active.

These statistics do not indicate whether the nursing females have newborn infants or older infants, which might affect the high levels of sexual
activity of most nursing females.

Rule 3. Prepubescent girls should not be sexually active.

As mentioned above, the youngest age category (0–10) includes most of
the pre-pubescent females, and only one female in this category is sexually active, a girl of nine years.

But 9 prepubescent girls in category 11–19 are having sex. There are
only 14 pre-pubescent girls in this second age category, so 64 percent of
them are violating the taboo.

Rule 4. Marriage for females is almost universal.

The table on page 236 indicates that some of the females in *all* age categories are married: 194 of 302 total females, or 64 percent. This count
includes infant females.

One of the reasons that Yanomamö females are "universally" married
is that, after about eleven or twelve years of age, they constitute a potential political problem in any village if they are unprotected by fathers or

husbands; that is, if there are no adult males to protect them from sexual harassment.

"Early marriage" can be seen as a father's way of shifting the responsibility of guarding the daughter to a younger man who is so eager to accept it that he pays the father-in-law for this onerous privilege by "bride service." Thus the young daughter is protected and guarded by the new husband, and the father-in-law also gains by having a young son-in-law produce game animals (meat) for the family.

The percentage of married females is lowest in the youngest age category—girls who range from newborn to ten years old. If we ignore this age category, the percentage of females over ten years of age who are married rises to 87 percent. The universality of female marriage is essentially correct (some women are "between" marriages due to the death or divorce of a spouse) if we confine this claim to females over age ten.

Women over fifty who lose their last husband are less likely to find a new one: only about half of the Yanomamö females in this sample (55 percent) over age fifty have husbands, compared to 80 percent of the women in the two younger age categories. Here we must consider "ultimate" versus "proximate" causes. The ultimate reason has to do, in a purely biological sense, with declining female reproductive value with age: older women are increasingly less likely to have children in the future. A shorthand way of expressing this would be the answer to the question "Would you risk your life to save your fifteen-year-old daughter when the ship sinks, or ignore the daughter to save your sixty-year-old mother?" While you share the same fraction of your genes with both, the fifteen-year-old daughter has high reproductive value and her potential output of offspring lies yet ahead. The mother's reproductive value has already been spent. (This answer regards the question in only an evolutionary sense, irrespective of emotional ties.) The traditional injunction apocryphally given when the ship is sinking "Women and children first!" really boils down to: "Women with higher reproductive value and all children first!" (Children of both sexes have high reproductive value.)

Percentage of Women That Are Sexually Active

Of the 302 females in this sample, 162 were sexually active at the time of this census: approximately 54 percent. Again ninety-one of these females are ten years old or younger, and only one female less than ten years of age was sexually active. If we remove the females who are in the first age category then the percentage of sexually active females jumps to 76 percent. It would be reasonable to say, therefore, that regular sexual activities by Yanomamö females do not begin until girls are older than eleven years of age. Only four of the youngest girls in the next age category (11–19 years) are not sexually active, and most of the older ones are pregnant or nursing newborns.

This high percentage (76 percent) surprised even me: what few comments I have published in the past about female sexual activities were based heavily on what the Yanomamö claimed were rather rigid proscriptions specified in their (unwritten) "rules" about sexuality, which led me to have the overall impression that the sexual activities of males in particular was extremely restricted by the scarcity of sexually active females (of the correct kinship category). These new data put Yanomamö male and female sexuality into a different statistical light: adult males have more opportunities to have sex than I presumed from how sternly they expressed the proscriptions about sex with pre-pubescent, lactating, pregnant, and postmenopausal women (see below for a discussion of the sexual activities of older women).

I once received a somewhat testy letter from a man who was certain that I had either overlooked or was reluctant to report on the amount of homosexuality among Yanomamö men. His argument was based on my statements that: (1) there was an excess of males in the younger age categories, which I have shown in many publications; (2) that this "scarcity of females" was compounded by Yanomamö proscriptions on sex by pre-pubescent, pregnant, and lactating women; and (3) therefore, men, he argued, would naturally turn to homosexuality to satisfy their sexual needs. He insisted that I either missed this or was concealing evidence of male homosexuality. But these data show that the alleged scarcity of sexually active females is not supported by what my informants say when asked about each individual female's sexual activities.

What about the older and postmenopausal women? The statistical answers to my inquiries about them also surprised me and differed from what my impressions were.

Sexual Activities of Yanomamö Women over Age Forty-five

Since the Yanomamö do not have numbers or calendars like we do, they cannot tell me how old they are. I had to guess their ages. The more often I went back to a particular village and the longer I had to know the people there, the more accurate my age estimates became. For example, I learned more about the deceased and living children of each woman and could adjust my age estimate of women's ages to be more consistent with their reproductive histories. A woman I initially estimated to be twenty years old is unlikely to have a child who is eleven or twelve years of age, so I would adjust her age upward on a subsequent visit to this village when I discovered that she had such a child.

Of the several age categories shown on page 236, ages of the women in the oldest category are probably less accurate than my age estimates in the other categories, and this should be kept in mind. I could be wrong by as much as eight to ten years for older women in some villages. But since my field research covered a span of some thirty years, my age estimates for people in their mid-40s and younger were likely to be more accurate.

Of the 40 women estimated to be forty-five years old or older, 25 of them were sexually active—about 63 percent. Seventeen of these were women under the age of fifty years.

Some of the related social patterns are interesting. For example, 4 of the 23 women over fifty years were "single," that is, had no living current spouse, but were actively engaged in sex, some of them with young men—*huyas,* as the Yanomamö call them. Several of my male informants, younger *huyas,* smirked and giggled when I asked about the oldest sexually active women, just as younger female informants giggled when they were asked to comment on marriages between young girls and old men.

None of the 40 women older than forty-five years was pregnant, but 3 of them were still nursing young children; all of these women were

younger than fifty years and might have been even younger than I estimated.

Finally, only 7 of the 23 women fifty years or older had a current
husband. My informants usually responded to my question "Who is
she married to?" with the following kind of answer: "She is too old . . ."
to have a husband. Although a fifty-year-old Yanomamö woman might
not remarry, her sexual activities do not end, as the data confirm. And a
small number of adult women in the 20–44 age category were said to be
unmarried or unable to bear children. Their sexual activities were said to
be mostly with men younger than they.

1986 Data on Infanticide

As I have mentioned, the Yanomamö engage in infanticide. This practice
is very difficult to document in a statistically acceptable way because
it is the mother who is most often the only reliable source of information on how many babies she killed and what the sex of each child was.
Mothers are extremely reluctant to discuss this topic because it causes
them enormous grief and anguish. And I was extremely reluctant to ask
them and their close relatives about it. Thus one must ask *others*—other
women and men in the mother's village who are not immediate close
relatives. Since most Yanomamö villages are highly inbred and most
people are closely related, the problem is compounded. Village members
of both sexes are usually knowledgeable about the numbers of births
of all the women and there is a high degree of consensus among them
in identifying the women who have committed infanticide. But there is
little consensus among informants of either sex regarding the *numbers* of
newborns terminated by each woman through infanticide and even less
consensus on the *sex* of the children that were terminated.

The sex of the deceased infant must be known to determine whether
infanticide is "sex preferential." It is sometimes alleged by anthropologists that more female infants are killed than male infants in tribes that
practice infanticide, a fact rarely documented in the anthropological
literature. My initial fieldwork drew attention to an important theoretical
problem: the Yanomamö population had an excess of males in the junior
age categories. For some areas I worked in the male/female sex ratio was

upwards of 135, that is, for every 100 females there were 135 males. I developed a theoretical model that attempted to explain how population variables like preferential female infanticide led to a shortage of women in the population, a shortage that was intensified by polygyny, and how these conditions in turn led to variations in the intensity of Yanomamö conflict. I called my model the Waiteri Complex ("Fierceness Complex"). My model rested on the demonstrable facts that the Yanomamö practiced infanticide, had high levels of polygyny, the population (all ages) sex ratio was upwards of 135, and warfare was an important phenomenon that entailed high adult male mortality rates. But the weakest link in my model was the question of whether Yanomamö infanticide was female preferential.

My attempts to collect more data on the sex of these dead infants continued, but by the mid-1970s I had begun reading more widely in the biological literature and started backing away from my initial Waiteri Complex model as I learned more about the complex issues that were involved in the theory of sex ratio selection. Males in some species, for example, kill all of the nursing offspring of females when they "take over" and replace the dominant male(s) in order to cause the females to go into estrus so they can mate with them. African lions, several species of rodents, and various prosimian, monkey, and ape species are notable examples. Humans appear to be unusual in that it is the females—the mothers—who commit infanticide. Reasons given for human infanticide include the mother's inability to care for two closely spaced highly dependent offspring, preference for a male offspring over a female, a taboo against twins, and other reasons.

One other reason I ceased my field efforts to collect more data on Yanomamö infanticide was that I was told that a Venezuelan *diputado* (a member of congress) had learned that some Venezuelan Indians killed newborns and threatened to punish the people who did these things.

The Yanomamö say that the mothers are the ones who actually kill the newborn, usually by placing a stick across the infant's throat and pushing down or standing on the stick to suffocate the baby. I have spoken to men who were angry that their wives killed a newborn without first discussing it with them. I had the impression that in many cases the mother decides sometime before the child is born to keep it or kill it and may not discuss her decision with others. On the other hand, informants have given me accounts that imply that some infanticides are decided *after* the infant is born, in particular those infanticides that were explained by saying that the newborn had an obvious defect at birth. For example, there was a man in one of the Shamatari villages who was an achondro-plastic dwarf—his head and torso were normal in size, but his arms and legs were very short. When I asked about his marriages, the Yanomamö chuckled and said he didn't have a wife because he was "ugly," that is, malformed. However, they did point out that one of his brothers allowed him to have sex with his own wife, but when she gave birth to a child that might have been sired by the dwarf, she decided to kill it because it might have been born with the same condition, which is difficult to iden-tify at birth.

Among some tribesmen, where the father plays some role in infanti-cide decision making, the suspicion that the wife has been impregnated by some man other than the husband might require that the newborn be killed. I know of no reliably documented cases of this situation for the Yanomamö. Some informants did tell me that they knew of cases where the mother killed an infant because the husband suspected cuckoldry, but they could not identify the women by name.

I knew of no cases of direct participation by adult male Yanomamö in infanticide from my own work. The eyewitness account by Helena Valero during her early captivity among the Yanomamö (in about 1938 or so) is exceptional in this regard. I have no reason to doubt it since I have veri-fied so many of her other observations while living in the same groups among whom she also lived. Here is one of her accounts on infanticide:

> One woman had a baby girl in her arms. The men seized the little child and asked: "Is it a boy or a girl?" and they wanted to kill it. The mother wept: "It's a little girl, you mustn't kill her." Then one of them said: "Leave her, it's a girl; we won't kill the females. Let's take the women away with us and make them give us sons. Let's kill the males instead." Another woman had a baby boy only a few months old in her arms. They snatched him away from her. "Don't kill him," shouted another woman, "he's your son. The mother was with you and she ran away when she was already pregnant with this child. He's one of your sons!" "No," the men replied,

"he's a Kohoroshiwatari child. It's too long since she ran away from us."
They took the baby by his feet and bashed him against the rock. His head
split open and the little white brains spurted out on the stone. They picked
up the tiny body, which had turned purple, and threw it away. I wept with
fear.

I did see two newborn infants that the mothers attempted to kill at
birth. Both were rescued by missionaries who happened to be living
in the villages at the time. The face and head of one of the infants was
badly bruised, suggesting that the infant had been taken by the ankles
and smashed against a tree or rock. The other had no obvious contusions
or bruises. Both infants were subsequently adopted by non-Yanomamö
families in large communities outside the Yanomamö area.

Thus detailed information about Yanomamö infanticide is not abundant and is difficult to obtain. When I did my short-term study of sexuality in 1986 (page 236), my main purpose was to get a cross-section at one
point in time of what was going on in the sexual and reproductive lives of
Yanomamö females at various stages in their life histories. My question-
naire was designed primarily with these specific objectives in mind and
included a column I simply called Comments. It was in this column that
I made notes on additional information my informants volunteered as I
discussed each female's reproductive attributes and sexual activities.

The Comments column was unstructured in the sense that it was not
intended to solicit any *specific* information about individual females, but
simply a column where I would write additional information that my informants gave me. My informants seemed to conclude that I wanted to
know about infant deaths and volunteered additional information about
some of the females that tended to center around two themes in particular: infant mortality and infanticide.

The information on page 246 is therefore not to be taken as a systematic survey of Yanomamö infanticide practices. Nevertheless, these data
give at least a partial view of the significance of infanticide in the lives of
some Yanomamö women.

At least 38 of the 211 females eleven years old or older have terminated one or more of their live births by infanticide: a rate of 18 percent.
This is almost certainly an underestimate of the number of females who

commit infanticide as well as an underestimate of the number of infants
so killed.

About 4 percent of women between 11 and 19 years are reported to
have killed at least one of their own infants at birth, and approximately
20 percent of females over age 19 have done so.

Number of Infants Killed by Mother, by Age of Mother

Mother's Age	0–10 yrs	11–19 yrs	20–44 yrs	45 yrs +
Number of Mothers	91	53	118	40
One	0	1	10	4
Two	0	1	5	4
More than Two	0	0	8	5
% of Mothers Who Have Committed Infanticide	0	3.8	19.5	32.5

Infanticide is an important subject in the comprehensive understanding of Yanomamö demographic and reproductive systems, but it is very
difficult to document accurately or reliably and cannot be done in Venezuela because the researcher's findings might be used to do harm to the
Yanomamö.

9

Fighting and Violence

The Several Forms of Yanomamö Fighting

The Yanomamö engage in several different kinds of fights or conflicts, increasing in seriousness and potential lethality. While one can rank their various forms of violence along a scale from "less serious" to "more serious," they do not necessarily follow that developmental progression in actual situations. Thus a particularly serious argument can immediately erupt into a potentially lethal club fight without first being preceded by more innocuous, less serious forms of fighting. Also, some forms of Yanomamö violence require a lengthy period of planning and preparation—like an agreement to have a chest-pounding duel at the next feast. This form of ritualized violence cannot happen spontaneously, that is, cannot break out immediately when some perceived wrong occurs.

Nevertheless, in a general sense, the Yanomamö can "scale" the nature of their fighting to the relative importance of the breach that provokes it and do not have to immediately escalate a dispute to lethal contests.

I will not consider the frequent verbal and sometimes angry disagreements that are constant in larger villages but will confine the discussion to events in which blows are exchanged.

Wrestling and Side-Slapping Melees

Wrestling combined with some side slapping is the least serious kind of fighting. The object is not to hurt someone seriously, but to show him that you are willing to fight, often just to save face, in other words, to protect your reputation or status or the reputation of your kin group or even your village.

The contestants usually take a squatting position at first, but this shortly turns into a kind of free-for-all as they slap each other with open palms, pull hair, and struggle for advantage in the dirt—or the mud if it is raining. Occasionally someone gets in a blow with a closed fist, but that is considered unfair. These fights are noisy and boisterous but only relatively minor injuries result from them.

Women mix with the bystanders, and add their screams and shouts as well, but in more serious fighting they tend to remain in the background to protect their children because serious fights sometimes lead to shooting with arrows. Women are never contestants in these or most other kinds of fights. They do, however, engage in vicious and animated shouting matches, and occasionally a woman will bash another woman on the head with a piece of firewood. But women's fights rarely get beyond the occupants of two or three households—or women from two or three families when a group is visiting. I would say that if you see 100 fights, 97 of them will involve only men.

In the side-slapping events the older men and other bystanders form a loose ring or gallery around the actual contestants, who are mostly boys in their adolescent years, teenagers, and a few of the *huyas*—younger men. These fights usually occur on the occasion of a visit by members of some neighboring village, such as a prearranged feast. Such fights are agreed to beforehand.

This kind of fighting is a form of expressing mild annoyance at something done by otherwise friendly neighbors, such as accusations of stinginess or suggestions that these neighbors are less than manly, perhaps even a bit timid or cowardly. This kind of gossip can spread to other villages and the Yanomamö are quick to take offense at allusions to their putative weakness or timidity. These offensive rumors can be easily squashed if they are immediately addressed by a "we'll show you" melee.

The few free-for-alls I've seen like this were preceded by the taking of hallucinogenic snuff by the older contestants, a few of them being rather high when they entered the brawl. It usually starts out slowly, with a pair of young men slapping or hitting each other on the chest and flanks from a squatting or kneeling position, with the other potential contestants milling around in a circle nearby, surrounded by the older men, who keep them within the circle of fighters lest they try to sneak out.

The older men usually brandish their bows and arrows, clacking and waving them over their heads, or if they have axes and machetes, wave them menacingly at the general assembly of fighters and onlookers and often pound them ominously on the ground as if they would pound them on someone's head with equal likelihood. This is, however, mostly bluff. They scream instructions to the young fighters of their own group, urging them to fight harder.

Some blows are obviously painful, and those who get slightly hurt angrily want to escalate the fighting to a more serious level. The older men try to prevent this . . . largely to avert the possibility that they themselves might have to fight if it escalates.

The fight eventually dies down after some thirty or forty minutes as the panting young men, often caked with dirt and mud, tangled together in pairs on the ground, grow increasingly exhausted. Nobody is declared a winner. The whole purpose of the fight just seems to be to set the record straight as far as rumors of cowardice or unwillingness to fight. When the young fighters regain their breath and composure, they quietly and unceremoniously get to their feet, go outside the *shabono* to clean up and wash their bodies, maybe even take a leisurely swim in the nearby creek. There seem to be no obvious hard feelings afterward and the more ceremonial events like eating, trading, chanting, and dancing proceed as though the fight had never happened.

But they have now sized up each other and are better informed regarding just how far they can push or intimidate each other in the future without triggering an unanticipated and more serious reaction. And they usually learn the possible costs of spreading false rumors about people who are feasting with them.

Formal Chest-Pounding and Side-Slapping Duels

Chest pounding and side slapping are more dangerous because, among other things, the contestants are older, mature men and usually experienced fighters. Men can get badly injured or even killed in these fights, although they are supposed to be nonlethal and designed to redress some affront that is normally not serious enough to settle by potentially lethal means.

Like the more harmless wrestling brawls described above, many of these fights are over somewhat more serious accusations of cowardice that one group has spread to the members of other villages. Such fights normally occur among members of two different villages and, like the above-described melees, are often prearranged and take place within the otherwise friendly atmosphere of feasting and trading.

This is not always the case. People from different villages can be angry with each other and agree to settle their dispute *immediately* in a chest-pounding duel without an associated feast, usually because they want to redress the immediate wrong and do not have the time or patience to wait for a feast. It takes a rather long time to plan, prepare, hunt for appropriate meat, and carry out a feast.

Ideally, the groups assemble at one or the other village on the chosen day. If there is no associated feast, usually the men from the visiting village arrive without their wives and children; they have come only to fight and are usually in a confrontational and belligerent mood.

The *patas* (the "big ones," the headmen) usually engage in long, vituperative arguments before the fighting begins, giving their respective points of view on the provocative incident or the offensive rumor. The accused party, if the dispute concerns a rumor of cowardice, denies having spread this rumor. The aggrieved party recites incidents, conversations, and events where people from other villages have confidentially related in detail these provocative accusations to them.

When it comes to rumormongering, the Yanomamö are experts—and experts at getting people in different villages all roiled up. They sometimes deliberately start rumors to provoke fights and instigate suspicion between neighboring villages. Often the rumors are spread to garner temporary favor with one of the groups, as in this hypothetical example: "Did you know that the Iwahikorobä-teri are telling everyone that you

A side-slapping duel

are cowards? We defended you against these vile accusations. We are your true friends!"

If the argument is over some specific incident that happened in the recent past and involved members of the two groups, nobody can deny that the initial disagreement or argument took place, but each insists that the other one started it.

Considerable bluffing and threatening punctuate these noisy arguments among the more senior and usually well-armed men—who normally are not engaged in the actual fighting when it begins. The *huyas*—strong, healthy, younger men in the prime of life—actually do almost all of the chest pounding. Cultivating a reputation of being a good fighter in these kinds of contests is a good thing, and most *huyas* are usually more than willing to take a few punishing blows on their pectoral muscles if they can, in turn, deliver as many on their opponent—and fell him. As the *huyas* get more fighting experience, their reputations as good fighters grow and the respect they command increases. Yanomamö men are incessantly trying to increase their social status through prowess in fighting, which usually leads to increased ability to sway public opinion and public action.

One man agrees to take the first blows from an opponent. He stands alone, arms held back, chest exposed, and stoically gazes into the distance, head held a bit upward. His opponent can make adjustments to the man's stance, tugging an arm forward, pushing an arm back a little, etc. When his opponent's body is adjusted and positioned to the satisfaction of the man who will deliver the blow, he may take a few practice runs to position his own body at just the right distance to deliver the most effective blow. Positioning the opponent may take several minutes and adds to the suspense and excitement.

The aggressor then delivers a powerful overhand blow to his opponent's chest—to one of his pectoral muscles—with a motion similar to that used by baseball pitchers. His powerful blow usually produces a dull thud sound and sets off howls and bursts of excited hooting by onlookers. The victim usually wobbles and reels from the blow or, if it was a particularly effective one from a strong fighter, he may actually be knocked down, usually to his knees, and sometimes from there collapses to the ground. The man who struck him usually lets out loud growls and shouts, and prances in place—or in a tight circle—like a ruffed grouse exhibiting his attractiveness in a mating display.

The victim may take two or three such blows in succession. For each blow he receives he can deliver as many back when it is his turn. The fighters usually alternate positions after three or four blows.

A fighter cannot simply hit someone without allowing his opponent to hit him back the same number of times. If his opponent is unable to hit back, the victorious man cannot retire from the fight—another man from the fallen victim's group will eagerly replace his downed comrade and take his turn for him. Particularly good, courageous replacement fighters might even allow the original fighter to strike more blows because the new fighter can then return the previous *and* the new blows while he is fresh. His opponent may be sore if earlier blows were inflicted to his chest by the now-fallen fighter.

Although it is against the rules, some men conceal stones in their clenched palms, which gives their blows even more force. In villages to the north of where I usually worked, I saw some men with multiple scars on their pectoral muscles. When I asked them about the scars, they said they got them in chest-pounding duels, implying that the use of stones is more common there and that the stones were large enough to protrude from their clenched fists and cut into the flesh of their opponents. This suggests that the stones were not concealed and their use was legitimate. However, none of the men where I normally worked had such scars, but almost all of them had been in many chest-pounding fights and some of them admitted they sometimes illegally concealed small stones in their clenched fists in these fights.

The blows delivered in chest-pounding duels are tremendous and sometimes do a considerable amount of damage to internal organs like the lungs and the heart. After such a fight all the participants are extremely sore and invariably have badly swollen pectoral muscles. Some of them even cough up blood for a period of time because lung tissue was damaged. A few men die from the blows they received, usually not immediately, but within a few hours or days, although such fights are not intentionally lethal. Deaths in chest-pounding duels almost always start wars.

A variant of the chest-pounding duel is side slapping. The fighters generally follow the procedures just described, but strike each other from a squatting or kneeling position. But in this kind of fighting, the opponents are supposed to slap each other on the flanks between the rib cage and the pelvis, with an open hand. But fighters sometimes deviate from the ideal rules and close their fists, and some even conceal stones in their clenched fists as described above.

More men get seriously injured in these kinds of fights because the blows are delivered to softer parts of their bodies, where no bones protect internal organs like the kidneys. As a consequence, fatalities are somewhat higher, although like the chest-pounding duels, the alternating side slapping by contestants is intended to avoid inflicting lethal blows.

Club Fighting

The next level of conflict is more severe and more likely to lead to fatal consequences: fighting with clubs. The Yanomamö call their clubs *nabrushi*. They are long saplings cut down to some seven or eight feet in length (see page 256). Club fights can be prearranged between the members of different villages or might break out spontaneously between two men in the same village. In the several villages where I lived, club fights

A side-slapping duel and wrestling match in a Yanomamö village

frequently started among the local men over such things as suspicion that some man was trying to seduce (or actually had) one of the other's wives, tobacco or food theft, a younger "low-status" man being impolite or sassy to an older "high-status" man, publicly insulting a man by giving him a small or undesirable cut of meat during a local ceremonial meat distribution, denigrating a rival by malicious gossip. Once started, club fights often escalate and involve more men. The contestants end up in a more chaotic fight where everyone tries to club opponents on any part of the body he can hit, sometimes breaking shoulder and arm bones.

"Clubs" might not be the best description of the *nabrushi*. They are thinner at the end the fighters hold in their hands, quite springy, shaped more or less like very long pool cues, and about the same or slightly larger diameter. Because poles like these are used to support the over-hanging roofs every thirty or so feet, they are immediately available if a club fight breaks out: a man simply pulls out a roof support pole, chops it with a machete to a suitable length, and then is ready for immediate action. I have never seen a section of a *shabono* roof collapse when support poles for the roof overhang are pulled out and used for an impromptu club fight, but I have seen the roof overhang sag conspicuously when too many support poles are pulled out, and I have heard Yanomamö express alarm that the roof might collapse if even more poles are pulled out. But more often they are concerned that if a wind were to develop during a club fight the roof might blow off—the support poles are buried several inches in the ground to prevent the roof from lifting up in a sudden wind and then blowing off.

Such fights sometimes escalate to fighting with even deadlier clubs, called *himo*, made of heavy, rigid, hard palm wood. They have sharpened edges on the business end of them, intended to cut flesh as well as fracture cranial bones. These *himo* clubs have to be fashioned before a club fight, and if the fight is slowly simmering, the man who makes such a weapon is basically announcing that he intends to inflict harm that is likely to be lethal, perhaps as a threat to dissuade his opponent. *Himo* clubs are only about six feet long, shorter than the wiry *nabrushi* clubs.

Club fights can even escalate to fighting with machetes and axes. If this happens the fights can result in severe chop wounds that can sever or badly damage a hand or arm, permanently crippling the victim. If delivered to the head they are almost always fatal.

As in the chest-pounding duels, the assailant is allowed to adjust the position of the man he will hit on the head with his club. (It is considered unfair to hit an opponent with a blow to the side of the head.) The assailant's club starts from behind him and is swung in a long arc and brought down with great force on top of the victim's head. Imagine someone grabbing the small end of a pool cue, putting it on the ground behind him, and then swinging it with all his might so that the thick part of it lands on top of your head. That is what happens in a typical Yanomamö club fight.

The victim is supposed to remain motionless during this process and expose his head to the assailant, usually bracing himself on his own club, stuck into the ground in front of him.

The resulting wounds to the scalp are nothing short of spectacular and grotesque (see page 256). I've seen men in such fights with large chunks of their scalp bashed loose, flapping up and down on their crania, and still fighting. Many accomplished and persistent club fighters have scalps that are crisscrossed with as many as a dozen huge, protuberant, lumpy scars two or three inches long after their scalps healed. Men with numerous club-fighting scars like these are not bashful about displaying

A clubfight in a large village that escalated to an ax fight in which one man was seriously injured when he was struck from behind with the blunt side of an ax

An example of clubfighting scars

them prominently. They shave the tops of their heads in a tonsure and then rub red pigment into their numerous deep scars, to exaggerate them. Such a man, if he lowers his face and head to you, is usually not showing deference: he is conspicuously advertising his fierceness.

Since the Yanomamö cremate their dead, nobody has had an opportunity to examine the crania of adult men to determine how many have depressed skull fractures that have healed, or to estimate how much damage might have been done to fighters' brains. One Yanomamö man I knew seemed to have a perpetual glazed-eye look and seemed a bit slow-witted. He had an extremely severe scar on the top of his head that made a visible indentation into his skull. One of my late colleagues, Phillip Walker, had at one time a large collection of Amerindian skeletal material from the immediate ancestors of the local Chumash Indians of Southern California. His studies of their crania indicated that they, too, must have been club fighters or fought with weapons that delivered severe blows to the top of the head. A large fraction of Chumash adult male crania indicated sustained blows severe enough that skull bones had been broken but had healed over.

I once heard a Yanomamö cynically comment that the *nabä* (non-Yanomamö) men they knew, like anthropologists and missionaries, would not be able to survive a Yanomamö club fight—their skulls were too thin and it would be like hitting birds' eggs with a *himo* club. Some, but not all, studies show that crania of American native peoples are more robust and thicker than the crania of most individuals in Caucasian populations.

Raiding

None of the fighting described above is *intentionally* lethal, despite the fact that fatalities sometimes occur. Indeed, one might classify these fights as *deliberately* sublethal "alternatives" to warfare.

The motive the Yanomamö give for lethal raids almost always has to do with revenge for the death of some person. As emphasized elsewhere, the previous killing is often a result of some fight over women. A much less common reason is revenge for deaths caused by sorcery or witchcraft, which involves blowing charms on distant people to kill them.

Some lethal raids occur for no logical reason at all. For example, one particularly aggressive headman led a raid on a very distant village and killed a man with a shotgun he had recently obtained from one of the Salesian missionaries. Rerebawä, one of my informants, told me, when I asked why the man did this, "When you give a fierce man a shotgun, he will want to use it to kill people. He killed this man *badao* [without reason, for no reason at all]."

In another strange case where I did almost all of my fieldwork, raiders attacked a distant village they had no previous contact with because they suspected them of harmful magic. It is noteworthy that the leader of this raid had also just recently obtained a shotgun from the Salesian missionaries. Although shotguns did not make the Yanomamö warlike, I believe that they probably caused an increase in mortality rates in areas near Salesian missions. Shotguns may have even made the Yanomamö more willing to attack their enemies because the shotguns were more efficient killing weapons than their bows and arrows.

Raiding is conducted with the explicit purpose of inflicting fatal injuries on people, almost always men, who live in other villages.

Some clarification is needed here regarding the usual definition in anthropology that warfare is armed conflict between people in different, territorially-defined, political groups with the intent of inflicting lethal harm on each other. This definition emphasizes the importance of "politically defined" groups, but the degree to which "warring" Yanomamö groups are territorially defined, politically distinct groups is a major problem.

Although Yanomamö villages are usually geographically separated from each other, their membership often overlaps because individuals in both groups have kinsmen in the other, and these individuals sometimes move back and forth between villages. Indeed, they may have all been members of the same village some years earlier as was the case with some villages I discussed earlier.

I've heard Yanomamö men say something like "If I see my 'brother' [or some other close kinsman] on this raid I won't shoot him." In only a few modern wars—the U.S. Civil War, for example—have members of the same nuclear or extended family ended up on opposite sides of a lethal conflict.

Some Yanomamö men refuse to go on raids against villages where they have many kinsmen and friends. They do not suffer any disgrace or stigma because of this decision. This is very different from, say, a "conscientious objector" in our society who would, on moral or religious principles, refuse to go on *any* raids or shoot *anyone* in *any* other group.

On the other hand, intervillage killings are not simply homicides comparable to killing someone in your own village, for example in a club fight, nor are they just blood feuds, because the Yanomamö also raid and kill people in other villages to whom they are not related and whose members may not have inflicted lethal casualties on their own village.

Finally, it would be difficult to characterize a Yanomamö village as a political entity that is "territorially defined" because defending a "territory" would be foreign to the Yanomamö, who move their villages from time to time and whose individual villagers move more often as noted above.

These definitional caveats should be kept in mind when comparing Yanomamö warfare to modern warfare.

But Yanomamö warfare exhibits many elements that are generally characteristic of primitive warfare in other tribal societies. One of these is the extensive use of deceit and subterfuge. It would be difficult to equate these practices with, for example, "intelligence" in our own recent wars. Military "intelligence" I take to mean the often clandestine, usually long-term acquisition of information that is potentially vital and/or useful to efforts leading to the successful defeat of some persistent opponent. Yanomamö deceit and subterfuge are more like practical tactics in a typical warfare incident. They are Machiavellian and, in general, these deceitful actions have short-term blunt and bloody outcomes, as in the occasional massacres of large numbers of men at "treacherous" feasts or *nomohoris*.

Nomohori

The word *nomohori* means something like "a malicious trick," a "deception," or "a dastardly, deceitful act." In the context of Yanomamö violence it means to invite someone to an otherwise friendly event, like a ceremonial feast or trading get-together, and then kill them. It is an extreme form of lethal violence and usually results in the deaths of upwards of a dozen men from the victimized village. Women are never the intended victims in a *nomohori*, although sometimes they may be taken captive during one.

If the captured women have older male children—usually older than about eight to ten years—they are sometimes killed, too. One man I knew shot and killed a young boy of about ten years of age with an arrow after he and his mother were captured during a raid and brought back to the village. The boy was swimming in the stream with the other children at the time. The man said that the boy reminded him of the death of his own close kinsman who was killed by raiders from the boy's village— the very reason for the raid that resulted in the capture of him and his mother. As he watched the boy play in the water, his anger welled, he nocked one of his arrows, and shot the boy dead.

Groups that instigate a treacherous feast for another group must often enlist a putatively neutral third party as accomplices. The neutral party must be on friendly terms with the intended victims and often hosts the fateful event at its own *shabono*. The others hide themselves in the nearby garden or forest and join in the killing once the hosts begin it. Needless to say, the "friendly" accomplices who hosted the feast immediately become mortal enemies of the victimized group and may suffer *more* retaliation than those who put them up to betraying their friends.

Thus groups allied to each other can suddenly turn on their former friends. One must be very cautious about accepting feast invitations when your presumed friends are known to be in regular contact with your known enemies. This caution gives a distinctly sinister quality to Yanomamö politics.

A more difficult way to trick some group to come to a *nomohori* is to engage in extremely persuasive but insincere assurances that former hostilities are now forgotten and it is time to resume friendship. Those invited, while being suspicious of foul play, then face a dilemma. If they decline the invitation they thereby indicate that they do not trust the hosts and risk offending them. This might provoke renewed hostilities at a time when the invited group needs allies and perhaps can ill afford more enemies. The alternative is to throw caution to the wind, go to the feast, and risk being massacred.

That the Yanomamö do not casually accept feast invitations and are usually wary of the motives of their allies is illustrated by the numerous examples I learned about during my field research where the intended victims refused to accept feast invitations. I recall one trip I made to Mishimishimaböwei-teri in the late 1960s when two young men from Mömariböwei-teri enthusiastically volunteered to come with me. I found this unusual because their respective villages were enemies at that time. They told me they wanted to invite the Mishimishimaböwei-teri to a feast in order to "resume friendship." I later discovered that their feast was to be a *nomohori*, instigated by one of the Bisaasi-teri groups, a third party, with whom I was then living!

Nomohoris are relatively rare, but when they occur, many fatalities result. Long-term political relationships between villages have, in most cases, been shaped by these rare but unforgettable events. The surviving victims never really forget about *nomohoris*, and their desire for revenge is sometimes very difficult to conceal, even after many years.

I did not witness the *nomohoris* that I describe below. These are eye-witness descriptions by individuals who were there when they happened.

The first of these accounts comes from New Tribes missionaries who have lived with members of these villages for many years. This example occurred in the lower Padamo River area some years before my fieldwork began, an area that fell outside the region where I usually worked. However, I knew many of the older people involved in this incident, whom I met some years later at Padre Cocco's Salesian mission at the mouth of the Ocamo River. They are known to their neighbors as the Iyäwei-teri and, less often, as Ocamo-teri.

The second example also happened before my fieldwork began but involved people and villages that I later studied in what I call the "fertile crescent" of Yanomamöland—the Upper Shanishani River area. This account comes from Helena Valero's captivity among the Yanomamö as documented by an Italian parasitologist, Ettore Biocca, who was doing research in the Rio Negro area of Brazil and interviewed Valero after she was repatriated in the mid-1960s.

Let me draw attention to the fact that these *nomohoris* incidentally mention steel tools like axes and machetes. The Yanomamö narrators or observers discuss them in matter-of-fact terms, indicating that they possessed steel tools many years prior to my first field trip. I mention this because a number of my persistent critics claim that I introduced or provided such tools, provoking the violence that I reported in my own publications.

I will briefly describe a third *nomohori*, this one among the Bisaasi-teri, that also took place before my fieldwork began.

Nomohori *on the Padamo River*

The first *nomohori* is described in Mark Ritchie's *Spirit of the Rainforest*. This *nomohori* on the lower Padamo River took place not far northwest from the villages I studied.

The informant is an old man from the village of Koshirowä-teri who related his life story to Ritchie through one of the local New Tribes missionaries, Gary Dawson. His father, Joe Dawson, was one of the first New Tribes missionaries to contact the Venezuelan Yanomamö in the early 1950s and was one of James Barker's companions in the early history of the New Tribes Mission in Venezuela. (Joe Dawson died in 2011.)

Ritchie apparently follows the Dawson family's use of an English translation of the Yanomamö village name Koshirowä-teri. This name can be translated as "Honey" or "Honey Village" because *koshiro* is the Yanomamö word for a type of honey made by a bee of that name.

The Koshirowä-teri found an accomplice from a friendly village, a man who was also on friendly terms with "Ocamo Village"—the village of the intended victims, known today as Iyäwei-teri. Members of this (unnamed) intermediary group invited the members of Ocamo Village to a feast at Koshirowä-teri, a feast that would also involve a mortuary ceremony during which the cremated and pulverized bones of recently deceased people would be consumed in a thick, sweet plantain soup. Afterward, they would all take *ebene* (*hisiomö*), an hallucinogenic snuff that is made from the seeds of a tree that grows abundantly in this region.

The Koshirowä-teri clandestinely sent invitations to some of their own close allies in other villages, revealing to them their sinister plan and inviting them to join in.

Ocamo Village had, a few years earlier, pulled the same kind of dirty trick on the Koshirowä-teri. This is noteworthy, since the Koshirowä-teri were closely related to at least some of the people of Ocamo Village. Both groups had been members of *the same village* some time in the recent past. They had subsequently fissioned into separate, now mutually hostile villages. But it is rare for recently separated related villages to *nomohori* each other. This is one of the few examples I know about. I got the impression from many different Yanomamö informants that villages whose members were related to each other should not *nomohori* each other, a proscription that appears to be, like other Yanomamö proscriptions, not always observed.

When the invitation was delivered, the people in Ocamo Village were immediately suspicious. The women frankly advised the men that they thought this would be a treacherous feast to avenge the deaths they had previously inflicted on the Koshirowä-teri in their own *nomohori*. Ultimately, the women decided to remain at home and only the men traveled to the *shabono* of the Koshirowä-teri.

I often wondered why the Yanomamö are willing to take such risks, but I concluded that part of the reason is that failure to do so communicates a message that could eventually lead to even more predation and intimidation. Other villages will begin to view the village that declines an invitation as timid or cowardly and will take advantage of them, that is, take their women. In addition, showing fear is an extremely dangerous thing to do if you are a Yanomamö. For example, one of my best Yanomamö friends, Kaobawä, asked me why I wouldn't bring shotgun shells for the people in his village who had, by then, begun to obtain shotguns from the Salesian missionaries at Mavaca. As a matter of principle, I refused to provide either shotguns or cartridges to the Yanomamö, but I didn't want to tell the Bisaasi-teri this. I made the excuse, on one occasion, that there were *policía* at the airport in Maiquetia, where I arrived in Venezuela. They had guns and searched my possessions carefully, and if they caught me with shotgun shells they would punish me. I mentioned that I was afraid of them, which I was. Kaobawä stopped me, somewhat angrily but showing genuine concern for my safety, and said: "Son-in-Law! Never ever show fear in the presence of your enemies. If they know you fear them, that is when they will kill you!"

The following is the conversation between the intermediary who delivered the invitation and the Yanomamö informant telling Gary Dawson his life story that Ritchie reports in his book.

"I don't think they believed me, but they said they would come," he told us when he came back. "Their women know it's a trap. They don't want their men to come. So even if the men come, the women might not."

"Of course the men will come," I said. "I told you they'd come. They won't want us telling everyone that they are cowards. But now that the women know it's a trap, we'll have to come up with a trick so we can catch the men off guard."

The men finally arrived after what appears to have been a several-day walk. They had no women or children with them and were tired from the long walk. They made their camp in the woods, just outside the hosts' *shabono*. As they approached the *shabono*, one of the local men, Tiger-Ear, whose father had been killed in the earlier *nomohori*, couldn't contain his desire for revenge and angrily approached the visitors with an ax, but the others disarmed him and calmed him down:

"When our enemies saw the axe-swinging vengeance in Tiger-Ear's eyes and our people holding him back, they knew that we were serious about wanting peace. We all feasted together like friends and drank the bones of our dead. They were tired from the long trip on the trail, but we promised them that we would all share ebene tomorrow. . . . 'Sleep well,' Shoefoot's father said, to make them feel comfortable. 'We'll all have a great time taking ebene tomorrow.' Our constant talk of ebene 'tomorrow' began to make them nervous. They knew that it was the ebene that had helped them kill us the last time. I saw the fear in their eyes as we talked about tomorrow. We knew they would be on their guard.

" 'We've had a great feast and shared the bones of our relatives,' I said to our new friends. 'Why don't you all stay with us here in the shabono tonight instead of going back out in the jungle? Then we'll end our festival tomorrow with ebene.' They decided it would be safe to stay with us because they knew that they would only pretend to take the ebene anyway. They weren't going to fall into the same trap as we had.

"So they hung their hammocks among ours all around our shabono and we talked together in small groups late into the night. We began to feel like friends again.

"I woke before dawn. It was so dark that it didn't help to open my eyes, I felt the hard dirt under my hammock and got up slow. I couldn't hear a sound. Our fires had died out. I knew right where all our hammocks were hung so I was able to keep from disturbing any of our visitors as I moved around the shabono waking our men. We all slept with a weapon in hand.

We had machetes, axes, clubs, and spears. I put my hand over each man's mouth and shook his head just a little.

"I moved one step at a time. It took a long time for me to get all the way around the shabono and back to my hammock. Then I gave the loud whistle of a tapir and each of us attacked the new friend in the hammock next to us. It was so dark we had to feel for our enemy with one hand. The other hand held a killing weapon. Jaguar Spirit was with us that morning, and a scream went up from our shabono that sent a charge of lightning through the body of every one of us. It was a slaughter that we will enjoy as long as we live.

"Some of them escaped in the dark, and because we couldn't see, we hid and waited until light to see how many we killed. In the early light of dawn we saw that most of them died in hammocks full of blood."

Shanishani Area

This second *nomohori* was witnessed by Helena Valero, a Brazilian woman who had been captured by the Yanomamö in about 1932, when she was just a young girl. She died relatively recently. I last saw her in 1991 when her oldest son, José, accompanied me on a trip into the village of Patanowä-teri, where he had been born. His father was the headman of Patanowä-teri, Husiwä, one of the several Yanomamö husbands Helena had over the course of her long captivity.

While José had been born in this area he had never returned there after his mother and her children were repatriated in about 1955. His closest Yanomamö relatives still lived in Patanowä-teri and I knew them well from my many trips there. José was very grateful that I had invited him to come with me on this trip. I was pleasantly amused when he took photographs of the Patanowä-teri with a Polaroid camera. They were only slightly more cooperative with him than they had been with me.

In about 1932 Helena and several members of her family were gathering forest products and hunting in an extremely remote area of Brazil, very near the southwestern corner of Venezuela, the spot where a mountain rises almost straight up, ten thousand feet into the clouds. U.S. military maps available in 1965 indicated "hazardous flying reported under 12,000 feet." They didn't specify the hazard, which turned out to be the highest point in Brazil: Pico da Neblina. Half of the peak lies in Venezuelan territory because its crest is the boundary between the two countries.

Helena's family, like most of the rural Brazilian backwoodsmen who lived in the Amazon Basin, was poor, eking out a living by cultivating small plots of cassava and other crops. They got much of their food and most of their necessities in general from the jungle, like poles and thatching for their houses. Her native language was Lengua Geral, an Amazon Basin language spoken in the Rio Negro region, a mixture of Portuguese, Spanish, and a native Amazonian language, Tupi. She subsequently learned a more standard form of Spanish by the time I first met her in the early 1970s at Ocamo, but I always spoke to her in Yanomamö. By then she lived with her son, José, near Padre Cocco's Salesian mission at Ocamo. Her Brazilian relatives seemed to shun her because, I was told by Venezuelan locals, she was tainted by her captivity among the Yanomamö. Many American women in our own history who had been captured as young girls by Native Americans were similarly rejected by their families in the few cases when they were returned to them.

On that fateful day the Valeros weren't aware that they had entered the southwestern edge of Yanomamö territory and were very far away from any outpost of Brazilian (or Venezuelan) culture. In fact, my settlement pattern research shows that the Yanomamö were slowly migrating in this direction and had only recently arrived in this area themselves.

Helena's family was attacked by a group of Kohoroshitari Yanomamö hunters. Her father was shot with some eight arrows, but he managed to pull all of them out. Helena herself was shot with an arrow that passed through the skin of her stomach and buried itself deep in her thigh. Her father tried to carry her, but his own wounds were too serious. He put her down and disappeared into the jungle, carrying Helena's younger brother. Her mother also escaped. The parents wandered separately through the jungle for two days before finding each other.

They came back some days later to where the attack had occurred after they found and got help from a group of Brazilian soldiers, but they could not find Helena. She was then just a pre-pubescent young girl, some twelve years of age.

She lived among the Yanomamö for the next twenty-four years as a captive and was able to get away from them only in about 1955, when a local Venezuelan man, Juan Eduardo Noguera, who worked for Padre Cocco, took her in his canoe and fled downstream to Padre Cocco's mission.

She subsequently told the history of her captivity to an Italian parasitologist, Ettore Biocca, who was doing research in the Rio Negro area. He published an account of her captivity in Italian in 1965, which immediately became a bestseller in Italy. It was later published in several other languages, including English in 1970.

Helena's account is remarkably detailed. The accounts of the same events my Yanomamö informants told me differ slightly from hers in a number of details. However, the remarkable richness of her eyewitness account conveys a sense of "participant observation" that very few anthropologists can duplicate.

Much of her captivity was spent among the same people I studied, the Mishimishimaböwei-teri in particular. I recognized most of the individuals by the names she used for them, although her spelling of most of them differs from mine, as does her (i.e., Biocca's) spellings of place names like Yanomamö garden and village names. Some of these differences stem in part from Biocca's attempt to render them into Italian (carried over into the English translation), but some stem from the fact that the last few years of Helena's captivity were spent in an area where the Yanomamö speak a slightly different dialect from the Shamatari dialect spoken by the people who first captured her—the dialect that I also learned. For example, she uses *Fusiwe* for the name of her long-time husband in the Patanowä-teri area, but his name (transliterated into my orthography and pronounced the way I spell it) was Husiwä. The *h* and *f* sounds in English are, to the Yanomamö, the same sound. In the Shamatari dialect it sounds more like *h* to English speakers, but in the Ocamo dialect, it sounds more like *f* to an English speaker.

By 1965 I had spent almost a year with the Yanomamö, who told me about this woman. My Yanomamö informants called her *Nabäyoma*— Woman From the Foreign People: *nabä*: foreigner, non-Yanomamö; *-yoma*: a woman from. By linguistic extension, the name *Shamatariyoma* means "a woman from the Shamatari people." *Aramamisiteriyoma*: a woman from the village of Aramamisi-teri. To me, Helena Valero was a "foreign woman," but I knew nothing at the time about her captivity or her roots—she could have been a Ye'kwana, Pemon, or Hiwi Indian. Women from all these tribes would be called *Nabäyoma* by the Yanomamö.

The Nomohori *According to Helena Valero*

Among the many fascinating things Helena discusses is a *nomohori* that resulted in the death of a prominent Shamatari headman named Ruwahiwä. This was, by Yanomamö standards, a rather small-scale *nomohori*, but it involved very prominent political leaders in villages that I later studied during many repeat visits.

I later got to know one of Ruwahiwä's sons, Möawä, intimately well. He was the nastiest man I have ever met in any culture anywhere. I will say more about him later.

Ruwahiwä was the headman of a village then called Konabumateri, some several days by trail south of the village of Patanowä-teri. Patanowä-teri is *still* a remote village, but in recent years has had an increasing amount of intermittent contact with missionary personnel at the Salesian mission at Platanal on the Orinoco, where the Yanomamö village of Mahekodo-teri is located.

The villages I initially studied included the Patanowä-teri, but it fissioned several times after the event described here occurred.

As mentioned, Helena Valero was an eyewitness to this *nomohori*. When this *nomohori* took place she had lived among the Yanomamö some fifteen or so years and by then knew their language with near-native fluency.

The *nomohori* took place prior to 1950, maybe several years earlier. One of the specific provocations of this *nomohori* was the accusation that a man from Ruwahiwä's village "poisoned" a brother of Husiwä (Fusiwe), the headman of Patanowä-teri, and Husiwä therefore wanted to avenge this death. "Poison" in this context most likely means to "blow magical charms" on a victim, who allegedly dies from this nefarious act.

Both Ruwahiwä and Husiwä were extremely accomplished warriors and each had killed numerous men by then. At the time of this incident both had well-earned reputations for violence.

There were rumors circulating in Konabuma-teri that the Patanowä-teri intended to kill Ruwahiwä on this visit, but he defiantly ignored this information and would show no fear. So, he and just a few others accepted the invitation to trade with the Patanowä-teri. They left their wives and children at home, implying that they were suspicious of possible Patanowä-teri treachery.

I will put into brackets some of the words used by Helena Valero that may not be familiar to most readers. Some of them are Portuguese words. I quote Valero's account starting after Ruwahiwä's group had arrived at Husiwä's village:

It must have been seven o'clock [A.M.] and still the Shamatari [Ruwahiwä's group] had not moved. Fusiwe's Aramamisiterignuma [Woman from Aramamisi-teri] wife said: "The Shamatari are still silent; they ought to leave at once, before they kill them." Fusiwe was still lying in his hammock; about eight o'clock Rohariwe [Ruwahiwä], the Shamatari tushaua [headman, "chief"], came up to him and asked him for tobacco. He did not answer, but made a sign; I got up, took a little tobacco from a box [most likely some kind of container made of leaves], put it in a piece of banana leaf and gave it to him. Fusiwe passed it to his enemy, still lying in the wide cotton hammock. Rohariwe asked him: "Shori, brother-in-law, are you ill?" "A little," he answered. "Your Hekura [personal spirits] are sad and is this why you feel ill?" and he began to blow upon him [to comfort him]. Fusiwe looked at him: "Get up, Shorï [brother-in-law]." "No," replied Fusiwe, "I am very ill." I was alarmed; I kept my head down low.

Another Shamatari came up to Fusiwe asking for arrows. Fusiwe's younger brother answered. "I don't give my arrows; with this I will kill you and keep the others to avenge myself if any one of our men dies." The Shamatari did not answer and his other companions looked at each other; perhaps they thought he was joking and they laughed—At last Rohariwe said: "Go there all of you, on the other side of the shapuno [shabono], where they told us they would give us the machetes." He too went; he was tall and strong, well painted all over and adorned with feathers; he had his son near him; his dogs followed him.—The tushaua [headman] Fusiwe took black urucú [a pigment worn by raiders or men who intend to kill or threaten to kill others] and rubbed it on his forehead and chest, then said to my companion: "Rub plenty of black on my thighs and calves." The Shamatari were on the other side of the square, squatting down, waiting for the machetes. Fusiwe approached them and said: "Here are the machetes," and he threw them towards them. "Now give me the dogs." He took the first and second dog . . . ; at that moment the tushaua's younger brother struck Rohariwe with a heavy axe-blow on the head. The axe did not cut, but split open his head. Beside him, the tushaua's brother-in-law struck on the head with another axe Rohariwe's brother, the very one who had come to warn them and whose name was Sherekariwe. I was bending down, cooking something on the fire and I heard the shout of the Shamatarignuma, wife of the tushaua's brother: "Ahi! They have killed him, my father!"

The two men fell. While their companions tried to take their bows and arrows, the Namoeteri [Namowei-teri, an earlier name for Husiwä's village] were ready and shot them. I saw a youth running with open arms and I saw an arrow transfix his back and quiver there, while he was running. Then another, with an arrow sticking in his chest, and yet another with an arrow in his flesh. . . . no wounded man shouted; only falling arrows and running people could be heard. . . . Rohariwe was not yet dead: he was full of arrows, he stood up, fell, stood up again. Fresh arrows, tak [a Yanomamö sound for an arrow piercing flesh], pierced his flesh, which trembled under the blows; the man did not die, and did not shout. They pulled the arrows out of his body and continued to strike him. He had arrows in his stomach, his chest, his face, his neck, his legs.

Meanwhile Sherekariwe, whose head was split open, was not dead and tried to stand up. . . . An arrow came and hit him in the stomach, passing through from one side to the other; the man fell again. . . .

The tushaua Rohariwe did not die; he fell and got up again. He tried to pull the arrows out of his body, but he was no longer able to do so. When a new arrow hit him, he only cried: "Ahh!" A man came up and stuck his bow into Rohariwe's body, as if it had been a spear. Rohariwe then slowly, very slowly, stood up; his body looked like a trunk with many branches. He walked ahead swaying, gave a horrid growl like a mad dog, lurched and fell forward on top of all those arrows. And so he died.

Fusiwe meanwhile had run in pursuit of the Shamatari who were fleeing. He told later how he saw a wounded youth under an embauba tree; it was the son whom Rohariwe had brought. The youth said to him: "Do not shoot me," but Fusiwe shot him. The youth repeated: "Do not shoot

me again, father; let me die, for you have already struck me a death blow."
He shot him again and killed him. Then he killed another in the forest. A
few days later vultures could be seen circling around; it was the corpse of
another which smelled.

Valiant leaders like Ruwahiwä sometimes sustain what are apparently—or even certainly—lethal blows to their heads from heavy axes,
but still rise, stagger forward, and somehow are able to keep on their feet
despite being mortally wounded. My own Yanomamö informants, who
were also eyewitnesses to Ruwahiwä's death, described the first ax blow
to his head as a fatal blow from which no man could possibly recover.
One of my informants was the man who delivered this fatal ax blow to
Ruwahiwä's head—a man named Mamiköniniwä, whose son was one of
my first regular informants. Yet Ruwahiwä managed to stand up and fall
down several times—all the while being shot multiple times with arrows
to his face, neck, stomach, and chest.

Many years later, one headman I knew—Matowä—was killed shortly
after I arrived, as described earlier. He probably also sustained as many
lethal arrow wounds as Ruwahiwä, but defiantly stood his ground and
cursed his assailants until he could no longer stand. He, too, never acknowledged the pain—nor the terror of knowing that his wounds were
fatal—but stoically taunted his assailants with defiant declarations of his
valor and fearlessness until he fell, dead, from his many wounds. He died
with many six-foot arrows stuck helter-skelter through or into his neck,
chest, and stomach. One of my informants, who was part of the raiding
party that killed him, told me in whispers that this valiant warrior Matowä bragged about his valor and ferocity even as the raiders continued
to shoot arrow after arrow into his body.

The Revenge Nomohori at Amiana

The *nomohori* for Ruwahiwä of course led to an inevitable retaliation: his
village was large and powerful and would seek retribution. They got their
revenge several years later, at a place called Amiana, in approximately
1948.

Amiana is the name of a mountain in the headwaters of the Washäwä

River, where some of the Shamatari, led by a headman named Riakowä, settled after the killing of their kinsmen Ruwahiwä and Sherekariwä. Several gardens were cleared by these new Shamatari arrivals.

The period from about 1948 to 1951 is a confusing one in the histories of both the Patanowä-teri and Konabuma-teri, since both populations split into multiple smaller ones, rejoined, then split again. One of the splinter groups of the large village of Patanowä-teri took the name Bisaasi-teri, another took the name Wanidima-teri, and yet a third one kept the original name. The Bisaasi-teri began moving farther to the west into the Washäwä drainage and eventually became neighbors of one of the Shamatari groups—relatives of Ruwahiwä—who had themselves just moved into and settled in that area.

Apparently the Bisaasi-teri faction had nothing to do with the previous *nomohori* in which Husiwä's group of the Patanowä-teri killed Ruwahiwä and Sherekariwä, but they were nevertheless now an inviting target for revenge: they were closely related to Husiwä and members of his faction but had fissioned away from his group and now lived in a much smaller and vulnerable village. Their culpability is one of the inevitable dimensions of "blood revenge" in tribes like the Yanomamö.

The Konabuma-teri—Ruwahiwä's group—had also fissioned into several smaller groups. As mentioned, Riakowä's group settled on the upper Washäwä near a small mountain called Amiana, but other Konabuma-teri splinter groups apparently remained in the Upper Shanishani drainage and began moving toward the Mavaca headwaters following a route to the south of the Washäwä. One of these groups was led by Sibarariwä—a younger brother of Ruwahiwä and a man I got to know very well. Sibarariwä, whom I discussed earlier, was considered by the Bisaasi-teri to have been the chief architect and instigator of the *nomohori* that followed.

My description of this *nomohori* is rather frugal because my information came from Bisaasi-teri informants who lost many close kinsmen in that event and who, quite understandably, were reluctant to discuss this fairly recent tragedy in detail with me because their fathers, brothers, and husbands died in this *nomohori*.

Sibarariwä persuaded his close relative Riakowä, who was friendly with the Bisaasi-teri, to invite them to a feast at his village near Amiana. Sibarariwä's men would lie in wait outside Riakowä's shabono, along with a group of men from Hasuböwä-teri, Sibarariwä's allies, who were already on hostile terms with the Patanowä-teri.

The Bisaasi-teri arrived at Riakowä's village for the feast. Shortly after they arrived Riakowä and his men began attacking them with clubs, axes, and arrows. Some managed to escape by breaking through the palisade, but many of those were then shot by archers from Sibarariwä's group and his Hasuböwä-teri allies. Kaobawä, one of the survivors and a man who eventually became the leader of the Upper Bisaasi-teri, told me that some of the Shamatari from Riakowä's group took pity on them and helped them escape through the palisade, saving their lives. Dedeheiwä, the renowned shaman of Mishimishimaböwei-teri and a dear friend of mine, was one of the men who helped some of the Bisaasi-teri escape.

Eleven Bisaasi-teri men were killed in that *nomohori* and many more were wounded but recovered. Kaobawä's father was killed in this incident. Seven Bisaasi-teri women were also captured.

The survivors retreated to their village and new garden a day or two to the northwest, Kreiböwei, where the wounded could recover.

While recovering from their wounds they were visited by the headman of Mahekodo-teri, who had learned about the *nomohori*. He invited them to live temporarily in his village on the banks of the Orinoco, some three days to the north. The Bisaasi-teri accepted his invitation and moved into Mahekodo-teri. As usual, this invitation was not altruistic: the Mahekodo-teri hosts had designs on the Bisaasi-teri's now poorly defended women.

James P. Barker had just established contact with the Mahekodo-teri a few months earlier. He told me he witnessed the arrival of the Bisaasi-teri survivors of the *nomohori* when they reached Mahekodo-teri. He said the year was 1950.

Scientific Summary of Yanomamö Warfare

In 1988 I published an article in the prestigious academic journal *Science* that summarized my twenty-five years of findings on Yanomamö warfare. My summary identified 137 living men in the villages I was studying who were *unokais*, that is, warriors who had killed someone.

Sixty percent (83 of the 137) of the *unokais* in this sample had partici-

Number of victims for which living killers *unokaied*

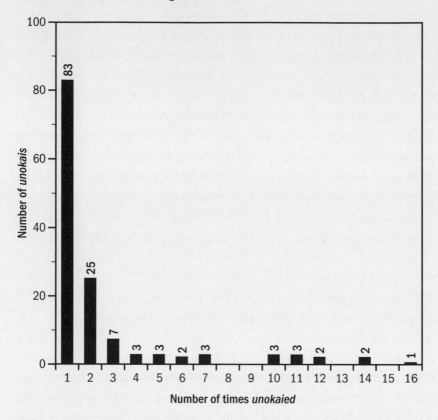

Number of times *unokaied*

pated in the killing of only one person (see above). The others had participated in the killings of two or more people. One man had participated in the killings of sixteen people. The most "accomplished" *unokai* in my records, Möawä, one of Ruwahiwä's sons, had participated in the killing of twenty-two people, but he is not included because he had died a few years earlier. There probably have been other *unokais* as successful at killing as Möawä.

I have meticulous data on how many kinsmen each person has in his/her village, the population bloc that village belongs to, and the overall area that I studied intensively—which contained nearly forty villages. In other words, my information on the prevalence of violence among the Yanomamö relies on extensive documentation. The Yanomamö may be the only warring tribal society in the world for which such data have ever been collected.

In my 1988 sample two-thirds of all living Yanomamö over the age of forty have lost one or more close genetic kinsman—a father, brother, husband, or son—to violence. This fact should underscore the importance that blood revenge plays in the Yanomamö population. I emphasized this point in my 1988 *Science* article to try to illustrate the percentage of people who are aggrieved at the violent death of "a kinsman" in their village.

Approximately 45 percent of all the living adult males in my study were *unokais*, that is, had participated in the killing of at least one person. That is an extraordinarily high percentage, but this statistic might not be unusual among pre-contact tribesmen had they been studied by anthropologists when they were demographically intact.

The Differential Reproductive Success of Yanomamö *Unokais*

My *Science* article included a number of additional findings that disturbed, even offended, a number of my colleagues in cultural anthropology, colleagues who clearly favored the Noble Savage view of tribesmen. But these findings were empirical.

Had I been discussing wild boars, yaks, ground squirrels, armadillos, or bats, nobody in the several subfields of biology would have been surprised by my findings. But I was discussing Homo sapiens—who, according to many cultural anthropologists, stands apart from the laws of nature. They say that the only "nature" Homo sapiens has is a "cultural nature."

In my article I first summarized the reproductive success of *unokais*

Marital success of *unokais* and non-*unokais*

Ages	Unokais			Non-*unokais*		
	n	Number of wives	Average number of wives	n	Number of wives	Average number of wives
20–24	5	4	0.80	78	10	0.13
25–30	14	13	0.93	58	31	0.53
31–40	43	49	1.14	61	59	0.97
>41	75	157	2.09	46	54	1.17
Total	137	223	1.63	243	154	0.63

compared to non-*unokais* of their same approximate age. Page 275 and the table below provide these results.

These two tables break down the adult males into four age categories. The age categories begin with men who have reached the approximate age when their active raiding careers begin—about twenty years old.

The numbers of men who are *unokais* in each age group are shown on the left and the non-*unokais* on the right. The numbers of wives these men have or have had and the average number of wives for their age category are in the two columns adjacent. Thus there were five *unokais* (page 275) between twenty and twenty-four years of age and these five young men had a total of four wives—yielding an average number of wives per man of 0.80. Continuing across the same row, there were seventy-eight same-age non-*unokais*, who had a total of ten wives among them, for an average of 0.13 wives each. The conclusion, for this row, a very small portion of the larger sample, is that men who are *unokais* have a higher average number of wives compared to their non-*unokais*, same-age peers.

This same pattern continues throughout the data table for all age categories: *unokais* have, on average, more wives than non-*unokais*. For all ages pooled, *unokais* have an average of 1.63 wives compared to an average of 0.63 for non-*unokais*.

The more interesting finding has to do with the comparative reproductive success of *unokais* and non-*unokais*. It should be intuitively clear that if *unokais* are more successful at acquiring wives, they are likely to have more children as well. This chart provides this comparison:

Reproductive success of *unokais* and non-*unokais*

	Unokais			Non-*unokais*		
Ages	n	Number of offspring	Average number of offspring	n	Number of offspring	Average number of offspring
20–24	5	5	1.00	78	14	0.18
25–30	14	22	1.57	58	50	0.86
31–40	43	122	2.83	61	123	2.02
> 41	75	524	6.99	46	193	4.19
Total	137	673	4.91	243	380	1.59

The bottom row reveals that *unokais* have, on average, 4.91 children compared to same-age non-*unokais*, who average only 1.59 offspring each, that is, *unokais* have three times as many offspring as non-*unokais*.

These findings are almost unique in cultural anthropology reports, not so much because the Yanomamö are unique but because they managed to survive demographically intact long enough for a Darwinian field working cultural anthropologist to document this aspect of their lives. It should have been done—and could have been done—among other groups by anthropologists even a generation earlier than me.

There have been some thirty or more anthropologists who began fieldwork among the Yanomamö after I began. They all could have easily collected comparable data on *unokais* and variations in reproductive success similar to the data just described. *Not one of them did this.* Yet some of these anthropologists claim that I have "exaggerated" Yanomamö violence even though they have not produced their own data, if they even collected these data, on causes of death among the various groups they studied. They could have demonstrated their statistical findings on how much violence and violent causes of death took place while they were studying the Yanomamö in the areas *they* worked in. Unfortunately, this is *not* how cultural anthropology now operates. Those among my anthropological colleagues who openly and frequently criticize my findings without providing comparable data on the Yanomamö groups they studied only convince academics in adjacent disciplines that cultural anthropology is not only not scientific, but it is not capable of being scientific. The finger, instead, should be pointed at those who *never collect* relevant data but simultaneously condemn their colleagues whose hard-won data sometimes lead to conclusions they find uncomfortable.

Neither field biologists nor intelligent laymen find my results strange or unusual. But a small, highly vocal number of cultural anthropologists seem to be very upset by my data. One anthropologist, as mentioned earlier, even accused me of suggesting that the Yanomamö "had a gene for warfare." In cultural anthropology, when you want to pour scorn on an adversary, you suggest that he is claiming that "genes" cause "culture" and he is therefore a "genetic determinist." For good measure, you can call him a "biological reductionist" as well. One of my former professors cynically observed that anthropologists really don't have colleagues—they just have co-conspirators.

My 1988 *Science* article led to a number of highly critical responses. Some ad hominem criticism of this article persists to this day. I will discuss the ramifications of this article later in this book.

10

First Contact with the Iwahikoroba-teri

In 1971 I contacted the village of Iwahikoroba-teri, northeast of Mishi-mishimabowei-teri and east of the Mavaca River. I had seen their trails next to the Mavaca River on several trips. On one occasion I saw one of their rickety pole-and-vine bridges where they had recently crossed the Mavaca.

It took me several attempts to contact this group. The Bisaasi-teri disliked them and had not seen them for twenty years. But the Bisaasi-teri had been wrong about how I would be received by the Mishimishimabowei-teri and I unconsciously dropped my guard when I decided to find the Iwahikoroba-teri, assuming they would be just as friendly as the Mishimishimabowei-teri had been.

First Attempt

In mid-January 1971, I learned that a hunting party from Bisaasi-teri had accidentally run into a group of Iwahikoroba-teri hunters about a half day inland from the middle course of the Mavaca River. It had happened in December 1970, a few weeks before I arrived for my annual fieldwork. Their meeting was nervous but peaceful, and the Iwahikoroba-teri indicated they would like to resume friendly contacts with the Bisaasi-teri.

I immediately decided to make an attempt to contact the Iwahikoroba-teri despite the hectic schedule planned for this year's biomedical fieldwork with Neel's group from the University of Michigan's medical school and from IVIC. I carefully questioned one of the Bisaasi-teri men who had made the initial contact. He described to me where it had occurred and where I should start inland from the Mavaca River. Surprisingly, three Bisaasi-teri men volunteered to come with me. They seemed less concerned about possible chicane from the Iwahikoroba-teri than they had from the Mishimishimaböwei-teri on the occasion of my first contact with them, some three years earlier.

One of the men wanted to bring his elderly mother along: Hubemi, an old woman who had been abducted from the Iwahikoroba-teri many years earlier. This was, they apparently assumed, their insurance that their hosts would not receive them with hostility and treachery. Hubemi wanted to visit her relatives there, people she had not seen since her capture in the late 1940s. I was very surprised that Hubemi's son, Shararaiwä, wanted to come—the Iwahikoroba-teri had killed his father's brother in the 1950 *nomohori* at Amiana Mountain, discussed in the previous chapter.

On January 16, we began to ascend the Mavaca River for nearly two days, made camp on the right bank, stored the canoe and gasoline, and started inland. Since none of the men had been in this area for some twenty years, they became disoriented and lost the faint trail they were following. We wandered in a meandering pattern for two days and found no fresh signs of Yanomamö travelers. Hubemi and two of the men then came down with severe diarrhea and were reluctant to go on. Thus we turned back and returned to my base at Mavaca—in part because I had to meet Neel's airplane at a mission airstrip in several days. Although I had to abort my first attempt to contact the Iwahikoroba-teri, I intended to make another try to contact them when my obligations to my biomedical co-researchers were done for the season.

After Neel's team arrived I spent the next ten or so days taking them to villages up the Ocamo River, where we collected blood samples in some half-dozen widely dispersed villages in that area.

An unusual thing happened that aggravated Neel, who was constantly concerned about something going wrong. We were on the way down the Ocamo River in our two dugout canoes to Padre Cocco's mission to get the blood samples on the airplane and out to Caracas to Layrisse's lab at IVIC. I was in the lead canoe because I knew the river better than anyone else. Neel was in the canoe behind me protecting the blood and other samples, worried about making the plane. Because we had hired that plane and the plane's owner would not get paid unless he could deliver the precious blood samples to Caracas, the pilot would remain at the airstrip until we arrived. But Neel still worried that something would go wrong.

As we rounded a bend in the river I spotted a tapir feeding quietly in a shallow pool on the inside of the curve. It didn't hear the motor as I idled it down and slowly picked up my shotgun and loaded two rifled slugs into the barrels.

Tapir is the most desirable meat in the Amazon Basin—red, juicy, and tender. A tapir can weigh up to 500 pounds and, accordingly, provides enough meat for a large number of people, even all the members of a village for example. If you have spent a long time in the Amazon Basin and are dependent on hunting to get your meat, you don't pass up a tapir. I would sear tapir steaks cut from the hindquarter in a small frying pan, cook them rare, and gobble them down. The Yanomamö always found this disgusting because blood from the steak would be dripping down my bearded chin. They would watch in horror and tell me that I "wanted to become a jaguar" because that's how jaguars eat their meat, adding that I also "wanted to become a cannibal" and eat human flesh like their mythical ancestors.

I knew I would be on the river or helping to collect various samples for the next weeks and that I wouldn't be able to eat the tapir, nor would Neel and any of his team, but I also knew that if I brought the tapir meat to the Yanomamö at Ocamo and Mavaca, they would very much appreciate this and reciprocate the favor at some future time. This was one of the reasons I got along well with the Yanomamö, even in villages I visited only occasionally—I always gave them most of the game I shot.

I cut the outboard engine and the momentum of my canoe glided me closer to the tapir. I shot once at its head and the tapir exploded out of the water, then fell back into it, motionless. I expected to see blood gushing from its head, but there wasn't a drop of blood on the tapir or in the water. We dragged the carcass to the shore and I began gutting it. When I tried to find the place on its skull where my slug had entered, all I could find was a small bruised area between its ears—the slug killed it just by shock. I began to hear someone shouting angrily at me, turned around, and realized that it was Jim Neel. His canoe was just pulling into the lagoon where I had killed the tapir. He was furious with me for having taken the time to shoot a tapir and then spend another fifteen minutes dressing it and butchering it into quarters to take with us. Didn't I realize that we had to make the plane and get the blood samples onto it? This wasn't a hunting expedition and I was being irresponsible and wasting precious time!

We made the plane with plenty of time to spare. The Iyäwei-teri at Ocamo, to whom I gave half the meat, were very grateful. I proceeded to my base camp at the mouth of the Mavaca River, about two hours up the Orinoco from Ocamo, when the plane left for Caracas carrying the precious blood samples. I gave the remaining half of the tapir to the Bisaasi-teri, who were likewise grateful for this bounty.

Neel decided to leave one of his Ph.D. students with me for several weeks while he accompanied the other members of his medical group to the Parima Mountains, where New Tribes missionaries would help him by translating for the various members of the group.

The student, Ryk Ward, was from New Zealand and was working on his doctoral degree in human genetics under Neel's supervision. Ryk wanted to travel with me and get some additional blood samples from a group of Shamatari (Mishimishimaböwei-teri) we had missed on our first trip to their village a year or so earlier. When Ryk learned I was going back up the Mavaca to try to contact the Iwahikoroba-teri he wanted to accompany me and collect blood samples from them. Neel immediately approved of this plan before he left for Parima because it meant that he would have two teams collecting blood samples at the same time.

I didn't think it was a good idea to show up in an uncontacted Yanomamö group and immediately begin sticking needles into their arms. By then, however, the Iwahikoroba-teri were probably aware of who I was and that I usually came with people who collected blood samples. The Iwahikoroba-teri regularly visited the Mishimishimaböwei-teri and exchanged news with them about this strange foreigner called *Shaki*, almost certainly including information about blood sampling.

I thought it over and decided that blood sampling would not constitute a problem for the trip into Iwahikoroba-teri because I always asked whether they were willing to provide blood samples for payment in *madohe*. They could always say no, and we would therefore not take samples.

I easily found several Yanomamö guides who were not only willing to come with me but seemed enthusiastic. We left on February 6 for Iwahikoroba-teri. My companions were Ward and four Bisaasi-teri men, one of whom had been in the original hunting party that accidentally ran into the Iwahikoroba-teri two months earlier.

We traveled up the Mavaca River in my large dugout canoe with a 33-horsepower outboard motor—a motor that was considerably more powerful than the 18-horsepower outboard motor I normally used. I carried my light aluminum boat and a smaller motor on top of the large dugout. We camped once on the banks of the Mavaca and, the next day, reached the mouth of *Örata Kä u* ("Jaguar River") not far below the place I used to begin my walk into Mishimishimaböwei-teri in 1968, when I made first contact with them.

We pulled the dugout a few yards into the *Örata Kä u* and unloaded what we would take with us: the blood-collecting equipment, food, our hammocks, and a few trade goods. We didn't know how far it was to their village so we left the bulkier trade goods. We would have the Iwahikoroba-teri accompany us back to the canoe, where I would pay them with these trade goods.

The following is a nearly verbatim transcription from my 1971 fieldbook:

We set off this morning (February 7, 1971) at 10:00 AM from the mouth of the *örata-u*, a few minutes above our camp. We managed to reduce our equipment down to three packs and one Styrofoam carton, but the packs are very heavy. In addition, Ryk and I each have a small side bag. The

Yanomamö managed to stick us with about 15 pounds of plantains each, which bounced around on our sides all day and were a nuisance to carry.

Our progress was slow. Ryk had a sunburn, so I carried his pack until 12:30, when we hit a large trail. Then I gave the pack to Koaseedema, who is our chief guide. He is the one who made personal contact with a *heniyomou* (an overnight hunting) party of Iwahikoroba-teri a few months ago. Shadadama was with him [on that trip]. He was to take us to the trail where he made contact, but unfortunately, he didn't tell me very clearly where it was. Half way in on the first day's walk I learned it was somewhere near the Bookona-u bora [a waterfall]. As it turns out, it will take us two days to reach these falls according to the prediction Koaseedema is now making, when we could have done it very easily in one day from my first camp [from my previous aborted trip]. In addition, Makaiyoböwei käkö (a mountain) is said to be very close to their village. Thus, today we wandered way to the south of our objective. [My notebook includes at this point a hand-drawn map of where we were and where we wanted to go.]

February 8, 1971. Woke up at 6:15 but lay in the hammock until 7:00. My ankle is sore from yesterday's walk; I hope it holds out for the trip.

. . . .

Last night I got a charley-horse from walking all day—so I guess I'm getting some exercise. I do not look forward to the day's march—it will be quite a shock to get into my soaked, cold clothing after sleeping in dry, clean ones.

. . . .

We walked until we hit a large, transverse trail that ran from Mishi-mishimaböwei-teri to Iwahikoroba-teri. At 4:00 we ran into a fresh *yano* (a temporary hut) that had been used this very day. The coals in the ashes were still hot enough for us to kindle our fire from. We camped there for the night and ate dehydrated soup. The first two nights we had [wild] duck and *paruri* [wild turkey] respectively. My arm was itching so I washed with Ryk's Dial soap.

February 9, 1971. We were up and away by 8:30 and ran into fresh tracks heading in the opposite direction. Shortly after leaving our camp we ran into a large herd of *boshe* pigs. I shot at one but only wounded it. Re-rebawä killed one [with arrows] and we took the lower back and hind legs with us. [The Yanomamö] complained about having to carry the meat—they were already tired. . . .

We made only about 5 to 6 hours actual walking this day—the third day inland. About mid-day I began feeling a little itchy under my left arm and had Ryk take a look at it to see if he could see anything unusual. He said that there were several small pustules, but also a large area of raised welts—hives—under both armpits. I then noticed that they appeared also between my legs where they were rubbing [together]. We camped early, having come by *Bookona bora* [Bookona Falls] late in the afternoon. That was the place I turned back after the first day's march several weeks earlier! We had, after 3 days, succeeded only in getting slightly further than the 1st day's march of my earlier trip.

That evening I began to break out all over with very itchy hives. They appeared up and down my arms and on my stomach. I could watch them move. A small blister would appear, then another and another until nearly my entire skin was covered. Then they would grow into each other and become hard, inflamed welts that burned and itched intensely. The sensation was excruciating. I could do nothing but writhe in my hammock and grit my teeth. That night all I could do was drink the broth of the wild pig . . . the only meal I had all day. I took *a* pyrabenzamine [tablet] at the time we camped and another at bed time. I woke up during the night intensely thirsty and nauseated. Mokahereiböwä went down to the creek to get me some drinking water, a whole bowl of which I drank in one attempt—about a quart-and-a-half. The night seemed like an eternity. I was dizzy—perhaps from the two previous pyrabenzamine pills. In any event, sometime during the night I took another one to relieve the misery. That was an error. I was stoned and delirious all night. . . . I also had contracted diarrhea. I dozed that way until dawn, when I had to defecate again. I could only stagger a few yards from the shelter before I discovered how weak and dizzy I was. I had to lean against a tree to keep from falling. I nearly fainted. . . . I told Ryk and the Yanomamö to plan to spend the day there; I couldn't move.

A couple of hours later the Yanomamö woke me to tell me there were some Yanomamö in the distance, hunting. They wanted to know if I should call to them. I managed to shout a loud *"Habo!"* [Come over here!] At that, Koaseedema began shouting to them that 'we were all foreigners [*nabä*] and friendly.' Soon two young men [nervous but stoical] approached our camp and entered. They were nearly stark naked, their penises tied tautly to their waist strings, large wads of tobacco stuck into their lower lips. I sat up and managed to talk with them a few minutes. They were Iwahikoroba-teri and were seeing their first foreigner, a not very awe-inspiring sight at the time. I told them I was sick because *hekura* spirits sent by my enemies had sprinkled charms on me, causing me to be weak and delirious. I told them that my Yanomamö companions were tired from walking for two days with very little food.

They disappeared and came back within a few minutes with a man who I was later able to identify as Sebredowä, one of the big wheels in their village. They were camped a few hours away and were hunting wild turkeys (*paruri*). I sat up and chatted half-heartedly with them for a while and told them to come back at mid-day with fresh carriers. They nodded in agreement and disappeared silently into the jungle. I collapsed back into a fitful sleep, waking up at noon when I heard a large group of men approaching whence our earlier visitors came.

What happened next was something I will remember forever. Some 20 young men, as naked as the first two were, slowly entered our camp and stood silently in a semi-circle around us. Like the first two, they had only their bows and arrows with them. Their penises were tied to their waist strings like the first two. Their pudding-bowl haircuts and tonsures—small shaved spots on the crowns of their intensely black raven-colored hair—contrasted starkly with their exceptionally white skin. It was as if they had never spent any time on or near even a small river and therefore had never been exposed to the sun for any appreciable length of time. They looked almost ghostly, even slightly sinister in the diminished light of the interfluvial jungle. In a strange way they looked majestic. I was witnessing the last human participants in a world that was about to disappear forever. It was a moment that was both exhilarating . . . and sad.

I felt weak as hell and I was not enthusiastic about moving, but it was out of the question to remain there in the hammock. I got slowly to my feet, packed up and took down our tarps. The Iwahikoroba-teri just continued to stand there with mouths full of tobacco wads, staring passively at us, their upright bows and arrows clutched in their hands.

We left for their camp shortly after noon. I was very weak, but pleasantly surprised that I could walk without fainting, as I had done in the morning. Still, I had a dizziness that was unpleasant. We stopped twice for long rests—the second time I actually fell asleep for a few minutes. I also stopped to defecate water several times. At 3:00 we reached their camp in the woods, and they stepped aside for me to enter first. Ryk was behind me. We walked into the clearing and struck our visitor's pose, but keeping a sharp eye peeled. I had enough energy left to turn on my small Sony tape recorder . . . to document the sounds of 1st contact.

They were a bit terrified at me, and I was a little apprehensive about them, in view of the rumors of the previous year that they intended to kill me. (In 1970 the Mishimishimaböwei-teri told me that the Iwakikoroba-teri were angry with me because I had not visited them when I visited the Mishimishimaböwei-teri. They said they would kill me and take my trade goods.) It was a very unusual welcome—it seemed as if they didn't quite know what to do with us. For a while there were no men to greet us. At last a few older, braver ones came forward with bows and arrows, remained at a safe distance and began growling and howling at us. None was brave enough to intimidate [by pointing their arrows in our faces] or come close until an old man—Dokonawä—approached me cautiously with bow and arrows conspicuously at rest and began to speak softly to me to welcome me. They knew which one of us was *Shaki,* and they were looking at me. I asked him where I was to set up my hammock, and at that they seemed to be relieved. The men in the distance heard me and, without speaking, clacked their arrows against the house in the middle of the clearing. In it was a rather young but serious-looking man who had the poise and demeanor of a headman. He was lying in his hammock taking it all in, quietly observing our every movement. I walked over to the hut and sat in the hammock next to his. Ryk and the others followed, but the hut was so small that there wasn't enough room for both me and Ryk. I then asked if we could use the hut across the way, which seemed larger. They agreed. It was also too small and very low . . . as are all of their temporary *yano* huts. I then asked them who the headman was so I could have a large hut made. They pointed to the young man in the hut I just left. I walked across [the clearing] and addressed him as *shoriwä* [brother-in-law], whereupon he "indignantly" cautioned me against using this kinship term, inviting me instead to call him younger brother.

I was pleased that he wanted to maximize kinship and friendship and immediately called him *owas* [my younger brother] to the approving clicks and hisses of the others. I asked him if he would have a large hut made for me. He barked out the command and very quickly several young men dashed off into the woods, one of them carrying a Brazilian-made machete. They reappeared in a few minutes with some large poles and vines for the hut. By then I had crawled back into my hammock in a state of near exhaustion and delirium. I vaguely remember the sounds of machetes hacking away at the poles and Mokaheriböwä laughing to himself at how clumsy they were with their dull machetes. Later, Ryk and Rerebawä put up our tarps and I went over and strung my hammock in the new hut. Someone had made a fire in it, and there was no way for me to hang my hammock without getting close to the fire, so I just resigned myself to my fate and lay there, roasting and half unconscious. I took a pyrabenzamine, the 3rd to the last one remaining.

I had eaten only a bowl of soup and a small piece of chocolate for two days. I told the Iwahikoroba-teri that I was sick and would "make friends" (*nohimou*) with all of them in the morning. They agreed that that was appropriate. I then fell asleep—into a very deep, restful sleep, waking only periodically for a few moments.

I did not wake up fully until dawn. I was very weak and very tired, but feeling good enough to chat with the Iwahikoroba-teri. I explained to the young headman what I was there for. I had advised Ryk a few minutes earlier to eat quickly and prepare to draw some blood samples.

[Here I skip over a long section of my notes on how the genealogies and names I had collected before getting to Iwahikoroba-teri were useless because of the Yanomamö name taboo . . . the names were in fact accurate, but I couldn't use them aloud. I had to rely, for identifying them, on numbers I put onto their arms with a felt tip marker and putting the same number on the Polaroid photos I then took of each individual. I could later have other informants tell me their names from the photographs and match them to my genealogies.]

I had enough strength to only number about thirty people before returning to and collapsing in my hammock. The Polaroid shots were next to useless [because of the poor light in the jungle], but they will later help me match the people to the 35mm shots I also took at the same time. Ryk had sampled two or three by the time I came back, so I paid them immediately, and lay back down again. I fell asleep for a while, and Ryk called to me to number more people. I still had diarrhea and had to relieve myself at least four times during the morning. I gave up trying to number people by [the numbers on] my genealogy. I numbered to 75 before growing too weak to continue, and had to lie down again. I started to itch all over and began perspiring intensely. The blisters began to appear on my arms and stomach again and I almost went insane with the pain and itching. I had to take another pyrabenzamine, the second-to-last one. Within a half hour the itching began to subside and the welts on my body started to disappear. In an hour I felt almost normal, but weak and dizzy from the pill, and very sleepy. [The pyrabenzamine pills] seemed to distort my time perspective— things seemed to last forever. On the trail the day before, I recall looking at my watch several times at what I thought was at least ½ hour intervals— but the hand had barely moved two or three minutes.

I dozed for a while. When I woke up Ryk was nearly out of people to sample and I mustered enough energy to begin numbering more. By then they had lost some of their timidity and the women began talking to me—I had called one of them "little sister" and that delighted them, so all began to call me "older brother." With that, I was able to number them all, up to 150. I missed a few babies, but not many. Ryk took blood samples from 133 people, so we got nearly 100% of the available people, mostly adults. They were separate from Hiakama's group, which was not far away from where we were. Hiakama's group is on the south side of the Washäwä-u, but I didn't know how large it was.

[A section of my notes has been eliminated here.]

Thus, on the night of the 11th we slept again with the Iwahikoroba-teri. I was feeling quite good until late in the afternoon, when Ryk was just finishing the blood sampling. I was worried that the hives might return. Sure enough I began itching and had to take a half of a pyrabenzamine, the last one I had. The pill seemed to have no effect on me, and the itching continued to grow worse, so I took the other half. This left nothing for the trip back—a very grim prospect. I imagined myself arriving at Ocamo, bloated up from the rash after having floated all night in excruciating pain. The whole pill worked and I fell asleep. But I woke up at 3:00 AM and tossed and turned until 5:30 AM when I began packing. I woke Ryk and the others and we were ready to go at 6:00 AM on the morning of the 12th.

February 12, 1971. The young headman [Börösöwä] asked me if I wanted him to accompany me back to my canoe and I assured him that I did since he seemed to be very knowledgeable. The day before, I took a half-hour or so to check some bearings with him on rivers and gardens, and he was amazed that I knew the names of so many of them in the area. The others were also amazed, especially when I began asking about old abandoned gardens that the younger fellow did not know about. At one point an older man jumped from his hammock in wild excitement, frustrated that the young guy didn't know where some of these places were. He rushed out to me and pointed to all of them.

We made a forced march on the 12th, stopping only very briefly and very seldom. The trail was very good for the first 3 hours—it was the same one we had taken into their camp. I knew before I even left camp that I would be strong on the trail that day, for when I rubbed my legs the muscles were hard and taut from the walk in, and the little food I had the night before had given my body a sufficient amount of energy. My first few steps assured me that I could take the marathon walk and my ankle felt rested. I guessed that I had lost about five pounds in the four previous days.

After about four hours we came to a spot where we rested. The young headman then told me from here on we would head straight for the mouth of the [Jaguar] river and we called for the more experienced men to come forward and *baröwo*—to lead the way on the trail. A particularly stocky and athletic man came forward and, without hesitating, plunged into the thicket, busting twigs [with his hands] as he went. There were at least 20 men with us. The next five and a half hours were pretty miserable, for we went through swamps up to our knees in mud, but more disagreeable, though, were the very low trees and brambles that hooked onto every part of your body.

We began our dead-reckoning at a spot where Bookona bora was audible, a spot that I reached in one day's walk a few weeks earlier.

At 4:30 PM we reached our canoe. The river had gone down at least two feet. I immediately took a refreshing bath in the Örata river with soap, and drank deeply of its clear, refreshing water. I took my own guides and equipment down to our camp, leaving the Iwahikoroba-teri sitting there until I came back with the machetes. Wakewä wanted to have me give his rags (clothing) to them, which I absolutely refused to do.

They assured me they would cut a trail to the Mavaca in ten days time so I could reach them without having to sleep en route from the river to their village. They are to mark the spot—at Boremaböwei-u—with an arrow shaft stuck into the bank, a sign I could not miss, and a very friendly gesture on their part.

I had planned on having the moon to light the way for us, but the sky was clouding up. I had some peanut butter and crackers before starting the motor on my canoe. We had enough daylight to get about an hour and a half to two hours downstream.

Just before dark I hit several logs with the foot of the motor and cracked the transom—the thick, flat, hand-hewn board onto which the motor is secured to the bongo [a large dugout canoe]. Then, before I knew what was happening, we were sitting right on top of two partially submerged tree trunks, high and dry. It took us a half-hour to get off. It was then that I noticed that the transom was so loose that the motor was about to break off. I told Ryk I couldn't take a chance—we might hit another sunken log and rip the whole back of the canoe out. So, we began floating and it began to rain. The moon never materialized.

Sometime about midnight Rerebawä shot at a caiman along the riverbank with one of my shotguns and it jumped into the water. We pulled up next to it and saw it with our flashlights lying under about a foot of water, refusing to surface. It was very big as *iwäs* [caiman] go—seven or eight feet long. Rerebawä got onto land and we shined our lights on it for a while. Finally it moved up and surfaced; I shot it in the head with my shotgun at five feet distance and it went wild, stood on its tail and began thrashing in every direction. I put in another cartridge and shot him again, and he rose up a second time, even more furious. Rerebawä got out of its way and Ryk seemed petrified as the monster began heading toward the canoe. I shot it yet a third time and still it would not die. Finally, it calmed down enough for Rerebawä to chop it behind the head and then at the base of its tail with a machete. It took two people to pull it into the canoe. It was big.

February 13, 1971. We floated with the current almost until dawn, when we were so exhausted that I just had to sleep for an hour. We pulled/

paddled our dugout under a mud cliff to try to get out of the rain, but were not very successful at avoiding the rain. Then we went downstream until we hit a sandbar, where I made a campfire and erected a very poor tipi of tarps and a few poles I found. I lay down in the drizzle under the tarps in my poncho. It was about 4:00 AM. The Yanomamö kept wrapping themselves in my tarp until they had appropriated nearly all of it. I found myself lying in the open, in the rain. I managed to get about 30 minutes of sleep. At about 5:00 AM I got up and Wakewä, Ryk and I began packing my aluminum *voladora*, which we had now reached, for the trip down to Mavaca.

I noticed that my lower lip had swollen up, as had my feet—the only two parts of my body that had not been affected with hives until now.

We set off in the *voladora* at 6:10 AM, in a very dense fog. It was nearly 7:00 AM before it was light enough to see through the mist and fog and a drizzle pelted us for the first three or four hours. I was shivering all the way downstream. We reached Mavaca at about 10:00 AM.

I took Ryk downstream to the Salesian mission at Ocamo, where he got on a small plane with the blood samples and took them out to Caracas.

The Yanomamö later told me that a *hekura* spirit sent by an enemy shaman had sprinkled "fire" onto my skin, and that is what caused me to break out with hives and itching. None of my Yanomamö companions on this trip developed this condition, although some of them said they later had diarrhea.

Disturbing News in 1972

On my next field trip to the Yanomamö I was given some alarming information by the older men in Mishimishimaböwei-teri when I visited them again. The information made me physically ill.

They told me in some detail that during my visit to Iwahikoroba-teri several senior men there had decided to kill me while I slept. They were instigated by a man named Boraböwä, who was supported by two of his adult brothers. They had attempted to crawl up to my hammock as I slept and smash my skull with an ax. They tried several times to do this, but I kept waking up and, when I did, I would shine my flashlight around

the camp as many Yanomamö had advised me to do when I visited a
new village I had not been to before. When I did this, Boraböwä and his
brothers realized that I was *moyawe*—alert, suspicious, and wary. I also
had my shotgun next to me. They had never seen one before but knew it
was a lethal weapon and they feared it.

There was apparently a difference of opinion within the village: the
young headman, Börösöwä, and his close male allies wanted to accept
me peaceably, but Boraböwä and his followers wanted to kill me because I was associated with the Bisaasi-teri and lived among them some
seven years by now. The Bisaasi-teri were their mortal enemies and they
wanted to kill as many of them as they could. Even the *nabä* who lived
with them was fair game. I also learned from the Patanowä-teri, who
joined the Iwahikoroba-teri on a raiding party at about this time, that
they made a *no owä* (an effigy used in the *wayu itou* ceremony) of me
and ceremoniously shot it full of arrows to symbolically kill me, further
evidence that they wanted me dead. When I expressed some anger at the
Patanowä-teri for participating in a *wayu itou* where I was the symbolic
victim, they vigorously assured me that they only went along with it.
Most certainly, *they* would not have shot me if they had seen me, they
said, but opined that the Iwahikoroba-teri *might* have. I kept the name
Boraböwä in my memory just in case I visited the Iwahikoroba-teri again.

11

Yanomamö Origins and Their Fertile Crescent

My field trips to the Venezuelan Yanomamö eventually resulted in stays in many different villages in different geographical zones. During these visits I collected meticulous data on the life histories of every person and their genealogies going back in time as far as the oldest people could recall. From these data I can fairly accurately reconstruct village histories for approximately 150 to 200 years. This was tedious, sometimes very boring work that, at any given time, seemed to yield just disconnected shreds of information. But patterns gradually emerged—for example, directions that people seemed to move—from the stories the old people told me. They passed their histories down to their children as they had learned them from their own parents and grandparents.

The overall picture was a fascinating story of the Yanomamö diaspora out of the Parima Highlands into the lower-lying regions to their south that offered new opportunities as well as new constraints affecting village size, leadership patterns, intensity of warfare, population growth, village fissioning, and the gradual development of increased political complexity as villages grew in size and were unable to fission into smaller villages. Key to everything was food and the concern for political security in a milieu of chronic warfare and each group's ability or lack of ability to remain in the more desirable area.

Yanomamö Slash-and-Burn-Cultivation

In the region where I worked the Yanomamö were similar to other tribal slash-and-burn cultivators in the Amazon Basin and, for that matter, all over the world. Slash-and-burn or "swidden" agriculture is found among tribesmen in all corners of the globe where the climate permits cultivation. There is a large anthropological literature on this practice. It is, as most anthropologists view cultural types, the mode of economic production that marked the transition from Paleolithic hunter/gatherers to full-blown dependence on agriculture and domesticated animals.

Swidden cultivators usually follow a general pattern. In Yanomamö practice, they select a forested site, fell the large timbers with axes, let them dry for several weeks to several months, and then burn the larger timbers and the branches attached to them. The burned timbers add ash to the soil, fertilizing it. Unburned larger logs are used for firewood. The women split off pieces of firewood daily and take them to the village to cook with, to keep warm at night, and to illuminate their living areas.

After the initial burning, both men and women plant their crops—mostly plantains, bananas, and tubers—among and between the fallen trees.

In most regions swidden agriculture follows a fairly regular pattern such that old areas re-grow and then are eventually cleared once again following a long fallow period. The Yanomamö were one of the few peoples in the world that were still practicing "pioneering" slash-and-burn agriculture when I studied them. They rarely cleared the same area twice because they normally moved a considerable distance away from their previous gardens, usually because they were pushed out by enemies. Warfare plays a significant role in the long-term settlement patterns of all Yanomamö groups.

Yanomamö pioneering slash-and-burn agriculture is comparable to the practices of, for example, the Iban of Borneo (Sarawak) who were described as historically having open, unoccupied frontiers into which they could expand.

In addition, the Yanomamö are somewhat unusual in the Amazon Basin in that their *primary* subsistence crops are bananas and plantains—cooking bananas of several varieties. Both of these crops were introduced into the New World after Columbus, after about 1500 AD. These introduced crops spread very rapidly thereafter, but so far as I know, no Amazon Basin tribesmen approach the Yanomamö in the degree to which they depend on banana and plantain crops.

All the Yanomamö groups I've visited—now some sixty-plus different villages in both Venezuela and Brazil—are highly dependent on cultivated foods, bananas and plantains in particular, but their food crops also include many indigenous Amazonian crops like maize, manioc, and a variety of tubers. They most likely cultivated some, possibly all, of these native crops well before bananas and plantains reached them. Their current economic emphasis probably goes back at least two hundred to 250 years in the histories of most Yanomamö groups . . . perhaps even longer.

Early casual visitors to the Yanomamö region thought that the Yanomamö were hunters and gatherers. One reason most observers believe that cultivation is, historically speaking, relatively "new" in their culture is that the Yanomamö have a technology—their collective repertoire of material items—that is more consistent with a hunting/gathering people than it is with an agricultural people. For example, they have so few material possessions that the members of even a large village—say some 150 people—can pack up and carry everything they own within a few minutes, completely and quickly vacating the village, effectively "abandoning" it. An archaeologist might easily and erroneously conclude that such an abandoned site was left by "typical" hunter/gatherers.

The men have just a bow and several arrows; a bamboo "quiver" to hold extra arrow points, which they carry on a neck cord behind their shoulders; a fire drill attached to the quiver; a small light hammock—made of split vines—that crumples and folds down to a small package not much bigger than their bamboo quiver; and perhaps a machete (or a piece of a machete). Male clothing consists of a few cotton strings—one to tie their penises to their waist string; string "bracelets" around their ankles, biceps, and wrists; and sometimes a string that is worn on the upper torso that crosses at the chest and goes over the shoulders and crosses in the middle of the back.

Women's possessions are only slightly more numerous and bulky—several kinds of baskets, also made from split vines. One kind is a shallow basket—like a platter—used primarily to serve food. The other kind of basket is much larger, a densely plaited and deep pack basket about 24 to 30 inches high and 18 to 24 inches in diameter. These larger baskets are used to carry firewood, garden produce like plantains, and large quantities of seasonal wild palm fruits from the jungle when these ripen. Women's clothing is basically like the men's: thin cotton strings around the wrists and ankles and, less commonly than men, the string that is worn on the upper torso that crosses at the chest and goes over the shoulders and crosses in the middle of the back. In addition to these strings, sometimes—usually on the occasion of a feast—girls and younger women wear a plaited cotton apron that covers their pubic area but is open at the back.

But the "garden produce" for the most part involves plants that have no seeds—just a lot of immediately perishable things like banana peelings, which decay quickly. Thus the several "garbage" piles just outside the houses in a typical *shabono* would yield very little preservable material, other than some animal skulls and bones, to cause an archaeologist who visited a Yanomamö village while it was occupied to realize just how dependent these people are on cultivated foods. Indeed, the relative abundance of animal bones after the village was abandoned would probably cause another archaeologist, who hadn't visited the village before it was abandoned, to overemphasize the importance of game animals—hunting—in their economy.

When I first arrived, most families also had a heavy clay pot used to boil food. It was pointed at the thick bottom and the 10- to 15-inch flaring sides tapered to almost nothing at the top edge. It was poorly fired, very fragile, and considerable care had to be taken when it was transported or even moved a few feet to cook food. The men were often reluctant to let the women use or even move the fragile pots—lest they break them in their alleged clumsiness. On camping trips the pots were invariably transported inside a large pack basket with vine hammocks used as padding, or with hand-plaited cotton hammocks. Or they were often left behind, hidden in the forest, when people left their *shabonos* for short periods of time. The pots would have been the only unusual item in a Yanomamö archaeological site, since shards of pottery usually imply some kind of sedentism and, in turn, sedentism implies food cultivation. Such an archaeological site would be ambiguous because the single unusual artifact, crude pottery, could have been left by typical hunter-gatherers that had sporadic contact with cultivators and had acquired a few pieces of pottery from them. Very little else would suggest that the Yanomamö were highly dependent on cultivated foods.

Within a few years of starting my fieldwork in 1965, I found their indigenous clay pots were rapidly replaced by aluminum cooking pots, even in the most remote villages. The aluminum pots came from either the Ye'kwana Indians or, more frequently, the missionaries, who gave them away in very large numbers. Constantly shifting trade networks quickly brought the pots to more remote villages. It is doubtful that any Yanomamö today have clay pots—or even remember how to make them anymore—an "art" and memory of that art that was lost in the brief span of fifty years, well within the span of the fieldwork of a single anthropologist.

When the clay pots broke, the men saved the larger pieces and used them either as a surface on which they ground their hallucinogenic snuff, or as "toasting platters" on which they prepared small manioc cakes about the size of large pancakes. For this they placed the larger pieces of broken pottery on the hot coals of a hearth and toasted the manioc cakes on *both* sides, very different from how these manioc cakes are produced in most other Amazonian tribes, who cook them on only one side.

Finally, there are a few optional material items in all villages, things that are so easy to make or produce that they are sometimes left behind when the villagers move. These include small plaited fire-fans, hollow bamboo tubes (called *toras*) men use to blow hallucinogenic drugs into each others' nostrils, gourds (or half gourds) used to hold water or as spoons, small cotton aprons worn by young girls, and other easily replaceable items.

In short, Yanomamö material culture—their worldly possessions—is more typical of Amazon Basin hunters and gatherers like, for example,

Yanomamö clay pots

the Siriono of Bolivia, than it is of Amazon Basin gardeners, who usually have elaborately decorated, well-fired pottery, a more elaborate food-processing tool kit, carved wooden objects, woven and decorated cotton garments, and dugout canoes that can be as long as sixty feet and can transport scores of people and their possessions along large and small waterways of the Amazon Basin.

But despite their limited repertoire of material items, in the Yanomamö villages where I worked in the lowlands, the people were highly dependent on their immense gardens. As elevation increased in the foothills, Yanomamö gardens seemed to become smaller—as did their villages.

The Yanomamö cultivate a very large number of varieties of both cooking plantains and eating bananas—which is basically how plantains are distinguished from bananas: you normally cook the former when they are green but eat the latter when they are ripe. The "banana soup" the Yanomamö use during feasts is actually "plantain soup" since it is prepared from ripe plantains. Most villagers where I worked had at least a half-dozen varieties of plantains and another half-dozen of bananas, and the Yanomamö, in general, over their entire distribution, must have upwards of 50 varieties of plantains and bananas. While these were all introduced into the Americas after 1500, the Yanomamö probably culti-vated a variety of indigenous crops well before 1500, particularly the two widely distributed Amazon basin varieties of manioc (cassava): "sweet" manioc and "bitter" manioc, the latter requiring the removal by leach-ing and squeezing out of a toxin, cyanic acid, before it is safe to eat. In addition to manioc, the Yanomamö also cultivated maize and a number of different potato-like tubers (*kabiromö* and *ohina*) indigenous to the Amazon Basin as well as sweet potatoes, various species of gourds, arrow cane, cotton, papaya, tobacco, the red pigment used to decorate their bodies (*Bixa orellana*), several varieties of hot peppers, and several spe-cies of "magical" plants.

The various Ecological Zones shown in the graph on page 302 indi-cate that village size is also a function of both elevation and the degree to which warfare is more likely to play a role in the politics of intervillage social relationships. In the lowlands the threat of war makes leaders seek out and find reliable allies, which necessitates holding elaborate feasts for them and this requires increased garden size in order to produce a "surplus" of plantains and bananas that are gluttonously consumed by the visitors in these feasts.

One region of the Yanomamö area far to the north was, according to a few evangelical missionaries I spoke with in the 1960s, populated by extremely small groups they called the Kobariwä-teri, who seemed to be much more dependent on hunting/gathering than the Yanomamö I knew. The missionaries said these people were more nomadic and had much smaller gardens that were barely visible from the air. The Kobariwä-teri were very poorly known at that time, and I am not sure if anyone has yet managed to study the small groups in this rugged area. If the frag-mentary reports are true, the Kobariwä-teri might still be living under circumstances that *all* Yanomamö lived under around two hundred or so years ago.

The Yanomamö Diaspora

I use the word *diaspora* advisedly to emphasize that a Yanomamö village is more of a temporary, plastic, and ephemeral *process* than some rigid and fixed entity that remains the same over long periods of time: village size and composition are in a constant state of flux because of the politics of upheaval, internal dissent, and fissioning.

The map below shows the general direction of Yanomamö migrations for approximately the past 150 years. Seven major populations are shown here, indicated by A–G. I established these migration patterns through interviews with Yanomamö informants on visits to villages in each area. What is not apparent from this map is that the Yanomamö have moved out of higher mountainous terrain into lower-lying adjacent areas.

The border between Venezuela and Brazil consists of a chain of low mountains known as the Parima Highlands or Parima Mountains. The Parima rises to elevations of approximately 2,500 to 2,800 feet and, in

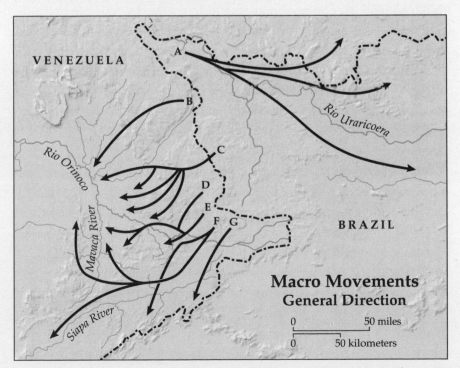

Yanomamö migrations from the 6th edition of my Yanomamö monograph, p. 82: Migration Patterns of Seven Clusters of Villages

the higher elevations includes some treeless savannas. The border also defines major watersheds: all rivers that flow to the east in the map eventually merge into the Amazon River and those that flow to the west drain into the Orinoco River. There is one exception, one geographical anomaly: the Orinoco splits into two parts in Venezuela's Amazonas territory and each part flows into the Atlantic by its own separate route, one part by way of the Amazon River, the other by way of the Orinoco River.

It was not until 1990 that I developed the final version of the geographical model shown below. I was able to arrive at this conception only after I had had opportunities to fly over the area and only after accurate maps that were based on satellite imagery began to appear. The ecological zones model below helps explain geographical and ecological aspects of recent population movements of large numbers of Yanomamö groups and sheds a great deal of light on why some villages are able to become larger and politically more complex.

The Ecological Zones Model is schematic in the sense that it distorts the horizontal aspects of Yanomamö terrain—the several regions (A, B, C, D, etc.) vary significantly in width and detail, depending on the location of each cross section of Yanomamö territory. The model best fits a cross section along a north-south axis passing approximately through the village of Patanowä-teri. (The vertical aspect showing elevation is more accurate than the more schematic width areas.) The model shows rea-

Ecological Zones Model

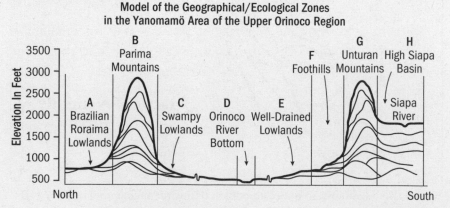

Model of the Geographical/Ecological Zones
in the Yanomamö Area of the Upper Orinoco Region

sonably well that different regions lie at different elevations and present different ecological, geographical, political, and economic opportunities and constraints to the Yanomamö groups living in them.

Once the Yanomamö left the Parima highlands and established themselves in the lowlands, some groups were forced by their enemies back into higher elevations in a different chain of mountains to the south, a group of mountains that lies immediately to the north of the Siapa River. This chain of mountains is called Sierra Unturan on some Venezuelan maps. As explained earlier, this narrow escarpment defines the boundary between the Orinoco watershed and the Siapa watershed, which eventually flows into the Amazon.

The historical origins of the populations I studied almost certainly lie in the Parima Highlands. The dozen or so villages that I knew best were from two different groups, each of which I could trace back to a single earlier village whence they fissioned within the past one hundred years.

People in these villages spoke slightly different but closely related dialects. One group was the Shamatari (Southern Yanomamö) and the other Namowei-teri. Their origins and migration routes are shown on page 301 as D, E, and F.

The key informants I spoke with in the 1960s were very old at that time and could reliably trace their political histories and genealogies back only to villages that were already approaching the banks of the Orinoco, that is, back to about 1850. In other words, their immediate ancestors had already left the Parima Highlands prior to 1850. Informant accounts of their settlement histories earlier than 1850 blend into the "mythical" past and are less reliable.

Two sites kept cropping up in their oral accounts. One was a mountain called Aramamisi käkö, where the Shamatari are said to have come from (shown on page 5 on the north side of the upper Orinoco River). The other was a place called Konata, where Namowei-teri informants said their ancestors originated. Konata lies just west of Aramamisi käkö. All informants said their ancestors came from farther to the northeast, in the direction of the Parima Highlands. They insisted that the Yanomamö already had "big gardens" at that time. In other words, my oldest informants in the mid-1960s believed that the Yanomamö had always been slash-and-burn cultivators and had no recollection of a time that this was not the case.

In the Parima Mountains, narrow strips of jungle immediately adjacent to the small rivers are called gallery forests. Yanomamö gardens in the highlands are cleared in these gallery forest areas.

Importance of Political Security in Yanomamö Culture

Contemporary villages in the Parima Highlands are usually located in or near these gallery forests, frequently just outside them where the open savanna offers clear vision for a long distance and the residents can see enemies approaching long before they reach them. Even here intervillage warfare is relatively frequent and the villages are often surrounded by stout palisades. As in all Yanomamö areas, political security appears to have been a major concern for a relatively long time. For example, when I first visited villages in 1967 at Parima B (the location in the highlands where a New Tribes mission was established in the 1960s), the local missionaries were already concerned about food shortages in the Yanomamö villages that were beginning to gravitate to their mission. By 1994 the food shortage was even more critical: there were over five hundred Yanomamö living near this one New Tribes mission!

This is a very large population concentration for the Yanomamö. The missionaries had turned to agricultural consultants to help solve the growing Yanomamö food problem there, a problem caused by choosing political security over subsistence needs. The missionaries explained to me that Yanomamö groups kept coming closer and closer to the mission to avoid raiding from other Yanomamö groups on their periphery, mostly from adjacent villages in Brazil whose residents were acquiring shotguns, first from missionaries, but later, in the late 1980s, from Brazilian illegal miners known as *garimpeiros*. The Yanomamö were willing to suffer hunger for the increased safety and security that the mission seemed to provide.

As one moves west from the Parima Highlands to lower elevations, one crosses rugged foothills that are very difficult to traverse. This area is occupied by villages that have left the highlands and are moving toward the more productive lower elevations, but their attempts are resisted by groups who have already established a foothold in the more desirable regions at lower elevations that do not flood.

As elevation decreases further, several important general changes seem to occur. First, villages become larger. Second, intervillage hostilities appear to increase, that is, warfare seems to become more frequent, more chronic, and more costly in terms of deaths. Third, the Yanomamö gradually become more dependent on cultivation because periodic "feasting" with allies appears to have begun. This means that gardening must do more than provide subsistence; it must also provide surplus cultivated food to feed large numbers of guests who arrive en masse from an allied village and who might stay for up to a week. Thus, gardens must become larger to accommodate the food costs of political alliances. In a sense the Yanomamö subsistence economy starts to become a political economy.

Lying at yet lower elevations are the river bottoms surrounded by lowlands, an area where gardening is more productive, where villages become even larger, and conflict between villages increases further. Although the lowlands seem, at first glance, to be more desirable places, living there entails a considerable degree of risk to cultivators. The river bottoms are subject to unpredictable but devastating flooding near larger rivers like the Orinoco and some of its larger tributaries, such as the Mavaca, Ocamo, and Padamo. I know of many groups whose gardens have been ruined periodically by floods during years of especially intense rains. I recall one year during my early field research actually being able to paddle my canoe right up to the entrance to the *shabono* I was visiting! The *shabono* is usually located on the highest ground, often within the garden. Needless to say, the gardens of the members of this village were underwater and their crops ruined. Hardship and hunger usually follow when the gardens are flooded. The residents then have to break up into smaller groups, move to higher terrain, and depend more extensively on wild foods and on garden produce obtained from their allied neighbors. Herein lies one of the more important aspects of intervillage alliances: food sharing between allied villages in times of privation.

Thus, the area labeled on page 302 as Zone D, "Orinoco River Bottom," is avoided because of unpredictable flooding and also because the Yanomamö cannot cross large rivers without canoes.

The most desirable area in the Ecological Zones model is "Well Drained Lowlands," Region E. Most of the lowland areas here are far enough inland from and at a slightly higher elevation than the larger rivers, so that the risk of flooding is greatly reduced. The most desirable lowland areas are gently sloping, well drained, and embrace a fairly large expanse. Food collecting and hunting are generally very productive in these areas and, combined with food cultivation, provide an excellent economic adaptation, one that spreads subsistence risks over a broader range of calorically productive subsistence activities.

What Yanomamö Land Might Tell Us About the Origin of Civilization

Even small amounts of food production confer military advantage on "transitional" societies. They can grow slightly larger in population size and therefore better resist incursions and potentially disastrous raids by their neighbors.

Jared Diamond argued that agriculture was "the worst mistake" in the history of the human race. I can agree with him only for the major civilizations, which depend heavily on starchy monocrop agriculture such as cultivation of rice, maize, potatoes, wheat, etc. However, the Yanomamö type of economic adaptation is an exception to Diamond's argument: food production enabled them to achieve larger, more defensible villages while retaining variety in their diets because of the ability to hunt and gather wild foods.

This Yanomamö type of economic adaptation was a crucial step in the development of more complex societies. People like the Yanomamö, historically speaking, moved step by subtle step from small-scale farming in order to maximize group size to thwart their aggressive neighbors. This historical/evolutionary direction ended, for many societies, with near complete dependence on just one or two staple cultivated foodstuffs that possibly lacked sufficient nutritional variability to maintain good health. Perhaps choosing the security of village size over the benefit of more nutritional variety is what drove people in Egypt, Mesopotamia, India, China, Mexico, and the Andes to take the nutritiously maladaptive step of cultivating only a few food crops.

The lowland area of Yanomamöland is flat enough that intervillage visiting is frequent because walking is easier. For the same reason intervillage raiding is also easier, so villages tend to be more widely spaced just in case the neighboring village turns hostile. This is especially significant in terms of adaptation to the social and political environments. Villages in these well-drained lowlands also claim and defend much larger areas of the lowlands than they need purely for subsistence. They create safe havens into which they can retreat if wars become frequent and costly (in deaths). These safe havens are areas they temporarily go to at a safe distance from their permanent *shabonos* to avoid raids. The sociopolitical strategy characterizing these movements is different from, but easily confused with, fighting over scarce resources such as cultivable land, where hunting and collecting are also highly productive. These are two different issues at the theoretical level: one view argues that human conflict, including war, reduces to somatic survival (food, nutrition). The other argues that human behavior and conflict are driven by an even more compelling issue, individual survival and the survival of one's kin group (close kin). When the bombs start falling—or the arrows—whom does one turn to for reliable support? Kinsmen, or the unknown strangers in the next valley over?

The "Fertile Crescent" of the Yanomamö Lowland

I did most of my fieldwork where there were at least three lowland regions south of the Orinoco River that comprised what we might call a Yanomamö fertile crescent. They were areas of expansive, gently sloping, well-drained lowlands where it was easy to clear gardens. They were characterized by an abundance of and a large variety of wild vegetable foods, game animals, and materials needed for *shabono* construction—especially roofing leaves, saplings, and vines (Zone "E" on page 302).

One of these special areas is the drainage of the Shanishani River, another is the upper reaches of the Washäwä and Örata rivers, and the third is the headwaters of the Mavaca River (see page 5).

When the first pioneering groups of Yanomamö entered this area over one hundred years ago their populations appear to have exploded. This region became the fertile crescent of Yanomamö culture, a veritable population pump that further dispersed the Yanomamö into the Siapa River basin and thence south into the headwaters of many of the rivers in Brazil's Amazonas State. I estimate that some 25 percent of all Yanomamö currently live in—or their parents or grandparents were born in—the villages whose members came from these three fertile crescent areas of Venezuela. Perhaps as many as 30 to 40 percent of the Brazilian Yanomamö are recent immigrants from this area and from the Parima Highlands, at least half of which lies in Venezuela. Many Yanomamö moved north and northeast into the Brazilian state of Roraima in very recent times.

The Shanishani kä u and Similar Micro-Niches in the Fertile Crescent

I was always surprised when I walked inland from the Orinoco River to villages located on or near the Shanishani River (near the village of Patanowä-teri in the map on page 5). At its mouth, where it drains into the Orinoco, this small river was always clogged with sandbars and fallen trees in the dry season, seemingly too shallow to navigate during *any* season. Yet upstream from there, even miles inland, the river seemed full of water, even in the dry season—almost enough water that one could ascend it in a small canoe. I even considered buying a small, collapsible boat for this purpose. It appeared to me that the adjacent terrain was bleeding its spill-off rainwater into the Shanishani, keeping the adjacent terrain relatively dry but the Shanishani full of water. I have never seen another small river in Yanomamöland that was impassable at its mouth yet potentially navigable by canoe in its middle and upper reaches. There was something very special and unusual about this river and the gently sloping lowlands it traversed and drained.

Several major Yanomamö populations passed through the Shanishani and the similar adjacent regions of this ecological zone. They made many gardens and *shabonos* here. The Namowei-teri occupied the easternmost portion of this area after about 1900 but, before they got there, several earlier populations had also been there—the Aramamisi-teri, a group that fissioned into what is now at least three major Yanomamö groups: the Karawatari, the Kohoroshitari, and the Shamatari. The first two multi-village groups are now located on the Brazilian side of the border far to the south, but several Shamatari villages I studied in this area might include large numbers of individuals who the others in the village claim are really Karawatari. One of my best Shamatari informants, an older man named Dedeheiwä, lived in Mishimishimaböwei-teri in the Mavaca headwaters and had many brothers and descendants through the male line there. He told me several times that he was actually an Aramamisi-teri as well as a Karawatari. Many of the gardens the Mishimishimaböwei-teri cleared where they lived during the past fifty years were at the same locations (and sometimes had the same names) of earlier gardens that the Karawatari originally cleared before they moved into and across the Siapa Basin and eventually into Brazil.

The fertile crescent area has had a long history of occupation by several major Yanomamö populations and through population growth has generated large numbers of villages. As we would expect, it has also been an area of comparatively high levels of warfare and violence.

Looking Back Up the Parima Mountains

Once migrating Yanomamö reached the fertile crescent area, their villages grew and subsequently fissioned. Initially the subgroups spread out within this desirable area, but as these groups grew and fissioned, not all of them could remain within the fertile crescent. Some of them were forced out of the area by their larger, more powerful neighbors, moving into the higher elevations of the foothills (Zone F on page 302), where conditions are harder due to the ruggedness of the terrain and the diminished resources.

It is a general rule in the biology of ecosystems that species variety and density diminish as elevation increases. Thus, as Yanomamö groups were forced to move higher up into the hills certain species of game animals and plants become less abundant—and some, like the caiman and tapir, are not found at all. In addition, it is much easier to clear gardens on relatively flat terrain in the lowlands than on hilly or mountainous terrain where fetching water and collecting firewood become energetically costlier tasks for both men and women.

Groups thus peripheralized try to get back into the lowlands, but their attempts are usually thwarted by the successful lowland occupants, whose villages are considerably larger. The peripheralized groups are sometimes forced to flee to even higher elevations, where making a living is even more difficult. Some are forced up the mountains separating the Orinoco drainage from the Siapa drainage (Zone G on page 302). It is clear from the village histories I collected that many groups crossed these mountains and moved into the Siapa Basin (Zone H on page 302). The Kohoroshitari and Karawatari did exactly this sometime in the recent past, perhaps as recently as 1900 to 1920. One large Shamatari group I visited in Brazil in 1995, the village of Abruwä-teri, moved to its location from the banks of the Siapa River in the early 1960s. They had fissioned from a village called Doshamosha-teri, presently located on the banks of the upper Siapa River. They had brothers and sisters still living in Doshamosha-teri and were extremely excited when I showed them Polaroid photographs of all the residents of Doshamosha-teri that I had taken some four years earlier. They could name all of the adults and tell me how they were related. In addition, they were sporadically visited by people from Doshamosha-teri, who lived several days' walk to the Abruwä-teri's northeast in Venezuela.

But the Siapa Basin is less desirable than the well-drained lowlands of the Orinoco Basin (Zone E on page 302) because important Yanomamö resources are less abundant. As I described earlier I was very surprised to discover that the Siapa River immediately south of the headwaters of the Shanishani River lies at an elevation of 1,800 feet, more than 1,200 feet higher than the Orinoco Basin at that latitude! Such a difference in elevation is very large for people who hunt, gather, and garden. Although I did not take an inventory of game animals the people here were hunting, I did notice that they ate snakes, which the lowland Yanomamö I had lived with *never* did. One man demonstrated his catch for me one day, a very large bushmaster, one of the most poisonous snakes in the Amazon Basin. The only other area I spent time in where the Yanomamö regularly ate snakes was in the Parima Highlands. There they also ate deer and jaguars—meat that the lowlanders I studied would find unpalatable, even a bit disgusting. It got much colder at night in the Siapa Basin because of the higher elevation. I had to wear my clothes, put on a wool sweater, use an insulated blanket, and sleep close to the hearth to keep warm at night. I also had to do these things when I visited villages in the Parima Highlands. There they also drape large banana leaves down from the *shabono* rafter poles to help retain warmth from the ever-tended hearth fires. But this practice also inhibited the escape of smoke, so in the mornings I smelled and felt like a partially cured Virginia ham.

Social Circumscription and Theories of Increasing Social Complexity

One of the first professional papers I presented at an anthropology meeting was an attempt to account for the reasons why some Yanomamö villages I was studying were larger, more warlike, and seemed to be politically more complex than the many other Yanomamö villages I had visited by 1968. I noted that villages tended to be larger and more warlike in what I call the fertile crescent. Headmen in these villages—the political leaders—were reluctant to move past or around neighbors on their periphery. I drew attention to the importance of the purely social component of their environment with regard to determinants of their overall settlement pattern strategies. This was an unusual theoretical distinction at the time because cultural-material theorists viewed the environment basically in terms of the material items found in it, not the social/political dimensions of the groups occupying it. I also noted that headmanship seemed to be more highly developed than in other areas. Although the Yanomamö fertile crescent was not sharply bounded by geographical barriers, the fact that the village leaders there were reluctant to leapfrog over neighboring groups suggested that these neighboring groups constituted, in effect, a kind of social wall or barricade impeding expansion. I argued that villages here were "socially" circumscribed, drawing a parallel to arguments first proposed by Robert L. Carneiro about the social and political effects of "environmental" circumscription in the Andean area.

Carneiro had earlier noted that societies that were environmentally circumscribed by mountains, deserts, and oceans, particularly in the western Andean area of Ecuador and Peru, eventually developed the political state. He argued that in these areas, the initial small communities of agriculturalists could simply retreat from neighbors in times of war and move elsewhere within the valley. Many Yanomamö groups do just this in their safe havens. As populations grew in Andean valleys, this option to move disappeared because the available land was used up. Over time, Carneiro observed, with increasing conflict and population growth, smaller communities were forced to amalgamate into fewer but larger communities for self-defense, a process that eventually culminated in the appearance of yet larger complex societies called chiefdoms, characterized by formal chiefs, hereditary rank, the appearance of specialized artisans, social classes, and the beginning of public works like temples and irrigation systems. Eventually one of the chiefdoms dominated the others by military conquest. Valley-wide political integration then took place: all outlying villages within the valley were now subordinate components in a larger political entity: the state was born. As these small states emerged in each valley, warfare *between* valleys began, culminating in the Inca Empire about 1000 AD. The Inca ultimately controlled an empire that ran 2,500 miles along the Andes Mountains.

Social circumscription contributes to increased political complexity by impeding population expansion and migration and forcing villages to deal with hostile neighbors by increasing village size and making alliances with some neighbors. For the Yanomamö fertile crescent region, populations were able to move westward while simultaneously remaining in the same kind of ecological niche—the more desirable lowlands.

Since 1968 I have done much more research on settlement patterns, village histories and size, social patterns, and, in particular, geography. Social circumscription could have only limited effects on the development of increased political complexity among the Yanomamö villages in the fertile crescent. Once the area of the Shanishani River had been filled with competing large villages, some of them left this desirable niche and moved into the basins of the Washäwä and Örata, thus relieving population pressure in the Shanishani Basin and reducing the effects of social circumscription. In turn, as these two new areas filled up, some of the groups then occupied the headwaters of the Mavaca—a similarly rich zone. From there they crossed the mountains into the Siapa Basin, moving southward across the high Siapa plateau and into Brazil, into the lowlands drained by affluents of the Amazon River like the Rio Negro. A few large villages remained in the high Siapa plateau, but these are very widely spaced, possibly because resources there are less abundant and less predictable.

In the early 1990s I collected some comparative sociopolitical data in eight villages that had been pushed out of the more desirable lowlands in the Shanishani drainage into the foothills and Unturan mountains separating the Orinoco and Siapa drainages. These are "refugee" villages, unable to successfully compete with the larger, more aggressive villages in the lowlands. Three of these eight villages have been pushed into higher elevations very recently and retain some statistical characteristics acquired in the lowlands (villages 71, 64, and 72 below). In general, these refugee villages are smaller, men have lower rates of polygynous marriage, there are fewer abducted women in these villages, and fewer men who are *unokais*—the honored men who have killed others.

The table below summarizes my findings, which support the social and political consequences of the general cultural-ecological model I just described. The average percent of abducted females in these villages that have been pushed out of the most desirable lowlands is 11.4 percent, and the average percent of *unokai* males is 22.3 percent. By comparison, in more desirable lowland villages approximately 17 percent of the women have been abducted and approximately 44 percent of adult males are *unokais*. The contrast between the fertile crescent lowlands and the less desirable highlands is striking.

Certain Characteristics of "Refugee" Villages Compared to Lowland Villages Found in Zones F and G on page 302

Village	Size	Number Men Polygynous	% Abducted Females	% *Unokai* Males
69	53	1	14.3	7.7
71	43	1	33.3	36.4
64	99	2	14.5	27.6
72	28	1	0.0	57.1
59	81	2	0.0	21.4
57	81	1	15.0	15.4
68	54	1	14.3	0.0
67	40	0	0.0	12.5
TOTAL:	479	9	–	–
AVERAGE:	59.9	1.1	11.4	22.3

12

Yanomamö Social Organization

Reproduction

The fundamental key to Yanomamö social organization and the social organization of all tribesmen is the *reproductive* success of adult men and women. In most tribal societies one will find that a few men have enormous numbers of offspring. They have (or have had) many wives because of polygyny.

By comparison, most women over their lives have pretty much the same number of children on average. If they start having children soon after their first menses and live to the age of menopause, all women in noncontracepting populations achieve about the same level of reproductive success.

The Yanomamö, like all tribesmen, also have ideas and notions about both kinship relationships—how one is related to people around them—and whether kin on father's side of the family are the same as or different from kin on mother's side. While kinship is very important in all tribal societies, descent through one line of relatives (males for example) is often more important than descent through the other line of relatives for many socially and reproductively important identities.

Anthropologists have studied and documented thousands of different tribesmen and, indeed, one prominent school of anthropology, associated with the anthropologist George Peter Murdock (1897–1985), has focused on the *frequencies* of various kinds of social arrangements that tribesmen have developed all over the world. For example, in how many societies is marriage with parallel cousins permitted? ("Parallel" cousins are cousins whose related parents are the same sex.) I have spent my entire professional career doing fieldwork in just one society, the Yanomamö. I report that the Yanomamö emphasize descent through the male line and have what I describe as patrilineal lineages. Researchers at HRAF draw on this sort of information to investigate more broadly into social arrangements, following Murdock's classic 1949 pioneering work, *Social Structure*. So, a researcher interested in how frequently "patrilineal" descent occurs in the ethnographic record, for example, consults the HRAF database.

I believe that patrilineal descent is far more common than matrilineal descent in the ethnographic record *because* warfare and intergroup conflict have been a chronic political condition in human history. In other words, I believe that the "Yanomamö model"—if we can say that the Yanomamö constitute a cluster of social, demographic, and military characteristics such that they represent a "type case"—was frequently found in human history and was probably common in the Paleolithic and Neolithic eras.

Patrilineal societies tend to keep the men in the same group they were born into, giving such groups advantages in hunting game animals because they have lived in the same general territory all of their lives and are intimately familiar with it and the movements of game animals.

But I believe the more important advantage that patriliny confers on groups of males who are closely related through the male line is that they tend to be able to cooperate more effectively and reliably in times of conflict. In short, they make a more cohesive fighting group because they are related closely. If anthropologists have learned anything from 150 years of studying tribesmen it is that closeness of kinship is a good predictor of social solidarity, cooperation, and amity. Indeed, it is closeness of kinship that appears to hold Yanomamö villages together when tensions develop and allows them to grow larger. Larger villages, of course, are better able to defend themselves when threatened by neighboring groups.

The fact that patrilineally organized societies are much more common in the ethnographic record is most likely the consequence of the constant threat of conflicts with neighbors that were very common in our Paleolithic and Neolithic past.

Differential Reproductive Success by Males Compared to Females

A man with ten wives can produce more offspring than a woman with ten husbands. Thus patrilineages can grow in size more quickly than can matrilineages. This fact has profound implications in a society organized by lineages. Another way of saying this is that there is very little variance in the reproductive success of women; all women who reach the age of forty-five will have about the same number of offspring, as I mentioned earlier.

By contrast, there is enormous variance in the reproductive success of Yanomamö men—one might even call it *spectacular* variance. Some men will successfully acquire many wives (polygyny), but many men will have only one (monogamy), a few will have to share a wife (polyandry), and some men will have none (celibacy). These anthropologically "standard" forms of marriage all occur among the Yanomamö so it is inaccurate to classify their marriage rules as either polygyny or monogamy or their culture as being characterized by just one of these various forms of marriage.

Regardless of their marital status, most Yanomamö men are trying to copulate with available women most of the time, but are constrained from doing so by the rules of incest and the intervention of some other man with proprietary interests in the same women.

This is why there is so much club fighting and why villages split into two or more groups so easily. Conflicts over the possession of nubile females have probably been the main reason for fights and killings throughout most of human history: the original human societal rules emerged, in all probability, to regulate male access to females and prevent the social chaos attendant on fighting over women. Males in this persistent kind of social environment sought the help of other related males—brothers, sons, cousins, uncles, nephews—and formed male coalitions to pursue their selfish reproductive goals as well as to minimize lethal conflicts within their own groups. Male access to females—usually "heroes" attempting to secure the love, affection, and proprietary reproductive potential of heroines—is the constant theme of myths, legends, and historical accounts of just about all cultures and societies known to historians and anthropologists.

Reproduction in the Yanomamö Fertile Crescent

Here is an example of what I have been discussing from the fertile crescent of Yanomamöland. In the beginning of Yanomamö habitation in the fertile crescent where I worked, a man named Matakuwä had ten siblings. His father was very successful at begetting. Matakuwä ("Shinbone") himself begat twenty sons and twenty-three daughters by eleven different wives. Shinbone probably died sometime in the late 1930s. I knew several of his children who were then in their late fifties when I began my fieldwork in 1964. For example, Sibarariwä was one of Shinbone's twenty sons and one of the few who were alive when I did my fieldwork. Another was Ruwahiwä, the Shamatari headman who was bludgeoned to death by the Patanowä-teri. One of my best informants, Dedeheiwä, was married to one of Shinbone's daughters, who was still alive during the years I was studying Mishimishimaböwei-teri, that is, between approximately 1968 and 1988.

So, following the narrative convention found in sacred texts and a few secular ethnographic monographs, Shinbone begat Sibarariwä, Shihewä, Shabreiwä, Shikomi, Shoshomi, Shiribimi, Shörökariwä—and thirty-six *more* children.

In turn, two of Shinbone's brothers had twenty-two children and nineteen children respectively, not because fecundity ran in their family but because they had many sisters and daughters to give away in marriage and they "traded" them to get extra wives for themselves and their sons. A Yanomamö without sisters and daughters to give away is most likely a bachelor and nobody's ancestor. People in the Stone Age to the time of the Bible had begetting as well as eating in mind.

How Does Such a "System" Start?

The short answer to this question is that it results from the long-term consequences of short-term decisions that tend to be made with immediate reproductive interests in mind. Yanomamö men probably do not consciously think about maximizing their reproductive success when they agree to give a young sister or daughter away in marriage. But Yanomamö men tend to give away females to men who can reciprocate by giving back their own sisters and daughters as wives. Think about this as investing in a capitalistic economy: deploying valuable resources (nubile females) in the most likely way to get an equal or better return on your investment, an equal or greater number of nubile females in return.

Once started, both parties benefit if they continue doing it every time a young man needs a wife and the other family has a young daughter to give away and vice versa. Soon the two "families" are locked into a marriage system wherein each gives marriageable females to the men in the other extended family.

While the concept of family is close to what I mean, the more precise word is *patrilineal descent group* (or *patrilineage*). It is a group of people who are descended from a particular man and can trace their genealogical relationship back to him exclusively through male links. On page 321 is an "ideal model" that represents the Yanomamö system of marriage and how two groups (X and Y patrilineages) reciprocally give marriageable females to each other over several generations.

The "ideal model" of Yanomamö society is a marvel of simplicity once the specific elements are understood. I will describe them here. These are also the basic elements that Claude Lévi-Strauss, the famous French anthropologist (1908–2009), identified in his approach to early human societies, an approach that is now widely known in anthropology as structuralism.

In Lévi-Strauss's approach, human societies can be described by a few general diagrams in which males are represented by triangles and females by circles (see Figure 1-A). A minimal number of elements is used. For example, the family has a father (triangle), a mother (circle), and one child of each sex (triangle for the son, circle for the daughter). A horizontal line above the two children indicates that they are genetically related as brother and sister. Marriages are shown by a horizontal line underneath the couple that connects the spouses, and a vertical line down from the marriage line shows the connection between the parents and their (two) children. (Parents can and often do have more than two children, but the "ideal model" shows only the minimal number of individuals needed to illustrate the important elements of the ideal models.) The parents constitute "generation 1" and the children "generation 2," a younger generation.

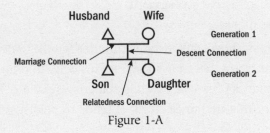

Figure 1-A

Let us now make the ideal model a little more complicated by showing that the "husband" in Figure 1-A has a sister, and the "wife" in Figure 1-A has a brother, as shown in Figure 1-B:

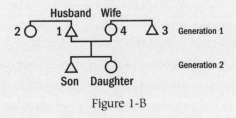

Figure 1-B

They are all in "Generation 1."

Things get a little bit complicated here: we are giving numbers to individuals, but the numbers appear to be illogical in the sense that instead of the expected 1, 2, 3, 4 order, I have put them in a different order: 2, 1, 4, 3. Thus, in Figure 1-B the husband is number 1 and his sister is number 2. The wife is number 4 and her brother is number 3.

Next, let us assume that people of marriageable age have siblings who are also of marriageable age, so, the sister of the husband and the brother of the wife in Figure 1-B are of marriageable age and both of them are married, as shown in Figure 1-C. Now the somewhat odd choice of numbers begins to make more sense:

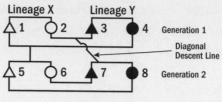

Figure 1-C

The Yanomamö make alliances with other families such that a man who marries takes another man's sister for his wife. In return he gives his sister to that man as his wife. This is sometimes called "brother/sister" exchange. Once this exchange starts, it tends to persist generation after generation.

As I said earlier, the Yanomamö have the most commonly found system of descent in the tribal world: patrilineal descent, which means that children are members of their father's patrilineage. So, to indicate this fact, I have darkened the circles and triangles of one of the patrilineages: all members of the "darkened" group, which I label as the "Y" patrilineage, are shown on one side of Figure 1-C. The other side of the figure represents a group that I have labeled the "X" lineage (they are not darkened).

Note that the "descent" line in the X lineage is perfectly perpendicular to connect the children (individuals 5 and 6) to their father (individual 1). But because the members of lineage "Y" all have to be in a different patrilineal group on the other half of the ideal model, their descent line has to be drawn diagonally to keep them on the other half of the diagram as shown.

What we have now is an "ideal" model that illustrates the following "rules" that guide many Yanomamö social actions, marriage in particular.

1. Men get their wives from some other lineage, i.e., a man must marry
   a woman who is not in his own lineage. Thus patrilineages are
   exogamous—meaning that both men and women must marry outside
   their lineage.

2. Men exchange their sisters to get wives from other men. Thus, these men are brothers-in-law—or as the Yanomamö say, "shori" or "shoriwa."

3. The most certain way to find a wife in a world where women are scarce (because some men have several wives) is to repeat this kind of "brother/sister" exchange generation after generation.

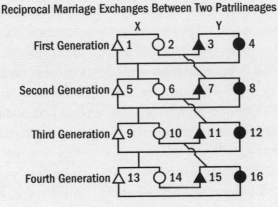

Figure 1-D

The logical and inevitable consequence of marriage exchanges, generation after generation, between males from two different lineages (lineage exogamy) is that every man will be marrying a woman who is simultaneously his mother's brother's daughter (MBD) as well as his father's sister's daughter (FZD), i.e., what anthropologists call his bilateral cross-cousin. This can be shown for every man in Figure 1-D after generation 1. Thus, individual 7 in generation 2 is marrying his mother's (individual 2) brother's (individual 1) daughter (individual 6). She is simultaneously his father's (individual 3) sister's (individual 4) daughter (individual 6).

This pattern continues for every male after generation 1 in both lineages in this diagram. See for yourself.

The resulting "ideal model" of Yanomamö society is a society that essentially has two "halves" because the Yanomamö rules about social behavior and marriage obligations imply that, ideally, villages are comprised of two lineages, i.e., they have what anthropologists call "dual organization."

However, the "ideal model" simplifies a more complicated real world.

For example, it assumes that each man has one wife and one sister, that each marriage has two offspring, one of each sex. Also that each man has one wife and each wife has one husband. Real villages deviate from the ideal village in the model. In the real world, families have more than one son, wives have more than one husband, individuals die before marriage, etc.

The short-term desire of men to acquire marriageable females develops into a long-term pattern of reciprocal marriage exchanges wherever men control the marital destinies of their sisters and daughters. Men give away their women in marriage in almost all tribal societies and have probably done so throughout human history. I know of no society where women give away their brothers in marriage, nor any human society where females from one group raid other groups and abduct males for husbands. Romantic love had nothing to do with mating and reproduction in the Stone Age. In the tribal world marriage was too important to be managed by lovestruck juveniles.

Reciprocal marriage exchange between two groups is probably the most effective marital strategy in a milieu where females are scarce and valuable—as they invariably are where polygyny occurs. In this situation the most common resulting pattern or system is the one shown on page 321—the system found among the Yanomamö in an ideal sense. This system was probably common in the pre-agricultural past and may have dominated most of human social evolution. Page 321 shows an "ideal model" of how things work. In reality things are more complex: people have more than two children each, both children do not always survive to age of marriage, not all families have one female and one male child, men often have more than one wife, and so on.

Dual Organization

The Amazon Basin is famous in anthropology for the frequency of societies characterized as having so-called dual organization.

What this generally means is that a large number of societies found there tend to have social halves, often two lineages like the ones shown on page 321. However, these lineages usually have social functions and attributes in addition to regulating marriages, such as the obligation of members of one of the groups to bury the deceased members of the other, privileges and responsibilities regarding the sponsorship of ceremonial events and feasts, a prescribed location within the village where they must live, etc.

These social accoutrements can be so elaborate and complex in some Amazonian tribes that an early prominent anthropologist, A. L. Kroeber, characterized them as "luxuriant developments" in the social calculus of the domestic, ceremonial, and political lives of native Amazonian tribesmen (Kroeber, 1948: 395–97). "Dual organization" is not confined to the Amazon Basin and is, in fact, commonly found in many tribal societies all over the globe where reciprocal exchange of marriageable females occurs.

If you examine page 321, you will discover that after the first generation of exchanges, continuation of reciprocal exchanges of women has what I consider to be profound social and political consequences.

First, everyone falls into one of two categories—"own group" and "other group"—with regard to where men get wives. Moreover, your wife's brothers (not shown on page 321) become your social, political, and reproductive allies because you and your brothers give them your sisters and they and their brothers give you theirs (also not shown on page 321). Consequently, your respective political and reproductive interests overlap. A male coalition whose members have their own reproductive self-interests in mind emerges. In a sense and at some analytical level, it is not "lineages" that should be viewed as the primary focal point in models of tribal social structure, but pairs of matrimonially bound lineages whose male members constitute a *coalition* with common reproductive interests and goals. These reproductive interests entail political and military interests.

Second, incest prohibitions probably develop quickly in an evolutionary sense: men cannot marry/mate with females in their own group, which basically includes their mothers, sisters, and daughters. Thus, men *must* get marriageable females from the other group.

To regulate the very important problem of making sure that men married (mated with) females who were young enough to bear offspring, in other words, females that had high reproductive value, the notion of generation developed.

The most logical categories for generations would be Parental, Own, and Offspring, or Older, Mine, and Younger. This becomes clearer if we focus for a moment on who arranges the marriages of whom. Adult males arrange the marriages of their (younger generation) children, largely through negotiations with adult males in the other group whose (younger generation) children are yet unmarried (or unpromised). Young females are easy to give away—all the males want them. It is more difficult for adult males to find young eligible females for their sons. In these negotiations, men who have some prominence do better than other men in getting their sons and other male dependents married off. This enhances the amity and solidarity between older and younger men: the latter are dependent on the former in finding a mate.

What makes a man "prominent"? It is not simply brute force and being fierce. Rather it is the number of kinsmen he has, which reflects how men in previous generations handled their own marriage negotiations, and which in turn depended on luck at having sisters to give away to get extra wives for themselves, who then reproduced large numbers of offspring, which in turn made it increasingly easy for any given male descendant to find wives for their own sons, and so on. This puts a premium on continuing to reciprocate women with as few reliable lineage heads as possible, thus keeping the marriage system as close to an efficient dual organization as possible.

The profound consequences of these patterns can be seen by examining more carefully the ideal model shown on page 321 of two lineages (X and Y) whose members give women to each other in marriage. If you pick any marriage that occurs after the first generation you will find that all males marry women who are related to them *simultaneously* as mother's brother's daughters (MBD) and father's sister's daughters (FZD). This fascinating outcome is empirically demonstrated in the statistical data I have collected for all Yanomamö marriages in all the villages I have studied. Thus, when two groups—patrilineages, for example—begin to reciprocally exchange females over several generations, this practice invariably leads to a system in which the males marry females who are *other group, own generation,* and not sisters. These women are a special kind of cousin that anthropologists call *cross cousins.*

Cousins are people in your own generation who are related to you because one or more of your and their parents are siblings. If the parents in question are of the same sex, then by anthropological convention the cousins are called "parallel" cousins. If the relevant parents are of the opposite sex, their children are called "cross" cousins.

Thus your mother's sisters' children and your father's brothers' children are your parallel cousins. By contrast, your father's sisters' children and your mother's brothers' children are cross cousins.

"Cousin marriage" has been significant in the history of anthropological theory as well as in the ethnographic descriptions anthropologists have made in their studies of tribesmen.

A number of mammal species expel sexually maturing young males from either the mother's territory if the species is nonsocial (for example, brown bears), or from the cooperative female group if they are highly social (for example, African lions). But, by contrast, in the large chimpanzee (*Pan troglodytes*) it is the females who disperse at sexual maturity while males tend to remain in the natal group. The result in the first two cases is the formation of "matri-focal groups" within which the incoming mate is a male from some other nearby group. If one were to draw a diagram of what happens, it would look just like the one on page 321 but the groups would be matrilineages and the males from one group mate with—"marry"—the females of the other, a kind of "husband" exchange system. The major difference between a human system and, say, the African lion system is that humans are able to assign names to the categories within which mating is legitimate and have, through language, developed more elaborate ways to constrain and limit sexual conflicts, such as by defining and prohibiting incest between close relatives.

In many primitive societies like the Yanomamö the rules that must be followed in marriage are often very specific and defined by the *kinship* terms that are used to address and/or refer to kinsmen—terms like *niece, cousin, brother* (of course, in the language used in the society). For example, the word we use for our genitor is *father*. The Yanomamö word is *habe*. Our word for our mother's brother's daughter is *cousin*. The Yanomamö word is *suaböya*. However, our word for our mother's sister's daughter is also *cousin*, but the Yanomamö word is *yaöya*. It is *identical* to their word for sister(s): they regard female parallel cousins as sisters. Like us, they cannot marry a female they classify as a "sister."

Here is where it becomes very interesting: the Yanomamö word for a female cross cousin, *Suaböya*, is also their word for wife. Thus they call female cross cousins "wife." Not only *can* they marry them, they *must* marry a woman they classify as *Suaböya*, wife.

Wherever various kinds of cousins are *legitimate* marriage partners in a society, the most common marriage rule found among tribesmen *all over the globe* is a rule or prescription that states, in effect, that males must marry their female bilateral cross cousins (females who are cross cousins through links via both the mother and the father). The reciprocal of this rule, from the female's vantage, is that females must marry their father's sister's sons or their mother's brother's sons. This is what the graphic on page 321 shows us.

One of the twentieth century's anthropological great works in fact focused on the marriage systems of primitive peoples all over the world. This is, of course, French anthropologist Claude Lévi-Strauss's *The Elementary Systems of Kinship*.

This work and the themes he raised in it about the inherent ability of "primitive societies" to hold together—to generate internal social solidarity—dominated the second half of the twentieth century in the cultural anthropology literature about tribesmen, and a great fraction of my own work focuses on this theme as well. Without what the French social scientists called "social solidarity" human societies tend to fall apart or fission into smaller groups.

One might liken the concept of "social solidarity" to some kind of "social glue." Marriage between groups provides one kind of glue, descent from a common ancestor another kind of glue, how closely you are related to your kinsmen a third kind of glue, and how you are related to your kinsmen (for example, through father or through mother) yet another kind of social glue.

Whereas Lévi-Strauss's "structural" approach largely concerned "ideal models" of tribal societies, his more fundamental interest had to do with the ability of social groups represented by these models to promote or hinder social solidarity, in other words, that somewhat mysterious quality that allowed social groups in the tribal world to grow in size and complexity. In my view, the evolution of social complexity in human societies was the result of increases in the *size* of local groups (villages, for example). The problem was how to develop more "glue" to enable increasingly larger groups to develop and hold together.

Under conditions of chronic warfare, there is safety in numbers. The proximate evolutionary end was to maximize group size, which in turn maximized individual reproductive survival—the ultimate end. The most persistent obstacle to the size to which local communities could grow was the sexual jealousy and proprietary ambitions of adult males within the group for the females in the group. The goal of men in tribal societies was to regulate such ambitions and jealousy.

Yanomamö Hypothetical Example of a "Little Bang" Theory

The development of the Bilateral Cross Cousin Marriage (BCCM) system was of sufficient moment in the evolution of human social systems that it might be regarded as the "big bang" in developing cooperation within human societies. It is *cooperation* that makes social life possible in all social species.

At the time Shinbone lived there were, of course, other men like him, men with immediate reproductive interests who wanted to marry and have offspring. Nobody knows the precise decisions made by these individuals to obtain wives and make sure there would be a reliable supply of them in the future for their sons, but I can draw attention to several of them because I spent many years collecting genealogies and documenting family sizes as meticulously as I could while I was trying to define and understand the Yanomamö reproductive rules. It is highly unlikely that these individuals had anything other than a short-term, even selfish, goal in mind: get women, copulate with them, and guard them from other men to make sure that only you fathered their offspring.

Cultural anthropologists like me arbitrarily refer to men like Shinbone as "lineage founders" because they are the male apex point of, for example, a patrilineal lineage from which all others in that lineage are descended. In the great scheme of things, of course, some Adam would be the "founder" if knowledge were perfect and anthropologists existed at the beginning of Homo sapiens, that is, at "Creation." All of this is to say that genealogies account for only the *most recent* historical sequence of individuals in any society. So in most societies, the "founder" turns out to be the first person in a long list of individuals who can be identified by a name, the most remote *named* ancestor about whom something is known (or believed). The founder of Shinbone's lineage, in my field records, is not Shinbone, but a man I have labeled "Shinbone's Father" because Shinbone had several known genetic/biological brothers and sisters who had the same father.

A man by the name of Yamirawä was an approximate contemporary of Shinbone, perhaps antedating him by a half or a full generation. Yamirawä was not demonstrably related to Shinbone, but he and his male relatives married Shinbone's female relatives. In my schematic, Shinbone could be considered the founder of lineage "X" and Yamirawä the founder of lineage "Y." Both men were major "founders" in the Shamatari—that is, southern—population of Yanomamö.

Yamirawä was one of three brothers whose immediate descendants married women in Shinbone's patrilineage and became matrimonially locked into marriage exchanges as represented earlier.

Initially, Yamirawä did not do as well reproductively as Shinbone did. He managed to marry two women and had six children by them. However, three of his sons did extremely well—and acquired multiple wives: one of them had 21 children, another had 32 children, and the third had 12 children. Indeed, by the time I began my field studies in 1964, Yamirawä's descendants were numerically the largest single lineage in half of the Shamatari villages and Shinbone's descendants the largest in the other half of the Shamatari villages. The political leaders in these villages came from one of these lineages, and in cases where both lineages were numerically predominant, there were two headmen—one from each lineage—and they were married to each other's sisters in most cases. That is what is implied by the term *shoriwä* or its abbreviation, *shori*—what we call "brother in law"—and why the men greet any strangers as *"Shori! Shori! Shori!"* to indicate intimacy and a desire for friendship.

It is in this somewhat random fashion that large lineages—almost accidentally at first—start, develop, and then dominate the immediate social and political destiny of whole tribes and nations. When they achieve their grandest scope and potential, they fundamentally shape just about every aspect of their tribal communities.

Shinbone's Descendants

In a patrilineage, the male founder has two kinds of descendants: lineal and cognatic. The first kind can trace their connection to the founder through male links only—sons of the sons of the sons, etc. of the founder. Daughters of the founder are his lineal descendants in the first generation, but their offspring are not lineal descendants and by definition, not members of his lineage. In patrilineages the *father's* lineal identity determines the lineage to which all of his children belong. Thus, when a female of lineage X marries, her children will belong to *her husband's lineage*, which cannot be X because both men and women must marry someone who is not in their lineage. This is called lineage exogamy by anthropologists and is a near-universal characteristic of marriage rules in societies that have lineages.

A simple way of thinking about patrilineal descent and lineage identity is the way most people of Western European ancestry pass on their family names through the father's line. My father's last name was Chagnon, and therefore my brothers and I are Chagnons and our immediate offspring are also Chagnons. Our sisters had the same last name as we did, but they changed their last names to their husbands' last names when they married. Their children's last names are no longer Chagnon because their fathers' last names are not Chagnon.

The children of our sisters are related to and can trace descent back to our father just as the children of my brothers and me can, but they are not his *lineal* descendants: they are what anthropologists define as *cognatic* descendants.

Shinbone's Other Descendants

The chart on page 330 is a truly remarkable empirical summary of how polygyny sets into motion the genealogical structures often found in demographically intact tribal populations, structures that are often unknown or even undocumentable in tribal populations that have been ravished by introduced diseases, depopulation, defeat by state-organized militaries, or forced resettlement, often with remnants of other tribes, on small reservations or mission posts. Anthropological research in these

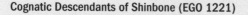

Cognatic Descendants of Shinbone (EGO 1221)

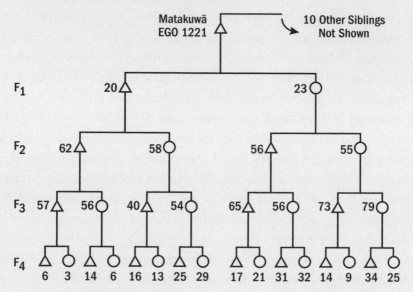

All descendants of 'Shinbone' (EGO 1221) grouped by sex. He had 20 sons and 23 daughters (F1 generation). The 20 sons in turn had 62 sons and 58 daughters, and so on. (Overlap in the F3 and F4 generations is not removed; descendants in generations F5 and F6 are not shown.)

kinds of refugee communities cannot, for obvious reasons, demonstrate the same principles I am discussing. Not all anthropological field research is equally useful to understanding the evolution of human societies because this understanding depends in large measure on genealogies obtained from demographically intact tribesmen.

The following discussion highlights the final component of Yanomamö marriage practices that persistently reinforce the social solidarity that enables their villages to grow larger than, say, one hundred people. The causal chain might be summarized as follows and explained in more detail below:

1. Their marriage rules prescribe marriage with bilateral cross cousins.
2. This form of marriage requires lineage exogamy (patrilineal identity).
3. High variation in male reproductive success implies strong competition for scarce females.

4. Men tend to continue to give their sisters and daughters to men in the same "other" lineage and expect to get the sisters and daughters of these men in exchange.

5. Within two generations some categories of the lineal descendants and the cognatic descendants will be eligible mates to each other, leading to "inbreeding," that is, closeness of kinship relatedness between spouses.

Look at Shinbone's grandchildren through his sons, the F_2 generation, 62 males and 58 females. As discussed above, the Yanomamö have a rule of "prescriptive bilateral cross cousin marriage," which means men are supposed to marry either their father's sister's daughters (FZDs) and/ or their mother's brother's daughters (MBDs) or a female who is simultaneously both. This means that the 62 males in the F_2 generation, for example, are eligible to marry any of the 55 females shown on the other portion of the diagram in the F_2 generation: they are *all* FZDs to these 62 males. By extension and Yanomamö kinship rules, the 58 females in the F_2 generation on the left portion of the diagram are also eligible as spouses to the 56 males on the right side of the diagram: these men are their father's sister's sons—the reciprocal of the above rule: if a man can marry his FZD, his wife is related to him as her mother's brother's sons.

This logic extends, of course, to all the generations depicted on page 330. For example, in the F_3 generation, the 57 great-grandsons of Shinbone can marry the 54 females shown on the left half of the diagram and the 40 males on the same side of the F_3 generation can marry the 56 females on that side of the generation because in the first case the females are related as FZDs to the males and, in the second case, the females are MBDs to the males.

Much of the "social glue" that keeps Yanomamö villages cohesive is the result of such marriages with bilateral cross cousins (FZD and MBD marriages). This practice explains why the Shamatari villages (dominated by Matakuwä's descendants) became larger than the Namowei-teri villages: more of the Shamatari individuals marry their "close" cross cousins because the Shamatari are more closely related.

Indeed, the genealogical structures set into motion by polygyny, high variance in male reproductive success, patrilineal descent, and lineage exogamy result in a situation in which the men in some villages might even find it difficult to locate a potential spouse who *is not* a bilateral cross cousin—unless they appropriate them by abductions in distant villages!

One of the first things that Christian missionaries usually do when they evangelize tribesmen is to prohibit polygyny and intervene wherever they can to discourage men from having two or more wives, as if monogamy were natural and polygyny were the "work of the Devil." The likelihood is that humans have been polygynous for most of their social evolution. Polygyny then is more natural in humans and the single most important element lying behind whatever social solidarity emerged in our prehistoric past. Marrying closely related cross cousins promotes cooperation between all members of a lineage. Polygyny explains why these descendants are able to cooperatively live in villages that exceed two to three hundred people.

Male Coalitions, Warfare, and the Distribution of Women

Despite the skepticism widely shared in the now politically correct anthropological profession, the ethnographic and archaeological evidence overwhelmingly indicates that warfare has been the most important single force shaping the evolution of political society in our species. Warfare has been chronic, with the few possible exceptions where humans migrated so far out from their home ranges that they had no neighbors. Probably the biggest threat to early human local groups came from neighbors—the people in the next valley over.

Because intragroup conflicts over local resources (such as females) increase with local group size, continued growth in community size was constantly limited by these conflicts. Such conflicts are most easily resolved by group fissioning: making conflicts less likely by reducing the size of the group. But since there is safety in numbers, there were countervailing pressures to continue to grow. The result was constant pressure for adult males to develop kinship-defined coalitions that peaceably distributed females and pooled their collective abilities to wield force against other groups.

As I see it, the most probable long-term evolutionary scenario in the development of human sociality was constant but slow growth of community size followed by fissions of communities once they reached sizes of 50 to 75 people—the numbers mentioned in Richard Lee and Irven DeVore's classic treatise, *Man the Hunter.*

It seems that the primary source of conflict within stateless human groups is young females of reproductive age who have neither fathers nor husbands to safeguard them. They constitute a major cause of potential instability and strife among the Yanomamö: aggressive adult males between the approximate ages of 15 and 40 constantly want to copulate with them and/or appropriate them for their exclusive reproductive interests. They are a source of conflict in Yanomamö communities and in many other tribally organized societies that lack the institutions associated with the political state—law, police, courts, judges, and odious sanctions.

I suggest that conflicts over the means of reproduction—women— dominated the political machinations of men during a vast span of human history and shaped human male psychology. It was only after polygyny became "expensive" that these conflicts shifted to material resources—the "gold and diamonds" my incredulous colleagues alluded to—and the material means of production. By that time, after the agricultural revolution, the accumulation of wealth—and its consequence, power—had become a prerequisite to having multiple mates.

13

Three Headmen of Authority

It is not clear to me if the Yanomamö political leaders are aware of how important lineages are to their authority in the fertile crescent region of Yanomamöland. But there is no doubt that much of their authority derives from the comparatively larger numbers of patrilineally related adult males—the members of their *mashi* (their name for patrilineal group)—on whom they are able to call to support and enforce their political decisions.

In a de facto sense, Yanomamö political leadership is hereditary. The heritability of headmanship becomes apparent only by collecting the genealogies of all village members. When you group the headmen into genealogically defined patrilineages, the fathers of the current headmen were also headmen, and the current headmen will be succeeded by their older (or oldest) son. Thus, when a headman dies or is killed, the next leader invariably comes from the same patrilineal descent group, usually the oldest son or a brother of the previous headman. The only clear exception I documented occurred when the headman in a village comprised of two large lineages, Matowä, was killed by raiders, as discussed elsewhere. There were approximately equal numbers of adult males in each of the two numerically prominent lineages. The headmanship devolved to the most senior leader of the other large lineage, one of Matowä's brothers-in-law. As I have mentioned several times, many villages have two prominent leaders and frequently both are considered to be "big."

The Emergence of Odious Sanctions and Headmanship

I knew several Yanomamö headmen who have, perhaps unconsciously, built on the kinship on which their authority rests. I will focus on two men, but I will also refer to other political leaders I knew very well. All of these men became considerably more "chiefly" than most other headmen I have known. Their personalities contributed to this prominence; they had a kind of social presence conspicuous even to non-Yanomamö.

Villages can become large if their political leaders are strong and they eagerly seize upon their opportunities to command others. While headmen mostly lead by example, a few deliberately become quite despotic: they order people to do things and expect them to comply. This is a subtle step in the direction of law.

Much of this kind of authority and power is based on the odious sanction that defiance of the headman's wishes will cause the disobedience. This comes close to what juridical scholars define as law: advisories issued by a sovereign authority who has the ability to legitimately punish offenders. The power behind law is almost always odious sanctions, that is, punishments like fines, stoning, beating, incarceration—even execution. The Yanomamö don't practice capital punishment, but in larger villages under stress and military threats from neighbors, they have come close.

The Yanomamö in the fertile crescent have taken a step in the direction of greater social and political complexity, a greater ordering and institutionalization of authority. Institutionalized authority brings the tribal social design closer to the political state. The almost imperceptible tiny steps that tribesmen like the Yanomamö have taken along that path are frequently visible only through the comparative study of the various social designs that ethnographers report in their firsthand studies of tribes—and even in different communities and bands of the same tribe. You have to look for these small changes to the tribal design, which depends on knowledge of multiple communities.

If you ask a Yanomamö what the ideal size of a village should be, the answer, if they had a numerical system, would be something like 30 or 40 people because it is easier to get along with others in small villages. They frequently complained to me that they "fight too much" when villages get larger than about forty people.

The Yanomamö prefer living in relatively small villages where the diffuse sanctions behind kinship rules are sufficient to maintain social order. But because you cannot trust your neighbors who live beyond the walls of the palisade not to take advantage of you, villages must remain large and attempt to avoid fissioning into smaller more vulnerable units. Thus the tendency for villages to fall apart when they become large is opposed by the need to remain large for security purposes. This is the central dilemma of Yanomamö life. And this is where the presence and personalities of the leaders matter: a strong headman can keep the village larger. He can make it cohesive as well as secure by virtue of his strong personality and the implied threats that his demeanor and his *waiteri* (fierceness) communicate.

Ironically, one of the more important Yanomamö myths accounting for why neighbors differ in the strength of their political and military resolve has to do with how they conceive of themselves as a people. I recounted their myth of the origin of man from the blood of *Peribo* (Moon) in chapter 2. The villages I have studied are in the heart of Yanomamöland and warfare is relatively intense here. As one moves away from the center of this area—particularly to the north, east, and south—warfare appears to diminish and becomes a more subdued dimension of their political relationships. To the west, however, the Yanomamö villages are recently fissioned groups from the more warlike central region and they seem to retain their belligerency.

Styles of Headmanship

I have visited and worked in some sixty or so Yanomamö villages and know a large number of Yanomamö headmen. They are sometimes called chiefs in popular articles written by journalists, especially Venezuelan and Brazilian journalists, but the word *chief* suggests a level of political organization and a formal election process that are absent in most tribal societies whose members live in small villages. The amount of authority and power a headman wields varies radically when village size is taken into consideration, as I have frequently emphasized. The integrative function of headmen in small villages largely emerges from the order and cohesion inherent in kinship amity and marriage ties—and the utter smallness of most Yanomamö communities. Many villages are comparable in some cases to large, extended families. In most of these smaller communities, as the saying goes, one word from the "chief" and everyone does as he pleases. But in larger villages, headmen often have considerable power and authority and can be quite tyrannical.

Political Status and the Myth of Primitive Egalitarianism

Pre-state societies—tribesmen like the Yanomamö—are described by many anthropologists as *egalitarian:* everyone is more or less interchangeable with any other person of the same age and same sex, so status differentials are essentially determined by age, sex, and occasionally the ephemeral characteristics of leaders. This is definitely not the case among the Yanomamö. If my teachers (and anthropology textbooks) got anything wrong, it was their misunderstanding of the notion of egalitarianism: they stubbornly insisted on tying it to "differential access to material resources." Among the Yanomamö, tribesmen differ in their ability to command and order others around because of differing numbers of kinsmen they can deploy in their service, whether they are *unokai*, and other nonmaterial attributes.

I concluded that this myth about differential access to resources was so pervasive and unchallenged in anthropological theory because anthropologists come from highly materialistic, industrialized, state societies and tend to project what is "natural" or "self-evident" in this kind of world back into prehistory. In our world, power, status, and authority usually rest on material wealth. It follows that fighting over resources is more "natural" and therefore comprehensible to anthropologists than fighting over women. The traditional anthropological view of egalitarianism is remarkably Eurocentric and ethnocentric, that is, the argument that tribesmen are egalitarian because nobody has "privileged" access to "strategic" material resources. Such a view erroneously projects our own political and economic views into the Stone Age. Two of the most celebrated anthropologists who held such views were among my teachers in graduate school, Marshall Sahlins and Morton Fried.

I was present at a scientific conference when the speaker, a prominent and distinguished social scientist who was then the president of a major national academic society, concluded his rather unpersuasive arguments in a plenary talk with the following remark: "And, Professor X, the leading authority in this field, reached the same conclusion as I do. And who are we to dispute his authority?" A very skeptical and no-nonsense biologist named Richard D. Alexander then got up and "innocently" made the following devastating comment: "I see. That clears up in my mind what the difference is between the social sciences and biology. Your conclusions seem to rest largely on the unquestionable authority of some Professor X. In biology we reach our conclusions on the basis of the evidence." He then sat down.

There are enormous differences in status among tribal communities. The differing abilities of headmen to govern does not rest on differential access to scarce strategic material resources, as it does in our society, but on differentials in the size of their respective kinship following. Because the general bias in anthropological theory draws heavily from Marxist sociopolitical theory, even "scientific" anthropological discussions of social status, primitive economics, political structure, and so forth tend to be viewed in terms of struggles over material resources (cultural materialism).

Struggles in the Stone Age, I am convinced, were more about the means of reproduction. That makes human biology and psychology central to a truly comprehensive scientific theory of how humans behave. Darwin's theory of evolution is a theory about reproductive survival.

Sources of Power of Yanomamö Leaders

I knew two headmen who, compared to other men in their own villages, had differential abilities to persuade members of their communities to follow particular courses of action: they had authority as well as power.

They came from large villages, they were polygynous, were middle-age adults, and had killed enemies in other villages. One of them, Krihisiwä, was from Patanowä-teri, which had a population of about 225 people during most of my study of it. The other, Möawä, was from Mishimishimaböwei-teri, where the village size was closer to 300 people. Both men also belonged to two of the largest patrilineal lineages (*mashi*) in their respective populations and had many biological (genetically related) kinsmen living with them within their village. Both villages were isolated and generally beyond the influence of the missions and the outside world. For much of my long-term study I was the only outsider who visited their villages on a regular basis.

Krihisiwä

I got along very well with Krihisiwä and found him to be likable, despite the fact that he was very dangerous and treacherous if you got on his wrong side.

I visited his remote village frequently between 1964 and 1987. His village was almost constantly at war with one or more neighboring villages during most of this time. Indeed, his village was raided more than twenty times by neighboring villages during the initial phase of my fieldwork, between 1964 and 1966. The raids seemed to follow the logic of a Machiavellian tactician: if your enemy is down and being harassed by all around, jump in and join the fray because he cannot possibly retaliate effectively against any particular village.

Krihisiwä was a headman who knew what Yanomamö wars were like because he started lots of them. From his perspective, they were no doubt "justified." A good case can be made that the hostility of his neighbors toward his group had much to do with his own "foreign policy."

One of the other prominent men in Patanowä-teri—a "co-headman"—was Krihisiwä's older brother, Kumaiewä. Quite obviously he was a member of Krihisiwä's patrilineal descent group, a man of the same *mashi,* as the Yanomamö would describe it. *"Yamakö mashi!"* means "We are all members of the same patrilineal descent group!" Kumaiewä and one of his adult sons were both killed by raiders with shotguns during my field studies (in about 1969), leaving Krihisiwä as the senior male member of that *mashi.*

Krihisiwä was only one of several prominent men in the village. Another was Rakoiwä, Krihisiwä's brother-in-law (and cross cousin). Their respective *mashis* exchanged marriageable females over a number of generations, so the political core of Patanowä-teri basically consisted of two large *mashis* tied together by several generations of marriage exchanges.

From my first visit, the people in Krihisiwä's village always welcomed me. One reason I was welcome was the fact that their wars had virtually cut them off from trading relationships with neighboring villages, particularly the village of Mahekodo-teri near the small Salesian mission post of Platanal. Krihisiwä's group had obtained most of their steel tools—machetes, axes, knives, fishhooks, and other Western goods—from the Mahekodo-teri, which obtained them from the resident Salesian priest or brother, and before the Salesians, James Barker of the New Tribes Mission, who could not afford many of these costly steel tools. I was a new source of these valuable tools.

They welcomed me for a number of additional reasons. First, I had made my home base in Bisaasi-teri, a village that had fissioned away from them some fifteen or so years earlier. The headman there was Kaobawä, a brother-in-law to Krihisiwä. Bisaasi-teri was far away and it was now hazardous to visit. There were a number of hostile villages whose territories the Patanowä-teri would have to traverse to get there. Still, a trickle of Patanowä-teri visitors continued to brave the risky trip and periodically came to visit Bisaasi-teri to spend time with Kaobawä's faction, which was still friendly to them.

But a sizable faction of the Bisaasi-teri—those living downstream from Kaobawä (Lower Bisaasi-teri)—were hostile to the Patanowä-teri and let it be known that they would kill them if the Patanowä-teri visited.

On one occasion that visitors arrived, I was lying in a hammock in Kaobawä's house next to several of the visitors from Patanowä-teri, chatting with them. There were rumors and threats that some of the hotheads from downstream Lower Bisaasi-teri were going to attack them with axes and shoot them with arrows. Suddenly, about twenty hotheads appeared in the village in war paint, brandishing axes, machetes, and arrows.

Kaobawä's brothers and supporters quietly picked up their bows and arrows and spread out, each standing in front of one of the house-posts adjacent to Kaobawä's area. They were stoic and silent, showing no outward fear. Their arrows were not yet nocked, but they were ready and they stood resolutely with solemn looks on their faces. Kaobawä didn't move a muscle, nor did the visitors. The hotheads pounded their axes on the ground and clacked their arrows against their bows as they walked swiftly across the plaza with their eyes fixed on the visitors. They had menacing looks on their faces. As they closed the last five yards the *browähäwäs* (politically important men) leading this pack raised their axes as if they were going to strike the visitors on their heads. Kaobawä and the visitors showed no fear and lay in silence. The would-be assassins then exploded with loud screams as they swung their axes down violently—stopping them just inches from the heads of the visitors. Kaobawä had told me once that you must never show fear, because if you do, that is when your enemies will kill you. I struggled to keep calm: I was now "representing" as an important political figure in Kaobawä's group simply by being among his visitors and not fleeing.

The assailants were bluffing and immediately went into *waiyamo* chanting—in this case a ceremonial way of relating why they were angry with the visitors. But moments earlier, had anyone moved a hand to protect themselves, it could have turned out much differently. Visiting can be an apprehensive experience because you are never certain how you will be received.

Palisades, Raiders, and Headmanship

When the Yanomamö have an "active" war, they surround the village with a stout palisade some ten to fifteen feet high that has only a few openings. The palisade is made from upright tree trunks, partially buried in the ground for support and lashed together with strong vines that provide additional support. It is intended to prevent raiders from sneaking up to the village at night and shooting people inside through the partially open spaces between the lower structural posts or through the thatched low-hanging roof whose leaves are easy to part by an archer. However, any tampering with the palisade alerts the village dogs, who start barking and noisily swarm to the area whence the noise came. Their barking alerts the villagers, and the men quickly grab their bows and arrows to investigate further.

Krihisiwä's village was almost always palisaded when I visited there. On one trip I made, not only had they erected a palisade, but they had meticulously removed every growing thing for an additional 150 to 200 feet outside the palisade and turned that area into barren ground. The stream where they got their water and bathed was also devoid of all growth for an additional hundred or so feet on the other side—and for several hundred feet along the course of the stream. I was very impressed with the amount of labor that must have been invested in this effort on behalf of security. The effort they expended was all the more remarkable because the Yanomamö don't do unnecessary work or expend effort on labor-intensive tasks without some compelling incentive. The clearing of this large area of all brush and tree stumps was a costly task, and the efforts of many people had to be mustered and coordinated, most likely by Krihisiwä.

I arrived at midday and put my backpack in the house, near Krihisiwä's, as was our custom. I spent the rest of the day visiting and chatting with the adults and explained what I wanted to do the next day when I went to "work" with my "leaves" (at first they called my notebooks and paper note pads "leaves").

The men were edgy, nervous, constantly alert for signs of raiders. They carried their bows and arrows with them even when they were crossing the plaza and had them close at hand if they were visiting someone in another house that was more than a few yards from their own.

As the afternoon sun got lower, the women gathered their gourd containers and assembled to go to the nearby stream to get water and to bathe their infants. The men, all armed, went out first and cautiously explored the area around the stream, their long arrows nocked in their six-foot palm-wood bows, which were partially drawn. The men spread out, stood on the near bank of the stream where the women and children were arriving, and looked intently into the surrounding forest. The women filled their water containers and quickly washed their children and themselves. No time was spent, as is usual, on leisure playing in the water because *wayu käbä* (raiders, assassins) might be lurking in the nearby jungle.

Nobody left the village after the water was collected. The several exits through the palisade were covered over with dry, noisy brush and secured for the night with vines.

As darkness came we all settled into our hammocks for the night. The Yanomamö insisted that I put my backpack against the low-hanging roof where it nearly touched the ground as an added security measure in case a raider got through the palisade and tried to shoot at me with his arrow. Maybe my backpack would stop an arrow. Some of my Bisaasi-teri informants said that this is how Krihisiwä's brother, Kumaiewä, was attacked and killed—his assailant shot him through the roofing leaves with his newly obtained shotgun.

Sometime during the night I was awakened when I felt a hand shaking me and a hoarse whisper urging me to be silent. It was Krihisiwä. He had crawled on the ground from his hammock to mine, some thirty feet away, because he heard a suspicious noise just outside the palisade. He whispered: *"Siboha wayu käbä kuwa!"* ("There are raiders just outside!")

I sleep very soundly and am very groggy when I'm awakened in the middle of the night. Krihisiwä wanted me to load my shotgun and chase away the would-be raiders. I really wasn't up to this, so I persuaded him that it would be enough for me to put one round into my shotgun and fire it up into the air. Any sane raider would immediately retreat on realizing that someone in the village had a shotgun. He agreed, so I loaded a round in my double-barreled twelve-gauge shotgun and fired a shot into the air. We listened. We heard no sounds from outside the palisade, and so we both went back to sleep, somewhat confident that there were no raiders lurking outside the village.

On a different visit, Krihisiwä asked me to go hunting with him for a tapir, one of the most desirable game animals in the Yanomamö cuisine. It tastes, to me, remarkably like beef—and I became fond of it. The tapir is distantly related to the horse and rhinoceros. It is a large animal, and can weigh as much as 500 pounds, with a longish snout, found in South and Central America and, a different species, in parts of Malaysia.

Krihisiwä had found a "lick"—a muddy wallow where the tapirs cover themselves with mud in order, I assume, to control ticks and other skin parasites. Tapirs also apparently eat some of the mud, which is said to contain salts and minerals. I've seen the Yanomamö bring quantities of this kind of mud back to the village, fling it up into the overhanging thatched roof, and let it dry out from the sun and the heat from the hearth. Then they eat it like smoked candy.

Again, the village was at war—and nobody wanted to go that far away from the village and spend the night waiting for a tapir to show up at the lick. It was dangerous to go hunting at all, let alone at night and so far from the village. (I can't refrain from mentioning that during much of my Yanomamö research a small but prominent group of anthropologists associated with Columbia University, interested in tribal warfare, kept insisting that the scarcity of game animals caused Yanomamö wars, although none of them had been to the Yanomamö region nor did they have any data from any Amazonian tribe that supported this theory. A better case could be made that war caused a dietary shortage of meat, not vice versa, because nobody wants to go hunting in these dangerous circumstances, either at night or during the day.)

Krihisiwä and I started out in the late afternoon. The lick was at least an hour from the village. We chatted quietly as we went along.

We found a cacao tree with a large pod. He pulled it off, broke it open, and leisurely ate it, taking huge bites out of it. The pods, when ripe, produce the beans that are turned into chocolate. The Yanomamö eat the flesh of the pod when it is immature. The edible flesh looks like what you might find inside an immature watermelon. The seeds are green and tender, not black as they are in ripe watermelons or dark like coffee beans. The flesh is bland, like an uncooked cabbage, but it fills you up. The same can be said of palm hearts, which we consider to be a delicacy but are regarded as a hardship food by the Yanomamö.

We later came across a *paruri*—a large, edible, turkey-like Amazonian bird—high in a tree. Krihisiwä positioned himself, moving slowly so as to not alarm the *paruri,* to get a clear shot at it with the low sun behind the bird, silhouetting it. He slowly drew his bow back, holding his aim steady for a very long time, and released his arrow. It struck the *paruri* dead center. The bird plummeted to the ground, flapping its wings, mortally wounded. Krihisiwä extracted the arrow, pulled down a piece of vine from a nearby tree, and tied the bird to the bamboo arrow-point quiver that dangled down his back between his shoulder blades.

The tapirs didn't come that night, although the lick was fresh and they had used it very recently. At dawn, shivering from the cold and damp-ness, we returned to the *shabono* with just a *paruri* bird. We had spent the long night peering into jungle, listening for tapirs and raiders, talking to each other in soft whispers.

On one visit to Patanowä-teri in 1968 I was surprised at how much authority Krihisiwä wielded. The incident grew out of a request I made to film the process of harvesting peach palm fruit, an activity that involved the use of a set of ingenious climbing frames the Yanomamö have in-vented for this purpose. The climbing unit consists of a pair of triangular frames made from strong, light wooden poles. One of the frames is placed above the other and loosely lashed to the thorny peach palm tree. The climber squats on the lower frame and pushes the upper one up the

Climb this tree or be banished.

trunk, then climbs onto the upper frame and pulls the lower one up, gets back onto that one and pushes the other one up higher, and so on. In this fashion the climber can slowly ascend the spine-covered tree, which can grow to forty feet tall.

Krihisiwä told a young man to make a pair of climbing frames and use them to climb the tree and harvest the now-ripe palm fruits. After Krihisiwä left, the young man refused to climb the tree, so I continued doing other work. Sometime that afternoon Krihisiwä asked me if I was satisfied with my filming of the young man climbing the peach palm tree. I said that the young man was unwilling to do it. Krihisiwä was furious and called the young man over and told him: "Either you climb that tree as I ordered you to or I will banish you from this village!" The young man promptly but nervously began to climb the tree as ordered. "Banishment" in this circumstance may have been a death sentence, since all the surrounding villages were at war with Patanowä-teri and the young man would have nowhere to go that would be safe.

Unokais

On a subsequent visit (in about 1986) I was checking details in a study I was doing on *unokais*. Long before then I knew the identities of every dead Yanomamö in my large sample of some four thousand people, and their causes of death as "diagnosed" by many informants in other villages. The Yanomamö attribute many deaths to various kinds of sicknesses and use a number of different words for these sicknesses. They also diagnose many deaths as the result of various forms of "harmful magic," but some of these deaths are caused by ordinary things like snakebites.

All observers agree when someone dies violently at the hands of another. Most of the time it is something like "he was shot by raiders." Less often, "He died in a clubfight" or "He died in a chest-pounding fight." Further questioning quickly reveals the village that the assailants came from and what weapons they killed him with—and often the names of one or more of the assailants. When an informant in Mishimishimaböwei-teri tells me that a man named Matowä was killed with arrows by raiders from Patanowä-teri and an informant in Mömariböwei-teri, many miles away, also knows this from the news of killings and wars and tells me the same thing, not knowing what the other informant said, or even whether I had asked someone else about how the same man died, this means that there is great consistency among informants from different, widely separated villages on violent causes of death. I am careful to make these kinds of inquiries of informants in private, always asking people who are not close relatives of the victim.

The men keep accurate tabs on these mortal events because it goes into their calculus of what they might expect from dealings with their neighbors. They need to know who among them is to be treated deferentially (because he is a known *unokai*) and who does not appear to be a threat. This kind of knowledge has obvious survival value. Members of a village in any given area know a great deal about the people in the next village over—and in many cases, had spent much of their lives living in the same village with the others before they split apart.

I eventually realized that the way I initially started collecting the information on causes of violent deaths did not permit me to exhaustively list the names of all of the assailants who shot fatal arrows into a victim. At the time I started doing this research I was primarily interested in documenting which village attacked which village and who was at war with whom. When I became interested in determining how many men were involved in the killing of every victim, my previously collected data listed only some of the killers. I had to fill in the missing names of all the killers of all the victims.

The task was relatively simple because I already knew the identities of who died at the hands of raiders, what village the raiders were from, and the names of at least some of the assailants. I had to revisit many widely separated villages by canoe and on foot to complete this work, but to have collected all of this data from scratch would have taken several years.

There is a Gary Larson cartoon that shows a couple of natives standing at the window of their thatched hut, grass skirts on, next to their TV sets. One says to the other: "Oh, damn! Here comes Margaret Mead. We'll have to put those old bones back into our noses and invent some new stories about our kinky sex habits." I could imagine a Gary Larson-style cartoon something like: "Oh, damn. Here comes that pesky Chagnon again . . . and this time his computer printout is three feet thick! He'll be asking questions for a month!"

Krihisiwä's Victims

Krihisiwä was easy to get along with and had indicated to me on previous visits that he was not reluctant to talk about the men he had killed. In fact, he seemed to be quite proud of these accomplishments.

When I began asking him privately about which men killed others he lit up and his eyes sparkled. This is how my conversation with him went that day.

Krihisiwä: Did I tell you how I killed three *huyas* from Ashidowä-teri?
[A neighboring village that had been chronically victimized and dominated by Krihisiwä's village. He had nothing but contempt for them.]

Chagnon: No, you never did tell me about that. What happened? (I suspected this would be a rather long story, so I settled in and got more comfortable in my hammock to take notes.)

Krihisiwä: These three *huyas* [holding three fingers up] showed up in our village wanting to trade for some of our things. They were all painted with *nara* pigment and decorated with their best feathers. They were very quiet and seemed to be nervous. My wife gave them some *date* [pronounced "dah-tay," a sweet, boiled ripe plantain soup, rather like banana pudding, customarily offered to visitors]. That seemed to make them more relaxed.

Chagnon: What happened next?

Krihisiwä: Okay. I'll tell you. They were sitting just under the roof overhang at the front of my house, squatting, and looking out over the plaza. They came to my house because I am the one who lives here! [A reference to himself as "the headman" here. He continued, becoming increasingly excited.] I could tell they were *moyawe* [alert, suspicious, apprehensive] and so I pretended that I was busy, straightening out my possessions, my hammock, my bow, cleaning the floor [ground] next to the hearth, rearranging things, etc. Without looking at them, I casually leaned my ax next to the front post . . . next to where they were sitting. [He stopped and looked expectantly at me, his eyes still flashing.] Well? Ask me what I did next!

Chagnon: [Going along with his request] Tell me, *shoabe* [father-in-law]: What did you do next?

Krihisiwä: I'll tell you what I did next! I worked my way over to where my ax was leaning against the front post, pretending to ignore them. They looked back a few times to see what I was doing, so I continued to straighten my things out and moved away from the ax. [He paused to remove the large wad of tobacco he had tucked between his lower lip and teeth and placed the slimy wad between the roof thatch and an overhead roof pole. He leaned over and put his face up close to mine and whispered hoarsely, spittle and tobacco juice hitting my face.] Ask me what I did next!

Chagnon: Okay . . . what did you do next?

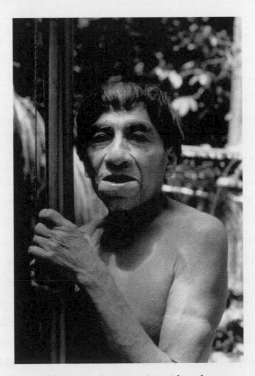

Krihisiwä, a Patanowä-teri headman

Krihisiwä: [Wiping the tobacco juice from his mouth and moving back
   where he had more room to act out the next scene, which would take
   more space] Let me tell you what I did next! Here's what I did! [He
   moved over to the front post of the house we were in and pretended
   to pick up a make-believe ax.] They had become more relaxed and
   stopped paying attention to me. I moved over to my front post and
   clandestinely grasped the handle of my ax, like this. When they weren't
   looking, I slowly raised it up! [He acted out the scene with great drama,
   and blurted:] Ask me what I did next!
Chagnon: [Feigning excitement and curiosity to go along with his
   increasingly dramatic actions, now sitting on the edge of my hammock]
   What did you do next?
Krihisiwä: [Taking a deep breath and then explosively shouting] *Kraaashii!*
   Kraaashi! Kraashi! I swung my ax down, burying the sharp edge of it
   into this *huya's* skull! That's what I did next! Kraaashi! Kraashi! [He
   paused, grinning excitedly.] Ask me what I did next!

When I asked him, he acted out, with equal drama, what he did to the
other two Ashidowä-teri *huyas.* He buried his ax into the skulls of each of
them in turn, as they frantically attempted to avoid his blows.

He killed all three of them where they were squatting, as visitors, in
front of his house. He apparently did so for no reason other than the fact
that he had contempt for their village because they were weaklings.

He calmed down after a few moments. We made small talk for a while,
and then we called it a day.

I was trembling when I got up to leave, thinking about how convincing
and deceptive a man like Krihisiwä could be while carefully calculating
how he could brutally kill three innocent visiting Yanomamö youths he
had put at ease—by treacherous deception—as they courteously visited
his house as his guests, trying to show no fear. In some cases, showing
no fear is fatal, even if it is prescribed by your culture and even admired
as something that leads to higher prestige.

Several years later, in 1990, I was visiting the Ashidowä-teri, located
several hours by trail upstream from the Dorita-teri (a Patanowä-teri faction). The Dorita-teri had threatened to kill me with axes on my last visit
because a Yanomamö from Mahekodo-teri (a village at the Salesian mis-

sion of Platanal) had walked into their village and told them I was killing their babies with my photographs and poisoning their water.

On this subsequent visit to Ashidowä-teri I had some six medical doctors and two of my graduate students with me.

About a dozen or so Dorita-teri (Patanowä-teri) men, bristling with bows and arrows, unexpectedly showed up and marched dramatically, if not arrogantly, across the village to the house where I was staying, which belonged to the local headman. They pointedly ignored the Ashidowä-teri headman, a remarkable breach of Yanomamö rules of etiquette. The Patanowä-teri had received information that I was visiting there and had come to invite me to their village. I accepted their invitation. Then they left. The Ashidowä-teri were trembling after their brief and unexpected visit, which lasted less than a half hour or so. The Patanowä-teri completely ignored them, as if they were servants or untouchables.

There is a conspicuous pecking order among villages where I have worked: some groups are bigger, stronger, and more feared than others, and the reputation of headmen like Krihisiwä is a big part of the reason. Krihisiwä and several other "big men" in Patanowä-teri had the power and authority to compel followers to obey them because they would use sanctions to compel them to do so.

Möawä: A Tyrannical Headman

My first contact with Mishimishimaböwei-teri, a very large, isolated village in the headwaters of the Mavaca River, came in 1968. There were several prominent leaders in this village, but the most feared was a man named Möawä, whom I described earlier. From the very beginning I could tell that I would eventually have difficulties with Möawä. The success of my work would depend very heavily on how I got along with him.

Möawä was the son of Ruwahiwä, the Shamatari headman whose death at the hands of Husiwä I recounted earlier.

Möawä was forceful, intimidating, and downright tyrannical even with his own co-villagers. He took what he wanted when he wanted it, and few people in his village would resist him. People feared him because he was capable of great violence. When he spoke or commanded, people listened and obeyed, albeit with little enthusiasm and often grudgingly.

When he threatened to take violent actions, everyone knew he meant what he said. When he was in a rare relaxed or happy mood, men obsequiously and cautiously gathered around him and directed their comments in his direction, as if they were hoping for—looking for—his approval. Men of great prestige and presence often command this kind of respect, but in this case it was more an expression of deference based on apprehension and genuine fear.

Möawä once visited Bisaasi-teri after the two groups made an uneasy peace in about 1968 or 1969. One incident that occurred then made his visit there remarkable.

It was not safe for some of the Mishimishimaböwei-teri to visit because many of the Bisaasi-teri could not forget their treachery at Amiana, where they held the 1950 nomohori—the treacherous feast—discussed earlier. After they had made peace on one visit by a small group of Mishimishimaböwei-teri, an enraged Bisaasi-teri man beat one of them so badly with the blunt end of an ax that he died en route back to Mishimishimaböwei-teri. Nobody avenged his death, which I found astonishing.

I was therefore stunned when Möawä showed up to visit Bisaasi-teri. Afterward, I asked the Bisaasi-teri headman, Kaobawä, why nobody molested him while he was there. Kaobawä explained that a notorious unokai like Möawä—who had killed twenty-one men—was fearless, and that other men, even his enemies, would be afraid to confront him face-to-face and would even cower in his presence.

As time went by I gradually came to know that Möawä's reputation and authority were firmly grounded in his accomplishments as an unokai. In fact, there is no Yanomamö in my extensive records who had killed more men than he. Some of his victims had even been former residents of his own village who fissioned away from his group.

Because of his forceful bearing and martial abilities, Möawä was able to attract a large following and hold it together. This is what I mean when I say that a strong headman can help keep a village large—adding cohesion where kinship and marriage alliances alone fail to do so. His reputation as an unokai provided an increased level of security, or at least a stronger sense of security, for members of his village.

But the security he added was relative. There were visits I made when

I had to put my pack and other containers between my hammock and the back of the roof lest raiders manage to get past the palisade and shoot me through the roof thatch. He might have been able to dominate men in his own village, but raiders from other groups were undeterred. He could not control the actions of enemies from other villages who would surreptitiously attack him when he was least able to deter their attack.

By 1972 Sibarariwä, a prominent man in Möawä's village, had formed a new group that was located several hours southwest by trail from the main Mishimishimaböwei-teri group. It took on the name Ironasi-teri to emphasize that it was no longer to be identified by neighbors as a temporary group of the Mishimishimaböwei-teri. It varied in size as the families within it went back to the main group but then decided to remain with the Ironasi-teri and moved back again. This is quite typical when groups fission and families are torn between allegiances to kin in both groups.

Life for the obedient in Möawä's village was secure but relatively apprehensive, but for the competitor, disobedient, or politically ambitious, residing in the same village with Möawä was dangerous. Competitors did not last long as co-residents because Möawä's overbearing manner led to frequent disputes, arguments, and constant strife. Men with some measure of self-esteem sooner or later fissioned away to form their own village, or packed up and left to join some other village where they also had kin, or they would simply head into the jungle with their immediate families to cool off and get away from Möawä for a while.

At least three prominent men in his village—Sibarariwä, Nanokawä, and Reirowä—were like him, but not nearly so tyrannical or personally offensive. All of these men were related to Möawä through the male line and, accordingly, all of them also had many kin in the village. Many of the men related through the male line in all lineages tend to be competitors—except for lineage members who are either full brothers or half brothers. More remote lineage members are competitors for women and political status.

There was a complicated history of these three men joining and leaving Möawä's village in recent years, a process of fission and fusion that hinged on how well they got along with Möawä.

My relationships to the village were largely predicated on my relationships with Möawä and his father-in-law, Dedeheiwä. Möawä called me "older brother" (abawä) and Dedeheiwä called me "son-in-law" (heka-maya). My relationships with Möawä were cold and strained, but with Dedeheiwä, friendly and relaxed. Dedeheiwä eventually became one of my most reliable informants as well as a good friend who frequently tried to smooth over my relationship with Möawä.

This was a situation unlike any other in my field experience. I was related as "brother" to many headmen in other villages and, with these headmen, I always enjoyed pleasant relationships. Möawä was a man I was never able to become friends with, but a man whom I could not avoid, even with deliberate attempts. He watched me constantly and de-manded that I sleep in his section of the shabono, right next to his ham-mock. I always take up residence next to one of the headmen in every village I visit, but none of them have ever demanded that I do this.

He had an annoying way of demanding things that others would sim-ply ask me to do, making it appear to others that I was obeying his com-mand when I intended to do it anyway.

It was clear from the outset that he would have it no other way: I had to sleep where he could watch my every move, and to force the issue would have precipitated a premature crisis. Indeed, toward the end, vir-tually every conversation or social encounter with him was of the nature of a tense crisis.

My growing awareness of how unpleasant Möawä was, how selfish and self-centered, came on the first day during my visit in 1970. I always brought with me tubes of antibiotic eye ointment when I visited remote villages, and made a point to check each child's eyes as soon as I ar-rived, treating those whose eyes were infected. When I left the village, I gave the leftover antibiotic tubes to selected adults around the village for future use by them and the children. Eye infections are very common among babies and, if untreated with antibiotics, cause great discomfort for months. Adults occasionally get the same infection, and the eye oint-ment was a welcome relief because it invariably cured the infections within a day or so.

On this visit Möawä had infected eyes and asked me to "cure" him as soon as I arrived. I did, and immediately the others began scurrying home to fetch their children. I began putting antibiotic ointment into the children's eyes right where my hammock was strung—in Möawä's house—whereupon Möawä barked a sharp, authoritative order and everybody scattered: "Get the hell out of here! That medicine is mine!"

He demanded all of the few tubes of eye ointment I had. At first, I thought he was joking, and I told him I was going to cure all the children and then give the adults the surplus tubes so they could continue to cure the children after I was gone. He was unflinching to the point of being obnoxious. He said he didn't care about the others or even if all of them went blind, and he forbade me to give the medicine to anybody but him. He repeated that he wanted it *all* for himself. "Let them all go blind!" he hissed: "That *mörösönö* [medicine] is mine!"

So I gave him several tubes of the ointment on the spot, but I concealed and saved a few tubes for my final day in the village when I surreptitiously gave them to more socially responsible men for their families and other children.

My reaction to Möawä's stinginess and cruel lack of concern for others in the village was not just my own appraisal of the situation. The Yanomamö themselves felt the same way about him and would privately let me know. Like parents everywhere, they are deeply concerned when their children are sick and when there is no available cure for the illness. They knew that my tubes of tetracycline ophthalmic ointment would cure their children and they were bitter when Möawä demanded it all for himself.

On another occasion I brought three triangular sharpening files with me on a trip to Möawä's village. The files are used to sharpen axes and machetes and they are much desired by the Yanomamö, who would otherwise have to sharpen their blades against a rock outcropping, a very time-consuming process that does not produce a satisfactorily sharp edge compared to what a steel file can do.

I intended to give one each to Möawä and Dedeheiwä (Möawä's father-in-law) and to keep the third one to loan to anybody who wanted to sharpen his machete. As soon as Möawä learned of the three files, he demanded that I give all of them to him—immediately. Seeing that this would possibly lead to a disagreement, I quickly gave one of them to old Dedeheiwä, to whom I had promised it, and one to Möawä, explaining publicly that the remaining one was mine, but I would happily loan it if someone wanted to borrow it.

Möawä immediately "borrowed" my file to sharpen his machete, even though I had just given one to him. After he finished sharpening his machete he announced publicly, with no small amount of authority and defiance in his voice, "This file now also belongs to me!" and stuck it into the rafters of his house above his head—next to the other one. He could not, however, appropriate the third one from Dedeheiwä because he was constrained by kinship prohibitions to respect his father-in-law.

Similar incidents developed around hallucinogenic seeds (hisiomö) whenever I brought them to the village to distribute among the prominent shamans. This was a very large village—over 250 people—and had a large number of shamans.

They use these drugs in their curing ceremonies almost daily. While another hallucinogen, called yakowana, is found in their area, hisiomö seeds are more powerful and more desirable. They are abundant only in the Ocamo River area, far to the north.

Möawä always demanded all of the hisiomö I would bring, and I was obliged to clandestinely give portions of these seeds away to others before he discovered that I had them. I knew, as did the others, that he would claim them all and refuse to share them fairly with the other shamans.

After my first two visits to his village, each suggestion or request he made was more like a command that had no alternative but compliance. The more often I visited his group, the more annoying and outrageous were the requests and demands he placed on me. My relationship to him, in response, was one of attempted avoidance and carefully calculated compromises that were geared to satisfy the substance of his request, but to indicate in a delicate way that there was a point beyond which I could not or would not go, at least on that particular occasion. This behavior is straightforward Yanomamö politics, and I was very much aware of it as an anthropologist who had spent a good deal of time living with them.

Möawä was no different from other Yanomamö in his persistent requests and demands for my madohe. What was different was that I felt that the probability of his doing something violent if disappointed was much higher than for other Yanomamö because of his reputation for hotheadedness, ill-temper, and impetuosity. It was a contest that I knew from the outset I would ultimately lose. All I wanted was to buy time on each visit in order to satisfy my curiosity about his village and collect the data I felt were required to adequately describe the political history, genealogical ties, and demography of this and adjacent groups.

From 1968 to 1971 I was able to conduct my field study in Mishimishimaböwei-teri with a tolerable degree of success despite a gradually accelerating feeling that things were not going well between Möawä and me.

Like all headmen, Möawä carefully weighed his requests and rarely made one that did not turn out the way he wanted it to. I was at first startled and then very intrigued by this consistent pattern among headmen, since it took consummate skill and ability to size up each situation, day after day, and consistently appear to have one's orders followed and requests satisfied. Kaobawä, the headman in Bisaasi-teri, where I began my work, was very accomplished at this and, in his dealings with me, he was very gracious and polite. Should there be any doubt in his mind that I might refuse one of his requests, it was never made in such a way that he asked for something and I refused. He would indicate, for example, that one of his friends from a distant village had arrived to visit and needed a machete, but he had none to give the man. Then he would pause, look at me, and say something like: "Dearest nephew, do you not have one lying around that you are not using?"

It worked every time, and I couldn't refuse such a gentle, polite, and sincere request. Möawä, on the other hand, would use a different style, harsher and more coercive. He would say something like: "Older brother! Give that man your machete and be quick about it! Do it right now!" (An unstated "or else" was always implicit.)

My routine field procedure was to distribute the majority of the trade goods I brought with me on the last day of my visit to that village. Before then I would usually dispense smaller items like fishhooks and fish line so both the adult men and the smaller boys could use them while I was there. It is primarily the adult men whom one must satisfy with trade goods. Giving fishhooks and nylon fishing line to the children when I arrived enabled them to bring additional food home, which pleased everyone in the family.

In 1972, the third time I lived in Mishimishimaböwei-teri, Möawä's patience had grown thin and he came to the point sooner than on previous trips: he bluntly ordered me, "Distribute all of your *madohe* right now and leave—but come back soon with more!" I was welcome in the village only so long as I had desirable items to give. Möawä insisted that I give them away *immediately* and almost all of them to *him*.

I tried to pace myself and nurse the situation along until it was time for me to leave the village so that my distribution of *madohe* came at a time when I had no more work projected and, therefore, I required no further approval from him or the people he could influence.

Even before my third trip to Mishimishimaböwei-teri, Möawä was constantly manipulating the status-establishing mechanisms, turning every conversation or personal interaction into a kind of contest to see if he could browbeat me into a new promise or to show me and, more important, show members of the village, where we both stood socially, demonstrating that he could order me and I would obey.

One annoying habit he fell into was to wait until a lesser individual made some request that I refused and then immediately make the same request. He seemed to seek out these opportunities, no matter how small and insignificant they were. They often began with my water supply. People would sit around my hut watching and listening to me interviewing people and periodically see what my reaction would be to a request for water. Nobody was thirsty, everybody had water, and the stream was just a few yards away. It was a pretext to test the relative status of individuals. If I complied with these innocent requests, the supplicant's status would rise and mine would decline: his presence and authority were such that I, by complying, endorsed his higher status and my inferior status. Then all the others would immediately try the same thing.

I usually refused to give in to requests for drinks, not because my water was scarce and valuable, but because I knew that after the water came my food, then my matches, then my hammock, then the clothing off my back, and so on.

Möawä had the annoying habit of waiting for me to casually refuse a drink of my water to someone, then coming over to me and asking not only for a drink, but also for my personal drinking cup from which to drink it. It seems irrational now, even to me, but tiny, chronic events like these took on larger proportions in the field, where I had long since become aware of the acceleration of demands that would follow.

Whenever I lived in Möawä's village (and in many other villages), I always had a crowd of cheerful, happy, and eager children in "my house" most of the day. They were a welcome contrast to the often-strained life in the adult world. I enjoyed chatting and joking with these cheerful children.

They became very fond of my salted crackers and other tidbits I gave to them. For example, I would ask them to wash my dishes and fetch water in the nearby stream and pay them with crackers. They enjoyed this and took turns. It didn't matter who actually washed the dishes or carried the water; they all shared in the crackers, and we were all quite pleased with this arrangement. But after several days of this on one of my stays, Möawä rose suddenly from his hammock and drove the children away with angry threats, pelting them with hard fruit seeds, sticks, and whatever he could find on the ground near his hearth. He then turned to me and hissed: "If you have any crackers to give away, give them to me! These crackers shall be mine from now on, and don't you ever give crackers to these brats again."

Möawä, too, had grown fond of my crackers and my other food, even though I was careful to share with him a portion of every one of the

Möawä, the Mishimishimaböwei-teri headman

meals I prepared for myself. He now insisted on exclusive rights to all of the food I might share with others.

Möawä and My 1972 Blood-Sampling Trip

The last straw took place in 1972 when as soon as I entered the village, Möawä demanded that I immediately give away all of the *madohe* I had brought and go back downstream to Mavaca (a two-day trip) to get more.

Nineteen seventy-two was the last year I would be associated with Neel's department and the team that did the blood sampling. I had decided to leave the University of Michigan at the end of this field season to take a position at Pennsylvania State University. But Neel had asked me to collect blood samples from about fifteen families of Mishimishimaböwei-teri who were not in the village when I took his biomedical team there a previous year. The missing people were primarily families living in Sibarariwä's group in Ironasi-teri and had not been present when Neel's team was with me.

I would do the sampling by myself and had brought with me the requisite number of Vacutainers, syringes, and disposable needles for this work, as well as "payment" to compensate the Yanomamö. The payment included some fifteen machetes for the male heads of the families from whom I would take blood samples. I had given machetes to the Mishimishimaböwei-teri male heads of families on the previous blood-sampling trip.

My plan on this trip was to visit Sibarariwä's village for a short stay to collect the blood samples. I would take the blood samples back downstream and then return again to Mishimishimaböwei-teri. A special bush pilot flight had been arranged specifically to transport these blood samples. That meant I had to plan carefully around the date of the pilot's arrival at the mission airstrip at Ocamo. Without a radio, I could not change this date. Taking the blood samples would require a long two-day trip from Mishimishimaböwei-teri downstream to Ocamo traveling ten hours per day in a *voladora*, a light aluminum boat powered by a relatively large outboard motor in the 25-horsepower range. And, after that, a long trip back up the same river to do my anthropological fieldwork.

My regular Yanomamö traveling companion was a young man named Rerebawä, as I have mentioned earlier. He enjoyed coming with me to visit the Mishimishimaböwei-teri—old Dedeheiwä was a renowned shaman, and Rerebawä was learning a great deal by just watching and listening to him. Rerebawä wanted to be a shaman as well and hoped that Dedeheiwä would be his mentor.

On our way to the village Rerebawä and I fortuitously encountered a number of Mishimishimaböwei-teri who were returning by trail from Iwahikoroba-teri, where they had just traded and participated in a feast. The feast had also included a large group of visitors from Yeisikorowä-teri, a remote and yet-uncontacted Shamatari village that lay several days to the south of Mishimishimaböwei-teri.

Since the returning visitors would reach Mishimishimaböwei-teri before we did, I asked them to inform Möawä and Dedeheiwä of my plans, and that I intended to "live" with them in Mishimishimaböwei-teri after I collected the blood samples from Sibarariwä's group. The visitors said they would also send young men in the morning to carry our equipment,

Dedeheiwä (center left), renowned shaman

for there was more than Rerebawä and I could carry in on one trip by ourselves. Although the medical research supplies were light, they were packed in very bulky Styrofoam containers.

It was already late in the afternoon so we decided to sleep next to the river to give us time to take the canoe, motor, and gasoline supplies out of the water, secure them, repack, and make camp. We gathered fire-wood, made a fire, strung our hammocks to trees, stretched a small tarp over them, and boiled some rice for dinner. I soon fell asleep. Rerebawä's task was to add more wood to our small fire and to keep vigil for jaguars.

At dawn a party of men and boys arrived, many of them from Sibara-riwä's group. I had arrived at a time when Sibarariwä's entire village was visiting Möawä's group for a mortuary ceremony. That was good news be-cause I would not have to walk another half day to reach their *shabono*. I could do the blood sampling in Möawä's village.

When we reached the village, I had the carriers, as usual, put all of my possessions in front of Möawä's house. Dedeheiwä's house was the next one over from Möawä's, which I always found somewhat puzzling because men should avoid their in-laws, particularly their mothers-in-law. Möawä was married to one of Dedeheiwä's daughters, yet their re-spective houses were side by side. His mother-in-law, Dedeheiwä's eldest wife, was already menopausal.

I explained my schedule and my plan to collect blood samples from the members of Sibarariwä's village who had not been sampled the year before, and told Möawä that I would be taking the samples downstream immediately, explaining that I would return shortly after that for a much longer stay.

He appeared to understand and seemed to endorse what I was tell-ing him, but his attention at that moment was fixed on the cluster of the fifteen machetes that were lying on the ground near my pack. The machetes were wrapped with vines to hold them together. He wanted to know what else I brought for him this year, whether I had any tobacco (their crop had failed) or any *hisiomö* seeds.

The machetes, I carefully and patiently explained, were intended for Sibarariwä and the others in his group, as payment for their blood samples, but I would immediately give one to him if he couldn't wait for my second trip. I had no tobacco with me, but I would surely bring large quantities back with me when I returned and I would also try to get *his-iomö* for them as well because the plane I would meet would be landing at Ocamo, the center for trade in *hisiomö*.

While I was helping a few young men construct a temporary palm-wood shelf for my packs and supplies, Möawä decided that he wanted to examine the machetes, so he cut the vine bindings that held the three small packages together and laid all fifteen of them out on the ground before his hammock, examining each one carefully and admiringly. It was a discourteous and insulting thing to do—you don't unpack and snoop through a visitor's belongings. I told him again that they were for the other group but that I would soon be back with many more machetes, like the ones he was looking at, after I took the blood samples downstream: "The plane would bring me many machetes," I said.

There was a crowd of men around his hammock, all of them from his group and none of them from Sibarariwä's. His face turned solemn at the third repetition of my intended disposition of the machetes. He looked at me coldly and then bluntly informed me that the machetes were to be distributed to the men *he* designated and *none of them* were to be given to people in Sibarariwä's group: they were thieves and liars, he said, and they were not to have *any* of these machetes.

I knew that matters were, after these several years, finally coming to a head. He went on. I was to give *all* of my *madohe* away *immediately* and not defer my distribution until I planned to leave. Moreover, the *madohe* was to be given to people that he named. If I had food to give away, he would see that it was eaten. He had also heard that in villages to the south, where the Yanomamö had foreigners living among them (from Brazil), the foreigners gave large numbers of shotguns to the Yanomamö. He informed me that he decided he wanted *my* shotgun and that I was to leave it and my ammunition with him when I left his village.

As he made demand after pointed demand I knew that this was going to be a delicate situation. I would not get any blood samples unless I was prepared to give trade goods in return, and I knew that as soon as I began paying for the blood samples according to my own plan, I might have a serious confrontation with Möawä.

Had I not promised Neel that I would collect these blood samples, the most appropriate course of action would have been to simply take my

things and leave the village on the spot in view of Möawä's outrageous demands and conditions. But I had too much medical equipment for me and
Rerebawä to take back to the canoe without carriers from Möawä's group.

To take blood samples or to make films with a filmmaking colleague, I
needed as many as eight or ten local carriers into and out of the villages I
visited. Collaborating with colleagues whose work entailed carrying large
quantities of the items had reduced my own research goals. All I needed
for myself was two backpacks and one guide.

That night Dedeheiwä and others again told Rerebawä of the attempt
on my life in Iwahikoroba-teri the previous year (discussed earlier). Rerebawä once again whispered the story to me from a distance, over the jabbering in the village. I again heard that the Iwahikoroba-teri—Boraböwä
and his brothers—had tried to kill me. It was annoying to be reminded
of how plausible the threats to my life had become. They could be easily
dismissed in the comfort and safety of Bisaasi-teri, but the Iwahikoroba-
teri were possibly just a day or two away on a well-traveled trail linking
them to the Mishimishimaböwei-teri.

I fell asleep worrying how I would be able to get the blood samples
and still remain on good terms with Möawä. The unsuccessful attempt
on my life by Boraböwä and his brothers the previous year had apparently impressed Möawä, and he had decided to drop any remaining veil
of diplomacy and patience. Not only was I to distribute my possessions
immediately, but I was to go back downstream to fetch tobacco and more
trade goods for him.

I visited with old friends the next day, took a new set of ID photos of
Sibarariwä's group, and worked in the garden with Dedeheiwä, having
him resolve questions that had arisen as a consequence of conflicting
information obtained from several other informants the previous year—
mostly informants from other villages. He also identified the Polaroid
photographs of those members of Sibarariwä's group—mostly children—
that I did not yet know well, and filled in genealogical gaps and omis-
sions in page after page of genealogies that I had converted to computer
printouts.

I avoided Möawä all the next day and went to bed long after he retired. Just to let me know he was around and keeping track of me, he
shouted at me occasionally to go to bed so he could get some sleep. I

assured him I would be doing so very soon. He had developed the habit on the occasion of my last two visits of ordering me to go to sleep when he was weary of observing me. It was just one more way of letting me know that he gave the orders in the village. Objecting to the disturbance I made was a fairly thin pretext, since the village often would be rocking with loud arguments, chatter, and chanting to the point of being a din. But that noise didn't bother him. The thin, silent beam of my flashlight on my notebook did.

Early the next morning Dedeheiwä told me that they were going to drink the remains of "someone" and I should get ready to take photographs if I wanted to do that. I was surprised by his suggestion because the Yanomamö don't like outsiders taking pictures or tape-recording the passionate wailing and sobbing during a funerary ceremony. They do not even like outsiders to get close to the mourners. I asked him if he thought it would be advisable, and he assured me that it would. He would even stay at my side to make sure nobody became unduly hostile to me. He had apparently decided to make a stand on my behalf and let everyone know that he would protect me if I filmed the funerary ceremony.

For the few mortuary ceremonies I witnessed, I always remained at a comfortable distance and just watched. I think that Dedeheiwä was deeply concerned about Möawä's unpleasantness toward me and did this to show me that he had considerable authority in this village, but perhaps more important, to remind Möawä and the others that he did.

The deceased had to be someone important. I asked Dedeheiwä in a soft whisper if the deceased were a man named Reirowä, a logical guess in view of the kinship ties among the assembled mourners, who were all prominent men in the same patrilineage. Dedeheiwä indicated quietly by nodding that my guess was correct.

Just before the ceremony began, Dedeheiwä came over to tell me to prepare my camera equipment. He told me he was increasingly concerned about the way Möawä was treating me and asked me privately to overlook it. He also urged me to take the blood samples in the afternoon, after the ceremony was over, because people would be dispersing and would not be going directly home. This was almost a full week earlier than I had planned to take the samples and would complicate the schedule for flying them out.

I quietly asked Dedeheiwä if he would come with me to Mavaca and work with me, away from the village, to reconcile a large number of questions that my premature departure would leave unanswered. He agreed to come.

I photographed and filmed the mortuary ceremony. Dedeheiwä remained at my side for most of it. A number of young men, emulating Möawä, made verbal objections while I filmed, but Dedeheiwä scolded them and told me to ignore them. Surprisingly, none of the *patas* (prominent men who were leaders) or *browähähä* (young men striving to be leaders but not as prominent as *patas*) objected. When it was over, Dedeheiwä conspicuously escorted me back to my section of the village.

I told them that I would begin to collect the blood samples late in the afternoon and continue this work the following morning. Luckily, some of those to whom Möawä ordered me to give machetes were men whose blood samples I intended to collect.

I told these men that I wanted samples from them, their wives and their children, and would give only the heads of households machetes, as my "younger brother had instructed me to do." The women would get small glass beads and the children fishhooks and fish line. While I prepared the equipment for sampling, most of the men of the village were by now busy taking hallucinogenic drugs and violently striking down *hekura* spirits sent from enemy villages. Everyone seemed to be in an unpredictable, surly mood after the mortuary ceremony.

There were over 400 people in the village at that time, the largest group of Yanomamö under one roof (*shabono*) I had ever seen in an isolated and unacculturated village.

It was one of the most volatile situations I have ever been in. To make matters more tense, a terrible fight broke out between Dedeheiwä's wife and several of the visiting women from Ironasi-teri. Dedeheiwä's wife screamed at the Ironasi-teri women across the village, "You ugly bitches! Always demanding more than your share of the meat! You come here and eat us out of house and home, and insult the people who feed you by demanding more than what they themselves eat! We work while you lie around flirting with our men. Your foreheads are filthy! You are all *shami* [filthy, polluted]."

They replied in kind, the insults growing hotter and more vitriolic until some of the women began picking up pieces of firewood and threatening to attack their adversaries. Dedeheiwä, reeling from the effects of the hallucinogenic snuff, staggered all the way across the village plaza and shouted at his wife: "Shut up! Stop insulting them! I'll have to beat you if you keep up that kind of talk!" He had to make several trips to convince her that he meant what he said.

He was well advised to stop the argument, for it was rapidly approaching the point where the women would start hitting each other with pieces of firewood, and then the fight would have extended to the men. In congregations of Yanomamö this large, and with most of the men high on drugs, such a fight would have been disastrous because there were many old, smoldering, personal grievances among the men, grievances that invariably involved previous illicit seductions or suspected seductions.

The fight among the women had to do with the distribution of the meat at the mortuary ceremony. The women from the visiting group felt that they had been slighted and had gotten less than the women from the local group, which was probably the case. There was a message in this manner of meat distribution, and it said that the visitors were no longer welcome and should return to their own village and eat their own food as soon as this event ended.

In the midst of this unhappy and volatile assembly, I pondered what to do about the blood samples. It seemed unlikely that I could persuade Sibarariwä and his group to remain at Möawä's for another week to accommodate my schedule. He and the members of his group were now being openly insulted by the locals. I could leave Möawä's village to go to Sibarariwä's village except that his group planned to split into several smaller groups and go in different directions. From this remote village, there was no way to contact the pilot and change the schedule I had earlier established with him. I would probably have to take the samples early, as Dedeheiwä suggested to me. I knew the mission downstream had refrigeration and could make ice. I would have to rely on that to keep the samples from spoiling.

As I was pondering what to do, Möawä and a few of the lesser leaders told me that they had invited the Iwahikoroba-teri to come for a feast, which they had not mentioned to me until now. The Mishimishimaböwei-teri told me that the Iwahikoroba-teri would have to pass by the spot at

the river where I had left my canoe and would then know that I was visiting Möawä's village. Möawä reminded me how angry the Iwahikoroba-
teri were with me, and how some of them might lie in ambush when I left
and shoot me with arrows as I descended the Mavaca.

The Yanomamö sometimes fire volleys of arrows at people—
strangers—in canoes even on the well-traveled Orinoco River. But, because the Orinoco is wide and the canoes are usually some distance from
the bank, nobody gets hit—neither the Yanomamö nor the Europeans
with them. I've been shot at this way a number of times, but it was likely
that the archers were only expressing their frustration that I was bypass-
ing their village to avoid the predictable begging from them. At least, that
explanation was comforting to me at the time.

But the Mavaca River at this distance from the mouth was a tiny
stream—hardly more than a canoe's length wide for the first day's travel.
It would have been difficult for an archer to miss at that range.

Möawä could tell that this information annoyed and disturbed
me. If I stayed for another week I would surely have to confront the
Iwahikoroba-teri visitors. Initially, when such a possibility seemed to
exist, Möawä and his supporters told me that they would make sure that
the Iwahikoroba-teri would not harm me. Then Möawä began hinting
around that while I might be safe within his village, there would be nothing he could do to prevent the Iwahikoroba-teri from ambushing me between the village and my canoe or downstream from it. When these hints
became more pointed I decided to collect the samples immediately and
leave Mishimishimaböwei-teri as soon as possible. Möawä calculated
that he would get the fifteen machetes, as he planned.

When I moved my blood-sampling equipment over to an unoccupied
section of the village, I was surrounded by about two hundred pushy,
impatient, squabbling people—mostly older men and *huyas,* each determined to get a particular item of which I had very few to distribute.

They jabbed and poked me constantly as I worked, each person
demanding items, while I methodically continued to draw the blood
samples. It was very hot that day and there was no breeze. They were
crowded in so close I could not move an inch in any direction. If I
hunched over to take a close look at a vein in someone's arm, the space
I just evacuated was immediately filled with sweaty Yanomamö bodies.

To make matters worse, everyone was breaking wind, a characteristic reaction to the food at feasts and mortuary ceremonies. A hundred or so men were farting at very close range. Anxious as my situation was, I recall breaking up with uncontrollable laughter at one point when I complained about the foul odor they were eliminating in such cramped quarters.

One of them, a young guy I knew well, immediately stood up defiantly and retorted cynically: "Farting? Who's farting? Why, we Yanomamö do not even have assholes in this village, so how could we fart?"

The genuine humor of his retort and my hilarious reaction started them all laughing, momentarily easing tensions. Tears were running down our faces we were laughing so hard.

When I began the blood sampling, Möawä had come over and repeated his instructions firmly: the machetes were to go to the men *he* specified, nobody else. He watched as I took the first few samples, so I deliberately chose local men that he had specified, but men whose samples I intended to collect anyway for the special paternity study. He seemed to be convinced that I was following his instructions and left to rejoin the drug taking, chanting, and calling to the *hekura*. He came back once again to check on me.

When I ran out of the men Möawä had chosen (and their wives and children), I then had to choose my patients very carefully. From my knowledge of past disputes in the group when Sibarariwä and his faction lived in the same village with Möawä, I knew who the men were that had stood up to Möawä in the past, men he could not easily dominate. I began calling them, in turn, gambling that Möawä would be less able to prevent me from giving my machetes to these men and hoping that these men would encourage the rest of their group to cooperate with me when the machetes ran out.

Instead of taking their families in turn, as I had done before, I quickly sampled the important men and paid them with machetes without sampling their wives and children at that time.

I was down to one machete when someone told Möawä what I had done. He trotted over in a rage and stared in disbelief at the single machete that was still lying on the ground at my feet. He glared at me with hatred in his eyes, and I defiantly glared back at him. He was clutching an ax in his hands and was trembling with anger. We stared at each other for some moments before he hissed: "You aren't following my orders, you son of a bitch! And don't you ever look at me that way!" He then raised his ax to strike, and I saw how white his lips and knuckles were. He hissed at me: "Either you give that machete to that man over there, or I'll bury this ax in your skull!"

Needless to say, I gave the remaining machete to the man he specified, but not before leisurely taking his unneeded blood sample to make it look as if it were part of my intended routine.

I worked late into the night and went to bed long after Möawä was sleeping. I remember feeling somewhat confident that he wouldn't try anything that night, since he was out of tobacco and he knew that I had promised to come back with a large quantity of it for him. After all, had I not invited Dedeheiwä to come along with me, and would I not have to bring the old man back up to the village?

The next morning I finished the blood sampling, but there were only odds and ends of trade goods left, so the crowd was much smaller. They were impatient to have me finish so that I could leave the village, go downstream, and collect more *madohe* for them. Möawä's blatant display of hostility had impressed the younger men and even some of the *yawäwä*—adolescent boys who had only recently begun tying their penises to their belly strings. These young guys were now emboldened and openly insulted me. I know of at least one war that started when boys this young openly insulted an adult prominent man—Kaobawä—when he visited their village to ask for plantains.

They repeatedly told me to hurry or else the Iwahikoroba-teri would surely catch me between the village and my canoe.

It was noon and raining before I stopped drawing blood samples. Möawä was so desperate for tobacco that he asked me for some of my pipe tobacco to chew. I refused, saying I had run out, but told him I would give to him a whole can of it that I had left at the river. He refused to walk out to collect it, but sent a youth along to bring it back for him.

We walked to the canoe in a dreary rain, not quite a downpour but more than a mere drizzle. Everything was soaked by the time we made it to the canoe some four hours later.

I carefully loaded my things into the canoe and asked Dedeheiwä to get in. Just as I was about to push out into the current, my canoe prow pointed downstream, the youth whom Möawä had sent stepped forward and asked for the can of tobacco I had promised to Möawä. I told him that I needed it and had decided not to give it. If Möawä wanted it that badly, he should have come to the river to get it himself.

I knew that when this remark was passed along, it would anger Möawä. I had no intention of coming back to the village so long as Möawä lived there.

When we reached the mouth of the Mavaca and the village of Bisaasi-teri, I worked with Dedeheiwä for longer than I told Möawä I intended to. I figured that if anybody were going to lie in wait along the riverbank to take potshots at me, they would have to wait for some time. It was foolish to follow a schedule that I had announced in advance. After I had worked for about a week with Dedeheiwä, Rerebawä told the Bisaasi-teri how Möawä treated us and how he threatened to kill me with an ax. They were angry and kept telling me, "We told you so!"

Seeing that the Bisaasi-teri were growing openly angry at his own fellow villagers, Dedeheiwä told me that he wanted to go home. Although the Bisaasi-teri liked him because he had helped some of them escape the horrible 1950 treacherous feast, he felt uncomfortable.

I dreaded the trip back upstream and worried about it all that week. At night I would dream about raiders behind every tree, of ambushes at every bend in the river where Iwahikoroba-teri hunters had been periodically seen in recent years. I would have to pass through this area for at least six or eight hours of river travel with the fastest boat I could find and chop my way through new deadfalls; the river would be very narrow from that point on. The Iwahikoroba-teri probably knew by now that I would be bringing Dedeheiwä back upstream soon.

For the long trip back upstream I decided to leave my heavy dugout behind and mount my 18-horsepower motor on my small sixteen-foot aluminum rowboat. The dugout was too heavy and too slow for this trip. I had already left supplies of gasoline hidden along the riverbank, the only way that such a small boat could make such a long trip because it could not carry enough fuel to travel upstream and back without additional fuel.

I again asked Rerebawä to come along. He had grown to hate Möawä.

He was very disturbed by Möawä's threat on my life and did not care if he ever saw him again. He told me that when Möawä raised his ax as if to strike me, he had grabbed my shotgun and was prepared to shoot him if he tried to hit me with the ax. He probably would have had no choice, because if Möawä had killed me, he would also have killed Rerebawä because he was my friend.

Rerebawä, Dedeheiwä, and I set off for Mishimishimaböwei-teri and the upper Mavaca, where I would let Dedeheiwä off. I did not tell him, but I knew I would not be seeing him for a very long time.

It was a long, anxious trip for me. The river had dropped markedly during the week, and that high up in its course it was again choked with logs and new deadfalls. After chopping our way through many of them we finally came to one that could not be passed without several hours of chopping. It was only a few minutes by boat below our final destination, so I put Dedeheiwä ashore at this point and gave him the tobacco I had obtained from the Bisaasi-teri.

It was difficult for me to watch my old friend disappear into the jungle, perhaps never to see him again. He also seemed very sad. I couldn't tell if it was because he suspected that I would probably not be back for a long time or because he accidentally dropped his large bundle of tobacco into the bottom of the canoe and got it wet. All he said when he got out of the canoe was: *"Ya nobreäö."* It means something like, "I'm really bummed out about this."

Sibarariwä

Sibarariwä was a legend among the Yanomamö in the Mavaca area. I knew quite a bit about him even before I met him because my local informants in Bisaasi-teri talked about him all the time. They despised him because he had engineered the infamous *nomohori* and, with his co-villagers and allies, killed many Bisaasi-teri, and abducted many of their women that day. Of all the Shamatari they wanted to kill, he was at the top of their hit list.

When I first decided to try to find his village and visit it, my local informants, genuinely concerned about my safety, tried to dissuade me. They assured me that he would kill me if I visited his group. He would probably kill me at night, when I was sleeping and off guard.

When I first contacted the Mishimishimaböwei-teri in 1968, Sibarariwä appeared from the forest, in a drizzle, and silently took up the hammock next to me. Nobody had to tell me who he was—I knew it was Sibarariwä by the hush that fell over the camp the moment he arrived and by the darting, nervous glances the other men made in his direction.

It took me almost twenty-five years to gain his confidence, probably because I started my field research career in a village whose members were his mortal enemies, Bisaasi-teri, and he identified me with these people and their headman, Kaobawä. I saw Sibarariwä periodically on my regular visits to his area after 1968, but he was always aloof and didn't warm up to me like the others did.

The last time I saw Sibarariwä was in 1991, after I had made several trips by helicopter into the unexplored Siapa area. In 1991 he surprised me because he had never been openly friendly with me until then. It was a brief, hurried encounter. I was just passing through his village on my way back by helicopter from several extremely remote villages in the headwaters of the Siapa River far to the east of Mishimishimaböwei-teri. This was the area where Sibarariwä had been born some seventy or more years earlier and whose residents and history he probably knew better than any man I had yet spoken with. He came up to me for the first time, happy and excited, and said he had been watching me a long time. I knew, because I watched *him* watch me for a long time and he usually said nothing. He just watched me with no expression on his face, avoiding conversations whenever I would ask him something. Whenever I spoke directly to him he usually gave a simple one-word answer and then moved farther away to watch me from a distance.

But on this occasion he knew I had just returned from the Siapa headwaters and had just spent a month living among several villages whose oldest residents were his boyhood friends—and most of whom were his kinsmen. Now, he announced enthusiastically, he wanted to tell me the "truth" about all the things he had heard me asking others for such a long time. He promised me he would do so the next time I came back, quickly rattling off a dozen extraordinary facts just to whet my appetite. Unfortunately, we never saw each other again after that.

The few facts he volunteered on that brief meeting made it clear that he knew much more than I suspected he did and that he had thoughtfully identified aspects of his group's history that he knew I didn't quite have straight. I was disappointed that my 1991 field season was ending but I eagerly looked forward to my 1992 trip and hoped to spend several weeks in Kedebaböwei-teri, his current residence, working intimately with him about the history of his people and the history of those in the surrounding villages—including villages that had long since migrated far to the south into Brazil.

But by 1992 the Salesians had turned against me after twenty-five years of generally cordial relationships for reasons I will explain in the next chapter. Because of their influence, for the first time in more than twenty-five years of field research among the Yanomamö I was denied a research permit for the following year.

This clash was, perhaps, inevitable. The Salesians had been attempting since 1973 to relocate the Shamatari villages I was studying. The Salesians at their Mavaca mission persuaded about half of the Mishimishimaböwei-teri to move out to a navigable portion of the upper Mavaca River. I visited them when I returned to the area in 1974 and was both surprised and annoyed that the missionaries had enticed them to move from their safer location deeper in the interior with a promise to feed them with plantains they would transport by boat from their distant mission at Mavaca. The Yanomamö moved out to a navigable stretch of the upper Mavaca River without first clearing gardens. Ordinarily a Yanomamö village moved only after its gardens at the new location were producing reliable quantities of food.

There was great anguish and mourning when I arrived in 1974 at the new village without a garden. Many of the older men were chanting passionately to their *hekura* spirits to drive off the sickness that had just killed several infants the night before. Two or three funeral pyres were burning the tiny bodies. I solemnly approached one of them to express my personal grief and squatted silently near it and lowered my head to mourn for the dead child. I could see the infant's tiny, lifeless hand and lower arm protruding from the stacked pieces of hastily gathered firewood that surrounded it. I watched the flames gradually grow, lick at, and then consume the little hand. It turned from talcum white to brown, split open, oozed bubbling fluid for a few seconds, and then disappeared in the flames.

It was Sibarariwä's newest child, his twenty-third offspring, about two months old at its death. Sibarariwä had tears streaming down his tired, drawn face. He danced methodically around the pyre, chanting in despair, his face rhythmically turning from the funeral pyre upward, to the sky, his outstretched arms pleading and supplicating his personal spirits with mournful injunctions, punctuated with quieter melancholy incantations.

Our eyes met for a brief instant, long enough for me to communicate my sadness to him and for him to acknowledge it in a seemingly understanding momentary glance. He turned away and continued to chant sorrowfully. I squatted motionless until the pyre burned down while he danced in his despair around it. I then quietly left.

Shabono with no garden at Mishimishimaböwei-teri

He would come back later, when the ashes cooled, and recover the unburned bones of his child and grind them into a fine powder. He and the infant's mother would solemnly consume them and weep. The child would never be mentioned again.

The short-lived group abandoned this place without a garden soon afterward for it portended sickness and death. They returned to their previous, more remote location, which could not be reached by boat.

Sometime in the early 1980s the Salesians again persuaded a faction of the Mishimishimaböwei-teri to move to a navigable portion of the Mavaca River and established a small mission post at a place they named Mavakita—"Little Mavaca." It was about halfway up the Mavaca River from where it joined the Orinoco River. This small group took the name Haoyaböwei-teri, the name of the tiny stream where they settled. This stream flowed into the Mavaca just across the river and slightly upstream from the Salesian satellite post of Mavakita.

At approximately the same time another large faction of the Mishimishimaböwei-teri had moved to the northwest into the headwaters of a small affluent of the Mavaca called Kedebaböwei kä u and took the village name Kedebaböwei-teri. (These were the former Ironasi-teri.) Sibarariwä and his large family lived in this group.

In 1987 the Salesians at Mavaca persuaded the 175 or so residents of Kedebaböwei-teri to move out to the banks of the Mavaca, a short way upstream from where the Haoyaböwei-teri were living. I spent about a week with them in 1987 at this new location. The Salesians had persuaded them to plant nothing but bitter manioc and planned to have them grind it into manioc flour with machines the Salesians provided so the Salesians would be free of their dependence on the Ye'kwana, who provided the manioc flour used by the missions.

By 1992 my long-term good relationships with the Salesians had come to an end. The Salesians wanted the Yanomamö and the Amazonas territory all to themselves. And a growing number of pro-Yanomamö advocacy groups and the anthropologists who worked for or with them wanted to be associated with the now-famous Yanomamö. Their interests overlapped with the interests of the Salesians.

The Salesians had removed Padre Cocco from the Ocamo mission in about 1975, against his wishes, and offered him an administrative post in Caracas. They replaced him with another Italian priest, Padre José Bórtoli. It broke Padre Cocco's heart to leave his beloved Yanomamö. He decided to go back to Italy. He was weary and in failing health from many years of exposure to malaria. I was a visiting professor at Cambridge University in 1980 when I received a handwritten note from a nun in Italy. She had been the mother superior of Padre Cocco's mission at Ocamo and his lifelong friend. She had retired immediately after the 1968 measles epidemic in Venezuela, which struck first at Ocamo. The measles epidemic exhausted her physically because of her heroic and time-consuming efforts tending to the sick Yanomamö there.

A visiting Italian biologist at Cambridge translated her letter. She informed me that Padre Cocco had died. She said that she wanted me to know that he was very fond of me and that I would want to know of his death.

The Italian biologist who orally translated her letter to me had tears in his eyes as he read her letter to me because her letter, handwritten in nineteenth-century script, moved him very much.

14

Twilight in Cultural Anthropology: Postmodernism and Radical Advocacy Supplant Science

How I Became a Sociobiologist

My theoretical views on the anthropology of human behavior became increasingly affected by new discoveries in theoretical biology, including the rapidly growing awareness among biologists and some anthropologists that the "unit" on which natural selection operated most effectively was the individual, not the group.

The traditional anthropological view of natural selection emphasized the importance of the "group," "society," and "culture." By the mid-1970s anthropologists in general were increasingly hostile to the works of E. O. Wilson, Richard Dawkins, George Williams, and William Hamilton, who represented the new thinking. In my research and publications, however, I became increasingly supportive of their work. Not surprisingly, a growing number of cultural anthropologists, including some prominent ones like Harris, Sahlins, and Clifford Geertz, began singling out my work for criticism because of my support for Wilson and the others.

By the 1980s and early 1990s, I began detecting a shift in the Salesian attitudes toward my fieldwork and my frequent returns to the Yanomamö area. While the Salesians had their own reasons to oppose me (such as my discovery of Yanomamö deaths caused by shotguns the Salesians provided and their concern that I might report this discovery to the authorities), I learned that they had begun using my "unpopularity" in academic circles for their own purposes. To the Salesians, subscribing to the theory of evolution meant, among other things, holding the view that humans could be compared to monkeys, apes, and other animals, and frequently were. They began to inform the Yanomamö at their missions that I wanted to show that the Yanomamö were comparable to monkeys. One of my long-time Yanomamö acquaintances at the Salesian mission at Ocamo angrily denounced me in the late 1990s, claiming that ". . . you think we Yanomamö are nothing but animals!" I was dumbfounded at this accusation and asked him what he meant by that claim. He replied, "Bórtoli showed us in your book where you said this about the Yanomamö!" Neither Bórtoli nor the Yanomamö understood English, so Bórtoli must have rather liberally reinterpreted something I said. Recall that the Yanomamö make a profound distinction between things that are wild, feral *(urihi tä rimö)* and things that are cultural, human *(yahi tä rimö)*. They find it offensive if you do not respect this distinction.

By the early 1990s, I was not welcome at the Salesian missions and took precautions to avoid them whenever I could. After all, a Salesian priest had announced in a prominent Caracas newspaper that the Salesians "could not guarantee Chagnon's safety if he were to pass through one of their missions."

Genealogies and Sociobiology

It was very clear to me that the Yanomamö were a "demographically pristine" population in the sense that they had not been subdued and decimated by some national military force, had not been forcibly settled on reservations, and had not been ravaged by introduced epidemic diseases. Moreover, their population was steadily growing, an indication of "demographic health." Thus, my routine collection of genealogies followed what I regarded as the universal anthropological tradition as described in many discussions of the "genealogical method."

My genealogical data could be used to express precisely what cultural anthropologists meant when they spoke of the intimacy and solidarity tribesmen felt for each other when they were "close kin" as distinct from "distant kin or non-kin." I could, in fact, express precisely how closely or remotely any pair of Yanomamö were related to each other because genealogies, like pedigrees used by animal breeders, were susceptible to precise quantification. Indeed, I was astonished that cultural anthropologists had failed to use these quantitative measures when almost all of them solemnly endorsed the anthropological truths that (1) social relationships in the tribal world were "embedded" in kinship institutions, that (2) closeness of kinship was the central component in "social solidarity," and (3) the political state emerged only when the "tribal design" based on kinship, descent, and marriage among related neighbors was supplanted by nonkinship institutions such as law, labor unions, police, armies, craft guilds, political parties, etc. In short, cultural anthropologists maintained that the political state and civilization were possible only when kinship-based social institutions were overthrown and replaced with these non-kin social institutions.

In my opinion there were two reasons why American cultural anthropologists in particular failed to take advantage of quantitative measure of kinship (and genealogies) and use them in their theoretical analyses.

One of the reasons—perhaps the more important one—had to do with the nature of the tribal populations that many of the founding theoretical figures in American anthropology studied. In general, they did their field studies in the Americas long after the tribes they studied had been decimated by epidemic diseases, defeated by the U.S. Army, forced to settle on reservations that often included remnants of other, unrelated tribes, had been exposed to the effects of colonial expansion and other forces of acculturation, and in the Southwest, hundreds of years of mission efforts by various orders of the Catholic Church whose practice was to attract Indians to live at their missions. Much of this work was "salvage ethnography"—a major attempt to document the last gasp of formerly large Native American tribes. Thus, in their own fieldwork it was probably futile to view kinship relationships as hardly more than a "polite" system of classifying mostly genealogically unrelated neighbors into categories that had, in most cases, no correspondence to genetic (biological) reality. The much touted "genealogical method" was, on closer inspection, more of a British colonial method: British anthropologists historically studied very large tribes in Africa that tended to be more demographically pristine than were the tribes in the Americas.

A good example of this comes from Marshall Sahlins's fieldwork in Hawaii in the 1950s, where the surviving native Hawaiians had suffered the ravages of introduced epidemics, decimation by the violence of colonial invaders, and the excesses of both Christian missionaries and colonial governments. While Sahlins's field research in Fiji and Hawaii occurred much later than that of the "founding" anthropologists just mentioned, it was similar in the sense that the culture he studied was basically in shreds and patches compared to pristine tribesmen. It is not surprising to me that Sahlins and other anthropologists concluded that in their own field studies of tribesmen, kinship did not seem to be very important. But why, in their theoretical claims, did they emphasize how central it was to understanding the tribal social design?

The second reason for not valuing kinship studies is that cultural anthropologists—as distinct from biological anthropologists—trained in the United States eschew quantitative measures of genetic kinship because of the widespread biophobia built into cultural anthropological theory, which results in deep suspicion and contempt for biological ideas. This peculiar contradiction has been characteristic of anthropology for over a century. For example, many undergraduate textbooks in introductory cultural anthropology go to considerable lengths in their discussions of kinship to emphasize the "nonbiological" dimensions of it by giving such examples "that in many African tribes, people call their mothers by the same term they use for their fathers." One of the acknowledged U.S. authorities on kinship, David Schneider, summed up this widespread attitude in anthropology by repeatedly arguing, in effect, that "whatever kinship is about, it is not about biology."

In 1975 Edward O. Wilson, a world-renowned specialist in ants and a distinguished biology professor at Harvard University, published his book *Sociobiology*. It rapidly became controversial in the social sciences especially among a small number of mostly Marxist academics. It was a masterful and comprehensive overview of the history of evolutionary thinking, explanatory milestones achieved by scores of researchers in the recent histories of biology, demography, ecology, taxonomy, theoretical genetics, animal behavior, psychology, sociology, anthropology, and other fields. Apart from being stunningly erudite, it was a politically innocent book in the sense that it simply illustrated how recent ideas in evolutionary theory had developed and how they might be applied to better understand how human beings in particular evolved to have the social capacities and characteristics we see in ourselves.

A few of the ideas discussed were found in some of Wilson's previous publications, but most of the book was about the accomplishments of others and how their findings and accomplishments were leading to a grand "synthesis of knowledge" that shed new light on human nature.

I remember having discussions with several senior anthropologists, Sherry Washburn among them, whose reaction to Wilson's book was initially enthusiastic. But once the implications of the last couple of chapters were publicly discussed, prominent academics in anthropology began to distance themselves from Wilson's book. One of the reasons was that Wilson over-simplified a number of features of tribesmen; this annoyed some anthropologists, but even more annoying to them was Wilson's claim that sociobiology would most likely become the overriding and comprehensive theoretical framework in the life sciences, one that would subsume other sciences—including anthropology and sociology—as subordinate components in a new field he called sociobiology.

But because anthropology—here I specifically mean *cultural* anthropology—had always been suspicious of theories and ideas from biology, a negative reaction against Wilson's new book spread swiftly in anthropology. The criticisms often had contemptuous undertones, almost as though Wilson had violated some sacred rule that cultural anthropologists held inviolate.

A classic example of anthropological arrogance and cynicism about Wilson's work was a book by Sahlins titled *The Use and Abuse of Biology: An Anthropological Critique of Sociobiology* (1976). After reading Sahlins's book I was embarrassed that he was one of my former professors.

Sociobiology soon became a term used by anthropologists as shorthand for almost everything hateful in the history of Homo sapiens: wars, fascism, racism, colonialism, capitalism, eugenics, elitism, genocide, etc.

The 1976 Meeting of the American Anthropological Association

As I mentioned, I left the University of Michigan in 1972 to join the anthropology faculty at Penn State. I was given considerable latitude in helping my new department develop a program devoted to the scientific approach in anthropology. Penn State already had outstanding scientific programs in archaeology, spearheaded by William Sanders, and in physical anthropology, chaired by Paul Baker, who founded the Penn State anthropology department and headed it for many years.

One of the first appointments I recommended to fill a vacant slot in cultural anthropology was Bill Irons, who had entered the graduate program in anthropology at Michigan in 1963 when I did. He had become a good friend who shared my view of anthropology as a science. We had both been trained to see "culture" as the prime determinant of human behavior, but we had become skeptical about this view and had begun exploring the new developments in theoretical biology, especially the works of George C. Williams and William D. Hamilton. I was particularly interested in Hamilton's theory of "inclusive fitness," also known as "kin selection," because it laid a new basis for understanding why kinship relationships provided the rock-bottom source of social solidarity. Our training had emphasized the role that culture played in human social relationships while completely ignoring the evolution of human behavior. The view from anthropology was that psychologists studied human behavior and anthropologists studied culture. Ever since Durkheim, cultural anthropology was skeptical about not only psychology and biology, but any theory that emphasized the biological underpinnings of behavior.

Both of us were avidly interested in potential applications of what Edward O. Wilson had called "sociobiology" to a number of problems in cultural anthropology. We organized what would turn out to be the first formal sessions devoted to this topic in the history of the American Anthropological Association (AAA). Among the scholars we asked to give papers in our symposium, held in 1976 in Washington, D.C., was Edward O. Wilson.

By now Wilson's book was widely condemned and denigrated by cultural anthropologists. Irons and I, plus all of the people we invited to give papers in our symposium, supported the ideas that constituted the field that Wilson defined.

Several anthropologists at Harvard University's anthropology department contacted me and Irons and asked us to make room for a series of papers by them and their advanced students and to split the sessions into primate and human sessions, which we did at the last minute.

An astonishing and unprecedented crisis developed just as the 1976 meetings of the AAA began. The business meeting of the AAA was held the night before our sociobiology sessions were scheduled to take place. The ballroom in which the business meeting was held was full beyond capacity. A motion had been placed on the agenda by opponents of sociobiology aimed at preventing the sessions that Irons and I had organized.

Because sociobiology was an effort to apply Darwinian—biological—principles to human behavior, Irons and I—and the speakers we had invited—were dumbfounded that such an anachronistic and organized opposition to Darwin's theory of evolution would blemish anthropology in 1976. It was as if the last two bastions of opposition to the theory of evolution by natural selection were fundamentalist fire-and-brimstone preachers and cultural anthropologists!

Heated debate and impassioned accusations of racism, fascism, and Nazism punctuated the frenzied business meeting that night. At one point I called for a vote to table the motion. Nobody heard me because Margaret Mead, the "Mother Goddess" of anthropology, stood up to address the motion to prohibit our sessions. A hush fell over the assembly. She began by expressing her opposition to Ed Wilson's book and his whole idea of a "science of sociobiology" that would possibly subsume anthropology as a subordinate discipline. However, she said, in spite of her opposition to Wilson's book and sociobiology, she felt that the motion as worded was essentially a "book burning" motion and, for that reason, she thought that it was not something our association should advocate and be identified with. She then sat down, somewhat regally, and the vote on the motion was taken almost immediately. The motion was defeated, but not by a wide margin. Our sessions on "sociobiology" were allowed to take place.

Nevertheless, anthropological opposition to sociobiology did not cease. It just operated from the shadows because many members of the

AAA realized that day that a sizable faction of the association was tolerant of biological views in cultural anthropology.

The papers in the sessions were published in 1979 in a volume titled *Evolutionary Biology and Human Social Organization: An Anthropological Perspective*. It was the first volume to attempt seriously to bridge the gap between ethnography (anthropology) and the new developments in theoretical biology.

The Sociobiological Debates on U.S. Campuses

Shortly after the AAA meetings a number of debates about sociobiology were organized on several major U.S. campuses. The general themes of these debates was something like "What's Dangerous About Sociobiology?"

I was invited to a number of these debates, as was Bill Irons. Two groups of academics debated each other: those who were opposed to sociobiology and those who defended it *and* the academic right to explore the scientific implications of this new approach. The "opposed" group had a larger pool to choose from because, by that time, the very word *sociobiology* had become a lightning rod in the social sciences on college campuses. The defenders were fewer (or less willing to debate this issue) but included some of the most distinguished academics in the field of biology and a much smaller number of social scientists.

One of the pro-sociobiology participants that I frequently ran into at these debates, Robert Trivers, said to me at one of them: "I've finally figured out what they mean by a 'balanced' debate. For every clear demonstration of how effective a sociobiological explanation is of some phenomenon, it must be 'balanced' by a completely nonsensical appeal to B.S., emotions and political correctness."

The Ultimate Debate Sponsored by AAAS

After several such debates, the American Association for the Advancement of Science (AAAS), one of the most prestigious and authoritative scientific bodies in the country, sponsored its own debate in 1978 hoping to put an end to the squabbling and to the unreasonable and false accusations against those who wished to study human behavior with new theoretical insights into natural selection, ideas resulting from the works of William Hamilton, George Williams, and Trivers, to name a few.

The two conveners—George W. Barlow, a biologist, and James Silverberg, an anthropologist—invited well-known opponents and proponents of sociobiology for a nationally sponsored debate under the auspices of the AAAS. Margaret Mead was scheduled to be the moderator of the session but a few weeks before the meeting she was diagnosed with terminal cancer. Her replacement was an anthropologist from Columbia University, Alexander Alland.

Bill Irons and I gave papers early in the meeting. While giving my paper I noticed that the first two rows nearest the podium were filled with mostly sullen-looking young men who showed no signs of interest in the papers.

Earlier that morning Irons and I had spoken briefly with Ed Wilson, who was to present last. He mentioned that he was scheduled to debate Marvin Harris of Columbia University that evening at the Smithsonian Institution. Harris was by now my most outspoken anthropological critic. His reason seemed to be that my research on the Yanomamö had become widely known, and I was now identified with and promoted sociobiology. Harris was attempting to establish a "materialist" (biology-free) science of anthropology, and Wilson's sociobiology was now a major rival to his theory. To have a prominent cultural anthropologist endorse sociobiology and include it in his papers about the Yanomamö was an added obstacle to Harris.

A number of heated arguments developed at the AAAS meeting before Wilson spoke. One of them focused on a recent publication by Hamilton that discussed pastoral nomads like the Mongols. One of the detractors in the audience pointedly and angrily demanded that Hamilton retract what he said in this paper. Hamilton, a very quiet, almost bashful man, solemnly replied: "I stand by what I published in my paper."

Richard Dawkins was also annoyed by some of the obviously political content of some of the criticisms, and to my surprise, he got up, stood on his seat where everyone could see him, and delivered from that commanding position well-considered and highly informed responses to the criticisms of his own work, especially his recent book *The Selfish Gene*.

Finally, it was Wilson's turn to speak. Wilson was a jogger and had taken a serious fall while jogging on an icy street in Cambridge. He had broken one of his legs and was now in a plaster cast from his foot to his hip. He was using crutches to get around with some noticeable difficulty. He got up from his seat and walked slowly with his crutches to the podium on an elevated stage some three feet high. He sat down, took out his paper, and began speaking. Suddenly the sullen people sitting in the first rows immediately in front of the podium exploded from their seats and jumped onto the stage, shouting angry insults at Wilson, jostling and pushing him around. They grabbed the pitchers of ice water from the table and poured them over Wilson's head, continuing to shout angry and ugly epithets at him. The moderator, Alland, tried to calm them down to keep order, shouting "Please stop! Please stop! I'm one of you people . . . I'm also a Marxist! This is unacceptable!" Maybe Marxists had some kind of secret code I didn't know about, but it didn't work: the "Marxists" continued to attack Wilson.

I was in the back of the room, trying frantically to get to the stage to help Wilson, but the crowd was heading in the opposite direction, anxiously attempting to get out of the auditorium as quickly as possible. It was the most hateful, frightening, and disgusting behavior I've ever witnessed at an academic assembly—and all the more shameful because it took place at a meeting sponsored by a venerable and prestigious association.

We subsequently learned that the sullen and cowardly people who attacked Wilson were from a radical organization known as the International Committee Against Racism (InCAR).

When Irons and I met with Wilson for dinner about an hour later, he was still wet from the dousing that the members of InCAR had given him, but was otherwise unscathed and remarkably calm. Wilson cheerfully announced that he wanted to share some good news with me. He said he and Harris had met for lunch and discussed how they would conduct their debate, who would go first, how long each would speak, how long they should leave for questions from the audience, and how the questions would be handled in an efficient way. The questions would have to be submitted in writing on small pieces of paper that would be handed out to the audience prior to the end of the debate. Anyone wishing to ask a question was instructed to identify on the paper the speaker—Harris or Wilson—to whom the question was directed. Audience members would pass their questions toward the aisle nearest the center of the auditorium, where ushers would collect them, divide them into two piles, and present these to each speaker, who could quickly sort them into topics and choose which ones to answer.

Wilson's "good news" for me went like this. He was certain he had done something in his discussion with Harris that would lead to greater understanding by Harris of what my publications on kin selection theory meant. He said that Harris believed that I was saying that the Yanomamö had specific genes for some of their social and political institutions and behavior, for example, their warfare and infanticide practices. Wilson beamed when he said that he explained to Harris that I made no such claims and went on to explain what the theory of kin selection meant. He added: "It was like seeing a lightbulb switch on inside someone's head, someone who had suddenly been made aware of something he didn't previously understand!" Wilson assured me that henceforth Harris and I would get along now that Harris understood what Hamilton's theory of kin selection and inclusive fitness meant and how I was applying it to the Yanomamö.

Irons and I looked at each other and smiled. I thanked Wilson for taking the time to explain kin selection to Harris, but added that I thought that this would make no difference in how we got along. His constant repetition of false claims that I believed in genes for warfare and other behaviors seemed to be a way that many anthropologists—among others—establish false truths. And, of course, by voting on what is and is not true.

At the Smithsonian Wilson was the first to speak. He gave his standard talk on what sociobiology was, how it developed out of the work of many researchers, and how it shed new light on the behavior of many different organisms, including higher primates and Homo sapiens. Wilson explained how it provided a new synthesis of many different fields of learning and brought them together in the advancement of greater understanding of the world around us. I had heard this talk several times at other venues.

Then Harris took the podium. He began by saying that he could recognize three different kinds of sociobiology. First, there was the "good" or "nondangerous" kind that people like Professor Wilson were doing, but he had misgivings about it because it didn't apply to humans, and those people who thought it did were simply wrong.

Then there was the second kind, the kind associated with several specific academics he named: David Barash, Mildred Dickemann, Richard D. Alexander, and others. This kind was badly misguided and bordered on being potentially dangerous.

Finally, there was the third kind, a kind that was not only wrong, but was also extremely dangerous. He paused, and then said dramatically: "Did you know that there is a certain anthropologist, a man who has become famous for his long-term studies of Amazon Indians, who claims, ladies and gentlemen, that this tribe not only has a gene for warfare, but he claims they also have genes for infanticide!" I looked at Wilson, who had visibly slumped into his chair on hearing Harris's false accusations. I think that it was then that Wilson understood that the battle over sociobiology in cultural anthropology was being played by rules and tactics unfamiliar to a biologist, tactics outside the realm of rational academic debate. Indeed, such accusations could provoke organized and dedicated radicals to attack people on the podium even in enlightened audiences.

I quickly looked for a piece of paper to submit a question to Harris. I took a sheet from, I recall, a yellow notepad, tore it into the approximate size of the sheets the ushers had several minutes earlier handed out to the audience except to those who were guests of the speakers, as I was.

My question to Harris was: "Identify the anthropologist who claimed that the people he studied had genes for warfare and infanticide." I passed it to the end of the aisle, where it was picked up by the passing usher. It was the only odd-sized piece of paper in the bundle passed to Harris and stood out also because it was the only one submitted on yellow paper.

Both Wilson and Harris took turns answering the questions on their sheets of paper, but there were far more questions than there was time to answer.

I could clearly see Harris repeatedly putting my question to the back of his package of questions as he looked for ones he preferred to answer. He had no intention of answering my question. Finally, the moderator called an end to the questions and began to thank the speakers for their participation in this wonderful, thought-provoking event.

I stood up and tried to get the attention of the moderator. A sizable number of people in the audience recognized me, probably from documentary films that I had made about the Yanomamö, and began to shout: "Let him speak! Let him speak!" The moderator finally gave me permission to speak. I demanded that Harris identify the anthropologist who had claimed that the people he studied had "genes for warfare and genes for infanticide." He was a little embarrassed, but self-righteously defiant. It didn't seem to bother him that his accusations were shameless lies. He replied something to the effect that if I actually don't claim these things, then welcome back to anthropology. By then I had climbed up on the stage to continue my defense. I assured the audience (and Harris) that I had never left anthropology and that sociobiology and the evolution of human behavior were legitimate ways to shed new light on humans and their behavior. My disagreement with Harris would continue and would in fact worsen.

Opposition to Sociobiology over the Next Decade

In 1975 I received a grant from the National Institute of Mental Health (NIMH) for a three-year project to investigate kinship, kin selection, and "group selection." I never used the word *sociobiology* to describe this project because the word was barely known to biology in 1975. But these are topics that sociobiology studied. Fortunately for me at that time cultural anthropology had not yet been systematically sensitized to the kinds of topics sociobiologists explored. In 1975, broad-minded cultural anthropologists would have found these topics rather typical research areas. Yet one of the NIMH administrators, a nonscientist, pointedly told me later that if they had known that I was doing "sociobiology" research, they would have tried to have my project terminated immediately. But prior to this remark, they invited me to Washington to discuss my funded research project before a group of administrators because it was an example of the kind of project that NIMH wanted to fund, one that they were proud of.

In 1981 I moved to Northwestern University in Evanston, Illinois, rejoining my friend and colleague Bill Irons, who had left Penn State and taken a position there in 1978. Both Irons and I left Penn State because sociobiological work apparently threatened faculty in our department who seemed to believe that cultural anthropologists should confine their interests to collecting anecdotes and myths and leave science (for example, biology) to "scientists."

This move also put me back in direct contact with biologist Richard D. Alexander of the University of Michigan because Ann Arbor was a relatively easy drive from Evanston. The three of us—Irons, Alexander, and I—had trained a number of graduate students who were now promising young scholars doing cultural anthropology with a sociobiological perspective.

By the early 1980s, sociobiological cultural anthropological research was being discriminated against in granting agencies like the anthropology division of the National Science Foundation (NSF). Referees who held strong prejudicial views against sociobiological research would fault sociobiological applications for "methodological" deficiencies and give them very low grades. One "poor" grade was enough to kill a research application.

Irons, Alexander, and I suggested to the NSF that they create a list of potential referees who would be neutral in their evaluations of research applications that were sociobiological. In 1981 Steven Brush, head of the anthropology branch of NSF, visited the three of us in Evanston to listen to our concerns. NSF complied with our suggestion that a list of academically competent reviewers be created to evaluate proposals that had sociobiological goals. Success rates of sociobiological proposals increased accordingly.

Prejudicial views against sociobiological research were also a problem in publications submitted to important peer-reviewed academic journals, but evidence for this is more difficult to prove.

Unjustified and prejudicial views of a colleague's research objectives also surfaced in tenure and promotion decisions in academia. Later, while I was on the faculty of the University of California, Santa Barbara, I was a member of a special committee that convened in cases where a faculty member was denied tenure and where there was some suspicion that prejudice was involved because of the theoretical perspective of the candidate. Several times I was called upon to participate in a specially appointed nondepartmental review committee to reconsider the candidate's credentials to be granted tenure. In at least one case it was very clear to me that the candidate, an Asian female faculty member, was denied tenure because her work was sociobiological in nature, and one of her previous academic advisors was now a controversial figure because of his own sociobiological views. He had written a letter of support for the candidate. Our committee reversed the decision of the committee from her department and she was awarded tenure.

My 1988 Article in *Science*

Sometime early in 1987 I received a telephone call from Daniel Koshland, the editor of the journal *Science*, the official publication of the American Association for the Advancement of Science (AAAS). He explained that subscriptions to the journal were flagging and some of the AAAS members were complaining that there were fewer articles of general interest, for example, articles that bridged disciplines. *Science* was constantly under pressure from project directors in prestigious medical schools to publish esoteric articles by their teams of researchers in order to justify their large grants from federal agencies. Hence there were lots of technical articles on medical research appearing in *Science*.

My name had been recommended as someone whose research might be of interest to a more general audience and it bridged disciplines like anthropology, biology, and demography. He asked me to submit an article to *Science* from my research among the Yanomamö on a topic of my own choosing, but warned me that it would have to go through the same strenuous review process that all articles were subjected to, meaning *Science* would not publish it unless the peer review process found it worthy.

I was just at the point in my research where I wanted to get certain kinds of data published before they would no longer reflect the ethnographic present. For example, one body of my data had to do with Yanomamö warfare and revenge killings. If I waited much longer, I would have to make it clear that these data no longer applied to the "ethnographic present" but, instead, were more characteristic of the "recent past." The introduction of shotguns at Salesian missions would most likely change traditional Yanomamö warfare patterns.

When I began organizing my data on differential reproductive success of male lineage members, I examined a number of possible variables that my earlier publications had identified—size of village, size of the lineage in the village and in the population, marriage success, etc. I also decided to check the possible correlation between a man's military success and his reproductive success and, much to my surprise, there was not only a correlation, but it was very strong. (I discussed this subject in Chapter 9.)

As my paper was going through the peer review process, a large number—upwards of forty thousand—of renegade Brazilian gold miners illegally entered Yanomamö territory in Brazil and began mining gold there, using hydraulic pumps that destroyed the pristine rivers and contaminated the water with mercury. There was great concern and outrage among native rights advocates and nongovernmental organizations that were advocating for the preservation of the pristine Amazon rain forests and the native people who lived there.

Almost all of the damage was being done in Brazil, where the history of the destruction of the rain forest was widely known in the international conservation community, as were the depredations inflicted on native Amazonian peoples, sometimes with the complicity of Brazilian "Indian protection agents" who worked for FUNAI, the Brazilian Indian Service, and its predecessor. By comparison, these kinds of destructive activities in Venezuela were more recent and also much less severe.

A small group of my persistent and academically jealous opponents in anthropology tried to link my research among the Yanomamö to the Brazilian gold rush. I found it astonishing because of my twenty or so different field trips to the Yanomamö by 1987, only one had been made to Brazil, in 1968. That one was a collaboration with a group of medical researchers who were working with Brazilian counterparts from distinguished Brazilian research centers. On that particular trip, my medical collaborator, James V. Neel, was able to show that the Yanomamö had no antibodies for measles, a disease that is especially lethal in isolated native populations. This single discovery probably saved hundreds if not thousands of Yanomamö because it led, the next year, to our efforts to thwart an epidemic of measles that broke out in the Venezuelan Yanomamö area (which I briefly discussed earlier).

One of my misdeeds, according to my detractors, was the fact that the subtitle of the first three editions of my college monograph was "The Fierce People"—a phrase the Yanomamö themselves frequently used to emphasize their valor, braveness, and willingness to act aggressively on their own behalf. My detractors claimed that this subtitle was demeaning and I was guilty of inflicting psychological harm on the Yanomamö and causing other evil people to do harm to them.

Thus, just at the moment that concerned anthropologists—particularly activist anthropologists associated with survival groups—were denouncing the *garimpeiro* invasion of Yanomamö territory, a lead article in the most influential American science journal appeared in March 1988 that documented the correlation between success at warfare and high reproductive success among Yanomamö men. To have the lead article in *Science* suggesting that "killers have more kids" was like pouring gasoline on a smoldering academic fire. My opponents argued and perhaps some of them actually believed that I was saying that "the Yanomamö have a gene for warfare and violence," as Marvin Harris had claimed. This accusation was not only illogical and false; it was being used politically to discredit me.

Lead articles in *Science* are automatically sent out to members of the press. A few of these journalists wrote what I considered to be inappropriate and even reprehensible headlines for their stories, such as "when they are not out collecting honey, the Yanomamö are murdering each other." They used words and phrases that my article (and all of my publications) carefully avoided, like *murder.*

My detractors immediately attempted to associate my article—and all of my work—with the depredations, real and imagined, that Brazilian gold miners inflicted on the Brazilian Yanomamö.

Outrageous Accusations of the ABA Published by the AAA

Shortly after my article in *Science* appeared a group of anthropologists drafted a list of accusations against me under the imprimatur of the

Associação Brasileira de Antropologia (ABA)—the Brazilian Anthropological Association. The accusations appeared in a document that was a formal complaint to the Ethics Committee of the American Anthropological Association. It was forwarded to Roy A. Rappaport, then president of the AAA and chairman of the anthropology department at the University of Michigan. By coincidence I happened to be in Ann Arbor attending the annual meeting of the Human Behavior and Evolution Society (HBES). When Rappaport learned where I was, he appeared quietly in the auditorium where I was listening to a paper by William D. Hamilton, whose 1962 paper on "inclusive fitness" constituted one of few major modifications to Darwin's theory of evolution by natural selection. Ironically, Hamilton was suggesting in this symposium, somewhat tongue-in-cheek, that we should become a "secret society" and not reveal our research findings to nonmembers and simply share our ideas among ourselves. Our findings, he said, simply annoyed and angered other academics, especially social scientists like Sahlins who earlier had written a scathing, book-length condemnation of what HBES was established to study: the applicability of Darwin's theory of natural selection to human behavior.

I was surprised to see "Skip" Rappaport, whom I considered to be a friend and good colleague. He whispered that he wanted to talk with me about something urgent and asked me to step out of the auditorium.

I was surprised and a little annoyed that I would miss some of Hamilton's talk, but I followed Rappaport out of the auditorium. He was clutching a letter-size document that I could see was addressed to the Ethics Committee of the AAA. He began by telling me that he had to get back to them by 3 P.M. I had no idea to whom "them" referred. I looked at my watch. It was about 2:40.

Rappaport asked me if I would agree to have the document he clutched in his hands published in the next issue of the official newsletter of the AAA. The deadline for submissions was three that afternoon. The next issue of the newsletter would not be published until after the summer break, several months from then.

He had not yet told me what was contained in the rolled-up document but I surmised that it was about me, most likely a new attack on me by my persistent detractors in cultural anthropology. He wanted my permission to approve publication in the AAA newsletter, adding: "The authors might send it to *Science* and we don't want *our* dirty laundry being aired in *Science* for others to read about."

I was dumbfounded. The president of my professional association and a former departmental colleague wanted me to approve the publication of something addressed to the AAA Ethics Committee, most likely a formal complaint about me, without even giving me a chance to read what it contained! What part of this laundry was dirty?

Needless to say, I told Rappaport that I would *not* give him my permission to rush this mysterious document into press where it might escape more serious scrutiny by scientists. He was disappointed, handed me the document, said he would be in touch soon, and departed.

The actual authors *did* send a "letter of complaint" to the editor of *Science* that was nearly identical to the one that reached Rappaport. It turned out that the complaint came from the Brazilian Anthropological Association, implying that a large group of Brazilian anthropologists were involved in drafting it. The document was signed by Maria Manuela Carneiro da Cunha, president of the Brazilian Anthropological Association. The complaint sent to the editor of *Science* had to be signed by the authors because *Science* does not accept anonymous complaints. That complaint was forwarded to me.

The authors turned out to be Bruce Albert, a French national, who was working among the Brazilian Yanomamö, and Brazilian anthropologist Alcida Ramos, who had earlier worked among a branch of the Yanomamö known as Sanema (Sanöma = Yanöma = Yanomamö). Albert sometimes worked among the Catrimani Yanomamö. His data came largely from Giovanni Saffirio, a Consolata priest who operated the Consolata mission on the Catrimani River. Both were known less for their ethnographic accomplishments than for their efforts as political advocates of Brazilian Indians in general and the Yanomamö in particular. Ramos once complained about me to the effect that "what Chagnon fails to understand is that doing anthropology in Brazil is a *political* activity."

The document was not published by the AAA's *Anthropology Newsletter* until January 1989 and was attributed solely to Carneiro da Cunha, who never worked among the Yanomamö. Carneiro da Cunha held an appointment in her Brazilian university as well as a courtesy appointment in the anthropology department at the University of Chicago. The article published by the *Anthropology Newsletter* was a mistake-ridden and intemperate condemnation of my 1988 article in *Science* and included the following accusations:

ABA Accusations

1. It was "racist," an accusation often used by radical cultural anthropologists to deprecate anything that can be construed as having been inspired by sociobiology;
2. I was guilty of complicity in genocide;
3. I had faked my data;
4. I had deliberately concealed the fact that diseases were the primary source of mortality among the Yanomamö in order to make violent deaths appear to be the most common cause of death among them;
5. I was encouraging and abetting sensational, negative press coverage of the Yanomamö at a time when they were being invaded by miners;
6. My *Science* article was a major reason why Brazilian officials set into motion a plan to separate the Yanomamö into twenty-one "micro" reservations, a false accusation that was subsequently repeated so often by my anthropological opponents that it has become an unchallenged "truth" in the community of activist anthropologists.

The editorial comments by Rappaport to the ABA critique and his comment on my response to the critique included a reference to an AAA policy that I found puzzling. I had never heard of the AAA "doctrine" that Rappaport cited when he asked my permission to publish the Brazilian document without my even being able to read it. Rappaport claimed that sister anthropology organizations had the right to object in writing to anything published in an AAA journal and would automatically receive space in that AAA journal to respond. I am unaware of any other occasion where this "policy" was invoked. I suspected that Rappaport invented it to appease Brazilian anthropologists who controlled access to tribes there that certain prominent U.S. anthropologists were studying.

A New Direction for American Anthropology

The subject matter of the "social" sciences is not as easily delineated as the subject matter of the "natural" sciences—and some observers even regard the very phrase "social science" as a contradiction in terms. For example, a "social fact" like, "You should not eat fruit bats if they are your clan totem" is not the same kind of fact as, "The temperature at which water boils at sea level is 212 degrees Fahrenheit." Nevertheless, most anthropologists attempt to follow rigorous conventions when they collect field data and publish them. They usually follow the procedures and methods of science to the extent they can. One fundamental rule is that you should not make claims that are not true and cannot be verified by independent researchers using the same or similar methods.

Archaeologists, physical anthropologists, and anthropological linguists are able to adhere more rigorously to the proposition that anthropology is a science because the stuff they deal with—pottery, house types, bones, grammar, etc.—are ontologically more factual than, for example, a taboo on eating your totem animal. They generally endorse the proposition that most disagreements can be resolved by independent observers collecting new data, by repeating the questioned observations, or by making sure that differences in results are not due to, for example, possibly real differences in the objects, items, communities, tribes, or whatever, that are the object of the disagreement.

However, *cultural* anthropology, as distinct from these other subbranches of the field of anthropology, contains two mutually incompatible and often contending factions. Many cultural anthropologists do subscribe to the methods and procedures associated with science and, historically, cultural anthropologists were comfortable with the word *science* as a general description of the kind of activity they engaged in. But many others—possibly the majority of cultural anthropologists today—prefer to look at themselves as nonscientists and, in many cases, are outspoken in their insistence that cultural anthropology is not a branch of science, but rather of the humanities. For example, David Maybury-Lewis, head of Harvard's Department of Social Relations, one of the outspoken advocates of anthropology as a branch of the humanities, nonetheless demanded an explanation from the National Science Foun-

of science, but rather of the humanities. For example, David Maybury-Lewis, head of Harvard's Department of Social Relations, one of the outspoken advocates of anthropology as a branch of the humanities, nonetheless demanded an explanation from the National Science Foundation's anthropology director when research proposals he and some of his students sent to the NSF were not funded in the 1970s. They were not funded *because they were not scientific*. When you want to do a "humanities" research project, you don't send the proposal to the National *Science* Foundation.

Today the many cultural anthropologists (or social anthropologists, as they are known in Great Britain) who prefer to think of what they do as a branch of the humanities regard their movement as "postmodernism." It is frequently associated with or said to have been inspired by several prominent French scholars, including Jacques Derrida and Michel Foucault. For some of them "truth" and "facts" are merely subjective categories, ideological constructs, inventions of a subjective observer. Science and the scientific method are viewed by these cultural anthropologists with skepticism, suspicion, and even disdain.

I was trained in the scientific tradition in cultural anthropology. Most of my fellow graduate students were also trained in that tradition and viewed the scientific method as an inseparable dimension of anthropological research. To most of us, science was not just something one did in laboratories with petri dishes, microscopes, and micrometers. Rather, it was a general way of viewing things that emphasized the collection and analysis of empirical data following the scientific method.

But respect for science and the scientific method was beginning to weaken in many universities and colleges by the end of the 1960s. The French thinkers, Derrida and Foucault in particular, began to influence curricula in several fields of the social sciences. Postmodernism was incompatible with and often antagonistic toward the scientific approach. The very notion that the external world had an existence independent of its observer was challenged. Moreover, the scientific view was usually said to be exploitative and designed to keep the poor, the disenfranchised, ethnic minorities, and women in subordinate social positions.

Those who adopted the postmodernist intellectual stance and who dis-

The very notion that the external world had an existence independent of its observer was challenged. Moreover, the scientific view was usually said to be exploitative and designed to keep the poor, the disenfranchised, ethnic minorities, and women in subordinate social positions.

Those who adopted the postmodernist intellectual stance and who disagreed with an observer reporting something that a postmodernist didn't like could denounce the observer as racist, sexist, biological determinist, and fraudulent. Or he could claim that the objective observer invented politically incorrect data.

Increasing numbers of American cultural anthropologists—and many academics in other disciplines—began to view their role in the academy as one of advocacy of various causes having to do with the harm that industrialized nations, especially capitalist ones, were inflicting on the earth's rivers, forests, ecological systems, and, most of all, the remaining tribesmen, ethnic minorities, illegal immigrants, the homeless, and others. In principle these genuine and meritorious concerns were not incompatible with the general historical traditions and accepted canons of ethics and behavior assumed by professionals in the sciences.

But somewhere along the way the anthropology profession was hijacked by radicals who constituted the "Academic Left," an aphorism coined by biologists Norman Levitt and Paul Gross in their superb book, *Higher Superstition.*

For example, an anthropology professor at the University of California, Berkeley, named Nancy Scheper-Hughes argued in the *Chronicle of Higher Education* that cultural anthropology should henceforth be viewed as some kind of forensic activity. Anthropologists should become "witnesses" and "name the wrongs" that have been done to the peoples that their predecessors studied, that is, the wrongs done by fellow anthropologists. Field research locations were no longer exotic, distant places where some anthropologist did his or her field research, but rather they were *crime scenes.* Scheper-Hughes suggested that today's cultural anthropologists should focus on the "crimes" committed by previous anthropologists and what they must now do to provide restitution to the victims of their "scientific" research.

Anthropologist Roy D'Andrade of the University of California, San Diego, in a prescient article in 1995 characterized these new anthropological trends in the following way: "The [postmodernist] model does not lead one to do anything positive about bad conditions. Instead it leads to denunciations of various social practitioners, such as social workers, doctors, psychiatrists, economists, civil servants, bureaucrats, etc. and especially other anthropologists. Isn't it odd that the true enemy of society turns out to be that guy in the office down the hall?"

These new and decidedly political views caused faculty members in some traditional anthropology departments to choose one of several options. For example, at Berkeley those who viewed their research as scientific simply sought appointments in other departments or took positions at higher salaries at other major universities, where they were able to continue their work without political harassment or distraction. Other major departments split into two smaller departments—the scientific anthropologists remaining in one, the postmodernists and political activists in the other, as happened at Stanford.

The denunciation of me in an official publication (the *Anthropology Newsletter*, 1989a) of the AAA was something of a turning point not only in my own professional career, but also, I believe, in American anthropology. It seemed to legitimize unprofessional attacks on me and my research and other researchers like me. The "New Anthropology" seemed to legitimize the view that anthropology should be a forensic enterprise, that the Ph.D. degree in cultural anthropology was the equivalent of a license to identify and hunt for the bad guys, "in offices down the hall," as D'Andrade observed.

As this trend became increasingly apparent, Paul Gross, a distinguished biologist from the University of Virginia, commented in 2001 on the damage that this trend was causing:

Thirty years ago the distinction between technical disagreements and moral-political warfare began to dissolve. A whole generation of students and teachers became convinced that *everything*, including scientific inquiry, is inextricably political because knowledge itself was inextricably a social—i.e., a political—phenomenon. Politics, meanwhile, is a matter too important for niceties. Berkeley anthropologist Nancy Scheper-Hughes exemplified these enthusiasms when she demanded from her colleagues, in 1995, a "militant anthropology, the education of a new cadre of 'barefoot anthropologists' that I envision must become alarmists and shock troopers—the producers of politically complicated and morally demanding texts and images capable of sinking through the layers of acceptance, complicity, and bad faith that allow the suffering and the deaths to continue . . ."

Gross concluded his essay by noting that "the barefoot anthropologists, the activists, will be teaching your children." And in fact they are.

The Gathering Storm

A storm was brewing in cultural anthropology by the late 1990s. This storm seemed to presage something ugly and unprecedented because parties had already begun to publicly and sometimes clandestinely denounce and denigrate each other, even essentially sabotaging research projects, and shamelessly trying to ruin opponents academically. These storm clouds were characterized by the following trends:

Biophobia: the chronic opposition in cultural anthropology to ideas from biology that purported to help account for what humans in all cultures did. This issue emerged when Wilson published *Sociobiology*, as I have noted. Many cultural anthropologists then had to reconsider and rethink the question, Why was cultural anthropology so opposed to the notion that humans had an *evolved* biological nature as well as a *learned* cultural nature? Many responded with the standard but thoughtless answer that genes don't determine culture. But the new biology (sociobiology) was more comprehensive and subtle than that, and perfunctory anthropological dismissals of it in the 1980s were ineffective.

Postmodernism and the notion that "facts" were merely "constructs" of the human mind and, consequently, that there was no "real world" independent of its observer. Objectivity could therefore not exist. What one person observed was not verifiable by another, and the repetition of empirically sound observations could no longer serve as the standard by which some kind of "truth" could be reached in anthropology. Thus science and the scientific method was just another arbitrary way to look at things, much like witchcraft, astrology, or dreams. Remarkable as it seems, many anthropologists seemed to prefer the latter approaches.

Activism and advocacy, the act of using your accumulated knowledge, prestige, education, deep commitment to some cause, and to direct the education, authority, and prestige normally associated with your position in society to advocate some *political* cause. This activism usually occurred with respect to causes that were "morally" or "ethically" correct in some absolute sense compared to the "immoral" or "ethically reprehensible" views of your competitors. Because your cause was moral and theirs was not, you could use false claims against competitors based on your presumed authority.

15

Confrontation with the Salesians

The Salesians Begin Their Opposition to My Fieldwork

In 1986 Joachim Bublath, a science producer for the ZDF television network in Germany, asked me to collaborate on a documentary film about my field research among the Yanomamö. The Yanomamö had become something of an international symbol of the last remaining "pristine" tribesmen, and many different groups had made films about them, or wanted to, for a variety of reasons. We agreed that he and his small film team would join me in the field in March 1988.

I met Bublath and his film crew at Padre Cocco's airstrip at Ocamo. As I mentioned earlier, Padre Cocco had left Venezuela permanently nearly a decade earlier and returned to Turin, Italy, where he had been born. For some reason Bublath was interested in Padre Cocco and his legacy as a cheerful and gracious host to his many guests and visitors, not only in Venezuela, but also in Europe—especially in Italy and Germany.

In 1988 ZDF aired a two-part documentary in Germany on the Yanomamö and my research among them. They included footage of several Yanomamö films that I had produced with Timothy Asch from our field

Jean Rouch, Napoleon Chagnon, John Marshall, and Timothy Asch at the Jean Rouch Film Festival on the Yanomamö in Paris

trip to MishimishimabÖwei-teri in 1971, including a film titled *The Ax Fight,* which was widely used in university classrooms. I was unaware that the ZDF film included, indeed *emphasized,* footage from *The Ax Fight.*

The ZDF film was shown on German television while one of the Salesian nuns from Mavaca happened to be in Germany visiting members of her family. She was furious with ZDF's portrayal of Padre Cocco as essentially a saintly tourist guide. She apparently wanted him portrayed in a more traditional priestly way. Her anger was directed especially at me for having helped the Germans make their film.

I learned about all this in August 1988 when I visited Mavaca for a novel project I had suggested to the Salesians. I was afraid that the *garimpeiro* invasion of Yanomamö territory in Brazil was threatening to spill over into Venezuelan territory and might lead to the abandoning of the Salesian missions there. If that happened, the Venezuelan Yanomamö would have to fend for themselves against the depredations of the miners.

I contacted Padre José Bórtoli, who was in charge of the Yanomamö Salesian missions in Venezuela, and urged him to begin a project with me, using my extensive genealogical data on families, to assign Spanish family names to all the Yanomamö at their missions. The Salesians were haphazardly giving the Yanomamö Spanish names, but with no regard to lineage. Thus five biological brothers might be given five different "family" names, especially if they did not all live in the same village. The Salesians often did not know, for example, that a man in the village right next to their mission had a full or half brother in the village just across the river. This haphazard way of assigning Spanish names disregarded one of the few sources of solidarity and cooperation the Yanomamö could rely on. These names would become legal and official on their identity cards as the Yanomamö were gradually incorporated into Venezuelan society. The Yanomamö would be required to carry identification papers if they ever went out of the area to Venezuelan towns and cities.

Bórtoli agreed with me. I had roughly four thousand Yanomamö in my data files arranged by lineage and sorted into the villages that were found in the immediate area of the Mavaca mission. I brought with me my computer programmer, Dante DeLucia, who could quickly add the recently assigned Spanish names to my computer file. The Salesians would provide these names, and I would correlate the Spanish names to the Yanomamö names in my census data.

There was something unusual about the way Bórtoli was treating me on this trip. I asked him if I could expect the mission to provide food and lodging while we were there, something I never had to ask Padre Cocco all the years I visited his mission. The answer from Bórtoli was that Dante and I could string up our hammocks in an old tool shed among the broken outboard motors and gasoline barrels and sleep there. He mentioned that the shed had no light because the mission generator was not wired to this outbuilding, which was a crude palm-wood and palm-thatch hut. This also meant that we would have to use the nearby jungle for our sanitary purposes instead of the mission's flush toilet. I mentioned that I no longer had cooking utensils because I had given them away to the Yanomamö on my last trip and asked if we could expect to be fed. Padre Bórtoli said we would have to provide our own food. He was definitely—if not deliberately—putting distance between us.

Up to this point, my relationships with the Salesians were still relatively amicable, but they were not as warm and friendly as they had been when Padre Cocco was in charge of the Salesian missions.

Although I never overnighted at a Salesian mission after Padre Cocco left the area, in this particular case I was traveling to Bórtoli's mission to do something that should have been of value to the missions. Bórtoli routinely provided food and lodging to European strangers, including a French anthropologist, Jacques Lizot.

Lizot had arrived in the Yanomamö area in 1968 with the French/IVIC medical group and spent about a year doing biomedical tasks for this group, but, like me, he was interested in ethnography, not biomedical research. His ethnographic field studies focused on villages north of the Orinoco while mine focused on villages south of the Orinoco. Our early relationships were generally cordial and cooperative, but by 1972 he became very hostile to me and seemed jealous of my research and that of my several graduate students. I felt that he resented them . . . and me for bringing them into the Yanomamö area. And that he was possessive with respect to the Yanomamö and regarded other researchers as a threat. Indeed, his behavior toward me seemed very unprofessional, antagonistic, and vindictive.

When Dante and I arrived at Mavaca, Bórtoli called me aside and recommended that I explain the role I had in the film shown on ZDF because the German nun was angry and offended. I explained that I simply took the filmmakers to villages where they could shoot film, and the point of view was theirs, not mine. Bórtoli also complained to me about using the names of dead Yanomamö when I investigated deaths and causes of death for my demographic work. I suspected that what he was actually concerned about was not the use of the names of the deceased but the fact that I would inevitably learn that the shotguns the Salesians were providing to lure Yanomamö to their missions were being used to kill other Yanomamö. I had also discovered deaths caused by new diseases: Yanomamö were now dying from diseases like hepatitis, a new source of mortality in the Mavaca area. The demographic aspects of my field research—collecting data on births, deaths, causes of deaths, and so forth were apparently now threatening to the Salesians—so much so that I learned from one of my better informants that Bórtoli had privately forbidden the Yanomamö to tell me the names of dead people. The Yano-mamö would clam up whenever Bórtoli or one of his favored Yanomamö was within earshot.

I remained focused on the task at hand and proposed to Bórtoli that we publish an article about the use of genealogies to assign names, hoping that other missionaries might be interested in doing something similar. He thought that was a good idea and suggested that one of the nuns be a co-author, a Spaniard named Maria Eguillor, who had published a monograph on the Yanomamö that drew extensively on my 1968 Yano-mamö monograph and, incidentally, on the work of Jacques Lizot. The Salesians apparently wanted to establish her as an anthropologist. When we ended our work that week, we submitted an article to the local Salesian journal, *La Iglesia en Amazonas* (*The Church in Amazonas*) based in the territorial capital, Puerto Ayacucho.

Salesian Nuns File a Complaint About Me

The German nun was not going to let go of her anger over the television program. She apparently convinced some of the other nuns to join her in filing a complaint against me with the Oficina Central de Asuntos Indigenas (OCAI)—the Venezuelan Indian Commission—sometime in 1988. It is unlikely that the Salesian priests were unaware of this action because they should have known this would lead to a major political incident.

Before they filed their complaint with the OCAI, the nuns published an article in *La Iglesia en Amazonas*, allegedly written by the leader they were grooming to be a chief and spokesman of the Yanomamö in the Mavaca area, César Dimanawä. Dimanawä's letter claimed, preposterously, that he spoke for "all the Yanomamö in the Mavaca area" and that they did not want me ever to come back there. He cited as the reason that I made films about Yanomamö warfare and violence "or so a friend of his told him." It wasn't hard to guess who his "friend" was.

The Nova/BBC Film Project

At about the same time in 1988, I was approached by documentary producers at BBC England and the PBS science program "Nova" in the United States. They wanted me to participate in a jointly produced documentary film about my research among the Yanomamö. I tentatively agreed. BBC/Nova then applied for and received a permit from OCAI to make this documentary among the Yanomamö.

When I passed through Caracas en route to the Yanomamö area that year, I was unexpectedly contacted by Charles Brewer-Carías, who had been a member of the IVIC/Michigan biomedical research project between 1966 and approximately 1970. I had seen Charles only intermittently since 1970, perhaps two or three times. He had turned to national politics and had become a minister in the Venezuelan government.

He wanted to meet me for dinner. That evening he told me that he had been chosen by the government to be the "spy" in the BBC/Nova project. He was being facetious when he said this, but there was an element of truth to it: ministries of the Venezuelan government wanted to know what outsiders were doing in their various filming and research projects in the remote interior of their country, especially major media players like BBC and PBS, and they would sometimes "attach" Venezuelan participants to these projects. Charles also took the opportunity to suggest that we resume our previous research after the BBC/Nova project ended: he would focus on the biodiversity of the Amazon jungle while I would continue piecing together the history of Yanomamö migrations and their geographical, genealogical, and ecological parameters. I agreed in principle to collaborate with him the following year.

Not long after that I was notified by one of the BBC producers that they were having difficulty reaching an understanding with their American counterparts at Nova on the subject matter of their joint scientific documentary. The Americans wanted to build the documentary around my longtime and widely known academic dispute with Marvin Harris (which I discussed earlier) about his allegation that scarcity of meat in the Yanomamö diet was a possible cause of their wars. The BBC wanted to focus on how I was using my genealogical and demographic data on the Yanomamö to test hypotheses generated from sociobiological theories, especially William Hamilton's theory of inclusive fitness (kin selection). Hamilton was an Englishman. The producer said this disagreement was causing a delay in their schedule and that he would contact me again when their disagreement was resolved.

Then I received a letter from Marcel Roche, who was the director of
IVIC and the host of the Michigan/IVIC biomedical research collabora-
tion between 1965 and 1972. He told me he was very concerned about
an article that appeared in *El Universal*, a prominent daily newspaper in
Venezuela, that he said described my participation in the forthcoming
BBC/Nova documentary. Roche said the wording seemed deliberately in-
flammatory and would stir up opposition to me and the project because
it described my return to the Yanomamö area to continue my studies of
"Yanomamö warfare, violence, and fighting." Roche knew how much
Venezuelan anthropologists resented me, giving as one of their reasons
that I exaggerated Yanomamö violence, even though no Venezuelan anthropologist had ever studied the Yanomamö.

Like Roche, I was surprised that the article emphasized these hot-
button issues. I sent the article to my BBC contact, who responded that he
also was surprised by this description of the project. He assured me that
it was not the description that he had sent to the Venezuelan embassy
in London and said that someone in Caracas must have deliberately dis-
torted the BBC description of the documentary.

By now, my 1988 lead article in *Science* demonstrating that Yanomamö violence and male reproductive success were correlated had been
published. It was getting a hostile reception from social-activist anthropologists because it described warfare, violence, and revenge in a Venezuelan tribe that they were trying to portray as peaceful and tranquil.
My article also raised the possibility that human violence had something
to do with the evolved nature of Homo sapiens.

Meanwhile, BBC and Nova were unable to reconcile their disagreement and notified OCAI that they were not going to make their proposed
joint documentary.

Since I had plans to continue my own field research regardless of the
BBC/Nova filming, I applied to OCAI for a new research permit. I received
a formal response from Maria Luisa Allais, a new director of OCAI, saying
that "OCAI could not grant me a research permit at this time" and listing the conditions under which they *might* grant me one. The conditions
were basically, When hell freezes over. Maria Luisa Allais was the official
whom the Salesian nuns had visited to file their complaint against me,
bringing Dimanawä and several other "leaders" with them.

This was the first time that I had applied for a research permit from OCAI and been turned down. I had been studying the Yanomamö for almost twenty-five years by then. However, between 1975 and 1985 it was clear to me that if I *had* applied for a permit from OCAI I would have been turned down, so I never applied for one and as a consequence, I did not visit Venezuela during this time period. I knew from Venezuelan colleagues that a permit would not be awarded because the people who ran OCAI then were widely known to be opposed to me and to American anthropologists in general.

President Pérez Becomes Involved

Shortly after getting the letter from Allais, I told Charles Brewer that my application for a research permit had been turned down. He became angry and told me he regarded the denial of my request as if it were a denial of a request that he had personally made. Brewer asked me to consider a new way to continue my research. He had just attended a meeting with a woman named Cecilia Matos, the "mistress" of the president of Venezuela, Carlos Andrés Pérez (known as "CAP" in the press).

Matos knew that CAP's political career was coming to an end soon and that he could not run for another term as president. She wanted to have some kind of visible social legacy after CAP left office and was attempting to create a charitable foundation to benefit the poor people of Venezuela, which included the country's indigenous tribesmen. She called her new organization Fundafaci, derived from *Fundación para las Familias Campesinas y Indígenas* (Foundation for the Families of Farmers and Indians).

At the meeting Brewer attended, she asked those present to recommend experts in their respective fields for her to consider as advisors. Brewer recommended me as a prominent international authority on the Venezuelan Yanomamö Indians. He was asked to invite me to Caracas to discuss how I might work with Matos and her new Fundafaci staff, a group of politically prominent and wealthy Venezuelan women who had fund-raising skills and extensive political networks.

Brewer and I met with Matos, who asked us to propose an idea that we could discuss with CAP that Fundafaci might later cultivate and expand. At our first and only meeting with President Pérez, Brewer and I introduced the idea of creating a biosphere reserve to protect the virgin forests of Venezuela's Amazon area and the Yanomamö and Ye'kwana people who lived there. The time to do this was *now* (1990). There was at present no pressure from Venezuelan colonists to enter this area. There were no commercial agricultural operations, no logging industries, no interest in cattle ranching, no known valuable subsurface minerals, and no mining operations. It would be relatively easy then for the Venezuelan government to simply declare this vast area as some kind of national park or special reserve because nobody would have to be removed from the area. The only people who seemed to be interested in this area were scientific researchers and missionaries to the indigenous people.

One of the first trips Brewer and I made to follow up on our proposal included a television crew from ABC. In November 1990, ABC aired a program hosted by Diane Sawyer about our new project among uncontacted Yanomamö villages. The program included footage of President Pérez promising to create a Yanomamö "reserve" of some kind within six months. ABC reran the program within a year and announced that the president had gotten his administration to approve the creation of a national park/biosphere reserve for the Yanomamö and Ye'kwana Indians—an area of some thirty-two thousand square miles. Shortly afterward, Brazilian president Fernando Collor de Mello announced that his government had also authorized an area about the same size intended for the same purpose for the Brazilian Yanomamö. The combined area was larger than the state of Florida.

This was a momentous event in the history of native peoples of the Amazon Basin, but my annoyed anthropological detractors claimed that my real intent in advocating for this reserve was "career aggrandizement," that is, an effort to exclude other anthropologists from studying the Yanomamö. They claimed that the area was intended for Charles Brewer and "other crooked politicians" to exploit gold and other minerals in this area. But neither Brewer nor I was ever asked our opinions about what policies or rules were to be followed in administering this area. Indeed, the Salesian Missions were given considerable authority in this reserve, something that Brewer and I would have resisted had we been consulted. We both hoped that this reserve would be purely secular in administration.

During our brief meeting with CAP, he asked us if there was any specific thing he could do to help us with any government problems. Brewer brought up the denial of my most recent research permit request. CAP asked what ministry was involved. Brewer replied, the Ministry of Education. CAP picked up the phone next to him, spoke for a few seconds, put the phone back, turned to us and said, "You have a meeting with the minister of education in thirty minutes." We then shook hands, thanked the president for meeting with us, and left for the offices of the minister of education.

The minister of education, Dr. Gustavo Roosen, was a courteous man, serious and professional. He asked us to explain the problem. After listening and asking a few questions, he asked that the head of OCAI be sent in. Maria Luisa Allais soon appeared, carrying an armful of files. She was well dressed, looked very nervous, and avoided eye contact with me and Brewer. The minister asked for the letter she had sent to me, read it, and diplomatically commented (apparently for her benefit) that her letter did not actually say that I would *never* get a research permit to continue my work among the Yanomamö, allowing her a face-saving way out of this situation.

Minister of Education Roosen made it clear to all of us that if the president of Venezuela approved of my request to continue my scientific studies of the Yanomamö, I had the permission, as did Brewer, of the highest authority of the Venezuelan government to proceed. The meeting then ended.

The Tragic Incident at Kedebaböwei

When we initiated our new research project in 1990, Brewer and I arranged to have a fuel depot cleared at a Yanomamö village called Kedebaböwei-teri some two hours up the Mavaca River from the main Salesian mission at the mouth of the Mavaca.

I knew the Kedebaböwei-teri people well. They had all formerly lived in Mishimishimaböwei-teri, a village I repeatedly visited after 1968. The

Salesians had persuaded them to break away from the main group in the headwaters of the Mavaca and settle downstream on a navigable portion of the Mavaca across from the relatively new Salesian satellite mission called "Mavakita" ("Little Mavaca"). The Salesians had earlier enticed the Haoyaböwei-teri, a much smaller faction, to settle at Mavakita.

Charles and I wanted our valuable supplies, like fuel for our outboard motors and the helicopters, to be in a safe location and away from a permanent Salesian mission.

We asked the Yanomamö at Haoyaböwei and Kedebaböwei to clear the brush and small trees close to the Mavaca River for a place to store our fifty-five-gallon barrels of fuel, which they enthusiastically did. In the process, they also took out a small hut that Hermano Finkers at the Mavaca Mission had asked them to construct for a beehive he wanted to place there. Finkers was trying to get the Yanomamö to keep bees and sell the honey as a cash crop.

This trivial incident ultimately led to lethal consequences for several of my Yanomamö friends.

When Brewer and I arrived at Kedebaböwei, we were greeted by a large number of Yanomamö men who were extremely angry with Finkers. He had just visited them earlier that day and, on discovering that they had taken down the beehive hut, he berated them angrily, a young man named Ushubiriwä in particular. His anger may have also been increased because they did this in order to create a storage area for fuel supply. I was now an "enemy."

There was a history of bad relationships between Finkers and Ushubiriwä. Ushubiriwä had been taught by the Salesians to read and was hired by Finkers to transport the local Yanomamö children daily across the river and downstream a short way to the recently established mission at Mavakita, where they learned reading and writing. The Salesians apparently gave or loaned Ushubiriwä a small outboard motor and canoe for this purpose, which he could also use for hunting and fishing when he was not transporting the children to and from the Mavakita mission. Ushubiriwä's young wife, Nonokama, was also hired by the Salesians to prepare breakfast for the children, which primarily consisted of heavily sweetened boiled oatmeal and powdered milk.

Ushubiriwä and Finkers were apparently on strained terms over the small motor the Salesians had given to him. The motor had stopped working, and Ushubiriwä had stopped transporting the children, whether because of the disabled motor or for other reasons.

The Yanomamö told me and Brewer that they told Finkers that he had promised to pay them for making the beehive shelter but had never done so, and since it was not paid for, did not have a beehive in it yet, was easy to replace, and was in the way, they simply removed it with the other brush. They were extremely angry with Finkers for berating them so unfairly—and also because during the argument Finkers had accused me and Brewer of being *garimpeiros*. They probably didn't know what a *garimpeiro* was and had never seen one, but they assumed it was something bad and was a slander against us.

Despite the disagreement, Brewer and I went to work. Brewer continued to collect animal, plant, and insect specimens, and I continued to collect data on Yanomamö village movements and genealogies.

In January 1992 I accompanied a medical research team from the Johns Hopkins University to the Mavaca area with the intent of taking them into Kedebaböwei-teri for a five-day research project on a "low-salt consumption" population. We were in a helicopter and landed at the Salesian mission at Mavaca. I didn't get out—the Salesians had already declared their hostility toward me in the Venezuelan press, and I believed that the Yanomamö at their three missions where I would pass through had been encouraged by the Salesians to steal anything they could from me—without concern over possible reprimands.

One of the participants in this medical expedition, a Venezuelan medical doctor named Teodardo Marcano, went to the Salesian mission to talk with Padre Bórtoli. Marcano explained what we were doing in the area, that we planned to do the medical study in Kedebaböwei-teri. When he returned to the helicopter he said that Bórtoli told him that there were rumors that the Kedebaböwei-teri had gotten "sick," but Bórtoli said that he didn't send anyone from the mission to Kedebaböwei-teri to check on this. He dismissed the rumor as just another Yanomamö attempt to get the Salesians to take a two-hour motorboat trip so the Yanomamö could beg items from them, knowing that the Salesians invariably brought trade goods each time they visited.

We then flew up the Mavaca to the large Kedebaböwei-teri *shabono*, which I could tell had been abandoned very recently—the packed earth in the central clearing was still devoid of green weeds, a sure sign that it had been inhabited recently. We circled it several times to see if anyone would come out of the nearby jungle and wave at us. We then flew due east to my "backup" village for the study, a splinter group of the Iwahi-koroba-teri that had been given the name Washäwä-teri by the Salesians, after the name of the small tributary of the Mavaca River on which their *shabono* was located.

Some hours after we had landed in Washäwä-teri two young men from Kedebaböwei-teri came into the *shabono* and headed straight for me. One of them carried a hand-scribbled note, which he gave to me. It was from Ushubiriwä. He addressed me as *habemi*—dearest father. It said that they were sick and dying and to please come and help them.

I immediately told Dr. Marcano what it said and asked him if he would walk out to Kedebaböwei-teri. Our helicopter had left right after we got out of it. One of the two Kedebaböwei-teri messengers would guide him to their *shabono*. Marcano quickly persuaded one of the other medical doctors to go with him, and they left immediately for the stricken *shabono* some five or six hours away.

I then asked the other young man, whom I had known since childhood, if he would stay with me and go through my recent census, name by name, to identify who was sick and who had died. When I asked if he would be upset if I said names of people who had died, he admonished me and said that he and all the others trusted me, I was now one of them, and this was an important life-and-death issue that involved our medical intervention. He would not get upset if I unknowingly whispered the names of dead people because he knew that I was trying to help them.

We found an isolated section of the *shabono* and got to work. After going through the list of names, I learned that twenty-one individuals had died within the span of the past week, all of them mature adults or older people. No children or infants had died, which I found very unusual for an introduced illness. Most depressing of all, one of them was their headman, Örasiyaborewä, and much to my shock and anguish, the fabled former headman, Sibarariwä, also died. This devastated me—and it angered me. A large number of the older political leaders in the villages immediately surrounding the Salesian mission at Mavaca had died in "epidemics" similar to this one, epidemics that spared the children but claimed the lives of the male political leaders.

The mortality in Kedebaböwei-teri amounted to 14 percent of a largely uncontacted Yanomamö village who perished in one week from some sort of upper respiratory infection, a sickness they might never have been exposed to if they had not been persuaded to move out to a navigable stretch of a large river. Here they could more easily be acculturated by the Salesian missionaries, who could now avoid the discomforts of walking inland to visit them. This was a continuation of a five-hundred-year-old colonial policy by the Catholic Church in the Americas to save the souls of native peoples by attracting them from the deep forest to living at their missions. When concentrated near the missions, the native people would, incidentally, be exposed to outsiders and new sicknesses. Such collateral damage began to be reported only when anthropologists like me started tracking these kinds of things, especially in demographically pristine tribes like the Yanomamö.

The most depressing and tragic aspect of this incident is that it appears that the Salesian missionaries at Mavaca, just two hours by boat from Kedebaböwei-teri, had heard rumors about the sickness shortly after it broke out a week earlier but had dismissed them. Yet it was they who urged the Kedebaböwei-teri to move to a site on the navigable lower Mavaca River where the Kedebaböwei-teri would be accessible and could more easily obtain medicines if they got sick.

I was also dumbfounded and anguished to learn that shortly after his argument with Finkers over the removal of the bee shelter, Ushubiriwä was killed by a small group of Yanomamö associated with the Washäwä-teri village and the Salesian post at Mavakita. In 1994 Finkers published an article in *La Iglesia en Amazonas* in which he publicly asserted that *I* was responsible for Ushubiriwä's death because Ushubiriwä had defended me, which allegedly made the other Yanomamö angry.

On October 4, 1993, an article appeared in a prominent Caracas newspaper quoting a Salesian priest saying that the Salesians could no longer guarantee my safety if I passed through one of their missions on future field research trips. I had repeatedly passed through Yanomamö villages near the missions without incident long before the current Salesian priests and brothers arrived.

Massacre at Hashimo-teri

In July 1993, Brazilian *garimpeiros* crossed the border into Venezuela near the Orinoco headwaters in the Parima Mountains and attacked and brutally massacred a Venezuelan Yanomamö group at Hashimo-teri that they had been feuding with for some time. They shot and hacked to death some sixteen or seventeen people, mostly women and children.

Astonishingly, the brutal deaths of these Yanomamö was not the story that attracted the attention of the Venezuelan press and the activist anthropological community. Instead, the story was the fact that Charles Brewer and I were named to the official Venezuelan commission to investigate the massacre at Hashimo-teri.

Brewer was among those Venezuelans who urged the new interim Venezuelan president, Ramón Velásquez, to create a special commission to investigate the massacre. Brewer was named as head of this commission and in that capacity could suggest names of other people with expertise whom the president should consider as members of the commission. Several Venezuelan anthropologists agreed to participate, but none of them were familiar with the Yanomamö and none spoke their language. Primarily for these reasons I was named as one of the members.

When Brewer and I were made official members of the Presidential Commission to investigate this massacre, the frantic opposition to this announcement came not only from Salesians but also my detractors in the radical activist anthropology community. For the first time my anthropological detractors united with the Salesians who dominated the politics of Venezuela's Amazonas and who were acquiring the secular functions of state in the entire Yanomamö/Ye'kwana area.

Some 600 articles were published in the major Venezuelan newspapers between August and December 1993 about this massacre, almost all of them sympathetic to the Salesians' presumed privileges in Venezuela's Amazon territory—which was on the verge of becoming a state. The Salesians strongly influenced much of the Venezuelan press and could suggest articles that the press would print. To me it was as if the Venezuelan press were just a widely distributed version of *La Iglesia en Amazonas*, the Salesians' official journal.

Shortly after being appointed Presidential Commission members,

Brewer and I were summoned to attend an urgent meeting in the office of the Fiscal General—the attorney general. The Salesians demanded this meeting and also demanded to be put on the Presidential Commission and that Brewer and I be removed from it. The attorney general defended the existing commission.

At one point during the meeting I was asked what I thought about having Salesians on the commission. I replied that I had no objections and would be happy to collaborate with whoever might be added. My response pleased the attorney general so much that he went out of his way to commend my statement and contrasted it to statements made at this meeting by the Salesians. (I must make an important point here, because it would come up repeatedly, usually in a false way: this commission was made official when its composition was approved by the president of Venezuela and then published as a presidential decree in the September 8, 1993, issue of Venezuela's *Gaceta Oficial*. No other commission was announced in the *Gaceta Oficial*.)

Complicating this entire situation was the fact that the interim government of Venezuela was teetering on the edge of a military coup.

The Commission was able to go into the Hashimo-teri area and begin our investigation only two months after the massacre had taken place and several weeks after a Brazilian investigation team had been to the scene of the massacre—illegally, in Venezuelan territory.

Not long after we got to the Hashimo-teri *shabono* we heard another helicopter approaching from Parima to the north. I was mapping the abandoned and burned *shabono* when the helicopter landed and its passengers exited. I was startled to see that the first several men to emerge were in civilian clothes and carrying submachine guns. A woman emerged whom I recognized from the meeting in the attorney general's office a week or so earlier. This group approached Brewer and me, and at gunpoint demanded that we leave the area because we were "contaminating" a crime scene. Brewer argued with the men with guns and a portly older man, who had been giving the others instructions. I later learned that he was the Salesian bishop of Amazonas, Bishop Ignacio Velasco.

While Brewer argued with them, I unobtrusively melted into the background and went back to our temporary campsite a few hundred yards away, next to a clear, sparkling creek. I had a Yanomamö companion with me who spoke a dialect of Yanomamö I could understand as well as the dialect of the Hashimo-teri. The Yanomamö in the Parima Mountains spoke a dialect that was difficult for me to understand at first, but after several days I could understand enough of it to be able to communicate with the people there.

At almost the same moment that we reached our makeshift camp, a small group of Yanomamö appeared—several young men and women—and followed us to our hammocks. They had come to harvest some of the local food that would now go to waste. They explained to us they were immediate neighbors of the Hashimo-teri and they knew them well.

I then spent the next several hours asking them for their version of the massacre, working without the distractions of the Salesian contingent and their armed guards. These Yanomamö told me that the Hashimo-teri and the miners had had several hostile interactions before the massacre and that the miners had killed five Yanomamö. The Hashimo-teri then retaliated and killed two miners. The Yanomamö informants said that when the massacre took place, the miners were guided to the Hashimo-teri *shabono* by Yanomamö from Brazilian villages to the east. They called them "Paapiu-teri" and "Vista-teri" (they probably meant "Boa Vista-teri").

A helicopter returned to pick us up late that afternoon and took us back to Parima B for the night. The bishop and the lawyers discovered my notebooks and maps and without asking my permission brazenly took them from me and photographed the several pages of maps I had drawn as well as my handwritten notes, demanding to know how I learned these things. I told them about the Yanomamö visitors I had interviewed. Meanwhile, the bishop and the lawyers had gathered no information that day except for collecting a few worn aluminum cooking pots with bullet holes in them and pieces of broken machetes.

The next day the unpleasant female lawyer, now acting "officially," asked me to appear at a room in the military compound where a desk had been provided for her. She demanded to know what I was doing there, a preposterous question in view of the fact that we had both met with the attorney general in his office a few days earlier. After I dutifully explained that I was an official member of the Presidential Commission, she claimed that I was not on the official commission, regardless of what the records showed.

She demanded my passport, which I provided to her. She looked it over very carefully, every page and every stamp, and there were many. She took an extraordinary amount of time. Most of the stamps were entry and exit stamps from Venezuela passport control at the Maiquetía International Airport. She then accused me of "illegally entering Venezuela." We had an unpleasant argument that ended only when I suggested that when we got back to Caracas we should take this up with both the attorney general's office and the U.S. embassy.

Brewer and I had requested that we be flown back to the massacre site on our second day, but our request was denied because, the military commander claimed, they didn't have enough fuel. But we learned that the Salesian bishop, one of his priests, and their Yanomamö interpreter *were* flown back to the massacre site to look for and question the same informants I had spoken to the previous day. However, they couldn't find them.

Brewer and I were sleeping at the New Tribes Mission facility at the other end of the airstrip from the military post at Parima B. I learned by accident that the helicopter we came in on was departing in a few minutes and the work of our commission was officially declared to be over by someone. The military commander didn't bother to tell either me or Brewer that the helicopter was leaving. I scrambled to gather my equipment and get to the helicopter. I barely made it in time to climb aboard—the rotors were already turning and the Salesian team was already on board. Brewer did not even know about the departure and was left behind.

When we landed in Puerto Ayacucho some two hours later, the commander, who had taken my field notes and was reading them in the helicopter, approached me to ask if he could photocopy my notes. He assured me he would get them back to me within an hour, well before the commercial flight I would be taking to Caracas. I agreed.

While we were talking I asked him about rumors that a military coup was about to take place and it might be difficult for anyone to leave Venezuela because commercial airline flights would all be canceled. I thought who better to ask about an impending military coup than a high-ranking officer in the Venezuelan air force? His response was something to the effect that if he were I, he would take the next available flight out of Venezuela.

Later, my detractors and activist opponents in anthropology would characterize this episode by saying that after being expelled from the Hashimo-teri massacre site, I was ordered to leave Venezuela on the next flight out of the country by a high-ranking military officer.

A very annoyed Venezuelan minister of defense had to send a plane to fetch Charles Brewer the next day.

Aftermath of the Salesian Interference in Hashimo-teri

Salesian control over Amazonas was now so pervasive that I was shocked to discover that major political protests against Brewer and me were held in Puerto Ayacucho. When I asked Brewer how the people of this small city knew anything about us, let alone enough to "protest" what we were doing, he told me: "They don't know *anything* about either of us. They were simply hired by the Salesians to carry already-made derogatory placards with anti-Chagnon and anti-Brewer slogans on them."

I even saw graffiti with anti-Chagnon and anti-Brewer slogans spray-painted on bridge abutments and buildings when I returned to Caracas the next day.

Apart from being amazed that political accusations could simply be invented in Venezuela and made to look as if they came spontaneously from informed citizens, I was very angry about how we were treated. But I was even more disturbed that the Hashimo-teri victims were of much less concern to the Salesians and the activist anthropologists than the legitimate presence of Brewer and me attempting to determine what had happened to the Hashimo-teri and trying to achieve some semblance of justice for them. The Salesians had decided that the Yanomamö land was theirs to administer, and they would not tolerate interference by anyone, including even the government of Venezuela.

16

Darkness in Cultural Anthropology

The Smear Campaigns Begin

In the spring of 1994 packages of derogatory hate mail were sent to officers of all of the granting agencies who had supported my Yanomamö research; editors of the several publishing companies who had published my books; the chancellor, several deans, and the chairman of my department at the University of California, Santa Barbara; and heads of anthropology departments of many other universities in the United States and some in Europe. Many of these people wrote to me expressing their disgust at receiving these packages, some saying they were simply revolting.

These packages contained self-serving cover letters from two Salesians, Father Enzo Cappelletti and Bishop Ignacio Velasco, as well as a highly critical letter about my Yanomamö research written by French anthropologist Jacques Lizot, who, Bishop Velasco's letter explained, was asked by the Salesians to write this letter.

Bishop Velasco's letter, dated January 20, 1994, was addressed to Father Cappelletti, director of the U.S. headquarters of the Salesian Missions in New Rochelle, New York, and explained the Venezuelan Salesian vicariate's alleged role in investigating the Hashimo-teri massacre that I wrote about in the previous chapter. Bishop Velasco denounced me and Charles Brewer, whom he described as members of the "so called Presidential Commission" appointed by Venezuelan president Ramón Velásquez. Bishop Velasco referred to two recent articles I had written about the massacre that were published in the *New York Times* and the London *Times* as among various articles in various parts of the world in which I "accused" the Salesians in "different ways." I took the main point of his letter to be the enclosed extraordinarily vicious attack on me and my research by Lizot. Lizot's letter emphasized that he, a Yanomamö expert, contested the demographic data I published that implicated Salesian policies in high death rates due to diseases. Lizot wrongfully said that my demographic data said "just the opposite."

Lizot also downplayed the Salesian tactic of luring the Yanomamö to their missions by offering them shotguns. He said that "the rifles (*sic*) arrive here from Brazil, crossing the border . . ." and were given out by the Venezuelan military, or were provided by the few Venezuelan creoles who visited the Salesian missions. (In fact, I had been told by some Yanomamö that Lizot himself provided them with shotguns and ammunition.) Lizot was one of my longtime academic detractors who also studied the Yanomamö for many years.

Among his several criticisms of me, Cappelletti refuted my claim that the 1915 Law of the Missions explained Salesian secular authority, because these privileges had long since been replaced by a real secular authority. Cappelletti's main point seemed to be that the presidential commission appointed by Venezuelan president Velásquez on September 9, 1993, to investigate the Hashimo-teri massacre "was repealed on September 14, five days later, due to the general outcry against the members of the Commission. The press, politicians, anthropologists, the Yanomami themselves and the Salesians objected to the persons chosen [by the president of Venezuela]."

This statement is not true. This presidential commission was the *only* legally authorized Venezuelan investigation of the Hashimo-teri massacre and was not dissolved until January 1997, over three years later.

The package also contained articles from recent Venezuelan newspapers that covered the Hashimo-teri massacre that criticized me and, to a lesser extent, Brewer, for our participation in the investigation. More articles in the Venezuelan news media were devoted to attacks on me and Brewer than to the tragic massacre of the Yanomamö at Hashimo-teri, as I mentioned in the previous chapter.

The packages reflected a considerable amount of sophistication in how they were assembled, the list of recipients, the hierarchy of administrative officials at my university, and the list of agencies and their addresses that funded portions of my research.

Shortly after the first packages of derogatory mail were sent out by the Salesians, my disgruntled former Venezuelan student Jesus Cardozo visited me at UCSB on March 23. He was already an anthropology graduate student at UCSB when I joined the faculty in 1984 and, since he indicated that he wanted to study Venezuelan natives, he was assigned to me as an advisee. I had taken him into the Yanomamö area in 1985. After a few days in the field on his first field trip with me, he angrily denounced me and my research colleague, Raymond Hames. Hames and I had left him at Haoyaböwei-teri, a small Yanomamö community across the river from the Salesian satellite mission post of Mavakita, while we went two days farther up the Mavaca River to Mishimishimaböwei-teri to work there. On our way back downstream several weeks later, we coincidentally slept on the riverbank at Mavakita some hundred yards downstream from Haoyaböwei-teri. Cardozo heard our motor and dispatched several Yanomamö in a canoe to take a message to us. The message said he wanted a ride back down to the main Salesian mission at Mavaca and needed my help in paying the Yanomamö for the work they had done for him. Early the next morning I left Hames at our camp and went back to the Haoyaböwei-teri *shabono* where Cardozo was staying. When I began "paying" the Yanomamö, he didn't like the way I proceeded: I gave the headman a machete, one of the most valuable trade items I had provided to Cardozo to pay informants for his work. He protested, saying that this man had done no work for him and didn't deserve a machete. I explained to him that it didn't make any difference: you must give the headman a big item, whether or not he did any work, simply because he was the headman.

Within two days of seeing his first Yanomamö when Hames and I took him to this village, Cardozo told us that he knew how to treat the

Yanomamö, because they were all Venezuelans like he was and his "brothers" and you have to treat them like children, like spoiled teenagers, if they misbehave. And he was apparently doing that, which annoyed and angered the Yanomamö headman. When we finished paying the Yanomamö, which took much longer than was necessary because Cardozo kept objecting to what I paid each informant, we returned to the camp. Hames and I had a subsequent confrontation with Cardozo over his behavior when we tried to load the canoe. When we reached Mavaca late that afternoon, Cardozo took refuge with the Salesian missionaries. I am aware of no meaningful research he has done among the Yanomamö since then. On his 1994 visit he tried—and failed—to have me removed from his doctoral committee. During my tenure there, he never did finish his Ph.D. at UCSB.

Cardozo, like a handful of other former graduate students and colleagues, seemingly found it easier to make a name for themselves in the ethnography of the Yanomamö by denouncing me rather than by expending the necessary time-consuming effort working in remote undesirable field conditions and producing academically acceptable research. On his 1994 visit, Cardozo informed me that it was a crime in Venezuela to make false claims about others, such as my claim that the Salesians had systematically provided shotguns to the Yanomamö over the years and some of these shotguns were used to kill other Yanomamö. Such a crime, he went on, involved a prison sentence. Then he made it clear that it was possible that I would be arrested if I were to return to Venezuela. He wanted me to know that the current attorney general of Venezuela was a good friend of the Salesian Bishop of Caracas (Ignacio Velasco, formerly Bishop of Amazonas) and, most likely, would favor the Salesians in a legal suit against me for libelous statements about them.

In May 1994 Fr. Cappelletti published a critical article about me in the Newsletter of the American Anthropological Association. To my surprise, the same issue of that newsletter also included a critical article about me by Terence Turner. I found it unusual that a prominent Salesian functionary and one of my long-term activist anthropological critics would coincidentally publish critical articles about me in the same issue of an anthropological journal because my disputes with these parties did not overlap. Turner had published occasional critical remarks about me over

a number of years and had publicly denounced me at a number of anthropology meetings. I had published nothing in response to his attacks.
In the *Anthropology Newsletter* in September 1994 Charles Brewer and I
responded to the attacks on us by Cappelletti and Turner.

Cappelletti's article in the AAA's newsletter repeated many of the same
arguments that Bishop Velasco had made. Turner's very long article in
the "Commentary" section of the newsletter cited a number of my alleged
misdeeds and reminded the reader twice that "Chagnon's sociobiological
theories" were a component in my dispute with the Salesians. My "sociobiological theories" had nothing to do with my dispute with the Salesians. Turner intended to remind the readers of the AAA newsletter who
opposed sociobiology about my unacceptable theories. Turner falsely
claimed that Charles Brewer was being investigated by the Venezuelan
government for his alleged illegal mining interests in tribal areas and repeated the false claim that Charles Brewer and I were not authorized to
investigate the massacre at Hashimo-teri:

> The President of Venezuela did in fact appoint such a commission on
> September 9, but dissolved it only five days later after massive protests by
> indigenous organizations, anthropologists and other academics, politicians,
> and missionaries against the presence of Brewer-Carías [Brewer was also
> known as Brewer-Carías] and Chagnon on the Commission. This was ten
> days before Chagnon and Brewer had themselves flown in an Air Force
> plane to Haximu, representing themselves as members in good standing of
> the Presidential Commission. Meanwhile, the President appointed a new
> Commission, which proceeded to the site, arriving . . . after Chagnon and
> Brewer-Carias.

This false statement would become a staple of the Salesians and the activist anthropologists. It would reappear again and again.

When Brewer and I responded to Cappelletti and Turner, we were
told by Susan Skomal, the editor of the *Anthropology Newsletter*, that
our response would appear in the correspondence section and had to be
limited to five hundred words. When I asked for space equal to that of
Cappelletti and Turner, Skomal held firm and added that Turner's long
article "was of general interest to the members of the association" and a

second article on the same topic would be unnecessary. I later learned that we should have been given equal space and that Skomal's advice was incorrect.

The 1994 Annual Meetings of the AAA

On November 14, 1994, an anthropologist named Frank Salamone, who taught "missiology" and anthropology at Iona College, phoned me saying that he was holding a session at the upcoming annual meetings of the AAA in Atlanta two weeks from then and wanted me to participate in it. He told me that Padre José Bórtoli, the head of the Salesian mission posts in Venezuela's Amazonas Territory, had come to New Rochelle, New York, and was staying with Father Enzo Cappelletti, the director of the Salesian Missions in the United States. Salamone said that he and Cappelletti were good friends and referred to Bórtoli by his first name. Iona College has no official connections to the Salesian order, but is in New Rochelle, New York, where the U.S. headquarters of the Salesian Missions are located. At the AAA meetings in Atlanta I was to discuss with Bórtoli my disagreements with some of the policies of the Salesian missionaries.

Salamone proposed a co-edited volume in which we would discuss what Salamone (and others) later characterized as the "ugliest war" between anthropology and the Catholic Church in the history of our discipline. He wanted to restrict the book to my dispute with the Salesians but I insisted on including other groups such as the New Tribes Missions. Salamone agreed to this suggestion. I had no difficulty finding an enthusiastic and reputable academic publisher for the proposed book—the publisher of my very successful monograph, *Yanomamö*, the most popular monograph ever used in introductory anthropology courses in American universities.

On the night before Salamone's session he, some Salesians, and I went out to dinner. Although the Salesians and I were now openly criticizing each other, I still hoped we could patch up our differences during the several discussions we would have at these meetings. Attending this dinner was an American-Irish Salesian priest whom I didn't know who worked for Cappelletti at the Salesian headquarters. His name was Donald Delaney. During the dinner he several times privately warned me in a stern and serious tone of voice to the effect, We will get back at you; the Salesians are not some trivial order of the Catholic Church that you can criticize with impunity. Salamone never mentioned when he first called me that he had just taken a trip to the Salesian mission at Mavaca, Bórtoli's home base, at the invitation of the Salesians. His traveling companion was Father Delaney. Salamone had also contacted Terence Turner, something else he did not inform me about.

In Salamone's AAA session Fr. Bórtoli and I made position statements about our respective disagreements with each other in a generally amicable way, focusing on the implications for the Yanomamö and Ye'kwana of the Biosphere Reserve that Charles Brewer and I were instrumental in helping create: Bórtoli acknowledged our role in persuading President Carlos Andrés Pérez to create this special area.

Near the end of the meeting Salamone called upon Turner, who was standing at the back of the small, crowded room. Turner denounced me angrily for, among other things, "undermining" the position of Davi Kobenawä, a Brazilian Yanomamö who was "emerging" as a politically prominent leader in Brazil.

I was annoyed that Salamone called on Turner to respond to what I had said. It was immediately clear to me that Salamone had arranged for Turner to be there and to make a provocative statement. When offered the opportunity to respond to Turner, I said, "you are goddamned right I want to respond, but this meeting is to attempt to establish some kind of détente between me and the Salesians and not to add more fuel to the existing flames . . . Turner's remarks are not contributing to that end."

After the 1994 AAA meetings, Salamone and I began exchanging the chapters we each had written for our proposed volume and made suggestions to each other. As we neared our publication date, Salamone added a chapter that was a list of the political accusations the Salesians had made in the Venezuelan newspapers intended to discredit me.

When I contacted our publisher and informed them that I intended to add a chapter to challenge the claims in Salamone's new chapter, the publisher decided to cancel our contract because it realized that the issues were political as well as academic and had no place in a volume intended for undergraduate courses in anthropology.

Salamone's several subsequent publications on my dispute with the Salesians indicate that his relationship with them was hopelessly biased in their favor. I had assumed that Salamone originally contacted me in the spirit of cooperation and professionalism, but his behavior thereafter led me to conclude that he had a hidden agenda intended to discredit me and make the Salesians look like victims of my allegedly unfair criticisms of them.

Over the next few months I also learned that Fr. Cappelletti was planning to advertise for a psychologist to "analyze" me from a distance and publish his results, known in advance, that I was a psychopath. Salamone states: "It was with some effort that Delaney and I persuaded Cappelletti to remain cool and not hire a psychologist to do a profile on Chagnon, for example. Cappelletti ranted that he would spend $20,000 on such a study."

Enter Patrick Tierney

In the spring of 1994 I began getting emails and telephone calls from colleagues all over the United States about a writer named Patrick Tierney, who had contacted them asking for information about me. It was clear to them that Tierney wanted information they might know that was uncomplimentary and derogatory.

About a year after I began getting these warnings I received a call from the UCSB legal office. One of the employees there informed me that Tierney had requested through the federal Freedom of Information Act (FOIA) a summary of the dollar amount of research support I had received from UCSB since I had joined the faculty. This person told me that "he was extremely surprised and insisted that the amounts simply *had* to be much larger."

On October 2, 1995, Tierney appeared in Campbell Hall on the campus of UCSB, where I was giving a lecture to a large class of undergraduates. When my lecture ended, he approached me, introduced himself as a journalist, and asked if he could talk with me. I bluntly replied that I knew about his attempts to get derogatory information about me and told him that I had no interest in talking to him. As I walked away from him I thought that this might be an opportunity to find out what he was up to, so I turned and invited him to my office the next morning.

When he appeared, I asked him for his press credentials. He didn't have any. I then confronted him about an error-ridden article he had co-authored with a Leda Martins on the op-ed page of the *New York Times* in April about the alleged environmental destruction that Charles Brewer had done to the Venezuelan environment by "his gold mining operation." We had a rather heated discussion about the inaccuracy of his information and the unsupported claims he and Martins had made about Brewer.

I then asked him about a "dossier" that I had heard about from a number of colleagues that he was allegedly putting together on me. He denied any knowledge of such a dossier. We spoke for only about a half-hour, at which point I told him I had work to do and indicated that our conversation was over.

Sabotaging My Trips to the Yanomamö

In 1995 I was approached by editors of *Veja* magazine, one of Brazil's most popular newsmagazines, to do a story on the Yanomamö Indians on the Brazilian side of the border. I had not been to the Yanomamö in Brazil since my first (and at that time only) trip there in 1967. *Veja* editors assured me that they could arrange the necessary research permits from FUNAI, the Brazilian agency that regulated access to areas where Brazilian Indians lived.

I was very interested in this invitation because it could inform some of my most recent field studies on several villages that were now on the Brazilian side of the border. Between 1990 and 1992 I had contacted and studied a cluster of new Yanomamö villages in Venezuela's Siapa River basin that were near the Venezuelan-Brazilian border and were closely related to several villages just over the border in Brazil. Indeed, the headman of Doshamosha-teri, a village I studied on Venezuela's Siapa River, was a brother to a headman in one of the Brazilian villages, Abruwä-teri. Immediately to the west of Abruwä-teri were many villages of the Kohoroshi-teri and Karawatari of the Cauaburi drainage, whose members had captured and held Helena Valero during the early years of her captivity.

I traveled to Boa Vista, Brazil, by way of Santa Elena, a small Venezuelan town near the Brazilian border. Boa Vista is the capital of the northernmost Brazilian state, Roraima, an area that was highly dependent on mining and cattle ranching. From Boa Vista I was able to fly by a local air taxi service directly to the Yanomamö village of Abruwä-teri, in the Amazonas state of Brazil. I spent some ten days or so in Abruwä-teri collecting genealogies that tied them to the people I had been studying in Venezuela and recording detailed information on how the villages had fissioned away from the several groups on the Venezuelan side of the border. Some of the villages the Abruwä-teri discussed were still, in 1995, minimally contacted, if at all, and still isolated in a very remote area of southern Venezuela. From the Venezuelan side, I had several months earlier flown over and photographed several of them, some of which were relatively large—in the 150-inhabitant range to judge from the sizes of their *shabonos*.

My activist opponents in Brazil had discovered that I had entered Yanomamö villages there and were now frantically attempting to interdict my research. They sent a protest message, a dossier, to FUNAI's office and contacted their resident Yanomamö "chief," Davi Kobenawä, urging him to intervene. Kobenawä "forbade" the pilot of my small plane from landing in an area where Kobenawä had influence.

The secret dossier I had been told about was used several additional times to sabotage my intended field trips. This was the first time. Alice Dreger, a historian of science who interviewed many of the major players in the scandal I am about to describe and later wrote an article about it, writes: "Curiously, when I first asked [Leda] Martins about the dossier, she told me she had written it: 'I wrote the dossier and gave it to Funai.' But she later changed her claim to me as follows: 'Patrick Tierney wrote the Chagnon dossier and I translated [it] to Portuguese. . . . I presented the dossier to Brazilian authorities (FUNAI employees) and human rights advocates who were looking for information on Chagnon who was seeking permission to go inside the Yanomami Territory in Brazil. I was the one who circulated the dossier in Brazil because people knew and trusted me. I trusted Patrick and did not check his references.'"

By some creative maneuvering of aircraft and swapping fuel supplies with other pilots, my pilot managed to get me out of Abruwä-teri and back to Boa Vista. When I landed late that day a Brazilian journalist introduced himself to me as the local correspondent of one of Brazil's most important newspapers, *O Globo*. He wanted to interview me. I was very tired and asked if he could see me in the morning.

The next morning he joined me for breakfast at my hotel. He pulled out a document that he said had just been given to him the day before. It had a list of accusations he wanted me to address and answer. I invited Antonio Mari, the Brazilian photographer whom *Veja* had assigned to this story, to join us to translate. The document turned out to be the dossier that I had been told about. This was the first time that I saw a copy of it.

The Brazilian journalist read me several of the charges from the document that, even to him, seemed preposterous and were clearly intended to discredit me politically. I had to laugh at some of them: for example, that I had been largely responsible for "destabilizing" the Venezuelan government and causing it to collapse in 1993. The journalist gradually realized that the questions were essentially all political attacks on me. His final question was something to the effect that, You are accused of saying that Davi Kobenawä is not the chief of the Brazilian Yanomamö and that his statements are largely constructed by his foreign mentors. I replied that it was true because I had visited and studied some sixty different Yanomamö villages, and the leaders in those villages had no authority outside their own villages unless they were being groomed by outsiders like missionaries, politicians, or leaders of NGOs. He said, "Most of us in the press also hold that view, but it is not something that is popular if you put it into your published articles." He thanked me for my time and then handed me his copy of the dossier.

I left Brazil the next day. I was later informed by Mari that the dossier had also been sent to the FUNAI office but arrived too late for them to withhold my permit, which was the intent of the senders.

My 1997 Lecture Trip to UFR

On my *Veja* trip to Brazil I had initiated contacts with administrative officials at the Federal University of Roraima (UFR) in Boa Vista. We began planning a formal long-term collaboration between UFR and the University of California, Santa Barbara. The Brazilian academics seemed enthusiastic and very pleased with this possibility and sent one of their administrators to Santa Barbara to begin discussions. The plan was to make possible exchanges of both anthropology students and faculty from the two campuses and develop a graduate anthropology program at UFR.

As part of the initiation of this program I agreed to give a series of free lectures—a "mini-course" in anthropology—at UFR and take a group of their anthropology students into one or more Yanomamö villages in Roraima to provide them with some hands-on fieldwork training.

I took a second trip to Boa Vista in March 1997, again by way of Santa Elena in Venezuela. I chose this route because it was much cheaper and faster than going via Brasilia, Rio, or São Paulo, the normal route most travelers coming from the United States would take. My visit coincided with a sensational denunciation of me on March 4, in *O Estado de São Paulo*, by Brazilian activist anthropologist Alcida Ramos, one of my longtime detractors and a coauthor of the attack on me in the 1989 *Anthropology Newsletter* following my 1988 article in *Science*. She had apparently been informed of my trip and timed her denunciation in a major Brazilian newspaper to correspond with my arrival. Her vitriolic article was sufficient to arouse several indigenous "leaders" in Roraima, including Davi Kobenawä, and their NGO advocates to protest. As a result of her article FUNAI immediately rescinded the permit that had been approved to allow a group of Brazilian anthropology students from UFR to visit any Yanomamö village for field training under my supervision. The "chief" of one indigenous group, the Makuxi, the tribe that Leda Martins was studying, sent a letter to the rector of UFR in Boa Vista *through his lawyer* protesting my presence in Roraima and urging the rector to suspend any collaboration with me.

The rector invited me to dinner to assure me that the cancellation of my permit was just a temporary setback and that FUNAI officials privately assured him that after the bad press subsided, the permit for me to take students into Yanomamö villages would quietly be approved. I gave two weeks of lectures at UFR and returned to Santa Barbara, convinced that doing traditional academic anthropological fieldwork in Brazil in collaboration with Brazilian anthropologists was not feasible. The exchange program with the UFR died and was never pursued further.

I also found the contrast in the forces affecting the native peoples of Brazil's Roraima area to be impossible to comprehend. The lands of the indigenous people were being invaded by merciless exploiters who were, in some cases, ruthlessly killing the native people. But instead of doing something useful and effective to stop this, the presumably "enlightened" anthropological forces in Brazil were forbidding most anthropologists even to visit the native people. Consequently the indigenous people now depended on the handful of radical anthropologists who jealously controlled their destinies. These same radical anthropologists informed the native people who the bad people were that they must vigorously denounce. The bad people turned out to be other anthropologists, mostly American anthropologists, and not the economic forces in Brazil and Venezuela destroying the lands and way of life of the indigenous people.

My 1998 Trip to Venezuela

In 1998 I again tried to continue my work among the Venezuelan Yanomamö. I had been approached by several medical researchers from the University of Cincinnati who wanted me to participate in a psychiatric study of the Yanomamö. I agreed to do so on the condition that their project would also include a practical public health component, namely, reliable long-term access by the Yanomamö to secular medical services that would meet the approval of the Venezuelan health authorities and would ultimately involve Venezuelan medical practitioners.

I had also been in contact with a number of State Department officials in Washington and in the American embassy in Caracas who were very cooperative and interested in helping the Yanomamö. Through them, one of the undersecretaries of state, Gare Smith, contacted me in Santa Barbara and asked if I could take him into the Yanomamö area as a visitor so he could see unacculturated Amazon Basin Indians first hand. At the same time the State Department was being pressured by American NGOs to take an interest in Amazon Basin tribes in response to frequent news reports of abuses of them by nationals in South American countries. He did not want to make the trip an "official" State Department visit, but since he had other business at the embassy in Caracas he wanted to combine his official trip with an unofficial visit to the Yanomamö.

When word of my arrangement with Smith became known in Venezuela, several Salesian priests showed up at the American embassy wanting an immediate meeting with Smith. Among them was my former UCSB graduate student Jesus Cardozo, who was now working closely with the Salesians.

In August the medical team from the University of Cincinnati and I traveled to Venezuela to carry out their study. I had earlier agreed to meet with Smith and other members of the State Department at my hotel that evening to discuss the details of our plans to go into the Yanomamö area. I didn't know about the officials' meeting with the Salesians that day. When Smith and a State Department colleague showed up at my hotel they told me that the Salesians were adamantly opposed to my going into the Yanomamö area and even more opposed to him or any State Department official traveling with me.

Smith said the Salesians had a long list of specific complaints about me and my research that had been produced by a group of supposedly internationally prominent anthropologists. They showed me a copy of a fax document that had just been sent to the Salesians and to Venezuelan officials that day. Its content was almost identical to the dossier that the Brazilian journalist gave me in 1995, but it also reflected specific complaints that appeared in the denunciation of me by Alcida Ramos in the Brazilian newspapers. Smith gave me the fax.

The Cincinnati medical doctors and I departed for home soon after. We were not allowed to go into the Yanomamö area. Once again, the "secret dossier" had successfully sabotaged my field plans.

A day or so later Smith and his State Department companions were taken on a Venezuelan air force helicopter trip to the Yanomamö area that was highly publicized in Venezuelan newspapers. Jesus Cardozo and his Salesian supporters were his guides and sponsors.

Smith later sent me a long note summarizing what had happened on the trip. Apart from concluding that Cardozo and the Salesians had a nearly fanatical hatred of me, he explained how Cardozo was adamant about having the State Department arrest me and put me in prison for crimes I had allegedly committed against the Yanomamö. When Smith asked him what crimes I committed, he said that Cardozo replied that I worked for the U.S. government and the Atomic Energy Commission (portions of my research had been funded by government agencies such as NIMH, NSF, and the AEC as I have discussed). Smith said he replied that he also worked for the U.S. government. Did that make him a criminal as well? He added that when the plane landed Cardozo angrily stalked off without saying good-bye and seemed annoyed that the State Department would not arrest me.

Retiring in 1999

In 1999 I decided to retire early from UCSB. My interest—indeed, my passion—in anthropology was field research, discovering new information about the people I studied, the Yanomamö, and where they fit into the evolving human saga. I taught the largest course my department offered—upwards of nine hundred students—and probably produced as many successful Ph.D.s as anyone in my department. I could have stopped doing research and taught small, specialized courses while continuing to publish articles that reported the results of my field studies. But I decided that if I could no longer continue my field studies of the Yanomamö, who were changing very rapidly—and I desperately wanted to document them before those changes were widespread—then remaining in academia would be unsatisfying and frustrating. What I loved most about anthropology was no longer possible. I was also very angry with those who were sabotaging my field research efforts, the preparation for which was very expensive and which I had to pay out of my own pocket.

My wife and I sold our modest home in Santa Barbara and moved back to Michigan.

An Impending Scandal

About a year after I moved to Michigan, Raymond Hames, one of my former students, sent me an email. He began by telling me how sorry he was that he had to be the one to send me this message, for it contained the text of one of the most hateful and despicable accusations a professional academic could possibly get.

This text was written by two anthropologists—Terence Turner and Leslie Sponsel—who had been longtime critics and detractors of mine. Their long email, sent in October 2000, was addressed to the president and president-elect of the American Anthropological Association and to a list of other people in the organization. Dated October 1, 2000, it began,

Madam President, Mr. President-elect:

We write to inform you of an impending scandal that will affect the American Anthropological profession as a whole in the eyes of the public, and arouse intense indignation and calls for action among members of the Association. In its scale, ramifications, and sheer criminality and corruption it is unparalleled in the history of Anthropology . . . This nightmarish story—a real anthropological heart of darkness beyond the imagining of even a Josef Conrad (though not, perhaps, a Josef Mengele)—will be seen (rightly in our view) by the public, as well as most anthropologists, as putting the whole discipline on trial. As another reader of the galleys put it, This book should shake anthropology to its very foundations. It should cause the field to understand how the corrupt and depraved protagonists could have spread their poison for so long while they were accorded great respect throughout the Western World and generations of undergraduates received their lies as the introductory substance of anthropology. This should never be allowed to happen again.

They were describing a book that was about to be published, Patrick Tierney's *Darkness in El Dorado: How Scientists and Journalists Devastated the Amazon.* The principal targets were me, James V. Neel, and other members of the team of researchers who participated in or had anything to do with our attempts to abort the 1968 measles epidemic that struck the Yanomamö, which I have earlier described. It was my highly successful monograph on the Yanomamö through which "generations of undergraduates received their [my] lies as the introductory substance of anthropology."

Not long after the incendiary Turner-Sponsel email circulated, sensational stories began appearing in the press. One of the first, in the British *Guardian*, made this claim on its front page: "Scientists 'killed Amazon Indians to test race theory.' " Then, on October 9, the *New Yorker* published an excerpt from the soon to be published book.

I began getting calls from journalists and reporters from all over the world representing major news outlets, clamoring to have my response to the astonishing claims, especially the central sensational claim that I and my colleagues had started a lethal epidemic of measles among the Yanomamö thirty-two years earlier.

I denied the accusations, but those who called were only interested in getting me to add some juicy comments they could use in their report. I recall one caller, a woman who worked for *Time* magazine, telling me, after I said the accusations were false, that it didn't really matter: *Time* simply had to publish something on this sensational story because *Newsweek* and other *Time* competitors were carrying the story. It didn't matter if the story was true or false it was sensational and involved allegedly suspicious activities of prominent scientists.

The American Anthropological Association Responds

The 2000 meetings of the American Anthropological Association were held November 17–20 in San Francisco. I had canceled my membership in the AAA in the late 1980s because the field of cultural anthropology had effectively become, in my estimation, an unintelligible mumbo-jumbo of postmodern jargon and a place where cynical assaults on the scientific approach were commonplace. I knew, however, that Tierney's book would be out soon, and that the Turner-Sponsel email and the sensational excerpt in the *New Yorker* made it likely that I would be a central issue at the AAA meetings. If anything were to be done by the professional community in response to the book, the 2000 annual meeting would most likely be where it would start.

I wasn't quite prepared for the call I got from Louise Lamphere, the president of the AAA, to whom the Turner-Sponsel memo was directed. She invited me to be on the panel that would discuss the accusations made in Tierney's book. I was astonished when she told me that Tierney had been invited to sit on this panel. In an open forum the panel would discuss the accusations Tierney made against me, Neel, and others about our 1968 Yanomamö expedition. (Neel had died about a year earlier.) I suddenly felt very uncomfortable, as if these accusations against me were already considered to be true by the officers of the AAA. Several others were also going to be on the stage with Tierney in the large hotel auditorium. Among those invitees were Jesus Cardozo and Nohely Pocaterra, a *diputado* (legislator) from the Venezuelan government who was also a Venezuelan Indian (Wayuú) and active in Venezuelan native rights movements.

I declined Lamphere's invitation to attend because I suspected that this forum would turn into a frenzy of acrimonious, self-righteous, politically correct denunciations, and I had no interest in becoming the bait in such a feeding frenzy. I informed her that I would ask Professor William Irons of Northwestern University, my longtime friend and colleague, to represent me at this meeting should that be necessary.

Remarkably, this was the only time that any official of the AAA invited me to participate in any discussion or invited my response to any accusation that Tierney, Turner, Sponsel, or their various committees said about me in the ensuing years during which the AAA "investigated" the accusations made against me and Neel. Yet this "investigation" lasted for over five years and whole sessions of AAA annual meetings were devoted to aspects of the investigation, the last as recent as 2011 at the New Orleans meetings of the AAA, in which three separate events were devoted to this theme.

Five of the speakers on the 2000 panel were critical of Tierney and challenged his accusations to the extent they were known from his *New Yorker* article (his book had not yet been published) and the Turner-Sponsel email. Two others (Cardozo and Pocaterra) were sympathetic to the several accusations Tierney made about Neel and me. More than eight hundred people crowded into the auditorium the first night.

The AAA organizers opened the second evening's session to questions from the audience in an open-mike discussion. This session was also filled to capacity: estimates of the size of the crowd on the second night were over one thousand, slightly higher than the estimates for the first night. Two of my former UCSB undergraduate students recorded the second session and sent me their recordings. What I heard on their tapes was shameful and depressing. For example, a female Peace Corps volunteer recalled bitterly and dramatically that she once visited Mavaca and I would not take her and her friends with me into the remote Shamatari region I was studying. She self-righteously claimed that I was discourteous to her. The audience applauded. A Ugandan man was recognized: he berated the U.S. government for introducing HIV/AIDS and the deadly Ebola virus into his African tribe back home. He also received loud applause. David Maybury-Lewis, head of Harvard University's Social Anthropology Department, denounced me for my alleged unacceptable and reprehensible field methods and the alleged harm I had done to the Yanomamö by subtitling the early editions of my college monograph "The Fierce People." He was also applauded. One of his books on the Xavante tribe in Brazil is entitled *The Savage and the Innocent*. It is not known how much psychological harm the Xavante suffered as a consequence of this book title.

In addition to his academic post at Harvard, Maybury-Lewis was also the founder (with his wife, Pia) and director of Cultural Survival, a major NGO advocating the rights of native peoples. In 1987 I had created my own NGO, which I called the Yanomamö Survival Fund, because I was worried that the 1987 gold rush in Brazil would lead to the occupation of Venezuelan mission posts by armed *garimpeiros* as had happened in Brazil. My Yanomamö Survival Fund was intended to provide medical aid to the Yanomamö for the new diseases that inevitably follow influxes of outsiders into isolated indigenous areas: upwards of forty thousand *garimpeiros* had invaded Yanomamö territory in Brazil and were approaching the Venezuelan border. Perhaps Cultural Survival regarded my nonprofit Yanomamö Survival Fund as a competitor for charitable donations because it attempted to denigrate me.

Another NGO, Survival International, also treated me hostilely. In the website *Evolutionary Psychology* in May 2002, Stephen Corry of the London office of Survival International said, among other things, that my data on Yanomamö violence was fabricated. The president of Survival International's American branch was Terence Turner, one of David Maybury-Lewis's former students.

The Peacock Committee

One of the first steps the AAA took during the November 2000 meeting in San Francisco was to set into motion a plan to investigate the charges that Tierney made against me, Neel, Charles Brewer, and others. But their attention was focused mainly on the accusations against me and, to a lesser extent, Neel. Patrick Tierney's *Darkness in El Dorado: How Scientists and Journalists Devastated the Amazon* was published in December 2000.

Former AAA president James Peacock, another former student of Maybury-Lewis, was asked to form a committee to do this. When I learned about the existence of this committee, I wrote to the AAA and asked to know who the members were. I was told that the committee's membership was confidential. This answer surprised me. In light of the legal principle called due process, I wondered how I, the accused, was not allowed to know who my accusers were or what, for that matter, my alleged crimes were.

The members of the Peacock Committee, I subsequently learned from a memo dated January 21, 2001, and sent to AAA president Louise Lamphere, included only one person I knew well, a physical anthropologist from my former department at UCSB.

The Peacock Committee's only role seems to have been to look into the accusations Tierney made against Neel, me, and others in his book and, from this, to advise the executive board of the AAA whether an "investigation" of Tierney's accusations warranted action. The Peacock Committee members considered Tierney's book chapter by chapter and then put together a list of issues they deemed worth investigating. The committee produced a report for the AAA executive board. Peacock submitted the committee's recommendations to AAA president Lamphere on January 21, 2001.

The Investigation That Never Was

Officers of the AAA repeatedly insisted that their investigation was not an investigation but an "inquiry" because the rules of the AAA Ethics Committee forbade the AAA to "investigate" accusations of misdeeds by its members. Yet the Peacock Committee several times described its mission in precisely these terms, seven times on the first page of Peacock's "Executive Summary" and many times elsewhere. For example,

> *This Task Force was charged to consider allegations in Patrick Tierney's Dark-ness in El Dorado (and related material) in order to recommend to the AAA President and Executive Board whether and, if so, how an investigation of these allegations be carried out by the AAA.*
>
> *The Committee recommends that the AAA carry out an investigation.*
> *This investigation would entail three levels. . . .*

A document issued by Jane Hill sometime in November 2001 (the date is not given) lists the members of the task force investigating the Peacock Committee's findings. The AAA's executive board established this task force, known as the El Dorado Task Force, "to conduct what the Board termed an 'inquiry' on the allegations . . . contained in *Darkness in El Dorado*, by Patrick Tierney. Such an 'inquiry' is unprecedented in the history of the Association. . . ." Note that the word *inquiry* is put in quotes.

Hill appointed various members of the task force to investigate the accusations made or suggested by Tierney or others:

1. Measles were introduced to the Yanomamö area in 1968 by Neel's team and followed Neel's team everywhere it went, spreading further;
2. The Edmonston B measles vaccine used by Neel's team was dangerous and contraindicated;
3. Neel's team withheld medical care from the Yanomamö;
4. Chagnon was a disciple of Neel and his "sociobiological" theories underpinned Neel's eugenics beliefs;
5. Chagnon subscribed to Senator Joseph McCarthy's right-wing political views;
6. Neel's objectives in his study of the Yanomamö over many years, especially his expedition in 1968, were scientific. The measles vaccination component of his study had nothing to do with humanitarian objectives;
7. Other anthropologists refute Chagnon's claims;

8. Chagnon and Asch "staged" their twenty-two films, and used fake sets. Yanomamö died because they acted out dangerous violent scenes at Chagnon's instructions;

9. Chagnon used enormous quantities of trade goods to bribe informants to reveal tabooed names of dead relatives, which he frequently spoke openly and loudly in their villages;

10. Chagnon had two German shepherd attack dogs that he used to intimidate large weight-lifter types in bars and regularly made his graduate students submit to training sessions as the targets of these attack dogs;

11. Chagnon had a pistol that he frequently used to intimidate the Yanomamö by firing it in their villages;

12. Chagnon associated in Venezuela with "criminal types" like Charles Brewer and Cecilia Matos, the longtime consort of Venezuelan president Carlos Andrés Pérez. They established an enormous "biosphere reserve" actually intended for gold mining and to prevent other anthropologists from studying the Yanomamö of Venezuela.

Various accusations were examined independently by Ed Hagen, Michael Price, and John Tooby at UCSB. They inspected the scientific literature, using both Tierney's cited sources and other relevant sources. The ethnographic film accusations were examined by two prominent ethnographic filmmakers, Peter Biella and Jay Ruby, who were familiar with the films Asch and I made. The "attack dog" claims were investigated by William Irons. Many people in the academic community have examined the claim that Neel's and my 1968 expedition to the Yanomamö started a measles epidemic.

Tierney's claims were also thoroughly examined by several national scientific publications and organizations, such as the International Genetic Epidemiology Society, the *American Journal of Epidemiology*, and the National Academy of Sciences. They found that the allegation regarding the measles epidemic was not supported by the evidence.

John Tooby, my former departmental colleague at UCSB, said that it took him only a few hours to determine that Tierney's measles epidemic allegation was patently false. Tooby describes how he did this:

I started putting in calls to the Centers for Disease Control and Prevention in Atlanta. Conversations with various researchers, including eventually Dr. Mark Papania, chief of the U.S. measles eradication program, rapidly discredited every essential element of the Tierney disease scenarios. For example, it turns out that researchers who test vaccines for safety have never been able to document, in hundreds of millions of uses, a single case of a live-virus measles vaccine leading to contagious transmission from one human to another—this despite their strenuous efforts to detect such a thing. If attenuated live virus does not jump from person to person, it cannot cause an epidemic. Nor can it be planned to cause an epidemic, as alleged in this case, if it never has caused one before.

Tooby's article about his investigation appeared in *Slate* on October 25, 2000. However, Terence Turner, who coauthored with Leslie Sponsel the sensational email warning the president of the AAA of the "impending scandal" that provoked the AAA to initiate its investigation, acknowledged in an email on September 28, 2000, to Samuel Katz, the co-developer of the vaccine used by Neel's team on our expedition, that the allegations regarding the measles epidemic in Tierney's book were inaccurate.

But if the central allegation in Tierney's book was false, why did his other accusations cause such a sensational scandal in the media and in academia? Part of the reason is that some people believe falsehoods and conspiracy theories because they like to think that their more esteemed colleagues got to the top by subterfuge. Another reason is that this scandal was simply too juicy a story for members of the press to ignore, including the editors of the *New Yorker*. But another and perhaps a more important reason was that my belief in a biologically evolved human nature—what Edward O. Wilson called sociobiology—was unacceptable to most cultural anthropologists and other academics. Tierney's book, the Turner-Sponsel warning to the AAA senior officers, and the subsequent witch hunt conducted by the AAA fit into an existing narrative opposing evolution in the field of cultural anthropology. I was one of the most visible figures in anthropology who espoused this despised view. Tierney's accusations gave opponents of my viewpoint an opportunity to discredit sociobiology.

The damage done to me and my work by the false accusations in this book devastated my research career, damaged my health, gravely distressed my family—and the family of James V. Neel, who died before Tierney's book was published. I was so overwhelmed by incessant calls from reporters during the first several weeks of the press coverage that, early one morning in October 2000, I collapsed from the stress and had to be hospitalized. Two of Neel's children are medical doctors like their father and were especially outraged at the distortion of medical science in the ugly accusations that Tierney, Turner, and Sponsel made about their father.

One of my colleagues, William Irons, mentioned to me that he had flagged all of Tierney's accusations against me in the margins of the book and they numbered some 106 separate accusations. That doesn't include additional accusations against Charles Brewer, Jacques Lizot, and documentary filmmaker Timothy Asch. Most of Tierney's accusations have been systematically repudiated by independent researchers. Any reader can check this for himself at http://www.anth.ucsb.edu /ucsbpreliminaryreport.pdf and at Douglas Hume's website at http:// anthroniche.com/. Hume's website is scrupulously neutral and includes materials supporting both sides of the controversy.

Darkness in *Darkness in El Dorado*

Tierney cites Yanomamö "eyewitnesses" (unnamed or untraceable) to the alleged crimes that Neel and I committed. But Tierney could not have received Venezuelan OCAI permission to enter Yanomamö territory when he says he did unless the Salesian Missions approved of his visits and invited him there, as they did with Salamone and others who are sympathetic to their viewpoints. Tierney had access to the health records of the Salesian missions, which could have happened only if the Salesians approved of him.

Tierney cites the death from measles at the Ocamo Salesian mission of a child named Roberto Balthasar. But Balthasar's father was a Brazilian, and although he was allegedly married to an Indian woman, Tierney provides no information that she was Yanomamö. Curiously, he does not document in the book the hundreds of deaths that he claims were caused by our use of the Edmonston B measles vaccine. If such deaths occurred, why don't the Salesian mission records confirm this? Why is the only measles death described that of the young Balthasar?

Similarly the Mavaca Salesian mission, upstream from Ocamo, recorded no deaths from measles during the period Tierney writes about. The Yanomamö community there, Bisaasi-teri, since its move to that location had been medically ministered to by members of the New Tribes Mission and, at the time of the 1968 measles epidemic, by the French medical doctors who arrived there with our expedition, and by Neel's medical team. To be fair, the Salesian mission at Mavaca was just getting under way in 1968 and may not have had any medical records yet because these were normally kept by nuns and nuns had not arrived there by 1968. The third Salesian mission, Platanal, had only a temporary priest from the Salesian mission at Esmeralda in 1968, Padre Sanchez, and no nuns. Tierney says we bypassed the Salesian mission at Platanal, but in fact we spent the night there and failed to vaccinate the local Mahekodo-teri only because they were not home: they were en route to Patanowä-teri to attend a feast, as I described earlier. We vaccinated most of the members of the large village of Patanowä-teri before the Mahekodo-teri arrived and used the last of our vaccine on the Patanowä-teri.

Tierney tells a very sad story of the reaction of the "elders" at Patanowä-teri and Mahekodo-teri (as if they were the same village) weeping when he showed them the film I made with Asch, *The Feast*, allegedly because they saw many of their dead kinsmen in the film, who Tierney implies all died of measles. I cannot think of anything more offensive and reprehensible than to show the Yanomamö motion picture film footage of their *deceased* relatives. For someone who faults me in such self-righteous, outraged, and moralistic terms for learning the true names of deceased people and whispering them back into the ears of my informants, Tierney displays blatant insensitivity and callousness.

Tierney's copious endnotes are often misleading and even inaccurate, as several investigators have demonstrated. In his chapter criticizing my 1988 lead article in *Science* and my "sociobiological" theories, Tierney refers to an incident that occurred in an extremely remote location in approximately 1950. I had pieced together this event from many hours of interviews with many informants because it was central to an account of their settlement patterns, yet Tierney cites a reference to the event as if he had found an eyewitness to it. Here is what Tierney said about this event on page 168 of *Darkness in El Dorado*: "The single biggest battle in Yanomami warfare occurred on February 3, 1951. It was a *nomohori*, a treacherous feast given by Riakowa, the Iwahikoroba-teri headman, in which eleven to fifteen men from Kreibowei-teri (the Bisaasi-teri's village at the time) were killed." Tierney cites an early visitor, Hector Acebes, author of *Orinoco Adventure*, page 242, as the source of this information. In that book, Acebes describes a very brief visit in Tama Tama in about 1951 with one Flora Trexel, an elderly missionary woman who told him the following: "She also said that a war had started on February 3 between the Guaicas of the Upper Siapa and those of the Orinoco, but she did not know if the fighting had ended or who was winning."

Trexel was a colleague of James Barker, the first American who lived among the Venezuelan Yanomamö long enough to become fluent in their language. Barker had only recently heard about this incident and most likely passed this information on to Trexel. It is very doubtful that Barker knew the exact date of this event because he told me in 1965 that he had learned about it from Shinanokawä, the headman of Mahekodo-teri, who had recently visited this area. The Yanomamö do not have any accurate means to specify the dates of events. Everything else in Tierney's discussion of this event was information that *I* had published based on my interviews with the Yanomamö survivors who were victims of this *nomohori*. That information is not contained in *Orinoco Adventure*. But of course Tierney could not cite me as the source of this information in the same book in which he was attacking me.

In the same chapter, titled "To Murder and Multiply," a cynical reference to my 1988 *Science* article reporting the reproductive success of *unokai* warriors, Tierney ends with this bizarre paragraph:

Yet there was something familiar about Chagnon's strategy of secret lists combined with accusations against ubiquitous Marxists, something that traced back to his childhood in rural Michigan, when Joe McCarthy was king. Like the old Yanomami *unokais*, the former senator from Wisconsin was in no danger of death. Under the mantle of Science, Tailgunner Joe was still firing away—undefeated, undaunted, and blessed with a wealth of offspring, one of whom, a poor boy from Port Austin, had received a full portion of his spirit.

Somehow my 1988 *Science* article illustrates my sociobiological bias, which in turn, is connected to my allegedly right-wing views in this ridiculous discussion of Senator Joseph McCarthy's alleged influence on that "poor boy" from Port Austin, Michigan.

Dawn after the Darkness

In May 2002 the AAA accepted the Final Report of the task force, a two-volume document. Among the findings the AAA included in the Final Report was an interview by anthropologist Janet Chernela of Brazilian Yanomamö Davi Kobenawä, who claimed that when I briefly visited his village in 1967 I commissioned the adult men to go out and kill neighboring Yanomamö: I would give the most pay to those who killed the most. Kobenawä was nine or ten years old when I briefly visited his village over thirty years earlier. He was, however, exposed to Brazilian activists after 1967, who told him this and similar stories. The story is absolutely false. The AAA at one point linked to a website on which young anthropology students taking their first classes in anthropology were encouraged by their instructors to express their opinions on my morality and ethics, and the harm my work inflicted on the Yanomamö. The AAA eventually removed the link.

The AAA's investigation had been opposed from the start by a small group of senior anthropologists for a variety of reasons, mainly because they knew such investigations were impermissible under the AAA's own rules and also because some of the accusations against me and Neel were unfair and likely to be untrue. *The Chronicle of Higher Education* summarized some of the reasons that senior anthropologists opposed this investigation in the July 2005 issue in the following words: "The report came under immediate and heavy criticism from several scholars. Those critics claimed that the panel's composition was biased, that Mr. Chagnon had not been afforded due process, and that the association's Web site had propagated (in 'comments' pages associated with the task-force report) a new stream of lurid and unsubstantiated allegations against Mr. Chagnon."

In November 2003, Thomas Gregor and Daniel Gross drafted a referendum on vaccine safety and managed to get it placed on a ballot that the entire membership of the AAA could vote on. They warned the members of the AAA about the dangers of having the AAA go on record as opposing the use of vaccines among the native inhabitants in third-world countries. Neel's group had used a vaccine, Edmonston B, that had been used successfully before—18 million times—and had never in its history caused measles as described in *Darkness in El Dorado.* Their referendum passed by a margin of more than 10 to 1. Gregor told me later that he suspected that many anthropologists viewed this referendum as an opportunity to express their opposition to the task force "investigation" and to Turner and Sponsel's role in it.

Gregor and Gross then published a meticulously researched and extremely critical article in the *American Anthropologist* in 2004 that elaborated the mistakes the AAA had made, calling attention to, among other criticisms, the violations of the association's own rules and guidelines.

They then placed a second referendum on the AAA ballot in June 2005. That referendum called for the rescission of the AAA's acceptance of the final report of the task force. Their second referendum also passed, but by a smaller margin: 846 to 338 (about 2.5 to 1).

These results clearly indicated that the leadership of the AAA was significantly out of step with the AAA membership. Gregor was of the opinion that Turner and Sponsel were probably caught unawares by the first vote on vaccine safety and may have organized and enjoined their supporters to cast their votes on the second referendum.

Nearly five years passed between the November 2000 annual meeting of the American Anthropological Association in San Francisco where Tierney's accusations were first aired and the rescission of the AAA's acceptance of the El Dorado Task Force report in June 2005.

Those five years seem like a blurry bad dream. What seems to stand out in this fog are the many articles that were published about this scandal and how ill-informed, misleading, or outright wrong many of them were, and how self-righteous, unkind, and cynical many were.

I spent a good deal of time contacting and exchanging information with colleagues in Venezuela, especially Ye'kwana leader Jaime Turon, who was the democratically elected *alcalde* (mayor) of the Alto Orinoco—elected by both the Ye'kwana and Yanomamö residents of that vast area. He was never interviewed by members of the AAA task force who went to this area, yet some of these same people were incensed about my "undermining" Davi Kobenawä, whose sphere of influence and whose authority in Brazil are much smaller. Turon was a democratically *elected* Native Amazonian leader.

At Turon's request, I sent at least two of his letters to the American Anthropological Association, Tierney's publisher, W. W. Norton, and the editor of the *New Yorker*, requesting that he and the Venezuelan Yanomamö be heard. None of them responded to me or to Turon. So I include here a letter he wrote to me:

La Esmerelda, 10/21/03

> Mr. Tierney's book has been translated into Spanish as The Plundering
> of El Dorado and we are [only] now able to read it. It is for this reason
> that we are annoyed with all his lies. Tierney describes events that took
> place 30 years ago and when he was in the Upper Orinoco he promised
> us various forms of medical aid, including hospitals. Some members of the
> AAA [task force] who visited Mavaca last year say they are participating in
> a medical program that we have not even heard of. One of the members of
> this commission claimed in a publication that she will be developing a public
> health program with the participation of a number of Yanomamö from the
> Mavaca region. They accuse Dr. James Neel, [Dr.] Marcel Roche, and you
> of manipulating us when, in reality, you were the only ones that helped us
> in your many visits in the 1960s and 1970s at a time when there were no
> medical programs or public health programs for us.

I spent a great deal of time during the *El Dorado* years providing information to colleagues here in the United States who were attempting to counter the false information that some journalists, anthropologists, and academics were putting into the various news outlets.

Finally, I spent years trying to write this book, scrapping much of the effort many times because of the anger that kept creeping into my writing, giving it a very depressing tone. Everything I wrote during this time was contaminated by the lingering stench associated with *Darkness in El Dorado*.

I also remembered what I did not do. I did not travel much, did not fish much, did not hunt grouse and pheasants over my German short-haired pointers, did not go to many concerts, did not read much fiction for pleasure, and did not spend more time with members of my family, all of which I had planned to do when I left Santa Barbara to come back to Michigan.

Cultural Anthropologists: The Fierce People

Cultural anthropology differs from the other subfields of anthropology such as archaeology, physical anthropology, and linguistics by being the only branch that has historically embraced and advocated explicitly nonscientific or even antiscientific approaches to explaining the external world. Yet throughout the history of anthropology and despite a wide range of variation in approaches and "styles" in cultural anthropology, there has always been a core group of anthropologists who maintain that anthropology—*all* branches of anthropology—is, in the final analysis, a *scientific* discipline. The National Academy of Sciences acknowledges this by making the discipline of anthropology a subdivision of the overall taxonomy of the sciences that it and other international academic organizations recognize.

But in the past twenty or so years the field of cultural anthropology in the United States has come precipitously close to abandoning the very notion of science. In 2010 the leadership of the AAA attempted to eliminate the very word *science* as a central component in the discipline. Science writer Nicholas Wade wrote this in the *New York Times* on December 9, 2010:

Anthropologists have been thrown into turmoil about the nature and future of their profession after a decision by the American Anthropological Association at its recent annual meeting to strip the word "science" from a statement of its long-range plan. The decision has reopened a long-simmering tension between researchers in science-based anthropological disciplines—including archaeologists, physical anthropologists and some cultural anthropologists—and members of the profession who study race, ethnicity and gender and see themselves as advocates for native peoples or human rights.

The schism is between those cultural anthropologists (like me) who regard cultural anthropology as a science and those who believe, as Brazilian anthropologist Alcida Ramos recently put it, that "to do anthropology" is to do something inherently political, or as Nancy Scheper-Hughes put it, anthropology is a "forensic activity" in which today's practitioners are expected to look for and denounce the wrongs committed to the native peoples by other anthropologists who have studied them. In a word, the schism in cultural anthropology is between those who do science and those whose exclusive goal is to speak on behalf of native peoples, an activity that they define as being incompatible with science. This latter view is not only wrong, it borders on irresponsibility.

Wade noted the immediate roots of the schism in cultural anthropology in the same article:

> During the last 10 years the two factions have been through a phase of bitter tribal warfare after the more politically active group attacked work on the Yanomamo people of Venezuela and Brazil by Napoleon Chagnon, a science-oriented anthropologist, and James Neel, a medical geneticist who died in 2000. With the wounds of this conflict still fresh, many science-based anthropologists were dismayed to learn last month that the long-range plan of the association would no longer be to advance anthropology as a science but rather to focus on "public understanding."

To their credit, some of the cultural anthropologists who still belong to the AAA did not complacently accept the decision of the AAA's executive board. They fought this new declaration, demanding that it be reconsidered. Four days later Nicholas Wade quoted Frank Marlowe, then president-elect of the AAA affiliate subsection the Evolutionary Anthropology Society: " 'We evolutionary anthropologists are outnumbered by the new cultural or social anthropologists, many but not all of whom are post-modern, which seems to translate into antiscience,' Dr. Marlowe said."

Those who narrowly define cultural anthropology as primarily an "advocacy" activity, that is, a political activity, as most Brazilian anthropologists view the field, are undermining the entire anthropological profession.

Final Comments

Alice Dreger, a historian of science at the Feinberg School of Medicine, Northwestern University, became interested in highly visible recent cases in which an academic was singled out by members of his own profession and in which his professional association not only did nothing to intervene on his behalf but seemingly acquiesced in the persecution that followed. She interviewed a large number of the major players in the *Darkness in El Dorado* scandal, including committee heads and officers in the AAA who played major roles in the investigation. Dreger writes:

What's really disturbing is that so many people who participated in the AAA's investigations of Neel and Chagnon seem to have understood what Tierney's book really amounted to. For example, Janet Chernela, who served on both the Peacock Commission and the Task Force, told me this: "Nobody took Tierney's book's claims seriously. I was surprised that James Peacock, who is a very careful and fair person, favored going forward with the Task Force." This begs the question of why Chernela went forward with an investigation that followed the path of Tierney. Compare the words of Jane Hill, the former president of the AAA who chaired the Task Force. On April 15, 2002, after [Raymond] Hames resigned from the Task Force, Sarah Hrdy wrote to Jane Hill objecting to the situation and got this response from Hill: "Burn this message. The book is just a piece of sleaze, that's all there is to it (some cosmetic language will be used in the report, but we *all* agree on that). But I think the AAA had to do something because I really think that the future of work by anthropologists with indigenous peoples in Latin America—with a high potential to do good—was put seriously at risk by its accusations, and silence on the part of the AAA would have been interpreted as either assent or cowardice. Whether we're doing the right thing will have to be judged by posterity."

So, even though Tierney's book was "just a piece of sleaze," Chagnon, the late Neel's legacy, the Chagnon and Neel families, and these two men's colleagues were put through a major investigation to preserve the field for other American anthropologists? Why did Hill not say publicly what she said to Hrdy? Why not admit that Chagnon must be publicly strung up to save anthropology from "just a piece of sleaze"?

Dreger concluded that so problematic were the AAA's actions, that "I can't imagine how any scholar feels safe" as a member.

Two of my colleagues, Jane Lancaster, editor of *Human Nature*, and Raymond Hames, wrote this editorial comment on the occasion of the publication of Alice Dreger's article in *Human Nature* in 2011 that criticized the AAA and several of its past and present officers for mishandling the *Darkness in El Dorado* scandal:

Science has a special place and currency in American society. Purging science from the AAA's Long Range Plan will lose us our credibility, the ability to testify and advocate for effective change, and hence our power to do good. We become just another special interest group by abandoning evidence-based testimony which trumps special interest group advocacy in the courts, public opinion, and the legislative process. So once again the status of science in anthropology has been challenged. Scientific anthropologists merit full respect and backing and should not be pushed into corners or swept under a rug or even worse, as Alice Dreger documents . . . come under attack by our own major professional organization to pacify those who initiated a witch hunt.

There are ways to discourage the behavior of self-righteous renegade anthropologists like Turner and Sponsel. They should be prohibited from holding any future office in the AAA or serving on any official AAA committee because of their reprehensible behavior in the *Darkness in El Dorado* scandal.

We should also recall at this point the warning that I quoted from Paul

Gross that "the barefoot anthropologists, the activists, will be teaching your children." One of the activists who played an important role in trying to sabotage my research, Leda Martins, *is* teaching your children in the Claremont College System (Pitzer College) in the Los Angeles area. I find it ironic, unfair, and shameful that her academic appointment seems to be a reward for her way of dealing with academics whose views she dislikes. I believe that most departments in an American university would neither grant her tenure nor promote her to a higher rank if they knew how she tried to prevent a senior anthropologist from conducting research. In his book, Tierney thanks her for preparing the infamous dossier used to sabotage the last three of my field trips.

Let me end by quoting Magdalena Hurtado's comments made at the 2000 annual meeting of the American Anthropological Association in San Francisco. She was an invited speaker at the AAA's *Darkness in El Dorado* panel. Hurtado is an American-trained Venezuelan anthropologist who has worked with several different Amazon Basin tribes in South American countries and has seen firsthand the deleterious consequences of governmental complacency and neglect of the human rights of Amazonian tribesmen not only in health issues, but also in land rights and even protection from lawless citizens who sometimes attack and kill them with impunity. She and her husband, anthropologist Kim Hill, have been to the Yanomamö area and have carefully followed the scandal discussed in this chapter. They are both on the anthropology faculty of Arizona State University.

Throughout South America, local governments allocate meager and inadequate resources to indigenous help programs and only a fraction of these resources is ever seen by native communities due to rampant corruption and embezzlement. Furthermore, laws that protect indigenous rights are infrequently implemented. For example, in 1986, I reported to the Direccion de Asuntos Indigenas of Venezuela that only 1 indigenous land title was legitimate out of 152 that had been initially decreed by President Rafael Caldera in 1972. Several months later, Peruvian government officials threatened to expel my husband and me from our field site because we had treated the sick during a massive respiratory epidemic in a remote Machiguenga village. In 1991 several of our Hiwi Indian collaborators were murdered without cause by Venezuelan nationals. All these events were reported to government officials with no response. They were ignored along with many other instances of wrongdoing observed by us and countless other anthropologists. *Darkness in El Dorado* did not come from actions of a geneticist, a sociobiologist and a filmmaker in one tiny corner of the Amazon. It has been produced through hundreds of years of racist colonialism and neglect. The devastation of the Amazon will only stop when governments and international agencies respond to human rights violations in an effective manner with the help of scientists.

I agree with Magdalena Hurtado that the harms inflicted on native Amazonians are caused primarily by actions and attitudes of "civilized" people, most notably the "Indian" policies—official or unofficial—of their national governments, Brazil and Venezuela in particular.

But what about those some 40-odd anthropologists who have spent anywhere from a few weeks to, in a few cases, a year or more among the Yanomamö? Let me conclude with this story, told to me by a Venezuelan anthropologist.

A man from Caracas was visiting Switzerland and witnessed a traditional maypole ceremony where contestants attempt to climb a greased pole to retrieve the flag on top to win the event. A large crowd of Swiss citizens was enthusiastically shouting at each contestant as he entered the ring, which was cordoned off by a stout rope and guards, preventing the onlookers from entering the arena. The Venezuelan man exclaimed: "We have the same kind of ceremony in Venezuela! And we, too, have to rope off the area to prevent people from rushing in and dragging the contestant down!" A puzzled Swiss official replied: "No. You have it all wrong. We cordon off the area to prevent the crowd from getting in to help the contestant get to the top!"

The Venezuelan could have meant cultural anthropologists from France, Brazil, Venezuela, and those American anthropologists who depend on them to keep others from climbing the maypole.

Acknowledgments

This book took a long time to write because an extraordinary academic scandal exploded in the national and international press shortly after I signed the contract to write this book in 1998 and before it appeared in print in 2013. Before I thank my academic colleagues let me first express my gratitude to Bob Bender, my editor at Simon & Schuster, for having had the patience of Job waiting for me to finish this book. His skillful editing has made the text more coherent than what I gave to him, and much of the success of this book, if it will have any, will be due in large measure to his editorial skills.

I will here simply call this academic scandal Darkness in El Dorado. Along with a number of medical colleagues and a few others, I was accused in 2000 of starting a lethal epidemic of measles among the Yanomamö Indians some thirty years earlier, native Amazonians among whom I spent my entire career studying and whom I had grown to love and admire. I discuss this scandal in the final chapters of the book, and what I say there is most likely not going to be the end of my end of this discussion.

I want to especially acknowledge my gratitude to my Venezuelan colleague Charles Brewer-Carías for making it possible for me to meet then-Venezuelan President Carlos Andrés Pérez in 1998, who made it possible for both of us to continue our research in Yanomamö villages we had recently discovered, villages in the Siapa River Basin that were yet uncontacted and demographically pristine. President Pérez acted effectively to follow our recommendation to create a Biosphere Reserve to safeguard the Ye'kwana and Yanomamö Indians who lived there, an area of some 32,000 square miles on the Venezuelan border with Brazil. I also want to thank another Venezuelan colleague, Issam Madi, for keeping me informed of events in the Venezuelan states of Amazonas and Bolívar that have affected the various groups of native peoples there after 1994.

Many of the people to whom I owe an incalculable debt are the friends, colleagues—and the academics in other fields I did not know personally—who effectively contested and challenged the accusations against me and the medical colleagues I worked with earlier in my research career.

John Tooby, Michael Price, and Edward Hagen immediately established a website associated with the Department of Anthropology at the University of California at Santa Barbara from which I had retired the previous year. Tooby was on the Anthropology faculty, and both Price and Hagen were then graduate students whom we both advised. Their website, still accessible at http://www.anth.ucsb .edu/ucsbpreliminaryreport.pdf, was started in 2000 and was periodically updated as new reports and investigations appeared. They themselves reviewed many of the primary published resources cited by my Inquisitors and showed that a large fraction of the citations were either wrong or had nothing to do with the accusations made against me or said just the opposite of what was claimed. Their website, no longer being updated, also preserves many of the original articles and emails that were central to accusations or repudiations in this scandal, some of which are cited in this book.

A similar but more immediate effort was made at the University of Michigan, where I earned all of my degrees in anthropology and where I subsequently served on the faculties of both the Anthropology Department and the Department of Human Genetics in the University of Michigan's School of Medicine. In 2000, when the Darkness scandal exploded in the press, two of my University of Michigan colleagues in the Anthropology Department, Kent Flannery and Joyce Marcus, conducted an investigation for the Provost's Office of the University of Michigan and concluded that the accusations against James V. Neel and me were without merit. Their investigation took place because the field research for my doctoral dissertation at Michigan was done among the Yanomamö, and James V. Neel, founder and longtime chairman of that department, joined me in the field in 1966 and, with a small team of medical doctors and advanced graduate students in medicine and/or human genetics, initiated a bio-medical research project among the Yanomamö. I was subsequently offered a position in the Department of Human Genetics by Neel. Our collaboration continued in annual field trips until 1972 when I moved to the Pennsylvania State University and Neel's interests turned to other research issues.

Several of my colleagues in anthropology, Thomas Gregor at Vanderbilt University, Daniel Gross at the World Bank, and William Irons at Northwestern University, were also concerned and alarmed by the enthusiasm with which elected officers and members of the Executive Board of my professional association, the American Anthropological Association (AAA), seemingly endorsed the accusations contained in *Darkness in El Dorado* and spoke out against them and repeatedly challenged them in publications and by their numerous direct communications with various officials in the AAA. Tom Gregor and Dan Gross also made very useful suggestions, especially to Chapter 16, where I described some of the committees the AAA created to conduct its investigation of me and James V. Neel, topics they themselves also investigated, wrote major papers on, and with which they were intimately familiar. Many other colleagues protested what the AAA did in a similar fashion, including Raymond Hames, who was asked to serve on the AAA Task Force on El Dorado charged with investigating me but who resigned when he discovered how biased and politically vindictive some members of this committee were. I am grateful for the long-term and costly efforts some of these colleagues put into their attempts to keep the public image of this association reputable at a time when many senior and influential academic leaders in other fields were becoming skeptical about the professional integrity of the AAA, as it was developing the reputation of being irrelevant to serious mainstream academic discussions of major issues of concern to the public. As one of my colleagues cynically commented, "It is no wonder that scientists in other fields view anthropologists as people who would eat their own offspring."

I also thank two of my former undergraduate students at UCSB, Amanda Grimes and Nathan Resch (now married to each other), for traveling from Santa Barbara to San Francisco at their own expense for the 2000 annual meetings of the AAA and for recording what every speaker said during the two major public open mike sessions about me and my alleged activities among the Yanomamö that were the major focus of the Darkness in El Dorado scandal and the then-impending AAA investigation of me. I also want to thank Betsy Myers of the Traverse Area District Library for her work in finding many references for me as this book neared completion.

I would like to thank those colleagues who read earlier drafts of some of the general material that appears in this book and made useful comments on them. Steven Pinker and Richard Dawkins read a very early draft of one of the chapters just as the Darkness scandal was breaking in 2000 and put a great deal of their time and effort into this, and I am grateful to them. Mary Ann Harrell, a former editor at the National Geographic Society and a dear friend, also read several of the earlier chapters and made useful editorial suggestions. I am grateful for her recommendations and for her longtime interest in my Yanomamö research and encouraging me to keep at it . . . and to ignore my detractors.

I also want to thank Edward O. Wilson for reading and making suggestions on the brief account I wrote about our participation in the 1976 "sociobiology" debate in Washington, D.C., when the InCAR radicals sullenly listened to the speakers, and then rose up and attacked Wilson, knocked him down, and poured pitchers of water on him while shouting ugly accusations of racism, facism, etc., about his research. Later that evening, at the Smithsonian, Wilson had a debate with one of my persistent anthropological critics, Marvin Harris, whose statements that night about me stunned Wilson. Wilson discovered that night just how treacherous anthropologists can be when they denigrate a competitor if their own "theories" are threatened by his research—as I discuss in Chapter 14. I also want to thank Ed Wilson for the regular phone calls he made to me to cheer me up and assure me of his support during the period immediately following the appearance of Darkness in El Dorado. He knew how depressing it can be when your own colleagues attacked you for some alleged political agenda they maliciously claim you are promoting, as Marxist biologists Richard Lewontin and Stephen J. Gould, his own departmental colleagues at Harvard, attacked him this way after his influential book Sociobiology appeared.

Finally, I want to thank Richard D. Alexander for not only reading most of the manuscript as it was nearing completion and making extensive comments on it, but also for the many conversations we have had since the early 1970s about the remarkable breakthroughs in theoretical biology that affected our respective research activities and theoretical interests and those of the several graduate students who worked with both of us—Mark Flinn, Laura Betzig, and Paul Turke in particular. I look forward to resuming my direct contact with Alexander as a consequence of my appointment in 2012 as an Adjunct Research Scientist at the University of Michigan, where I will be putting my many years of data on the Yanomamö into an archive to be managed and ultimately distributed by the University of Michigan's Inter-University Consortium for Political and Social Research (ICPSR) in the Institute of Social Research (ISR) to qualifying universities that subscribe to their programs.

Notes

3 *It was this aspect of Yanomamö cultural geography*: This means they had not been ravaged by epidemic diseases and their population was distributed among the expected numbers of children, adults, old people, etc. Most tribes are so demographically disrupted when anthropologists reach them that the kinds of fieldwork I discuss in this book cannot be done there.

7 The Social Contract *(1762)*: See Ellingson, 2001, for an erudite history of the Noble Savage idea; see Keeley, 1996, for a summary of how anthropologists and archaeologists have used the noble savage concept, and Pinker, 2002, for how it has been used in general social science thinking.

9 *biological and evolutionary matter*: Alexander, 1979

10 *who laid down his life*: The anecdote was reported by English geneticist John Maynard Smith, who claims to have heard J. B. S. Haldane say this or something very similar. Maynard Smith was the editor of the *Journal of Theoretical Biology*, in which Hamilton's two theoretically important papers appeared. Even now major issues are reappearing in evolutionary theory. For example, E. O. Wilson's 2012 book, *The Social Conquest of Earth*, raises once more the issue of group selection versus individual selection, and what he says seemingly calls into question Hamilton's eloquent solution to this problem laid out in his two 1964 papers on *inclusive fitness* or, as John Maynard Smith called it, *kin selection* theory. As Richard Dawkins said in 2012 in a highly critical review of Wilson's book with reference to Hamilton's work: "It truly is a beautiful theory." Dawkins, 2012.

In my view, and I agree with Dawkins, it is *the* theory that best explains the importance of genetic kinship in all forms of life, including social insects, social animals, humans in the environments of history, and tribesmen like the Yanomamö. It is the key to understanding the question that Alexander caused me to start thinking about in the first place because nepotism lies at the heart of understanding cooperation and sociality in human societies.

Needless to say a large fraction of major theoreticians in evolutionary biology reject Wilson's arguments for group selection, but one of them, David Sloan Wilson, an advocate of group selection, argues, somewhat regretfully, that the empirical and theoretical issues are so complex that neither Dawkins nor Wilson has gotten them right (2012). He argues that these individuals are simply two luminaries among a much larger group of experts and there is more consensus among this group than meets the eye. But other luminaries, Steven Pinker among them, are now voicing their disapproval of E. O. Wilson's attempted resurrection of group selection. Pinker, 2012. D. S. Wilson essentially dismisses the conflict by arguing that the days of pitting kin selection against group selection are over, largely because many things that have been taken as examples of group selection are now being usefully framed in terms of inclusive fitness theory and many things that were formerly explained in terms of kin selection are being framed in terms of multilevel or group selection. But lurking uncomfortably in my memory is the comment I once heard W. D. Hamilton make: in almost all cases where group selection is said to work these have been reduced to a solution in which individual-level selection has been also shown to be operating. That is not the same thing that D. S. Wilson is saying.

Finally, it is appropriate in thinking about these issues to recall the pithy anecdote by George C. Williams (1966) that a herd of fleet deer is not the same thing as a fleet herd of deer.

10 *kinship rules*: Chagnon, 1982.

12 *toward increased social and political complexity*: These developments can also go the *opposite* way, toward decreasing complexity: the important issue is that, through long-term studies, one can identify which developments do what to social trends.

13 *general reading audience*: My 1992 book, *Yanomamö: The Last Days of Eden*, is largely an expansion on my original textbook, *Yanomamö*, but with the more difficult and technical material on kinship and social organization eliminated and sections of new text added.

Chapter 1. Culture Shock: My First Year in the Field
PAGE

16 *evangelical missionaries*: These were members of the New Tribes Mission. Although most of them were Americans, those working in Venezuela included missionaries from Canada, England, Denmark, and other countries.

16 *Venezuelan Yanomamö in 1950*: Several other New Tribes missionaries may have made contact with the Yanomamö at Platanal in 1948. Dan Shaylor, personal communication.

17 *lots of* bareto: The wet season begins in early April and lasts until October or November, the heaviest rains falling in May and June when any travel—by foot or by open canoe—is very unpleasant.

26 *foreboding presence*: Some thirty-five to forty anthropologists have now done fieldwork among the Yanomamö since I started. By the mid-1970s

things had changed radically and it is not surprising that some anthropologists who choose to be critical of some of my findings say that they never saw any of the things that Chagnon reports. They probably stayed with the Salesian missionaries, who by the mid-1970s, had missions with cement floors, flush toilets, screened windows, electricity, tables and chairs, kerosene refrigerators, and running water.

27 *in my doctoral thesis*: Chagnon, Napoleon A. 1966. *Yanomamö Warfare, Social Organization and Marriage Alliances*. Ph.D. dissertation, University of Michigan. University Microfilms. Ann Arbor, Michigan.

28 *Englishman named Ashley Montagu*: Born in London, his name at birth was Israel Ehrenberg.

29 *evolution of biological organisms*: See White, 1949.

31 *a "primitive stage" in human social history*: Harris, 1968, p. 197.

32 *living expenses for one year*: NIMH was one of two major federal agencies that funded research by advanced graduate students in most universities and was a major source of funding in anthropology. The other agency, a more common funder, was the National Science Foundation. Few universities provide research funding for their graduate students. Instead they expect them to find research funds on their own by applying to NSF, NIMH, or other agencies and private foundations.

33 *survivors of the atomic bombings*: Neel and Schull, 1991.

33 *research among the Xavante*: Neel et al., 1964.

33 *from James Spuhler*: Spuhler also had a joint appointment in Neel's Human Genetics Department.

33 *members in Neel's department*: Some people seem to assume that Neel was one of my professors at Michigan—a mentor of sorts. This is not true. I took no courses from Neel and met him only on the eve of my departure to do my first fieldwork. By that time almost all of my formal course work for the Ph.D. degree was completed, as I describe in the text.

34 *anthropologist Johannes Wilbert*: Wilbert joined the faculty of the University of California, Los Angeles, in 1962 and remained there for his entire career.

34 *variations found among them*: Wilbert, 1966.

35 *Venezuelan Waika Indians*: The German anthropologist Otto Zerries (Zerries, 1964) had spent some months among the Yanomamö in Barker's first village, Mahekodo-teri, studying material culture. His research assistant, Meinhard Schuster (Schuster, 1958), published generally accurate but superficial observations on Yanomamö social organization.

36 *from the University of Michigan*: Seriously ill individuals were normally flown out to Puerto Ayacucho by the missions who, in the villages we visited in 1966, had already been seen by doctors before we arrived.

Chapter 2. Discovering the Significance of the Names
PAGE

42 *a system of writing*: *All* languages have structure and grammar, but only some of them are written.

43 *Yanomamö, and German*: I had learned German in my freshman year at Michigan Tech and continued to learn it on my own after transferring to the University of Michigan. Ann Arbor was largely settled by Germans and several of my favorite restaurants had German-speaking personnel, so I had frequent opportunities to speak German and improve my skill in this language. In addition, the research institute in Venezuela, IVIC, had many German-speaking scientists and while I was there I spoke German more frequently than I spoke Spanish.

44 *Venezuelan Malarialogía:* The men who worked for the Malarialogía systematically dispensed antimalaria pills to the Yanomamö who lived in villages on or close to the rivers and periodically sprayed their *shabonos* with DDT. In this area of Venezuela most of the Malarialogía employees were called *creoles.*

44 *about 120 pounds*: For detailed anthropometric data see R. Spielman, 1971. See also Hames, Chagnon, and Oliver on Kedebaböwei-teri children, 2005.

49 *first menstrual period*: There are few features of Yanomamö culture that can be used to measure time. The place of a female's first menstruation is one of them. For example, if a female had her first menstruation in the same place she was born, then most likely her mother's group lived there at least twelve years, perhaps longer.

49 *what garden*: Over time the names of *shabonos* change, but the names of gardens are almost never forgotten. *Shabonos* have to be reconstructed periodically—usually about every three years. Sometimes the Yanomamö call the new *shabono* by a different name. Babies, when due, are normally born in the garden, where the mother and her female attendants have more privacy. They almost always give me the name of the garden when I ask where a child was born. There will be many more gardens and garden names than *shabonos* and *shabono* (village) names.

49 *people to study*: Some of the Ye'kwana I got to know well chastised me for studying the Yanomamö and invited me to study them instead. One of the reasons was that the Yanomamö are secretive about their names and genealogies, whereas the Ye'kwana were extremely willing to talk about these topics—and would not lie to me about them.

51 *blood relative to everyone else*: I will discuss in more detail what "being related" means. In most Yanomamö villages the vast majority of individuals are related to upwards of 90 percent of all other individuals no matter how many 'families' there are in the village. See Chagnon, 1979a, fig. 4–5, pp. 129–31, "Quartiles of Village Population Relatedness."

51 *"female cross cousin"*: This is a simplified discussion of Yanomamö kinship classification and marriage rules. I will expand on this material in chapter 12. For an even more detailed discussion of Yanomamö kinship, see Chagnon, 1997, ch. 4. A sixth edition of this monograph is scheduled to appear in 2012.

52 *a nabä: a subhuman*: The Yanomamö are extremely ethnocentric and believe that all non-Yanomamö are subhuman.

53 *Individuals of the same age*: Sahlins, 1968; Fried, 1967.

54 *within the group*: See Chagnon, 1979a, 1979b, and Chagnon and Bugos, 1979.

54 *to calculate approximate ages*: They also have rich vocabularies to describe the various growth stages of plants, insects, animals, and other living things.

54 *his waist string*: Boys are eager to begin tying their penises to their waist strings and would be ridiculed if they failed to do so when they reached the "appropriate" degree of maturity.

55 *their political system*: Politics and political activities are almost everywhere the domain of males. The name taboo for females is observed more to avoid drawing attention to them when they are sick and/or very old or for incest prohibitions—sons-in-law are not supposed to use the names of their mothers-in-law.

56 *the less angry* (hushuwo): The word *hushuwo* has several meanings. It is used to describe ordinary anger, but in the context of grief after the death of a close relative, it means something like: *an emotional state of intense sadness and grief, associated with unpredictable and uncontrollable emotions that verge on acts of violence.* It is, therefore, potentially dangerous to casually say the name of someone who is recently deceased in the presence of his or her close kin . . . especially adult males.

58 *beg for steel tools*: Even the Yanomamö villages I contacted that had never before been visited by outsiders had machetes and axes, often badly worn ones, but also sometimes relatively new ones obtained in trade with other, distant Yanomamö villages.

59 *generation of ancestors*: I always avoided using young informants because they didn't know as much as older people. On the few occasions I had to use young female informants—captives from other villages I wanted to know about—I would have another person in my hut to chaperone the session.

60 *an agouti-tooth knife*: Agoutis are small rodents whose sharp incisors are used by the Yanomamö as small cutting tools—"knives"—when an incisor is affixed to a short stick with pitch and vine wrapping.

62 *presentable as a visitor*: When I traveled with the Yanomamö I normally wore a T-shirt, swimming trunks, and tennis shoes, all of which got soaked within an hour of travel, either by perspiration or by my wading through rivers and streams. However, I always carried a piece of red cloth in my backpack that I used as a loin cloth to "ceremoniously" enter a village. The Yanomamö encouraged me to do this to put on a display as they did.

65 *the main group had*: See Chagnon, 1979, pp. 86–131, for statistical details and discussion of village composition by patrilineages.

Chapter 3. Raids and Revenge: Why Villages Fission and Move

PAGE

70 *peaceful terms with the Bisaasi-teri*: The village name "Monou-teri" derives from *mono u* meaning "lagoon." "Bisaasi-teri" derives from the commonly

found roofing palm plant, called *bisaasi*. The suffix *teri* means "people" or "people of."

72 *gardens began producing*: When a group moves, it clears new gardens and, once these begin producing, the group moves into them and builds its permanent *shabono*. Meanwhile, people build and sleep in simple temporary *yanos*—"camping" huts—which can be made in less than an hour.

73 *their leader, their* waiteri: *Waiteri* means "fierce one." They had several *waiteris*, but Matowä was the most *waiteri* in the village, the headman, and an *unokai* (see below).

78 *in this particular war*: As my association with the Bisaasi-teri continued I became more and more identified with them and this affected how some of their enemies viewed me.

78 *two Patanowä-teri headmen*: Very large villages often have two (or more) headmen, usually the senior men from the largest patrilineages in the village. Very often these men are cross-cousins and are married to each others' sisters. (See chapter 12 on Yanomamö social organization.)

78 *firewood and my backpacks*: I carried one of the packs and my guide carried the other.

78 *blocked shut for the night*: I obliged them, but thankfully no situation ever arose in which I had to consider taking this kind of action.

78 *all men are Yanomamö*: One of my critics would later accuse me of being the "classic" example of the Heisenberg principle, i.e., unwittingly influencing what I was there to observe. In short, he accused me of causing the "wars" I witnessed, like this one, because I allegedly had such a "vile" personality and communicated this to the Yanomamö, thus causing them to become vile, aggressive, and warlike. (Cockburn, 1991.) This accusation was too bizarre to respond to. However, I and all other anthropologists are aware that simply by being in a relatively uncontacted village we have an effect on what we report.

80 *with the bark removed*: In other raid rehearsals I witnessed, the *no owa* was made from thatch—bunches of vegetation tied together to look like a human with legs and a head.

88 *after they killed an enemy*: Several years after this raid, Matarawä, even then just a youth, was killed by raiders from the village of Daiyari-teri. He went fishing at night too close to their village, they caught him, and riddled his neck and chest with many arrows. But his assassins did what I consider an honorable thing. His body fell into the river. Lest it disappear forever, they dived in, recovered it, and tied it with vines to the riverbank so his kinsmen would find it and be able to cremate it. His assassins knew him well, liked him, but they were now on opposite sides of a new war, and so they killed him.

92 *the sexual lives*: I once had an amusing conversation with Meyer Fortes, a distinguished British anthropologist renowned for his fieldwork among several African tribes. After we got to know each other well (he had invited me to spend my 1980 sabbatical leave at King's College, Cambridge University,

where we had many conversations), he whispered to me: "How often have you seen the Yanomamö copulate?" I whispered back: "Never." He then said to me that in his years among the Tale, one of the African tribes he was famous for studying, "I've never seen the Tale do it either."

96 *the* shabono *on their lagoon*: They finally abandoned this *shabono* a few months later when their new gardens across the Mavaca were producing.

96 *snuff tube with* ebene: *Ebene* is a generic word used for Yanomamö hallucinogens, all of which are of vegetable origin. In this area the two most commonly used hallucinogens are *hisiomö* and *yakowana*. Of the two, the first is the more desirable and comes from the tiny seeds of a large tree. The other comes from the inner bark of a different tree. See Chagnon, LeQuesne, and Cook, 1971.

98 *EEA*: Symons, 1979.

98 *Environments of History*: Alexander, 1979.

98 *ARE*: Irons, 1998.

Chapter 4. Bringing My Family to Yanomamöland and My Early Encounters with the Salesians

PAGE

100 *his generous offer*: Both my wife and I came from large and relatively poor families. Both of us remember that as children our families lived, at times, in houses that did not have indoor plumbing and we were familiar with the discomforts of having to use an outhouse.

102 *Barker had developed*: Barker did not reveal to me the extensive materials he had on the Yanomamö language, perhaps because he mistrusted me because I told him that I had been raised Catholic. He was suspicious of Catholics because of the problems he had had with the Salesian missionaries. In any case, I think the only way to learn Yanomamö is to live with the Yanomamö themselves, something Lizot and I both did, but which the Salesians did not do.

102 *female cross-cousins*: Cousin, sibling, and other kinship terms are explained in chapter 12, p. 324.

108 *by the Catholic Church*: Chagnon, 1986. *Newsweek*, where I described Venezuela as "the last Theocracy in the Western Hemisphere."

109 *Venezuela's remote areas*: This policy has been going on in Latin America since the Spanish conquest. When I moved to Santa Barbara, California, in 1984 and saw the chain of Catholic missions along the Pacific coast, I knew I was witnessing this same longtime policy among the Yanomamö, with its devastating effects on their health.

109 *colleague named Gene Higdom*: Dan Shaylor, personal communication, January 13, 2010.

110 *sites was occupied in 1950*: This was probably true in 1950, but either late in 1950 or early in 1951 a New Tribes missionary by the name of Flora Troxell lived for a time with one of the groups on the lower Ocamo, possibly at the mouth of the Ocamo. Remarkably, she had a wooden leg. Dan Shaylor,

personal communication, January 13, 2010. In 1954 Hector Acebes said he met her at Tama Tama in 1951.

110 *as Mahekodo-teri*: One Yanomamö name for the uppermost reaches of the Orinoco River is *Mahekodo kä u*. But, in fact, this river is a branch that splits away from the main stream of the Orinoco at the rapids known as *Raudal Peñascal*, very near the headwaters of the Orinoco and the Brazilian border.

112 reduce *them to living there*: The practice, as I mentioned above, was widespread in the Spanish colonization of the Americas: a *reducción* is a word that means, historically, a community of Native Americans who have been "converted" to Catholicism, usually by being forced to settle at or near a Catholic mission and required to attend the mission school. The native people are dissuaded from (and in some cases, punished for) speaking their native language.

112 *months at a time*: I was prevented from returning to the Yanomamö by a small group of Venezuelan anthropologists for a ten-year period from 1975 to 1985 that included establishment in the Upper Orinoco of these Salesian policies. I did not learn about them until these policies were discontinued at least for the Yanomamö. See Lizot, 1976.

112 *effectively amounted to purchasing*: From 1975 to 1985 opposition to my study of the Yanomamö by Venezuelan anthropologists had become so intense that they succeeded in having a policy passed that no "foreign" (meaning American) anthropologists were given permits from the Venezuelan "Indian Bureau," the Oficina Central de Asuntos Indigenas (OCAI). The head of this group was an anthropologist named Eddie Romero, whose wife was an archaeologist at IVIC. OCAI was controlled by Venezuelan anthropologists until about 1985, when it was moved into the Ministry of Education. See Lizot, 1976.

115 *alliances, and warfare*: Chagnon, 1974, pp. 180–82.

115 *films on the Yanomamö*: *The Feast* and *Yanomamö: A Multidisciplinary Study*.

116 *beginning to annoy the Salesians*: After 1975 the Salesians began criticizing me and my work to Venezuelan authorities because I was "violating the Yanomamö name taboo"—that is, I was asking about deceased individuals who might possibly have died from their introduced shotguns. I believe they were using the name taboo to hide the shotgun deaths. However, by the early 1970s most of my fieldwork was being done among the Yanomamö villages known collectively as Shamatari, where the Salesians had no knowledge of my field procedures. The only Salesian who might have had firsthand knowledge of my interview procedures was Padre Cocco. Padre Bórtoli did not arrive in the area until about 1975.

Chapter 5. First Contact with New Yanomamö Villages
PAGE

131 *my valuable trade items, or* madohe: *Madohe* means "material possessions" but in the context of the possessions of foreigners, it means their "trade goods."

132 *give valuable* madohe *to them*: The Yanomamö do this to *every* foreigner. My critics dishonestly claim or naïvely seem to believe that only my trade goods had special properties such that my paying informants with my *madohe* made them "dependent" on me and caused wars among Yanomamö because they coveted the novel steel tools I brought into their area. However, long before I arrived, the Salesian Missions, especially Padre Cocco's mission at Ocamo, had distributed *thousands* of steel tools to the Yanomamö. See Chagnon and Asch, *Ocamo Is My Town*. The Yanomamö were engaged in wars long before either I or the Salesians arrived, as I describe throughout this book.

134 *from Mömaribowei-teri*: As I explained in chapter 1, he was the first Yanomamö I met as I passed through Tama Tama into their area.

135 *to find Sibarariwä's village*: The Mavaca River seemed to have an aura of mystery and danger in 1965. For example, the creole men who worked for the Malarialogía seemed to be reluctant to ascend it more than a half hour by motorized dugout from where it flowed into the Orinoco. They had also heard of "Shamatari treachery."

140 *Amerindian populations*: Measles also decimates other, non-indigenous, isolated populations whenever long periods of time elapse between exposure to the illness. In such isolated demographic situations the entire population, when exposed to measles, contracts the disease and everyone becomes sick, including adults, thus leading to high death rates because adult caregivers cannot help the children and infants.

142 *didn't feel like coming*: Karina had gotten a measles vaccination from one of the medical doctors in our group some ten days earlier and was at the end of his period of reaction to the vaccination. Our expedition had fought the measles epidemic for weeks. By this time the Venezuelan government was sending in medical doctors, more vaccines, and other medical supplies, and had taken over the work of containing the 1968 measles epidemic. One tragic new outbreak did occur at about this time, caused I believe by the failure of a Salesian priest at Platanal, Padre Sanchez, to evacuate a Brazilian man who had recently arrived at his mission sick with measles. This man caused many of the Yanomamö there and in neighboring Patanowäteri to contract measles and numbers of them died.

157 *"He got it right!"*: This is how I routinely used Yanomamö personal names all during my sixty months of fieldwork. My use—or alleged misuse—of personal names would later become the topic of an investigation of my "ethical misconduct" by the American Anthropological Association. Most anthropologists probably never worked among people who had a name taboo, but many of them acted as though they knew and understood how the taboo worked.

Chapter 6. Geography Lesson
PAGE

179 *was called Bisaasi-teri*: Since the Yanomamö frequently rename their villages, any maps with current village names would soon be out of date. The
names of the Yanomamö villages at the mouth of the Mavaca, for example,
have changed numerous times since I first went there in 1964 because the
villages have subdivided many times, even though they have remained
within sight of each other.

181 *in the local jungle*: I've spoken to many fieldworkers who studied tribes in
other parts of the world whose experiences were comparable: their native
informants invariably had an exceptional sense of direction and distance
between places familiar to them.

182 *child-bearing, death, etc.*: Anthropology also has had a theoretical interest in
what is generally known as "rites of passage" and these phenomena are also
nongeographical.

182 *early in my fieldwork*: Chagnon, 1974, p. 160.

Chapter 7. From Fieldwork to Science
PAGE

197 *other universities as well*: Paul and Beatty, 2000; Baur, IGES-ELSI Committee, et al., 2001.

204 *We spent many days*: Neel et al., 1970.

206 *"inbreeding coefficient"*: The "f" statistic is a measure of how much genetic
material is shared by two people who are related. A mating of these two
people would produce an "inbreeding coefficient" for their offspring that is
half the value of the "relatedness coefficient."

207 *"zoological perspective"*: Tiger and Fox, 1966.

209 *this interesting issue*: Chagnon, 1966; 1967; 1968a; 1968c; 1972.

209 *hours upstream by large dugout*: The Venezuelans use the name *bongo* to refer
to a large native dugout canoe used to transport loads of heavy cargo, like full
fifty-five-gallon gasoline barrels, cement, etc. They are often "planked up" by
adding boards along both gunwales to carry larger loads. Palm-thatched or
sheet-metal roofs are sometimes added for comfort and rain-proofing.

209 *children in the village*: Neel and I would later be accused of deliberately
withholding gamma globulin when we vaccinated the Iyäwei-teri at Ocamo.

Chapter 8. Conflicts over Women
PAGE

214 *Females appear*: Keeley, 1996.

214 *Crow Creek site*: Zimmerman and Whitten, 1980; Zimmerman, 1981; Zimmerman, J. Gregg, and P. S. Gregg, 1981; Zimmerman and Bradley, 1993.

214 *reached the Americas*: This date is significant because it eliminates the frequently invoked argument that "colonial influence after Columbus" made
the American Indians warlike: before that, they were allegedly peaceful and
among whom war and violence were rare or nonexistent.

216 *Or, perhaps, these injuries*: See P. L. Walker on forensic studies of different groups of North American skeletal remains that show many wounds and injuries: 1989; 1997; 2001; Walker et al. 2005.

217 *John Morgan*: Morgan, 1852.

218 *"Don't ask"*: Chagnon, 1974, p. 82.

219 *inseminated by other men*: See Dickemann, 1979, and on claustration.

219 *films ever made*, Dead Birds: Gardner, 1964.

219 *"Among the sources"*: Heider, 1970, p. 100.

219 *University of Michigan*: Larson, 1987.

220 *accounting for only 6 percent of it*: Ibid., Tables 8 and 9. While there is significant variation in "causes" of war in the New Guinea Highlands, fighting over women is among the more frequently reported ones. The relationship of women to warfare and conflicts in other Highland tribes neighboring the Ilaga Dani is less clear.

Kapauku: While revenge for homicides is common, among the Kapauku "most wars start because of violations of the husband's sexual exclusive rights, the delict of adultery, as well as the rape of a married woman is considered the most heinous of crimes. The penalty is execution." Pospisil, 1958, p. 167.

Western Dani (Konda): Here, disputes over women are the most frequent causes of "brawls" (22 cases out of 52:42.3 percent). About 19 percent of Konda wars start over women, but twice as many start to avenge previous killings. About 22 percent of the wars were over "property," mostly resulting from disputes over pigs. O'Brien, 1969, Table 11.

Western Dani (Wanggulam): Dutch anthropologist Anton Ploeg (Ploeg, 1969) documents 131 cases of "trouble" over the course of twenty-five years. Seventy-five were bow-and-arrow fights in which 142 people were killed. The second most frequent cause of wars was conflicts over women; theft of property was the most frequent.

Lower Grand Valley: Myron Bromley, a mission linguist and anthropologist, lived among the Dani for thirty-eight years (1954–92). His observations are particularly valuable because they include a period of time before the government established political control over the Grand Valley in 1958. Warfare was perpetual, especially at boundaries separating large confederacies or alliances of many groups. He discusses twenty cases of "a system of seizure, particularly of married women and pigs." Bromley, 1981, p. 10. Eight of these cases were over women, six were over pigs, and six over theft.

221 *and reproductive resources*: This theme is explored more systematically in Chagnon, 1990; see also Chagnon, 1988.

222 *and some of the British sociologists*: This approach goes back to F. Barth and some of the British sociologists. Irons and I have discussed this approach frequently in private, and I have published about it in articles about Yanomamö "wars."

223 *Sex ratio deviations*: The sex ratio is expressed as the ratio of males to females multiplied by 100, thus, 107/100 x 100 equals a sex ratio of 107.

223 *my early publications*: Chagnon, 1968c.

224 *warfare and politics*: I believe I was the first anthropologist to observe, document statistically, and draw attention to this striking phenomenon among tribesmen, making it a theoretically important issue for the first time.

224 *"lurid activity"*: Harris, 1968.

225 *including humans:* See Alexander, 1979.

225 *abduction is greatly reduced*: This has important implications for theories about the origin and evolution of cooperation. One of the best known theories, tit-for-tat (Axelrod and Hamilton, 1981), is based on the assumption that interacting individuals or groups are able to inflict the *same* amount of punishment on each other. The Yanomamö—and probably all societies— are constantly trying to achieve the ability to inflict *more* harm on competitors than the competitors can reciprocate: they constantly try to violate the assumptions in tit-for-tat. For the Yanomamö, this means trying to achieve larger village size compared to those of their immediate neighbors and enemies.

228 *treat them better*: My data on *shuwahimou* women are largely anecdotal. I cannot give an accurate estimate of what percentage of women among the Yanomamö have succeeded in fleeing from husbands but my guess would be that it is in the range of 5 percent. Many more, of course, attempt to flee but are recovered by their angry husbands and his friends—and severely punished.

230 *they never before did*: Alexander Cockburn (Cockburn, 1991), claimed that I had such a "vile personality" that it somehow infected the otherwise peaceful Yanomamö, who then became vile in turn and began engaging in acts of violence, which I then dutifully observed and described—thereby exemplifying a stunning instance of the Heisenberg principle. R. B. Ferguson (Ferguson, 1995) also claimed that I caused animosity, jealousy, and conflicts by the way I gave metal tools to the Yanomamö.

230 *Ritchie visited*: Ritchie, 1996, p. 10.

231 *central role in Yanomamö culture*: For example works by both missionaries and anthropologists. See Jank, 1977; Peters, 2000; Ales, 1984. Lizot's 1976 book, *Le Cercle de Feux* (Circle of Fires), denounces me in the preface for "overemphasizing Yanomamö violence" in some of my publications and then ironically proceeds to report even *more* violence among the people Lizot lived with.

232 *established by faith*: One article of faith is that Noble Savages don't abduct women from their neighbors. During a talk I gave in 1999 at a major research university in Wisconsin to faculty members and graduate students in science (including anthropology) a young female faculty member objected to my discussion of abductions among the Yanomamö on the grounds that "we females in anthropology do not like to hear about things like this. It is demeaning to women."

232 *but rule* breakers: Many social scientists emphasize the difference between humans and other animals by drawing attention to the fact that only hu-

mans make "rules" (and laws) about the appropriateness of their behavior. For them a culture hero is someone like Moses—the lawgiver. But humans not only make rules; we develop complex schemes to break these rules (Alexander, 1979; Chagnon, 1982). The truly distinctive thing about humans is not that we make rules, but that we make rules in order to break them, a kind of educational message for others to heed when the rule breaker is punished.

236 *response to a male*: Male and female anthropologists studying the same tribe sometimes come up with radically different characterizations of the "realities" they report. Perhaps the most widely known case involves Margaret Mead's work. For example, one of her husbands was a prominent English anthropologist, Reo Fortune, who had studied, among other peoples, a Melanesian tribe known as the Arapesh (Mountain Arapesh). One of his publications was a straightforward account of their warfare. Mead later visited the same people. Her publications on the same tribe seem to deny the very existence of the warfare Fortune described. She portrayed them as friendly, peaceable people.

239 *rises to 87 percent*: To get this percentage, we must subtract the 91 females who are less than eleven years old from the total number of females: 302 − 91 = 211. This must be divided into the number of married females eleven years or older (194 − 9 = 185). 185/211 = 88.7, which I rounded down to 88 percent.

240 *jumps to 76 percent*: The math: 302 − 91 = 211; 161/211 = 76 percent.

241 *such a child*: This is a particularly important issue in my fieldwork because I try to visit and learn about the people in many different and widely dispersed villages and doing this takes an enormous amount of travel time and cost. This is a chronic problem faced by anthropological field researchers. The trade-off is this: is it better to get more in-depth knowledge about a smaller, and possibly unrepresentative village, or try to get data on a more comprehensive sample and be able to document the variability that always exists in a larger number of small, widely dispersed villages?

243 *there were 135 males*: Sex ratios can be, and often are, measured at different levels of the population—such as the point of conception, point of birth, average age at marriage of females (or males), people over age fifty, etc.

243 *("Fierceness Complex")*: In my 1968c publication I described the "Waiteri Complex" as a new model suggesting how preferential female infanticide led to a shortage of females and how this, in turn, led to fighting among men and eventually to intervillage warfare. Divale and Harris (1976) then appropriated this idea and called it the "male supremacist complex" without mentioning that their model derived from mine. Harris was the co-editor of the volume in which my original article was published, so it was highly unlikely that he didn't know about my article.

243 *are notable examples*: Blaffer-Hrdy, 1977.

243 *did these things*: In 1985 a Venezuelan official from the Indian Commission (OCAI) came to the Yanomamö area to find me. He wanted me to make an

official, formal, notarized statement about the Yanomamö practice of infanticide. A female member of the Venezuelan congress had heard that some Indians in Venezuela killed infants and she vowed to find the perpetrators, try them for murder in a court of law, and advocate harsh punishments for them. She was obviously referring to the Yanomamö and my publications on them. In my formal statement to OCAI about Yanomamö infanticide practices I said that I had never witnessed an infanticide and that these reports therefore might be inaccurate. I added that the compassionate and effective teachings of many missionaries had probably resulted in the abandonment of this vile practice. The first part of my statement was factually correct and that ended the matter. However, from that point onward, I stopped collecting systematic data on Yanomamö infanticide. Much to my dismay, Marvin Harris (then of Columbia University) accused me of "withholding data on infanticide" because it would support his theory that Yanomamö were adjusting "land-man ratios" through infanticide, that is, they were making the world safe for peccaries, armadillos, and monkeys, etc. by controlling their population growth through selective female infanticide to ensure that future Yanomamö would have enough protein in their diets. This was a component in the "great protein debate" that Harris and I had from the 1970s through the 1990s and part of a larger, but infrequently discussed, theoretical issue of whether Marxist or Darwinian theory would eventually prevail in American scientific cultural anthropology.

244 *the women by name*: Intense mate guarding by Yanomamö husbands leads to a relatively high degree of paternal certainty, as previously discussed.

244 *One woman had*: Biocca, 1996, pp. 34–35.

Chapter 9. Fighting and Violence
PAGE

251 *opinion and public action*: The Yanomamö represent a kind of tribal horticultural society that most anthropologists consider to be egalitarian. See Fried, 1967.

252 *to the ground*: I filmed one of these fights in 1965. This footage can be seen in the film *Yanomamö: A Multidisciplinary Study*. Neel, Asch, and Chagnon, 1971.

255 *even deadlier clubs, called* himo: Since *himo* clubs take hours to make and must be prepared in advance of a club fight, they clearly cannot be used in spontaneous club fights, as most club fights are. There are, however, club fight challenges sent to neighboring villages and participants have time to make *himo* clubs before appearing for a club fight. But since steel machetes and axes are always found in most villages due to trade, these can also be used to intimidate or threaten opponents that the one who wields the weapon might escalate a club fight to a fight with weapons that are potentially lethal. A *himo* club visibly displayed in a *nabrushi* club fight is, however, more likely to be used than a machete or an ax—which are definitely more likely to be lethal. A *himo* club does ensure that injuries will be more severe than those caused by *nabrushi* clubs.

257 *individuals in Caucasian populations*: Lahr and Wright, 1996; Lahr, 1996. South American Indian crania from the Fuegians and Patagonians are extremely robust, but there is some debate about whether this can best be explained by allometry (big skulls are more robust) or by genetic/environmental effects. Rolando González-José, personal communication.

257 *death of some person*: See Chagnon, 1988.

257 *particularly aggressive headman*: His name was Heawä and he lived in Mahekodo-teri. One of the victims of his Salesian-provided shotgun was the headman of Makorima-teri, a man named Säsäwä, but he also shot and killed several men in other villages, including in the Ashidowä-teri area far to the south of his village.

258 *Although shotguns*: My informants provided other examples. As I relate elsewhere, Padre Cocco was initially skeptical of my information that the Yanomamö were using shotguns to kill one another until a Yanomamö he called Carlito told both of us about a raid on an isolated village on the Harota River in which several people were killed. Heawä, a son of the headman of the Mahekodo-teri, shot and killed the headman of Makorima-teri during my fieldwork. His older brother Asiawä killed a young woman in Upper Bisaasi-teri. Both men obtained their shotguns at the Salesian mission at Platanal, according to my Yanomamö informants.

261 *these villages for many years*: Ritchie, 1966, provides a translation of an account that happened in a village that was subsequently evangelized by the Dawson family, who were initially associated with the New Tribes Mission but later became an independent nonaffiliated mission.

261 *in the mid-1960s*: Biocca, 1996.

262 *with "Ocamo Village"*: This village was known from at least 1965 to the present as Iyäwei-teri, the village whose members lived at Padre Cocco's Salesian mission at the mouth of the Ocamo.

263 *which I was*: Venezuelan police are frequently poorly educated trigger-happy goons with automatic weapons and unquestioned authority to shoot to kill for trivial reasons. One of them once shoved the barrel of his machine gun into my belly because I was wearing a Boy Scout belt with a brass buckle, which he claimed was a piece of "military" equipment. During one of my trips to Venezuela, American Peace Corps workers were summarily shot dead in downtown Caracas with their hands high above their heads, pleading and saying who they were in fluent Spanish. So far as I know, their assassins were never investigated, punished, or reprimanded.

266 *this area themselves*: See Chagnon, 1966; 1991, for my discussion of the Kohoroshitari and Karawatari Yanomamö.

267 *including English in 1970*: Biocca, 1996. Quotations are from the Kodansha Press paperback edition, which I used as a text in my anthropology courses at the University of California, Santa Barbara.

268 *headman named Ruwahiwä*: My own monograph, widely used in college courses in anthropology, begins with a prologue that describes this *nomohori* according to what my Yanomamö informants told me (Chagnon, 2011).

269 *possible Patanowä-teri treachery*: This *nomohori* did not involve a third neutral or friendly village. See my comments above where I explain how a convincing deception can sometimes lure members of a village to a trick.

269 *It must have been*: Helena Valero, *Yanoáma* (New York: Kodansha, 1996).

272 *yet a third one kept the original name*: Much confusion arises because the Yanomamö frequently change their village "identities" and take on new—sometimes temporary—village names. I ultimately resorted to using the names of the headmen of each group in an attempt to resolve this kind of confusion. Village names might change frequently, but the Yanomamö remember who was the "founder" or who were the prominent leaders of these newly named subgroupings. This tribal name confusion is commonplace in the historical ethnology of almost all native South American peoples, especially those located in the Amazon drainage.

272 *tribes like the Yanomamö*: In the 1970s when more contact between the Yanomamö and Venezuelan culture was developing, one Yanomamö man was being trained in practical nursing in the town of Puerto Ayacucho, where he learned about police and law. He excitedly told me about this when he realized that "law" would deal with homicides and this meant the end of blood revenge—and his worry that he might be a legitimate target of revenge for killings that his brothers had been involved in. Chagnon, 1988.

273 *with the Patanowä-teri*: Some of my older informants claimed that the Hasuböwä-teri were originally part of the "Aramamisi-teri" population and therefore relatives of the Shamatari. While there was considerable intermarriage between the Namowei-teri and ancestral Hasuböwä-teri, many of the latter may in fact be more closely related to the Shamatari. If so, their complicity in the *nomohori* at Amiana in about 1950 is not surprising.

273 *wounded could recover*: The Bisaasi-teri were also called Kreiböwei-teri at this time and assumed the name Bisaasi-teri only later.

275 *close genetic kinsman*: The meticulous genealogies I collected over the course of many years were intended to be as close to genetic pedigrees as I could make them. See Chagnon, 1974, for a discussion of the genealogical methods I used to collect these genealogies.

275 *a "cultural nature"*: See my discussion in Chagnon, 1982, and in this book. The prominent English mathematical geneticist John Maynard Smith, at the project's final meeting in King's College, Cambridge University, stopped his presentation, looked directly at me, and asked: "I can't understand why you anthropologists think this theory applies to 'chaps' [Homo sapiens]." He later endorsed the position that it did—presumably because he would have looked very silly as a biologist who claimed that natural selection theory did *not* apply to humans. See Chagnon, 1982, and my discussion of the paper I gave at the end of the King's College research project that provoked Maynard-Smith's remarkable question.

276 *an average of 1.63 wives*: These comparisons are statistically significant for all age categories. See my original 1988 article for the statistical tests. The same is true for the data given on p. 277.

278 *persists to this day*: For a sampling, see Carneiro da Cunha, 1989; Lizot, 1989; 1994; Ferguson, 1989; Albert, 1989; Moore, 1990; Kemp and Fry, 2004; Borofsky, 2005.

Chapter 10. First Contact with the Iwahikoroba-teri
PAGE

281 *"become a jaguar"*: See Chagnon and Asch, 1976.

282 *under Neel's supervision*: Ward went on to a successful career in human genetics in several U.S. universities and eventually Oxford University.

283 *not take samples*: After Neel's medical team worked with me the first time in 1966, word spread quickly and widely that I took medical people with me into villages, people who cured their sicknesses and who also took blood and other tissue samples. By 1966 I had also developed a reputation among the Yanomamö for being honest, fair, and "amusing" that was independent of my association with medical researchers. Nevertheless, the good reputation I had among the Yanomamö—even in villages I never visited regularly—made their acceptance of the medical researchers with me much easier.

284 *holds out for the trip*: I had recently broken my left ankle in Ann Arbor when a ladder I was standing on collapsed while I was cleaning leaves out of the gutters of my house.

285 *several weeks earlier*: I mistakenly said "first day's march" when it was the second day's march on my previous trip.

287 *growling and howling at us*: This is part of the ritual intimidation that visitors are exposed to when they arrive at a village, but in this case, they seemed ꞏꞏꞏꞏ nervous and apprehensive.

287 *demeanor of a headman*: I learned later that they that his name was Börösöwä.

288 *carrying a Brazilian-made machete*: The machete had a wooden handle, tightly wrapped with braided copper wire. They can be found only in Brazil. The Iwahikoroba-teri were obviously trading with villages far to their south, whose members in turn were in trade contact with other Yanomamö located near or at mission posts in Brazil. The Iwahikoroba-teri were at war with the Yanomamö villages to their north and no Venezuelan-made machetes were reaching them.

289 *didn't know how large it was*: We had contacted the main group of Iwahikoroba-teri, which probably numbered 170 or so people. Hiakama's group had recently fissioned away from them. It probably contained another sixty or seventy more people. Later, in the mid-1980s, I managed to contact all the Iwahikoroba-teri subgroups, which by that time consisted of four separate villages that numbered approximately 350 people. By then three of these groups were living *he borara*, that is, in separate *shabonos* that were within a few hundred yards from each other.

292 *my aluminum voladora*: In the Venezuelan Amazonas this means any aluminum boat on which you can put an outboard motor and travel fast. The word comes from *volar*, to fly.

292 *out to Caracas*: Ryk Ward and I kept in contact periodically for the next thirty years. We resumed correspondence when the *Darkness in El Dorado* accusations against me and James V. Neel erupted in 2000. Ryk started writing a book to repudiate Patrick Tierney's astonishing claims. He died of a heart attack while bicycling to his office in 2003.

Chapter 11. Yanomamö Origins and the Fertile Crescent

PAGE

295 *timbers with axes*: Today they use steel axes they obtain by trade from other Indians and, more recently, from missionaries and other outsiders. Very old informants have told me that before steel tools, much of the felling of trees was accomplished by placing firewood at the base of large trees and burning the base of the tree to kill it. As trees die, they lose their leaves and sunlight reaches the ground. No Yanomamö ever told me that he used a stone ax to fell trees, although stone axes are commonly found in the Yanomamö area, presumably made and used by the native peoples who preceded the current inhabitants. It is not known if these people were ancestors of the contemporary Yanomamö. On one of my field trips (1975) I invited two senior anthropologists to join me to advise several of my graduate students in potential field methods they might use. One of them, Robert L. Carneiro, did an experiment with a young Yanomamö man and had him haft a stone celt (a polished stone ax) by securing it to a piece of wood with vines. The celt was found locally and was an archaeological artifact, presumably once used to chop wood. Carneiro estimated how efficient the stone ax was compared to a modern steel ax (Carneiro, 1979). Not surprisingly, the stone celt was much less effective at chopping down even small trees than a steel tool—an ax or a machete—was.

295 *a fairly regular pattern*: Carneiro, 1961; Conklin, 1961.

296 *into which they could expand*: Freeman, 1955.

296 *"typical" hunter/gatherers*: Just before I retired from UCSB in 1999, I was attempting to get one of my archaeology graduate students, Nathan Craig, into an abandoned Yanomamö village site that I had lived in and had documented extensively in my 1974 book (Chagnon, 1974). The plan was to test various archaeological hypotheses having to do with social status differentials that could possibly be inferred by an archaeologist who later discovered this site and who examined the refuse heaps that were left by the inhabitants. I was unable to get Craig the necessary permission.

298 *on only one side*: Contemporary tribes like the Ye'kwana, who live to the north of the Yanomamö, now use very large toasting pans made from steel, which they purchase in Caracas.

301 *here, indicated by A–G*: Page 301 originally appeared in my doctoral dissertation (Chagnon, 1966). It was subsequently reproduced in all of the editions of my college textbook on Yanomamö culture (1968, 1977, 1983, 1992, 1997, and 2011). More details on Yanomamö settlement histories,

village fissions, and geography in this region can also be found in Chagnon, 1974a; Chagnon, 1991.

303 *"big gardens"*: See Chagnon, 1991, for more details.

304 *the mission seemed to provide*: The Yanomamö avoid raiding mission posts, knowing or assuming that at least some of the Yanomamö there might have firearms.

305 *rivers without canoes*: A few areas along the Orinoco, however, are high enough above the river that flooding is a much smaller risk. The few groups of Yanomamö who have moved to these areas appear to have chosen them because of this feature.

306 *"the worst mistake"*: Diamond, 1987.

306 *potatoes, wheat, etc.*: See also Diamond's popular 1997 book, *Guns, Germs, and Steel*.

306 *lacked sufficient nutritional*: By that time in human history socioeconomic classes and social stratification had emerged so that it is likely that only the lower (but numerically predominant) classes actually "paid" this price.

307 *leaves, saplings, and vines*: My longtime disagreement with Marvin Harris about the "cause" of Yanomamö warfare was in large part a product of Harris's view that the only important scarce strategic material resource in Yanomamöland was animal protein, a shortage he simply invented and never empirically documented. One could have made a better case that the Yanomamö may have been fighting over scarce supplies of roofing leaves and poles used in *shabono* construction. This scarcity, as distinct from Harris's speculations about protein, can be documented empirically. But it, too, does not explain the causes of warfare and violence among the Yanomamö.

308 *fertile crescent areas of Venezuela*: Chagnon, 1991.

308 *and the Shamatari*: Chagnon, 1991.

309 *as well as a Karawatari*: On one of my visits to Mishimishimaböwei-teri I noticed that a friend of mine, one of the younger political leaders, was not there. When I asked where he was they told me there had been a fight and he left in anger. The way they said it was *"Karawatari hamö a koraiyoma,"* which translates as "He went back home to his own people, the Karawatari." He was about as "Shamatari" as any Yanomamö.

310 *upper Siapa River*: I made first contact with the Doshamosha-teri in 1990 with Venezuelan naturalist Charles Brewer-Carías, with whom I had worked many years earlier in several of the biomedical expeditions that involved Drs. Neel, Roche, and Layrisse.

311 *had visited by 1968*: Chagnon, 1968b.

311 *circumscription in the Andean area*: Carneiro, 1961; 1970.

312 *along the Andes Mountains*: In 1970 Carneiro published an important theoretical paper presenting a more general theory of the origin of the state. He further elaborated his earlier arguments on environmental circumscription and how in the presence of warfare and increasing population density, it set into motion social processes leading to increased social and political com-

plexity and, ultimately, to the origin of states and empires in both the New World (Aztecs and Incas) and the Old World (Egypt, Mesopotamia, China, and India). His revised theory added two new variables: social circumscription and resource concentration. His model for social circumscription was my 1968 account of what was happening to Yanomamö groups in this "fertile crescent" area. Carneiro notes: "Thus, while still at the autonomous village level of political organization, those Yanomamö subject to social circumscription have clearly moved a step or two in the direction of higher political development." Carneiro, 1970, p. 737.

312 *into the Siapa Basin*: They also crossed over the Unturan Mountains, where the headwaters of the Shanishani come very close to the upper Siapa near Doshamosha-teri.

313 *The table below summarizes my findings*: From Chagnon, 1997, p. 88.

Chapter 12. Yanomamö Social Organization
PAGE

314 *because of polygyny*: By this I mean demographically intact tribes, not those that have been decimated by recently introduced diseases, militarily oppressed by states who attempt to control them, and forcibly relocated on "reservations" with other tribal groups to whom they may or may not be related. Almost all anthropological research in North American tribes has been done in groups like this.

314 *level of reproductive success*: The highest "natural" female fertility in a noncontracepting population is found among the Hutterites and is slightly higher than ten children per woman.

315 *I report*: I also report that the Yanomamö kinship system is of the "bifurcate-merging" type with the "Dravidian" cousin classification and, specifically, this is what other anthropologists define as the Iroquois kinship system. Humans have developed only six distinct kinds of kinship systems. All human societies have one of these six.

316 *than can matrilineages*: I demonstrated this in a computer analysis of Yanomamö kinship and descent, using achieved completed fertility of both sexes in a large group of Yanomamö villages (Chagnon, 1979b).

322 *lovestruck juveniles*: This is not to say that something we might classify as love does not exist among the Yanomamö. The Love Hypothesis does not, however, adequately account for who marries whom and who actually does the work of begetting in primitive societies. There is a large literature on romantic love and many of my good colleagues who are members of the Human Behavior and Evolution Society (HBES) and I have serious arguments about this issue. The subject is often discussed in the field called evolutionary psychology—a collection of psychologists, biological anthropologists, sociologists, and other evolutionary social scientists who originally called themselves (or were called by others) sociobiologists. The cultural anthropologists who were initially sociobiologists now mostly belong in a group called "evolutionary ecology."

323 *Amazonian tribesmen*: Kroeber, 1948 and Maybury-Lewis, 1979, on "dual organization" societies in the Amazon Basin.

323 *marriageable females occurs*: See Murdock, 1957, for frequencies and types of cross-cousin marriages cross-culturally.

324 *efficient dual organization as possible*: To illustrate why this is so would make this discussion extremely complicated. One can imagine a third patrilineage named "Z" wanting to intrude into the ideal system shown on page 321, causing one of the existing two lineages to have to give women to a third group to the displeasure of its "regular" exchange partners.

324 *villages I have studied*: For some statistical data see Chagnon, 1979, chapter 4, and summarized in Chagnon 1997, chapter 4.

325 *"husband" exchange system*: Matrilineal human societies in fact do just this.

325 *primitive societies*: In the field of anthropology, the word *primitive* is a technical term and has been used to characterize a particular kind of social organization that dominated hunting and gathering bands and early agricultural (slash-and-burn) societies. It is not a pejorative term unless someone wants to deliberately denigrate a social competitor by associating the word *primitive* with ideas from outside the context in which this word has been traditionally and technically used in anthropology.

326 The Elementary Systems of Kinship: This influential work was published in English by Beacon Press in 1969. The original 1949 edition was in French.

327 *lineage are descended*: Human geneticists like my late longtime collaborator James V. Neel also refer to "founders" or "founder effect," but rely in most cases on anthropologists or sociologists to provide specific empirical demographic and genealogical data where human societies are concerned.

328 *sisters in most cases*: Headmen are almost always polygynous and in most cases one or more of their spouses come from the other numerically dominant lineage(s).

329 *societies that have lineages*: The major exception is the *bint amin* marriage rule in some Arab-speaking communities, where men can marry their *parallel* cousins.

331 *their "close" cross cousins*: Chagnon, 1979, chapter 4, fig. 4.13; 1997, 5th ed.

332 *"work of the Devil"*: Padre Cocco explicitly cited this goal in the Salesian "attract and reduce" agenda. He believed that monogamy would render the Yanomamö "civilized, desirable" but would be accomplished in time only with persistent efforts. See Chagnon and Asch, Film: *Ocamo Is My Town*.

332 *evolution of political society in our species*: See Alexander, 1979, for arguments of a theoretical biologist who has a consummate interest in human social evolution.

Chapter 13. Three Headmen of Authority
PAGE

337 *described by many anthropologists as* egalitarian: See Fried, 1967, on tribal egalitarianism.

338 *Marshall Sahlins and Morton Fried*: Several of the works of both have had an enormous impact on anthropological theories and views of the tribal world and are now canonical texts. Sahlins, 1965; 1968; 1972; Fried, 1967.

339 *as well as* power: Fried's discussion of the differences between these two concepts is very good. He points out that a dictionary has authority, which is different from what a police force or army has: power, especially over life and death. The sanctions lying behind and underpinning what a police force can legally do are "odious"—like being legally authorized to kill someone who refuses to comply. The sanctions lying behind "law" are almost always odious. That distinguishes "law" from "customs"—what most tribesmen have. There is a large literature on whether or not the "customs" of tribesmen are sufficiently similar to "law" to regard them as such. See Fried (1967) for references to these works.

339 *closer to 300 people*: Village size in all the examples below fluctuated during the thirty-five years of my fieldwork. The figure I use is the approximate median size during these years.

340 *member of that* mashi: Both men are shown in my 1975 film (most of the footage was shot in 1968) with Timothy Asch, *The Feast*. They were later killed with a shotgun obtained from someone at a Salesian mission.

340 *always welcomed me*: In 1990 one of the Salesian (Catholic) missionaries' "converts" went into Patanowä-teri and told them I was killing their babies with my photographs and "driving their game away with the noise of my helicopters" on my most recent field trip. The latter allegation is made by anthropologists who denounce illegal Brazilian gold miners (*garimpeiros*) who entered their area after 1987. After 1987, Salesians also repeatedly told the Yanomamö I was a *garimpeiro*. Thus the new headman threatened to kill me with his ax as a consequence of these astonishing and sinister accusations. See the discussion of my relations with the Salesians in the following chapters.

342 *most likely by Krihisiwä*: In *The Feast* there is a memorable scene where Krihisiwä is cleaning and scraping the village plaza, urging all the others to join in and help. Headmen sometimes must lead by example.

343 *water was collected*: When they are confined inside the palisade they urinate at the back of their houses and defecate onto leaves, then throw the package over the wall or take it out the next day to discard in the woods.

344 *Amazonian bird*: It is known as *pajui* in Spanish and *mutum* in Portuguese. *Guan* is also used in the English language.

348 *"asking questions for a month!"*: Morton Fried, in his preface to Chagnon 1974a, wrote: "It blows the mind, mine at least, to know that Chag does not live among the Yanomamö merely with canoes and outboard motors and Coleman lamps and boxes of soft pencils and specifically selected notepaper, but with reams of IBM printouts!"

350 *leads to higher prestige*: Cultural success does not always lead to biological success, an exception to the general theoretical proposition developed by William Irons (Irons, 1979a).

351 *Yanomamö rules of etiquette*: This group of Patanowä-teri visitors had separated from Krihisiwä's group and by then was living a considerable distance away from Krihisiwä's people. By 1990 Krihisiwä had died, some say from an infected arrow wound he sustained sometime after my last visit to his village.

352 *away from his group*: Several of these victims were dispatched with assistance from others in the raiding party, but most of these killings were attributed to Möawä alone.

353 *More remote lineage members*: See Irons, 1979b; Chagnon, 1982.

356 *respect his father-in-law*: In-law avoidance is part of the prohibition against incest.

358 *my water supply*: Yanomamö family water supplies were usually kept in open cooking pots and contained debris, insects, fish scales, animal hair, etc. For sanitation reasons, I kept my own water supply in plastic jugs with screw-on tops.

359 *most of the day*: By "my house" I mean the section of the *shabono* they had provided for me, next to the headman.

361 *Dedeheiwä would be his mentor*: Dedeheiwä is shown in *Magical Death*, a film I shot in 1971. It is a dramatic documentation of Yanomamö shamanism and drug use.

361 *south of Mishimishimaböwei-teri*: I subsequently contacted the Yeisikorowä-teri by helicopter in 1990. They were in an extremely remote area in the then unknown Siapa River valley. They were also volatile and aggressive and were divided into at least three groups living *he borara*. I took a complete census with ID photographs of all three groups.

362 *was already menopausal*: The mother-in-law avoidance taboo seems to be intended to minimize the possibility that a young son-in-law might become sexually attracted to his wife's mother. Many women have marriageable daughters when they are in their early to mid-thirties and still sexually attractive.

366 *in an isolated and unacculturated village*: Mishimishimaböwei-teri always had 275 to 300 inhabitants during my studies and must have been close to 450 people a few years earlier before Sibarariwä and his followers fissioned away. In other areas, years after sustained contact with missionaries, formerly smaller villages now approach 500 or more inhabitants in some regions. They do not, however, all live under one roof in these changed circumstances but, generally, in smaller, nontraditional mud huts that are sometimes widely scattered up and down the river adjacent to the mission post. One can hardly call them a "single" community now.

366 *screamed at the Ironasi-teri*: Sibarariwä's community took the name Ironasi-teri for their group, which they later changed to Kedebaböwei-teri.

367 *he meant what he said*: A similar argument between women was filmed in 1971 when Asch and I documented an ax fight that broke out in this village. Asch and Chagnon, 1975.

370 *at least one war*: See Chagnon, 1990.

371 *so long as Möawä lived there*: After Möawä died in the late 1970s, a group of Mishimishimaböwei-teri men approached me in Mavaca to inquire if I would again start coming back to their village, explaining that Möawä had died and that they knew he was the reason I had stopped visiting them. They also went on to say that after his death, many Yanomamö from other villages had resumed visiting them. "Everybody is now happy with us and friendly again," they explained. Möawä was good at making war but bad at making peace.

Chapter 14. Twilight in Cultural Anthropology
PAGE

379 *precise quantification*: I specifically mean "any pair of related Yanomamö" who have at least one ancestor in common. The vast majority of Yanomamö are related in this way. See Chagnon, 1979, chapter 4, "quartiles of relatedness."

380 *political parties, etc.*: There are many theories about how this transformation occurred. Only a few of them focus on the social institutions that had to change for this to happen. One in particular that was seminal in my own thinking was Morton Fried's 1967 book, *The Evolution of Political Society*. Ironically, Fried was very much opposed to what I was doing with my "biological" analysis of Yanomamö genealogies and told me so when I asked him to write the foreword to my 1974 book, which he did. When Fried was a visiting professor at Michigan I took two courses from him that helped me refine my own views of the importance of kinship and its biological underpinnings in and its role in the evolution of political society.

381 *"it is not about biology"*: Sahlins (1976) and Alexander (1979) also refer to this characterization of Schneider's view of kinship, especially as presented in a 1972 article "What is kinship all about?" W. D. Hamilton gave a hypothetical scenario at a talk I attended in Ann Arbor to the effect that if people like Sahlins believed that kinship had nothing to do with biology, then he'd like to see their reaction to the nurse in charge of the pediatric ward when they came to claim their own baby: "Just take any one of them—they're all alike. Kinship has nothing to do with biology."

381 *his book* Sociobiology: Wilson, 1975.

384 *subordinate discipline*: She also expressed her cynical views of sociobiology at about this time. She said of Wilson something to the effect that when you study bugs you think like a bug.

385 *Evolutionary Biology*: Chagnon and Irons, 1979.

385 *"I've finally figured out"*: See Trivers, 1971; 1972; 1974 for some of the most important papers on evolutionary theory he has written.

386 *new theoretical insights*: Darwin's theory of evolution by natural selection was developed before the concept of the gene was known, that is the units through which natural selection operated. The concept of the gene revolutionized Darwin's theory of evolution by natural selection. Lamentably, the rediscovery of Mendel's work and the awareness of the gene had almost no

impact on anthropological theories of cultural evolution. Darwin's theory of evolution by natural selection applied only to living, reproducing, organisms. Cultures, which cultural anthropologists studied, were not living organisms. This led to fanciful arguments about analogy versus homology, that cultures "behaved" like living organisms, that the equivalent of "genes" might be some cultural element called "memes," etc. Perhaps the best solution was to simply look at culture change as an historical process different from biological evolution of living reproducing organisms.

386 *the auspices of the AAAS*: Some of the prominent biologists there included Richard Dawkins, George C. Williams, William D. Hamilton, and Stephen J. Gould. All but Gould were supporters of Wilson and sociobiology.

386 *rival to his theory*: This was abundantly clear in a later debate that Harris had with Harvard anthropologist Irven DeVore, who led the 1968 Harvard group's participation in the Chagnon-Irons presentations at the AAA meetings in Washington, D.C., in 1976. Harris's position was essentially if we don't stop sociobiology from spreading in anthropology, we will only have ourselves to blame! In Harris's view, sociobiology was likely to replace the extreme cultural determinism on which most of cultural anthropology "theory" was based.

386 *his recent book: The Selfish Gene*: Dawkins, 1976.

389 *extremely dangerous*: Cultural anthropologists never seem to tell us what is dangerous about any idea. Those who agree seem to take it on the authority of the speaker that the mere assertion that something is dangerous makes it dangerous.

393 *possible correlation*. William Irons proposed in his 1976 paper that "cultural success" in humans might be correlated to "biological success," presumably reproductive success especially in males. My 1988 paper in *Science* was a dramatic illustration of Irons's hypothesis.

393 *water with mercury*: Mercury was used to amalgamate the gold particles and cause them to drop to the bottom of the slurry, where they could more efficiently be recovered. The mercury killed fish and other wildlife and, of course, was toxic to humans.

394 *my college monograph*: The first edition was published in 1968, the second in 1977, and the third in 1983. I dropped this subtitle in the fourth edition, published in 1992. Subsequent editions were published without the subtitle.

394 *do harm to them*: The translation of the word into other languages caused problems because in some other languages the equivalent of "fierce" was more easily applied to animal-like behavior.

395 *Brazilian Yanomamö*: In 1993, six years after the Brazilian gold rush began, a group of Brazilian *garimpeiros* attacked and massacred many of the residents of Hashimo-teri, a Yanomamö village just inside Venezuela on the Venezuelan/Brazilian border. This is the only reliably documented case of lethal violence caused by the 1987 Brazilian gold rush directly affecting a group of Yanomamö in Venezuelan territory. See Chagnon, 1993a; 1993b.

397 *the following accusations*: The complete text of the ABA accusations and my

response to them were published in the newsletter of the AAA in 1989 and are available on Doug Hume's website.

397   *activist anthropologists*: Brazilian plans to divide the Brazilian Yanomamö into multiple small, isolated reserves were publicly revealed years before my *Science* article appeared or my ethnographic work became known outside the field of anthropology. This policy was never enacted, but the plan was said by my opponents in Brazil and the United States to have been *caused* by my anthropological publications on the Yanomamö. See *Survival International*, "Yanomami Timeline": "1978: Brazilian government proposes to split Yanomami area into 21 separate pockets of land; the plan would mean the destruction of the Yanomami if approved. Under pressure from NGOs supporting the Indians, the plan is shelved."

398   *object of the disagreement*: To this date not one of my anthropological critics has provided any evidence of empirical findings differing substantially from mine by providing comparable data from their own field research. No critic has provided mortality statistics on causes of death due to violence on the Yanomamö groups he has studied.

399   *the scientific approach*: See Gross and Levitt, 1994, for their concerns about the growing attacks on science and the scientific method by what they characterized as "the academic left."

400   *"The [postmodernist] model"*: R. D'Andrade, 1995. "Moral Models in Anthropology," *Current Anthropology*, 36:399–408.5.

Chapter 15. Confrontation with the Salesians
PAGE

404   *for a variety of reasons*: As early as the mid-1970s there were enough films about the Yanomamö made by filmmakers from several different countries that Jean Rouch, the famous French filmmaker and pioneer in cinéma vérité, held an international film festival in Paris. Since Timothy Asch and I had, by then, made some twenty films on the Yanomamö, we were invited to his festival, where our films occupied a central place.

404   *Italy and Germany*: In the late 1960s and 1970s a Spanish Salesian priest, Padre Gonzalez, attempted to establish a "tourist destination" in Platanal, the most remote Salesian mission on the Orinoco River. International flights from several European cities to "The Stone Age in Platanal" with a stopover in Caracas, were advertised in some tourist brochures. Padre Cocco was opposed to tourism on such a grand scale but seemingly went along with a more discreet version of it. Padre Cocco brought Hioduwä, the headman of the Iyäwei-teri at Ocamo, to Rome to meet the pope in the early 1960s, perhaps one of the first Yanomamö not only to leave Amazonas, but to travel to Europe.

405   *in university classrooms*: This film was distributed in 1975 and remained in its original format until 1997, when it was released as a much more elaborate 'interactive' film on CD-ROM, *Ax Fight Interactive*, in 1997 (Biella, Chagnon, and Seaman). The 1997 version included an immense amount of data

I had collected in Mishimishimaböwei-teri after the original film was shot. In 2012 a revised version of this film will be distributed by Pennsylvania State University's Media Sales Division.

405 *depredations of the miners*: In 1987 John Saffirio, a Consolata priest and anthropologist I had helped for several years, was visiting me in Santa Barbara, California. He received an international telephone call at my house from Dom Aldo Mangiano, the Consolata bishop of Roraima, who informed him that he could not return to his Yanomamö mission on the Catrimani River because *garimpeiros* had taken it over. He said that the government had also informed him that he had to withdraw his missionary staff from several of the Yanomamö villages where the Consolata order had missions. They had to be shut down because of the invasion by miners.

406 *Salesian missions in Venezuela*: Bórtoli was Padre Cocco's successor in about the mid-1970s.

408 *Puerto Ayacucho*: Chagnon, Bórtoli, and Eguillor, 1988.

410 *anthropologists resented me*: According to one of the IVIC researchers who attended an IVIC-wide meeting in the early 1970s, someone asked, "Why is it that the IVIC anthropologists dislike Chagnon so much?" She told me that Roche replied to the question with a brief retort: "They are all jealous of his academic accomplishments."

410 *other "leaders" with them*: In 1991 I took James Brooke, Latin American bureau chief for the *New York Times*, into one of the new Yanomamö villages that Charles Brewer and I had just contacted. When we left the Yanomamö area we passed through the Salesian mission at Ocamo. Brooke was asking questions in Spanish to one of the Yanomamö, a man I had known since he was a child. Padre Cocco had given him the Spanish name Francisco. While repacking I was listening as he related to Brooke how he and several other "leaders" accompanied a group of nuns to the OCAI office in Caracas to file a complaint against "Shaki"—my Yanomamö name. He said that a woman he did not know actually wrote out the complaint against me. He mentioned that the nuns asked *all* the Yanomamö in the party to sign their names on the complaint. He claimed that he and most of the others refused to sign the complaint, but that Dimanawä signed it with no hesitation.

411 *the "mistress"*: She was the lifetime consort of Carlos Andrés Pérez, by whom she had had several children, who were duly baptized in the Catholic Church. President Pérez's wife appeared at state functions with him but would typically discreetly withdraw after her official presence was no longer required. However, in a Catholic country it was politically unwise for a prominent politician to attempt to divorce a spouse to whom he was legally married in an official wedding ceremony in the Catholic Church and that, I was told, was why Pérez lived with Cecilia Matos and did not divorce his legal wife.

412 *mining operations*: There were, of course, many Venezuelan scientists who knew a great deal about Venezuela's mineral, lumber, ranching, etc. potential, but the national population at large was basically uninformed

about these and there were no popular calls to open up the frontiers of Venezuela's Amazonas . . . except for the short-lived program in the mid-1970s
known as Conquista del Sur.

412 *scientific researchers and missionaries*: Various groups of Venezuelan anthropologists had made two proposals to designate the area a reserve for
Indians but officials in the Venezuelan government appeared to have been
very skeptical about both of them and no action was taken. I was told that
one reason was that both of the proposals included suggestions or proposed
requirements that seemed to put the Venezuelan anthropologists in strategically important administrative positions that were not integrated into the
apparatus of the national bureaucracy. Venezuelan politicians were fearful
that the anthropologists were likely to turn this area into a political entity,
like some kind of indigenous "nation" that operated independently from the
Venezuelan government.

412 *some thirty-two thousand square miles*: ABC's *Prime Time Live* accompanied
me and Charles Brewer to this area and filmed CAP, who promised to establish a "protected" area in Venezuela. ABC produced a film that was shown
on U.S. television in 1991 and repeated six months later when the Venezuelan president established this protected area.

412 *minerals in this area*: The infamous "dossier" that Tierney and Martins circulated makes this charge.

414 *permanent Salesian mission*: After 1989 many at the Salesian Missions were
openly hostile to me and encouraged the Yanomamö at their missions to
steal from me. They began spreading lies about me—how I was now working for *garimpeiros*, that my ID photos were killing Yanomamö babies, etc.

414 *the Salesians to read*: See Chagnon, 1997, for a discussion of my "discovery"
that Ushubiriwä could read. In 1985, during the first year of a three-year
NSF project, I stopped at the village he then lived in. To my immense surprise, he could read the file I opened on my laptop computer that included
the names of everyone in his village . . . and the names of their deceased
parents, including his own father! He simply jabbed me in the ribs and giggled about it—we both now knew what the secret of "writing" was capable
of. He was not disturbed by the fact that I knew his dead father's name.
Indeed, he and everyone else assumed that I knew the names of every one
of their dead relatives, but I was extremely circumspect about using them
unless the circumstances permitted—as they sometimes do.

415 *during the argument*: One of the Venezuelans with Brewer filmed this discussion with an 8 mm camera.

415 *Teodardo Marcano*: Marcano was affiliated with a Venezuelan medical
program called Parima-Culebra. They were trying to start a local health
program for the Yanomamö and I periodically collaborated with them. I
hoped to help them create a successful rural health program for all of the
Yanomamö.

416 shabono *was located*: This was the village to which I had taken the German
ZDF-TV film crew five years earlier.

417 *they got sick*: Salesian attempts to "attract and reduce" this and other, related Shamatari groups of the Upper Mavaca began in the early 1970s, as
I explain in the fifth edition of *Yanomamö* (Chagnon, 1997). The tragic fate
of the Kedebaböwei-teri is spelled out in more detail in chapter 8 of *Yanomamö*.

417 *Yanomamö angry*: Finkers, 1994. The Salesians know that I will investigate
Ushubiriwä's death if I ever get back to the Mavaca area and find out what
the circumstances were and who was responsible for his death. This time,
the intent of my inquiry will be personal, not simply demographic. Finkers's article also gratuitously claims that I had promised Ushubiriwä a "new
outboard motor." This is a lie. When the Salesians give a Yanomamö a complicated item like an outboard motor, as they did in this case, they thereby
assume the responsibility of replacing parts and keeping it in good repair.
Salamone (2001) found this attack on me by Finkers to be detrimental to
my attempts to make peace with the Salesians at that time.

418 *shot and hacked to death*: Chagnon, 1993.

418 *one of the members*: Brewer later told me that this was the first time a non-
Venezuelan was included in a Venezuelan presidential commission.

418 *becoming a state*: Statehood for the Venezuelan Amazonas was officially
granted in 1996.

418 *the Salesians' official journal*: The Salesians have considerable control over
the printed news and the televised news. In the heated debate that took
place in 1993 one of the major Venezuelan television channels, Venevision,
scheduled a repeat broadcast of a recent documentary their film crew made
of the Charles Brewer, and some of the medical people we worked with
among the Yanomamö. When the Salesians learned of this, they pressured
the top executives of Venevision to kill the scheduled broadcast, outraging
the woman who produced and directed it, Marta Rodríguez. She tearfully
called Charles Brewer while I was there to explain that the repeat program
had been suddenly canceled, and she explicitly blamed the Salesians for
pressuring the Venevision executives to cancel the broadcast.

419 *Venezuela's Gaceta Oficial*: This Commission remained official for at least
three years. I want to emphasize this point because in the utter madness
that followed, one of the false claims made by both the Salesians and some
of my anthropological detractors was that this "presidential commission"
was *immediately* dissolved a day or so after being created and replaced
with a new one headed by the Salesian Missions and the Salesian bishop
of Amazonas. That is simply not true. In fact, the alleged replacement
presidential commission could not have been official without being so designated in the *Gaceta Oficial de Venezuela*, which it never was.

419 *a military coup*: A military coup by members of the air force was in fact
attempted in 1992 while I was living among the Yanomamö and I had difficulty getting out of Venezuela as a result. Many of the officers involved in
the failed coup had to flee and take refuge in other Latin American countries like Peru and Ecuador. Some were eventually allowed to come home

and resume their rank and activities in the Venezuelan Air Force, but at a price: Brewer told me that he believes they were compelled to give false testimony against us as part of a plan to impeach CAP and discredit his consort, Cecilia Matos. Some of them claimed, for instance, that they saw us doing "mysterious things," like paying undue attention to and guarding a large metal cylinder in one of their helicopters. This was taken as evidence that we were "guarding" a container filled with gold that we had illegally collected. The fact of the matter was that the top of a large cylinder of liquid nitrogen needed by the medical team had gotten lost, and the liquid nitrogen was slopping around and spilling out of the cylinder. If any liquid nitrogen had gotten onto our skin it would have instantly frozen the flesh. Some of us were trying to prevent that from happening.

420 *for the night*: Parima B had been, since the early 1960s, a very remote New Tribes Mission post very close to the Brazilian border. At about the time of the *garimpeiro*/Brazilian penetration of the immediately adjacent Brazilian territory in 1987, the Venezuelan military established a military post at Parima B and lengthened the dirt airstrip there. The military personnel were persistently attempting to seduce the Yanomamö women and their presence was a constant threat to the Yanomamö.

Chapter 16. Darkness in Cultural Anthropology
PAGE

423 *some in Europe*: See Salamone, 1997, pp. 97–98, for confirmation that the Salesians sent these.

424 *"just the opposite"*: Neither Lizot nor Eibl (Iranaeus Eibl-Eibesfeld) was able to provide data on Yanomamö mortality rates due to new diseases to refute my findings.

426 *no meaningful research*: I have heard from anthropology colleagues and journalists who work in southern Venezuela that Cardozo spends almost all of his time at the Salesian mission at Boca Mavaca and rarely spends time in villages that are not within the regular visiting orbit of the Salesians. Father Enzo Cappelletti (1994) asserts that there are three anthropologists among the Salesians who work among the Yanomamö. If Cardozo published anything in an anthropological journal in either Venezuela or the U.S. and other centers where anthropological research papers are normally published, I am confident I would know about it.

426 *by Terence Turner*: See Salamone, 1997b, for discussion of the development of the Chagnon-Salesian disagreement and the Salamone session of the 1994 AAA meetings and phone discussions with Turner.

427 *The President of Venezuela*: Turner, *Anthropology Newsletter*, May 1994, p. 48.

428 *Skomal's advice was incorrect*: William Irons was later told by John Cornman, Executive Director of the AAA, that giving equal space in the Newsletter was the "implicit policy" of the AAA. Cornman told Irons that they violated their policy of allowing a victim to respond in the same issue where s/he has been attacked, and said the AAA made a mistake in this case.

429 *did not inform me*: See Salamone, 1997b, for his discussion about having a phone discussion with Turner prior to the meetings.

429 *prominent leader in Brazil*: See Winkler, 1994, for the article she wrote that covered Salamone's session at the 1994 AAA meetings in Atlanta.

430 *Salamone's several*: Salamone, 1997a, 1997b, 2006. Michael D'Antonio interviewed Salamone in 2000 and reported: " 'The Salesians have educated every Venezuelan president in history and most of its other leaders,' explains Frank Salamone, an anthropologist at Iona College in New York. Salamone has worked for the Salesians and the order refers journalists with questions about the Yanomamo issue to him." Some of the most unprofessional and demeaning comments Salamone has made about me can be found in the interview he gave to Andrew Brown, author of *The Darwin Wars,* in the *Daily Telegraph Magazine* (March 3, 2001). These comments were made after Patrick Tierney's *Darkness in El Dorado* was published. Salamone supported Tierney's claims. Salamone, in short, represents the Salesians.

430 *Salamone states*: Salamone, *The Yanomami and Their Interpreters.*

431 *"his gold mining operation"*: Sometime between 1972, when I last collaborated with Brewer in the IVIC/University of Michigan biomedical research project, and about 1990, when we resumed our collaboration with the support of the Venezuelan president, Brewer had purchased an interest in a gold mining operation in Estado Bolivar, well outside of the Yanomamö area and where gold mining was legal. He was in the process of selling his interest in this mining concern when our collaboration began again in 1990. He never discussed his gold mining interests with me, but I became aware of them when an extremely critical and very political article by Leda Martins and Patrick Tierney appeared in the op-ed section of the *New York Times* in 1995 that attacked Brewer for alleged illegalities and destructive consequences of this gold mining operation.

432 *"forbade" the pilot*: The air taxi service that brought me into Abruwä-teri did not want to jeopardize their status as the only officially approved air taxi service for the Yanomamö area. Kobenawä's threat to make trouble for them was taken seriously by both the air taxi service and by the FUNAI office in Boa Vista. However, there were literally scores of bush pilots who would eagerly fly *garimpeiros* or anyone else into Yanomamö territory illegally.

432 *"Curiously, when I first"*: Dreger goes on to say that I wrote Raymond Hames an email about asking Tierney if he knew anything about this secret dossier, which he denied. Dreger had by then interviewed both Martins and Turner and references her following remarks to these interviews: "Notably, right about the time Chagnon was writing this to Hames in 1995, Patrick Tierney was introducing Leda Martins to Terence Turner, at the Pittsburgh airport (Martins 2009; confirmed in Terence Turner 2009). The three—Tierney, Martins, and Turner—would continue to meet several times there over the next few months. Within a few years, Martins went on to earn her Ph.D. in anthropology under Turner, and to publish criticisms of Chagnon." Dreger, 2011, p. 7.

435 *quietly be approved*: Unknown to the UFR rector, Alcida Ramos had been recently named as head of an important national council that controlled permissions for researchers, including anthropologists, to work in *any* indigenous tribal areas. It was highly unlikely that I would be allowed into the Brazilian Yanomamö area so long as she held this position.

435 *medical practitioners*: I had repeatedly tried to develop such a program with various Venezuelan medical groups, but there always seemed to be obstacles.

439 *the* New Yorker *published*: Tierney, 2000.

440 *hotel auditorium*: Others included Yvonne Maldonado, Magdalena Hurtado, Susan Lindee, Trudy Turner, and Sharon Kaufman.

440 *Jesus Cardozo*: Cardozo's "affiliation" is given as Venezuela's Office of Indigenous Affairs (OCAI) by at least one journalist, D. W. Miller, who writes for the *Chronicle of Higher Education*. He says "[Cardozo] announced that his agency was declaring a moratorium on permits for research in that nation's hinterland. . . . Some audience members gasped, as if realizing for the first time that the conflict over anthropological ethics is hardly academic." http://anthroniche.com/darkness_documents/0286.htm. It is doubtful that Cardozo officially represented OCAI or was an employee of OCAI.

440 *for the first night*: Most people who attend the large anthropology meetings like this one are practicing anthropologists, mostly employed by colleges and universities, but anyone who belongs to the American Anthropological Association by paying for a membership can attend.

441 *"The Fierce People"*: Terence Turner is a former student of Maybury-Lewis as is James Peacock, a former AAA president who was soon commissioned to investigate Tierney's accusations.

441 *denigrate me*: I heard from a former president of the World Wildlife Fund and the wife of a U.S. congressman about derogatory comments that a senior officer of Cultural Survival made to them about me.

442 *Peacock Committee*: The members of the Peacock Committee were Janet Chernela, Linda Green, Ellen Gruenbaum, Joe Watkins, Linda Whiteford, and Philip Walker. Although Peacock seemed to be the chair of the AAA Task Force, the chair was ultimately Jane Hill from the University of Arizona. Hill might have become chair after Peacock's report was written.

442 *Louise Lamphere*: This memo became known to the general public only in 2011 when Douglas Hume obtained a copy of it and posted it on his website: http://anthroniche.com/darkness_documents/0612.pdf.

442 *produced a report*: http://anthroniche.com/darkness_documents/0612.pdf.

443 *members of the task force*: They are Janet Chernela (Florida International University), Fernando Coronil (University of Michigan), Raymond Hames (University of Nebraska), Trudy Turner (University of Wisconsin, Milwaukee), and Joe Watkins (University of Oklahoma). http://anthroniche.com/darkness_documents/0577.pdf.

443 *El Dorado Task Force*: The Members of the El Dorado Task Force and the

justification for creating it are spelled out in an AAA document entitled "Working Papers of the American Anthropological Association El Dorado Task Force Submitted as a Preliminary Report" and can be accessed at http://anthroniche.com/darkness_documents/0577.pdf. The confidential Peacock Report members, what they considered, and their recommendations can be found at http://anthroniche.com/darkness_documents/0612.pdf.

444 *relevant sources*: Hagen, Price, and Tooby, 2001, and Tooby, 2000.

444 *were examined*: See Appendices VII and VIII in Hagen, Price, and Tooby, 2001.

444 *"attack dog"*: http://anthroniche.com/darkness_documents/0511.htm.

444 *not supported*: See especially Alberts, 2000, for the statement made as president of the National Academy of Sciences.

445 *patently false*: Tooby, 2000.

445 *I started putting*: Tooby, 2000, *Slate*, October 25, 2000.

445 *were inaccurate*: Reprinted in Appendix II, p. 60, of Hagen, Price, and Tooby, 2001.

447 *the young Balthasar*: William Oliver, former Chairman of the Pediatrics Department at the University of Michigan and a participant in several of our expeditions, sent a letter to the *New Yorker* challenging the data in Tierney's article, "The Fierce Anthropologist." Oliver's letter was published in a subsequent issue of the *New Yorker* and can be found also in the UCSB Preliminary Report as Appendix X, pp. 81–86. It is a concise and accurate listing of the critical medical events, including Tierney's fanciful and dishonest account of Roberto Balthasar. Oliver flatly says, "His report is factually incorrect." Oliver then writes, "On February 13, 1968, Baltasar [sic] brought his one-year-old son, Roberto, to the Ocamo Mission for treatment. Neel wrote that the infant had a very high fever, intense conjunctival infection, extreme shortness of breath and findings of pneumonia but no rash. He was given penicillin, tetramycin, a cardiac stimulant and quarantined in the infirmary. Following a short phase of improvement, his condition deteriorated. He died on February 15, 1968. There is no record of Vitalino Baltasar [sic] or his son receiving measles vaccine. In retrospect, it is likely that both had wild measles, but atypical for absence of a classical rash."

449 *investigators have demonstrated*: See, for example, Tooby, 2000, Hagen et al., 2001, and Dreger, 2011.

449 *following words*: http://chronicle.com/article/National-Academy-of-Sciences/9116/.

450 *They warned*: Some of the dangers of spreading false information about the safety of vaccines in third-world countries are spelled out in the Referendum: http://anthroniche.com/darkness_documents/0438.htm.

450 *10 to 1*: See Tooby, 2000, Katz, 2000, on the safety record of the Edmonston B vaccine.

450 *critical article*: "Guilt by Association: The Culture of Accusation and the

American Anthropological Association's Investigation of Darkness in El Do-rado," *American Anthropologist* 106, no. 4 (December 2004).

450 *task force*: http://anthroniche.com/darkness_documents/0438.htm.

450 *smaller margin*: http://chronicle.com/article/Anthropologists-Rescind -Report/121225/.

451 *who visited Mavaca*: The AAA Task Force who visited the Mavaca area to investigate Tierney's claims prevented a legitimate AAA task force member from going there, Raymond Hames, who resigned as a consequence. But among the AAA visitors to Mavaca was Terence Turner, who was *not* a mem-ber of the AAA Task Force and had not done ethnographic work among the Yanomamö. But he, as a concerned advocate of Native Rights, seemed to be able to ignore AAA rules and policies with nobody raising issues.

454 *"Marlowe said"*: Nicholas Wade, *New York Times*, Science section, Dec. 13, 2010.

454 *Dreger writes*: Dreger, 2011, pp. 12–13.

454 *"Burn this message"*: Obtained via email from Hrdy, November 6, 2009; used with Hill's permission from November 6, 2009; emphasis in original.

455 *"I can't imagine"*: Mann, 2009.

455 *article in* Human Nature *in 2011*: Dreger, 2011.

455 *witch hunt*: Lancaster and Hames, 2011.

456 *preparing the infamous dossier*: While Martins initially acknowledged to Dreger in 2009 that she wrote the dossier, she subsequently changed her story and told Dreger that Tierney wrote it and explained that all she did was translate it into Portuguese and then clandestinely made it available to FUNAI and activists who were trying to prevent me from conducting re-search among the Brazilian Yanomamö. This raises the question of whether she lied to Dreger and that the actual reason for changing her story was that she was soon to go up for a tenure review and if it was on record (in Tierney's book) that she wrote the dossier, this might jeopardize her bid for tenure at Pitzer College.

Bibliography

Albert, B. 1989. "Yanomamö 'Violence': Inclusive Fitness or Ethnographer's Representation?" *Current Anthropology* 30:637–40.

Alberts, B. 2000. A statement from Bruce Alberts, President of the National Academy of Sciences: "Setting the Record Straight regarding Darkness in El Dorado." Washington, DC: National Academy of Sciences. (November 9.) Available at http://www.nku.edu/~humed1/darkness_in_el_dorado/document/0538.htm.

Ales, C. 1984. "Violence et ordre social dans une société amazonienne: Les Yanomami du Venezuela." *Etudes Rurales* 89–114.

Alexander, Richard D. 1974. "The Evolution of Social Behavior." *Annual Review of Ecology and Systematics* 5:325–83.

Alexander, Richard D. 1977. "Natural Selection and the Analysis of Human Sociality." In *The Changing Scenes in Natural Sciences, 1776–1976* (pp. 283–337). Academy of Natural Sciences, Special Publication 12.

Alexander, Richard D. 1978. "Natural Selection and Societal Laws." In *The Foundations of Ethics and Its Relationship to Science.* Vol. 3, *Morals, Science, and Society.* T. Engelhardt and D. Callahan, eds. (pp. 138–82). Hastings-on-Hudson, NY: Hastings Institute.

Alexander, Richard D. 1979. *Darwinism and Human Affairs.* London: Pittman. Also published by University of Washington Press.

Alexander, Richard D. 1987. *The Biology of Moral Systems.* New York: Aldine de Gruyter.

American Society of Human Genetics. 2002. "Response to Allegations against James V. Neel in *Darkness in El Dorado,* by Patrick Tierney." ASHG Commentary. *American Journal of Human Genetics* 70:1–10.

Asch, Timothy, and Napoleon A. Chagnon. 1970. *The Feast.* Film/DVD. Penn State Media Sales, University Park, PA.

Asch, Timothy, and Napoleon A. Chagnon. 1975. *The Ax Fight.* Film/DVD. Penn State Media Sales, University Park, PA.

Axelrod, R., and William Hamilton. 1981. "The Evolution of Cooperation." *Science* 211:1390–96.

Bailey, Frederick G. 1969. *Stratagems and Spoils: A Social Anthropology of Politics.* Schocken Books. New York.

Banton, Michael B., ed. 1965. *Political Systems and the Distribution of Power.* A.S.A. Monographs 2. Tavistock Publications. London.

Barnes, John. 1971. *Three Styles in the Study of Kinship.* Berkeley: University of California Press.

Barth, Fredrick. 1966. *Models of Social Organization.* Royal Anthropological Institute, Occasional Paper No. 23. London: Royal Anthropological Institute.

Barth, Fredrick. 1967. "On the Study of Social Change," *American Anthropologist,* 69:661–69.

Becher, Hans. 1960. *Die Surára und Pakidái: Zwei Yanomámi-Stämme in Nordwestsbrasiliens.* Mitteilungen aus dem Museum für Völkerkunde. Hamburg.

Bertram, B., et al, eds. 1982. *Current Problems in Sociobiology.* Cambridge: Cambridge University Press.

Betzig, Laura. 1986. *Despotism and Differential Reproduction.* New York: Aldine.

Biocca, E. 1996. *Yanomama: The Story of Helena Valero, a Girl Kidnapped by Amazonian Indians.* [As told to Ettore Biocca.] New York: Kodansha International. [First English translation, 1970, E.P. Dutton.]

Borofsky, Robert, with Bruce Albert et al. 2005. *Yanomami: The Fierce Controversy and What We Can Learn from It.* Berkeley: University of California Press.

Bromley, Myron. 1981. "A Grammar of Lower Grand Valley Dani." *Pacific Linguistics,* Series C, No. 63.

Brown, Andrew. 2000. *The Darwin Wars.* London: Touchstone.

Brown, Andrew. 2001. "The Fierce Anthropologists." *Daily Telegraph,* March 3, 2001.

Brown, Donald. 1991. *Human Universals.* New York: McGraw-Hill.

Campbell, B., ed. 1972. *Sexual Selection and the Descent of Man, 1871–1971.* Chicago: Aldine.

Carneiro, Robert L. 1961. "Slash-and-Burn Cultivation Among the Kuikuru and Its Implications for Cultural Development in the Amazon Basin." In *The Evolution of Horticultural Systems in Native South America: Causes and Consequences: A Symposium.* Johannes Wilbert, ed. Caracas: Anthropologica, Supplement Publication 2:47–67.

Carneiro, Robert L. 1970. "A Theory of the Origin of the State." *Science* 169:733–38.

Carneiro, Robert L. 1979. "Tree felling with the stone ax: An experiment carried out among the Yanomamo Indians of Southern Venezuela." In *Ethnoarchaeology: Implications of Ethnography for Archaeology.* C. Kramer, ed. (pp. 21–58). New York: Columbia University Press.

Carneiro, Robert L. 1987. "Further Reflections on Resource Concentration and Its Role in the Rise of the State." In *Studies in the Neolithic and Urban Revolutions: The V. Gordon Childe Colloquium, Mexico, 1986.* Linda Manzanilla, ed. BAR International Series, 349.

Carneiro, Robert L. 1998. "What Happened at the Flashpoint? Conjectures on Chiefdom Formation at the Very Moment of Conception." In *Chiefdoms and*

Chieftaincy. Elsa Redmond, ed. (pp. 18–42). Gainesville: University Press of Florida.

Carneiro da Cunha, M. M. 1989. "Letter to the Editor." *Anthropology Newsletter, American Anthropological Association.* January, p. 3.

Chagnon, Napoleon A. 1966. *Yanomamö Warfare, Social Organization and Marriage Alliances.* Ph.D. dissertation, University of Michigan. University Microfilms. Ann Arbor, MI.

Chagnon, Napoleon A. 1968a. *Yanomamö: The Fierce People.* Case Studies in Cultural Anthropology. New York: Holt, Rinehart & Winston.

Chagnon, Napoleon A. 1968b. "The Culture-Ecology of Shifting (Pioneering) Cultivation Among the Yanomamö Indians." In *Proceedings, III International Congress of Anthropological and Ethnological Sciences.* Tokyo, 1968. 3:249–55.

Chagnon, Napoleon A. 1968c. "Yanomamö Social Organization and Warfare." In *War: The Anthropology of Armed Conflict and Aggression.* Morton Fried, Marvin Harris, and Robert Murphy, eds. (pp. 109–59). Garden City, NY: Natural History Press.

Chagnon, Napoleon A., P. LeQuesne, and J. Cook. 1971. "Yanomamö Hallucinogens: Anthropological, Botanical, and Chemical Findings." *Current Anthropology* 12:72–74.

Chagnon, Napoleon A. 1972. "Social Causes for Population Fissioning: Tribal Social Organization and Genetic Microdifferentiation." In *The Structure of Human Populations.* G. A. Harrison and A. J. Boyce, eds. (pp. 252–82). Oxford: Clarendon Press.

Chagnon, Napoleon A. 1973. *Magical Death.* Film/DVD, Penn State Media Sales, University Park, PA.

Chagnon, Napoleon A. 1974a. *Studying the Yanomamö.* New York: Holt, Rinehart & Winston.

Chagnon, Napoleon A. 1974b. "Yanomamö." In *Primitive Worlds.* National Geographic Society Special Publication Series 127:141–83.

Chagnon, Napoleon A. 1975. "Genealogy, Solidarity, and Relatedness: Limits to Local Group Size and Patterns of Fissioning in an Expanding Population." In *Yearbook of Physical Anthropology,* vol. 19 (pp. 95–110). American Anthropological Association, Washington, DC.

Chagnon, Napoleon A., and Timothy Asch, 1976. *Jaguar: A Yanomamö Twin-Cycle Myth.* Film/DVD. Penn State Media Sales, University Park, PA.

Chagnon, Napoleon A. 1977. *Yanomamö: The Fierce People.* 2nd ed. New York: Holt, Rinehart & Winston.

Chagnon, Napoleon A., and William Irons, eds. 1979. *Evolutionary Biology and Human Social Behavior: An Anthropological Perspective.* Scituate, MA: Duxbury Press.

Chagnon, Napoleon A. 1979a. "Mate Competition and Village Fissioning Among the Yanomamö Indians." In *Evolutionary Biology and Human Social Behavior: An Anthropological Perspective.* Napoleon A. Chagnon and William Irons, eds. (pp. 86–132). Scituate, MA: Duxbury Press.

Chagnon, Napoleon A. 1979b. "Is Reproductive Success Equal in Egalitarian Societies?" In *Evolutionary Biology and Human Social Behavior: An Anthropological Perspective.* Napoleon A. Chagnon and William Irons, eds. (pp. 374–401). Scituate, MA: Duxbury Press.

Chagnon, Napoleon A., and Paul E. Bugos, Jr. 1979. "Kin Selection and Conflict: An Analysis of a Yanomamö Ax Fight" In *Evolutionary Biology and Human Social Behavior: An Anthropological Perspective.* Napoleon A. Chagnon and William Irons, eds. (pp. 213–38). Scituate, MA: Duxbury Press.

Chagnon, Napoleon A. 1980. "Highland New Guinea Models in the South American Lowlands." *Working Papers on South American Indians, Studies in Hunting and Fishing in the Neotropics.* Kenneth Kensinger, Bennington College, series ed. Raymond Hames, issue No. 2.

Chagnon, Napoleon A. 1982. "Sociodemographic Attributes of Nepotism in Tribal Populations: Man the Rule Breaker." In *Current Problems in Sociobiology.* Brian Bertram et al., eds. (pp. 291–318). Cambridge: Cambridge University Press.

Chagnon, Napoleon A., and James R. Bryant. 1984. "KINDEMCOM: The Fourth Style in the Study of Human Kinship Relationships." [An MS/DOS computer program and user's manual for analyzing genealogies and kinship relationships. Originally distributed privately as floppy disks at cost, but discontinued in about 1990.]

Chagnon, Napoleon A., and Raymond Hames, 1984. "The Social Effects of Mortality and Divorce on the Yanomamö Nuclear Family: Kinship, Fosterage, and Marriage Implications for Tribal Societies." *National Science Foundation Research Grant BNS83-19644, 1984–1987.*

Chagnon, Napoleon A. 1988. "Life Histories, Blood Revenge, and Warfare in a Tribal Population." *Science* 239:985–92. http://www.nku.edu/%7Ehumed1/darkness_in_el_dorado/documents/0606.pdf.

Chagnon, Napoleon A., José Bórtoli, and Maria Eguillor. 1988. "Una Aplicación Antropológica Práctica Entre Los Yanomami: Colaboración Entre Misioneros y Antropólogos." *La Iglesia En Amazonas* (pp. 75–83). Vicariato Apostolico de Puerto Ayacucho, Venezuela.

Chagnon, Napoleon A. 1989. "On Yanomamö Violence: A Reply to Albert." *Current Anthropology* 31:49–53.

Chagnon, Napoleon A. 1989a. "To the Editor" [Response to ABA denunciation of 1988 *Science* article] *Anthropology Newsletter,* 12 January 1989a, pp. 3 & 24. American Anthropological Association. Washington, D.C. See text of the ABA statement and my response: http://anthroniche.com/darkness_documents/0560.pdf.

Chagnon, Napoleon A. 1990. "Reproductive and Somatic Conflicts of Interest in the Genesis of Violence and Warfare Among Tribesmen." In *The Anthropology of War.* J. Haas, ed. (pp. 77–104). Cambridge: Cambridge University Press.

Chagnon, Napoleon A. 1991. "GIS, GPS, Political History and Geo-demography of the Aramamisi Yanomamö Expansion." In *Applications of Space-Age Tech-*

nology in Anthropology. C. A. Behrens and T. Sever, eds. (pp. 35–62). Stennis Space Center, MS: NASA, Science and Technology Laboratory. John C. Stennis Space Center.

Chagnon, Napoleon A. 1993a. "Covering Up the Yanomamö Massacre." *New York Times*, op-ed, October 23, 1993 (p. 13). Available at Doug Hume's website, http://www.nku.edu/~humed1/.

Chagnon, Napoleon A. 1993b. "Killed by Kindness?" *Times Literary Supplement*, December 24, 1993 (pp. 11–12). [Invited essay by TLS editors.] Available at Doug Hume's website, http://www.nku.edu/~humed1/.

Chagnon, Napoleon A., and Charles Brewer-Carías. 1994. "Response to Cappelletti and Turner." *Anthropology Newsletter*, September 1994.

Chagnon, Napoleon A. 1995. "L'ethnologie du déshonneur: Brief Response to Lizot." *American Ethnologist* 22(1):187–89.

Chagnon, Napoleon A. 1996. "Chronic Problems in Understanding Tribal Violence and Warfare." In *Genetics of Criminal and Antisocial Behaviour* (pp. 202–36). Ciba Foundation Symposium 194. New York: John Wiley.

Chagnon, Napoleon A. 1997. *Yanomamö*. 5th ed. Fort Worth, TX: Harcourt, Brace.

Chagnon, Napoleon A. 2012. *Yanomamö*. 6th ed. Wadsworth. CENGAGE Learning. Belmont, CA. [Copyright is given as 2013.]

Cocco, Luiz. 1972. *Iyëwei-teri: Quince años entre los Yanomamos*. Librería Editorial Salesiana. [Caracas.]

Clausewitz, Karl von. 1832. *On War*. Berlin: Dummlers Verlag.

Cockburn, Alexander. 1991. "Beat the Devil: Half Century: Half Full? Half Empty? Full of it Anyway," *Nation* 252(24):839.

Conklin, Harold. 1961. "The Study of Shifting Cultivation." *Current Anthropology* 2:27–61.

Cooper, James Fenimore. 1826. *The Last of the Mohicans*.

Daly, Martin, and Margo Wilson. 1988. "Evolutionary Social Psychology and Family Homicide." *Science* 242:519–24.

D'Antonio, Michael. 2000. "Napoleon Chagnon's War of Discovery." *Los Angeles Times Magazine*, January 30, 2000.

Da Rocha, F. J., R. S. Spielman, and J. V. Neel. 1974. "A Comparison of Gene Frequencies and Anthropometric Distance Matrices in Seven Villages of Four Indian Tribes." *Human Biology* 46: 295–310.

Davis, Shelton, and Robert Mathews. 1976. *The Geological Imperative: Anthropology and Development in the Amazon Basin of South America*. Cambridge, MA: Anthropological Resource Center.

Dawkins, Richard. 1976. *The Selfish Gene*. Oxford: Oxford University Press.

Dawkins, Richard. 1979. "Twelve Misunderstandings of Kin Selection." *Zeitschrift für Tierpsychologie* 51:184–200.

Dawkins, Richard. 1986. *The Blind Watchmaker: Why the Evidence of Evolution Reveals a Universe Without Design*. New York: Norton.

Dawkins, Richard. 2012. "The Descent of Edward Wilson," a review of *The Social Conquest of Earth*, by Edward O. Wilson in *Prospect*, 2012, May 24, Issue 195.

D.E.R. (Documentary Educational Resources). Film Distributor. Watertown, MA.

Diamond, Jared M. 1987. "The Worst Mistake in the History of the Human Race." *Discover Magazine* 8:64–66.

Diamond, Jared M. 1997. *Guns, Germs, and Steel: The Fates of Human Societies.* New York: Norton.

Dickemann, Mildred. 1979. "Female Strategies, Reproductive Strategies, and Social Stratification: A Preliminary Model." In *Evolutionary Biology and Human Social Behavior: An Anthropological Perspective.* Napoleon A. Chagnon and William Irons, eds. (pp. 321–67). Scituate, MA: Duxbury Press.

Dickemann, Mildred. 1981. "Paternal Confidence and Dowry Competition: A Biocultural Analysis of Purdah." In *Natural Selection and Social Behavior: Recent Research and New Theory.* Richard D. Alexander and Donald W. Tinkle, eds. (pp. 417–38).

Dimanawä, César. 1990. "Open Letter to Napoleon Chagnon." In *La Iglesia en Amazonas* 11(49): 20.

Divale, William T. and Marvin Harris. 1976. "Population, Warfare, and the Male Supremicist Complex." *American Anthropologist* 78:521–38.

Dreger, Alice. 2011. "*Darkness's* Descent on the American Anthropological Association: A Cautionary Tale." *Human Nature,* February 16, 2011, http://www.springerlink.com/content/1936-4776.

Dreger, Alice. Unpublished ms. *Galileo's Middle Finger: Science and Identity Politics in the Internet Age.*

Durkheim, Emile. 1893. *Division of Labor in Society.* G. Simpson, trans. New York: Macmillan (1933).

Durkheim, Emile. 1895. *The Rules of the Sociological Method.* S. Solovay and J. Mueller, trans. New York: Free Press (1938).

Durkheim, Emile 1897. *Suicide.* J. Spaulding and G. Simpson, trans. New York: Free Press (1951).

Edwards, Elizabeth. 2010. "Napoleon Chagnon, Anthropologist, Discusses His Dramatic Career from Northern Michigan." In *My North,* August 3, 2010, http://www.mynorth.com/My-North/August-2010/Napoleon-Chagnon-Anthropologist-Discusses-Controversial-Career-from-Northern-Michigan/.

Ellingson, Terry J. 2001. *The Myth of the Noble Savage.* Berkeley: University of California Press.

Ember, C. R. 1975. "Residential Variation among Hunter-Gatherers." *Behavior Science Research* 10:199–227.

Ember, C. R. 1978. "Myths about Hunter-Gatherers." *Ethnology* 17:439–48.

Engels, Friedrich. 1884. *Origin of the Family, Private Property, and the State.* Ernest Untermann, trans. Moscow: Foreign Languages Publishing House (1954).

Ferguson, B. 1989. "Do Yanomamö Killers Have More Kids?" *American Ethnologist* 16:564–65.

Ferguson, B. 1995. *Yanomami Warfare.* Santa Fe, NM: School for American Research Press.

Finkers, Juan. 1994. "Acclaraciones al Sr. Chagnon." *La Iglesia en Amazonas*, December 1994.

Fisher, R. A. 1930. *The Genetical Theory of Natural Selection.* Oxford: Clarendon Press (pp. 136–37).

Fortes, Meyer. 1969. *Kinship and the Social Order: The Legacy of Lewis Henry Morgan.* Chicago: Aldine.

Fox, Robin. 1967. *Kinship and Marriage.* Baltimore: Penguin.

Freeman, Derek. 1955. *Iban Agriculture: A Report on the Shifting Cultivation of Hill Rice of the Iban of Sarawak.* London: H. M. Stationery Office.

Freeman, Derek. 1983. *Margaret Mead and Samoa: The Making and Unmaking of an Anthropological Myth.* Cambridge, MA: Harvard University Press.

Fried, Morton. 1967. *The Evolution of Political Society.* New York: Random House.

Gardner, Robert. *Dead Birds.* 1964. Sound, color, 84 min. Massachusetts: Documentary Education Resources.

Glenn, D. and T. Bartlett, 2009. "Rebuttal of Decade-Old Accusations Against Researchers Roils Anthropology Meeting Anew." *Chronicle of Higher Education*, December 3, 2009.

Gregor, Thomas A., and Daniel R. Gross. 2002. "Anthropology and the Search for the Enemy Within." *Chronicle of Higher Education*, July 26, 2002.

Gregor, Thomas A., and Daniel R. Gross. 2004. " 'Guilt by Association': The Culture of Accusation and the American Anthropological Association's Investigation of *Darkness in El Dorado.*" *American Anthropologist* 106(4):687–98.

Gross, Daniel. 1973. *Peoples and Cultures of Native South America: An Anthropological Reader.* Garden City, NY: Natural History Press.

Gross, Paul. 2001. "Exorcising Sociobiology," pp. 24 ff, *New Criterion*, vol. 19, February 2001. New York, N.Y.

Gross, Paul, and Norman Levitt. 1994. *Higher Superstition: The Academic Left and Its Quarrels with Science.* Baltimore: Johns Hopkins University Press.

Haas, Jonathan. 1990. *The Anthropology of War.* School of American Research. Cambridge University Press. Cambridge, U.K.

Hagen, Edward, Michael Price, and John Tooby. 2001. Preliminary report, Department of Anthropology, University of California, Santa Barbara, http://www.anth.ucsb.edu/ucsbpreliminaryreport.pdf.

Hames, Raymond. 1979. "A Comparison of the Efficiencies of the Shotgun and Bow." *Neotropical Forest Hunting, Human Ecology* 7:219–52.

Hames, Raymond. 1989. "Time, Efficiency, and Fitness in the Amazonian Protein Quest." *Research in Economic Anthropology* 11:43–85.

Hames, Raymond. 1996. "Costs and Benefits of Monogamy and Polygyny for Yanomamö Women." *Ethology and Sociobiology* 17:1–19.

Hames, Raymond, William Oliver, and Napoleon Chagnon. 2005. "Growth, Development, and Health of Yanomamö Orphans in Relation to Parental Loss." Paper presented at the 14th Annual Meeting of the Human Behavior and Evolution Society, Austin, Texas, June 6, 2005.

Hamilton, W. D. 1964. "The Genetical Evolution of Social Behaviour I and II." *Journal of Theoretical Biology* 7:1–16, 17–52.

Harner, M. 1962. "Jívaro Souls." *American Anthropologist* 64:258–72.

Harner, M. 1968. "The Sound of Rushing Water." *Natural History* 77(6):28–33, 60–61.

Harner, M. 1972. *The Jívaro: People of the Sacred Waterfalls.* New York: Natural History Press.

Harris, Marvin. 1968. *The Rise of Anthropological Theory.* New York: T. Y. Crowell.

Headland, Thomas N. 2000. "When Did the Measles Epidemic Begin among the Yanomami?" http://www.sil.org/~headlandt/measles.htm.

Heider, Karl. 1970. *The Dugum Dani: A Papuan Culture in the Highlands of West New Guinea.* Viking Fund Publications in Anthropology No. 49. New York: Wenner-Gren Foundation.

Heider, Karl. 1997. *The Grand Valley Dani: Peaceful Warriors.* Case Studies in Cultural Anthropology. New York: Holt, Rinehart & Winston.

Hobbes, Thomas. 1981. *Leviathan.* New York: Penguin English Library (1651).

Hölldobler, Bert, and Edward O. Wilson. 1990. *The Ants.* Harvard University Press. Cambridge, MA.

Hrdy, Sarah Blaffer. 1977. "Infanticide as a Primate Reproductive Strategy." *American Scientist.* 65:40–49.

Hurtado, Magdalena. 2000. Statement read by Professor Magdalena Hurtado at the AAA Meetings, San Francisco, November 16, 2000. In Hagen, Price, and Tooby, *UCSB Preliminary Report* (pp. 89–90). Appendix XII.

Irons, William. 1979a. "Cultural and Biological Success." In *Evolutionary Biology and Human Social Behavior: An Anthropological Perspective.* Napoleon A. Chagnon and William Irons, eds. (pp. 257–72). Scituate, MA: Duxbury Press.

Irons, William. 1979b. "Investment and Primary Social Dyads." In *Evolutionary Biology and Human Social Behavior: An Anthropological Perspective.* Napoleon A. Chagnon and William Irons, eds. (pp. 181–213). Scituate, MA: Duxbury Press.

Irons, William. 1998. "Adaptively Relevant Environments Versus the Environment of Evolutionary Adaptedness." *Evolutionary Anthropology* 4:194–203.

Jank, Margaret. 1977. *Mission: Venezuela.* Florida: Brown Gold Publications Bookroom.

Katz, Samuel. 2000. Open email to recipients of the Turner-Sponsel 2000 email. In: Hagen, Price, and Tooby, Appendix I, p. 59.

Keeley, Lawrence H. 1996. *War Before Civilization: The Myth of the Peaceful Savage.* Oxford: Oxford University Press.

Keesing, Roger M. 1975. *Kin Groups and Social Structure.* New York: Holt, Rinehart & Winston.

Kemp, G., and Douglas P. Fry, eds. 2004. *Keeping the Peace: Conflict Resolution and Peaceful Societies Around the World.* New York: Routledge.

King's College Sociobiology Group, eds. 1982. *Current Problems in Sociobiology,* Cambridge, Cambridge University Press.

Knauft, Bruce. 1987. "Reconsidering Violence in Simple Human Societies," *Current Anthropology*, vol. 28, pp. 457–500.

Kroeber, Alfred. 1948. *Anthropology.* New York: Harcourt, Brace, & Co.

Kroeber, Alfred L. 1949. "The Chibcha." In *Handbook of South American Indians,* Julian Steward, ed., vol. 2 (pp. 899–910). New York: Cooper Square (1963).

Lahr, Marta M. 1996. *The Evolution of Modern Human Diversity: A Study in Cranial Variation.* Cambridge: Cambridge University Press.

Lahr, Marta M., and Richard V. S. Wright. 1996. "The question of robusticity and the relationship between cranial size and shape in *Homo sapiens." Journal of Human Evolution* 31:157–91.

Lancaster, Jane B., and Raymond Hames. 2011. "Statement on the Publication of Alice Dreger's Investigation, 'Darkness's Descent on the American Anthropological Association: A Cautionary Tale.'" *Human Nature,* February 19, 2011, http://www.springerlink.com/content/1936-4776.

Larson, Gordon F. 1987. *The Structure and Demography of the Cycle of Warfare Among the Ilaga Dani of Irian Jaya, Volumes I and II.* Ph.D. dissertation, University of Michigan, Ann Arbor. University Microfilms International.

Leach, Edmund, 1954. *Political Systems of Highland Burma.* Boston: Beacon Press.

Lee, Richard B., and Irven DeVore, eds. 1968. *Man the Hunter.* Chicago: Aldine.

Levi-Strauss, Claude. 1949. *The Elementary Structures of Kinship,* 1969 English translation. Boston: Beacon Press.

Levi-Strauss, Claude. 1956. "Les organisations dualistes existent-elles?" *Bijdragen tot de Taal-, Land-, en Volkenkunde* 112:99–128.

Lizot, Jacques. 1976. *Le Cercle de Feux.* Paris: Editions du Sueil. Published in English in 1985 as *Tales of the Yanomami.* Cambridge: Cambridge University Press, Cambridge Series in Social Anthropology.

Lizot, Jacques. 1976. "The Yanomami in the Face of Ethnocide." Copenhagen, IWGIA.

Lizot, J. 1989. "Sobre la guerra: Una respuesta a N. Chagnon (*Science,* 1988)." *La Iglesia en Amazonas* 44:23–34.

Lizot, J. 1994. "On Warfare: An Answer to N.A. Chagnon." *American Ethnologist* 21:841–58.

McCombe, Leonard, Evon Z. Vogt, and Clyde Kluckhohn. 1951. *Navaho Means People.* Cambridge, MA: Harvard University Press.

McLennan, John F. 1865. *Primitive Marriage.* Edinburgh: Adam & Charles Black.

Malinowski, Bronislaw. 1929. *The Sexual Life of Savages in Northwestern Melanesia.* London: George Routledge.

Mann, Charles. 2009. "Chagnon Critics Overstepped Bounds, Historian Says." *Science* 326: 1466, December 11, 2009.

Martins, Leda, and P. Tierney. 1995. "El Dorado, Lost Again?" *New York Times,* Op-Ed. April 7, 1995.

Maybury-Lewis, D. 1965. "Prescriptive Marriage Systems." *Southwestern Journal of Anthropology* 21:207–30.

Maybury-Lewis, D. 1965. *The Savage and the Innocent.* Boston: Beacon Press.

Maybury-Lewis, D. 1979. *Dialectical Societies: The Gê and Bororo of Central Brazil.* Harvard Studies in Cultural Anthropology. Cambridge, MA.

Maynard-Smith, John. 1964. "Group Selection and Kin Selection." *Nature* 20(4924):1145–47.

Meggitt, Mervyn. 1977. *Blood Is Their Argument: Warfare Among Mae Enga Tribesmen of the New Guinea Highlands.* Palo Alto, CA: Mayfield Press.

Moore, J. H. 1990. "The Reproductive Success of Cheyenne War Chiefs: A Contrary Case to Chagnon's Yanomamo." *Current Anthropology* 31:322–30.

Morgan, John. 1852. *The Life and Adventures of William Buckley, thirty-two years a wanderer amongst the aborigines of then unexplored country round Port Phillip, now the province of Victoria,* Tasmania: A. Macdougall. [See also the 1979 reprint of this work by Caliban Books, Sussex, UK]

Morgan, Lewis Henry. 1851. *The League of Ho-de'-no-sau-nee, or Iroquois.* Rochester: Sage & Brother.

Morgan, Lewis Henry. 1870. *Systems of Consanguinity and Affinity of the Human Family.* Washington: Smithsonian Institution.

Morgan, Lewis Henry. 1877. *Ancient Society.* New York: World.

Murdock, George P. 1951. *Outline of South American Cultures.* Behavior Science Outlines, vol. 2. New Haven, CT: Human Relations Area Files.

Murdock, George P. 1957. "World Ethnographic Sample." *American Anthropologist* 59:664–87.

Murdock, George P. 1967. "Ethnographic Atlas: A Summary." *Ethnology* 6:109–236.

Murdock, G. P. 1968. "The Current Status of the World's Hunting and Gathering Peoples." In *Man the Hunter.* Richard B. Lee and Irven DeVore, eds. (pp. 13–20). Chicago: Aldine.

Murdock, George P. 1983. *Outline of World Cultures,* 6th ed. New Haven, CT: Human Relations Area Files.

Murdock, George P., Clellan S. Ford, Alfred E. Hudson, Raymond Kennedy, Leo W. Simmons, and John W. M. Whiting. 1987. *Outline of Cultural Materials.* 5th rev. ed. New Haven, CT: Human Relations Area Files.

Needham, Rodney. 1960. *Structure and Sentiment: A Test Case in Social Anthropology.* Chicago: University of Chicago Press.

Neel, James V. 1994. *Physician to the Gene Pool: Genetic Lessons and Other Stories.* New York: John Wiley.

Neel, James V., and William J. Schull, eds. 1991. *The Children of Atomic Bomb Survivors: A Genetic Study.* Washington, DC: National Academy Press.

Neel, J. V., W. R. Centerwall, N. A. Chagnon, and H. L. Casey. 1970. "Notes on the Effect of Measles and Measles Vaccine in a Virgin-Soil Population of South American Indians," *American Journal of Epidemiology* 91, pp. 418–29.

Neel, J. V., F. M. Salzano, P. C. Junqueira, F. Keiter, and D. Maybury-Lewis. 1964. "Studies on the Xavante Indians of the Brazilian Mato Grosso." *American Journal of Human Genetics* 16:52–140.

Neel, James V., Timothy Asch, and Napoleon Chagnon. 1971. *Yanomamö: A Multidisciplinary Study.* DVD, Penn State Media Sales, University Park, PA.

Nicholas, Ralph W. 1965. "Factions: A Comparative Analysis." In Banton, Michael, ed. pp. 21–61.

O'Brien, Denise. 1969. *The Economics of Dani Marriage: An Analysis of Marriage Payments in a Highland New Guinea Society.* Ph.D. dissertation, Yale University.

Peters, John F. 2000. *Life Among the Yanomami.* Peterborough, Ontario: Broadview Press.

Pinker, Steven. 2002. *The Blank Slate: The Modern Denial of Human Nature.* New York: Viking.

Pinker, Steven. 1997. *How the Mind Works.* New York: Norton.

Pinker, Steven. 2012a. "The False Allure of Group Selection," The Edge Foundation, Monday, June 18, 2012.

Pinker, Steven. 2012b. Commentary on Pinker's "The False Allure of Group Selection," The Edge Foundation, Thursday, July 12, 2012.

Ploeg, Anton. 1969. "Government in Wanggulam." *Verhandlingen van het Koninkimk Instituut Voor Taal-, Land-, en Volkenkunde,* 57. The Hague: Martinus Nijhoff.

Pospisil, Leo. 1958. *Kapauku Papuans and Their Law.* New Haven, CT: Yale University Publications in Anthropology, No. 54.

Ritchie, M. A. 1996. *Spirit of the Rainforest: A Yanomamö Shaman Story.* Chicago: Island Lake Press.

Rivière, Peter. 1972. *The Forgotten Frontier: Ranchers of Northern Brazil.* Case Studies in Cultural Anthropology. New York: Holt, Rinehart & Winston.

Rousseau, Jean-Jacques. 1938. *The Social Contract.* New York: E. P. Dutton (1762).

Sahlins, Marshall D. 1961. "The Segmentary Lineage: An Organization of Predatory Expansion." *American Anthropologist* 63:322–45.

Sahlins, Marshall D. 1963. "Poor Man, Rich Man, Big Man, Chief: Political Types in Melanesia and Polynesia." *Comparative Studies in Society and History* 5:285–303.

Sahlins, Marshall D. 1965. "On the Sociology of Primitive Exchange." In *The Relevance of Models for Social Anthropology,* A.S.A. Monographs No. 1. Michael Banton, ed. (pp. 139–236). London: Tavistock.

Sahlins, Marshall D. 1968. *Tribesmen.* Englewood Cliffs, NJ: Prentice-Hall.

Sahlins, Marshall D. 1972. *Stone Age Economics.* Chicago: Aldine Atherton.

Sahlins, Marshall D. 1976. *The Use and Abuse of Biology: An Anthropological Critique of Sociobiology.* Ann Arbor: University of Michigan Press.

Salamone, Frank A. 1997a. *The Yanomami and Their Interpreters: Fierce People or Fierce Interpreters?* Lanham, MD: University Press of America.

Salamone, Frank A. 1997b. "Theoretical Reflections on the Chagnon-Salesian Controversy." In *Explorations in Anthropology.* Frank A. Salamone and W. R. Adams, eds. (pp. 91–112). Lanham, MD: University Press of America.

Salamone, Frank A. 2001. Interview with Andrew Brown, *The Daily Telegraph, Magazine,* March 3, 2001.

Salamone, Frank A. 2006. "Yanomami: The Fierce Controversy and What We

Can Learn From It." (Review of Robert Borofsky's book by the same title) *Americas*, 62 (4): (April 20–26) (pp. 660–662). Academy of American Franciscan History.

Schneider, David. 1972. "What Is Kinship All About?" In *Kinship Studies in the Morgan Centennial Year.* P. Reining, ed. (pp. 32–62). Anthropological Society of Washington, DC.

Schuster, Meinhard. 1958. "Die Soziologie der Waika." In *Proceedings of the 32nd International Congress of Americanists* (pp. 114–22). Copenhagen.

Service, Elman R. 1962. *Primitive Social Organization: An Evolutionary Perspective.* New York: Random House.

Service, Elman R. 1985. *A Century of Controversy: Ethnological Issues from 1860 to 1960.* New York: Academic Press.

Simpson, George G. 1980. *Splendid Isolation: The Curious History of South American Mammals.* New Haven, CT: Yale University Press.

Spielman, Richard. 1971. *Anthropometric and Genetic Differences among Yanomama Villages.* Ph.D. dissertation, University of Michigan, Ann Arbor.

Steward, Julian. 1949. "Cultural Causality and Law: A Trial Formulation of Early Civilization." *American Anthropologist* 51:1–27.

Steward, Julian. 1955. *Theory of Culture Change.* Urbana: University of Illinois Press.

Stirling, M. W. 1938. *Historical and Ethnographical Material on the Jivaro Indians.* Bureau of American Ethnology Bulletin 117. Washington, DC: Smithsonian Institution.

Symons, Donald. 1979. *The Evolution of Human Sexuality.* New York: Oxford University Press.

Survival International. [PDF Document]. Yanomami_timeline-3.pdf

Thomas, Elizabeth Marshall. 1959. *The Harmless People.* New York: Knopf.

Tierney, P. 1994. *Last Tribes of El Dorado: The Gold Wars in the Amazon Rain Forest.* New York: Viking. Apparently never officially published; page citations are from a typeset, bound copy marked "advanced uncorrected proofs."

Tierney, P. 2000. "The fierce anthropologist." *New Yorker,* October 9, 2000, 50–61.

Tierney, P. 2000. *Darkness in El Dorado: How Scientists and Journalists Devastated the Amazon.* New York: Norton.

Tiger, Lionel, and Robin Fox. 1966. "The Zoological Perspective in Social Science." *Man* 1:75–81.

Tooby, John. "UCSB Preliminary Report." See Hagen et al.

Tooby, John. 2000. "Jungle Fever: Did two U.S. scientists start a genocidal epidemic in the Amazon, or was *The New Yorker* duped?" *Slate,* October 25, 2000, http://www.slate.com/?id=91946.

Turner, T., and L. Sponsel. 2000. Email to Louise Lamphere, President, American Anthropological Association. Retrieved from Doug Hume's *Darkness in El Dorado* website, http://anthroniche.com/darkness_documents/0055.htm.

Trivers, Robert L. 1971. "The Evolution of Reciprocal Altruism." *Quarterly Review of Biology* 46:35–57.

Trivers, Robert L. 1972. "Parental Investment and Sexual Selection." In *Sexual*

Selection and the Descent of Man, 1871–1971. B. H. Campbell, ed. (pp. 136–79). Chicago: Aldine.

Trivers, Robert L. 1972. "Parent-Offspring Conflict." *American Zoologist* 14:249–64.

Trivers, Robert L. 1985. *Social Evolution*. Menlo Park, CA: Benjamin/Cummings.

Trivers, R. L., and D. E. Willard. 1973. "Natural Selection of Parental Ability to Vary the Sex Ratio of Offspring." *Science* 179:90–92.

Tylor, E. B. 1871. *Primitive Culture: Researches into the Development of Mythology, Philosophy, Religion, Language, Art and Custom*. London: J. Murray.

Van Creveld, Martin. 1991. *The Transformation of War*. New York: Free Press.

Van den Berghe, Pierre. 1979. *Human Family Systems*. New York: Elsevier.

Wade, Nicholas. 2010. "Anthropology a Science? Statement Deepens a Rift." *The New York Times*, Science section. Dec. 9, 2010.

Wade, Nicholas. 2010. "Anthropology Group Tries to Soothe Tempers After Dropping the Word 'Science.'" *The New York Times*, Science section. Dec. 13, 2010.

Walker, P. L. 1989. "Cranial Injuries as Evidence of Violence in Prehistoric Southern California." *American Journal of Physical Anthropology* 80(3):313–23.

Walker, P. L. 1997. "Wife beating, boxing, and broken noses: Skeletal evidence for the cultural patterning of interpersonal violence." In *Troubled Times: Violence and Warfare in the Past*. D. Martin and D. Frayer, eds. (pp. 145–75). London: Gordon & Breach.

Walker, P. L. 2001. "A Bioarchaeological Perspective on the History of Violence." *Annual Review of Anthropology* 30:573–96.

Walker, P. L., A. Andrushko, K. Latham, D. Grady, and A. Pastron. 2005. "Bioarchaeological Evidence for Trophy Taking in Prehistoric Central California." *American Journal of Physical Anthropology* 127:375–84.

Weitkamp, L. R., and Napoleon A. Chagnon. 1968. "Albumin Maku: A New Variant of Human Serum Albumin." *Nature* 217:759–60.

White, Leslie A. 1949. *The Science of Culture: A Study of Man and Civilization*. New York: Grove Press.

White, Leslie A. 1957. "How Morgan Came to Write Systems of Consanguinity and Affinity." *Papers of the Michigan Academy of Science, Arts, and Letters* 42:257–68.

Wilbert, Johannes. 1966. *Indios de la region Orinoco-Ventuari*. Monografias de la Fundacion La Salle de Ciencias Naturales, No. 8. Caracas.

Williams, George C. 1966. *Adaptation and Natural Selection: A Critique of Some Current Evolutionary Thought*. Princeton, NJ: Princeton University Press.

Williams, George C., ed. 1971. *Group Selection*. Chicago: Aldine Atherton.

Wilson, David Sloan. 2012. "This View of Life: Richard Dawkins, Edward O. Wilson, and the Consensus of the Many." *The Evolution Institute*. State University of New York at Binghamton.

Wilson, Edward O. 1975. *Sociobiology: The New Synthesis*. Cambridge, MA: Harvard University Press.

Wilson, Edward O. 2012. *The Social Conquest of Earth*. New York: W. W. Norton.

Winkler, Karen. 1994. "A Fragile Peace in Dispute Over Indians." *Chronicle of*

Higher Education, December 14, 1994, http://chronicle.com/article/A-Fragile
-Peace-in-Dispute/82373/.

Wrangham, Richard, and Dale Peterson. 1996. *Demonic Males: Apes and the Origins of Human Violence.* Boston: Houghton Mifflin Company.

Wright, Sewall. 1922. "Coefficients of Inbreeding and Relationship." *American Naturalist* 56:330–38.

Zerries, Otto. 1964. *Waika: Die Kulturgeschichtliche Stellung der Waika-Indianer des oberen Orinoco im Rahmen der Völkerkunde Südamerikas.* Band I. Ergebnisse der Frobenius-Expedition 1954/55 nach Südost Venezuela. Munich.

Zimmerman, Larry. 1981. "Digging Ancient Burial: The Crow Creek Experience." *Early Man* 3(3):3–10.

Zimmerman, Larry J., and Lawrence E. Bradley. 1993. "The Crow Creek Massacre: Initial Coalescent Warfare and Speculations About the Genesis of Extended Coalescent." *Plains Anthropologist* 38:145.

Zimmerman, L. J., J. B. Gregg, and P. S. Gregg. 1981. "Para-mortem Osteopathology in the Crow Creek Massacre Victims." *South Dakota Journal of Medicine* 34(2):7–12.

Zimmerman, Larry J., and Richard G. Whitten. 1980. "Prehistoric Bones Tell a Grim Tale of Indian v. Indian." *Smithsonian* 11(6):100–109.

Index